The Thirties in America

The Thirties in America

Volume II
Goodman, Benny—
Prohibition repeal

Editor
Thomas Tandy Lewis
St. Cloud State University

SALEM PRESS
Pasadena, California
Hackensack, New Jersey

Editor in Chief: Dawn P. Dawson

Editorial Director: Christina J. Moose   *Photo Editor:* Cynthia Breslin Beres
Project and Development Editor: R. Kent Rasmussen   *Production Editor:* Andrea E. Miller
Manuscript Editor: Christopher Rager   *Graphics and Design:* James Hutson
Acquisitions Editor: Mark Rehn   *Layout:* William Zimmerman
Research Supervisor: Jeffry Jensen

Title page photo: *Standing atop a fictionalized Empire State Building, film monster King Kong swats at biplanes pelting him with bullets and traps one in his massive left paw, in a scene from the 1933 motion picture classic* King Kong. (Hulton Archive/Getty Images)

Cover images: (pictured clockwise, from top left): The *Hindenburg* disaster (The Granger Collection, New York); Superman comic book (The Granger Collection, New York); Babe Ruth trading card (The Granger Collection, New York); "Migrant Mother," by Dorothea Lange (The Granger Collection, New York)

∞ The paper used in these volumes conforms to the American National Standard for Permanence of Paper for Printed Library Materials, Z39.48-1992 (R1997).

Library of Congress Cataloging-in-Publication Data

The thirties in America / editor, Thomas Tandy Lewis.
     p. cm.
Includes bibliographical references and index.
  ISBN 978-1-58765-725-2 (set : alk. paper) — ISBN 978-1-58765-726-9 (vol. 1 : alk. paper) — ISBN 978-1-58765-727-6 (vol. 2 : alk. paper) — ISBN 978-1-58765-728-3 (vol. 3 : alk. paper)
  1. United States—Civilization—1918-1945—Encyclopedias. 2. United States—History—1933-1945—Encyclopedias. 3. Nineteen thirties—Encyclopedias. I. Lewis, Thomas T. (Thomas Tandy)
  E169.1.T475 2011
  973.917—dc22
                                                  2010049260

■ Table of Contents

■ Complete List of Contents

Volume I

Volume II

Volume III

The Thirties in America

■ Goodman, Benny

Identification American jazz clarinetist and
bandleader
Born May 30, 1909; Chicago, Illinois
Died June 13, 1986; New York, New York

A creative improvisor and a virtuoso of the clarinet, Goodman set a high standard for ensemble precision in swing bands. As the leader of one of the most popular bands during the swing era, he was extremely influential in American culture. By including African American performers and arrangers in his performances, he also played a role in overcoming racial barriers in the United States.

Although Benny Goodman's closely knit family lived in poverty, his parents, who were immigrants, made sure that he and his brothers received some training in music. This started when Goodman and his brothers were given instruments on loan through a music program at Kehelah Synagogue in their Chicago neighborhood. Goodman, who was ten years old at the time, developed a great love for the clarinet and was given lessons in classical technique with Franz Schoepp. He immersed himself in music and was fortunate to be able to hear the great New Orleans jazz musicians who came to Chicago to play during this period. He learned their rhythmic language, their subtle blues inflections, and the special techniques of clarinetists such as Jimmie Noone. Soon, Goodman was playing professionally, working with, among others, cornet player Bix Beiderbecke. He joined the band of drummer Ben Pollack, who moved the group to New York in 1928.

Goodman became a freelance musician after leaving Pollack's group in 1929 and began playing on radio broadcasts. As the Depression worsened, radio became an important medium for musicians, and Goodman's early contacts in this field were valuable. Most of these jobs, however, were commercial, and for a time Goodman, who had to work under tight stylistic constraints, drifted away from jazz. This problem was remedied in 1933 by John Hammond, a wealthy jazz enthusiast who booked recording sessions for Goodman that included jazz artists such as vocalist-trombonist Jack Teagarden, drummer Gene Krupa, violinist Joe Venuti, and vocalist Billie Holiday. With fresh enthusiasm for jazz, Goodman formed his own big band, which played in ballrooms in 1934 with mixed success. Goodman and his band were hired to play on the popular *Let's Dance*

radio program, which provided many young people with evening entertainment that they could otherwise not afford. The jitterbug dance craze was just starting, and Goodman, who used exciting, driving jazz arrangements by Fletcher Henderson and others, selected music that was perfect for this kind of dancing.

This connection was affirmed when Goodman and his orchestra arrived in California in the midst of an otherwise disappointing tour in 1935 and were met by crowds of young people who had heard them on the radio. Momentum built quickly, and Goodman was catapulted to fame. In 1938, he and his band gave a highly successful concert at Carnegie Hall in New York. In addition to his big band, Goodman continued to play and record with small combos, which were usually racially integrated and included at various times prominent African American musicians such as pianist Teddy Wilson, vibraphonist Lionel Hampton, and guitarist Charlie Christian. He was also joined by his tireless colleague from Chi-

Benny Goodman. (Library of Congress)

cago, Krupa, who also played in Goodman's big band. All the while, Goodman continued to grow musically and explored many musical forms. After the 1930's, however, Goodman maintained the basic elements of his playing style, even while expanding his repertoire.

Impact Goodman's professional relationships with African American musicians eventually expanded to live performances, making it easier for continued integration in music, long before sports and other fields followed suit. This also allowed white jazz musicians to acknowledge their connections to African American musical traditions. Along with other prominent bandleaders of the 1930's, Goodman helped to establish the standard large jazz ensemble instrumentation, which included reeds, trumpets, trombones, and a rhythm section. Because of his continued involvement with Western classical music and jazz, he also encouraged the cultivation of bimusicality, or fluency in more than one musical language, among jazz musicians. He was the subject of a Hollywood feature film, *The Benny Goodman Story*, made in 1956, and he remained a popular figure in American music, even after his death in 1986.

John E. Myers

Further Reading

Collier, James Lincoln. *Benny Goodman and the Swing Era.* New York: Oxford University Press, 1989.

Firestone, Ross. *Swing, Swing, Swing: The Life and Times of Benny Goodman.* New York: Norton, 1993.

Tumpak, John R. *When Swing Was the Thing: Personality Profiles of the Big Band Era.* Milwaukee, Wis.: Marquette University Press, 2008.

See also Dance; Great Depression in the United States; Holiday, Billie; Miller, Glenn; Music: Jazz; Music: Popular; Recording industry; Recreation; Shaw, Artie.

■ Graham, Martha

Identification Dancer and choreographer
Born May 11, 1894; Allegheny (now in Pittsburgh), Pennsylvania
Died April 1, 1991; New York, New York

Graham developed much of her distinctive dance style during the 1930's, choreographing and performing more than fifty works. Her angular, athletic, and sometimes provocative use of the human body contrasted strongly with the fluidity of traditional ballet movements and helped to define the essential vocabulary of modern dance throughout the twentieth century.

Martha Graham began her study of ballet in 1916 at the Denishawn dance school. In 1926, she founded the Martha Graham Center of Contemporary Dance

Dancer Martha Graham (standing) with her partner Charles Weidman beside her. (©Condé Nast Archive/CORBIS)

in New York City. Graham earned fame for her unique approach to dance, breaking away from the traditional themes and movements of classical ballet. From the late 1920's through the 1930's, Graham continued to develop and teach her experimental dance language, which used sharp, angular movements; sexually suggestive body language; symbolic gestures; and series of contractions and releases of the dancers' muscles.

Graham's work of the 1930's was strongly influenced by ideas of primitivism, seen both in her 1930 interpretation of Igor Stravinsky's *Le Sacre du Printemps* (*The Rite of Spring*, 1913) and in her creation of works such as *Primitive Mysteries* (1931) and *Two Primitive Canticles* (1931). Thematically, her dances frequently centered on American topics, such as current events and architecture, folklore, and Native American culture, and often used the music of American composers, such as George Antheil and Henry Cowell. Her ballet *Chronicle* (1936) was based on the events of the Great Depression and the pervasive poverty and suffering that ensued from it. In 1937, at the invitation of First Lady Eleanor Roosevelt, Graham became the first dancer to perform at the White House.

Impact Martha Graham's distinctive approach to dance and choreography helped to define the development of modern dance throughout the twentieth century. She continued to teach dance and perform on stage into her seventies and choreographed works until her death in 1991.

Joanna R. Smolko

Further Reading

Bird, Dorothy, and Joyce Greenberg. *Bird's Eye View: Dancing with Martha Graham on Broadway*. Pittsburgh: University of Pittsburgh Press, 1997.

Deane, John, and Nan Deane Cano. *Acts of Light: Martha Graham in the Twenty-first Century*. Gainesville: University Press of Florida, 2006.

Graham, Martha. *Blood Memory*. New York: Doubleday, 1991.

Morgan, Barbara. *Martha Graham: Sixteen Dances in Photographs*. Rev. ed. Dobbs Ferry, N.Y.: Morgan & Morgan, 1980.

See also Art movements; Dance; Music: Classical; Roosevelt, Eleanor; Theater in the United States.

■ Grand Coulee Dam

The Event Gravity dam on the Columbia River in Washington

Date Construction begun on September 8, 1933

The largest concrete structure in the United States, the Grand Coulee Dam generates an enormous amount of electricity and approximately one-half billion dollars worth of hydroelectric power annually. The dam also supplies the water for a large part of the arid western United States, and it created two artificial lakes, which are used primarily for stabilization, water reserve, and recreational purposes. The irrigating system made possible by the dam created arable land out of former waste areas.

As early as 1920, Washington State officials had studied the possibility of harnessing what was, at that time, the largely uncontrollable Columbia River, but these plans lay dormant for years because of both political feuds and insufficient state funding. Finally, in 1929 the U.S. Senate requested the U.S. Army Corps of Engineers study development possibilities. The ensuing report advocated building a dam on the Columbia River, but again real action toward construction was delayed, this time by the Depression.

In order to build the dam, officials had to deal with numerous problems. Native Americans were fervently opposed because they believed, correctly, that the dam would greatly harm fish-spawning areas and put a substantial amount of their land, including burial grounds, under water. In addition, state and local utility companies resented what they considered to be unfair federal usurpation of their potential markets. Nevertheless, President Franklin D. Roosevelt ordered construction to begin in 1933. Four government agencies were directly involved, as were the Canadian government and some local dispensers of patronage. The project grew even larger when, in 1935, Secretary of the Interior Harold Ickes ordered an enlargement of the dam in order to increase electricity generation and provide jobs.

Impact The Grand Coulee Dam has drastically altered and changed the lives and cultures of the people of the Pacific Northwest and British Columbia. On the positive side, it provides huge amounts of electricity, employment, industry, and tax revenues.

Grand Coulee Dam

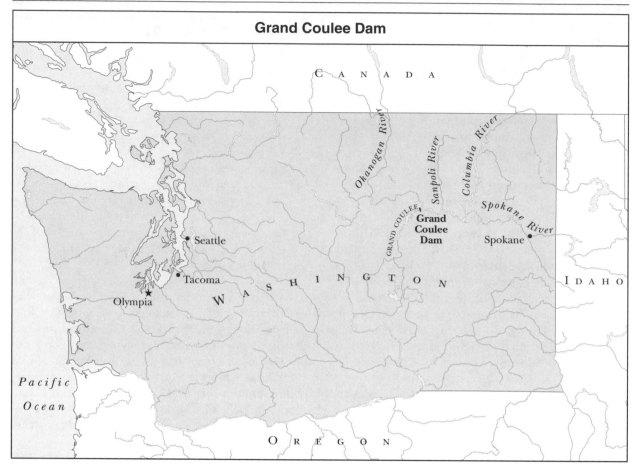

Others see it as an unnatural, giant, concrete eyesore that was and is disastrous to local communities, regional autonomy, and wildlife.

Thomas Buchanan

Further Reading

Billington, David P., and Donald C. Jackson. *Big Dams of the New Deal Era: A Confluence of Engineering and Politics.* Norman: University of Oklahoma Press, 2006.

Lowitt, Richard, ed. *Politics in the Postwar American West.* Norman: University of Oklahoma Press, 1995.

Pitzer, Paul C. *Grand Coulee: Harnessing a Dream.* Pullman: Washington State University Press, 1994.

See also Architecture; Boulder Dam; Hoover, Herbert; Roosevelt, Franklin D.; Rural Electrification Administration.

■ *Grand Hotel*

Identification Motion-picture drama about interactions of guests in an opulent Berlin hotel in the early 1930's

Director Edmund Goulding

Date Released on September 11, 1932

Known as the film in which Greta Garbo uttered her signature line, "I want to be alone," Grand Hotel won the Academy Award for best motion picture of 1932, its sole nomination. Based on the popular 1930 novel by Vicki Baum, Menschen im Hotel *(people in a hotel), the film's screenplay was adapted from a stage play by William A. Drake, which opened on Broadway on November 13, 1930, and ran for 459 performances.*

Grand Hotel brought together seven of Metro-Goldwyn-Mayer's brightest stars—Garbo, John Barrymore, Joan Crawford, Wallace Beery, Lionel Barrymore, Lewis Stone, and Jean Hersholt—in a legendary production that enjoyed the premiere of the year at Grauman's Chinese Theatre in Hollywood. The famously jealous Garbo and Crawford were never on screen at the same time. The Barrymore brothers had several moving scenes together.

The film's lavish Art Deco design by Cedric Gibbons and the elegant costumes designed by Adrian Adolph Greenberg (better known as Adrian) were a perfect example of classic Hollywood style. A West German film with the title of Vicki Baum's original 1930 novel, *Menschen im Hotel*, was made in 1959.

Impact   Life in five-star hotels fascinated the public of the era. The Grand Hotel of the title was ostensibly based on the Hotel Excelsior in Berlin, where the elite of the pre-Nazi years met. The film's impact is noteworthy from the remakes, one of which was *Week-End at the Waldorf* (1945) with Ginger Rogers, Lana Turner, Walter Pidgeon, Van Johnson, and Edward Arnold. It was also made into two stage musicals, *At the Grand* (1958) and *Grand Hotel: The Musical* (1989). *Grand Hotel* was the first of the vehicles to showcase a studio's top talent. This trend continued during the 1960's and 1970's but later grew too expensive.

Richard J. Rundell

Further Reading

Baum, Vicki. *It Was All Quite Different: The Memoirs of Vicki Baum.* New York: Funk & Wagnalls, 1964.

Eames, John Douglas, and Ronald Bergan. *The MGM Story: The Complete History of Sixty-nine Roaring Years.* London: Hamlyn, 1993.

Flamini, Roland. *Thalberg: The Last Tycoon and the World of M-G-M.* New York: Crown, 1994.

Kobler, John. *Damned in Paradise: The Life of John Barrymore.* New York: Atheneum, 1977.

Paris, Barry. *Garbo: A Biography.* New York: Knopf, 1995.

Robinson, David, and Paul Duncan. *Greta Garbo.* London: Taschen, 2007.

See also   Academy Awards; Film; Garbo, Greta.

■ Grapes of Wrath, The

Identification   Novel about a family of Oklahoma farmers forced to leave their land and travel to California
Author   John Steinbeck
Date   Published in 1939

Upon publication, The Grapes of Wrath *became a lightning rod for controversy. Its stark portrayal of the poverty and predation in the Oklahoma Dust Bowl and the growing fields of California's Salinas Valley launched it to the top of best-seller lists. It won the Pulitzer Prize for fiction, but praise was not universal; the book was burned publicly in the author's hometown and banned from the state of Oklahoma.*

The Grapes of Wrath was John Steinbeck's ninth book and is considered by many to be his best work. First published in 1939, the book has never been out of print, and it is a mainstay on public school reading lists. Upon publication it received critical literary praise and even elicited a response from the U.S. Senate, which considered changing federal labor

---

The Causes of Revolt

In The Grapes of Wrath, *Steinbeck included "interchapters" in which he ruminated on the migrants' plight in order to distance readers from the main plot and allow a longer perspective on the social machinery that drove it. One famous passage concerns the evolution of farming from a family occupation to an industry to which the Joads were clearly in thrall:*

And the great owners, who must lose their land in an upheaval, the great owners with access to history, with eyes to read history and to know the great fact: when property accumulates in too few hands it is taken away. And that companion fact: when a majority of the people are hungry and cold they will take by force what they need. And the little screaming fact that sounds through all history: repression works only to strengthen and knit the repressed. The great owners ignored the three cries of history . . . and every effort of the great owners was directed at repression. The money was spent for arms, for gas to protect the great holdings, and spies were sent to catch the murmurings of revolt so that it might be stamped out. The changing economy was ignored, plans for the change ignored; and only means to destroy revolt were considered, while the causes of revolt went on.

Source: John Steinbeck, *The Grapes of Wrath* (New York: Random House, 1939).

Actor Henry Fonda atop the roof of the Joad family truck in the film version of T h e Grapes of Wrath, *as the Joads load up their belongings before heading to California.* (Hulton Archive/Getty Images)

law to correct some of the iniquities Steinbeck documented.

The Grapes of Wrath opens as its protagonist, Tom Joad, returns to his boyhood home in Oklahoma after he is paroled from prison, where he had been incarcerated for homicide. When he arrives, the family farm is abandoned. He travels to a nearby farm owned by his uncle and finds his family loading their few remaining belongings in a truck as they prepare to leave Oklahoma for California. The farm had been foreclosed after crops were lost to drought, and the destitute family is planning to travel to California, where they have heard there are high wages and sufficient jobs. Tom Joad joins his family even though it means breaking his parole, and they leave for California with all of their possessions latched to a rickety truck.

While traveling to California, the Joads encounter many other families in their same circumstance,

some of whom are returning from California with news that there are no jobs to be had there. The Joads continue, even as members of their party flee and others die, because they have nowhere else to go.

In California the family cannot find decent jobs because there is an oversupply of field labor, and large agricultural growers are colluding to keep wages low. They are reduced to living outdoors in camps filled with other itinerant workers. The conditions they live in are squalid and subhuman. The only well-maintained camp they find is subsidized by the federal government, but it does not have the capacity to help all of the needy.

Because working conditions are so poor, the migrant workers begin to form unions. The family become involved in the labor struggle and then, inadvertently, take jobs as strikebreakers. They are caught in a violent conflict, and Tom Joad is forced to kill a man and subsequently flee. Before he leaves, he promises his mother he will remain an advocate for the oppressed wherever he travels.

Impact Steinbeck's portrayal of the Dust Bowl and itinerant farmers in California's Salinas Valley remains among the most enduring images of the Great Depression. The book was controversial for both its subject matter and its language, which is profane at times. Steinbeck was attacked from both ends of the political spectrum. Some thought he had written a piece of communist propaganda, others that his realistic portrayal of itinerant farmers was insulting and stereotypical. Criticism was heaped on him, in part, because of the book's high profile and incredible popularity.

The Grapes of Wrath was a best seller and was reviewed in dozens of papers and magazines. In 1940, it was adapted for the big screen. The film version was directed by John Ford, and the lead character, Tom Joad, was played by Henry Fonda. As time passed, the characters Steinbeck created became part of popular culture, and they have been featured in songs written by Woody Guthrie, Kris Kristofferson, and Bruce Springsteen, among many others. Decades after its initial publication, *The Grapes of Wrath* is still read widely and continues to define the way many think about the Great Depression.

Colin Asher

Further Reading

Johnson, Claudia, and Vernon Johnson. *The Social Impact of the Novel: A Reference Guide.* Westport, Conn.: Greenwood Press, 2004.

Saxton, Alexander. "In Dubious Battle: Looking Backward." *Pacific Historical Review* 73, no. 2 (2004): 249-262.

Zirakzadeh, Cyrus Ernesto. "John Steinbeck on the Political Capacities of Everyday Folk: Moms, Reds, and Ma Joad's Revolt." *Polity* (2004).

See also Book publishing; Dust Bowl; Ford, John; Great Depression in the United States; Homelessness; Migrations, domestic; National Labor Relations Act of 1935; Steinbeck, John.

■ *Graves v. New York ex rel. O'Keefe*

The Case U.S. Supreme Court ruling that removed the immunity of state employees from paying federal taxes and federal employees from paying state taxes

Date Decided on March 27, 1939

The Supreme Court found no constitutional requirement of tax immunity, nor did any act of Congress specifically grant immunity to federal or state employees in paying taxes. The Court thus concluded that salaries of such employees were subject to regular federal and state taxes.

In *Graves*, the state of New York imposed an income tax on a New York resident and federal employee of the Federal Home Owners' Loan Corporation. This resident paid the tax but then appealed his payment based on a long history of Supreme Court cases stating there was a tax immunity for federal employees. Overruling those previous cases, the Supreme Court held that there was nothing in the Constitution that required such immunity, nor did any act of Congress specifically grant immunity to federal employees, and denied the appeal. In those overruled previous cases, the Court held that income taxes were a tax on the source of that income. This meant that taxing government employees was like taxing the government, which was not allowed. The Supreme Court's new rule stated there was no basis for the assumption that a nondiscriminatory state income tax on the salary of a government employee or of a governmental agency imposed a burden on the national government tantamount to an unconstitutional interference with government functions.

Impact The *Graves* case demonstrated the rising power of the federal and state governments during the 1930's. Later, income taxes represented a major source of government revenues. The growth of state and federal governments to try to lessen the impact of the Great Depression called for a greater need of revenue to fund their efforts. This opinion specifically overruled a long line of cases supporting the tax immunity and the doctrine that a tax on income constitutes a tax on the source of that income.

Eric T. Bellone

Further Reading

Currie, David, P. *The Constitution of the United States: A Primer for the People.* Chicago: University of Chicago Press, 2000.

Kurland, Philip B. *The Supreme Court and the Judicial Function.* Chicago: University of Chicago Press, 1975.

Swinford, Bill, and Eric N. Waltenburg. *Litigating Federalism: The States Before the U.S. Supreme Court.* Westport, Conn.: Praeger Greenwood Press, 1999.

See also Civil rights and liberties in the United States; Great Depression in the United States; Income and wages in the United States; Supreme Court, U.S.

■ Great Depression in Canada

The Event Large-scale economic downturn
Dates 1929-1941

The Great Depression marked a significant change from the economy that had characterized the 1920's. During that decade, business had boomed, Canada's exports rose to previously unknown levels, and investment soared. The break, marked by the collapse of the stock market in New York, ushered in a decade that was, in many respects, the opposite of the decade of the 1920's.

One of Canada's major twentieth century historians, Harold Adams Innis, famously characterized the country's economy as a "staples economy." By that he meant that in the world economy, and especially in world trade, Canada was a major producer of raw materials and that these products were then exported to other countries, where they were manufactured into products that ordinary people could use. Canada's major export, wheat, was turned into bread and other food products by other countries. Canada was a major producer of aluminum ore; other countries turned the aluminum ore into more elaborate manufactured goods. Canada was one of the world's major miners of gold, and the trees that it harvested from the woodlands in northern British Columbia provided the raw materials for a large number of the houses built in the United States.

These products earned a return only if they were in demand elsewhere in the world. All of them—even the wheat cascading off the Prairie Provinces—depended on a vibrant world economy. Many of them could find a consumer market only if there were businesses able to take the raw materials and fashion them into products consumers needed.

During the 1920's, vigorous investments had been made in many industries, predicated on the availability of the raw materials needed for manufacturing; as a result, many businesses carried a heavy load of debt. As long as demand kept rising and financing continued to be available, these businesses prospered; but with the collapse of the stock market in the United States, demand for the raw materials that Canada produced fell dramatically. When the 1930's began, the entire world market declined to a fraction of what it had been in the 1920's. In 1930, the Canadian economy descended into the Great Depression. It continued to decline until 1933, after which it began a modest recovery that lasted until 1937. That year a major drought occurred in the Prairie Provinces, and the collapse of the wheat market hurt the economy. The Canadian economy began a slow recovery in 1938, but only with the outbreak of World War II, in 1939-1940, did a full-scale recovery occur.

Regional Effects of the Great Depression The Maritime Provinces—Nova Scotia, New Brunswick, and Prince Edward Island—were less affected by the Great Depression than other parts of Canada, but this was largely because they had not shared as much in the prosperity of the 1920's. Nova Scotia lost some of its ocean trade simply because there was less of it; the demand for the coal and iron deposits in Nova Scotia and Cape Breton Island dropped sharply, resulting in a rise in unemployment. Prince Edward Island was largely agricultural, and it remained so; however, farms were small, and their owners fell back on subsistence. For the most part, New Brunswick had small businesses except for the newsprint industry, which had grown dramatically in the 1920's because of the small trees growing in the local forest. During the Depression, this industry had to scale back its output dramatically, often to only 50 to 60 percent of capacity.

The central provinces, Quebec and Ontario, had more diversified economies than the Maritime Provinces. Quebec's French farmers went on with their subsistence agriculture, but other jobs, especially in the textile industry, were hard to come by. Ontario had become an ally of the U.S. auto industry, and the job shortages there led to considerable unrest. How-

Indigent Canadians line up for food outside a mission in Toronto during the height of the Great Depression.

ever, Canadian auto workers earned a major victory when a strike against General Motors in Oshawa led to recognition of the auto workers' union as the legitimate representative of those workers; this matched the achievements of the U.S. auto workers.

The most drastic effects of the Great Depression were felt in the Prairie Provinces. During the 1920's, Canada had become one of the five great wheat exporters in the world—the others were the United States, Argentina, Australia, and the Soviet Union. World demand for wheat plummeted in the 1930's, and Canada, whose wheat farmers produced far more wheat than could be consumed at home, lost out enormously. Wheat that had sold for one dollar per bushel in the late 1920's fell in price, first to fifty-three cents, and then below that figure. At the same time, the wheat farmers were hammered by persistent droughts, especially in 1933 and in 1937. Farm income fell by at least one-half and by as much as

four-fifths in the three Prairie Provinces. In parts of southern Saskatchewan, planting or harvesting wheat became impossible. Many of the prairie farmers had made significant investments in agricultural machinery in the late 1920's, and they became saddled with debts they could not repay. Significant numbers gave up their farms and joined a great army of unemployed all across Canada.

With so little agricultural land, British Columbia was chiefly affected by the decreased demand for wood products and some minerals. Because of this, left-wing activism flourished in the province, attempting to energize either the provincial government or the national government into doing something about the economy.

Government Response to the Great Depression   As unemployment rose, so did the readiness of the government to respond. Among local, provincial, and national levels of government, disagreement existed over responsibility toward the poor and unemployed. In the end, relief was provided for families but not for individuals. The dominion government made substantial loans to the provinces, which in turn passed on the financing to the municipalities. The latter struggled throughout the Depression, because the cost of relief had to be borne at a time when local income, which came largely from real estate taxes, was itself depressed. Many families feared the social impact of relying on relief payments and relied on them only when desperate.

In the first half of the 1930's, the national government was dominated by the Conservative Party, which was headed by Richard Bedford Bennett. He felt his responsibility was to cement the national foundations of the country, and relief in some of the early efforts he sponsored was a by-product. Under Bennett, the dominion government took responsibility for projects that appeared to enhance Canada's national reach, sponsoring such programs as the creation of a national airline and the establishment of what later became the Canadian Broadcasting Corporation.

When the dominion government had taken over the privately owned eastern railroads and formed them into the Canadian National Railways during the 1920's, it had guaranteed the group's debt. During the 1930's the government had to pay the interest charges on this debt, which rose from $1/3$ of federal revenues in 1929 to $33^2/3$ by 1933-1934; it had even tapped the provinces for part of these payments. Given Canada's immense geographic size, the railroads proved to be both national integrators and sources of employment.

As the decade progressed, the fact that the Great Depression was far more than a temporary phenomenon became clear. Prime Minister Bennett felt great pressure to adopt more detailed measures to help the unemployed. The dominion government shepherded through parliament a Minimum Wages Act, the Limitation of Hours of Work Act, the Weekly Rest in Industrial Undertakings Act, the Unemployment and Social Insurance Act, and the Natural Products Marketing Act. These efforts proved unavailing, because the British Privy Council, which had granted self-government to Canada in 1931, declared all these acts to be unconstitutional.

Local authorities refused to assume economic responsibility for single men. As the Depression wors-

ened, this army of vagrants generated widespread unease, and the federal government created some "relief camps," more or less army camps, for these single individuals. The bulk of these camps were located in the West; and unrest grew among the residents during the summer of 1935. Some of the leaders organized a march on Ottawa that managed to get from Vancouver to Regina, Saskatchewan. There they were confronted by the Royal Canadian Mounted Police and forced to disband. The William Lyon Mackenzie King government closed the camps in early 1936.

The one financial instrument still available to the dominion government was the tariff. The U.S. government had responded to the enormous falloff in economic activity by passing the infamous Hawley-Smoot Tariff, which sharply reduced Canadian exports (especially of agricultural products) to the United States. European countries had raised their duties on wheat, so that Canadian exports to the continent dropped off dramatically. Even Great Britain resuscitated an earlier tariff that taxed imports of agricultural products and raw materials. Canada responded to these measures by increasing its own tariffs, but because its economy was a net exporter, it lost more than it gained. In 1932, at the Ottawa Conference, Great Britain gave Canada preferential treatment for a number of major Canadian exports, notably wheat, lumber, apples, and bacon. The United States-Canada trade agreement of 1935 returned the duties on major Canadian exports to the U.S. to the levels at which they had been before Smoot-Hawley.

Impact of Business and the Growth of Radicalism Although the Great Depression impacted all parts of Canadian society, it affected businesspeople the least. Businesses that had made substantial investments during the 1920's experienced difficulties, and some were forced to go out of business. However, if they were able to retrench and had not acquired too much debt, they were able to survive. Their chief problem was a significant decline in prices, which impacted their ability to secure a profit. Workers who retained their jobs benefited from the decline in prices. Estimates indicate that of those who managed to keep their jobs, as many as 20 percent had incomes of at least $1,500, and such people survived well. Canada's economy had started the conversion to service jobs, and for those who had entered the service economy, the downturn was survivable. The chief victims were the wage workers and those whose careers depended on their own labor, such as farmers.

By the mid-1930's, the Depression had generated a significant labor movement. The unions, some of which were represented by the Trades and Labour Congress of Canada, began organizing a series of strikes in 1936 and 1937. Although most of these union actions were directed at preventing wage cuts by industrial employers, the strike called against the General Motors operation in Oshawa led to recognition of the union's right to represent the workers.

The distress of the unemployed provided a healthy stimulus for radical ideas. Formal adherence to communism was banned in section 98 of the criminal code, and some agitators were jailed under this provision. There was a fear of the danger of communism in the business community. The majority of Canadians who found radical ideas attractive professed allegiance to the socialism advocated by the British Labour Party; drawing on the interest of many farmers in cooperative organization, these forces found formal expression in the program of the Social Credit League, chiefly in Alberta. In August of 1935, the voters of Alberta elected the Co-operative Commonwealth Federation to lead the province. However, when the party attempted to enact legislation to put some of its ideas into practice, the dominion government disallowed the legislation. The Liberal Party repealed section 98 of the criminal code, so that advocates of communism could no longer be prosecuted under it, but otherwise they did little to put into action some of the socialist theories that had won a radical following.

Impact   The period of the Great Depression in Canada has sometimes been referred to as "the lost decade." Although its impact was felt throughout the country, the most dramatic effect was seen in the Prairie Provinces, where the wheat economy was battered by a loss of foreign markets and by devastating drought. Canada was capable of producing far more wheat than the world was prepared to buy, and the loss of that business reverberated throughout the country. Things reached their lowest point in 1933. In 1934, a slow recovery began, which took a hit when drought struck the prairies once more in 1937. In the end, only the outbreak of World War II,

and the resulting need for agricultural products and raw materials, restored the Canadian economy to health.

Nancy M. Gordon

Further Reading

Campbell, Lara. *Respectable Citizens: Gender, Family, and Unemployment in Ontario's Great Depression.* Toronto: University of Toronto Press, 2009. Focuses on the impact that the Great Depression had on working-class citizens of Ontario and how the economic conditions of the time fostered activism and protest.

Creighton, Donald Grant. *Dominion of the North: A History of Canada.* Boston: Houghton-Mifflin, 1944. The last chapter of this book gives an excellent summary of the Great Depression.

Finkel, Alvin. *Business and Social Reform in the Thirties.* Toronto: Lorimer, 1979. An analysis of the reaction of business to the Great Depression, giving business credit for its role.

Horn, Michiel. *The Great Depression of the 1930's in Canada.* Ottawa: The Canadian Historical Association, 1984. This pamphlet-size account is useful, as it compresses all the important details.

_____, ed. *The Dirty Thirties: Canadians in the Great Depression.* Toronto: Copp Clark, 1972. Substantial compendium of events related to the Great Depression.

Marr, William L., and Donald G. Paterson. *Canada: An Economic History.* Toronto: Macmillan of Canada, 1980. Fact-filled account of Canada, with a plethora of economic details, graphs, and lists.

Safarian, A. E. *The Canadian Economy in the Great Depression.* Toronto: University of Toronto Press, 1959. A statistics-based account of the Great Depression in Canada.

Watkins, M. H., and H. M. Grant, eds. *Canadian Economic History: Classic and Contemporary Approaches.* Ottawa: Carleton University Press, 1993. This volume contains articles by numerous scholars on various aspects of twentieth century Canadian economic history.

See also   Agriculture in Canada; Business and the economy in Canada; Canada, U.S. investments in; Great Depression in the United States; Income and wages in Canada; Ottawa Agreements; Recession of 1937-1938.

■ Great Depression in the United States

The Event Large-scale economic downturn
Dates 1929-1941

The Great Depression in the United States has been re-
garded as the worst national crisis in American history
since the American Civil War. The Depression, which was
worldwide, had profound economic, political, and social ef-
fects on the United States during the 1930's. It was the lon-
gest and most significant economic downturn in U.S. his-
tory, and the government efforts to address it shaped
American society.

The Great Depression of the 1930's was the result of several causes. Although economic mini-depressions, or "panics," had been part of the American economic cycle for at least a century, this depression was deeper and lasted longer than any previous economic downturn. The Depression followed the unprecedented economic prosperity of the 1920's.

The event that symbolized the beginning of the Great Depression was the stock market crash of October, 1929, which ended an unprecedented rise in the stock markets that included a doubling of the Dow Jones Industrial Average between 1928 and 1929. Because most of the growth was fueled by purchases made on margin, however, the growth was unsustainable. Trouble was exacerbated by the response of the Federal Reserve, which raised credit rates and tightened the money supply, at a time when lowering interest rates and easing credit would have helped borrowers to pay back lenders. These factors led to a downward spiral of bank and business failures. The nation's economy continued downward between 1929 and 1932, and the expected sources of relief—families, private organizations, and the state—proved inadequate.

Beyond the cost to American business and the financial infrastructure was the human cost. People lost not only jobs but also homes and savings; even previously middle-class people were reduced to scavenging for food and coal. Many, forced out of their homes, constructed campsites of shoddily built shanties in public places that quickly earned the nickname "Hoovervilles." In the early Depression era, most Americans, shell-shocked but believing firmly in self-reliance, were initially fairly passive and focused on surviving. Not until later, as economic conditions improved marginally and the people's hopes were raised, did active political restiveness emerge.

The Hoover Administration and the Great Depression, 1929-1933 The president at the time of the onset of the Depression, Herbert Hoover, quickly proved unequal to the task of addressing the severe economic downturn. A genuinely compassionate man whose long career had included heading the Food Administration in World War I, Hoover nonetheless believed firmly that the federal government should not take a leading role in administering aid, fearing that it would undermine human initiative and self-reliance. Hoover had no such qualms about aiding businesses, believing that supporting business would help stimulate the economy. For that reason, in 1932, Hoover authorized the first governmental body specifically designed to address the economic conditions, the Reconstruction Finance Corporation (RFC), which made $2 billion available as loans to banks and corporations that were willing to build low-cost public housing and public works, displaying Hoover's emphasis on public-private partnerships. The Hoover administration also created the Home Loan Bank Board to support mortgage companies and savings and loans corporations.

Hoover's political undoing was his treatment of the Bonus Army marchers, who were veterans of the World War I American Expeditionary Force. Feeling the economic effects of the Depression, they gathered throughout the country and rode boxcars to Washington, D.C., to demand early payment of service bonuses that were not due until 1945; they set up camp at the Anacostia Flats, near Capitol Hill. Fearing what might happen if he gave in to the demands, Hoover refused to meet with the marchers, so they camped outside the White House. Hoover then sent troops, led by Army Chief of Staff Douglas MacArthur and General George Patton, to drive them out. The troops set fire to shacks and tents, and in the melee, one hundred veterans were wounded and one infant was killed. The sight of veterans driven out by the Army did not look good, and it played a significant role in Hoover's defeat in the 1932 election.

Roosevelt Administration and the Great Depression, 1933-1941 The American people found a savior of sorts in Franklin D. Roosevelt, the aristocratic New York governor and the fifth cousin of President Theodore Roosevelt. As New York governor, Roosevelt had created successful statewide relief programs that he adapted for the nation as president. As a candidate for president, he promised "a new deal for the American people," and this message resonated with the voting public. Between the election and Roosevelt's inauguration on March 4, 1933, the economy continued to worsen; even the banks that had been saved by the RFC were closing.

Roosevelt and his administration spent their first one hundred days attempting to restore American confidence by taking emergency measures against total economic collapse. During this time, Roosevelt set a record for political activity, taking actions that ranged from partially repealing Prohibition to declaring a bank holiday that closed the nation's banks long enough for the government to determine which ones were worth saving. Roosevelt also authorized the establishment of the Federal Emergency Relief Administration, which administered $500 million in direct relief, and the Home Owners' Loan Corporation to prevent widespread mortgage foreclosures. In an effort to boost the nation's morale, Roosevelt also began a series of radio addresses that became known as the "fireside chats," which were effective for their relative infrequency (four times per year) and their direct address to the people through their home radios, a practice that gave Americans the sense that their president cared about their problems. In return, the sheer volume of letters written to the president and First Lady Eleanor Roosevelt displayed the immediate success of Roosevelt's efforts to reach out to the American people.

Once the immediate crisis was under control, Roosevelt took more definitive regulatory action through a series of programs and agencies that became known as "The New Deal." Technically speaking, however, there were two New Deals. The first, enacted between 1933 and 1935, focused primarily on shoring up and regulating American business and restricting output to address overproduction. A key piece of legislation was the National Industrial Recovery Act (NIRA), which created the National Recovery Administration. The NIRA, a voluntary program, encouraged industries to get together to agree on fair codes of competition. The NIRA also included unprecedented prolabor provisions that recognized the right of workers to organize and the responsibility of employers to bargain in good faith. More controversial programs of the first New Deal included the Agricultural Adjustment Act, which paid farmers to not only reduce production but also destroy existing produce and livestock in order to bring prices back up, and the Tennessee Valley Authority, a government program that provided flood control and cheap hydroelectric power for the multistate Tennessee River Valley. The latter initiative was popular with the public because it brought unprecedented improvements for the people of the region. The first New Deal also included early, and controversial, work relief programs, such as the Civil Works Administration (CWA), the Public Works Administration (PWA), and the Civilian Conservation Corps (CCC).

By contrast to the first New Deal, the second New Deal, enacted between 1935 and 1937, shifted the focus from addressing overproduction to addressing underconsumption. The purpose of the second New Deal's was to enable Americans to earn and consume again, through methods ranging from social welfare to employment at public works to collective bargaining rights for workers. The task of employing many of the unemployed was accomplished through an expanded public works program, the Works Progress Administration, that built on the efforts of the CWA and PWA and expanded them to include the employment of artists to paint public murals, writers to produce travel guides, and actors and other theater professionals to produce low-cost theatrical performances for the public. Paying for all of this involved deficit spending and a break from balanced budgets in order to "prime the pump," following the theories of British economist John Maynard Keynes, which rejected the classical idea that the free market should be left alone to function without governmental assistance or interference.

Politics and Society in the Great Depression   Both New Deals were shaped by the politics of the time, which were, in turn, greatly affected by the economic conditions. Desperate times brought out political extremes from both the left and the right. On the left, the decade represented a resurgence of influence, including electoral, from radical third parties, both socialist and communist. Labor parties were popular among the working poor, as was the Communist Party USA, which by this time had shifted from preaching world revolution to emphasizing a "Popular Front" strategy of making alliances with labor and political organizations, ostensibly against fascism. In California, Upton Sinclair, the au-

(continued on page 411)

Roosevelt Reassures the Nation

Franklin D. Roosevelt was elected to an unprecedented four terms as U.S. president, serving during two of the nation's greatest crises, the Great Depression and World War II. In his first inaugural address, delivered on Saturday, March 4, 1933, he discussed the first order of business: to bolster a people breaking under the burdens of the Depression.

I am certain that my fellow Americans expect that on my induction into the Presidency I will address them with a candor and a decision which the present situation of our Nation impels. This is preeminently the time to speak the truth, the whole truth, frankly and boldly. Nor need we shrink from honestly facing conditions in our country today. This great Nation will endure as it has endured, will revive and will prosper. So, first of all, let me assert my firm belief that the only thing we have to fear is fear itself—nameless, unreasoning, unjustified terror which paralyzes needed efforts to convert retreat into advance. In every dark hour of our national life a leadership of frankness and vigor has met with that understanding and support of the people themselves which is essential to victory. I am convinced that you will again give that support to leadership in these critical days.

In such a spirit on my part and on yours we face our common difficulties. They concern, thank God, only material things. Values have shrunken to fantastic levels; taxes have risen; our ability to pay has fallen; government of all kinds is faced by serious curtailment of income; the means of exchange are frozen in the currents of trade; the withered leaves of industrial enterprise lie on every side; farmers find no markets for their produce; the savings of many years in thousands of families are gone.

More important, a host of unemployed citizens face the grim problem of existence, and an equally great number toil with little return. Only a foolish optimist can deny the dark realities of the moment.

Yet our distress comes from no failure of substance. We are stricken by no plague of locusts. Compared with the perils which our forefathers conquered because they believed and were not afraid, we have still much to be thankful for. . . . The money changers have fled from their high seats in the temple of our civilization. We may now restore that temple to the ancient truths.

The measure of the restoration lies in the extent to which we apply social values more noble than mere monetary profit. . . . Restoration calls, however, not for changes in ethics alone. This Nation asks for action, and action now.

Our greatest primary task is to put people to work. . . .

Hand in hand with this we must frankly recognize the overbalance of population in our industrial centers and, by engaging on a national scale in a redistribution, endeavor to provide a better use of the land. . . .

Finally, in our progress toward a resumption of work we require two safeguards against a return of the evils of the old order; there must be a strict supervision of all banking and credits and investments; there must be an end to speculation with other people's money, and there must be provision for an adequate but sound currency.

These are the lines of attack. I shall presently urge upon a new Congress, in special session, detailed measures for their fulfillment, and I shall seek the immediate assistance of the several States. . . .

If I read the temper of our people correctly, we now realize as we have never realized before our interdependence on each other; that we cannot merely take but we must give as well; that if we are to go forward, we must move as a trained and loyal army willing to sacrifice for the good of a common discipline, because without such discipline no progress is made, no leadership becomes effective. We are, I know, ready and willing to submit our lives and property to such discipline, because it makes possible a leadership which aims at a larger good. This I propose to offer, pledging that the larger purposes will bind upon us all as a sacred obligation with a unity of duty hitherto evoked only in time of armed strife.

With this pledge taken, I assume unhesitatingly the leadership of this great army of our people dedicated to a disciplined attack upon our common problems. . . .

thor of *The Jungle* (1906), the early twentieth century exposé of the meatpacking industry, ran for governor of California as part of his End Poverty in California program. He did not win, but he came close. The most significant left-leaning political challenge to Roosevelt came from the eccentric, populist Louisiana senator Huey Long, who preached nothing less than a complete redistribution of U.S. wealth and won enough support to be considered a serious challenger for the presidency before he was assassinated in 1936.

Political challenges to Roosevelt and the New Deal did not come solely from the left. The other major figure to challenge Roosevelt publicly was Father Charles E. Coughlin, a Catholic priest from Michigan who earned the nickname "the Radio Priest" for his regular addresses and sermons on the radio. Coughlin began as a supporter of Roosevelt and the New Deal until he realized that Roosevelt was not listening to his advice, at which point he became a virulent critic of what he labeled "the Jew Deal." He founded the National Union of Social Justice, a proto-political party that increasingly leaned toward fascism. Also, like the industrialist Henry Ford, Coughlin became increasingly anti-Semitic and obsessed with Jewish conspiracies. By 1939, many radio stations refused to air his programs. In the middle of these extremes, Francis E. Townsend also achieved public prominence through his promotion of an old-age pension plan that was economically and politically unfeasible, but one that Roosevelt later co-opted to create the Social Security system.

As a net result of this labor and political unrest, Roosevelt took a rhetorical left turn, as he publicly attacked the "economic royalists" in the 1936 election, in which he was reelected by a landslide. Substantively, however, Roosevelt's politics remained relatively unchanged, and while the programs of the two New Deals created significant economic and social reforms, few did anything to seriously redistribute wealth in the United States or otherwise attack economic inequality. By 1937, when the economy appeared to be picking up, Roosevelt began cutting back on some New Deal programs, which led to another economic downturn. "The Roosevelt Recession," as it was labeled, contributed to a decline in Roosevelt's popu-

larity, as did his attempt to "pack" the Supreme Court by a failed effort to introduce legislation to expand the number of justices on the Court.

Social and Cultural Aspects of the Great Depression

Beyond politics, the Great Depression left other lasting effects on American society. Economically, it undermined the traditional American business culture severely. Conversely, for a time, the Depression promoted a uniquely prolabor environment in which even popular culture was sympathetic to the goals and aspirations of workers' movements and the common man was a subject of celebration and sympathy.

The Depression had a profoundly disruptive effect on the American family or, at least, the accepted middle-class ideal of the family. Because most of the

In a scene not unfamiliar during the Depression, an unemployed, elderly man hawks fruit on a New York City street. (Archive Photos/Getty Images)

job losses were in industries traditionally associated with men, women were more likely to maintain employment and often ended up as the primary breadwinners of their families. These changes in gender roles were not easily accepted, which led to family breakups and desertions for those who could not afford divorce. Marriage rates and birthrates also declined. Because of these consequences, many states and localities fired or refused to hire married women, and subsequent New Deal efforts to help "the forgotten man" forgot or never considered that many women, regardless of marital status, were often the sole supporters of their families. Even some of the early New Deal work-relief programs, such as the CCC, were designated for men only.

Minorities also suffered disproportionately from the effects of the Great Depression. African Americans had enjoyed comparatively little of the prosperity of the 1920's, and when the Depression hit, they were the most likely to be fired and pushed out of jobs that Caucasians would not have considered in better times. During the New Deal, the obstructionism of southern Democrats prevented Roosevelt from doing more for African Americans; if anything, many of the relief programs reinforced existing patterns of discrimination. The situation for Mexican Americans was in many ways worse than that of African Americans. Many were victimized by repatriation schemes designed to give more jobs to American citizens, and many were caught up in citizenship raids in which even American citizens were deported. State and local governments forced out many more, and by 1935, an additional 500,000 left voluntarily. The New Deal alleviated the worst of this discrimination, but legal harassment and discrimination in the distribution of relief remained, and only Latinos who worked in the construction trades genuinely benefited from the New Deal.

Culturally and psychologically, the national mood became one of darkness and cynicism. Depression was a literal phenomenon for many, with a marked increase in the suicide rate. Reflecting a loss of faith in the norms of polite society, the films and popular culture glorified gangsters and "hardboiled" heroes who lived by their wits—even outside the law, if need be. Accompanying the darker outlook on life was a yearning for escape, which Hollywood provided through films that presented visions of glamour. The popular culture of the period also reflected a yearning for heroes, which was most visibly expressed by the creation of the character of Superman.

Over time, Americans developed social solidarity, which was expressed in a general willingness to provide food and work for hoboes—jobless men (and occasionally women) who wandered the country both to search for work and to escape the shame of unemployment. Finally, the culture emphasized that those who had once worked and served their country should be treated not as beggars but as upstanding citizens down on their luck. This sentiment was most powerfully expressed in Yip Harburg's classic song "Brother, Can You Spare a Dime?" and shaped subsequent politics and policy.

Impact Although the Great Depression ended with the U.S. entry into World War II, effects of the Depression, and the efforts implemented to address it, had a lasting impact on the American government and on American society. Most immediately, there were numerous regulations of business and banking, which kept the American economy essentially sound through the end of the century. Regulations that created minimum standards for labor conditions and a minimum wage came about, though both were only later extended to agricultural and domestic labor. Organized labor was legalized through the Wagner Act, but at the price of compliance with subsequent legal measures that were the product of a less prolabor political climate. Finally, the Social Security system addressed the issue of poverty and the aged, long after industrialized European nations had established old-age pension systems.

Beyond these concrete measures, the Great Depression led to a mostly permanent expansion of the federal government, in terms of both structure and function. For much of subsequent history, it led to a greater understanding of the limits of capitalism and the free market as well as the idea that the government could be the solution to American problems. For that reason, by the end of World War II, most citizens accepted that the government would have an economic regulatory role, albeit one that was mainly indirect and advisory. During the Depression, poverty became a national issue, and old distinctions between the "deserving" and "undeserving" poor were largely, though never entirely, erased. The Americans who lived through the Great Depression, and subsequently World War II, saw many dreams lost or at least deferred, but for the most part, they displayed a resourcefulness and resilience that earned them the nickname the "Greatest Generation."

Susan Roth Breitzer

Further Reading

Brinkley, Alan. *Voices of Protest: Huey Long, Father Coughlin, and the Great Depression.* New York: Alfred A. Knopf, 1982. Comparative study of the lives and careers of two of the most prominent critics of the New Deal from the political fringes.

Cochrane, Thomas C. *The Great Depression and World War II, 1929-1945.* Glenview, Ill.: Scott, Foresman, 1968. Part of a larger series on the history of the United States, providing a general overview of the Great Depression and the New Deal and connecting both with World War II.

Gordon, Colin. *New Deals: Business, Labor, and Politics in America, 1920-1935.* New York: Cambridge University Press, 1994. This significant reinterpretation of the New Deal emphasizes the role of big business in shaping the direction of governmental economic planning and policy.

Himmelberg, Robert F. *The Great Depression and the New Deal.* Westport, Conn.: Greenwood Press, 2001. Part of the Greenwood Press Guides to the Historical Events of the Twentieth Century series, this book provides a general overview of the major themes, issues, and political players in the Great Depression and New Deal.

Steindl, Frank G. *Understanding Economic Recovery in the 1930s: Endogamous Propagation in the Great Depression.* Ann Arbor: University of Michigan Press, 2004. An economic history of the Great Depression that spotlights the understudied significance of economic recoveries during the 1930's.

Terkel, Studs. *Hard Times: An Oral History of the Great Depression.* New York: Pantheon Books, 1970. Classic collection of first-person reminiscences of the Great Depression.

See also Bank of United States failure; Breadlines and soup kitchens; Business and the economy in the United States; Coughlin, Charles E.; Great Depression in Canada; National Industrial Recovery Act of 1933; New Deal; Recession of 1937-1938; Roosevelt, Franklin D.; Roosevelt's first one hundred days; Unemployment in the United States.

■ Great New England hurricane

The Event Atlantic storm that devastated New England
Date September 21-22, 1938
Places Long Island, New York; New England

The Great Hurricane of 1938 was the strongest and most destructive storm ever to hit New England. The loss of lives and property exceeded that of the 1906 San Francisco earthquake and the 1871 Chicago fire. One of the most powerful natural events in recorded history; it was a disaster from which many communities never recovered.

Weather forecasters noted a storm forming in the Azores on September 4, 1938. It took the traditional path, appropriately named "Hurricane Alley," across the Atlantic, and by the night of September 16, people in Florida were warned that a hurricane was headed their way. However, the storm passed them by, and many assumed the storm would follow the usual path north and die out. As the storm began heading north, warnings were posted, and on September 21, the Washington, D.C., weather bureau downgraded the storm to a tropical disturbance.

However, a "Bermuda high" was in an unusual position, and there was a second front over the Allegheny Mountains; between the parallel systems was a valley of moist, low pressure. After four days of rain and excessive humidity, New England's weather resembled the tropics. At a noon meeting of the weather bureau, Charles Pierce, a junior forecaster, expressed concern that the storm could be funneled up the coast and into New England. Experienced forecasters said the chances of the storm striking land were one hundred to one. New England had experienced only two major hurricanes in its history, and the last had occurred more than a century before. Similarities between the 1815 hurricane and the one in 1938 were remarkable. They followed identical paths from the Azores to Long Island and made landfall within ten miles of each other. In both cases, New England was waterlogged from an excessively wet summer, and both hurricanes struck during the autumnal equinox, during high tide.

Traveling up the Atlantic coast at speeds between fifty and seventy miles per hour, the hurricane covered 425 miles in seven hours, earning the nickname the "Long Island Express." It made landfall at Patchogue, Long Island, striking with such force that it set off seismographs in Alaska. People living along the shore had no warning. The two o'clock weather advisory from Washington, D.C., had no mention of a hurricane, yet by 3:30 P.M. the storm was destroying homes and trees on Long Island. At about four o'clock the sea surged, washing houses into the sea. Long Island felt the first shock of the storm and protected most of coastal Connecticut, but eastern Connecticut and Rhode Island were in the storm's path. Oceanside towns such as Misquamicut and Napatree Point, Rhode Island, were completely obliterated. Westerly and Charlestown lost 659 homes. The storm surge forced the high tide up the Narragansett River, flooding Providence under seventeen feet of water.

Normally, once a hurricane hits land, it begins to lose its strength. However, this storm gained intensity. At 500 miles across, it was double the width of a typical hurricane. Winds were sustained at 121 miles per hour, and gusts were recorded in Milton, Massachusetts, at 186 miles per hour. The eye of the storm passed over Connecticut between Bridgeport and New Haven, then traveled up the Connecticut Valley, flooding tobacco fields and mill towns. The storm hit New Hampshire, Vermont, and upstate New York, raising the water of Lake Champlain by two feet; finally, the hurricane blew itself out in Canada the next morning.

The hurricane of 1938 could not have been prevented, but people might have had more of a chance to prepare or evacuate if they had been warned. Once the hurricane arrived, communication failed, as did power. The loss of lives is estimated at 680 people and property loss at $400 million, but there were other losses, such as centuries-old trees.

Impact   The initial impact of the hurricane was loss of lives, homes, businesses, and a way of life. People who experienced the hurricane were forever changed, as were many communities. At that time, the U.S. weather bureau lagged behind European counterparts that had pioneered methods of forecasting. The 1938 hurricane prompted advances in weather tracking and communication to guarantee that the country would never again be caught off guard by such a storm.

Marcia B. Dinneen

Further Reading

Burns, Cherie. *The Great Hurricane: 1938.* New York: Grove, 2005.

Scotti, R. A. *Sudden Sea.* Boston: Little, Brown, 2003.

See also   Labor Day hurricane; Long Beach earthquake; Natural disasters.

■ *Green Pastures, The*

Identification   Film about God's engagement with humanity

Directors   Marc Connelly and William Keighley

Date   1936

Released during the Great Migration and Harlem Renaissance, The Green Pastures *idealized both black religion and black rural life in the South as simple and pure. The film purported to provide an interior view of black spirituality. Its racial vision inspired mixed reviews: Some praised the drama as a positive portrayal of African American culture, while others criticized its assumptions about black primitivism as racist.*

The Green Pastures, like the successful Broadway play on which it was based, presents a series of scenes drawn from the Hebrew Bible in a modern, racialized setting. The film opens with Mr. Deshee (George Reed) escorting Carlisle (Philip Hurlic) and several other children to church for Sunday school. Mr. Deshee begins the Sunday school lesson by reading the genealogies recorded in Genesis to his pupils, but their questions soon lead the preacher to abandon his recitation from the text and offer an imaginative description of God and heaven instead. The remainder of the film follows De Lawd (Rex Ingram) as he interacts with the angelic inhabitants of heaven and sinful humanity on Earth.

Throughout the film, De Lawd departs from traditional Protestant conceptions of God, proving himself to be a highly improvisational and sometimes bumbling deity. He interrupts a heavenly fish fry to create the Earth in order to resolve a culinary problem. Dissatisfied with the amount of firmament in his custard, De Lawd miraculously produces more of this substance and then creates the Earth to make use of the excess. De Lawd later destroys his rebellious and sinful human subjects in the Flood and teaches Moses (Frank Wilson) magic tricks to help him free the captive Hebrews from bondage in

Actor Oscar Polk, playing archangel Gabriel, holds a child in a scene from The Green Pastures, *a 1936 film that reinterprets Old Testament tales from an African American perspective.* (Hulton Archive/Getty Images)

Egypt. De Lawd repents of his creation when he discovers human beings have fallen into flagrant sin yet again in the New Orleans- and Harlem-inspired nightclubs of Babylon. Ultimately, Hezdrel (also played by Ingram) teaches De Lawd about human faithfulness and divine mercy in an apocryphal scene. *The Green Pastures* ends with De Lawd and his angels discerning a mysterious figure on Earth who is suffering on a cross.

Marc Connelly, a white playwright and member of the Algonquin Round Table, adapted *The Green Pastures* from a local "color" tale written by Roark Bradford, titled *Ol' Man Adam an' His Chillun* (1928). He won the Pulitzer Prize in drama in 1930 for the play. Although both the stage and screen versions of *The Green Pastures* were generally well received, critics objected to the drama's romanticization of black religion and black rural life in the South. Connelly's claims to have crafted a work true to the African American perspective proved especially controversial among black intellectuals.

Impact   The vision of race and religion advanced by *The Green Pastures* profoundly shaped American culture during the 1930's and beyond. Audiences judged the film—like the play that preceded it—regarding its claims to both racial and religious authenticity. Many critics praised the film for its all-black cast and its attempt to incorporate African Americans within the framework of a biblically grounded drama. They interpreted *The Green Pastures* as a sincere tribute to black folk religion. However, others argued that the childlike representations of African Americans and the theologically conservative view of African American religion promoted within *The Green Pastures* ignored the cultural accomplishments of African Americans and narrowed the scope and complexity of African American religious life. The widespread appeal *The Green Pastures* held for its white admirers indicates the film also spoke to broader concerns about rapid black migration to the North, Jim Crow restrictions, scientific racial theories, and changing social norms. The interpretation of black religion articulated in *The Green Pastures* served as a medium in which to engage the race debates of the day.

Tammy Heise

Further Reading

Connelly, Marc. *The Green Pastures.* Madison: Wisconsin Center for Film and Theater Research/University of Wisconsin Press, 1979.

Evans, Curtis J. *The Burden of Black Religion.* New York: Oxford University Press, 2008.

Weisenfeld, Judith. *Hollywood Be Thy Name: African American Religion in American Film, 1929-1949.* Berkeley: University of California Press, 2007.

See also   Civil rights and liberties in the United States; Film; Harlem Renaissance; Jim Crow segregation; Migrations, domestic; Racial discrimination; Religion in the United States; Urbanization in the United States.

■ Greenfield Village

Identification Living history outdoor museum
Also known as Edison Institute; Henry Ford
Museum and Greenfield Village
Dates Dedicated on October 21, 1929; opened to
public on June 22, 1933
Place Dearborn, Michigan

Greenfield Village was the first open-air, outdoor village museum in the United States. The village served as a model for the development of similar museums throughout the country and remains one of the largest and most popular.

In 1929, Henry Ford, with the help of his friend Thomas Edison, dedicated Greenfield Village on the fiftieth anniversary of the invention of the incandescent light. Ford named it for the nearby town in which his wife had grown up and opened the village to the public in 1933. It contained historic buildings that had been taken from their original historical context and brought to the site in Dearborn. The buildings were typical of nineteenth century American architecture or were connected to famous Americans. Ford wanted to reproduce "American life as lived."

The village drew on well-established open-air museums in Europe, but it also reflected conditions of the Depression in the United States. Ford excluded banks, upper-class homes, and lawyers from his village to avoid discussions about bankruptcies, disclosures, and unemployment. The village idealized the rural, agricultural past, a time when people depended on themselves for employment rather than on others.

A unique feature of Greenfield was the real schools it housed from 1929 to 1969. Classes covered kindergarten through college level. The Greenfield Village Schools conformed to the standards of the Michigan State Department of Public Instruction, although the focus was on learning by doing more than reading.

By 1930, Ford was an atypical capitalist. Ford Motors remained a family firm, although it grew quite large. Greenfield Village became a retreat from protesting employees and the untrustworthy financiers and Wall Street bankers.

Impact The methods of costumed staff and craft demonstrations at Greenfield influenced other outdoor museums to adopt these educational methods.

Greenfield also represented a dramatic departure from earlier preservation efforts, which had been led by patrician elites and women.

Linda Eikmeier Endersby

Further Reading

Upward, Geoffrey C. *A Home for Our Heritage: The Building and Growth of Greenfield Village and Henry Ford Museum, 1929-1979.* Dearborn, Mich.: Henry Ford Museum Press, 1979.

Watts, Steven. *The People's Tycoon: Henry Ford and the American Century.* New York: Alfred A. Knopf, 2005.

See also Ford, Henry; Great Depression in the United States; Travel.

■ Gropius House

Identification Modernist residence designed by
Walter Gropius of the Bauhaus school
Date Built in 1937

During the 1930's, when industrial technology and mass production were becoming more prominent, Walter Gropius, the famous founder of the German Bauhaus school and master architect, built a house in Lincoln, Massachusetts. This was instrumental in bringing the revolutionary Bauhaus style of architecture to the United States.

Using mass-produced materials, the Bauhaus style, also known as the International Modern style, epitomized rationality, functionality, and economy by bringing together elements of the Arts and Crafts movement with industrial technology to produce simple, unadorned buildings. The Bauhaus school thrived in Germany from 1919 until 1933, when Adolf Hitler and the Nazi regime rose to power. The Nazis viewed the bare, basic forms of the Bauhaus as reflective of communist and Jewish influences and closed Gropius's school in 1937. After the school was shuttered, Gropius fled to England and then moved to the United States, where he became chairperson of the Harvard University Graduate School of Design and settled in Lincoln, Massachusetts.

Somewhat incongruous with its quintessential New England setting, Gropius's box-style house was built in 1937 in what was once an apple orchard. More than just a domestic dwelling, the house was an experimental model that fused traditional New England architectural elements with machine-made materials not commonly used in construction at the time. Mass-produced fittings, chrome banisters, cork floors, recessed lighting, a glass wall supported by a wood frame, and exterior floodlights coexisted with New England clapboards, brick, and fieldstone. Stark rather than ornamental, the minimalist color scheme of the house's interior featured gray, black, white, and earth tones, broken up by an occasional spot of red. The furniture fashioned by Bauhaus craftsman Marcel Breuer also embodied the functional principles of the school's aesthetic, as did artworks scattered throughout the house, many of which were created by important modernist artists.

Exterior view of the Gropius House in Lincoln, Massachusetts. (Library of Congress)

Impact The simple, utilitarian design features of the Gropius House had an enormous and long-lasting influence on American architecture. In weaving together art, craft, and technology, the house reflected one of Gropius's deeply held beliefs—that cheap, mass-produced materials could be used to provide cost-effective housing for the general population, an attractive idea during the Depression era. Gropius's legacy lived on in his students, some of whom became prominent twentieth century architects, including Philip Johnson, I. M. Pei, and Lawrence Halprin.

Pegge Bochynski

Further Reading

Ford, James, and Katherine Morrow Ford. *Classic Modern Homes of the Thirties: Sixty-four Designs of Neutra, Gropius, Breuer, Stone, and Others.* New York: Dover, 1989.

Gropius, Walter. *The New Architecture and the Bauhaus.* Cambridge, Mass.: MIT Press, 1965.

Lupger, Gilbert, and Paul Sigel. *Walter Gropius, 1883-1969: The Promoter of a New Form.* Los Angeles: Taschen, 2005.

See also Architecture; Art movements; Great Depression in the United States; Housing in the United States; Wright, Frank Lloyd.

■ *Grosjean v. American Press Co.*

The Case U.S. Supreme Court overruling of a Louisiana tax on newspapers

Date February 10, 1936

The Supreme Court determined that some state taxes on newspapers could constitute a form of prior restraint on a free press. The Court ruled that newspaper companies could be subject to nondiscriminatory economic regulation, but measures such as Louisiana's law were attempts to control the press posing as taxation. The decision reaffirmed the protections of the First Amendment despite states' rights to tax.

In July of 1934, Louisiana passed a state license tax targeting newspapers with circulations of more than twenty thousand, taxing their revenue at the rate of 2 percent on gross advertising receipts. Louisiana had 163 newspapers in publication, but only 13 were affected. Twelve of them opposed policies of former governor Huey Long, who had pushed for the measure, which was to be enforced by the state tax supervisor, Alice Lee Grosjean. Nine companies that published the 13 newspapers sought to overturn the law, alleging that the tax violated the First and Four-

Dangers of a "Fettered" Press

Below is an excerpt from the Supreme Court decision in Grosjean v. American Press Co. *written by Justice George Sutherland.*

This is not an ordinary form of tax, but one single in kind, with a long history of hostile misuse against the freedom of the press . . . The First Amendment . . . was meant to preclude the national government, and, by the Fourteenth Amendment, to preclude the states, from adopting any form of previous restraint upon printed publications, or their circulation . . . Th[is] tax . . . is bad because, in light of its history and its present setting, it is seen to be a deliberate and calculated device in the guise of a tax to limit the circulation of information to which the public is entitled in virtue of the constitutional guarantees. . . . A free press stands as one of the great interpreters between the government and the people. To allow it to be fettered is to fetter ourselves.

teenth Amendments, abridging freedom of the press and denying equal protection because smaller newspapers were not affected. The District Court of the United States for the Eastern District of Louisiana granted an injunction against collecting the tax, and the case was appealed to the U.S. Supreme Court, which heard arguments on January 14, 1936. On February 10, 1936, the Supreme Court issued its unanimous decision, finding solely on First Amendment grounds that newspapers are not immune from ordinary taxation, but that Louisiana's statute was an extraordinary measure that targeted certain newspapers.

Impact The First Amendment does more than guard against censorship prior to publication, the Court ruled, affirming that "the predominant purpose of the grant of immunity was to preserve an untrammeled press as a vital source of public information." Nonetheless, the Court's ruling has occasionally been ignored by states trying to impose comparable restrictions.

Bill Knight

Further Reading

Cortner, Richard C. *The Kingfish and the Constitution: Huey Long, the First Amendment, and the Emergence of Modern Press Freedom in America.* Westport, Conn.: Greenwood Press, 1996.

Epps, Garrett. *The First Amendment, Freedom of the Press: Its Constitutional History and the Contemporary Debate.* Amherst, N.Y.: Prometheus Books, 2008.

"Free to Print Without Taxation: Supreme Court Outlawry of Louisiana Levy on Newspaper Earnings." *Literary Digest* 121 (1936): 17.

Witt, Elder. *Congressional Quarterly's Guide to the U.S. Supreme Court.* Washington, D.C.: Congressional Quarterly, 1990.

See also Civil rights and liberties in the United States; Long, Huey; Newspapers, U.S.; Supreme Court, U.S.

■ Gross national product

Definition Measurement of the annual dollar value of the nation's production of goods and services

The concepts and measures of the gross national product (GNP) were under development during the 1930's but did not become widely used until later. However, these techniques have helped subsequent analysts understand what was going on in the United States at the time.

To measure the value of a nation's output, each product or service as it reaches the final buyer must be included. Each is valued at current market price. The value of output (nominal GNP) is equivalent to the flow of expenditures to buy that output. This flow represents aggregate demand and is, in the short run, the driving force leading output to rise or fall.

Increase in nominal GNP represents some combination of increase in output and increase in prices. The increase in output is normally a positive occurrence, raising people's potential consumption and employment. By valuing the quantity of each output by its price in a fixed base period, analysts derive measures of GNP in constant prices; this known as "real" GNP.

The GNP data indicate the catastrophic downswing of 1929-1933 with stark clarity. From the business-cycle peak value of $104 billion in 1929, nominal GNP declined steadily to $56 billion in 1933. The decline affected output and prices almost equally; each fell by about one-fourth. The decline in output translated directly into a decline in employment, so that by 1933, one-fourth of the labor force was unemployed. The decline in prices magnified the burden of debts and led to a vast increase in bankruptcies and property foreclosures.

After 1933, the economy moved into vigorous expansion, raising real output and employment rather than prices. By 1937, real output was greater than it had been in 1929. However, recovery was interrupted by a painful recession in 1937-1938. The data for 1939 show only a slight improvement over those for 1937.

The publication in 1936 of John Maynard Keynes's groundbreaking *The General Theory of Employment, Interest and Money* led economists to direct much more attention to the behavior of aggregate demand. Keynes gave special emphasis to investment spending—mainly business purchases of capital goods such as buildings, machinery, and inventories. He argued that, while consumption might be the largest component of GNP, its behavior was rather passive and it followed the stimulation pro-

Nominal and Real Gross National Product (GNP)

(billions of dollars)

Year	Nominal GNP	Real GNP	Price Index in 1929 Prices
1929	104.4	104.4	100
1933	56.0	74.2	75
1937	90.8	109.1	83
1939	91.1	111.0	82

Source: U.S. Bureau of the Census. *Historical Statistics of the United States: From Colonial Times to 1957.* Washington, D.C.: U.S. Government Printing Office, 1960, p. 139.

vided by investment spending. The seriousness of the Great Depression is well depicted in the collapse of investment spending, which fell from $17 billion in 1929 to less than $2 billion in 1933. The government's lack of success in bringing about recovery is represented by the fact that investment in 1939 was still lower than in 1929. Many New Deal measures worked to discourage private investment, notably the frequent tax-rate increases and the formation of labor unions.

Money and Velocity   As a measure of total expenditure, nominal GNP can be expressed as the quantity of money (M) multiplied by its velocity (V), where V is the average annual number of times each dollar is spent each year to buy current output. Decline in the money supply was a major cause of the great contraction of 1929-1933. Bank failures contributed to the loss of large amounts of bank deposits. Hoarding contributed to the decline in velocity. By 1937, the money supply had returned to its pre-Depression level, but velocity remained far lower, reflecting low interest rates that led the risk-averse public to hold large amounts of idle cash.

As aggregate demand fell after 1929, workers' incomes declined from $51 billion to $30 billion, dragging down their consumption spending. Business profits nearly vanished in that downswing, explaining the drop in investment spending. The recovery between 1937 and 1939 was

Important Income Components of Gross National Product (GNP)

(billions of dollars)

Component	1929	1933	1937	1939
GNP	104.4	56.0	90.8	91.1
Capital consumption	8.6	7.2	7.8	7.8
Indirect business taxes	8.0	8.6	9.4	10.5
National income	87.8	40.2	73.6	72.8
Employee compensation	51.1	29.5	47.9	48.1
Business income	24.9	3.6	18.9	17.3
Rent and interest	11.8	7.0	6.8	7.3

Source: U.S. Bureau of the Census. *Historical Statistics of the United States: From Colonial Times to 1957.* Washington, D.C.: U.S. Government Printing Office, 1960, pp. 139-141.

Disposable Personal Income, Consumption, and Personal Saving

(billions of dollars)

Year	Disposable Income	Consumption	Personal Saving	Savings Increase (percentage)
1929	83.1	79.0	4.1	4.9
1933	45.7	46.4	–0.7	–1.5
1937	71.0	67.3	3.7	5.2
1939	70.4	67.6	2.8	4.0

Source: U.S. Bureau of the Census. *Historical Statistics of the United States: From Colonial Times to 1957.* Washington, D.C.: U.S. Government Printing Office, 1960, pp. 139-141.

Note: First three columns are billions of dollars; fourth column is percentage

incomplete in part because the rise in total income went into government tax receipts instead of employee pay.

Disposable Income, Consumption, and Saving Keynes stressed the relationship between saving and investment. Saving drew money out of the expenditure flow, while investment spending put it back. After 1929, the big drop in investment spending meant that a lot of total income did not find its way back into expenditures. National-income totals were adjusted to remove personal taxes and undistributed corporate profits and to add back transfer payments. This adjustment generated data for disposable personal income—income available to spend or save. A measure of the severity of the contraction after 1929 was the fact that household savings became negative by 1933—households were spending more than their disposable incomes, by drawing down savings and borrowing. The percentage of income consumed had returned by 1937 to its 1929 level, implying that if incomes had risen more, consumption would also have risen more.

Impact Development of the United States GNP accounts, which became widely available during the 1940's, enabled economists to diagnose the Great Depression and subsequent recovery. These accounts provided the statistical parallel to Keynesian economics. By the 1940's, econometricians were us-

ing the GNP data to try to find causal interconnections, particularly between income and different types of expenditures. The GNP data verified that the downswing following 1929 reflected the decline in aggregate demand.

One conjecture as to why the different GNP components responded as they did emphasized the fact that consumers experienced a huge decline in wealth, arising from the stock market decline, the fall in the market value of housing, and the increase in the burden of debts. This accentuated the consumption decline, which would be predicted by the Keynesian "multiplier" effect. The GNP estimates also tracked the response of output and prices, which was different from the depression of 1920-1921, when price drops absorbed a much larger part of the fall in aggregate demand.

The GNP accounts and Keynesian analysis also combined to show how inappropriate were the federal government's responses under Presidents Herbert Hoover and Franklin D. Roosevelt. Both presidents pushed for higher taxes to balance the budget, cutting into household incomes and reducing business profit expectations.

The new data and theories also led to drastic change in attitudes toward monetary policy. The balanced budget and the gold standard became discredited. Emphasis shifted to demand management, built up from monetary and fiscal policies. On repeated occasions after the 1930's, momentary decreases in aggregate demand were reversed by monetary and fiscal responses, extending through the major financial crisis of 2008-2009.

Paul B. Trescott

Further Reading

Atack, Jeremy, and Peter Passell. *A New Economic View of American History from Colonial Times to 1940.* 2d ed. New York: W. W. Norton, 1994. Chapters 21 and 22 give a clear review of the causes and consequences of the Depression, relying extensively on GNP data.

Carson, Carol S. "The History of the United States National Income and Product Accounts." *Review of Income and Wealth* 21, no. 2 (June, 1975): 153-

181. Discusses how Clark Warburton invented the system of GNP accounting during the 1930's and how Simon Kuznets became a pioneer in measuring GNP.

Chandler, Lester V. *America's Greatest Depression, 1929-1941.* New York: Harper & Row, 1970. Clear and simple analysis of the causes and consequences of the Depression. Chandler uses GNP data and analysis extensively.

Historical Statistics of the United States: Earliest Times to the Present. New York: Cambridge University Press, 2006. Includes readable review of national income accounting. Extensive GNP data.

Trescott, Paul B. *Money, Banking and Economic Welfare.* New York: McGraw-Hill, 1960. The description and analysis of the Depression presented in chapter 16 is centered around the GNP and its components.

See also Business and the economy in the United States; *General Theory of Employment, Interest and Money, The*; Great Depression in the United States; Housing in the United States; Income and wages in the United States; Recession of 1937-1938; Revenue Acts.

■ Group Theatre

Identification   Theater company that introduced method acting
Date   Established in the summer of 1931
Place   New York, New York

The Group Theatre presented contemporary plays with social significance while also refining an American style of acting through its dissemination of Stanislavski-based acting, which evolved into method acting.

The Group Theatre was formed in New York City in 1931 by Lee Strasberg, Harold Clurman, and Cheryl Crawford. Wishing to have a "no-star" system, the Group Theatre was composed of twenty-eight actors, directors, playwrights, and producers banded together to produce plays they felt had immediate social impact. They produced new works throughout most of the 1930's, among them 1933's *Men in White*, which later won the Pulitzer Prize for Drama, and Clifford Odets's *Awake and Sing!* (1935), *Golden Boy* (1937), and *Waiting for Lefty* (1935).

Members of the Group Theatre, and Strasberg in particular, studied with famous Russian acting teacher Constantin Stanislavski. Upon returning to the United States, Strasberg refined Stanislavski's system into something called the method, whose basic tenets are that an actor must draw upon both sense and affective memory to best portray another character. The Group Theatre popularized this internal approach to acting throughout its productions, and Strasberg opened his own actor training school, the Actors Studio, to develop it further.

During the Group Theatre's heyday in the mid-to-late 1930's, the organization included notable stage and film stars Elia Kazan, Stella Adler, Will Geer, John Randolph, Odets, Sanford Meisner, and Lee J. Cobb. Despite the group's impact on American theater, the war, financial struggles, the beckoning of Hollywood, and interper-

Actor Stella Adler (left) and playwright Clifford Odets, key members of the Group Theatre, at London's Paddington Station in 1938. (Hulton Archive/Getty Images)

sonal frictions led to the disbanding of the company in the spring of 1941. Its influence continues to be felt in acting programs and conservatories across the United States.

Impact Through both its productions and its adherence to the method, the Group Theatre changed American actor training forever. Its members taught the method's emotional and internal-based tenets to the following generation of actors and acting teachers, and it remains the most prevalent actor-training technique in the United States. The group also worked with artists who went on to shape Hollywood and the American film industry.

Tom Smith

Further Reading

Clurman, Harold. *The Fervent Years: The Group Theatre and the Thirties.* New York: Da Capo Press, 1983.

Hull, S. Loraine. *Strasberg's Method as Taught by Lorrie Hull: A Practical Guide for Actors, Teachers, Directors.* New York: Hull-Smithers, 2004.

Smith, Wendy. *Real Life Drama.* New York: Grove Press, 1994.

See also *Awake and Sing!*; Federal Theatre Project; Film; Odets, Clifford; Theater in the United States.

■ Grovey v. Townsend

The Case U.S. Supreme Court ruling on voting rights of African Americans in Texas

Dates Argued on March 11, 1935; decided on April 1, 1935

The U.S. Supreme Court determined that the Texas Democratic Party had the right to prohibit black people from voting in the state's Democratic Party primary election. This decision was based upon the fact that the Democratic Party had established itself as a nongovernmental, private, whites-only organization. This court decision was a major setback for the civil rights movement in the South and the entire United States.

For many years, the Democratic Party was the dominant party in Texas; the candidate who won the Democratic primary election was a virtual shoo-in to win the general election. The Democratic Party attempted to use several strategies to exclude black people from voting in its primaries. These strategies were all turned down by the Supreme Court because they violated the Fourteenth Amendment's equal-protection clause and the Fifteenth Amendment's nondiscrimination-in-right-to-vote clause of the U.S. Constitution. In the *Grovey* case, the Texas Democratic Party established itself as a private, all-white organization. Then, the party allowed only members of the private organization to vote in its primary elections.

R. R. Grovey, a black man, sued because he was not allowed to vote in the Texas Democratic Party primary election. The Supreme Court ruled nine to zero against Grovey on the theory that the constitutional amendments applied to governmental organizations but not to private organizations. In 1944, the Grovey decision was overturned by the *Smith v. Allwright* case.

Impact The *Grovey v. Townsend* decision was a major setback for the civil rights movement in the United States. Many people decried the ruling. However, other people, particularly in the South, were highly supportive of the decision. For years, they had attempted to disenfranchise black voters. They thought the *Grovey* decision provided a legal method for doing this. The *Smith v. Allwright* decision overturned the *Grovey* decision and facilitated black people voting in state primary elections.

David M. Brown

Further Reading

Levey, M. L. "The Texas White Primary Cases." *Thurgood Marshall Law Review* (Spring, 2008).

Stephenson, D. Grier. *The Right to Vote: Rights and Liberties Under the Law.* Santa Barbara, Calif.: ABC-Clio, 2004.

See also African Americans; *Nixon v. Condon*; Racial discrimination; Supreme Court, U.S.

■ Gunther, John

Identification American author and journalist

Born August 30, 1901; Chicago, Illinois

Died May 29, 1970; New York, New York

Gunther's series of "Inside" books, begun with Inside Europe *in 1936, provided general readers with insightful overviews of the history and geography of the rest of the world, with information gleaned from interviews with everyone from average citizens to business and political leaders.*

As a well-known international correspondent for the *Chicago Daily News* and the London *Daily News* during the 1920's and 1930's, John Gunther was well positioned to undertake the lengthy project that became the "Inside" books. The series that eventually covered Asia, Latin America, the United States, Africa, Russia, and South America began with the five-hundred-page *Inside Europe* in 1936. Gunther was stationed in Vienna from 1930 to 1935, and in London during 1935-1936, with temporary assignments in Berlin, Moscow, Rome, Paris, and other cities. He was an experienced researcher and interviewer, and he was both a holistic and a detail-oriented thinker. With his insider's perspective, his was an important voice, warning Americans of the dangers posed by Adolf Hitler, Benito Mussolini, and Joseph Stalin.

Inside Europe was an instant international success, and it made Gunther both famous and respected. He became something of an informal counselor to Winston Churchill and Franklin D. Roosevelt, as well as an official enemy of the Gestapo. The success of *Inside Europe* enabled Gunther to quit newspaper reporting and to spend much of 1937 and 1938 preparing *Inside Asia* (1939), the second book in his series. That same year he also published *The High Cost of Hitler.*

Impact　During the approach to World War II, *Inside Europe* was an important source of information for readers trying to decipher what was happening on the continent. The book was updated in 1938 and 1939; a fourth edition, which included a major rewriting that reflected the influence of Hitler's Germany, was released in 1940. It provides a fascinating look at attitudes during the prelude to war.

Cynthia A. Bily

Further Reading

Cuthbertson, Ken. *Inside: The Biography of John Gunther.* Chicago: Bonus Books, 1992.

Gunther, John. *A Fragment of Autobiography: The Fun of Writing the Inside Books.* New York: Harper & Row, 1962.

Pridmore, Jay. *John Gunther: Inside Journalism.* Chicago: University of Chicago Library, 1990.

See also　Asia; Europe; Germany and U.S. appeasement; Newspapers, U.S.; Roosevelt, Franklin D.; Soviet Union.

■ Guthrie, Woody

Identification　American folk singer and songwriter

Born　July 12, 1912; Okemah, Oklahoma

Died　October 3, 1967; Queens, New York

Guthrie is widely considered one of the founding fathers of American folk music and arguably represents the genre's most important figure from the first half of the twentieth century. Guthrie's influence as a songwriter and interpreter and his significant contribution of original folk songs greatly impacted the folk revival of the 1960's and continue to dominate folk music into the twenty-first century.

Woodrow Wilson "Woody" Guthrie was the third child of Charley Guthrie, a local politician and land speculator in the oil boomtown of Okemah, Oklahoma, and Nora. Early in his life, Guthrie was plagued by a series of economic and medical hardships that affected his family, including several fires, the death of his younger sister Clara, and his mother's struggle with the symptoms of undiagnosed Huntington's disease. Throughout these formative years, Guthrie was exposed to music though folk songs introduced by his mother, his own desire to learn the harmonica, and the union songs he absorbed while listening to the leftist politics of his father and uncle.

In 1927, a kerosene fire injured Guthrie's father gravely, and this event marked a significant change in young Guthrie's life. His father left the family and moved to Pampa, Texas; his mother was committed to the state hospital for the insane in Normal, Oklahoma; and Guthrie, then age fifteen, was left to fend for himself.

Guthrie lived with family and embarked on the first of what became a lifetime of extended hitchhiking and train-hopping hobo trips across the country. In 1929, he reunited with his father in Pampa, working odd jobs and studying guitar with his uncle Jeff Guthrie. In Pampa, Guthrie began his first serious musical endeavors, forming the Corncob Trio and later joining the Pampa Junior Chamber of Commerce Band. Music was not Guthrie's only inspiration, and his creativity spread to drawing, painting, and writing.

Guthrie wrote approximately one thousand songs, and his activities as a songwriter began in earnest during 1932. Despite marrying Mary Jennings in 1933 and welcoming his first child, Gwendolyn Gail,

Folk singer Woody Guthrie, who gave voice to many disillusioned by the economic and social conditions brought on by the Great Depression. (AP/Wide World Photos)

in 1935, Guthrie drew inspiration for his songwriting from the hardships of the people and places he encountered throughout his life and travels. In particular, Guthrie was drawn to natural disasters such as the drought and subsequent dust storms that devastated subsistence farming across the Great Plains. During this time, Guthrie wrote "So Long It's Been Good to Know Yuh," which became a de facto anthem for the displaced victims of the storm.

After five years of domesticity, Guthrie took to the road again in 1936, finally settling in California. In Los Angeles, he connected with his cousin, and the two launched the *Oklahoma and Woody* show in 1937, which was broadcast on local radio stations. Guthrie's cousin left the duo and was replaced by singer Maxine Crissman, who carried the stage name "Lefty Lou." The *Woody and Lefty Lou* show was popular with relocated Dust Bowl migrants, also known as "Okies," scattered throughout California's agricultural areas. Guthrie began writing songs directed at this poor and disenfranchised audience.

Despite the show's success, a restless Guthrie resigned in late 1938, left his family, and once again began traveling the country. By late 1938, Guthrie's reputation began to grow and his songs, including "Pretty Boy Floyd" and "Vigilante Man," had assumed an increasingly political tone, a trend that continued into the 1940's. Moreover, in 1939, Guthrie took his political expression one step further and started writing a column in the communist newspaper *People's World.*

Impact   As a songwriter and cultural icon, Guthrie had a wide-ranging impact on the American musical landscape of the twentieth century. His songwriting style of infusing political rhetoric into accessible lyrics has become a stylistic benchmark for the genre. Despite decades of inactivity, due in large part to his own bout with Huntington's disease, Guthrie was deeply influential to the folk revival of the 1960's, and his songs propelled the careers of artists such as Bob Dylan and Joan Baez. Many of his songs, such as "This Land Is Your Land" and "Do Re Mi," became genre standards and American cultural anthems.

Andrew R. Martin

Further Reading

Guthrie, Woody. *Bound for Glory.* New York: Plume, 1983.

Jackson, Mark Allan. *Prophet Singer: The Voice and Vision of Woody Guthrie.* Jackson: University Press of Mississippi, 2007.

Yurchenco, H. *A Mighty Hard Road: The Woody Guthrie Story.* New York: McGraw-Hill, 1970.

See also   Communism; Dust Bowl; Leadbelly; Music: Popular; Recording industry; Robeson, Paul; Socialist parties.

H

Hague v. Congress of Industrial Organizations

The Case   U.S. Supreme Court ruling protecting the right of organizations to meet and distribute printed matter in public places

Date   June 5, 1939

The decision lent support to labor unions but more broadly held that local officials could reasonably regulate, but could not arbitrarily stop, public gatherings for the exchange of ideas merely out of disapproval of the ideas presented.

Jersey City, New Jersey, had an ordinance requiring the sponsors of public meetings in parks, on sidewalks, or in other public spaces to obtain permits from the chief of police. The ordinance imposed similar restraints on the distribution of leaflets or other printed materials and was used aggressively against labor unions denounced by Mayor Frank Hague as communist.

When a federal district court enjoined enforcement, the city appealed to the Supreme Court. With two justices not participating in the case and two more in dissent, the majority upheld the injunction but split on the reasons. The plurality argued that the streets and parks are held in trust for the use of the public and may be used for purposes of assembly, communicating thoughts among citizens, and discussing public questions. Protection of the public peace might require reasonable regulation of the use of such public spaces, but such regulation could not be a pretext for an absolute ban on free-speech activities.

Impact   The decision established the doctrine of the public forum, holding that governments were obligated to set aside public spaces for citizens to gather and to exchange ideas. This doctrine was refined during the civil rights protests of the 1960's and remains a staple of First Amendment law.

John C. Hughes

Further Reading

Bollinger, Lee C. *The Tolerant Society.* New York: Oxford University Press, 1986.

Farber, Daniel A. *The First Amendment.* New York: Foundation Press, 1998.

Lewis, Anthony. *Freedom for the Thought That We Hate: A Biography of the First Amendment.* New York: Basic Books, 2007.

Smolla, Rodney A. *Free Speech in an Open Society.* New York: Random House, 1992.

See also   Civil rights and liberties in the United States; Congress of Industrial Organizations; Supreme Court, U.S.; Unionism.

Hairstyles

Female hairstyles of the 1930's incorporated an elegance that was absent from the boyish styles of the 1920's. Both women and men kept their hair close to the head in clean, stylish lines consistent with the sophisticated dress of the day. Waves and curls were the fashion of the day for women, who could emulate their favorite stars with little cost.

Though most women were unable to afford the current styles of clothing during the 1930's, they could approximate the hairstyles of their favorite stars. As Hollywood became an American center of fashion, the hairstyles of the stars were copied by ladies locally and abroad. Claudette Colbert's short and curled bangs were widely imitated. Greta Garbo's bob haircut influenced the many versions of this adaptable hairstyle. Women began to part their hair and wave or curl it down to their shoulders. The long bob was created by pinning up the front and sides, while leaving the back loose or curled under, which was reminiscent of a long, pageboy hairstyle. Gone were the shorn, boyish bobs of the 1920's; these were replaced by artfully dressed feminine coiffure. The longer shingled bobs were carefully styled with finger waves or artfully arranged in flat pin curls.

Woman with a wavy hairstyle popular during the 1930's. (Retrofile/ Getty Images)

Women who chose to wear their hair longer kept it shoulder length and trained into soft waves on the nape of the neck or curled around the neckline. The longer hair also allowed for rolls at the back of the neck or small chignons at the nape. Upswept hair was also trendy. For evening, women often smoothed the front of the hair and carefully curled it at the nape of the neck, or they brushed upward and curled the hair at the crown of the head.

Sales of peroxide skyrocketed when Jean Harlow appeared as a platinum blond in *Hell's Angels* (1930). To create the super-blond look, layers of peroxide were applied to the hair until the desired lightness was achieved. Ladies with grey hair often used home rinses to give the hair a blue or mauve hue. The stigma attacked to dying one's hair was gone. Many advances had been made in dying agents, and the U.S. Food and Drug Administration certified many colorings and perm chemicals. A great number of dyes, rinses, and colors were available for use in both salons and the home.

To help create these hairstyles, women could perm their hair, which helped hold curls. With the aid of setting lotions, women were able to set their hair without the use of falls or additional hairpieces. Home catalogs—such as Sears, Roebuck and Company's—sold a wide variety of curlers, wave combs, and aids for creating up-to-date hairstyles.

In response to the impending world war, around 1938, magazines started pushing a "factory" look. Hair was pinned up and hidden under scarves, safely put away, or net snoods were worn to contain the hair, while curls fell from the sides. The lacquered pompadour also had a resurgence with women at this time, which eliminated the time-consuming waves and curls.

Men's hair was worn short and smoothed with hair oil. Any natural wave was allowed to show. Hair was brushed back from the forehead, creating a slightly raised front. Brushing the hair from the sides toward the back to create a blunt point was also popular. During the late 1930's, men's hair was normally not parted and was cut to contour to the shape of the head. By 1939, creating slightly raised wings by brushing the hair up from the temples was popular.

For the most part, men were clean shaven in the early 1930's. Mustaches were out of style for all but the older, conservative set. During the mid-1930's, both beards and mustaches started to become acceptable again.

Young girls copied the hair of Judy Garland and Shirley Temple, who wore long curls, or ringlets. A styling product marketed at girls, called Curly Top, claimed to encourage the hair to curl. Young boys copied the hairstyles of men. Curls were cut off, and hair was kept short.

Impact Hairstyles of the 1930's revived elegance. Women, especially, enjoyed the long, artful hairstyles, forgoing the shorn styles of previous years. Advancements in hair-styling products helped to bring about new, carefully arranged styles. These safer products continued to influence hairstyles after the 1930's.

Hannah Schauer Galli

Further Reading

Blum, Stella, ed. *Everyday Fashions of the Thirties as Pictured in Sears Catalogs.* New York: Dover, 1986.

Costantino, Maria. *Fashions of a Decade: The 1930s.* New York: Chelsea House, 2007.

Robinson, Julian. *Fashion in the '30's.* London: Oresko Books, 1987.

Wilcox, R. Turner. *The Mode in Hats and Headress: Including Hair Styles, Cosmetics, and Jewelry.* New York: Charles Scribner's Sons, 1959.

See also   Fads; Fashions and clothing; Garbo, Greta; Harlow, Jean; Magazines; Temple, Shirley.

■ Haiti occupation

The Event   End of American military occupation of the Caribbean nation of Haiti

Date   Last American troops left August 15, 1934

Place   Haiti

The withdrawal of U.S. troops from Haiti signaled the temporary end of an era of American intervention in the domestic affairs of Latin American nations. Through the 1930's, the United States sought to use beneficial trade agreements instead of "gunboat diplomacy" to maintain influence.

The U.S. occupation of Haiti began in July, 1915, following the assassination of the president of Haiti. U.S. president Woodrow Wilson sent the Marines into Haiti to restore order and protect American interests. The United States formulated the Haitian-American Treaty of 1915, in which the United States was given the right to intervene in Haiti at any time and control over the economy of Haiti. The occupation lasted from 1915 until 1934, when President Franklin D. Roosevelt withdrew the last of the Marines from the island nation.

Prior to Roosevelt's election, Haitians had begun to demonstrate for greater independence from the United States. Workers and students engaged in mass protests and were met by violence from U.S. troops. Following an incident in late 1929, President Herbert Hoover set up a commission to investigate the situation in Haiti. The commission found that the majority of Haitians wanted

the United States to end the occupation. The commission recommended that the United States withdraw its forces, and negotiations with the newly elected Haitian government began.

Before the troops could be withdrawn, Roosevelt was elected president. He propagated what became known as the Good Neighbor Policy, essentially stating that the United States would not intervene or interfere in Latin American nations. The concept was welcomed throughout Latin America. The United States began to remove troops from Haiti in an effort to restore sovereignty. Finally, on August 15, 1934, the last of the Marines left Haiti. The United States left behind what they believed to be a bulwark of democracy and order in Haiti.

During the occupation, the United States controlled Haiti's economy, ensuring that debts to other nations were paid. Additionally, U.S. troops trained a Haitian national guard and formed it into an effective police force. One Marine wrote that the United States enabled Haiti to have its first election in years in which the sitting president and the newly elected president each attended the inauguration ceremony without violence.

Impact   The end of the U.S. occupation of Haiti was a tangible representation of the Good Neighbor Policy. However, immediately after announcing the policy, Roosevelt sent an official to interfere in the domestic affairs of Cuba. Though U.S. forces left Haiti, the U.S. maintained supervision over Haiti's econ-

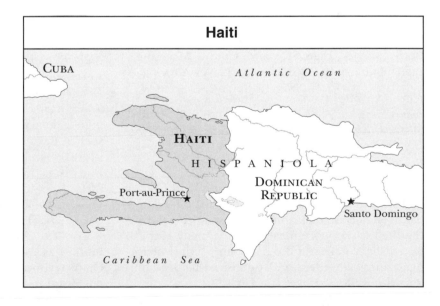

omy until 1942. A by-product of the U.S. control of the Haitian economy was that the majority of domestic societal issues were ignored in order to remove or reduce the debts Haiti owed to other nations. However, orienting Haiti's economy toward paying its debts made the country unable to provide the social structures it needed to support and improve the lives of its people. Also, most Americans stationed in Haiti believed that they helped to provide Haiti with a sustainable and functional government. However, for decades after the United States left, Haiti remained in turmoil with numerous coups, and the United States sent troops back into Haiti in 1994 to restore peace.

Michael W. Cheek

Further Reading

Langley, Lester D. *The Banana Wars: United States Intervention in the Caribbean, 1898-1934.* Wilmington, Del.: Scholarly Resources, 2002.

Renda, Mary A. *Taking Haiti: Military Occupation and the Culture of U.S. Imperialism, 1915-1940.* Chapel Hill: University of North Carolina Press, 2001.

Schmidt, Hans R. *The United States Occupation of Haiti, 1915-1934.* New Brunswick, N.J.: Rutgers University Press, 1995.

See also Butler, Smedley; Good Neighbor Policy; Great Depression in the United States; Latin America and the Caribbean; Roosevelt, Franklin D.

■ Hammett, Dashiell

Identification   American detective-fiction writer
Born   May 27, 1894; St. Mary's County, Maryland
Died   January 10, 1961; New York, New York

Hammett created the hard-boiled detective genre with his novels, specifically The Maltese Falcon *(1930) and* Red Harvest *(1929), turning from the more intellectual mystery genre previously published while introducing a more urban culture to the mystery-reading public.*

After contracting tuberculosis during World War I and leaving his employment with a national detective agency, Dashiell Hammett began writing during the 1920's to support himself and his family. He published short stories in the many pulp, crime-fiction magazines of the era and published his first full-length novel, *Red Harvest*, in 1929.

Dashiell Hammett. (Library of Congress)

By 1930, Hammett had gained a significant following as the result of the novels that focused on the Continental Op, a character based on Hammett's experience working for the Pinkerton National Detective Agency. He decided to introduce a new character, Sam Spade, in his most influential work, *The Maltese Falcon.* Spade also appeared in three short stories, published in pulp magazines, but *The Maltese Falcon* was the only novel in which Spade appeared. *The Maltese Falcon* became the quintessential hard-boiled detective novel, influencing other authors such as Raymond Chandler. The book was adapted into a film in 1931, starring Ricardo Cortez and Bebe Daniels, and into a lighter and comedic film, *Satan Met a Lady*, in 1936, before it was adapted into the Humphrey Bogart classic in 1941.

In 1931, Hammett published his favorite of all his works, *The Glass Key*. The protagonist, Ned Beaumont, was modeled closely on Hammett himself; characteristics that he shared with Hammett were a tall and thin physique, tuberculosis, and a propensity for gambling. Like other novels published during the Great Depression, *The Glass Key* emphasized the role of luck in life. It focused on an investigation of the death of a senator's son and, like many of Hammett's other novels, was also adapted for film, first in 1935 and again in 1942. Like Sam Spade in *The Maltese Falcon*, Ned Beaumont did not appear in any additional novels Hammett published.

Hammett published his final novel, *The Thin Man*, in 1934, featuring the detective couple Nick and Nora Charles. He based the characters on himself and his lover, Lillian Hellman; the characters share witty banter and consume large quantities of alcohol during the course of their investigation. No one is quite sure why Hammett retired as a writer after this novel, but *The Thin Man* was adapted into a film that same year, featuring Myrna Loy and William Powell, and went on to spawn a film series.

After retiring from writing, Hammett began to focus on politics. Vehemently antifascist, he joined the Communist Party USA in 1937 and devoted the rest of his life to political activism. His involvement with communism led him to be blacklisted by the House Committee on Un-American Activities during the 1950's.

Though Hammett had married and had two daughters, he divorced his wife, Josephine, a split caused primarily by their enforced separation because of his tuberculosis. He had an affair with author Nell Martin from 1929 to 1930 and dedicated *The Glass Key* to her. After ending that relationship, he engaged in the relationship with Hellman, which lasted from 1931 until his death.

Impact   Hammett introduced a new kind of detective fiction to the United States, one that focused less on the intellectual musings of detectives, as seen in such characters as Sherlock Holmes, and more upon the hard work and difficulties inherent in investigating crimes. He also introduced the seedy side of urban culture to a predominantly rural population. His depictions of the hard-boiled detective have influenced mystery writers ever since.

Emily Carroll Shearer

Further Reading

Gregory, Sinda. *Private Investigations: The Novels of Dashiell Hammett*. Carbondale: Southern Illinois University Press, 1985.

Johnson, Diane. *Dashiell Hammett: A Life*. New York: Random House, 1983.

Layman, Richard. *Dashiell Hammett*. Detroit: Gale Group, 2000.

_____. *Shadow Man: The Life of Dashiell Hammett*. New York: Harcourt Brace Jovanovich, 1981.

See also   Communism; Great Depression in the United States; Hellman, Lillian; Literature in the United States; *Thin Man, The*.

■ "Happy Days Are Here Again"

Identification   Popular song identified with President Franklin D. Roosevelt
Composers   Jack Yellen and Milton Ager
Date   Copyrighted in 1929

"Happy Days Are Here Again" became synonymous with the hope inspired by the administration of Franklin D. Roosevelt. First used early in his 1932 presidential campaign, the song represented the optimism of Roosevelt's unique ideas and active stance in combating the Great Depression. The song became a standard after 1932 at the quadrennial Democratic National Convention until replaced by Bill Clinton in 1992.

"Happy Days Are Here Again" was a collaboration between lyricist Jack Yellen and composer Milton Ager written and published in 1929. Ben Selvin and His Orchestra first recorded it February 3, 1930, for Columbia-American Records; however, it was recorded by many of the best-known artists of the era. In was first featured in film as the finale in Charles Reisner's *Chasing Rainbows* (1930) and was subsequently used in thirty-eight additional films throughout the decade. The refrain of the song was also the theme to radio shows sponsored by Lucky Strike cigarettes.

Typical of a Tin Pan Alley popular song, "Happy Days Are Here Again" is a mostly strophic song in a 4/4 time signature. Although the introduction starts in minor, the song quickly progresses to major. The bouncy rhythm and upbeat lyrics, as well as the accompaniment, reminiscent of those typically used in polka and drinking songs, contribute to the mood of the song.

Impact   Listed forty-seventh on the Recording Industry of America and the National Endowment for the Arts Songs of the Century list, "Happy Days Are Here Again" is one of the most popular songs to originate in the twentieth century. It has been recorded many times and continues to invoke the feelings of exuberant hope exemplified by Roosevelt, the New Deal, and the return of good times.

Amanda M. Pence

Further Reading

Brylawski, Samuel S. "Ager, Milton." In *The New Grove Dictionary of Music and Musicians*, edited by Stanley Sadie and John Tyrrell. New York: Oxford University Press, 2004.

Neal, Steve. *Happy Days Are Here Again: The 1932 Democratic Convention, the Emergence of FDR—and How America Was Changed Forever.* Waterville, Maine: Thorndike Press, 2004.

See also   Elections of 1932, U.S.; Music: Popular; New Deal; Recording industry; Roosevelt, Franklin D.

■ *Harlem on the Prairie*

Identification   Musical film with an all-African American cast
Director   Sam Newfield
Date   1937

Harlem on the Prairie is known as the first B-musical Western starring an all-African American cast. It was publicized as the first black film to play in a first-run theater.

Although there had been Westerns with all-black casts in silent films, the 1937 African American musical Western *Harlem on the Prairie* was presumably the first of its kind. It starred the tall, handsome, Detroit-born, baritone singer Herbert Jeffrey, who was later sometimes billed as Herb Jeffries. The film was produced by Associated Features and was shot on a dude ranch in the high desert of Southern California.

As was the common practice with African American films in those days, the director, Sam Newfield, and all of the production executives were white. The producer, Jed Buell, may have codirected the film as well. Also common practice was for the word "Harlem" to be inserted in titles of all-black films. Jeffrey played the hero, Jeff Kincaid. Of mixed parentage, Jeffrey was light-skinned and could easily portray Latino characters. As was sometimes done, darkening makeup was applied to make him look more African American, and he almost always wore a hat onscreen to conceal his straight, light-brown hair.

Comic relief in the film was supplied by the stage and vaudeville star Flournoy Miller and comedian Mantan Moreland, later better known as the chauffeur Birmingham Brown in many Charlie Chan films. Miller was also credited with adapting the script from one of his own specialty pieces. Also in the cast was Spencer Williams, an actor and director whose later fame came as Andy in the television series *Amos 'n' Andy*. The de rigueur musical interludes were supplied by the musical group The Four Tones, the female lead was played by Connie Harris, and the menacing gangster villain was Maceo Sheffield. The plot involved the search for a cache of hidden gold that had been stolen by a gang of outlaws.

Though *Harlem on the Prairie* was a short feature film, it managed to incorporate comedy; music, including the title song and the popular "Romance in the Rain"; horseback chases; and gunfights. The film was originally intended to be released mainly in the South, where numerous theaters showed so-called race films, that is, those intended for black audiences only. However, cowboy-actor Gene Autry supposedly arranged to have Sack Amusement Enterprises distribute the film to a wider audience.

Because the rights to the lead character's name were held by the original production company, Jeffrey played Bob Blake in the three remaining installments in the series: *Two-Gun Man from Harlem* (1938), *The Bronze Buckaroo* (1939), and *Harlem Rides the Range* (1939). Apparently, more films had been planned for the series, but they were never made. Jeffrey went on to have a noted singing career with the Duke Ellington Band, and he had a major hit in 1941 with the ballad "Flamingo," his theme song for many years. Other successful recordings of Jeffrey included "Angel Eyes" and "Satin Doll."

Impact   Although *Harlem on the Prairie* broke no new ground in the Western genre in terms of production values or plot, it is significant as the first all-black musical Western. Its reach extended beyond African American audiences of the day to the wider audiences who flocked to these bottom-of-the-bill "horse operas."

Roy Liebman

Further Reading

Berry, S. Toriano, and Venise T. Berry. *The Fifty Most Influential Black Films: A Celebration of African-American Talent.* New York: Citadel Press/Kensington, 2001.

Green, Douglas B. *Singing Cowboys*. Salt Lake City, Utah: Gibbs Smith, 2006.

Sampson, Henry. *Blacks in Black and White: A Source Book on Black Films*. Metuchen, N.J.: Scarecrow Press, 1997.

See also African Americans; Charlie Chan films; Film; McDaniel, Hattie; Western films.

■ Harlem Renaissance

The Event Significant era in African American cultural and artistic history

Dates 1918-1937

The Harlem Renaissance marks a period that paradoxically venerated both intellectualism and the working class. The early years brought an onslaught of African American publications, dramatic productions, and musical innovations, while the last decade generated strong philosophical commentaries that shaped later political and literary movements.

The Harlem Renaissance, also referred to as the New Negro movement or the Black Literary Renaissance, began around 1918 and lasted approximately two decades. It was an era when African American philosophers, politicians, writers, and artists became recognized by the world. Important publications in 1930 included S. Randolph Edmonds's *Shades and Shadows*, Charles S. Johnson's *The Negro in American Civilization: A Study of Negro Life and Race Relations*, James Weldon Johnson's *Black Manhattan*, and Langston Hughes's *Not Without Laughter*. The Harlem Renaissance's artistic output during the 1930's also included the production of *The Green Pastures* (1931), a Broadway musical with an all-African American cast.

Philosophy and Politics In the early years of the Harlem Renaissance, artists and writers sought to create "high" cultural works, often ignoring the stories of the common people. However, during the 1930's, with the problems caused by the Great Depression, the focus turned to raising the status of the working class. As the government implemented programs to help poverty-stricken Americans, leaders of the Harlem Renaissance recognized that black citizens were not included in the aid. Because the Republican Party refused to acknowledge the needs of these citizens, large numbers of African American began to desert the party.

A number of key Harlem Renaissance figures joined the communist and Marxist parties and promoted their political ideas as necessary for African Americans to gain recognition as equal citizens. One important idea of this group was that the early participants of the Harlem Renaissance had fully accepted and participated in racial compromise by following the dictates of white publishers and patrons. In June, 1932, a group of twenty young African Americans, including Hughes, set sail for the Soviet Union with the intent of making a film about the black experience in the United States beginning from the days of slavery. The intended title for the uncompleted film was *Black and White*.

The Federal Writers' Project, funded in 1935 by Franklin D. Roosevelt's New Deal, was a program that encouraged writers during the Great Depression. The program employed a number of Harlem Renaissance writers, including Claude McKay, Zora Neale Hurston, Margaret Walker, Dorothy West, Frank Yerby, Richard Wright, and Ralph Ellison. Many of the writers used the jobs provided to promote their own political agendas, focusing primarily on socialist and communist ideals.

Literature Figures in the literary world of the 1930's included George S. Schuyler, McKay, Countée Cullen, and Hurston. Schuyler's works *Black No More* (1931) and *Slaves Today: A Story of Liberia* (1931) are satires on the issue of race in American life, and characters were often recognizable figures from the previous decade. McKay was a Jamaican immigrant whose works during the 1930's include the short story collection *Gingertown* (1932) and novel *Banana Bottom* (1933). In *Banana Bottom*, his last novel, he confronts the racial problems inherent in Jamaican culture. Cullen's *One Way to Heaven* (1932) and *The Medea and Other Poems* (1935) share the division between self and society that Cullen, who had been a teen during the Jim Crow period, dealt with much of his life. Hurston was one of the most prolific writers of the decade. Her career during the 1930's included the novels *Jonah's Gourd Vine* (1934) and *Their Eyes Were Watching God* (1937), the folklore collection *Mules and Men* (1935), and an anthropological study, *Tell My Horse* (1938). She closed the decade with *Man of the Mountain* (1939). Hurston is known for strong characterization, African American vernacular, and confrontation of issues of race and class.

The idea of high culture that was popular in the first decade of the Harlem Renaissance was less appealing to writers after 1935. The change in direction began as early as 1933, when Sterling A. Brown, a poet and professor at Howard University, argued against the stereotypes that many of the earlier popular African American writers had borrowed from white tradition. His contention against lifeless African American writing was part of an emerging intellectual trend that urged black writers to craft their own style and expectations.

Three writers whose works reflected these ideals included Hughes, Wright, and Ellison. Hughes, who is known mostly for his poetry, centered his work on the plight of the lower class. His use of African American dialect, lower-class experience, and the ugly side of African American life affirmed the equality of African Americans. Hughes used religion and folklore as the basis for much of his poetry, introducing a combination of jazz and blues into the genre. His works during the decade include four volumes of poetry. In the middle of the decade, Wright wrote that the main flaw of his predecessors was that they had not acknowledged the problems of working-class African Americans. His works during the 1930's were mostly nonfiction, but he did write a number of short stories toward the end of the decade, including the collection *Uncle Tom's Children* (1938). His novels of the 1940's reflect the political influences from the 1930's. Strongly swayed by Wright's philosophies, Ellison also began writing nonfiction and short fiction during the 1930's, beginning his fiction career with the publication of a short story titled "Heine's Bull" in 1937. In the last few years of the decade, he focused his writing on African American folklore. The issue of ethnic identity induced both Ellison and Wright to write strong novels in the following years.

Decline of the Harlem Renaissance   Although the end of the Harlem Renaissance resulted from a variety of events, including the Great Depression, historian David Levering Lewis suggests that the March 19, 1935, riot on Lennox Avenue was the terminal point. This riot—which ended with deaths and hospitalizations of, and jail time for, many African Americans—followed a 1934 announcement by African American socialites Roscoe and Clara Bruce

that it was time to discontinue the written fight. However, many historians feel the movement continued through the end of the decade.

Harlem intellectuals had hoped this period would provide a link between African Americans and Caucasians through an interest and ability in the arts. However, despite the progress made during the years of the Harlem Renaissance, some see it as the expression of socially powerless African Americans. In the following years, the importance of its advancements were often disregarded even by those who contributed during its highest points.

Impact   The Harlem Renaissance was an era of prolific work by African Americans. Seminal figures emerged during the time, and their work, though discounted and even forgotten for a time, has greatly influenced the work of later African American writers. In the second decade of the period, African American writers harshly critiqued the works of the early Harlem Renaissance writers. This group forged an angry literary tradition that laid the foundations for some of the strong writings of the Civil Rights movement and gave rise to the powerful forms used by African American writers in the later years of the twentieth century.

Theresa L. Stowell

Further Reading

Carroll, Anne Elizabeth. *Word, Image, and the New Negro: Representation and Identity in the Harlem Renaissance.* Bloomington: Indiana University Press, 2005. Discusses the use of images and text in African American magazines and anthologies published during the early years of the Harlem Renaissance.

Fabre, Genevieve, and Michel Feith, eds. *Temples for Tomorrow: Looking Back at the Harlem Renaissance.* Bloomington: Indiana University Press, 2001. Seventeen essays on varying perspectives of the Harlem Renaissance. Content includes commentary on art, literature, and international perspectives of the period.

Higgins, Nathan Irvin. *Harlem Renaissance.* Updated ed. New York: Oxford University Press, 2007. Revision of a groundbreaking study of the period. Includes historical information and literary explication of key texts.

Hughes, Langston, and Joseph McLaren. *Autobiography: The Big Sea.* Columbia: University of Missouri

Press, 2002. Autobiographical account of the poet's life and experiences during the Harlem Renaissance. Hughes's inclusion of both the positives and the negatives of the movement provides a foundation for any study of the period.

Hutchinson, George, ed. *The Cambridge Companion to the Harlem Renaissance*. New York: Cambridge University Press, 2007. Comprehensive coverage of the period includes sixteen essays on the foundations and literature of the period. Includes a closing essay that reflects on the era.

Lewis, David Levering. *When Harlem Was in Vogue*. New York: Penguin, 1997. Offers full historical perspective and analysis of the period's philosophical and literary movements.

See also African Americans; Art movements; *Black Empire*; *Black No More*; Du Bois, W. E. B.; Literature in the United States; Music: Jazz; Racial discrimination; Schuyler, George S.; Theater in the United States.

■ Harlow, Jean

Identification American film star, for whom the term "platinum blond" was coined
Born March 3, 1911; Kansas City, Missouri
Died June 7, 1937; Los Angeles, California

Harlow was a Hollywood sex symbol but did not possess the vanity often associated with such status. Lacking any formal training, she learned on the job and became a gifted comedian, with a unique talent for portraying "bad" girls with compassion and wit. The mysterious suicide of Harlow's second husband, Paul Bern, and her own sudden death fueled much public speculation; this, as much as her too-brief film career, has kept the actor alive in the public's memory.

Born Harlean Carpenter, Jean Harlow had no "rags-to-riches" back story; she was born into a comfortable upper-class family and attended a finishing school. Her domineering mother left her father and moved young Harlow to Hollywood, hoping to break into films herself. However, it was Harlow who started as an extra at Twentieth Century-Fox, then appeared in Hal Roach's comedy short subjects, after eloping at the age of sixteen with Charles McGrew. After two years of marriage, Harlow divorced McGrew, then got her big break when Howard Hughes cast her in *Hell's Angels* (1930).

Though Harlow's wooden performance was panned by critics, her star quality was obvious, and her "platinum blond" hair—a phrase coined for her by a press agent—caused U.S. sales of peroxide to skyrocket.

In 1932, Harlow played the lead in Metro-Goldwyn-Mayer's (MGM's) *Red-Headed Woman*, which proved to be a major turning point in her career. Not only did she discover her natural gift for comedy, but she also played for the first time the role that became her trademark: a "bad" woman transformed into a comic character.

In July, 1932, Harlow married Bern, Irving Thalberg's right-hand man. A few months later, Bern was found dead, apparently by suicide, leaving behind a cryptic note that fueled much speculation, suggesting impotence and sexual humiliation. However, Harlow maintained a dignified public silence throughout the subsequent investigation and came through the scandal with her popularity intact.

Red Dust, released November, 1932, further established Harlow's image as a hard-boiled girl with a heart of gold, and critics praised her performance.

Jean Harlow. (AP/Wide World Photos)

Her costar Clark Gable, who made more films with Harlow than any other actor, became a close friend and remained so throughout Harlow's life.

In September, 1933, Harlow married MGM cameraman Harold Rosson and made several more films, notably *Bombshell* and the classic *Dinner at Eight*. Divorced in 1934, she began dating actor William Powell, with whom she remained romantically involved for the rest of her life—though the two never married.

In March, 1937, Harlow began to exhibit signs of ill health. As the shooting of her final film, *Saratoga*, neared completion, Harlow became so ill that she had to stop working. Within days she was dead; she was twenty-six.

The cause of Harlow's death was a topic of public conversation for decades afterward. Some wondered if her death was the result of a botched abortion, peroxide poisoning, or injuries sustained from a beating by her former husband Bern. Others blamed her mother for hastening her death by refusing medical attention, citing her Christian Science beliefs. In actuality, Harlow died of acute nephritis, better known as kidney failure. Her kidneys had been failing for years, stemming from a bout of scarlet fever in her teens. She received constant medical attention from the moment she left the set of *Saratoga* (1937). There simply was no treatment available in 1937 that could have saved her. Harlow was laid to rest at Forest Lawn, in Glendale, California, in a crypt paid for by Powell. The inscription reads "Our Baby."

Impact   The original "blond bombshell," Harlow was an icon of American pop culture. A great Hollywood sex symbol and a gifted comedian, she was number twenty-two on the American Film Institute's list of the greatest actors of the Golden Age. In May, 1937, she was the first female film actor to appear on the cover of *Life* magazine. Her early death only heightened her popularity, leading to endless speculation about what might have been.

Jennifer Davis-Kay

Further Reading

Conway, Michael, and Mark Ricci, eds. *The Films of Jean Harlow*. New York: The Citadel Press, 1965.

Golden, Eve. *Platinum Girl: The Life and Legends of Jean Harlow*. New York: Abbeville Press, 1991.

Jordan, Jessica Hope. *The Sex Goddess in American Film, 1930-1965: Jean Harlow, Mae West, Lana Turner, and Jayne Mansfield*. Amherst, N.Y.: Cambria Press, 2009.

Marx, Samuel, and Joyce Vanderveen. *Deadly Illusions: Jean Harlow and the Murder of Paul Bern*. New York: Random House, 1990.

Stenn, David. *Bombshell: The Life and Death of Jean Harlow*. New York: Doubleday, 1993.

See also   *City Lights*; Film; Gable, Clark; Hairstyles; *Hell's Angels*; Hughes, Howard; Screwball comedy; Thalberg, Irving.

Hart, Moss. See **Kaufman, George S., and Moss Hart**

■ Hatch Act

The Law   Federal law restricting the political activities of federal and civil service employees

Also known as   Act to Prevent Pernicious Political Activities

Date   August 2, 1939

The Hatch Act of 1939 and its subsequent amendments constituted a significant achievement in American political development by eliminating abuses against the general public by civil service workers in political campaigns. The act extended to the state level if the relevant positions were supported with federal funds.

Concerns emerged after the 1938 elections that the Franklin D. Roosevelt presidential administration and the Democratic Party had violated civil service rules by using funds and employees of the Works Progress Administration to intimidate voters and businesses in Kentucky, Tennessee, and Maryland to secure the election of Democrats. In addition, Republicans throughout the United States expressed fear that the impact of New Deal funds was corrupting American politics by way of illegal and unethical involvement in the election process. After the specific accusations were documented, Senator Carl A. Hatch, a Democrat from New Mexico, introduced "An Act to Prevent Pernicious Political Activities," which became known as the Hatch Act. This act forbade the intimidation of voters and bribery, the use of federal funds to affect elections, and the promise of jobs or job security to gain support in an election.

It severely restricted political activities by federal workers who were not involved in policy decisions—that is, almost all federal employees. Initially, the penalty was immediate loss of employment; later, it was amended to a thirty-day suspension. While the Hatch Act succeeded in eliminating most abuse, it created an environment in which federal employees were restricted from the full practice of a fundamental civil liberty—the freedom of political expression. During the ensuing decades, the Hatch Act was amended several times and altered as a result of court decisions.

Impact The Hatch Act and its amendments serve as an exemplary model of bipartisanship on behalf of the common good and ethical electoral politics. It has succeeded in eliminating the abuse of the vast majority of civil service employees in federal elections by manipulative political party leaders.

William T. Walker

Further Reading

Eccles, James R. *The Hatch Act and American Bureaucracy.* New York: Vantage Press, 1981.

Rosenbloom, David H. *Federal Service and the Constitution.* Ithaca, N.Y.: Cornell University Press, 1971.

Smith, Jason Scott. *Building New Deal Liberalism: The Political Economy of Public Works, 1933-1956.* New York: Cambridge University Press, 2006.

See also Civil rights and liberties in the United States; Congress, U.S.; Roosevelt, Franklin D.; Works Progress Administration.

■ Hawk's Nest Tunnel disaster

The Event Tunnel-drilling accident in which about fifteen hundred workers were exposed to potentially lethal concentrations of silica dust

Dates June, 1930, to December, 1931

Place Gauley Bridge, West Virginia

The drilling of the Hawk's Nest Tunnel through West Virginia's Gauley Mountain was completed in record time at what was later determined to be an unacceptable cost in lives. As many as one-half of the workers on the project may have died of fibrotic lung disease and its complications; about three-quarters of the workers were African American

men who had come to West Virginia from all parts of the South seeking work during the early years of the Great Depression. Vital statistics were not reported from West Virginia until 1933, and the dispersion of workers after completion of the tunnel made determining the full extent of the tragedy impossible.

The Hawk's Nest Tunnel was a hydroelectric power project by one subsidiary of the Union Carbide and Carbon Corporation, the New Kanawha Power Company at Gauley Bridge, for another, the Electro-Metallurgical Company of Alloy, West Virginia. The latter made ferrosilicon for carbon steel. The purpose of the 3.75-mile tunnel was to divert water from the New River to operate turbines, but when drilling began in the summer of 1930, the crew discovered that the rock was exceptionally rich in silica that was more than 90 percent pure. This made the mineral both valuable to the alloy plant and dangerous to the workers, who did not have respirators to prevent inhalation of the silica dust. Dry drilling techniques increased the hazard, with dozens of workers dying during the eighteen-month construction project. Litigation resulted in limited compensation to some workers and their heirs.

Impact The Hawk's Nest tragedy and subsequent litigation brought silicosis to public attention via the press and congressional hearings. Although not even West Virginia compensated workers for silicosis when litigation began in 1932, all but two of the forty-eight states had workers' compensation provisions for dust diseases by 1937.

Rachel Maines

Further Reading

Cherniack, Martin. *The Hawk's Nest Incident: America's Worst Industrial Disaster.* New Haven, Conn.: Yale University Press, 1986.

Rukeyser, Muriel. "The Book of the Dead." In *The Collected Poems of Muriel Rukeyser.* Pittsburgh, Pa.: University of Pittsburgh Press, 2006.

Spangler, Patricia. *The Hawks Nest Tunnel: An Unabridged History.* Proctorville, Ohio: Wythe-North, 2008.

See also African Americans; Great Depression in the United States; Racial discrimination; Unemployment in the United States.

■ Hawley-Smoot Tariff Act of 1930

The Law   Raised U.S. Tariffs on imported goods
Also known as   Smoot-Hawley Tariff Act of 1930, Tariff Act of 1930
Date   June 17, 1930

The Hawley-Smoot Tariff Act, which raised U.S. tariffs to their highest levels in history and has been cited as a significant contributor to the Great Depression, marked the decline of tariffs as a means of furthering protectionist economic policy and as a major source of income for the U.S. government.

By the time U.S. president Herbert Hoover signed the Hawley-Smoot Tariff Act in June, 1930, the United States was experiencing the early effects of what became the longest and most devastating economic depression in American history and the catalyst for a global depression of unprecedented proportions. However, the inspiration for the act originated in issues and debates that predated the events leading to the Great Depression.

Willis C. Hawley (left) and Reed Smoot. (Library of Congress)

Protective tariffs, favored by midwestern farmers and northern manufacturers and opposed by laborers and southern planters, had been a source of both revenue and controversy throughout the nineteenth and early twentieth centuries. The economic growth of the 1920's had been a boon to manufacturers, but the global economic ramifications of World War I had encouraged overproduction of American agricultural goods, leading to falling prices and prompting farmers to increase their calls for government intervention in international trade. The Fordney-McCumber Tariff of 1922 raised tariff rates to their highest levels in American history, but pressure from farmers' organizations to raise tariffs persisted further during the late 1920's. During the presidential campaign of 1928, Hoover, then a candidate for president, promised to raise tariffs on farm products if elected. Following the election of Hoover, Congressman Willis C. Hawley, a Republican from Oregon, and Senator Reed Smoot, a Republican from Utah, introduced a bill in April, 1929, that would have increased tariff levels on agricultural and other imported goods.

By the time debate of the bill began, the U.S. economy had already begun a downturn that intensified following the stock market crash of October, 1929; this heightened pressure on Congress from farmers and industrialists to pass the bill. It passed rapidly through the Republican-dominated House of Representatives but stalled in the Senate because of opposition from a minority of progressive Republicans who opposed the protectionist aims of the bill. Debate of the bill continued in the Senate through 1929 and into 1930 as the economy worsened. Many economists opposed the bill, fearing reprisals from foreign governments. Pressure from constituents led many midwestern progressives to abandon their opposition, and a final version of the bill passed both houses in June, 1930. Hoover signed it into law on June 17.

The Hawley-Smoot Tariff Act took effect just as the U.S. economy was showing signs of possible recovery. However, as its effects rippled throughout international markets, domestic production and international trade resumed a downward trend. Many foreign countries responded to the act by enacting retaliatory tariffs and other restrictions on trade with the United States; in 1930, the Canadian parliament passed legislation raising tariffs on certain products imported from the United States to levels commensurate with those set forth in the Hawley-Smoot Act. Between 1929 and 1932, U.S. imports of European goods declined more than 70 percent, and U.S. exports of goods to Europe declined more than 65 percent, contributing to an overall decline of more than 60 percent in world trade between 1929 and 1934. Although much of this decline was the result of other economic forces, many economists estimate that around 20 to 25 percent of these declines were attributable to the effects of the Hawley-Smoot Tariff Act.

Impact Although the true effects of the Hawley-Smoot Tariff Act remain the subject of debate, the act is commonly regarded as a contributor to the decline of the global economy during the Great Depression. By contributing to a general decrease in international trade, the act harmed the U.S. agricultural and industrial interests that it was designed to protect and hampered the recovery of European economies ravaged by the effects of World War I. The effects of the act upon global markets during the Great Depression discredited the concept of tariffs as effective economic policy, fueling twentieth century trends toward free trade and reciprocal treaties among global trading partners. The Reciprocal Trade Agreements Act of 1934, a response to the Hawley-Smoot Act, authorized the U.S. government to negotiate with other countries for bilateral tariff reductions, setting a precedent for free trade agreements that defined subsequent international trade. The act led to the decline of tariffs as a major source of revenue for the U.S. government, increasing the role of federal income taxes as a revenue source.

Michael H. Burchett

Further Reading

Eckes, Alfred. *Opening America's Market: U.S. Foreign Trade Policy Since 1776.* Chapel Hill: University of North Carolina Press, 1995.
Koyama, Kumiko. "The Passage of the Smoot-Hawley Tariff Act: Why Did the President Sign the Bill?" *Journal of Policy History* 21, no. 2 (2009): 163-186.
McElvaine, Robert S. *The Great Depression: America 1929-1941.* New York: Times Books, 1993.
Termin, Peter. *Lessons from the Great Depression.* Cambridge, Mass.: MIT Press, 1989.

See also Business and the economy in the United States; Farmers' organizations; Foreign policy of the United States; Great Depression in the United States; Hoover, Herbert; International trade; Reciprocal Trade Agreements Act of 1936.

Hays Code. See **Motion Picture Production Code**

■ Health care

The Great Depression presented many challenges for Americans, one of which concerned the ability to acquire quality health care. High unemployment and limited financial resources caused many Americans to bypass medical care, resulting in decreased receipts for doctors and hospitals. As a result, insurance plans emerged, along with government programs. Despite these difficult times, medical advances continued.

At the onset of the Great Depression the United States had a first-rate medical system that included at least as many hospital beds and medical and nursing schools per capita as it has in the twenty-first century. However, as the Depression progressed, fewer and fewer Americans had the financial resources to pay for medical services. Because a high percentage of the public forwent health care, hospitals and physicians lost revenues, and some went out of business. To avoid these problems in the future, health insurance programs formed to maintain a more constant flow of revenues. Additionally, the federal government attempted, unsuccessfully, to intervene by trying to create a government-run health care system. At the same time the country was struggling with financing health care, many advances were made in health care, including the development of organizations such as the National Institutes of Health and the March of Dimes, blood banks, and the yellow fever vaccine.

Health Insurance Hospitals suffered dramatically from the large drop in receipts. In an effort to de-

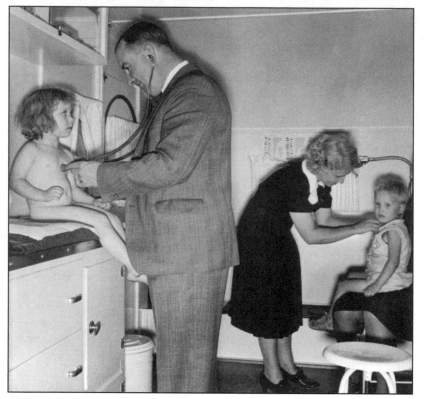

Children of migrant workers are examined by a doctor and nurse in a mobile clinic in Oregon in 1939. (The Granger Collection, New York)

velop a steadier inflow of funds, hospitals developed the first insurance programs. The first recorded plan was at the Baylor University Medical Center in Dallas, Texas. A group of schoolteachers contracted with the hospital by paying a monthly fee, and the hospital agreed to care for them if they needed medical attention. Soon groups of hospitals in large cities joined together and formed hospital insurance plans. These plans were attractive because they gave participants more options, which in turn generated more subscribers and stabilized those hospitals. In contrast to modern-day health care plans, these programs were not to protect individuals from catastrophic expenses but to protect the hospitals from revenue drops that could put them out of business.

The multiple-hospital programs evolved into the first true health insurance company in 1932, when Blue Cross was established in Sacramento, California. Subscribers could choose their physicians and hospitals and have their medical expenses paid by Blue Cross. California state law allowed Blue Cross to operate as a nonprofit corporation, exempting it

from taxes and insurance regulations. Blue Cross soon expanded to other states that allowed similar exempt status. With the support of the American Medical Association and the American Hospital Association, Blue Cross/ Blue Shield became a major health insurer, commanding at least 40 percent of the health insurance market into the 1980's.

In the mid-1930's a different medical care plan evolved. The Kaiser Company, started by Henry J. Kaiser, was building the Los Angeles Aqueduct in the Mojave Desert. Sidney Garfield, a young physician, was caring for the sick and injured workers at a small hospital he built near the construction site. However, he had difficulty getting paid by the company's insurance carrier because the costs were variable and unpredictable. Afraid of losing all nearby medical services, Kaiser helped to get the insurance companies to pay Garfield a fixed amount of money per covered worker per day. This agreement helped keep the hospital running and provided the companies with a known cost. This became the first major prepayment system. After the aqueduct was completed, Garfield ran similar programs across California, which culminated in the Kaiser Shipyards at the beginning of World War II. After the war ended and the shipyard's workforce dropped dramatically, Kaiser opened the prepaid medical care program to the public, which evolved into Kaiser Permanente.

Government Efforts Health care for Americans was not left out of the New Deal development. President Franklin D. Roosevelt pushed for social security, unemployment insurance, and national health care insurance by creating the Committee on Economic Security (CES). President Roosevelt wanted compulsory health insurance included in the Social Security bill. However, the CES was concerned that the American Medical Association's opposition to national health insurance would doom the entire bill. While

Congress passed the Social Security Act and the Federal Unemployment Tax Act in 1935, health care reform was temporarily dropped.

In 1937, President Roosevelt formed the Tactical Committee on Medical Care as an effort to revisit national health care. The committee's recommendations were incorporated into legislation proposed by Senator Robert F. Wagner of New York, which became known as the National Health Act. The proposed bill would have provided federal grants to states and localities to administer the insurance program. However, the 1938 election resulted in a loss of power for the progressives and a more conservative influence in Congress. The Wagner National Health Act of 1939 was defeated. The movement for national health care was soon overshadowed by World War II and faded for many years.

Advances in Health Care Despite the severe economic depression of the 1930's, health care advanced in many ways. There were medical breakthroughs in treatments and procedures as well as the formation of new medical organizations.

In 1930, the Ransdell Act created the National Institute of Health (NIH). Built with $750,000 of government funds on ninety-two acres of land in Bethesda, Maryland, donated by Luke I. Wilson and his wife, the NIH expanded on the Hygienic Laboratory that was established in 1887. Senator Joseph E. Ransdell sponsored the bill to support medical research for the cure of diseases. The NIH later became known as the National Institutes of Health, comprising more than twenty institutes and centers; it is one of the leading medical research agencies in the world.

Yellow fever was one disease on which progress was made during the 1930's. Wilbur Augustus Sawyer at the Rockefeller Institute in New York City and Max Theiler at Harvard College in Boston were both researching a yellow-fever vaccine. This was dangerous work because often researchers contracted the disease accidentally, as both Sawyer and Theiler did. In 1932, Theiler first cultured a

strain of the virus. In 1936, he developed a weakened form of the virus that could be used as a vaccine, called 17D, with minimal side effects. By 1937, field studies had begun, and a successful vaccine for yellow fever was produced.

Events during the 1930's led to the formation of Alcoholics Anonymous by William G. Wilson and Robert Smith. In 1934, after his finance career was ruined by his alcoholism, Wilson received treatment at a hospital. During his stay he had a spiritual revelation and was able to quit drinking. A year later, when he had an urge to drink alcohol again, he sought help, this time from Smith, also an alcoholic. To-

Canadian Movement for National Health Insurance

During the Great Depression, large numbers of Canadians were unable to afford needed medical care, and while private charity was helpful, it was unable to meet the large demand. Doctors and hospitals experienced a substantial decline in paying patients, and this resulted in a variety of experiments aimed as reducing costs. In 1934, several hospitals in the provinces of Ontario and Alberta pioneered prepaid hospital insurance plans. Hospital associations in other provinces experimented with similar arrangements. However, such programs provided little help to those who were unemployed and poor.

The decade of the 1930's saw Canada's first significant movement in favor of public health programs like those provided in some European countries. Despite widespread support for such programs, governments were hesitant to respond because of the large funding requirements at a time when increased deficits were considered unacceptable. In 1935, Alberta's government, led by the United Farmers of Alberta (UFA), passed a bill creating a tax-supported insurance program. A few months later, however, the UFA was defeated in an election, and the program was scrapped. The next year, a similar bill was enacted in British Columbia, but it was never implemented, for financial reasons. At the national level, Prime Minister William Lyon Mackenzie King said that he supported a government program of universal medical care, but he waited until 1945 to introduce a bill. It was not until 1947 that the Saskatchewan legislature initiated Canada's first near-universal program of health insurance.

Thomas Tandy Lewis

gether they helped each other stop drinking alcohol and developed a twelve-step rehabilitation program to help others quit. By the end of the decade Wilson began writing his book, *Alcoholics Anonymous* (1938), which also became the name of their program and has helped millions of people around the world quit drinking alcohol.

During World War I the value of storing donor blood for future transfusions to save lives became apparent. In the early 1930's, the Soviet Union developed a nationwide system of blood stores and distribution. Upon hearing this news, Bernard Fantus developed the first "blood bank" in the United States at Chicago's Cook County Hospital in 1937. Seeing the lifesaving opportunities of storing blood, many medical facilities across the United States began developing blood banks of their own.

In 1938, Roosevelt created a nonprofit organization he called the National Foundation for Infantile Paralysis. By then, Roosevelt was stricken with what was believed to be poliomyelitis, or polio. The foundation's purpose was to raise funds for polio research and help those afflicted by the disease. Many entertainers joined the president in his effort to promote the charity. Eddie Cantor encouraged his radio audiences to send a dime to the White House to help fight the disease. This campaign became known as the March of Dimes, and in 1979, the organization adopted the moniker as its name.

Prior to the 1930's, most children were born at home. However, medical specializations and health insurance increased during the decade. The American Board of Obstetricians and Gynecologists was formed in 1930. Obstetricians who delivered babies in hospitals began displacing midwives who delivered babies at home. The growth of health insurance made hospital deliveries more affordable. By 1939, 50 percent of all babies in the United States and 75 percent of all urban babies were born in hospitals.

Impact The economic challenges of the 1930's forced the U.S. government to consider changing the health care system. Although national health insurance was dropped from the Social Security Act of 1935 and the Wagner National Health Act of 1939 did not pass, the great private health insurance and prepaid medical care programs developed during the Depression era. One success the federal government had was the creation of the NIH, which developed into a top health organization that has assisted in many health care breakthroughs.

Nongovernment efforts also progressed during the Great Depression. Many organizations founded during the 1930's have continued to develop and become leaders in helping people with various health issues by raising funds for research and assisting individuals with disease management. During this time progress was made in developing vaccines to fight diseases. The 1930's were a difficult time in American history, but the perseverance of the people was rewarded with continued advances in health care.

Bradley R. A. Wilson

Further Reading

B, Dick. *Real Twelve Step Fellowship History: The Old School A.A. You May Not Know.* Kihei, Hawaii: Paradise Research, 2006. Using the Alcoholics Anonymous tradition of name anonymity, Dick B gives a history of the organization beginning with its origin in 1935.

Crosby, Molly Caldwell. *The American Plague: The Untold Story of Yellow Fever, the Epidemic That Shaped Our History.* New York: Berkeley, 2006. A history of yellow fever in the Americas; chapter 26 focuses on the vaccine that was developed during the 1930's.

Cunningham, Robert, III, and Robert M. Cunningham, Jr. *Blues: A History of the Blue Cross and Blue Shield System.* De Kalb: Northern Illinois University Press, 1997. History of the oldest American health care insurer, beginning with its hospital prepayment plan, which began during the 1930's.

Murray, John E. *Origins of American Health Insurance: A History of Industrial Sickness Funds.* New Haven, Conn.: Yale University Press, 2007. A discussion of the history of health insurance in the United States; chapter 9 focuses on the Great Depression.

Rose, David W. *March of Dimes.* Mount Pleasant, S.C.: Arcadia, 2003. Written by the archivist of the March of Dimes, this book documents the organization, beginning with its founding in 1938 by President Roosevelt.

See also Alcoholics Anonymous; Blood banks; Elixir sulfanilamide scandal; March of Dimes; Medicine; Polio; Social Security Act of 1935; Typhus immunization.

■ Hearing aids

Definition   Sound amplification devices assisting
people with hearing loss

*During the 1930's, advancements in vacuum-tube technol-
ogy made hearing aids more practical and wearable than
they had been previously. However, the devices were powered
by large, costly batteries. Bone-conductor hearing aids were
also invented. In general, hearing aids became more compact, efficient, and wearable during the decade.*

Loss of hearing produces communication difficulties and social isolation. Speaking tubes and ear
trumpets were some of the first hearing aids, but
these devices could only assist people with mild hearing loss. Microphones convert acoustic energy into
electrical currents, which are far more easily amplified than acoustic or mechanical energy. Therefore,
electrical or carbon hearing aids provided significantly better acoustic amplification than tubes and
trumpets. Such hearing aids, however, required
large, cumbersome six-volt batteries to run them,
and they were only powerful enough to assist people
with moderate hearing loss.

During the 1930's, custom earmolds that carried
acoustic energy directly into the ear canal were introduced. These earmolds replaced the earlier, impractical hand-held earphone receivers. Also, bulky
batteries were camouflaged as purses, camera cases,
or even headbands. Also in the 1930's, the replacement of carbon hearing aids by vacuum-tube hearing aids assisted people with severe hearing loss.

In 1932, the Sonotone Corporation introduced
the first wearable bone-conduction hearing aid that
transmitted sound waves through the side of the
skull into the inner ear, thus bypassing defective
middle ears. In 1935, A. Edwin Steven made the first
"wearable" hearing aid, which weighed only 2.5
pounds.

Impact   Advances in hearing-aid technology made
during the 1930's provided the framework for the invention of transistor hearing aids during the 1950's;
these needed only one small battery and were substantially smaller. The invention of bone-conducting
hearing aids, coupled with research conducted during the 1930's by Americans and Russians that
showed that direct electrical stimulation could
substitute for middle-ear activation of the cochlea,
gave rise to the invention of cochlear implants decades later.

Michael A. Buratovich

Further Reading

Dillon, Harvey. *Hearing Aids*. New York: Thieme,
2001.
Myers, David G. *A Quiet World: Living with Hearing
Loss*. New Haven, Conn.: Yale University Press,
2000.
Vonlanthen, Andi, and Horst Arndt. *Hearing Instrument Technology for the Hearing Health Care Professional*. Florence, Ky.: Delmar Cengage Learning,
2006.

See also   Inventions; Medicine; Roosevelt, Eleanor.

■ Heart-lung machine

Definition   Machine used during surgeries to
pump blood while the heart is stopped

*Beginning in 1930, John H. Gibbon, Jr., and his wife per-
formed seminal experiments that established and perfected
the basic design of the heart-lung machine. They solved several significant problems and established the fundamental
model of the heart-lung machine that others improved upon
in later decades. In 1953, Gibbon used the heart-lung machine to perform the first open-heart surgery.*

On October 3, 1930, Gibbon was assigned to a female patient who eventually died from a blood clot
in her pulmonary artery. Gibbon postulated he
could have saved her if the oxygen-poor blood from
her veins was removed from her body, filled with oxygen and purged of carbon dioxide, and then reintro-
duced into her arteries. At the time, however, no machine existed that could do such a task. Gibbon
determined to design, build, and test a machine that
could. He received little encouragement from his
colleagues, who tried to dissuade him, but Gibbon
pressed forward nevertheless. Such a machine
would temporarily substitute for the heart and the
lungs, and therefore was called a "heart-lung machine."

While at Massachusetts General Hospital in Boston, Gibbon surmised that there were four components to a heart-lung machine: a reservoir tank to
store blood from the patient's veins, an "oxygen-

ator" that infused the venous blood with oxygen, a heater to keep the blood warm while outside the body, and a pump to move the blood through the machine and back into the patient's body. Gibbon, in collaboration with his wife, Mary, designed several experimental heart-lung machines and tested them on cats. Because blood has a marked tendency to clot if it comes into contact with glass, metals, and other surfaces, Gibbon needed to use an anticoagulant to prevent the blood from clotting while in the machine. By mixing the blood with heparin, a chemical that was invented in 1916 but became commercially available during the 1930's, Gibbon solved the clotting problem.

In 1934, the Gibbons succeeded in blocking blood flow from the heart to the lungs in a laboratory animal on an experimental heart-lung machine without observing any changes in the animal's blood pressure. However, the lab animals died soon after the procedure. By May, 1935, the Gibbons found that a continuous, pulsating pump, rather than an intermittent pump, allowed lab animals that had been on the machine for more than two hours to recover and survive for several days after the procedure. By 1938, adjustments to the flow rate and better postoperative care strategies boosted to 30 percent the survival rate of laboratory animals that had been on the heart-lung machine for twenty-five minutes.

Impact Many researchers raced to perfect the heart-lung machine in the decades that followed the 1930's. However, the Gibbons had already solved the most pressing problems in the design of the heart-lung machine. Their basic design greatly influenced all subsequent machines. Those produced after the 1940's continued to improve the oxygenator, filters, pumps, and machine-cleaning procedures. Such refinements greatly increased the survival of lab animals that had been placed on the heart-lung machine for up to thirty minutes.

During the 1940's, Gibbon collaborated with the engineers at IBM Corporation, and their mechanical expertise substantially improved the efficiency of the heart-lung machine. This collaboration produced the Model II heart-lung machine, which solved many major problems, such as low oxygen levels, an inability to properly adjust the flow rate, and blood clots. On May 16, 1953, Gibbon used the Model II heart-lung machine to sustain the life of an eighteen-year-old girl during open-heart surgery

while he repaired a septal defect in her heart. This unprecedented medical treatment, which had been unimaginable twenty years before, began with the seminal work conducted by the Gibbons during the 1930's.

Michael A. Buratovich

Further Reading
Cohn, Lawrence H. "Fifty Years of Open-Heart Surgery." *Circulation* 107 (2003): 2168-2170.
Edmunds, L. H. "Cardiopulmonary Bypass After Fifty Years." *New England Journal of Medicine* 351, no. 16 (2004): 1603-1606.
Fou, Adora A. "John H. Gibbon: The First Twenty Years of the Heart-Lung Machine." *Texas Heart Institute Journal* 24, no. 1 (1997): 1-8.

See also Health care; Inventions; Medicine.

■ Heat wave of 1931

The Event Period of abnormally high air and soil temperatures that afflicted much of the continental United States
Dates Late spring through early autumn, 1931, peaking from June 18 to July 2, 1931
Place Continental United States

The heat wave set unprecedented air and soil temperature records and worsened conditions for wind erosion of topsoil by killing both ground plant cover and the supporting root systems. This initiated a massive loss of marginal soils, the slow collapse of much of the U.S. farming industry in the Great Plains and the Midwest, and the massive dust storms that began in 1932 and created the "Dust Bowl."

The impact of long-term drought on the continental United States during the 1930's was foreshadowed in 1931. The winter of 1930-1931 had insufficient rainfall, and the Mississippi and other rivers were at record low levels in January, 1931. Rainfall levels for February were below normal for more 50 percent of the country, while temperatures continued to be above expected ranges. While the spring of 1931 had relatively more moisture, a marked shift in temperature across most of the interior United States began on June 17.

An area of increasing heat, augmented by dry westerly winds, set in over the southern Great Plains and the interior valleys, gradually widening its scope until virtually all of the United States between the Rocky Mountains and the Appalachians was engulfed by it. Temperatures of more than 100 degrees Fahrenheit were recorded in every state, with the central and northern plains reporting extreme readings ranging between 107 and 115 degrees, the latter in South Dakota. The high temperatures continued for much of July, with lower-than-normal humidity levels. Many areas reported readings of more than 110 degrees. The rain returned in August, but excessively high heat continued until nearly the end of the month, with all areas in the East except New England experiencing unusually high temperatures, up to 105 degrees. The West peaked at 123 degrees in California. September, 1931, was the warmest September on record, with a temperature range between four and ten degrees above normal.

The intense heat presented different problems for major urban areas; their populations experienced cases of heat prostration, canned liquids reached explosive temperatures, and water supplies were challenged. On June, 29, Chicago reported forty-four deaths; by July 2, 1931, the total number of deaths from heat-related causes across the United States stood at 1,016. In many cities, lawns in public parks were opened to provide spaces for relief, and record crowds flooded coastal beaches, with an estimated one-half million people at Coney Island in one day. On July 1, a low-pressure area moving eastward across the Great Plains brought rain to Iowa, Minnesota, and the Dakotas, dropping temperatures between twenty and forty degrees. By late October, colder air had moved into the Great Plains and Midwest, breaking the grip of the extreme heat and bringing vitally needed rains across most of the damaged interior of the country.

Impact Already damaged by a drought that had begun in 1930, the American agricultural industry was hit hard by the heat wave of 1931. Primary water sources shrank noticeably, depriving farmers of the water necessary to stave off the effects of the heat on both crops and livestock. Unrelieved high soil temperatures also killed grasses and other essential components of the ground cover vital to maintaining stable soils in marginal environments, resulting in a rise in wind erosion across much of the southern Great Plains. The failure of small farmers' fields directly impacted the economies of twenty-two states, forcing many communities into or close to bank-ruptcy and pushing many families off land that literally was crumbling beneath them. Shrinking water supplies also had an effect on the national health. Many people were forced to take untreated water directly from springs, wells, and rivers, thus increasing the risk of typhoid. In some of the affected states, the losses of regular sources of standard foods such as milk and meat caused a high number of malnutrition-related illnesses. By late June, 1931, some farmers in the Corn Belt were sleeping in the daylight and tending their fields by moonlight, and in many towns regular church services were held to pray for rain. Crops most heavily impacted were tobacco, corn, oats, and fruit grown in orchards. The dust storms of 1932 and succeeding years forced substantial changes in farming and soil conservation strategies across much of the American grain belt.

Robert Ridinger

Further Reading

Egan, Timothy. *The Worst Hard Time: The Untold Story of Those Who Survived the Great American Dust Bowl.* Boston: Houghton Mifflin, 2006.

Hunter, Herbert C. "The Weather of 1931 in the United States." *Monthly Weather Review* (December, 1931): 483-484.

Worster, Donald. *Dust Bowl: The Southern Plains in the 1930's.* New York: Oxford University Press, 1979.

See also Agriculture in the United States; Business and the economy in the United States; Dust Bowl; Great Depression in the United States; Natural disasters.

■ Hell's Angels

Identification Film about aerial combat in World War I

Date Released on May 27, 1930

Producer-director Howard Hughes used expensive and dangerous stunt flying for the combat scenes. After completion of the silent version in 1928, he reshot much of the film to accommodate sound and used innovative color sequences in one of the most expensive Hollywood films to that time.

Even before its release, *Hell's Angels* generated public interest. Shooting began in October, 1927, and continued until early 1930. Twenty-one-year-old

Hell's Angels, *produced by Howard Hughes, was lauded for its innovative action sequences and was heavily promoted, as evidenced by this neon sign advertising the screening of the film.* (Hulton Archive/Getty Images)

multimillionaire Hughes was the producer and directed many scenes. He was fascinated by airplanes and spent much of the nearly four-million-dollar budget on risky sequences involving depictions of aerial combat. He placed extraordinary demands on stunt work. Two pilots and one mechanic died during filming. Hughes insisted on technical accuracy and purchased several vintage World War I aircraft. Committed to his own visual preconceptions, Hughes removed the first two directors and directed most of the aerial sequences himself.

Hughes was keenly aware of changes in motion-picture technology. His production of the silent version of *Hell's Angels* was near completion when he realized that *The Jazz Singer* (1927) had revolutionized film. Audiences now expected sound and dialogue.

Hughes decided to reshoot the dramatic sequences with sound. The thick accent of the original female star prompted Hughes to replace her with eighteen-year-old Jean Harlow. Though she was awkward at first, Harlow relied on the coaching of the film's third director, James Whale. Her performance improved, and her appearance in *Hell's Angels* launched her career. The premiere at Grauman's Chinese Theater was a dramatic event. The audience, including Hollywood stars and moguls, was disappointed by the pedestrian plot that revolved around the lives of two British brothers and their German friend whose lives are interwoven in World War I air combat with tragic consequences. However, the aerial sequences found resounding approval among film-industry professionals.

Impact Hughes became famous because of his erratic, expensive production methods that resulted in a film that was flawed in plot and performances but admired for its editing and special effects. The popular success of *Hell's Angels* confirmed the public's affinity for films about aviation and pushed the limits for stunt flying and special effects.

John A. Britton

Further Reading

Crafton, Donald. *The Talkies: American Cinema's Transition to Sound, 1926-1931.* New York: Charles Scribner's Sons, 1997.

Dooley, Roger. *From Scarface to Scarlett: American Films in the 1930's.* New York: Harcourt Brace Jovanovich, 1981.

Higham, Charles. *Howard Hughes: The Secret Life.* New York: G. P. Putnam's Sons, 1993.

Marrett, George J. *Howard Hughes: Aviator.* Annapolis, Md.: Naval Institute Press, 2004.

See also Corrigan's wrong-way flight; Earhart, Amelia; Film serials; Harlow, Jean; Hughes, Howard; Motion Picture Production Code.

■ Hellman, Lillian

Identification American playwright
Born June 20, 1905; New Orleans, Louisiana
Died June 30, 1984; Martha's Vineyard, Massachusetts

Hellman was the nation's first female playwright to achieve both commercial and critical acclaim. Her Broadway hits The Children's Hour *(1934) and* The Little Foxes *(1939) tackled the taboo subjects of lesbianism and women's economic rights, respectively, while her offstage relationship with mystery novelist Dashiell Hammett ranks among the most celebrated public romances of the 1930's.*

The scion of a genteel New Orleans family, Lillian Hellman was raised in New York City and attended New York University before dropping out to work as a book reviewer for the *New York Herald Tribune*. She also read plays for director Leo Bulgakov and later evaluated scenarios for Metro-Goldwyn-Mayer in Los Angeles, before her partner, detective-turned-mystery-writer Dashiell Hammett, encouraged her to write serious theatrical fare of her own.

Hellman's major breakthrough came with *The Children's Hour* in 1934. Drawing on a Scottish case from 1810, Hellman's account of a malicious schoolgirl who falsely accuses two schoolteachers of lesbianism shattered taboos and ran for 691 performances. The play was banned for indecency in several American cities, including Boston and Chicago, as well as in Great Britain. Its success garnered Hellman $125,000 from the first run alone and elevated her to literary stardom. However, the Pulitzer committee passed over the play in favor of *The Old Maid* (1935), by Zoë Akins.

After working briefly on scripts for the Hollywood films *Dead End* (1937) and *The Dark Angel* (1939) and writing a play about a labor action, *Days to Come*, which ran on Broadway for one week in 1936, Hellman traveled to Europe and immersed herself in Soviet theater. She also lent her public support to the Loyalist forces during the Spanish Civil War and returned to the United States as a determined antifascist. These experiences later formed the background for her 1940 play *Watch on the Rhine*.

Hellman's second major hit of the 1930's, *The Little Foxes*, opened in 1939 with Tallulah Bankhead in the starring role. Set in a small southern town at the beginning of the twentieth century, the drama depicts the internecine struggles of the Hubbard family as they battle over plans to finance a cotton mill. The work's brutal indictment of the economic dependence of women marked a political turn in the author's work. It ran for 410 performances but also was passed over for the Pulitzer Prize.

Hellman's relationship with Dashiell Hammett, author of *The Maltese Falcon* (1930), was among the most publicized literary romances of its time. Hammett acknowledged that Hellman was the model for the sharp and sassy wife, Nora Charles, in *The Thin Man* (1934). The couple's stormy partnership lasted for thirty years, until his death in 1961. They presided over dinner parties attended by the nation's leading artists and intellectuals, including friends Dorothy Parker, Nathanael West, and George Gershwin. Hellman also gained public attention for her leftist activism, which increasingly led to feuds with colleagues, such as a thirty-year spat with Bankhead over Hellman's support for the Soviet Union in its 1939 invasion of Finland.

Impact At the close of the 1930's, Hellman ranked alongside Eugene O'Neill, Thornton Wilder, and

Clifford Odets as one of the dominant American dramatists of the era. However, her reputation suffered after she refused to incriminate fellow leftists before the House Committee on Un-American Activities in 1950, famously stating, "I cannot and will not cut my conscience to fit this year's fashions." She also became embroiled in bitter public feuds with writers Diana Trilling and Mary McCarthy, the latter leading to a multimillion-dollar slander lawsuit that became the basis for Nora Ephron's play *Imaginary Friends* (2002). The publication of Hellman's well-received memoirs and a series of revivals starring such luminaries as Elizabeth Taylor, Stockard Channing, and Lauren Marcus solidified Hellman's reputation after her death.

Jacob M. Appel

Further Reading

Feibelman, Peter. *Lilly: Reminiscences of Lillian Hellman.* New York: Chatto & Windus, 1989.

Hellman, Lillian. *An Unfinished Woman: A Memoir.* New York: Back Bay Books, 1999.

Martinson, Deborah. *Lillian Hellman: A Life with Foxes and Scoundrels.* Berkeley, Calif.: Counterpoint, 2005.

Mellen, Joan. *Hellman and Hammett: The Legendary Passion of Lillian Hellman and Dashiell Hammett.* New York: HarperCollins, 1997.

See also *Children's Hour, The*; Hammett, Dashiell; Homosexuality and gay rights; Literature in the United States; Theater in the United States; *Thin Man, The.*

■ *Hellzapoppin'*

Identification Broadway musical revue
Dates November 26, 1938, through December 17, 1941

With 1,404 performances, Hellzapoppin' *was the longest running Broadway musical to that time.*

Written by the comedy team of John "Ole" Olsen and Harold "Chic" Johnson, with music and lyrics by Sammy Fain and Charles Tobias, *Hellzapoppin'* presented a wacky, unpredictable night of songs, sight gags, audience participation, and adult-laden humor and double entendre. The show drew large audiences that were in need of an escape. The show ran more than three years, for 1,404 performances, and was the longest running Broadway musical in history at its time.

Hellzapoppin' opened at the Forty-sixth Street Theatre on September 22, 1938, before transferring to the much larger Broadway's Winter Garden Theatre on November 26. Less than a month before closing, it moved to the Majestic Theatre. Later, it toured the United States extensively, albeit in a much smaller production.

More akin to vaudeville and burlesque than a traditional Broadway musical, *Hellzapoppin'* was rewritten throughout its run to remain current and topical. Its comic sketches were the highlight of the evening; these included scenes with clowns, trained pigeons, planted audience members, and even Adolf Hitler speaking in a Yiddish accent. Perhaps its most famous contributor was Oscar Hammerstein II, who wrote a song later added to the run.

The anything-goes atmosphere encouraged audiences to return, helping boost the three dollar ticket sales. The rotating cast of entertainers was also popular and included the Radio Rogues, the singing group the Charioteers, identical-twin dancers Bettymae and Beverly Crane, and the Lindy Hop dance troupe Whitey's Steppers. Magicians, Hawaiian music, comedy teams, impersonators, clowns, and stuntmen filled out the cast.

Impact *Hellzapoppin'* benefited from the need for escapism during the late 1930's. After years of economic depression and uncertainty in the United States, the musical offered audiences a chance to experience a place in which chaos was entertaining and unexpected.

Tom Smith

Further Reading

Bordman, Gerald, and Thomas S. Hischak. "Hellzapoppin'." In *The Oxford Companion to American Theatre.* New York: Oxford University Press, 2004.

Hinckley, David. "Modern Mildew. *Hellzapoppin'* 1938." *New York Daily News*, September, 2005.

See also Broadway musicals; Film; Great Depression in the United States; Kaufman, George S., and Moss Hart; Theater in the United States.

■ Hemingway, Ernest

Identification Iconic American writer
Born July 21, 1899; Oak Park, Illinois
Died July 2, 1961; Ketchum, Idaho

Journalist, author of several classic novels, and winner of the 1954 Nobel Prize in Literature, Hemingway was a "writer's writer" and a supreme stylist. His sparse, understated prose, which was heavy on nouns and verbs and shunned display of emotion, influenced the development of twentieth century American fiction and has come to be recognized as the Hemingway style.

In poet Archibald MacLeish's often quoted praise, Ernest Hemingway was famous at twenty-five, at thirty, a master. However, during the 1930's, Hemingway was struggling for inspiration and artistic direction, while savagely resenting the critical success of writers such as John Dos Passos, who in 1936 became the first of his generation to make the cover of *Time* magazine. Hemingway had not published a novel since *A Farewell to Arms* (1929) and, even as he churned out more commercially successful short fiction, he feared that his talent was burning itself out, settling into a dull glow.

The self-doubts and the doubts of critics vanished for good with *For Whom the Bell Tolls* (1940), but in the 1930's, both remained strong. Pilloried by Max Eastman and other leftist and Marxist critics for indulging in rich man's safaris or fishing off forty-foot, oceangoing yachts at the time when people all over the United States were suffering from the Great Depression, his only novel during the decade was *To Have and Have Not* (1937). Even here, however, questions about his originality lingered. The first third of the book, for example, was stitched together from two previously published stories—"One Trip Across," published in *Cosmopolitan* in 1934, and "The Tradesman's Return," published in *Esquire* in 1936—in a semblance of narrative continuity.

Hard-boiled in style and more socially engaged than any of his previous publications, *To Have and Have Not* was written to bring him commercial success. In fact, his first appearance on the cover of *Time* coincided with the publication of the novel. In 1945,

the story was turned into a Hollywood film with Humphrey Bogart and Lauren Bacall, with the screenplay developed by William Faulkner and Jules Furthman.

If there is a theme that unites Hemingway's writings, it is the continuous presence of, and the need for response to, aggression and violence. Although he frequently focuses on the subtlety of human relationships and on the importance of the individual's conduct in society, he is sometimes stigmatized as an aficionado of machismo brutality. The picture that emerges from Hemingway's novels, and especially from *To Have and Have Not*, is that of the world at war. It is a harsh, indifferent place into which people are brought only to take a beating from life. What saves them, in the end, is their code of conduct: The saving grace of all those doomed to suffer may be the style with which they go down.

In 1937, second-guessing himself, Hemingway lobbied his publisher to issue *To Have and Have Not*

Novelist Ernest Hemingway working on For Whom the Bell Tolls *at Idaho's Sun Valley Lodge in Idaho in 1939.* (AP/Wide World Photos)

in an omnibus volume together with his previously acclaimed short stories "The Short Happy Life of Francis Macomber," "The Snows of Kilimanjaro," and "The Capital of the World." The first two originated from his experiences on a 1933 African safari that also gave him the material for the nonfictional *Green Hills of Africa* (1935). In the end, released as a stand-alone novel, *To Have and Have Not* was snapped up by a public titillated by reports of the succession of his failed marriages, health problems, literary feuds, and verbal attacks on his erstwhile friends and supporters. The book went through four printings in the first two months, stayed on the best-seller lists from October to December, 1937, and sold thirty-six thousand copies in the first five months.

Hemingway's previously off-the-shelf political awareness became markedly more sophisticated and personal during the 1930's. It owed in particular to his intense involvement in the Spanish Civil War and his agitprop work for the Loyalists, including the short 1937 film *The Spanish Earth* (narrated by Dos Passos and Hemingway). His more mature grasp of the political reality behind the slogans of proletarian revolution and the brotherhood of working men found its way into his longest and most ambitious novel. Commenced in March, 1939, and released the following year, *For Whom the Bell Tolls* cemented Hemingway's reputation as perhaps the most influential prosodist of the twentieth century.

Impact   For decades Hemingway's life and art have been at the center of a storm of critical controversy, largely owing to the writer himself and the larger-than-life personality he strove to create and then struggled to live up to. The decade of the 1930's may have been less successful artistically than others, but it marked his elevation to the rank of a modern classic in American literature.

Peter Swirski

Further Reading

Bruccoli, Matthew J., and Robert W. Trogdon, eds. *The Only Thing That Counts: The Ernest Hemingway-Maxwell Perkins Correspondence 1925-1947.* New York: Charles Scribner's Sons, 1996.

Grissom, Edgar. *Ernest Hemingway: A Descriptive Bibliography.* New Castle, Del.: Oak Knoll, 2010.

Hemingway, Ernest. *By-Line: Ernest Hemingway. Selected Articles and Dispatches of Four Decades.* Edited by William White, with commentaries by Philip Young. London: Collins, 1968.

Lynn, Kenneth S. *Hemingway.* New York: Simon and Schuster, 1987.

Mellow, James R. *Hemingway: A Life Without Consequences.* Boston: Houghton Mifflin, 1992.

Wagner-Martin, Linda, ed. *A Historical Guide to Ernest Hemingway.* New York: Oxford University Press, 2000.

See also   Faulkner, William; Fitzgerald, F. Scott; Hammett, Dashiell; Literature in the United States; West, Nathanael.

■ Hepburn, Katharine

Identification   American film and stage star
Born   May 12, 1907; Hartford, Connecticut
Died   June 29, 2003; Old Saybrook, Connecticut

Hepburn's fifteen films during the 1930's included more failures than successes, but her determination to succeed in Hollywood, along with her unusual talent, natural beauty, and independent spirit, led to a long and memorable career, inspiring generations of women.

When Katharine Hepburn arrived in Hollywood in 1932, she came with an arrogance and fierce ambition that stemmed from her New England background. Both of her parents were involved in social issues: Her father was a doctor concerned with venereal disease, and her mother campaigned for legal contraception. Debate was encouraged among their six offspring; thus, Hepburn was never reluctant to speak her mind. Her happy childhood was marred in adolescence by the tragic death of her older brother Tom. He was fifteen, she was thirteen, and it was she who discovered his body. Whether his hanging was a deliberate act or an accident was never determined.

After appearing in three plays while an undergraduate at Bryn Mawr College, Hepburn acted in summer stock and advanced to New York. She was fired from five Broadway productions; however, she was still determined to act and played bit parts in almost a dozen other plays. In her first leading role, in 1932 in *The Warrior's Husband*, a play by Julian Thompson, Hepburn, in a spectacular silver costume, bounded down the stairs with a stag slung over her shoulders; she caught the attention of Irene Selznick. She and husband David O. Selznick were seeking an unknown to play John Barrymore's daughter in *A Bill of Divorcement* (1932). Hepburn's screen test for the role was not particularly impressive; however, something about her manner attracted director George Cukor, and she was cast.

Hepburn later admitted that she was in the right place at the right time. The advent of sound in film in 1927 had thrown the industry into a state of turmoil that continued into the years of the Great Depression. Many stars of the silent film era could no longer be employed because of their inability to speak well. Studios anxiously sought fresh faces to fill this void. Young Hepburn appeared on the scene.

A Bill of Divorcement began shooting in July of 1932 and opened about two months later to great success. Hepburn was considered rather odd but engaging. RKO Pictures, delighted with its new ingenue, lined up more projects. Hepburn's following film, in 1933, was *Christopher Strong*, which failed financially but provided raves reviews for Hepburn, who played a fearless aviatrix. Next she fought for and won the role of the budding actor in *Morning Glory* (1933), for which she won her first Academy Award. The same year, *Little Women* was released; Hepburn thought she was born to play Jo March, and the public agreed. The film broke box-office records at Radio City Music Hall, and Hepburn's star position seemed to be secure.

Little Women was followed by seven forgettable films, although *Alice Adams* (1935) was nominated for an Academy Award and earned Hepburn good reviews. However, the financial failures reflected upon her ability to draw audiences, and despite *Stage Door* (1937), *Bringing Up Baby* (1938), and *Holiday* (1938), all of which later became favorites, she was labeled "box-office poison" by the end of the decade.

In 1938, she left Hollywood to appear in *The Philadelphia Story*, a play Philip Barry had written especially for her. She played a spoiled Main Line divorcee about to marry again. Her friend Howard Hughes advised her to buy the film rights even before the play opened. It opened in March, 1939, and ran for four hundred performances; Hepburn's star never dimmed again.

Impact In an era in which women could anticipate little beyond a home and children, Hepburn offered enticing alternatives. Her films of the 1930's presented a female character as the central figure, whether as an aviatrix, an aspiring writer, a gypsy, a queen, a scam artist, or a society snob. Whatever the persona, she was always smart, attractive, independent, unique, and assertive. She battled hard for her position, paving the way for other determined women both on and off the silver screen.

Joyce E. Henry

Further Reading

Berg, A. Scott. *Kate Remembered*. New York: G. P. Putnam's Sons, 2003.

Hepburn, Katharine. *Me: Stories of My Life*. New York: Ballantine Books, 1991.

Mann, William J. *Kate: The Woman Who Was Hepburn*. New York: Picador, 2007.

Pierpont, Claudia Roth. "Born for the Part." *The New Yorker* (July 14, 2003): 53-63.

See also Academy Awards; *Bringing Up Baby*; Film; Hughes, Howard; *100,000,000 Guinea Pigs*; Tracy, Spencer.

■ *Hindenburg* disaster

The Event Fire and explosion of dirigible
Date May 6, 1937
Place Lakehurst, New Jersey

The highly publicized fire and explosion of the Hindenburg *dirigible as it landed after a transatlantic flight terminated interest in dirigibles and effectively ended the era of the global commercial use of rigid airships in transporting passengers.*

Rigid dirigible balloons were first built on a large scale by Ferdinand von Zeppelin. On July 9, 1928, the Luftschiff Zeppelin 127 (LZ-127) was christened the *Graf Zeppelin*, and it quickly made several flights that set aviation records.

The LZ-129, named the *Hindenburg* for Paul von Hindenburg, the famous World War I German field marshal and second president of the Weimar Republic, was built according to a design intended to use the nonflammable gas helium, which, although twice as heavy as highly flammable hydrogen, possessed 92 percent of its lifting power. However, the dirigible operated with hydrogen because the U.S. Helium Control Act of March, 1925, prohibited the export of this rare gas, of which the United States possessed a virtual world monopoly.

The airship Hindenburg *bursting into flames.* (Courtesy, Navy Lakehurst Historical Society, Inc.)

With the appointment Adolf Hitler as German chancellor on January 30, 1933, the zeppelins were used as propaganda tools and symbols of the Third Reich's preeminence in commercial air travel. The *Hindenburg* flew over the Opening Ceremony of the 1936 Olympic Games in Berlin. The dirigible was the largest aircraft constructed up to that time. At 93 feet longer than the largest battleship, it was to Nazi Germany what the largest ocean liners, the *Queen Mary* and the *Normandie*, were to Great Britain and France.

The *Hindenburg*'s length was 804 feet, its height was 147 feet, and its weight with necessary equipment and fuel was 215 tons. Its berths, seats, dining room, lounges (complete with an aluminum grand piano and gourmet meals), and promenades were much more spacious than first-class accommoda-tions on most modern jumbo jetliners. Its relatively low fare and its luxurious accommodations contrib-uted to its popularity during the Great Depression.

Every conceivable precaution against fire was taken. The *Hindenburg* was considered the safest air-craft ever built, and Lloyd's of London insured it for 500,000 pounds, equivalent to about $2.5 million, at the low rate of 5 percent. When it departed from Frankfurt on May 3, 1937, en route to Lakehurst, New Jersey, on its first scheduled demonstration flight of the season, no one dreamed that this levia-than of the skies was destined to become the *Titanic* of lighter-than-air craft. At approximately 7 P.M. on May 6, 1937, Captain Max Pruss began the landing maneuver. At 7:25 P.M., as the giant airship de-scended to approximately 150 feet, the first flames were observed and were followed by an explosion.

Within thirty-four seconds the ship's main body crashed to the ground, a tangled wreckage of aluminum and burned fabric. Herbert Morrison, a radio journalist sent to cover the mooring of the airship live on the air, gave an eyewitness account of the crash to millions of radio listeners.

In the conflagration, twenty-two crew members, thirteen passengers, and one ground crew Navy linesman were killed. Sixty-two persons aboard the craft, many of whom were burned or injured, survived. Both U.S. and German commissions that investigated the catastrophe found no evidence of sabotage and concluded that the cause of the accident was ignition of a mixture of hydrogen and air resulting from a gas-cell leak. The Germans attributed the ignition to a spark, and the Americans, to brush discharge (St. Elmo's fire). The disaster terminated interest in rigid airships everywhere in the world. Since that day not a single dirigible has carried a paying passenger.

Impact Although the flammable lifting gas and not the structure of the airship caused the accident, the catastrophe strengthened the claims of critics who had long maintained that these aerial dinosaurs were dangerous and could never compete successfully with airplanes. Helium-filled blimps, the great dirigible's smaller cousins, are used for advertising, reconnaissance, scientific studies, and observation of sporting events; these remain the only vestige of those halcyon days of the 1930's when dirigibles captured the world's attention.

George B. Kauffman

Further Reading

Dick, Harold G., with Douglas H. Robinson. *The Golden Age of the Great Passenger Airships: Graf Zeppelin and Hindenburg.* Washington, D.C.: Smithsonian Institution Press, 1985.

Lace, William W. *The Hindenburg Disaster of 1937.* New York: Chelsea House, 2008.

Robinson, Douglas H. *Giants in the Sky: A History of the Rigid Airship.* Seattle: University of Washington Press, 1973.

Toland, John. *The Great Dirigibles: Their Triumphs and Disasters.* New York: Dover, 1972.

See also Airships; *Akron* disaster; Aviation and aeronautics; Great Depression in the United States; Nylon.

■ Hobbies

Definition Avocational activities pursued out of personal choice, often influenced by cultural and social attitudes

During the 1930's, several hobbies won widespread public attention and acceptance. Helping boost them to higher prominence was their positive economic impact during difficult times. Hobbies supported large numbers of manufacturing companies, distributors, and stores.

Early in the Great Depression, several companies whose products were important to American hobbyists permanently shut their doors. The general unavailability of cash also made the prospect dim for those who wished to pursue avocational interests. Other developments during the first half of the 1930's, however, created conditions for an unprecedented flourishing of hobbies in general.

Although many events helped counterbalance the negative impact of the stock market crash of 1929, none had so widespread an effect as the Chicago World's Fair held in Chicago in 1933 and 1934. In its reshaping of public attitudes toward the possibilities of commerce and industry, the exposition exerted considerable influence on daily life. The strong showings made by many manufacturers sharpened interest in mechanical progress, with automobiles, airplanes, and railroads commanding special attention. One hobby that benefited directly was model railroading. At least one million fairgoers visited the extensive model-railroad layout offered by American Flyer Manufacturing Company of Chicago. The crowd-pleasing display was initially located at the exposition's Enchanted Island and then within the heavily visited Travel and Transport Building.

While several manufacturers who had helped make model railroading a standard hobby of the 1920's had failed by the time of the exposition, others continued, with their numbers boosted by the fair. Ranking among the most important makers of model railway systems during the 1930's were American Flyer and Hafner Manufacturing of Chicago; the Lionel Corporation, Hoge Manufacturing, and Louis Marx and Company of New York; A. C. Gilbert of New Haven, Connecticut; Knapp Electric of Indianapolis; and William K. Walthers of Milwaukee. The hobby grew to the point that many smaller manufacturers produced railroad-system accessories, such as miniature buildings and metal figures. At the end of the decade, for example, at least seven national companies were manufacturing tunnels for use with model railroad systems.

Model Airplanes, Boats, and Race Cars Public interest in aviation spurred what was perhaps the fastest-growing hobby of the decade. The making and flying of model aircraft, which had become increasingly popular in the middle and later 1920's, became a significant, all-ages activity across the United States by the middle of the 1930's. At that point, more than fifty companies were involved in producing model aircraft and kits. Manufacturers of accessories and parts proliferated. The hobby's popularity continued increasing to the end of the decade. An example of this growth was Model Craft Hobbies of Toronto.

Starting with a single model in 1928, the company produced dozens of models by the end of the 1930's, with individual kits numbering approximately one million per year.

Making model boats also became widespread in the United States during the 1930's. Model-boat shows grew to sizable proportions, with one in 1934 sponsored by J. L. Hudson Co. of Detroit attracting more than three hundred entries. The Detroit Model Yacht Club encouraged the event, in a typical demonstration of the role that small, established clubs played in turning the minor hobby into one of national scope. Increasing numbers of model-kit manufacturers also helped its popularity. Thornecraft of Chicago, for example, made sailboat kits that appealed to model-sailboat-racing enthusiasts. One

A young family enjoys a model train, a popular collectible of the 1930's, during Christmas time. (©Camerique/ClassicStock/ CORBIS)

of the most successful companies throughout the 1930's was New York's Boucher Playthings Manufacturing. Boucher first emphasized miniature power- and sailboats but soon offered kits for constructing historic ships.

Another hobby that gained popularity at the end of the decade was the building and racing of gas-powered race cars. The kits for these model cars, which were often made of aluminum and other metal parts, were produced in some cases by model-airplane manufacturers. Other companies, such as Dooling Brothers of Los Angeles, specialized in fully assembled, streamlined aluminum racers.

Natural-History Hobbies   Alongside these hobbies, natural-history activities flourished. These interests required little or no money, a fact that aided their popularity. Encouragement also came from retail establishments. Displays organized by the education department of the University of Chicago at the Marshall Field Company store, often featuring natural-history materials, were typical of the times in that they reflected a progressive attitude concerning the educational importance of hobbies. Even model railroading was promoted as "practical" because it taught children about the operating conditions of real railroads. Rock and fossil collecting, butterfly collecting, flower-pressing, and astronomy were heavily promoted along educational lines and were pursued by youth and many adults.

Perhaps because of interest spurred by the Chicago World's Fair, the year 1933 was marked by the arrival of the inexpensive microscope as an item available to the natural-history hobbyist. Companies such as Goetz, Gans, and Orenstein of New York experienced increasing sales of items such as field glasses, microscope sets, dissecting kits, and telescope-based "transit sets," all of which were fully functional and were marketed not to the scientific establishment but to hobbyists and youths.

Educational sets that introduced people to more technical hobbies increased in use. These "outfits," as they were called, included mechanical and electrical kits that encouraged home-shop activities. Partly as a result of this, home radio-making and operation was a widely pursued pastime. Photography was steadily growing in popularity among the general public.

Many activity hobbies thrived, with companies such as Indian Archery Toy Corp. of Evansville, Indiana, taking advantage of growing interest in archery and darts games. On a different economic level, woodworking with discarded crates or cartons also became commonplace. The resulting "tramp art" picture frames or ornate boxes were not always made by tramps, although among hoboes the activity provided a vital means of making items for barter.

Collecting Hobbies   While stamp collecting had attracted some attention during the 1920's, during the 1930's the activity became more widespread. Some interest derived from the notion of philatelic investment, because of the rapid rise in values of U.S. stamp issues from the 1920's. Through the 1930's, an increasing number of collectors pursued stamp issues in order to hoard them in mint condition.

Several events stimulated interest in coin collecting. The change in design for the quarter coin contributed to this hobby. The 1930 last minting of the Standing Liberty quarter was not followed by the new design, featuring a bust of George Washington, until 1932. Other gaps occurred in minting series during this period. Mintings of the Lincoln penny were low from 1931 to 1933, after the large minting numbers of 1929 and 1930, which also prompted some collector interest. Late in the decade, the 1938 change from the Indian-head nickel to the Jefferson nickel again stimulated interest in coins. However, probably the most significant event of the decade that affected public interest in coins, and encouraged their collection, was the cessation of silver-dollar production in 1935.

An accident of history impacted the usually quiet realm of doll collecting. The birth of the Dionne quintuplets in 1934 provided the stimulus. A sign at a New York City department store, accompanying a display of dolls in sets of five, was typical in reflecting general interest; it read: "If you haven't a baby of your own Bloomingdale's will sell you one." The collection of not only five-doll sets but also the accompanying caps, outfits, bottles, cradles, and strollers became widespread in the summer of 1934. When the Dionne quintuplets were one year old, the release of dolls to reflect the rising popularity of child screen star Shirley Temple had a similar effect among collectors.

Manufactured Goods and Distribution Centers
Other all-ages hobbies in the early and later 1930's relied heavily upon manufactured goods. For example, New York's Blackstone Art Embroidery Com-

pany provided stamped and tinted items for embroidery, while Chicago's Molter-Reinhard Company catered to the art-needlework hobby, providing stamped linens and accessories. During the later decade, interest grew in crafts related to Native American beads and Native American weaving, aided by kits made by manufacturers such as New York's Indian Bead Company.

The growing numbers of dedicated distribution centers and stand-alone stores that appeared during the 1930's reflected the growing impact of hobbies on the American economy. Hobbycraft Model Supply of Detroit, established in the mid-1930's, was a distributor to more than five hundred retail outlets. It grew to occupy a three-floor building by the end of the decade. Some businesses that started as hobby shops, such as H. F. Auler's basement shop supporting model-building in Milwaukee, became established retail outlets. Auler opened Wisconsin Hobby Craft Shop and also engaged in manufacturing and distribution during the 1930's.

Department stores also began establishing hobby departments. Combined businesses became more commonplace. Gene Bloch's Paint Store, established in Allentown, Pennsylvania, devoted half of its space to hobbies, which accounted for the fastest growing aspect of its business.

Some nontraditional hobbies had significant economic impact, as was the case with the home-casting of lead or pewter items from manufactured molds. This activity was popular during the last half of the decade. Many individuals approached the casting of toys and novelties as a hobby business, with some of their basement efforts giving rise to small companies large enough to offer employment to others.

Impact   One indication of the impact of hobbies within the larger economy was the plans to unify the model-related sectors at the end of the 1930's. These efforts led to the establishment of the Model Industry Association, which became a major force in the hobby sector in the 1940's.

Mark Rich

Further Reading

Allen, Frederick L. *Since Yesterday: The 1930's in America, September 3, 1929 to September 3, 1939.* New York: Harper Perennial, 1986. Examination of both political and daily life in the United States.

Blom, Philipp. *To Have and to Hold: An Intimate History of Collectors and Collecting.* New York: Penguin Books, 2003. A far-ranging and engaging study of collecting that covers influences and trends in the collecting hobbies.

Dilworth, Leah, ed. *Acts of Possession: Collecting in America.* Piscataway, N.J.: Rutgers University Press, 2003. Provides historical perspective on the development of American collecting hobbies.

Featherstone, Raymond, Jr. *Naptown Memories: One Boy's Life Growing up in Indianapolis, 1930s and 1940s.* New York: iUniverse, 2006. A memoir of midwestern, middle-class life.

Kyvig, David E. *Daily Life in the United States, 1920-1940: How Americans Lived Through the Roaring Twenties and the Great Depression.* Chicago: Ivan R. Dee, 2004. Well-researched, lucid, and readable account of most aspects of American domestic life.

Young, William H. *The 1930s (American Popular Culture Through History).* Westport, Conn.: Greenwood Press, 2008. Concise, useful survey of the decade's popular culture; includes time line.

See also   Bingo; Coinage; Contract bridge; Fads; Homelessness; Marathon dancing; Monopoly; Radio in Canada; Radio in the United States; Recreation.

■ Holiday, Billie

Identification   African American jazz singer
Born   April 7, 1915; Philadelphia, Pennsylvania
Died   July 17, 1959; New York, New York

Holiday's ability to interpret a song with depth and profundity was unparalleled during the swing era of the 1930's and 1940's. Her impeccable sense of timing and melodic phrasing transcended her vocal limitations, consequently affecting the approach of subsequent generations of jazz singers.

Billie Holiday was born Eleanora Fagan to Sadie Fagan and Clarence Holiday. Her mother, a domestic worker, moved to New York City in 1928, leaving her teenage daughter in Baltimore in the care of Martha Miller, whom Holiday called "grandmother."

Holiday was drawn to the Baltimore nightlife at an early age and began singing in speakeasies such as Club Paradise by the end of 1928. Her burgeoning career was brief, as her mother requested she

Jazz singer Billie Holiday performing at the Offbeat Club in Chicago in 1939. (Archive Photos/Getty Images)

join her in Harlem. They resided at 151 West 140th Street between bustling Lenox Avenue and Seventh Avenue.

Holiday performed in small cabaret bars throughout the boroughs of New York in 1930. Disenchanted with her birth name, she adopted the stage name of Billie Holiday, hoping the change would enhance her job prospects.

During the early 1930's, Holiday continued to perform in Harlem nightclubs such as The Bright Spot and Connie's Inn. Her stint at Connie's Inn proved to be invaluable. In 1933, record producer John Hammond discovered Holiday during one of her appearances at Connie's Inn. A tireless advocate for Holiday, Hammond managed to procure a commitment from England's division of Columbia Records for a November 27, recording date with the Benny Goodman Orchestra. Holiday's commercial

debut with Goodman consisted of two songs: "Your Mother's Son-in-Law" and "Riffin' the Scotch."

In 1934, Hammond was working for the office of Irving Mills, a leading impresario who represented several top bands, including those of Duke Ellington and Cab Calloway. He persuaded Mills that Holiday was destined for stardom. Mills increased Holiday's exposure by including her in an Ellington short film entitled *Symphony in Black*.

Ellington treated Holiday as a featured star instrumentalist. He composed an accompaniment to suit the characteristics of her style. Holiday's performance in *Symphony in Black* underscored the centrality of her art, creating an inseparable link between lyrics, music, and singer.

In 1935, Holiday had several recording engagements with ensembles led by pianist Teddy Wilson. These sessions resulted in worthy renditions of "What a Little Moonlight Can Do" and "Miss Brown to You."

In 1936, Holiday left the management of Mills in favor of Louis Armstrong's manager, Joe Glaser. He procured a contract with the Fletcher Henderson Orchestra, the hottest swing band of the time. Holiday gained national exposure through radio broadcasts of Henderson's orchestra. She was offered a recording contract with Vocalion, a subsidiary of Brunswick Records.

By the spring of 1937, Count Basie, under the urging of Hammond, signed Holiday to join his band. She was the female complement to the powerful vocals of Jimmy Rushing. The association lasted less than one year; Basie cited the financial strain of carrying two vocalists on his payroll.

The move actually temporarily benefited Holiday. Less than one month after leaving Basie, she was hired by Artie Shaw's popular band. She began singing with the group in February of 1938, representing one of the first instances of a black female singer appearing with a white ensemble. In July of 1938, Holiday made her only known recording with Shaw's band, "Any Old Time."

In November of 1938, perhaps tired of the hard-driving tour schedule and the strain of racial oppression, Holiday left the Shaw orchestra. The bandleader ultimately replaced Holiday with Helen Forrest, who became one of the greatest singers of the swing era.

Holiday's decision to leave Shaw provided her the freedom to headline in a Greenwich Village nightclub called Café Society. Billed as "the Right Place for the Wrong People," Café Society was a "black and tan" club, a cabaret that advocated racial integration among its performers and clientele. In 1939, in the safety of this environment, Holiday introduced a song written by a teacher named Abel Meeropol. The antilynching protest song was entitled "Strange Fruit." Holiday credited Café Society with her success: "I opened as an unknown and I left two years later as a star."

During the 1940's, Holiday experienced critical acclaim and personal demise. She succumbed to heroin addiction, and her downfall was hastened. She died while under house arrest for possession of narcotics on July 17, 1959. By then, she was virtually penniless.

Impact   Holiday's impact on jazz and popular singing is immeasurable. Her influence and artistic expression can be heard in vocalists such as Sarah Vaughan, Frank Sinatra, and Tony Bennett.

Michael Conklin

Further Reading

Blackburn, Julie. *With Billie.* New York: Pantheon Books, 2005.

Holiday, Billie, with William Dufty. *Lady Sings the Blues.* Garden City, N.Y.: Doubleday, 1956.

Margolick, David. *Strange Fruit: The Biography of a Song.* New York: HarperPerennial, 2001.

Nicholson, Stuart. *Billie Holiday.* Boston: Northeastern University Press, 1995.

O'Meally, Robert. *Lady Day: The Many Faces of Billie Holiday.* New York: Arcade, 1991.

White, John. *Billie Holiday: Her Life and Times.* New York: Neal, 1987.

See also   Basie, Count; Ellington, Duke; Music: Jazz; Shaw, Artie.

■ Home Building and Loan Association v. Blaisdell

The Case   U.S. Supreme Court ruling on the impairment of the contract clause of the Constitution and on state powers to confront an economic emergency

Date   June 8, 1934

The decision upheld a Minnesota law that provided relief to hard-pressed debtors in the form of a two-year moratorium on mortgage foreclosures in the context of a national economic emergency.

Responding to the Depression-era plights of beleaguered home owners and farmers, the Minnesota legislature enacted a law enabling a Minnesota court, when litigating mortgage foreclosures, to exempt the properties from foreclosure during the period of economic emergency, not to exceed two years. The Home Building and Loan Association sought to foreclose on the home of John H. Blaisdell, but the Court denied foreclosure during the authorized period provided that regular, court-approved monthly payments continued to be made.

The bank appealed to the U.S. Supreme Court, citing Article I, section 10 of the Constitution, which states "No State shall . . . pass any . . . Law impairing the Obligation of Contracts." A bare majority of the Supreme Court, in an opinion by Chief Justice Charles Evan Hughes, declined to read the clause literally, or as it had been understood by the Court during the early nineteenth century. Instead, the Court construed the contract clause in the light of contemporary experience and the needs of a new society, especially in the context of an economic emergency. The Minnesota law left intact the fundamental regime of contract, including the binding obligation of the parties. Only a limited extension of the schedule for repayment had been affected, a reasonable adjustment to preserve the economic well-being of the community. The dissent, by Justice George Sutherland and three of his colleagues, argued that the contract clause had a singular and timeless meaning, and so must be understood as the framers of the Constitution understood it.

Impact   The decision signaled a departure from past readings of the contract clause as an absolute prohibition on the revision of contracts. With the rise of state police powers, the clause would henceforth be read as balancing the interests of contracting parties with reasonable considerations of the public good.

John C. Hughes

Further Reading

Friedman, Barry. *The Will of the People: How Public Opinion Has Shaped the Supreme Court and Shaped the Meaning of the Constitution.* New York: Farrar, Straus and Giroux, 2009.

Lewis, Thomas T., ed. *U.S. Supreme Court.* Pasadena, Calif.: Salem Press, 2007.

Schwartz, Bernard. *A History of the Supreme Court.* New York: Oxford University Press, 1993.

See also   Business and the economy in the United States; Congress of Industrial Organizations; Credit and debt; Great Depression in the United States; Hughes, Charles Evans; Supreme Court, U.S.

■ Home furnishings

Definition   Lighting, furniture, appliances, and accessories for domestic interiors

The 1930's was a period of rebellion against traditional design in home furnishings. A modernist design aesthetic developed, using new technologies and materials. The kitchen became more functional and efficient and was filled with beautiful, scientifically advanced appliances and gadgets. The economic turmoil of the decade led manufacturers to establish industrial design departments to create distinctive and competitive modern products. Many of these designs and innovations have had a lasting impact.

The Great Depression of the 1930's was an economic reversal of the prosperous 1920's. A design revolution also occurred during the 1930's. A rebellion against conventional or traditional design aesthetics led to Moderne, or modernistic, design, expressed in the Art Deco style at the beginning of the decade and then later as a style called Streamline Moderne. Instead of using traditional ornamentation, home furnishings in the Moderne style had streamlined shapes and clean lines, suggesting the movement and speed of machines. The style also made use of newly developed technologies and materials, such as plastic, aluminum, and wood laminates. Most of the products were mass produced and affordable for the middle class. The average home had some traditional-style rooms. The typical living room had an upholstered sofa and chairs. Most rooms had rugs or linoleum floors and flowered wallpaper and curtains. However, furnishings in the Moderne style were popular and widespread.

New Design, Materials, and Technologies   The Art Deco style was introduced at the 1925 Exposition Internationale des Arts Décoratifs et Industriels Modernes. This style emphasized a basic geometrical structure, typically including repeating lines, rounded corners, steps, and symmetry. Rich colors, black, and metallics were used frequently. Stylized sun rays, animals, and foliage were common motifs. Materials included chrome, glass, and Bakelite, a chemically resistant plastic. Natural materials such as silver, rock crystal, ivory, and jade also were popular.

Streamline Moderne was a more radical transformation in design, allowing no ornamentation and little applied decoration. The style emphasized pure lines and simplified, abstract forms with rounded corners. New materials such as chrome, plastics, stainless steel, and aluminum were used to construct home furnishings such as chairs, vacuum cleaners, telephones, sewing machines, electric clocks, and lamps. The three-piece seating suite, an invention of the 1930's, often had chrome hardware. Bakelite was used for countless home furnishings, including radios, light switches, and telephones.

Magazines such as *Better Homes and Gardens*, *Woman's Home Companion*, *House Beautiful*, the *Ladies Home Journal*, and *Home and Garden* provided advice on how to modernize the home and included advertisements for Veltone Sealex flooring, Armstrong linoleum, appliances, furniture, and other home products. In 1933, Sears promoted its 1933 "top-operator" washer, which had controls on a top panel and chrome bands, as a Moderne style improvement on earlier models.

One of the most influential innovators of the 1930's was Finnish architect and designer Alvar Aalto. An internationally known modernist, he aimed to humanize mechanical forms and technology to assert cultural values. Named for the town where Aalto designed a tuberculosis sanatorium, the revolutionary Paimio, or scroll, chair was developed from 1930 to 1933. Made of molded plywood, solid birch, and bent laminated birch, the chair was sculptural, organic, and sturdy. The curved seat was a thin piece of plywood bent into scrolls at the top and bottom. It was held between ribbonlike loops of bent laminated birch veneers serving as both arms and legs. Other famous pieces of furniture included the three-legged stacking stool (1933) and the Zebra Tank Chair (1935-1936).

In 1935, Artek Ltd. was established to manufacture Aalto's furniture, and in 1936, the company began exporting products to the United States. In 1936, Aalto designed the world-famous Savoy vase, a glass vase with a free-form, organic design and wavy lines. In 1938, the Museum of Modern Art in New York City presented an exhibition of Aalto's designs.

Industrial Design Another 1930's phenomenon was the rise of the industrial designer, a profession that the U.S. Patent Office had recognized in 1913. During the Great Depression, department stores and manufacturers realized that to be competitive and increase sales, they needed design departments to give their products a distinct identity and to develop compelling advertising. In 1931, Montgomery Ward established its bureau of design, and in 1934, Sears, Roebuck and Company formed its Merchandise Testing and Development Laboratory. Pioneers of the industrial design profession in the United States included Henry Dreyfuss, an ergonomic designer for Thermos, Hoover, and Bell Telephone; Donald Deskey, known for his Moderne interiors and furniture; and Raymond Loewy, an appliance designer for Sears, Roebuck and Company.

Art schools, such as the School of the Art Institute of Chicago and the University of Illinois at Urbana-Champaign, added industrial design programs to their curricula. Professional organizations, such as the American Designers Institute (1938), were formed to unite design professionals. Further endorsement of industrial design came from the fine-art establishment. In 1932, the Museum of Modern Art (MoMA) in New York started a department of architecture and design. In 1934, MoMA presented *Machine Art*, an exhibition of industrial design, and the Metropolitan Museum of Art in New York presented the exhibition *Contemporary American Industrial Art*.

American industrial designer Russel Wright was instrumental in popularizing the Moderne aesthetic. Using new technologies and materials, he designed visually distinctive furniture, dinnerware, and tex-

tiles that were mass produced and inexpensive. Between 1935 and 1939, Conant Ball Company manufactured Wright's celebrated line of Art Deco American modern "blond" wood furniture. In 1937, he created his classic American Modern ceramic dinnerware for Steubenville Pottery, which manufactured the tableware from 1939 until 1959. The appealing colors, glazes, and organic design helped make the ceramic dinnerware the best selling in history. During the 1930's, Wright also introduced spun aluminum oven-to-tableware, spherical vases, cocktail shakers, planters, ice buckets, and other housewares in spun aluminum. Combining form and function in his designs, Wright promoted his concept of informal, "easier living" instead of formal etiquette.

Another influential designer was Gilbert Rohde, who in 1931 designed the first Moderne style furniture produced by the legendary Herman Miller Company. He explored the use of chrome for furniture and created electric clocks made of chrome-plated metal and glass. Another significant industrial designer was Norman Bel Geddes, whose commercial designs included chrome-plated brass cocktail shakers, radio cabinets, and the classic, sleek Cobra Lamp.

The Transformation of the Kitchen During the 1930's, the North American kitchen was transformed into the Streamline Moderne style kitchen. In the typical 1920's kitchen, the sink, table, stove, and icebox were freestanding, separate pieces. There was also a "Hoosier," the freestanding cabinet and counter combination with drawers. During the 1930's, built-in cabinets and countertops and large appliances placed ergonomically became the norm. The kitchen was organized and efficiently laid out. In 1930, Freon was introduced as a refrigerant. Unlike previous refrigerating mediums, Freon was not flammable and was nontoxic, so refrigerator leaks were no longer dangerous. Refrigerator sales jumped. By the middle of the decade, Sears, Roebuck and Company and General Electric were manufacturing Streamline refrigerators. By 1935, eight million refrigerators using Freon had been sold in the United States.

Moderne kitchen accessories were readily available from stores such as Montgomery Ward and Sears. These companies sold colorful bread boxes, canister sets, cake servers, and other kitchenware. One of the most popular colors was "Depression green," often combined with cream. Depression glass or "tank glass" was inexpensive, mass-produced kitchenware that came in pink, amber, burgundy, and various greens. In 1936, Fiestaware table settings, available in five mix-or-match colors, came on the market. Other kitchen essentials included enameled steel products and large cookie jars in various shapes, such as penguins or clowns.

The Great Depression changed social activities and eating habits. Instead of formal dinners, less expensive, casual, or potluck parties were in vogue. Gatherings often combined meals with popular activities such as playing cards. Eating and entertaining at home were more convenient and affordable than dining out, and the 1930's kitchen was full of electric gadgets and small appliances that made cooking relatively easy. In contrast to the utilitarian designs of the 1920's, many kitchen devices were shiny, beautifully designed pieces that could be used at the dining table too.

In 1930, the amazing Sunbeam Mixmaster, designed by Ivar Jepson, was introduced. Unlike earlier mechanical mixers, the Mixmaster had two detachable beaters with interlocking blades and a motor encased in a pivoting perpendicular arm reaching over a bowl. Affordable, durable, and versatile, the Mixmaster was an instant success. It could peel, grind, juice, mash, slice, chop, shred, whip, grate, open cans, and sharpen knives. Coffeemakers, chafing dishes, hot plates, Waring blenders, waffle irons, pop-up toasters, and electric snack servers also helped simplify cooking and entertaining. The electric roaster, a freestanding portable oven, was one of the best-selling kitchen aids.

Impact　During World War II, many industrial designers worked on aircraft, naval, cartographic, and other war projects. After the war, corporate design staffs grew to meet the increased consumer demands. During the 1980's, as global competition grew and companies restructured, many internal design departments were eliminated. A trend toward outsourcing design and product development needs continued into the twenty-first century.

Aalto revolutionized furniture design and technology. Along with innovators Rohde and Deskey, Aalto laid the foundation for future designers such as George Nelson and Charles and Ray Eames. Aalto's Artek furniture collections and his legendary handcrafted vases continued to be popular and were eventually marketed on the Internet.

Wright, with help from his wife Mary Wright, made his name a recognizable trademark. They invented personality driven, lifestyle marketing, which laid the groundwork for future lifestyle empires such as those of Ralph Lauren, Martha Stewart, and Oprah Winfrey. Russel Wright Studios continued as an industrial design licensing firm.

The efficient 1930's modern kitchen with the latest appliances and gadgets has remained the ideal. The classic Sunbeam Mixmaster, the original food processor, was manufactured and sold until 1967. It remained a cultural icon and symbol of the 1930's.

Alice Myers

Further Reading

Abercrombie, Stanley. *A Century of Interior Design 1900-2000.* New York: Rizzoli, 2003. Illustrated sourcebook using a time line format to describe yearly developments in technology, culture, architecture, and furniture and furnishing design.

Bayer, Patricia. *Art Deco Interiors: Decoration and Design Classics of the 1920s and 1930s.* London: Thames & Hudson, 1998. An informative chronicle of the modern and exotic Art Deco style, including its evolution in the United States. Includes more than three hundred illustrations, more than one-half of which are in color. Includes bibliography and index.

Fiell, Peter, and Charlotte Fiell. *30s, 40s Decorative Art: A Source Book.* New York: Taschen, 2000. Almost six hundred pages of illustration and commentary covering architecture, interiors and furniture, metalwork, ceramics and glass, lighting, and textiles.

Mielke, Rita. *The Kitchen: History, Culture, Design.* Berlin: Art Books International, 2005. With more than four hundred illustrations, this comprehensive history describes the design trends, furnishings, and technological evolution of the kitchen through the centuries. Includes appendix.

Parissien, Steven. *Interiors: The Home Since 1700.* London: Laurence King, 2009. This history of home interiors analyzes the middle-class homes and the impact of technology in Western Europe and North America. Includes bibliography and index.

Troy, Virginia Gardner. *The Modernist Textile: Europe `and America, 1890-1940.* Aldershot: Lund Humphries, 2006. A scholarly work covering textile design in the United States, including constructivism, modernist impulses, and pictorial tapestry during the 1930's. Mostly color illustrations. Includes bibliography and index.

Wilson, Kristina. *Livable Modernism: Interior Decorating and Design During the Great Depression.* New Haven, Conn.: Yale University Press, 2004. Analysis of the marketing of the livable modernism products for middle-class homes during the Great Depression. Illustrated. Includes bibliography and index.

See also   Advertising in Canada; Advertising in the United States; Freon; Housing in Canada; Housing in the United States; Recreation; Refrigerators; Telephone technology and service.

■ Homelessness

Definition   The state of existence in which families or individual persons have become unable to secure and maintain stable residence in dwellings

During the 1920's, people often became hoboes because they desired the freedom from material concerns that homelessness, travel, and adventure afforded them. In the 1930's, the number of hoboes—men, women, and youth—increased exponentially as a result of the Great Depression. No longer were most hoboes seeking travel experiences and adventure; rather, they tended to be consumed with the grim realities of economic survival.

Prior to the Depression, homeless people and hoboes were perceived as single men who desired the freedom that homelessness, travel, and adventure afforded them. In his 1923 book *The Hobo: The Sociology of the Homeless Man*, Nels Anderson called them "itinerant casual workers." Hoboes migrated, seeking seasonal work, and they depended mainly on rail transportation, usually secured through unpaid passage.

In the 1930's, however—as a result of their economic marginalization—homeless persons included not only traditional hoboes but also women, children, and youth. The numbers of homeless persons increased exponentially as migrants began to seek work wherever they could find it. Many of the homeless families traveled to seek employment that would sustain their livelihoods. The migration of families during the 1930's differed from earlier internal migrations because of the advent and private ownership of the automobile. Many families in the east and south headed north and west.

The numbers of those economically marginalized into homelessness probably began rising as early as the American stock market crash and banking industry failure in the fall of 1929. Specific information on the human impacts of the first few years of the Great Depression is clouded by the official stance of President Herbert Hoover's administration, which was to assure Americans that the economy and job market soon would rebound to levels that had preceded the stock market crash and bank failures. What is known is that at least 20 percent of American families and individuals were estimated to be homeless by 1933 and 1934. Some historians speculate that 30 percent of the American workforce was unemployed during those years.

A homeless mother carries her child while searching for work along Highway 99, near Brawley, California. (Library of Congress)

For fathers of families, for single young men and young women, and even for teenagers migrating to find employment, the open boxcars of freight trains and the rod undercarriages of passenger trains beckoned, offering free travel. These individuals formed the ranks of a new type of hobo: characterized by the frustrations of finding little or no work, ever hoping to find lucrative employment so that the homeless life of travel could come to an end. There was, among these hoboes of the 1930's, little of the excitement of travel for travel's sake or the eagerness for adventure that had characterized hoboes of the earlier period.

Citizens of the states and of the cities of destination frequently protested the migrations and lobbied governments to exclude outsiders from seeking local employment. Those migrating did not find the sustaining employment opportunities they expected: While hoboes of the era between 1865 and 1930 found ready employment in helping to build the superstructures of Western industry and in providing the work required for labor-intensive agricultural production, the migrants of the 1930's found few jobs available after arriving at their destinations, because labor-saving technologies, in both industry and agriculture, had been developed in the interim.

Impact With marches by the homeless on the nation's capital, with food riots in the larger cities, with the growing strength of underemployed workers' organizations demanding aid, and with the common sight of destitute families sitting barefoot, dressed in rags, beside the road or begging in residential neighborhoods door-to-door, the U.S. government was compelled to respond. Hence the homelessness of the 1930's impacted, and was in turn impacted by, two major governmental actions: the New Deal programs set in place by President Franklin D. Roosevelt and, eventually, the decision of the U.S. Congress to enter into war with Germany and Japan in World War II.

The social services and welfare programs set up under President Roosevelt's guidance offered new options for homeless families. With the institution of the social welfare and works projects programs, marginalized families and individuals no longer felt absolutely driven to migrate to sustain themselves.

When the United States entered into warfare with Germany and Japan, the huge scale of World War II required that every American be involved in some way to ensure American success. While the military operations demanded the participation of every available healthy male for combat and many women for support in the field, war production demands required the labor of many older or less healthy males, and many women were recruited as industrial laborers.

Therefore, the social welfare programs of President Roosevelt ended much of the American internal labor migration of the 1930's, while the demands of World War II effectively ended the era of hoboes as migrant seasonal laborers, as practiced before 1930, or as itinerant pursuers of work, as practiced during the 1930's.

Edward J. Schauer

Further Reading

Allsop, Kenneth. *Hard Travellin'*. New York: New American Library, 1967.

Anderson, Nels. *The Hobo: The Sociology of the Homeless Man*. Chicago: University of Chicago Press, 1923.

_____. *Men on the Move*. Chicago: University of Chicago Press, 1940.

Bruns, Roger A. *Knights of the Road*. New York: Methuen, 1980.

Cresswell, Tim. *The Tramp in America*. London: Reaktion Books, 2001.

Mathers, M. *Riding the Rails*. Boston: Gambit, 1973.

Minehan, Thomas. *Boy and Girl Tramps of America*. New York: Farrar and Rinehart, 1934.

Reitman, Ben L. *Boxcar Bertha: An Autobiography—as Told to Dr. Ben L. Reitman*. New York: Amok Press, 1988.

Terkel, Studs. *Hard Times: An Oral History of the Great Depression*. New York: Pantheon, 1970.

Watkins, T. H. *The Hungry Years: A Narrative History of the Great Depression in America*. New York: Henry Holt, 1999.

See also Breadlines and soup kitchens; *Grapes of Wrath, The*; Guthrie, Woody; Hoovervilles; Housing in the United States; Migrations, domestic; Oklahoma Welfare Act of 1936; Scottsboro trials; Sinclair, Upton; Unemployment in the United States.

■ Homosexuality and gay rights

During the 1930's, the concept of homosexuality was seldomly discussed neutrally. In the public mind, it was affiliated with a range of behaviors disruptive to basic social concepts such as the family and morality. Furthermore, open discussion of sexuality in general was taboo during this time.

Public mention of homosexuality in the United States was limited almost exclusively to the literatures of medicine, psychiatry, and law. Reprints of translated articles from European professional journals of psychology conveyed the view that homosexuality was a condition responsive to various therapeutic techniques. The first major studies of the nature of sexuality by U.S. researchers appeared in 1933 and 1934.

In a society that had abandoned the more flexible social attitudes of the 1920's, homosexuality was regarded as an abnormality that threatened the stability of traditional social structures and conservative mores. Although Sigmund Freud privately assured an American mother in 1935 that homosexuality was "no advantage . . . but nothing to be ashamed of," this was a minority view in psychology circles. In 1935, the American Psychological Association issued a report documenting the use of aversion therapy using electricity to treat a male homosexual; this case was the first appearance of a technique that became widely applied.

In the field of law, sodomy regulations, which had been part of the law codes of every state since colonial times, were joined by the new category of sex crimes, a designation that grouped homosexuality with violent criminal behaviors such as rape and child molestation. This allowed men and women identified as homosexual to be prosecuted as part of efforts to maintain community moral standards. Confusion stemming from what constituted the range of crimes covered by sodomy laws was clarified in a January, 1939, ruling by the Georgia Supreme Court. The case at issue was an appeal by Ella Thompson of a conviction on the grounds that the Georgia sodomy law as written did not include acts between two women, a strategy that resulted in the overturning of her previous judgment.

The portrayal in literature of homosexual people and their relationships mirrored the illness model offered by medicine and psychiatry. Many of these characters either died or were abandoned in the course of the plot. The use of this theme reinforced the idea that stable and lasting homosexual relationships for either gender were doomed or were an unhealthy parody of the mainstream nuclear family. Nonetheless, works celebrating same-sex unions continued to appear on the American market, including those from such notable writers as André Gide, Radclyffe Hall, and Christa Winsloe. American expatriate author and poet Gertrude Stein added to the complexity of the picture with her 1933 work *The Autobiography of Alice B. Toklas*. The use of lesbianism as a plot element by American writers was so frequent that by the end of the decade the topic was not nearly as controversial. For example, the public reaction to Gale Wilhelm's 1938 novel *Torchlight to Valhalla* was tepid, which was a sharp contrast to the reception of her first lesbian novel, *We Too Are Drifting* (1935), which had been described as dealing with "potentially disturbing subject-matter." The decade ended with the publication of Diana Frederics's *Diana: A Strange Autobiography* (1939), in which the main character atypically accepts her lesbian orientation and works to achieve a satisfying life.

The theater pushed the limits of sexual censorship in subtle ways with plays such as Noël Coward's *Design for Living* (1932) and Lillian Hellman's *The Children's Hour* (1934). A set of standards adopted by the Motion Picture Producers and Distributors Association in 1930 called for films to conform to "the wholesome instincts of life" and stated that "sex perversion or any inference of it is forbidden on the screen." Films such as Greta Garbo's *Queen Christina* (1933) and *Mädchen in Uniform* (1931) used the themes of cross-dressing and same-gender affection within traditional social structures such as the school and public life.

In contrast to the active homosexual rights movement in Germany led by Magnus Hirschfeld and his colleagues, the United States possessed no organizations advocating similar social change. The characterization of homosexuals as persons suffering from psychological disorders worked against any open affiliation of individuals whose formal mission involved civil rights for an already marginalized population.

Impact   The classification of same-sex affections as a subject both unmentionable and controversial effectively isolated homosexual men and women. The absence of any means of secure communication among homosexuals resulted in the creation of informal social networks in the larger cities but prohibited the formation of a larger sense of community identity.

Robert Ridinger

Further Reading

Freud, Sigmund. "Sigmund Freud on Homosexuality (1935)." In *Gay and Lesbian Rights in the United States: A Documentary History*. Westport, Conn.: Greenwood Press, 1983.

Griffin, Sean. *Hetero: Queering Representations of Straightness*. Albany: State University of New York Press, 2009.

Katz, Jonathan, ed. *Gay American History: Lesbians and Gay Men in the United States*. New York: Thomas Y. Crowell, 1976.

_____. *Gay/Lesbian Almanac*. New York: Harper & Row, 1983.

Potter, La Forest. *Strange Loves: A Study in Sexual Abnormalities*. New York: Robert Dodsley, 1933.

Segall, James Leo. *Sex Life in America, Its Problems and Their Solution*. New York: B. Marks, 1934.

See also   *Children's Hour, The*; Civil rights and liberties in the United States; Hellman, Lillian; Medicine; Psychology and psychiatry; Sex and sex education.

■ Hoover, Herbert

Identification   President of the United States, 1929-1933
Born   August 10, 1874; West Branch, Iowa
Died   October 20, 1964; New York, New York

The thirty-first president of the United States, Hoover was embroiled in the Great Depression. The inability of his administration to cope with the worst economic crisis in the nation's history resulted in a massive repudiation of his Republican Party at the voting booth in 1932. Hoover spent the rest of the 1930's attempting to vindicate his record and to make another run at the presidency.

Herbert Clark Hoover was the second of three children of Jesse Clark and Hulda Minthorn Hoover and was a member of one of the Quaker families that founded rural West Branch, Iowa. His father died of pneumonia in 1880, and his mother died in 1884. After their mother's death, the orphaned Hoover sib-

lings separated for four years, living with different relatives. Hoover was raised in a devoutly religious environment, a fact that affected him throughout his career.

From 1891 to 1895, Hoover attended Stanford University, graduating with a degree in geology. He was forced by economic circumstance to take a job beneath his educational qualifications as a mine laborer in Nevada City, California. Within months he had worked up to an engineering position, and in 1897, he secured a post with the British mining and engineering firm of Bewick, Moreing Company. He was sent to Western Australia and was soon promoted to manager. He married a former Stanford classmate, Lou Henry, in 1899; eventually, the couple had two sons: Herbert Clark, Jr., and Allan Henry.

"The Great Engineer"   Hoover was so successful in turning moribund Australian mining operations into profit-generating enterprises that he was sent by Bewick, Moreing and Company to China. In 1900, he and his wife were among the members of the foreign community besieged by the Boxers in the city of Tianjin. Hoover took an active role in military operations, designing the city defenses and guiding a contingent of U.S. Marines. Surviving this brush with death, he returned to Australia in 1901, becoming a full company partner and a millionaire by the time he left the company in 1908. From 1908 to 1917, he served as a mines and engineering consultant, author, and itinerant lecturer. He began to earn the sobriquet of "the Great Engineer," a title that henceforth defined him.

Shortly after the start of World War I, Hoover grew concerned about the plight of the Belgian population, many of whom were threatened with starvation under the German occupation. His work with the Committee for Relief in Belgium earned him recognition as a notable humanitarian and a superb organizer and catapulted him to international fame. In 1917, after the U.S. entry into the war on the Allied side, Hoover was designated the director of the U.S. Food Commission. In the immediate aftermath of the war, he directed the American Relief Organization and dispatched emergency food shipments to Germany and the former Austro-Hungarian Empire.

Political Career to 1929   So respected was Hoover by 1920, he was courted by individuals within both parties for the presidential nomination. However, he

President Hoover's 1931 State of the Union Address

Reproduced below is an excerpt of President Herbert Hoover's address to Congress on December 8, 1931, given in the midst of the Great Depression.

If we lift our vision beyond these immediate [economic] emergencies we find fundamental national gains even amid depression. In meeting the problems of this difficult period, we have witnessed a remarkable development of the sense of cooperation in the community. For the first time in the history of our major economic depressions there has been a notable absence of public disorders and industrial conflict. Above all there is an enlargement of social and spiritual responsibility among the people. The strains and stresses upon business have resulted in closer application in saner policies, and in better methods. Public improvements have been carried out on a larger scale than even in normal times. The country is richer in physical property, in newly discovered resources, and in productive capacity than ever before. There has been constant gain in knowledge and education; there has been continuous advance in science and invention; there has been distinct gain in public health. Business depressions have been recurrent in the life of our country and are but transitory. The nation has emerged from each of them with increased strength and virility because of the enlightenment they have brought, the readjustments and the larger understanding of the realities and obligations of life and work which come from them.

was by family and regional conviction a Republican, and so entered the race for the Republican nomination. A reluctance to campaign aggressively and a rather dull and pedantic oratorical style slowed his campaign's momentum: He experienced successive primary election losses in Minnesota, Michigan, Montana, and his adopted home state of California. Though he entertained vague hopes that a convention deadlock might bring about his nomination, Hoover's 1920 run for president had ended.

In 1921, Hoover was appointed secretary of commerce by President Warren G. Harding, serving through the Calvin Coolidge administration until August 21, 1928, when he accepted the Republican nomination for president. By then his reputation as a humanitarian and efficiency expert had been enhanced by his handling of relief to Russia from 1921 to 1923, again under the auspices of the American Relief Administration, and by his energetic tenure as the most productive of the cabinet secretaries during the 1920's. Buoyed by the unprecedented economic prosperity of the "New Era" of the 1920's and by his own standing as the organizational genius of his day, Hoover easily beat his Democratic adversary, New York governor Alfred E. Smith, by roughly 58 to 41 percent of the popular vote and by 444 to 87 in the electoral college.

Presidency The auspicious beginning to Hoover's presidency was shattered by the collapse of the stock market in 1929, the extreme contraction of the economy known as the Great Depression, and the Dust Bowl of the Midwest. After making predictions during the early months of his term about the imminent disappearance of poverty, Hoover never recovered his credibility with the American people. This was aggravated by his continual optimism in the face of a worsening situation and by his slowness to realize the horrific nature of what the general populace was facing. His persistent adherence to a policy of volunteerism and individual private initiative and his attempts to persuade business leaders to reinvest, to keep employment and wage levels up, and to provide loans to buttress smaller financial institutions through the National Credit Corporation all faltered in the face of an extreme economic situation that he failed to grasp fully.

One of Hoover's most misguided efforts to revive the economy was the Hawley-Smoot Tariff Act of 1930, which tried to protect American businesses and jobs by imposing a high import duty on foreign products. The measure backfired when foreign governments responded with their own increased duties, igniting a tariff trade war and deepening rather than improving the Depression. Hoover committed another monumental blunder when he ordered General Douglas MacArthur to clear the Bonus Army marchers out of Washington, D.C., on July 28,

1932. Exceeding his orders, MacArthur ordered an attack on the demonstrators' tent city, causing deaths and injuries. Though Hoover disapproved of the Army's assault on civilians, he never reprimanded the general and so was viewed as complicit by some.

Disheartened, visibly tired, and with reelection prospects bleak, Hoover was renominated by the Republican Party in June, 1932. The Democratic nominee, New York governor Franklin D. Roosevelt, hammered the president for both his lackluster early response to the economic crisis and the radical nature of the relief legislation he had later introduced. In the 1932 election, Roosevelt won the presidency in a landslide, and Democrats won a majority in the Senate and the House of Representatives. Hoover was ousted by a popular percentage total of 57.4 to 39.7 percent (Norman Thomas garnered 2.2 percent of the votes, and other candidates accounted for the remaining 0.7 percent of the votes) and by 472 to 59 in the electoral college.

In July of 1932, which by then was far too late to salvage the elections, Hoover had enacted the Emergency Relief and Construction Act, which set into motion the allocation of funds through the Reconstruction Finance Corporation into job-creating building projects. Ironically, though this measure would be incorporated into the New Deal, at the time the Democrats denounced Hoover for going back on his self-help principles and introducing elements of socialism. The Norris-La Guardia Act, which marked a departure from noninterventionist principles by prohibiting employer contracts requiring permanent nonunion membership as a condition of employment, likewise did little to help Hoover's candidacy.

For many years, the Depression obscured the accomplishments of the Hoover administration, which included the construction of both the Hoover Dam (originally the Boulder Dam) on the Colorado River and the San Francisco Bay Bridge; a softening of U.S. policy regarding Latin America, which was later appropriated by the Roosevelt administration in the Good Neighbor Policy; the London Naval Treaty to reduce naval and submarine armaments; and the Pratt-Smoot Act of 1931, which established the Books for the Blind program.

Aftermath of Hoover's Presidency   Hoover took his electoral defeat much to heart; he had been sub-

jected to a degree of invective and denunciation for which his previously highly successful career had ill-prepared him. Tent cities were dubbed "Hoovervilles," and turned-out pockets were called "Hoover flags." Roosevelt rebuffed all overtures from Hoover to meet and cooperate in making the five-month transition of presidential administrations as smooth as possible. Bitterness grew between the two men, which lasted until Roosevelt's death, until which time Hoover was frozen out of any major role in the public sphere. Defying those who proclaimed him to be a broken man who would not survive long after his term of office, Hoover remained proactive in political affairs, roundly attacking the New Deal, writing books, and placing himself in readiness for another try at the Republican nomination for the election of 1936, where he hoped that a deadlocked convention might turn to him. However, the possibility was never seriously entertained by most of the delegates, who nominated Kansas governor Alf

Former U.S. president Herbert Hoover posing with his pet dog in 1935. (Archive Photos/Getty Images)

Landon. A similar fate awaited Hoover's candidacy in 1940, when the Republicans nominated business executive Wendell Willkie. Thereafter, Hoover ceased all efforts to recapture the presidency.

After Harry S. Truman ascended to the presidency, Hoover's reputation began to be rehabilitated. Truman first called upon Hoover to advise and oversee relief efforts and food distribution in Allied-occupied areas of what later became West Germany. From 1947 to 1949 and again from 1953 to 1955, he chaired the Hoover Commission, which was charged with examining the workings of the executive branch of government and offering suggestions on measures aimed at increasing its efficiency and economy of operations.

Impact Hoover has been seen as a well-meaning individual whose fixation on his self-help philosophy kept him from discerning the desperate nature of the plight of the average American until the Depression had progressed too far. His tardy response left him open to invective and vilification from his political opponents. His failure thus subjected the Republican Party to demoralizing electoral defeats from 1930 to 1936. Ironically, certain measures that he passed and advocated toward the end of his administration were incorporated into the New Deal agenda—thereby inadvertently contributing to the detriment of his own reputation and to the legend of Roosevelt as the "miracle worker" of the 1930's.

Raymond Pierre Hylton

Further Reading

Best, Gary Dean. *Herbert Hoover: The Postpresidential Years, 1933-1964*. Stanford, Calif.: Hoover Institution Press, 1983. Detailed reading, emphasizing the president's emergence from his personal limbo during the Roosevelt administration to attain status as an "elder statesman."

Kennedy, David M. *Freedom from Fear: The American People in Depression and War, 1929-1945*. New York: Oxford University Press, 1999. Focuses on the factors of Hoover's upbringing and the inflexibility of his philosophical principles as contributing to his response to the economic crisis.

Pietrusza, David. *1920: The Year of the Six Presidents*. New York: Basic Books, 2007. Includes a basic biography and a highly sympathetic view of Hoover, at the expense of Roosevelt, who is depicted as cunning and devious.

Schwarz, Jordan A. *The Interregnum of Despair: Hoover, Congress, and the Depression*. Urbana: University of Illinois Press, 1970. Hoover emerges as a tragic, largely sympathetic figure who actually anticipated some significant New Deal and Great Society initiatives.

Shlaes, Amity. *The Forgotten Man: A New History of the Great Depression*. New York: HarperCollins, 2008. Elucidates Hoover's basically liberal economic philosophy and why he was unable to realize it during the crisis years of the early 1930's.

Wilson, Joan Hoff. *Herbert Hoover: Forgotten Progressive*. Boston: Little, Brown, 1975. Thorough but slow-moving biography that portrays Hoover as a sincere, misunderstood reformer who was out of step with his times.

See also Bank of United States failure; Bonus Army March; Breadlines and soup kitchens; Elections of 1930, 1934, and 1938, U.S.; Elections of 1932, U.S.; Great Depression in the United States; Hoovervilles; Insull Utilities Trusts collapse; London Naval Treaty; Manchuria occupation; Roosevelt, Franklin D.; *Stromberg v. California*.

Hoover Dam. See Boulder Dam

■ Hoovervilles

Definition Makeshift shantytowns that arose during the Great Depression

During the Great Depression, more than one million Americans were forced into homelessness; some became transients, but others settled in shantytowns that became known as Hoovervilles, a mocking reference to President Herbert Hoover. By the mid-1930's, there were Hoovervilles in most major cities.

Between 1930 and 1941, shantytowns sprang up in cities throughout the United States as refuges of last resort for the newly homeless. Called Hoovervilles, these camps contained buildings of all varieties. Some were merely shacks constructed of tin, tar paper, salvaged lumber, and canvas that offered little protection from the elements. Others were constructed by out-of-work masons and carpenters, who built solid structures that stood for years.

New York City's Central Park was home to one of

A shantytown in Seattle, Washington, that was typical of Depression encampments that were often "Hoovervilles." Similar encampments arose in most major urban areas in the United States. (The Granger Collection, New York)

the country's largest Hoovervilles. Located in the drained Central Park reservoir, the shantytown was founded in 1930. Like most Hoovervilles, it was intermittently broken up by the police and parks department, which were concerned about sanitary conditions. However, as the Great Depression continued, the camp was unofficially sanctioned by officials who did not have the heart to fine the homeless for sleeping outside. By 1932, the camp was known as Hoover Valley and contained a 20-foot-long stone structure with a roof and tile floor.

Some Hoovervilles were so stable they elected their own sanitary committees and even mayors. There were Hoovervilles in New York, St. Louis, Washington, D.C., Seattle, Chicago, and Denver. These shantytowns proved nearly immune to efforts by agencies at all levels of government to eliminate them because there was no housing or work for their occupants. Not until 1941, as unemployment

eased, did Hoovervilles begin to disappear from major cities.

Impact Homelessness proved to be one of the more intractable problems for government during the Great Depression, and Hoovervilles were a constant visible reminder of that problem. Even wealthy residents of major cities were forced to see the plight of the least fortunate when they camped outside in city parks and thoroughfares. Hoovervilles became a cultural touchstone and common visual reference for the Great Depression.

Colin Asher

Further Reading

Anderson, Nels. *On Hobos and Homelessness.* Chicago: University of Chicago Press, 1998.

Crouse, Joan M. *The Homeless Transient in the Great Depression: New York State, 1929-1941.* Albany: State University of New York Press, 1986.

Rauchway, Eric. *The Great Depression and the New Deal: A Very Short Introduction.* New York: Oxford University Press, 2008.

See also Great Depression in the United States; Homelessness; Hoover, Herbert; Migrations, domestic; Unemployment in the United States.

■ Horror films

Definition Feature films about terror and the supernatural

The 1930's marked the golden age of horror films as audiences sought relief from the economic hardships of the Great Depression and found solace in fictional cinematic frights. The decade came to be recognized as a high-water mark for Hollywood horror, with the creation of iconic monsters and beautifully crafted films.

While most genre films enjoy brief popularity and then disappear from the screen, horror films have existed since the beginning of cinema and have endured throughout the decades. Their popularity has regularly coincided with wars, national disasters, and catastrophic events, coming either during or after the event itself. Therefore the cultural, economic, and political climate of the Great Depression was the backdrop for the first significant talking horror film in the United States: *Dracula* (1931), starring Bela Lugosi.

Dracula was followed by the equally iconic *Frankenstein* (1931), with Boris Karloff. Universal Pictures became famous for its horror output, employing the gifted James Whale to direct *The Old Dark House* (1932), *The Invisible Man* (1933), and *Bride of Frankenstein* (1935). Universal also produced *The Mummy* (1932) with Karloff, a film about an ancient Egyptian seeking his reincarnated love, and *Murders in the Rue Morgue* with Lugosi (1932), a loose adaptation of Edgar Allan Poe's short story. Universal even introduced the werewolf to the screen in *Werewolf of London* (1936), which predated the much more popular *Wolf Man* series with Lon Chaney, Jr., by five years.

While Universal produced some of popular culture's most iconic monsters of the 1930's—Frankenstein's monster, Dracula, the Mummy, and the Invisible Man—other studios were quick to catch on to the appeal of horror as well. Paramount Pictures produced the best-known version of *Dr. Jekyll and Mr. Hyde* (1931), with Fredric March in the title roles; special effects used to achieve the onscreen transformation were kept secret for decades until director Rouben Mamoulian's death. Perhaps the most visually spectacular horror film of the decade was *King Kong* (1933), RKO Pictures' tale of a giant ape run amok.

Disturbing Films and Censorship Horror films have always been magnets for censors, but there were some films produced during the 1930's that went beyond frightening to genuinely unsettling. Based on H. G. Wells's novel *The Island of Doctor Moreau* (1896), *Island of Lost Souls* (1932) from Paramount is a truly perverse film. Dr. Moreau, played by Charles Laughton, creates semihumans from animals through vivisection—audiences glimpse an operation in progress with no anesthetic used. Further, Moreau plans to mate a stranded seafarer with Lota, the panther woman who is his most perfect creation yet. In another example of the unsettling impact of horror films in the 1930's, director Tod Browning's career was almost destroyed because he used real deformed circus performers in making *Freaks* (1932) for Metro-Goldwyn-Mayer (MGM).

Another controversial film was Universal's *The Black Cat* (1934). Starring Karloff and Lugosi, its mix of Satanism, mysticism, hints of necrophilia, and sadism was too much for the censors to bear, and the resulting cuts left an otherwise highly regarded film somewhat incoherent at times. The Motion Picture Production Code reined in any potential excesses: A rat was changed to an owl in *Bride of Frankenstein*; the same film edited shots of Elsa Lanchester's "scandalously" low-cut dress; the cuts rendered some of the dialogue incomprehensible in the process. Removal of suggestions of incest and suicide not only made elements of MGM's *Mark of the Vampire* (1935) puzzling but also reduced its running time to a mere sixty minutes. It is common to think of horror films of the 1930's as tame, but quite a few were surprisingly sadistic and perverse for their time.

Decline As the 1930's wore on and economic conditions improved, tolerance for horror began to decline. *The Raven* (1935), from Universal, roused calls for banning horror films, despite the fact that the film is extremely tame even by the period's standards. Milder fare and watered-down sequels became the order of the day. Universal's *Dracula's*

Daughter (1936) was a pale shadow of the grandiose sequel originally planned. *Son of Kong* (RKO, 1933) showcased a lovable giant white gorilla that endears itself to audiences by saving the lead characters at the end, sacrificing itself. By 1939, Karloff had decided that the Frankenstein monster's story line had been exhausted; *Son of Frankenstein* (1939) was his last turn playing the part.

Impact The 1930's left cinema with a legacy of iconic, well-made, classic horror films. Distracting Depression-weary audiences from their real-life problems, the horror films of the 1930's were alternately frightening, fantastic, disturbing, and disappointing, but they gave audiences an experience that has endured for decades with the eventual release of these films in home video and later formats.

Charles Lewis Avinger, Jr.

Further Reading

Clarens, Carlos. "Children of the Night." In *The Horror Film*, edited by Stephen Prince. New Brunswick, N.J.: Rutgers University Press, 2004. A concise commentary on Universal's classic horror films of the period, focusing on a handful of the most significant entries.

Curtis, James. *James Whale: A New World of Gods and Monsters.* London: Faber and Faber, 1998. A substantial biography of Universal's most notable horror film director of the 1930's.

Marriott, James, and Kim Newman. *Horror: The Definitive Guide to the Cinema of Fear.* London: André Deutsch, 2006. Exploration of horror cinema from the nineteenth century to the twentieth century, highlighting the best and most prominent films in each decade, along with thematic analyses.

Rigby, Jonathan. *American Gothic: Sixty Years of Horror Cinema.* London: Reynolds and Hearn, 2007. Narrow in scope, this overview contains a substantial analysis of films of the 1930's.

Skal, David J. *Hollywood Gothic: The Tangled Web of Dracula from Novel to Stage to Screen.* New York: W. W. Norton, 1990. An extensively researched volume with exhaustive information about the 1931 production.

See also *Dracula*; Film; *Frankenstein* films; *Freaks*; *Invisible Man, The*; *King Kong*; Motion Picture Production Code; Science fiction; Thalberg, Irving; Wray, Fay.

■ Horse racing

Definition Commercial and recreational activity of racing thoroughbred horses ridden by jockeys

Horse racing has always played a significant role in American life. Thoroughbred horse racing's Triple Crown is a major tradition in American culture. The three Triple Crown winners of the 1930's were instrumental in establishing that tradition.

During the 1930's, horse racing became a popular sport in the United States. The number of states in which horse racing was legal increased from fifteen to twenty-one. Also during this decade, winter racing began in Florida and California, which played a significant role in the horse-racing industry. In 1930, the first American Totalisator machine, which calculated betting odds and displayed them on an electronic board, was set up at Pimlico Race Course in Baltimore, Maryland. The use of such machines improved the accuracy of calculation of bettors' winnings, thereby increasing the confidence of bettors and resulting in greater attendance at the races. In 1933, the pari-mutuel system of legalized wagering was introduced in the United States at Arlington Park in Chicago and significantly contributed to another increase in attendance at the racetracks. Horseracing attracted both individuals who enjoyed the competition of horses and those who were attracted by the opportunity to gamble.

While the actual process of wagering became more reliable, other problems plagued the sport during the 1930's. Because no sure means of identifying individual horses existed, unscrupulous trainers and owners substituted slower horses for fast ones and vice versa in order to fix the outcome of races. During the 1940's, this practice was curtailed with the development of tattooing horses. There were also few rules of conduct for jockeys, both on and off the racetrack. Fighting and scuffling were everyday occurrences during races—even prestigious ones—and in the jockey room. In the 1933 Kentucky Derby, jockeys Don Meade and Herb Fisher, aboard Head Play and Broker's Tip, fought all the way down the stretch. This helped bring about the formation of associations, and rules were established to eliminate such encounters.

Triple Crown Winners and Other Great Horses The 1930's was one of the two great decades for the Triple Crown, a feat in which one horse wins all three major racing events—the Kentucky Derby, the Preakness Stakes, and the Belmont Stakes—in one calendar year. In 1919, Sir Barton won the three major races, but during the 1920's, no horse accomplished this feat. Then in 1930, Gallant Fox won all three races. The term "Triple Crown" was introduced into racing vocabulary by Charles Hatton, who used the term in his *Daily Racing Form* column in reference to Gallant Fox. In 1935, Gallant Fox's son Omaha became the second Triple Crown winner of the 1930's. Gallant Fox is the only Triple Crown winner to sire another Triple Crown winner. In 1937, War Admiral won the Triple Crown and was chosen horse of the year. This gave the decade three Triple Crown winners and ranks the decade as second only to the 1940's in number of Triple Crown winners.

The three triple crown winners were certainly three of the greatest horses of the decade. Gallant Fox was so fast that a relay of horses had to be used with him when he trained. A graceful, even-tempered, and well-mannered horse, he was a favorite of racing fans, who referred to him as "the Fox of Belair." After winning the Triple Crown, Gallant Fox's son Omaha raced with great success in long-distance races in England. He won the Victor Wild Stakes and the Queen's Plate and finished second by a nose in the Ascot Gold Cup and second by a neck in the Princess of Wales Stakes. Omaha returned to the United States to stand at stud, where he founded a strong distaff line; his great-granddaughter was the dam of Nijinsky.

The most memorable horses of the 1930's, however, are Man o' War's son War Admiral and his grandson Seabiscuit. Although their racing careers were different, both War Admiral and Seabiscuit were exceptional horses. Match races had regained popularity during the decade, and War Admiral and Seabiscuit caught the attention of not only racing fans but also the American public. The two met in a match race on November 1, 1938, which Seabiscuit won.

Impact   For an American public suffering from the Great Depression and unemployment, horse racing provided escape, hope, and a folk hero in Seabiscuit. Going to the races was enjoyable and exciting, and there were always winners. Also, the opportunity to wager offered a possibility of quick financial pros-

perity. Seabiscuit and his jockey Red Pollard, who had risen from obscurity to become a sensational winning team, reaffirmed the idea that success was always possible. Horses such as War Admiral, Seabiscuit, and Gallant Fox helped launch racing as a popular sport appealing to a wide cross section of Americans. Omaha started a distaff bloodline that made a significant contribution to horse racing in the twentieth century.

Shawncey Webb

Further Reading

Beckwith, B. K. *Seabiscuit: The Saga of the Great Champion.* Reprint. Yardley, Pa.: Westholme, 2004. Originally published in 1940, an eyewitness account of Seabiscuit's immense impact on the American public. Excellent illustrations and photographs.

Bowen, Edward L. *War Admiral: Man of o' War's Greatest Son.* Forestville, Calif.: Eclipse Press, 2007. Excellent biography of War Admiral. Discusses his accomplishments and support he received as the greatest progeny of Man o' War.

Drager, Marvin. *The Most Glorious Crown: The Story of America's Triple Crown Thoroughbreds from Sir Barton to Affirmed.* Chicago: Triumph Books, 2005. Detailed account of Triple Crown winners, including Gallant Fox, Omaha, and War Admiral.

Hillenbrand, Laura. *Seabiscuit: An American Legend.* New York: Ballantine Books, 2003. Excellent coverage of Seabiscuit and his owner, trainer, and jockey and the problems they overcame.

Lefcourt, Blossom, and Eric Rachlis, eds. *Horse Racing: The Golden Age of the Track.* San Francisco: Chronicle Books, 2001. Primarily photographic coverage of thoroughbred racing as a sport that crossed social designations.

Simon, Mary, and Mark Simon. *Racing Through the Century: The Story of Thoroughbred Racing in America.* Irvine, Calif.: BowTie Press, 2002. Good overview of horse racing. Highlights the contribution that racing made during the 1930's to the sport's development through the twentieth century. Discusses both accomplishments and problems involved in racing.

See also   Gambling; Recreation; Seabiscuit; Sports in the United States; Unemployment in the United States.

■ House Committee on Un-American Activities

Identification   U.S. congressional committee
  charged with investigating subversion
Also known as   House Un-American Activities
  Committee; HUAC
Date   Established on May 26, 1938

*The House Committee on Un-American Activities origi-
nally was formed by Congress to investigate political organizations that were considered extreme or radical and therefore "un-American." Pro-Nazi German individuals were
its first targets of investigation during the late 1930's, but
the committee soon broadened its scope. It would reach the
peak of its influence during the late 1940's and 1950's, as
fear of communism grew and McCarthyism spread.*

The House Committee on Un-American Activities
was established in 1938 as a special investigating
committee under the chairmanship of Texas congressman Martin Dies, Jr., to investigate suspected
left-wing and right-wing subversive activities. Formally called the House Special Committee on Un-
American Activities, the body was also known as the
House Committee on Un-American Activities and
the House Un-American Activities Committee and
would later become best known by
the latter's acronym, HUAC. Original members of the committee included Democrats John J. Dempsey
of New Mexico, Samuel Dickstein
of New York, and Joe Starnes of Alabama and Republicans Noah M.
Mason of Illinois, Harold G. Mosier
of Ohio, and J. Parnell Thomas of
New Jersey.

The 1930's was a period during
which American fear of plots to
overthrow the existing social and
political order of the United States
grew rapidly. In June, 1938, the
committee began holding hearings to seek out subversive activities against the government of the
United States. The committee was
initially interested in uncovering
fascist subversion, particularly Nazi
spies and collaborators among
branches of the Ku Klux Klan
(KKK), German American organi-
zations, and other groups with pro-German or fascist
leanings. However, the committee did not carry its
investigation of fascist activities very far. Indeed,
when its members were urged to investigate the violent racist activities of the KKK, Chairman Dies refused to taken action. Dies himself was known to
have been a supporter of the KKK and had even spo-
ken at the group's rallies. Meanwhile, the committee
was switching its focus to the other end of the political spectrum, looking for evidence of communist,
rather than fascist, activity.

At the top of the committee's new list for investigation were the Federal Theatre Project and the
Federal Writers' Project. Created by New Deal legislation, these Democrat-inspired programs were targets of Republican strategists in the congressional
electoral campaigns of 1936 and 1938. Representative Thomas led the attack, claiming that the committee found clear evidence that the Federal Theatre Project was a branch of the Communist Party
USA. However, tangible evidence for his allegations
was never produced.

The committee then turned its attention to labor
unions. One of its key witnesses was John P. Frey, the
president of the Metal Trades Department of the
American Federation of Labor (AFL). In August,

*Wallace Stark testifies before the House Committee on Un-American Activities about al-
leged communist influence in the Federal Theatre Project.* (Library of Congress)

1938, he spent three days testifying before the committee that all but one of the top leaders of the rival Congress of Industrial Organizations (CIO) were either Communist Party USA members or communist sympathizers, exempting only United Mine Workers president John L. Lewis of this charge. Frey eventually charged 280 CIO union leaders with communist activity. Despite the gravity of Frey's charges, he was never cross-examined. There was little corroborating material to support his allegations, and the committee never subpoenaed any of the alleged communists. Frey himself later amended his testimony to state that the rank and file of the CIO were not being accused, only their leaders.

Another important early witness was chairman of the American Coalition Committee on National Security, Walter S. Steele. He claimed to have documents proving that millions of Americans were criminally conspiring against the U.S. government. However, he was never asked to produce his evidence. By the end of the committee's first hearings, 640 separate groups, 483 newspapers, and 280 labor unions had been labeled as communist organizations.

Included in the list of accused organizations was the American Civil Liberties Union (ACLU), which had recently been involved in the Senate Civil Liberties Committee hearings. The Senate's committee had been organized by Robert M. La Follette, Jr., to investigate official abuses of civil rights in trade-union organizing activities during the decade. According to HUAC, both the Senate committee itself and the ACLU had fallen under communist influence. Also, the targets of HUAC censure were pacifist organizations that the committee saw as communist dupes, media supporters of trade unionism, and colleges and universities that the committee regarded as overrun by communists and radicals. The film industry received special attention because of its perceived power to influence public opinion. Among the actors and screenwriters investigated were James Cagney, Clark Gable, Dorothy Parker, Robert Taylor, and even child star Shirley Temple.

Despite HUAC's assurances that all those accused would be given a chance to clear their names, only a small number received that opportunity. For example, writer Heywood Broun was allowed to read a prepared statement and then asked to leave. Between June and October, 1938, numerous witnesses testified before the committee. Their sheer numbers seemed to support the idea that communists held important positions in government, higher education, the media, and labor. By the elections of November, 1938, public opinion was dividing on the committee's methods but not on the idea that the committee served an important purpose. In the elections, the Republican Party scored its first major successes in almost a decade, bringing down such New Deal leaders as Michigan governor Frank Murphy and Wisconsin governor Philip La Follette. The party also gained eight U.S. senate seats and eighty-eight seats in the House of Representatives.

Impact In times of crisis—real or imagined, foreign or domestic—when national security appears threatened and fear is widespread, even democratic societies that pride themselves on protecting individual rights and due process tend to become overly suspicious and sometimes sacrifice their most precious principles in order to defend them. The HUAC investigations and hearings are a prime example of this phenomenon. In the name of uncovering radical or treasonous activities, HUAC itself engaged in blatantly un-American tactics, abusing its authority through threats and intimidation, recklessly labeling people subversive, and substituting guilt by association for real evidence.

Dies chaired the committee until 1945, when he was succeeded by Edward J. Hart. In September, 1947, the committee launched an investigation of Hollywood, holding nine days of hearings in which it interviewed forty-one people who worked in the motion-picture industry. HUAC would also investigate whether communists held positions of influence in the federal government. Eventually, the committee's influence declined, in tandem with the downfall of red-baiting senator Joseph McCarthy. In 1969, HUAC was renamed the Internal Security Committee. In 1975, it was abolished and its functions transferred to the House Judiciary Committee.

Further Reading

Bentley, Eric, and Frank Rich. *Thirty Years of Treason: Excerpts from Hearings Before the House Committee on Un-American Activities, 1938-1968.* New York: Nation Books, 2002. Alternately hilarious and sobering, this volume remains the best introduction to the things said and done in HUAC's name.

Dies, Martin. *Martin Dies' Story.* New York: Bookmailer, 1963. Memoir of the first chairman of committee, providing personal insight into Dies's life. Includes informative appendixes.

Gladchuk, John Joseph. *Hollywood and Anticommunism: HUAC and the Evolution of the Red Menace, 1935-1950*. New York: Routledge, 2006. Thorough study of HUAC's years of investigating the film industry.

Goodman, Walter. *The Committee: The Extraordinary Career of the House Committee on Un-American Activities*. New York: Farrar, Straus and Giroux, 1968. Written in a lively, journalistic style, this is the standard history of HUAC's first three decades. Goodman criticizes both the committee, for its inquisitorial and sensationalist style, and the investigated, for their dissident politics and confrontational posturing.

O'Reilly, Kenneth. *Hoover and the Un-Americans: The FBI, HUAC, and the Red Menace*. Philadelphia: Temple University Press, 1983. Drawing on Federal Bureau of Investigation (FBI) and other government agency files secured under the Freedom of Information Act, this book explores the uncomfortable relationship between the FBI and HUAC, emphasizing the ways in which HUAC publicized information from FBI files on dissident individuals and groups.

See also   Civil rights and liberties in the United States; Communism; Foreign Agents Registration Act of 1938; Foreign policy of the United States; Hellman, Lillian; Soviet Union.

■ Housing in Canada

Prior to the twentieth century, housing was considered a concern of the private, rather than the public, sector in Canada, and legislation and regulation were handled on local or provincial levels. However, with the widespread upheavals caused by World War I and the Great Depression, the Canadian federal government was forced to take action in an attempt to alleviate a variety of social issues related to housing.

The Canadian government initially became involved in housing on a national scale following World War I, when it was anticipated that unoccupied dwellings would be filled by soldiers returning from the European battlefields. As part of the War Measures Act of 1918, $25 million was made available to the provinces for municipal loans aimed at residential construction or mortgages for the purchase of new housing. Under the plan, loans up to $4,500, at 5 percent annual interest, were to be allocated to individuals or construction corporations. Interest would be paid quarterly or semiannually, and the principal would be due upon maturity, usually after a period of five years, with the possibility of renewal for additional five-year increments. Ill-conceived and indifferently administered, and coming into effect during a time of building material shortages and inflated prices, the plan was not successful. Before the funding ran out in 1924, fewer than sixty-three hundred housing units had been built under the scheme.

As it turned out, the feared housing shortages did not materialize. The 1920's represented a boom time, during which the Canadian economy grew at a rapid rate. Returning war veterans were eventually reabsorbed into society. The home-building industry completed dwellings at an unprecedented, though haphazard, rate across the provinces, as more than fifty thousand units were built per year; lenders had no trouble finding takers for mortgage loans at 10 percent interest or higher.

The spate of construction brought with it new problems. Land speculators bought up fertile agricultural plots to create suburban subdivisions, causing communities to develop unevenly. This result paved the way for the rise of urban planners, who initially were more concerned with the technical aspects, rather than with the human impact, of their work.

The Great Depression and Canadian Housing   The Great Depression halted Canada's booming economy. Canada was affected more severely than virtually any other country in the world because of its significant dependence on resource-based industries such as mining, farming, and logging. Almost overnight, the gross national product began falling, and by 1933 it had plunged by 40 percent from pre-Depression highs. Hundreds of businesses were forced to close, putting thousands of employees out of work. By 1933, nearly one of three Canadians was unemployed, and in some communities unemployment topped 50 percent. Construction was hit particularly hard: Home building plummeted by more than 80 percent, and two out of three construction workers were unemployed.

Exacerbating the already desperate situation were such factors as the American Hawley-Smoot

Tariff Act of 1930, which imposed stiff tariffs on Canadian goods imported into the United States, causing exports to be cut in half over a four-year period. The weather, particularly in the agriculturally oriented Prairie Provinces, was bad, and crops failed in the hot, dry, rainless seasons of the early 1930's. Wheat, a mainstay crop, suffered its own depression: Between 1928 and 1932, the price of a bushel dropped by two-thirds.

In the wake of the Depression, Canadian society changed dramatically and adversely. As in the United States, the poor and those who were already in debt were most affected by the economy. Canadian farmers lost their farms. Many homeowners had their property foreclosed for failure to meet mortgage terms. Duplicating the hardships of their American neighbors, armies of rootless Canadians wandered from city to city seeking work and descended into overcrowded urban skid rows in search of cheap shelter.

In Vancouver, British Columbia, homeless men and women congregated in a sizable hobo jungle along the waterfront. In Calgary, Alberta, a vast tent city of those who had lost their residences was erected. In places like Saskatoon, Saskatchewan, and Montreal, Quebec, work-for-wages camps were set up, offering jobs on city infrastructure projects for small wages (twenty cents per day). In Nova Scotia and elsewhere, private citizens created housing cooperatives that pooled the resources of members to build housing. Tens of thousands had to rely on poverty-level government relief or charitable handouts.

Such stopgap measures provided only short-term solutions to the housing problem. By the mid-1930's, when the economy had begun to improve slowly, many realized that the Canadian government would have to become involved to speed up the recovery process.

Governmental Responses to the Housing Crisis Beginning in 1935, the Canadian parliament passed a series of bills designed both to alleviate low-cost housing shortages and to jump-start the languishing construction industry. The first and most significant of these was the Dominion Housing Act (DHA) of 1935, which provided $20 million to establish joint mortgages between the government and private trust and loan companies. Home buyers would make a 20 percent down payment, while 70 or 80 percent of the remaining value of the property would come from the private lender at 5 percent interest over a ten-year period, renewable for an additional ten years. Twenty percent of the lender's risk would be covered by government funds, guaranteed against loss and loaned to the lender at 3 percent, producing a yield of at least 5.7 percent interest on the investment. Unlike previous such agreements, these loans were amortized, made prepayment possible, and included provisions for minimum construction standards. While the forty-nine hundred loans created under the DHA represented less than 5 percent of all housing construction between 1935 and 1938, they set the pattern for future federal and conventional mortgage-lending programs.

In 1936, the DHA was supplemented with the Mortgages Act, which gave priority to DHA mortgages in litigation claims. The following year, the Federal Home Improvement Plan provided funds under similar terms to the DHA for the purpose of repairing, refurbishing, or remodeling owner-occupied homes. The Home Improvement Plan gave construction a tremendous boost between 1937 and 1939; nearly sixty-seven thousand homes from New Brunswick to British Columbia were rehabilitated—though the bulk of the work was carried out in urban areas of Ontario and Quebec. Finally, in 1938 the National Housing Act was passed, which replaced the DHA and focused on construction of low-rent housing, additional loans for home buying, and improvements to existing housing. Together, the various acts supplied needed infusions of government concern and money, which helped tide over Canadians until the outbreak of World War II, when the national economy again surged forward to pre-Depression levels.

Impact By 1937, some 40 percent of all residential construction and renovation was funded through government assistance. The trend toward significant government involvement in housing continued during World War II and beyond, with new legislation that built upon the strengths of previous laws. The National Housing Act (1944) retained joint lending provisions, introducing guaranteed twenty-year, fixed-rate, government-subsidized mortgages. The Central Mortgage and Housing Corporation Act of 1945 founded a Crown corporation to administer federal loans made directly with homeowners and developers. Subsequent amendments refined loan-to-value ratios, the determination of interest rates, and other technical aspects. These culminated in the National Housing Act of 1954, which, with additional amendments to account for changes in immigration, home buyers' incomes, and other factors, is the determining factor in a healthy Canadian housing market.

Jack Ewing

Further Reading

Bacher, John C. *Keeping to the Marketplace: The Evolution of Canadian Housing Policy.* Montreal: McGill-Queen's University Press, 1993. Thorough overview based on primary sources concerning the conditions and personalities that led to the development of modern Canadian housing legislation.

Campbell, Lara A. *Respectable Citizens: Gender, Family, and Unemployment in Ontario's Great Depression.* Toronto: University of Toronto Press, 2009. Examination based on media sources of the period, public records, family memoirs, and oral accounts of how individuals in Ontario dealt with hardship and changing roles during the Depression.

Harris, Richard. *Creeping Conformity: How Canada Became Suburban, 1900-1960.* Toronto: University of Toronto Press, 2004. Study of how industrialization, shifting demographics, and government actions changed Canadian society during the first half of the twentieth century.

Safarian, A. E. *The Canadian Economy in the Great Depression.* Montreal: McGill-Queen's University Press, 2010. Focuses on the causes and effects of Canada's economic collapse of the 1930's, comparing and contrasting conditions from that era to the economic woes of the early twenty-first century.

Wade, Jill. *Houses for All: The Struggle for Social Housing in Vancouver, 1919-1950.* Vancouver: University of British Columbia Press, 1994. Study of the actions and reactions of the citizens of Vancouver to the sweeping societal changes affecting living conditions during the crucial periods following World War I, the economic boom of the 1920's, the Great Depression and economic recovery, and during and after World War II.

See also Agriculture in Canada; Architecture; Business and the economy in Canada; Federal National Mortgage Association; Great Depression in Canada; Hawley-Smoot Tariff Act of 1930; Income and wages in Canada; Unemployment in Canada.

■ Housing in the United States

The Great Depression caused a housing crisis for many Americans throughout the 1930's. In some cities, unemployment rates were nearly 50 percent and many Americans lost the ability to make their rent and mortgage payments. As a result, the federal government created a series of New Deal policies to help Americans find affordable housing.

The housing realities of the 1930's had roots in the housing policies of the 1920's, which in fact played a large role in the onset of the Great Depression. In the mid-1920's, Secretary of Commerce Herbert Hoover strongly believed that the housing market should be left in the hands of private developers. Through a series of programs such as the Own Your Own Home program, the Architects Small House Service Bureau, and the Home Modernizing Bureau, Hoover encouraged private developers to create high-quality, single-family homes in suburban communities. These programs promoted the customization of homes through the use of architectural detail. Where new construction was not possible, Hoover encouraged the renovation of existing units to include the latest conveniences of modern life.

However, such customization was not cheap, and as a result, developers built too many homes at prices that few Americans could afford. After 1925, the construction industry came to a halt as many new homes sat on the market. The downturn in the housing market deeply affected the economy of the United States, contributing to the stock market crash of 1929 and ultimately the Great Depression. As with all other aspects of American life in the 1930's, the Great Depression had a major effect on the housing market, particularly for people in the middle class. The rich were slightly more insulated from the effects of the Depression, while the struggles of the poor only increased.

Housing Policy Under President Herbert Hoover In 1931, President Hoover gathered a wide range of housing specialists to the National Conference on Home Building and Home Ownership to discuss ways of addressing the housing crisis. Many experts were extremely hesitant to allow the federal government to intervene, even though the crisis continued to grow exponentially. In general, the conference participants agreed that ownership of single-family homes would be the best way for people to escape destitute housing arrangements and that the private real estate market should provide most of the initiative and funding for future homeownership.

After the conference, Congress passed the Federal Home Loan Bank Act of 1932 in order to allow the federal government to provide credit for mortgage lenders. The idea behind this act was to reduce the risk that banks faced when lending money in a shaky housing market. However, in reality, very few people met the requirements for mortgages backed by the act. Most Americans who were desperate for government support believed that Hoover was indifferent to the housing crisis, because his reform policies did not appear to be working. The average American only saw that his own circumstances had not improved. Furthermore, between 1929 and 1933, construction of residential property declined by 95 percent, which left thousands of workers in the construction industry without jobs.

The Great Depression's Effect on Housing By the beginning of 1933, approximately 50 percent of the people who possessed mortgages were unable to pay them, and nearly one thousand homes went into foreclosure daily. Some banks calculated that repossession was more trouble than it was worth, because the real estate market was unlikely to attract buyers for the foreclosed properties. As a result, some people were able to stay in their homes even though they were in default. Nevertheless, as many as one in six people who could not afford their rent or mortgage moved in with friends or relatives. This situation created crowded living conditions, and entertaining in the home became increasingly uncommon. Some people also resorted to building makeshift homes on vacant land out of such materials as cardboard, scrap lumber, and tarpaper. Entire communities of these shacks came to be known as Hoovervilles. Other people simply moved from place to place and many developed a "hobo" lifestyle riding as stowaways on trains.

Housing Policy and the New Deal By the time President Franklin D. Roosevelt took office in 1933, Americans were more desperate than ever to get back to work and live in decent housing. Within the first one hundred days of Roosevelt's presidency, Congress passed the National Industrial Recovery Act. The law stipulated that a new agency, the Public Works Administration (PWA), would oversee public

Works Progress Administration poster advertising a low-rent housing project in Cleveland. (Library of Congress)

housing construction projects in major cities. Although the concept of public housing was controversial, the president urged Congress to pass the act quickly. Because of the urgency of the economic crisis, the bill passed with little debate.

The main purpose of the bill was to create jobs, not solve the housing problem, and Roosevelt viewed the projects as temporary housing for working-class people who were down on their luck. The PWA faced many obstacles, especially after a 1935 Supreme Court ruling that the administration could not take land under eminent domain. Therefore, the federal government had to pay market rates for properties, and it faced difficulties in securing enough space for development. Many of the sites that were feasible for construction were isolated from employment opportunities and other communities. Furthermore, because the main goal of the PWA was to provide jobs, labor costs made development more expensive. As a result, the PWA could not produce nearly as much public housing as it had originally anticipated.

In addition to the Industrial Recovery Act, in 1933 Congress passed the Homeowners Refinancing Act (also known as the Home Owners' Loan Act), which established the Home Owners' Loan Corporation (HOLC). This institution bought defaulted loans from banks and refinanced them so that homeowners would be able to make smaller monthly payments over a longer period of time. Before the Homeowners Refinancing Act, the average mortgage lasted five years. Under the new program, the typical loan term was fifteen years.

The National Housing Act of 1934 established the Federal Housing Administration (FHA), which also gave more Americans the opportunity for homeownership. The FHA began insuring many qualifying mortgages with funds from the U.S. Treasury. The administration gave banks confidence that they could provide low-interest mortgages with little financial risk. Generally speaking, buyers had to make a down payment of 30 percent of a home's price in order to qualify for an FHA loan. Previous programs had required a down payment of at least 50 percent. The creation of the FHA opened up lending markets, and in many instances, buying a home became cheaper than renting.

Public Housing Revisited: The Wagner Act Although the New Deal policies enabled more Americans to afford homeownership, the debate about public housing continued in Congress. Most legislators agreed that the PWA was not living up to the expectations for it and discussed whether to expand public housing to a wider segment of the market or to eliminate it altogether.

From 1935 through 1937, Senator Robert F. Wagner of New York worked closely with Catherine Bauer and other reformers to advocate for the expansion of public housing. Bauer's book *Modern Housing* (1934) outlined the achievements of European public housing policies, which she regarded as highly successful. The book served as a template for a possible public housing strategy in the United States. Single-family townhouses or condominiums, clustered in groups, would allow for maximum open space. These places would encourage communal forms of living and provide residents with amenities such as public gardens, day care facilities, and recre-

ational areas. Bauer supported the idea that public housing was a viable option for people in the middle class, not just the poor. She argued that the cornerstone of the successful European housing model was its focus on creating homes for utilitarian purposes rather than their ability to generate profit.

Conservative members of the legislature strongly resisted the idea of federally operated communities, no matter how well designed, claiming that public housing would lead to a welfare state and communism. A common sentiment was that the higher-density housing of the European model would lead to many vices, including sexual promiscuity, drunkenness, the breakdown of family values, laziness, and perpetual poverty. Furthermore, powerful lobbyist groups such as the National Association of Real Estate Boards, the National Association of Home Builders, the Mortgage Bankers Association, and the U.S. Building and Loan League saw the potential for a huge threat to their interests in the private housing market and therefore opposed the creation of large-scale public housing.

By the time Congress completed negotiations on the issue, very few elements of Bauer's original vision remained intact. For example, instead of creating a universal form of public housing that could cater to middle-class Americans, Congress's public housing strategy primarily focused on helping the most desperate people in society. In 1937, Congress approved the United States Housing Act, which allowed the federal government to build public housing only for the poorest citizens. The act also established the United States Housing Authority (USHA) as the primary agency to oversee the construction of public housing, but the program was severely underfunded. Because of budget constraints, builders used low-quality materials and left off nonessential architectural details, such as closet doors. As the years passed, these dwellings quickly deteriorated, and the concept of public housing became highly stigmatized in American society.

Another shortcoming of public housing policy was that it confused slum clearance with urban renewal. Critics of the USHA argued that slum clearance projects merely displaced former residents into new ghettos. Once they made the move, residents typically did not return to their former neighborhoods, in part because the new units were far too expensive. Furthermore, the demand for public housing far exceeded supply, which meant many

Americans continued to struggle to find adequate housing.

Impact Because the HOLC labeled many city dwellings as risky or undesirable investments, the FHA backed loans primarily in suburban locations. Roosevelt also encouraged Americans to move out of the cities and reacquaint themselves with the land. Therefore, once Americans could afford homeownership through the FHA, they were likely to move out of the cities and into sprawling suburban communities. These homes contained all of the latest advancements in technology, including appliances from companies such as General Electric. Throughout the Great Depression, marketing strategies such as model homes and advertising in magazines such as *Ladies' Home Journal* kept single-family, detached homes in the suburbs at the forefront of consumer attention.

Many of the new suburban houses featured adequate ventilation, indoor plumbing, and safe electric outlets in convenient locations, features that were lacking in many homes just a decade earlier during the Better Homes Movement. Furthermore, car ownership was practically a prerequisite for living in many suburban communities, which provided a boost for the automobile industry. This suburban style of living continued to dominate the American landscape throughout the twentieth century. However, despite these advances in housing for the middle classes, the lack of funding for public housing created a two-tiered housing system characterized by vast housing inequalities that persisted into the twenty-first century.

Jill Eshelman

Further Reading

Jackson, Kenneth. *Crabgrass Frontier: Suburbanization of the United States.* New York: Oxford University Press, 1985. Examines the social, political, cultural, and economic factors involved in the development of the American suburb.

Mason, Joseph B. *History of Housing in the U.S., 1930-1980.* Houston, Tex.: Gulf, 1982. This insightful source covers housing, housing policy, and domestic architecture from 1930 to 1980.

Mitchell, J. Paul. *Federal Housing Policy and Program: Past and Present.* New Brunswick, N.J.: Rutgers University Press, 1985. Examines the political philosophy of postwar housing policies.

Radford, Gail. "The Federal Government and Housing During the Great Depression." In *From Tenements to Taylor Homes: In Search of an Urban Housing Policy in Twentieth Century America,* edited by John F. Bauman, Roger Biles, and Kristin M. Szylvian. University Park: Pennsylvania State University Press, 2000. Describes and analyzes the effects of Roosevelt's New Deal housing policies.

Squires, Gregory D., ed. *Urban Sprawl: Causes, Consequences and Policy Responses.* Washington, D.C.: Urban Institute Press, 2002. Excellent collection of twelve articles on the legacy of suburbanization and its largely negative impacts.

Weiss, Marc. *The Rise of Community Builders: The American Real Estate Industry and Urban Land Planning.* New York: Columbia University Press, 1987. Useful history of tract housing and the landmark changes in American housing that unfolded during the 1940's and 1950's.

Wright, Gwendolyn. *Building the Dream: A Social History of Housing in America.* Cambridge, Mass.: MIT Press, 1983. An important work on the rich diversity of American architecture and housing from the colonial era through 1980.

See also Federal Housing Administration; Federal National Mortgage Association; Great Depression in the United States; Homelessness; Hoovervilles; New Deal; Urbanization in the United States; Wagner, Robert F.; Wagner-Steagall Housing Act of 1937.

■ How to Win Friends and Influence People

Identification Nonfiction book designed to help people develop and maintain positive personal and professional relationships
Author Dale Carnegie
Date First published in 1936

In the midst of the Great Depression, How to Win Friends and Influence People *offered people a number of ideas to improve their interpersonal skills and thereby improve the quality of their lives. In this context, it was the first self-help book to become a best seller.*

How to Win Friends and Influence People was written by Dale Carnegie, a self-made man who rose from an impoverished farming family to become a prime mover in the self-improvement publishing movement. As published in 1936, the book contained six

Examples of Advice Offered in *How to Win Friends and Influence People*

- Don't criticize, condemn, or complain
- Give honest and sincere appreciation
- Become genuinely interested in other people
- Smile
- Remember that a person's name is to that person the sweetest and most important sound in any language
- Be a good listener
- Make the other person feel important—and do it sincerely
- The only way to get the best of an argument is to avoid it
- Show respect for the other person's opinions
- Try honestly to see things from the other person's point of view

Source: Carnegie, Dale B. *How to Win Friends and Influence People.* New York: Simon and Schuster, 1936.

sections: "Fundamental Techniques in Handling People," "Six Ways to Make People Like You," "Twelve Ways to Win People to Your Way of Thinking," "Be a Leader: How to Change People Without Giving Offense or Arousing Resentment," "Letters That Produced Miraculous Results," and "Eight Rules for Making Your Home Life Happier." Subsequent editions were published without the last two sections.

Impact   Carnegie's easy-to-read writing style, commonsense advice, and frequent use of anecdotes made this book a popular read among many people across the social spectrum of the 1930's. It helped improve people's ability to interact with others and led to improvements in people's self-esteem, increasing the likelihood that their own needs were met. This book provided a positive outlook during the period of the Great Depression.

Stephen W. Brown

Further Reading

Carnegie, Dale. *How to Win Friends and Influence People.* New ed. New York: Simon & Schuster, 2009.

Duke, Allison, and Milorad M. Novicevic. "Historical Foundations of Social Effectiveness? Dale Carnegie's Principles." *Social Influence* 3, no. 2 (June, 2008): 132-142.

See also   Book publishing; *Functions of the Executive, The*; Literature in the United States; *Modern Corporation and Private Property, The*; Philosophy and philosophers; Psychology and psychiatry.

■ Hughes, Charles Evans

Identification   Chief justice of the United States
Born   April 11, 1862; Glens Falls, New York
Died   August 27, 1948; Osterville, Massachusetts

Hughes served as chief justice through a decade that included several landmark decisions about the New Deal, civil rights, and other issues.

Charles Evans Hughes was a moderately progressive Republican politician who served as a reform-minded governor of New York; associate justice of the Supreme Court, resigning after his 1916 nomination for the presidency, which he narrowly lost; secretary of state; and World Court judge. He also spent time in a private law practice. He wrote several books about American government, including one on the Supreme Court. Herbert Hoover nominated him for chief justice and after a brief, bitter fight primarily from antibusiness progressives complaining about his private practice, he took office on February 24, 1930.

Return to the Supreme Court   Hughes was an excellent administrator and maintained strict punctuality on the Court. He and Justice Owen J. Roberts occupied the center between the conservative and liberal wings. He maintained collegiality between them, often arranging common ground for them to agree on and assigned opinion-writing fairly and carefully. In his own 350 opinions, he sought to be accurate, clear, and concise but was not always consistent.

Hughes opposed double taxation, though he upheld a West Virginia law taxing out-of-state property of a company headquartered there, and state taxation of interstate commerce, though he upheld a Minnesota law taxing cattle shipped interstate but held in stockyards in the state for resale. He accepted federal taxation of state employees, but not profits from state bonds, and upheld state taxation of federal contractors.

From 1930 to 1936, the Court overturned state regulations in a third of the cases it reviewed. Hughes wrote many of these decisions and joined in many others. In key cases, he joined in overturning, on due process grounds, an Oklahoma law requiring a license to sell ice, but he upheld Minnesota's temporary moratorium on foreclosure executions and joined in upholding New York's milk-pricing law. He dissented from a decision overturning a state minimum wage, a decision he reversed in 1937, ending the use of substantial due process to invalidate state regulations. He repeatedly upheld state utility rates restricting utility profits to 7 percent, but not less. He joined in denying the existence of any federal general common law, reversing an 1842 precedent. Skeptical of administrative law, Hughes defended the Court's right to examine facts independently in a federal injured workers' compensation case and rejected Justice Louis D. Brandeis's distinction between property and personal rights in another case.

Hughes led the Court in incorporating all the First Amendment rights into the Fourteenth Amendment in a long string of decisions, starting in 1931, when he overturned a law banning red flags and a press-gag law. He also overturned an abuse of martial law in Texas. His Court reversed racist judicial convictions, including the accused Scottsboro rapists twice; reversed convictions garnered from confessions induced by the third degree; and overturned some racial discriminations. His dissent in a naturalization case was cited later in reversing it.

Hughes and the New Deal   Hughes was personally friendly with President Franklin D. Roosevelt, but his Court clashed frequently with the administration. He overturned a Department of Agriculture ruling on commission rates based on a lack of a fair hearing. He concurred in a decision overturning a reduction in pay for retired lower-court judges because they could be recalled and thus still hold office. He ruled that the president could not remove a member of the Federal Trade Commission without proper cause. Hughes strongly supported anti-trust action and union collective bargaining, though he did not support union violence and sit-down strikes.

In the first case overturning major New Deal legislation, the Court almost unanimously overturned the Petroleum Code for delegating too much discretionary regulatory power to the executive branch. Then simultaneous unanimous decisions struck down the National Recovery Administration, both for excessive delegation and excessive extension of the regulation of interstate commerce and for farm debtor relief as a seizure of private property without just compensation. The Court unanimously overturned the Homeowners Refinancing Act (also known as the Home Owners' Loan Act) as a violation of the Tenth Amendment. It overturned the first Agricultural Adjustment Act for trying to use taxation to regulate agricultural production. Hughes dissented from a decision overturning the Municipal Bankruptcy Act on Tenth Amendment grounds and concurred separately and partially with a decision to overturn bituminous coal regulation. All of this happened in 1935 and 1936.

The Court often upheld the administration, and most of the New Deal stayed intact, but not enough to assuage the imperious Roosevelt, who tried to turn the Court into a "rubber stamp" for his policies. Both progressives and conservatives opposed him, as did Hughes in a somewhat controversial letter refuting Roosevelt's claim that the Court was behind in its duties. Hughes retired in 1941 and thereafter mostly avoided public life.

Impact

Regarded as one of the greatest chief justices in American history, Hughes played a major role in expanding civil liberties, worked hard to maintain separation of powers against a centralizing executive, and influenced economic policy.

Timothy Lane

Further Reading

Powell, Jim. *FDR's Folly.* New York: Three Rivers Press, 2003. Libertarian critique of the New Deal, including two chapters on major Supreme Court decisions.

Ross, William G. *The Chief Justiceship of Charles Evans Hughes, 1930-1941.* Columbia: South Carolina University Press, 2007. Scholarly study of the place of Hughes and his Court in judicial history, linking his judicial votes and political philosophy.

Smith, Jean Edward. *FDR.* New York: Random House, 2007. Reasonably objective, sympathetic biography, including Roosevelt's relations with Hughes and the Court.

White, G. Edward. *The Constitution and the New Deal.* Cambridge, Mass.: Harvard University Press, 2000. Scholarly study of the Supreme Court in the New Deal era effectively arguing that its adaptation to regulation was evolutionary rather than sudden and revolutionary.

See also   Brandeis, Louis D.; *Brown v. Mississippi*; *Carter v. Carter Coal Co.*; Civil rights and liberties in the United States; *De Jonge v. Oregon*; *Erie Railroad Co. v. Tompkins*; *Four Horsemen vs. Three Musketeers*; *Gold Clause Cases*; *Home Building and Loan Association v. Blaisdell*; *Humphrey's Executor v. United States*; *Lovell v. City of Griffin*; *Missouri ex rel. Gaines v. Canada*.

■ Hughes, Howard

Identification   American business tycoon, aviator, and film producer
Born   December 24, 1905; Houston, Texas
Died   April 5, 1976; In an airplane en route from Acapulco, Mexico, to Houston, Texas

A filmmaker and trailblazing aviator, Hughes inherited a gigantic personal fortune and added a touch of dash and glamour to the 1930's Hollywood scene. His concrete achievements in aeronautical engineering and cinematic innovations were counterbalanced by erratic behavior and clashes over censorship issues.

Howard Robard Hughes, Jr., was born to Allene Gano and Howard Robard Hughes, Sr. The elder Hughes was an inventor who had capitalized on the oil drill-bits he had designed to make the transition to corporation owner, founding Hughes Tool Company. As a child, Howard, Jr., underperformed in school, struggling academically, but he demonstrated a mechanical and mathematical aptitude. His parents both died abruptly while he was in his teens: his mother from pregnancy complications in 1922, and his father from a heart attack in 1924.

In 1924, Hughes was in full control of the family company, though he was only nineteen years of age. One year later, he married Ella Botts Rice and left for Hollywood to pursue filmmaking. Appointing the talented Noah Dietrich to manage this new enterprise, Hughes was able to focus on his foray into the entertainment industry. His notorious infidelities with Hollywood starlets and peculiar personal habits resulted in his first marriage ending in divorce in 1929.

Afterward, he went through multiple mistresses, the most substantial proving to be a long-term live-in relationship with actor Katharine Hepburn.

Hughes's films of the 1920's had some success: *Two Arabian Knights* (1928) won an Academy Award. However, during the 1930's, Hughes achieved his greatest cinematic success. In 1930, he produced the hugely expensive but innovative *Hell's Angels*, a tragic romance-drama about World War I aerial combat. This established him as a major player in the film industry. His next blockbuster was *Scarface* (1932), which was based on the life of the mobster Al Capone. The production and release of this film were marred by conflicts between Hughes and the censors over what were excessively violent scenes.

Speaking before the Press Club in Washington, D.C., in 1938, aviator and filmmaker Howard Hughes discusses his vision for the future of aviation, which he said would eventually see aircraft as large as ocean liners. (Library of Congress)

Shortly thereafter, Hughes decided to devote himself to aviation and aeronautics and established Hughes Aircraft Company, another subsidiary of Hughes Tool. Hughes, more often than not, piloted his own planes. He engaged in such daredevil escapades and aerial feats of bravado involving competition and bets that he was nearly killed on several occasions and was once severely injured. His manly image and glamorous good looks made him one of the great public heroes of the 1930's. In 1934, he designed and constructed the world's highest performing racing plane, the H-1. One year later, he broke the international speed record. His most spectacular performance was his epic around-the-world flight from July 10 to 14, 1938. The official time of his flight was three days, nineteen hours, and seventeen minutes, which broke the record previously set by Wiley Post. In 1939, Hughes took over the management of Trans World Airlines (TWA) as the major shareholder. As the 1930's ended, he was a well-connected, influential, and glittering icon on the American scene.

Impact An individual whose accomplishments made him a genuine hero and who personified success in the midst of an era defined by despair, poverty, and uncertainty, Hughes filled a necessary niche for those enduring the pangs of the Great Depression. The public perception of Hughes and other larger-than-life figures who were "making good" in spite of the negative socioeconomic climate offered a model to emulate and helped to fuel hopes for better times ahead.

Raymond Pierre Hylton

Further Reading

Bartlett, Donald L., and James B. Steele. *Howard Hughes: His Life and Madness.* New York: W. W. Norton, 2004.

Brown, Peter Harry, and Pat H. Broeske. *Howard Hughes: The Untold Story.* Cambridge, Mass.: Da Capo Press, 2004.

Higham, Charles. *Howard Hughes: The Secret Life.* New York: G. P. Putnam's Sons, 1993.

See also Aviation and aeronautics; Davis, Bette; Gangster films; Harlow, Jean; *Hell's Angels*; Hepburn, Katharine.

■ Hull, Cordell

Identification American statesman
Born October 2, 1871; near Byrdstown, Overton (now Pickett) County, Tennessee
Died July 23, 1955; Bethesda, Maryland

During the 1930's, Secretary of State Hull was instrumental in the development of the Good Neighbor Policy, an American diplomatic initiative in which the United States made a commitment to treat Latin American states as equal partners in the maintenance of peace and in the economic development within the Western Hemisphere. Hull opposed the imposition of high-tariff barriers and promoted access to markets. During the late 1930's, Hull advocated collective security in opposing fascist aggression.

In 1933, President Franklin D. Roosevelt appointed U.S. Senator Cordell Hull from Tennessee as the secretary of state. Hull had served as a U.S. Representative in Congress from 1907 to 1921 and 1923 to 1931 and had been elected to the Senate in 1931. Hull was the longest-serving secretary of state in American history and, later, played a leadership role in the development of the United Nations. He did not possess charisma, but he was recognized as a statesman of integrity.

Hull's first major assignment was to represent the United States at the London Monetary and Economic Conference in July, 1933. Hull maintained that economic recovery could be realized through low tariffs, access to more markets, and stabilization of major currencies. His efforts in London were undermined by Roosevelt's changing attitudes on stabilizing the value of the dollar. As a result, nothing meaningful emerged from the London Conference. However, Hull did succeed in developing trade agreements with many nations that resulted in reduced tariffs and expanded trade.

Hull was more successful in implementing the new American policy in Latin America. As head of the American delegation to the 1933 Pan-American Union meeting in Montevideo, Uruguay, Hull initiated a process that led to the Good Neighbor Policy. American Marines were withdrawn from Haiti and Nicaragua in 1934; in the same year, Roosevelt annulled the Platt amendment, which had curbed the exercise of Cuban independence. In 1936, at the Inter-American Conference for the Maintenance of Peace in Buenos Aires, Argentina, Hull and the representatives of twenty other nations agreed to the

Good Neighbor Policy. This agreement was affirmed at subsequent meetings—the 1938 Eighth Pan-American Conference in Lima, Peru, and the meeting of the 1940 foreign-affairs ministers of American Republics, in Havana, Cuba.

After 1936, Hull recognized the impending collapse of order in Europe with the rise of Adolf Hitler and Benito Mussolini. Unlike others in Roosevelt's government, Hull warned of the coming dangers and called for rearmament of the American military and for the Western democracies to join in collective security. Hull was an "internationalist" and opposed the American isolationist view of the world. Hull had condemned Japanese expansion in Manchuria during the early 1930's; his criticism of Japanese policies intensified with the outbreak of the Sino-Japanese War in 1937 and the later attacks on Indo-China.

As the relationship between the United States and Japan deteriorated during the late 1930's, Hull initiated efforts to resolve the principal sources of disagreement; these undertakings failed. With the outbreak of World War II in September, 1939, Hull continued his deliberations with the Japanese, but to no avail. During these same months, Roosevelt expanded the White House's activities in foreign policy—sometimes without Hull's knowledge. Long before the Japanese attack on Pearl Harbor, Hull's State Department sent messages to American military installations in the Pacific to prepare for surprise attacks by the Japanese.

Impact   In spite of President Roosevelt's personal control over American foreign policy, Hull succeeded in implementing some of Roosevelt's initiatives during the 1930's. These included the development of the Good Neighbor Policy and his opposition to aggression in Europe and Asia. His efforts to resolve the mounting tensions between the United States and Japan were not successful; Japan's aggression in China and its expansionist policies throughout Asia threatened American interests in the Philippines and American access to trade in China. Later, in 1945, Hull was awarded the Nobel Peace Prize for his efforts in the development of the United Nations.

William T. Walker

Further Reading

Butler, Michael A. *Cautious Visionary: Cordell Hull and Trade Reform, 1933-1937.* Kent, Ohio: Kent State University Press, 1998.

Gellman, Irwin. *Secret Affairs: FDR, Cordell Hull, and Sumner Welles.* New York: Enigma Books, 2003.

Pratt, Julius W. *Cordell Hull.* 2 vols. New York: Cooper Square, 1964.

See also   Asia; Foreign policy of the United States; Geneva Disarmament Conference; Germany and U.S. appeasement; Inter-American Conference for the Maintenance of Peace; Isolationism; Japanese military aggression; London Economic Conference; Manchuria occupation; Neutrality Acts; *Panay* incident; Philippine Independence Act of 1934; Reciprocal Trade Agreements Act of 1936; Roosevelt, Franklin D.

■ *Humphrey's Executor v. United States*

The Case   U.S. Supreme Court ruling upholding the constitutionality of the Federal Trade Commission Act

Date   Decided on May 27, 1935

The Federal Trade Commission (FTC) Act of 1914 limited presidential powers to remove an executive official who performed legislative and judicial duties. By upholding that act, the Supreme Court's ruling in Humphrey's Executor *recognized the independence of government regulatory agencies that exercised legislative and judicial functions by denying the president of the United States the power to remove an agency official because that offiicial disagreed with the president's political views and by requiring the president to comply with the removal provisions of the statute creating the agency.*

In 1931, President Herbert Hoover appointed, and the Senate confirmed, William Humphrey to serve a seven-year term as a federal trade commissioner. President Franklin D. Roosevelt dismissed Humphrey in 1933, because the latter disagreed with his New Deal policies. Humphrey brought suit to recover the salary owed him but died before the Supreme Court heard his case. The suit was brought by the executor of Humphrey's estate.

In a unanimous decision written by Justice George Sutherland, the Supreme Court held that the FTC Act limited the president's power to remove FTC commissioners during their terms in office, because Congress intended to create a body of experts free to exercise their judgment independent of presidential control. The FTC Act did not, however, interfere unconstitutionally with the president's executive power. Unlike in *Myers v. United States* (1926), which involved a postmaster who was an executive official, and therefore removable at the discretion of the president, Congress had limited the president's power to remove a commissioner of an independent regulatory agency who performed principally legislative and judicial duties.

Impact The decision in the *Humphrey's Executor* case was announced the same day as two other decisions that struck down major New Deal recovery programs: *Schechter Poultry Corp. v. United States*, which nullified the National Industrial Recovery Act, and *Louisville Bank v. Redford*, which struck down the Frazier-Lemke Farm Bankruptcy Act. In response to this Black Monday for the New Deal, President Roosevelt denounced the decisions and began to design his plan to "pack" the Supreme Court. *Humphrey's Executor* liberated independent regulatory commissioners from political control, and *Weiner v. United States* (1958) extended its holding when the Supreme Court overturned President Dwight D. Eisenhower's removal without cause of a member of the War Claims Commission, a quasi-judicial agency.

William Crawford Green

Further Reading

Ellis, Richard J., ed. *Judging Executive Power: Sixteen Supreme Court Cases That Have Shaped the American Presidency.* Lanham, Md.: Rowman & Littlefield, 2009.

Leuchtenburg, William E. "The Case of the Contentious Commissioner: *Humphrey's Executor v. U.S.*" In *Freedom and Reform: Essays in Honor of Henry Steele Commager,* edited by Harold M. Hyman and Leonard W. Levy. New York: Harper & Row, 1967.

See also Federal Trade Commission; Hoover, Herbert; New Deal; Roosevelt, Franklin D.; Roosevelt's court-packing plan; *Schechter Poultry Corp. v. United States*; Supreme Court, U.S.

■ Hutton, Barbara

Identification American socialite
Born November 14, 1912; New York, New York
Died May 11, 1979; Beverly Hills, California

A fabulously wealthy heiress who had been traumatized as a child, Hutton came of age during the 1930's, when the news media began tracking her life. She spent the rest of her life fruitlessly attempting to find happiness, traveling the world, spending her fortune, and marrying and divorcing a succession of men of dubious reputation.

Barbara Woolworth Hutton was the granddaughter of five-and-dime store magnate F. W. Woolworth. She was the only child of Woolworth's daughter Edna and stockbroker Franklyn Hutton, the cofounder of the E. F. Hutton investment firm. Despite the circumstances of her birth, Hutton grew up in

Heiress Barbara Hutton in 1935. (Hulton Archive/Getty Images)

turmoil. Her father was often absent because of numerous sexual escapades, and his affairs were the primary reason for her mother's suicide: At the age of five, Hutton discovered Edna's lifeless body. Lonely and withdrawn, Hutton subsequently stayed with relatives before attending several exclusive finishing schools.

In 1924, Hutton inherited millions of dollars, which were held in trust. The money was shrewdly invested, and when she came of age was worth several billion dollars in spending power, making her the world's richest woman. Hutton had many love affairs and married the first of her eight husbands in 1929. After divorcing him in 1933, she relocated to Europe, where she met and married an impoverished Russian aristocrat, Prince Alexis Mdivani. Their union lasted less than two years, during which time she spent millions of dollars on cars, jewels, and property and began her descent into alcohol and drugs. Afterward, she married an abusive Danish aristocrat, Kurt von Haugwitz-Reventlow, father of her only child, Lance Reventlow, who died in a plane crash at the age of thirty-six. From 1942 to 1945, Hutton was married to film star Cary Grant—the only one of her husbands who did not take advantage of her. Always surrounded by hangers-on and gold diggers, Hutton had an unfortunate tendency to marry them, wedding and divorcing four more times between 1947 and 1966. Having squandered her fortune, Hutton died alone and almost penniless at the age of sixty-six.

Impact   Dubbed the "poor little rich girl" by the media during the 1930's, Hutton was often derided for her excesses. Others believe she was deserving of sympathy, as a classic case of an adult who tried unsuccessfully to buy the love and nurturing she was denied as a child.

Jack Ewing

Further Reading

Heymann, C. David. *Poor Little Rich Girl: The Life and Legend of Barbara Hutton.* New York: Pocket Books, 1990.

Pitrone, Jean Maddern. *F. W. Woolworth and the American Five and Dime: A Social History.* Jefferson, N.C.: McFarland, 2007.

See also   Crimes and scandals; Fashions and clothing; Hairstyles; Hughes, Howard; Newspapers, U.S.

■ I AM movement

Identification   Esoteric, theosophical religious
movement

Date   Established in 1930

*One of the most popular religious organizations offering
Americans an alternative to mainstream Judeo-Christian
traditions during the 1930's, the I AM movement began
during the first year of the decade and all but ended in its final year, when its founder, Guy Ballard, died in 1939. Synthesizing aspects of traditional Christianity, alchemy, Theosophy, Spiritualism, and various Eastern religions, the
movement attracted thousands of adherents.*

Ballard's early years are shrouded in scandal. Supposedly, he had once been charged with operating a
confidence scheme and had to flee to California
from Chicago, where he had been living with his
wife, Edna, and where both of them had been practicing as mediums in a Spiritualist church. During
walks on Mount Shasta in California in 1930, he
claimed he encountered three times the Count St.
Germain, an eighteenth century alchemist and ad-
venturer who had become an Ascended Master, that
is, a perfectly enlightened, all-but-immortal spiritual
being. The concept of Ascended Masters was a major
element of Theosophy, an admixture of Eastern and
Western religious thought expounded initially by
Helena Petrovna Blavatsky in 1875, which was a synthetic religious philosophy popular in Europe and
the United States in the late nineteenth and early
twentieth centuries.

After these alleged encounters with St. Germain,
Ballard began to formulate a religious creed similar
to that of Theosophy; it revered Christ and took its
name from the identification of God in the book of
Exodus in the episode of Moses and the burning
bush. However, it also advocated belief in reincarnation and other tenets of Hinduism and Buddhism,
such as adoration of numerous spirits and gurus.
The strictest adherents to the I AM movement practiced vegetarianism, maintained celibacy, and re-
frained from using tobacco and drinking alcohol.
Central to the tenets of the I AM movement was a
spiritual force or entity that Ballard called the Violet
Consuming Flame, which was supposed to be able to
neutralize bad karma or effectively negate the effects of greed, desire, and violent impulses. When
the Violet Consuming Flame had carried out this
cleansing function, souls would be free from endless
reincarnation in the material world and endurance
of lives of desperation and suffering—a concept similar to nirvana in Hinduism and Buddhism. Ballard
encoded the basic beliefs of the I AM movement in
Unveiled Mysteries (1934), which he wrote under the
pseudonym Godfré Ray King.

The worship services and devotional meetings of
the I AM movement were colorful, and perhaps
therein lay much of the appeal the group had
among Depression-era Americans. The Ballards
dressed exclusively in white and pink, and most of
their publications were bound in various shades of
purple. Audiences were regaled with stories of Guy
Ballard's visits with various Ascended Masters—including some from the planet Venus. Attendees
were instructed in how to summon the Violet Consuming Flame and were encouraged to chant "decrees," prolonged mantras. Outside the halls where
the sessions were held, vendors sold religious tracts
and recordings of Ballard's lectures. The popularity
of the movement quickly waned in late 1939 when
Ballard lost his life to arteriosclerosis. Though Edna
Ballard announced that her husband had gone to
join the Ascended Masters, it was apparent to all but
the most credulous adherents that he had simply
died. During the 1940's, Edna Ballard and Donald
Ballard, her son, were twice convicted of fraud, but
both convictions were overturned.

Impact   Although the heyday of the original I AM
movement ended with the death of Ballard in 1939,
the organization continued into the twenty-first century, though as a smaller group, renamed the I Am
Activity. Its popularity during the 1930's represents a

populist redaction of various transcendental and theosophical trends of the nineteenth century made palatable and accessible for Depression-era Americans searching for explanations and remedies for their plight.

Thomas Du Bose

Further Reading

Ballard, Guy [Godfré Ray King, pseud.]. *Unveiled Mysteries.* Chicago: Saint Germain Press, 1934.

Godwin, Joscelyn. *The Theosophical Enlightenment.* Albany: State University of New York Press, 1994.

Partride, Christopher, ed. *New Religions: A Guide— New Religious Movements, Sects, and Alternative Spiritualities.* New York: Oxford University Press, 2004.

Whalen, William J. *Minority Religions in America.* Staten Island, N.Y.: Alba House, 1972.

See also   Father Divine; Fundamentalist-Modernist conflict; Nation of Islam; Religion in Canada; Religion in the United States.

■ Ice hockey

The 1930's marked the birth of the National Hockey League (NHL). Although a number of franchises were lost in major American and Canadian cities, the league was able to survive and retain its fan base despite a cap on players' salaries, a reduction in ticket prices, and significant changes to the way the game itself was played.

By the end of the 1920's, the NHL was the premier professional hockey league in North America, with ten franchises, six of which were in U.S. cities. With rule changes that allowed forward passing in all three zones of the rink and radio broadcasts of games in both the United States and Canada, professional hockey was creating a fan base that was beginning to rival those of baseball and boxing. By 1931, however, the Great Depression had led to the departure of the Philadelphia Quakers and the Ottawa Senators from the league, although Ottawa returned for the 1932-1933 season. By the end of the 1930's, only the two franchises in New York (the Rangers and the Americans), the Boston Bruins, the Toronto Maple Leafs, the Montreal Canadiens, the Detroit Red Wings, and the Chicago Blackhawks remained. Nonetheless, the 1930's was a remarkable decade for

professional hockey in terms of how the team owners kept the league solvent and how the game changed to attract increasing numbers of fans.

Labor Relations, Business, and the NHL   In 1931, the board of governors of the NHL approved an increase in the number of games played from forty-four to forty-eight for each franchise in an effort to ensure that players would be better compensated during the economic downturn that affected both the United States and Canada. However, with revenues continuing to shrink, the board established a salary cap, mandating that no team's payroll could exceed $70,000 per year and that no individual player could receive more than $7,500 per year. Stars such as Frank Boucher of the Rangers, Lorne Chabot of the Maple Leafs, and Aurel Joliat of the Canadiens resisted the move by refusing to play, but the board gave team owners the power to suspend any of the holdouts. Eventually, all of the dissidents capitulated. Ticket prices were slashed as well. In 1933, the top price for a ticket to an NHL game was three dollars, and in many arenas, fans could see a game for fifty cents. While such measures had negative effects on the NHL—the Montreal Maroons and Ottawa Senators folded—the league avoided the fate of rival professional hockey leagues such as the American Hockey League, which was forced to suspend activity altogether.

The Great Depression made it increasingly difficult for sports franchises to attract investors. As economic conditions worsened, only the teams in major American markets with large arenas—such as in New York, Detroit, and Chicago, which had a new 16,500-seat arena—seemed viable. However, Conn Smythe, the owner of the Maple Leafs, was able to attract some of Canada's largest banks to fund the construction of a 13,500-seat arena. He convinced the International Brotherhood of Electrical Workers to accept 20 percent of their pay in Maple Leafs stock while building the new arena. In return, Smythe pledged to use only union labor. Thus, the "original six" franchises remained solvent throughout the Great Depression.

Rule Changes   To attract more casual sports fans to hockey games, the NHL instituted a few controversial changes to the rules of the game. In 1929, the rules allowing increased forward passing were instituted. In 1934, the league instituted the penalty shots, taken thirty-eight feet from the goaltender and employed when an offensive player is fouled in scoring position. By 1937, the icing rule, which made it illegal for a player to pass an untouched puck from the defensive zone to the offensive zone, had been adopted. As a result, hockey became more dependent on passing and team play and an arguably faster-paced game than it had been previously. The changes also led to the development of semipermanent forward lines for teams. The result was healthy attendance for all of the original six franchises throughout the 1930's. However, these innovations were not considered improvements to the game by all fans. Longtime Canadian hockey fans bemoaned the "Americanization" of the game, claiming that the rule changes catered to an American audience that did not completely understand the game. Further, these changes coincided with the league's quest for American investors to ensure financial solvency. While many Canadian fans voiced feelings of disenfranchisement from their national game, the rule changes and the partnerships with investors did much to ensure the survival of the league during the 1930's.

Professional Stars and Top Teams Despite the salary caps, the NHL did much to attract and keep the dominant amateur hockey players of the time by signing them to long-term contracts. Toronto's Frank "King" Clancy was probably the most popular defensive player of the decade. Montreal's Joliat was perhaps the most popular francophone player of the decade. Boucher of the Rangers was the most dominant center of the period. However, Eddie Shore of the Boston Bruins was the most talked-about player of the 1930's. A player of great intensity, Shore was known as much for his physical style of play as he was for his pregame antics, which included skating onto the ice wearing a black and gold cape with a "valet" in tow.

Members of the Canadian national ice hockey team taking a break during the 1936 Winter Olympics, at which the team won a silver medal. (Hulton Archive/Getty Images)

The dominant teams of the 1930's were the Canadiens, the Blackhawks, and the Red Wings; each won two Stanley Cup championships during the period. The Maple Leafs appeared in six Stanley Cup series, losing five and winning one. During the 1930's, the Stanley Cup championship was changed to a best-of-five-games format and, later in the decade, to a best-of-seven-games format, the system that is still in use. Radio broadcasts of this league championship led to even greater popularity for the game in the United States. Thus, the league survived the Great Depression and readied itself for the expansion it experienced over the following fifty years.

Impact The 1930's established ice hockey as one of the premier professional sports in North America. Initially a Canadian pastime, hockey enjoyed tremendous success in the United States during and after the 1930's. The rule changes adopted by the NHL during the ten-year period from 1929 to 1939 were designed to entice the casual fan to follow hockey, and this notion of expanding the fan base provided a model for rule changes in other major sports.

William Carney

Further Reading

Askin, Mark, and Malcolm G. Kelly. *The Complete Idiot's Guide to the History of Hockey.* Toronto: Pearson Education Canada, 2000. Concise overview of the history of ice hockey, including the pivotal decade of the 1930's.

Houston, William. *Pride and Glory: One Hundred Years of the Stanley Cup.* Whitby, Ont.: McGraw-Hill Ryerson, 1992. History of hockey's professional championship, which began during the 1890's.

McKinley, Michael. *Hockey: A People's History.* Toronto: Canadian Broadcasting Corporation, 2006. Charts hockey from its beginning and discusses teams, rules, and equipment.

Pincus, Arthur, with David Rosner, Len Hochberg, and Chris Malcolm. *The Official Illustrated NHL History: The Story of the Coolest Game.* Chicago: Triumph Books, 2001. Comprehensive coverage that includes statistics and other information. Numerous historical and contemporary photographs.

See also Great Depression in Canada; Shore, Eddie; Sports in Canada; Sports in the United States.

■ Ickes, Harold

Identification U.S. secretary of the interior
Born March 15, 1874; Frankstown Township, Pennsylvania
Died February 3, 1952; Washington, D.C.

Ickes was a strong Progressive reformer and political leader in Chicago and an avid conservationist who served as secretary of the interior longer than any predecessor or successor. He oversaw and administered some of the greatest triumphs of New Deal reforms through the National Park Service (NPS), the Public Works Administration (PWA), and the Bureau of Indian Affairs (BIA).

Harold Ickes was born to Martha McCune and Jesse Ickes in a rough and often uncaring rural household of seven children. Ickes saw his father rarely but was extremely close to his mother; her death in 1890 forced him to move to Chicago to live with his aunt and uncle. Although removed from his father's household, life for the young Ickes was hardly ideal. Assisting his adoptive family, Ickes worked in the family's drugstore, opening the store at six in the morning, then attending school, and afterward returning to work until ten at night. Despite such hardships, Ickes obtained a solid education and graduated in the top of his class. His boyhood experiences along with his working-class education instilled in him a respect for workers, the poor, and the indigent and shaped his political outlook within the Progressive movement of the late 1890's and early twentieth century.

Ickes entered the University of Chicago in 1893 and graduated in 1897, afterward working with local Chicago political campaigns and reformers. Returning to the university in 1903 to pursue a law degree, Ickes maintained his political friendships and campaign connections with leading Chicago and Illinois politicians throughout his school years; he graduated in 1907. Ickes used his law profession as a basis to invoke political change and became a significant force behind the Chicago scene through his leadership of local, state, and nationwide elections for Progressive politicians through the 1920's. During this time, Ickes was first introduced to the problems facing Native Americans, a factor that impacted his career as secretary of the interior.

In 1923, Ickes attended a meeting led by John Collier, who later served as commissioner of the Bureau of Indian Affairs under Ickes. Collier spoke about the land and water rights threats against the

Secretary of the Interior Harold Ickes, leaving the White House in late 1938, flashes two fingers to indicate he has two days to decide whether to run for mayor of Chicago. (Library of Congress)

Pueblo tribe. Ickes immediately joined the organization, and, despite some hostility with Collier over management, he became an important advocate of Native American rights. When President Franklin D. Roosevelt assumed office and appointed Ickes as secretary of the Department of the Interior in 1933, Ickes and Collier worked to implement a series of reforms aimed at ending allotment and assimilation and improving land resources, economic stability, and education with the 1934 Johnson O'Malley Act, the 1935 Indian Arts and Crafts Board, the creation of the Civilian Conservation Corps, Indian Division, and the preeminent Indian Reorganization Act (IRA) of 1934. Ickes' endorsement of the tribal sovereignty outlined under the IRA won him many political enemies; nonetheless, he remained a staunch supporter of Native American rights after he left office in 1946.

Other areas where Ickes implemented Progressive ideals were in the realms of forest conservation with the NPS, the PWA, and the Bureau of Reclama-

tion. From 1933 to 1939, Ickes used the PWA to fund construction projects and reclamation efforts with the All-American Canal, the Grand Coulee Dam, and others and to channel money toward NPS efforts for scenic parkways and the addition of millions of acres for new parks. Ickes moved beyond the limitations of his fellow Progressives in the field of civil rights. He advocated for African Americans, creating jobs within PWA projects and standing against the Daughters of the American Revolution in 1939, who barred contralto singer Marian Anderson from performing in Constitution Hall. In return, Ickes introduced Anderson at a concert in front of the Lincoln Memorial.

Following his 1946 departure from the Department of the Interior, Ickes remained a voice for conservation and civil rights as a newspaper columnist and an author of several books, including *The New Democracy* (1934), *The Third Term Bugaboo* (1940), *Fightin' Oil* (1943), *The Autobiography of a Curmudgeon* (1943), and the three-volume, posthumous *The Secret Diary of Harold Ickes* (1953-1954).

Impact   Ickes's impact and significance in the areas of conservation and civil rights were one of the hallmarks of New Deal democracy and reforms. Even though many of the victories of Native American reform were reversed immediately following Ickes's departure and some conservation projects, such as the Wilderness Act, were not implemented until the 1960's, Ickes was one of the most powerful voices of Roosevelt's cabinet and oversaw the transformation of the federal government as an agent of social change for the American people.

Nathan Wilson

Further Reading

Clarke, Jeanne Nienaber. *Roosevelt's Warrior: Harold L. Ickes and the New Deal.* Baltimore: Johns Hopkins University Press, 1996.

Watkins, T. H. *Righteous Pilgrim: The Life and Times of Harold L. Ickes, 1874-1952.* New York: Henry Holt, 1990.

White, Graham J., and John Maze. *Harold Ickes of the New Deal: His Private Life and Public Career.* Cambridge, Mass.: Harvard University Press, 1985.

See also   African Americans; Collier, John; Grand Coulee Dam; Indian Reorganization Act; National parks; Native Americans; New Deal.

■ I'd Rather Be Right

Identification Broadway musical satirizing 1930's politics
Creators Richard Rodgers and Lorenz Hart
Date November 2, 1937

I'd Rather Be Right was a Depression-era musical satire in the mold of George Gershwin's Of Thee I Sing *(1931), which was premiered six years earlier.* I'd Rather Be Right *featured fifty-nine-year-old George M. Cohan playing the role of President Franklin D. Roosevelt.*

During the 1930's, popular entertainment made many allusions to politics, and the Great Depression in particular. Many Broadway musicals were fashioned as political satires, and the greatest Broadway composers and lyricists of the era all produced socially relevant musicals: George and Ira Gershwin created *Strike Up the Band* (1930), *Of Thee I Sing* (1931), and *Let 'Em Eat Cake* (1933). Irving Berlin wrote *Face the Music* (1932). *I'd Rather Be Right* was Richard Rodgers's and Lorenz Hart's contribution to the genre. The book of *I'd Rather Be Right* was written by George S. Kaufman and Moss Hart.

I'd Rather Be Right concerns the story of two young lovers—Peggy Jones and Phil Barker—who cannot marry until they secure pay raises. Their salaries cannot be raised, however, until President Roosevelt balances the budget. During a dream sequence, the president enters the characters' lives and concocts many farcical strategies in an attempt to balance the budget. Although he never succeeds in balancing the budget, Roosevelt ultimately encourages the couple to marry anyway.

I'd Rather Be Right opened at the Alvin Theater in 1937 and ran for 290 performances. One of the major factors in the show's success was the casting of an aging Cohan in the role of Roosevelt. Substantial portions of *I'd Rather Be Right* are featured in the Cohan biopic *Yankee Doodle Dandy* (1942).

Impact *I'd Rather Be Right* was representative of the political edge taken by many Broadway musicals of the 1930's. With a nine-month run, it was the second most successful political musical of the decade, next to *Of Thee I Sing*, and remains one of the most memorable shows written by Rodgers and Hart.

Matthew Hoch

Further Reading

Everett, William A., and Paul R. Laird. *Historical Dictionary of Broadway Musicals*. Lanham, Md.: Scarecrow Press, 2008.

Green, Stanley, and Kay Green. *Broadway Musicals: Show by Show*. 6th ed. New York: Hal Leonard, 2007.

Mordden, Ethan. *Sing for Your Supper: The Broadway Musical in the 1930's*. New York: Palgrave Macmillan, 2005.

See also Broadway musicals; Cohan, George M.; Gershwin, George; Roosevelt, Franklin D.

■ Imitation of Life

Identification Film about American racism
Director of film John M. Stahl
Author of book Fannie Hurst
Date Novel published in 1933; film released on November 26, 1934

One of the first big-budget Hollywood films to treat racial discrimination in the United States, Imitation of Life *was a box-office success that garnered three Academy Award nominations, including one for best picture.*

Directed by John M. Stahl from a script by William Hurlbut, *Imitation of Life* was based on the best-selling 1933 novel of the same name by Fannie Hurst, which dealt with racial prejudice. Specifically, the film addressed the unsure position of light-complexioned African Americans and the temptation some might feel in the era of segregation to "pass," that is, deny their African heritage and present themselves as of European descent. Heading the cast was Claudette Colbert, who had a breakthrough year in 1934, appearing in the historical spectacle *Cleopatra* and the classic screwball comedy *It Happened One Night*, for which she won an Academy Award for best actress. Fredi Washington played Peola, a light-skinned young black woman who "passes" for white. Washington had had a varied career, working with such highly respected African American performers as Duke Ellington, Josephine Baker, and Paul Robeson.

Imitation of Life deals with two single mothers, Bea, who is white, and Delilah, who is black, who market Delilah's family recipe for pancakes. The women become successful in business, but their daughters bring them grief, especially Delilah's daughter,

Louise Beavers (left) and Fredi Washington in a scene from Imitation of Life, *a film in part about African Americans "passing" for white.* (©Bettmann/CORBIS)

Peola, who rejects her mother and her race. Meanwhile, Bea's daughter Jessie falls in love with her mother's fiancé. The climax of the film is a melodramatic but genuinely touching funeral scene in which Bea and Jessie bury Delilah. Peola rushes into the service and penitently throws herself on her mother's coffin.

Impact   *Imitation of Life* was revolutionary during the 1930's for its forthright portrayal of racism. A remake of the film starring Lana Turner was a hit in 1959, overshadowing the original for decades afterward. However, during the early twenty-first century, the 1930's version came to be reevaluated by critics, resulting in its entry in the U.S. National Film Registry in 2005. In 2007, *Time* magazine proclaimed it one of the top five films in its list of the twenty-five most important films on race.

Thomas Du Bose

Further Reading

Black, Cheryl. "Looking White, Acting Black: Cast(e)ing Fredi Washington." *Theatre Survey* 45, no. 1 (2004): 19-40.

Bogle, Donald. *Bright Boulevard, Bold Dream: The Story of Black Hollywood.* New York: One World, 2006.

Hurst, Fannie. *Imitation of Life.* New ed. Durham, N.C.: Duke University Press, 2004.

See also   African Americans; Anderson, Marian; Ellington, Duke; *Green Pastures, The; It Happened One Night;* Race riots; Racial discrimination.

■ Immigration to Canada

The Great Depression was a period of mass unemployment and economic hardship for a vast majority of Canadians. Almost all immigration to Canada during this period was halted because of the lack of jobs in the country. Even as the economy began to recover slowly in the late 1930's, severe immigration restrictions remained intact.

The depressed economic conditions of the 1930's resulted in immigration controls that were even more restrictive than ones from previous years. Exclusionary policies directed at Chinese, Japanese, and Asian Indian people continued to be upheld. Refugees, a vast majority of whom were Jews, were faced with closed-door policies that denied them refuge. Nonpreferred immigrants, such as southern and eastern Europeans, also were targets of tight immigration restrictions. Between 1921 and 1931, 1,166,000 immigrants came to Canada; the number of immigrants to Canada between 1931 and 1941 dropped to a total of 140,000. The precipitous decline in the number of immigrants was partly the result of mass deportation used by the government to rid the country of the foreign-born indigent and impoverished people and immigrant labor leaders with little, if any, opposition by the Canadian public. For every three immigrants allowed into Canada in this period, one immigrant was deported.

Immigration Controls and Deportations During the Great Depression, 1930-1935   By August, 1930, the Depression was well under way in Canada. Richard Bedford Bennett won the federal election that year and within months of coming to power initiated a series of immigration policies that led to the most restrictive immigration controls in Canadian history. By March, 1931, the only immigrants allowed to enter Canada were white American and British subjects who had sufficient funds to support themselves until they could obtain secure employment, agriculturalists with enough resources to farm in Canada, and the wives and minor children of Canadian residents. All activities to promote immigration from abroad were stopped, medical examinations of potential immigrants were strictly enforced, and various immigration offices in the United States were closed.

The Canadian government also actively engaged in deportation as a means of inexpensively and quickly removing unemployed immigrants and foreign-born labor leaders who challenged the status quo. Between 1930 and 1935, approximately 30,000 immigrants were deported from Canada, an average of about 5,700 deportations annually. Government records show that approximately 60 percent of the deportations were the result of a public charge; criminality accounted for 15 percent, medical reasons for 10 percent, family members of a deported immigrant for 10 percent. The remaining 5 percent were deported for "other civil causes," which was a broad category used to deport labor radicals and union organizers. These deportations received widespread support from the Canadian public, who held anti-immigrant sentiments and blamed immigrants for unemployment, and from government officials, who tended to think of unemployed immigrants as troublemakers that would create social unrest.

Immigration Restrictions and Slow Economic Recovery, 1936-1939   In 1935, the same year that William Lyon Mackenzie King was elected to replace Bennett as prime minister, the economy began to recover slowly. While King maintained the same tight restrictions on immigration that had been enforced during the first half of the 1930's, the number of deportations drastically declined largely in response to the wider demands of Canadians that various labor movements had helped to cultivate.

Immigration policy during the late 1930's was shaped primarily in response to overseas events, notably the devastation of Europe that resulted in enormous numbers of refugees, and focused specifically on prohibiting the entrance of displaced persons and other immigrants. The more than four hundred anti-Jewish laws passed in Germany shortly after the election of Adolf Hitler as chancellor of Germany in 1933, the enactment of the Nuremberg Laws in 1935, and the event of Kristallnacht in 1938 created mass numbers of mostly Jewish refugees. Despite a recovering economy and pressure from big business to allow more workers, the Canadian government refused to lessen its tight immigration restrictions. The most notable aspect of the policy was the government's refusal to liberalize immigration controls primarily to ensure that Canada did not become a place of refuge for those who had been displaced by fascist regimes in their countries of origin.

Between 1933 and 1939, Canada admitted a total of 4,000 refugees from Nazi Germany, a number that

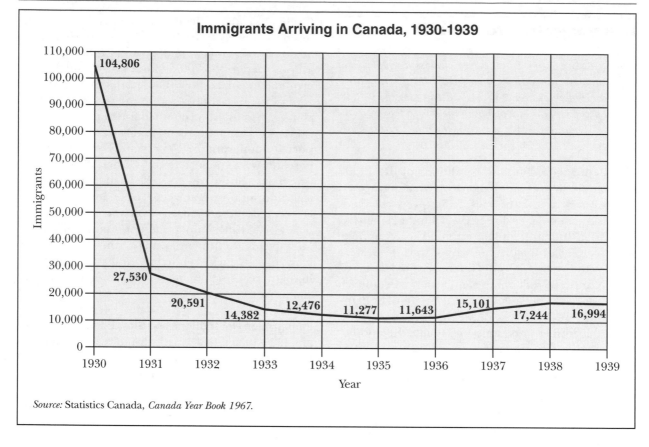

Immigrants Arriving in Canada, 1930-1939

Source: Statistics Canada, *Canada Year Book 1967.*

is considered inadequate when compared to other Western nations during the same period. A particularly sad example of Canada's antirefugee position was the government's refusal in 1939 to allow the *St. Louis* ship, carrying 907 Jewish refugees from Germany, to dock at a Canadian port, forcing those aboard to return to Nazi Germany to face the death camps. King's government chose to ignore the pleas for a more humanitarian policy toward the growing numbers of European refugees that came from a few members of parliament, the Canadian Jewish community, some church groups and humanitarian organizations, and a small number of journalists. King's decision reflected the political atmosphere of the time, in which widespread anti-immigrant and anti-Semitic sentiment was held by a majority of Canadians, particularly in Quebec.

Impact Canada's immigration policy during the 1930's is one of the bleakest and most repressive in Canada's history. Although Canadian immigration policy had historically restricted non-European set-

tlement, the period of the Depression is marked by indifference toward displaced persons who, in many cases, faced death upon their return home. Similarly, the mass deportations of impoverished, unemployed immigrants and foreign-born labor leaders and union organizers displayed the anti-immigrant, antilabor sentiments of the Canadian public that were echoed by the Canadian government through its policies. Although the Canadian economy began to recover slowly in the period after 1935, albeit with a temporary setback in 1937-1938, the door to immigration remained shut. Not until the 1950's were immigration restrictions reduced, but even then only with respect to European immigrants.

Kelly Amanda Train

Further Reading

Abella, Irving, and Harold Troper. *None Is Too Many: Canada and the Jews of Europe 1933-1948.* Toronto: Lester, 1991. Detailed discussion of Canadian government policies toward Jewish refugees prior to, during, and after World War II and the political efforts of the Canadian Jewish community.

Bialystok, Franklin. *Delayed Impact: The Holocaust and the Canadian Jewish Community.* Montreal: McGill-Queen's University Press, 2000. Critical analysis of Canadian anti-Semitism, Canadian immigration policy, Jewish refugees, and Canadian Jewish community responses from the 1930's to the 1990's.

Dirks, Gerald E. *Canada's Refugee Policy: Indifference or Opportunism?* Montreal: McGill-Queen's University Press, 1977. Examines the evolution of refugee policy in Canada and how policy makers failed to address the enormity of the refugee problem prior to, during, and after World War II.

Kelley, Ninette, and Michael J. Trebilcock. *The Making of the Mosaic: A History of Canadian Immigration Policy.* Toronto: University of Toronto Press, 1998. A detailed examination of Canadian immigration policy, exclusionary acts, and discriminatory practices aimed at various immigrant groups from pre-Confederation to the 1990's.

Knowles, Valerie. *Strangers at Our Gates: Canadian Immigration and Immigration Policy, 1540-2006.* Toronto: Dundurn Press, 2007. Examines Canadian immigration policy and how it has historically been shaped by social, economic, and political factors.

Tulchinsky, Gerald, ed. *Immigration in Canada: Historical Perspectives.* Toronto: Copp Clark Longman, 1994. Edited collection that explores specific events in the history of Canadian immigration policy from pre-Confederation until the post-World War II era, including a chapter discussing the deportations of foreign-born immigrants between 1930 and 1936.

Whitaker, Reg. *Canadian Immigration Policy Since Confederation.* Ottawa: Canadian Historical Association, 1991. Presents a clear and concise critical overview of Canadian immigration policy from 1867 until the 1980's.

See also Bennett, Richard Bedford; Canadian minority communities; Great Depression in Canada; Great Depression in the United States; Immigration to the United States; King, William Lyon Mackenzie; Unemployment in Canada; Unemployment in the United States; Urbanization in Canada.

■ Immigration to the United States

During the 1930's, restrictive immigration laws and the Great Depression resulted in the lowest U.S. immigration numbers in fifty years. Between 1932 and 1935, more people emigrated from than immigrated to the United States, and the United States gained a net increase of only 68,639 immigrants during the decade.

Between 1881 and 1920, more than twenty-three million immigrants came to the United States, and one-half of these new arrivals entered the country during the first two decades of the twentieth century. In 1909, nativist reaction to this new mass immigration demanded immigration quotas. In 1924, Congress passed the Immigration Act, which introduced national quotas and limited the number of immigrants allowed into the United States each year. Combined with the impact of the Great Depression, this law was instrumental in reducing immigration during the 1930's to the lowest level recorded in any decade since 1881. Even though the 1924 law exempted Mexicans and Filipinos from the quota system, federal and local legal measures were used to repatriate hundreds of thousands to Mexico and to introduce a small quota for the Philippines.

Great Depression and European Immigrants Congressional efforts to limit immigration focused primarily on European immigrants because Asian immigrants were barred entry into the country, with minor exceptions. The first law that established a yearly immigration limit of 350,000 was passed in 1921; each year, Congress continued to expand the stringent U.S. immigration policies and passed the 1924 Immigration Act sponsored by Representative Albert Johnson and Senator David A. Reed. Johnson characterized Russian and Polish Jews as "filthy un-American." In 1929, Congress established the final national quota system, which discriminated against southern and eastern Europeans much more than the original 1924 plan had and limited annual immigration to 150,000. The Western Hemisphere was excluded from the quota system. Opinion polls revealed strong public support for the new law. Between 1924 and 1930, almost 1.8 million immigrants came to the United States, but only 55 percent arrived from Europe; the remainder came primarily from Canada and Mexico.

The economic collapse after 1929 caused American officials to question all immigration. In December, 1930, President Herbert Hoover informed the nation that because of economic conditions and unemployment, the United States had to limit immigration further; two years later, he demanded rigid immigration restrictions. In a speech in San Francisco on September 23, 1933, presidential candidate Franklin D. Roosevelt insisted that the country could not afford additional European immigrants. Roosevelt's election programs between 1932 and 1944 did not include the topic of immigration. Even Louis Adamic, an immigrant who had helped get a bronze copy of Emma Lazarus's poem "The New Colossus," welcoming the world's poor, attached to the Statue of Liberty, wanted Europeans to remain at home.

Several factors helped to reduce immigration during the 1930's to a mere trickle compared to earlier patterns. First, President Hoover authorized consular officials, who had to issue visas to potential immigrants in Europe, to apply the "likely-to-be-a-public-charge" (LPC) clause more rigorously. Consequently, government officials could bar the less affluent or those without sponsors. Visa issues declined from twenty-four thousand to seven thousand a month after 1930. In addition, the federal government deported to Europe and Canada between six thousand and eight thousand people each year during the early 1930's. In order to pressure aliens in the United States to leave the country, local and state relief agencies discriminated against them. Federal relief in 1933 was available to aliens, but they were excluded from employment with the Works Progress Administration in 1936, and relief was administered by local agencies. Even Fiorello Henry La Guardia, the mayor of New York City, whose father had Italian roots, accused aliens of obtaining Home Relief while being "idle," while citizens had to work to obtain relief support.

The lack of work during the Great Depression induced thousands of immigrants, particularly those who came to the United States after World War I, to return to their native countries. Between July, 1931, and June, 1935, more people left the United States than entered. The lack of employment in the United States was another factor that caused many potential immigrants to remain in Europe. By 1930-1931, more immigrants came from the "New World" than from Europe. On average, during the 1930's, only 6,900 immigrants entered the United States each year. Before 1914, more people than that arrived in the country every two days. Between 1931 and 1940, a total of 528,400 immigrants came to the United States. European immigrants accounted for 347,000 of that total, while the

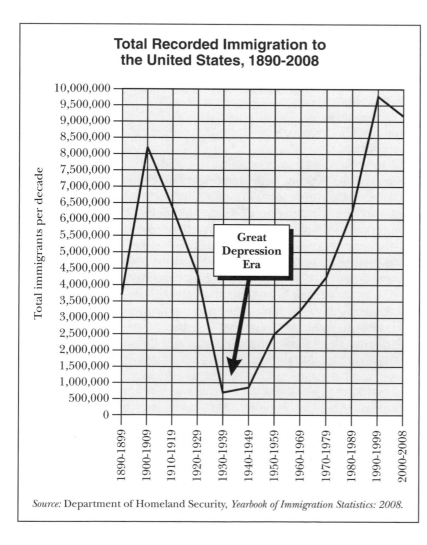

Total Recorded Immigration to the United States, 1890-2008

Source: Department of Homeland Security, *Yearbook of Immigration Statistics: 2008.*

Immigrant women with a child arriving in New York from Czechoslovakia on the SS President Harding in 1939. (©Bettmann/CORBIS)

remainder arrived from the Americas, primarily Canada and Mexico.

Mexican and Filipino Immigrants The 1924 quotas did not apply to Mexicans, but government administrative and legal measures during the 1930's dramatically reduced immigration from Mexico. Between 1901 and 1930, almost 750,000 Mexicans came to the United States, primarily to California and Texas. From 1929 to 1930, the number of Mexican immigrants dropped from 40,000 to 13,000 after the American government started used the LPC clause more rigorously. Between 1931 and 1940, only 22,319 visas were issued to Mexican immigrants.

President Hoover also introduced a program of "repatriation," which resulted in the return of nearly 500,000 Mexican immigrants to Mexico. The peak of this repatriation occurred between 1930 and 1934. President Roosevelt ended repatriation, but an average of nine thousand Mexicans were de-

ported annually between 1934 and 1940. Local authorities such as a Los Angeles committee that coordinated unemployment relief used the relief system to convince Mexicans to leave the country. In a similar fashion, the Dearborn, Michigan, welfare department deported unemployed Mexican Ford workers. In many cases, Mexican American citizens were among the deported. Pablo Guerrero, who came to the United States in 1905 and had five children who were American citizens by birth, was forced to leave Los Angeles in 1932 and return to Mexico. In 1936, the governor of Colorado declared martial law in the southern regions of the state to turn back Mexicans attempting to enter the state. Reflecting the prejudice of the time, Vanderbilt University professor Roy Garis informed John Box, a Texas congressman, that the mental capacity of Mexicans was close to that of an animal.

In 1930, Filipinos were the only Asians who were not barred by American law to immigrate into the United States because the American occupation of the Philippines made them U.S. "nationals." In 1920, about forty-five thousand Filipinos were living in the United States, and many more worked on sugar plantations in Hawaii, which was then a U.S. territory. Prejudice, based on racism and economic fear, against these Asian immigrants was widespread. For example, David P. Barrows, the president of the University of California, told a congressional committee that Filipinos were drawn to both vice and crime, and Charles Goethe, a businessman in Sacramento, California, worried that Filipinos would breed with morons. California included the Filipinos in the state's antimiscegenation law.

Organized labor, represented by the American Federation of Labor (AFL), also campaigned to bar Filipinos from entering the country. In 1934, the U.S. Congress passed a law accepted by the Philippine legislature that promised independence to the Philippines by 1945. This enabled Congress to add Filipinos to the quota system, which allowed only fifty Filipino immigrants to enter the country. Congressman Samuel Dickstein, a supporter of European immigration, made a special effort to return unemployed Filipinos to the Philippines. In 1935, 2,190 Filipinos accepted free transportation to return to Manila.

Mexican immigrants wait at the border in El Paso, Texas. (Library of Congress)

Jewish Refugees The Immigration Law of 1924 did not include a section on refugees, a void that had a devastating impact on German Jews attempting to emigrate en masse after the November, 1938, party-organized pogrom known as "crystal night." During the 1930's, European Jews faced a national quota system and the need to prove that they would not become "public charges" when applying for a visa. For German Jews the quota system was not an obstacle because only 45,952 slots were used out of a total of 157,155 places available for Germans between July, 1932, and June, 1938. German Jews faced increasing discrimination under the Nazi regime, and in 1938 and 1939, there was a mass exodus of Jews from Germany. By 1939, the German, and Austrian, quota was overfilled by ll9.7 percent.

More important than the quota system in hindering German Jewish immigration into the United States was the difficulty of proving that the applicant for a visa had sufficient funds or a sponsor to avoid public support. The Nazis were willing to allow Jews to leave Germany until early 1940, but they robbed Jews of much of their financial wealth before allowing them to exit the country. In addition, many American consular officers in Europe granted few visas to Jews. Furthermore, the assistant secretary of state, Breckinridge Long, was an anti-Semite. When Hebrew Union College attempted to bring two additional Jewish scholars to the campus, the State Department's visa division used a technicality to bar the scholars. Both scholars were eventually confined to a concentration camp, where one died. In May, 1939, a Coast Guard ship prevented the German ship *St. Louis,* carrying hundreds of Jews, from docking in Miami. In 1939, Congress also failed to act on a bill that would have allowed twenty thousand German children to enter the United States regardless of the quota.

In 1938, public-opinion polls revealed that 71 to 85 percent of Americans did not want to change the quota system to assist refugees. In early 1939, two-thirds of the American public did not want to admit children outside the quota system. Ironically, the *News and Courier,* a negrophobic paper in Charleston, South Carolina, wanted white German Jews to settle in the state. Only in 1938 did President Roosevelt establish an Advisory Committee on Political Refugees, and he sent a representative to an international meeting in Évian-les-Bains, France, in July, 1938. He also ordered Frances Perkins, the secretary of the Department of Labor, to renew temporary or tourist visas to allow Jews to stay in the country. In addition, he permitted 150,000 refugees, mostly Jews, to enter the country before December, 1941. The United States could have done more to rescue Jews before 1941, but its record was much better than that of Canada, which only admitted five thousand Jewish refugees between 1939 and 1943.

Impact   In late 1940, the Roman Catholic journal *America* lamented the fact that during the decade of the 1930's the U.S. population increased by only 0.8 percent. By 1940, only 8.8 percent of the population was foreign born, compared to 14.7 percent in 1910. The historian Otis L. Graham, however, considered this to be a "demographic blessing" because it allowed the United States to amalgamate its immigrants, increase wages, and provide job opportunities to African Americans. On the other hand, Henry Kissinger, a Jewish refugee, remembers the elation he felt when coming to New York City in 1938. Also, many Jewish refugees able to escape Europe before 1939 made major scientific and scholarly contributions to the United States.

Johnpeter Horst Grill

Further Reading

Daniels, Roger. *Guarding the Golden Door: American Immigration Policy and Immigration Since 1882.* New York: Hill & Wang, 2004. Solid survey by a specialist on Asian immigration that includes a chapter on the 1930's. Massive notes, bibliography, and index.

Fermi, Lauri. *Illustrious Immigrants: The Intellectual Migration from Europe, 1930-1941.* 2d ed. Chicago: University of Chicago Press, 1971. The author left fascist Italy in 1939 with her scientist husband Enrico Fermi.

Garland, Libby. "Not-Quite-Closed Gates: Jewish Alien Smuggling in the Post-Quota Years." *American Jewish History* 96 (2008): 197-224. Examines Jewish illegal immigration from Cuba. Exhaustive footnotes.

Hoffmann, Abraham. *Unwanted Mexican Americans in the Great Depression—Repatriation Pressures, 1929-1939.* Tucson: University of Arizona Press, 1974. Focusing on the greater Los Angeles region, the author reviews efforts to deport or repatriate Mexican immigrants. Appendix and notes.

Kraut, Alan, and Richard Breitman. *American Refugee Policy and European Jewry, 1933-1945.* Bloomington: University of Indiana Press, 1988. Balanced account of American reactions to Nazi treatment of European Jews. Scholarly bibliography.

Ngai, Mae M. *Impossible Subjects: Illegal Aliens and the Making of Modern America.* Princeton, N.J.: Princeton University Press, 2004. Focusing on Asians and Mexicans, this work describes in great detail illegal immigration and U.S. immigration laws.

Thatcher, Mary Anne. *Immigrants and the 1930's: Ethnicity and Alienage in Depression and On-coming War.* New York: Garland, 1990. Examines the treatment of immigrants by welfare and relief agencies, particularly in New York.

See also   Anti-Semitism; Asian Americans; Evian Conference; Hoover, Herbert; Mexico; Perkins, Frances; Philippine Independence Act of 1934; *St. Louis* incident.

■ Income and wages in Canada

By the 1930's, the transition from subsistence to employ-ment for wages or salaries had already begun in Canada, as it had elsewhere in the developed world. In fact, employ-ment had reached a peak in Canada in late 1929, only to experience a drop of approximately 30 percent by 1933, when the economy reached its lowest point since the end of World War I. In fact, world trade fell by as much as 50 per-cent between 1929 and 1933, and Canada's foreign trade had fallen by nearly as much. Inevitably, this drop had its effect on income and wages.

The income and wages varied by region. The lowest wages and income were in the East, followed by the Maritime Provinces and progressing toward the West. Overseas trade dropped off dramatically; how-ever, the other sources of individual support had not developed in the Maritime Provinces to the extent they had elsewhere in Canada, and as a conse-quence, they had less to lose.

The central provinces, Quebec and Ontario, had a large commitment to manufacturing, and employ-ment did drop among the manufacturing centers in that region. Nonetheless, both provinces still en-joyed mixed economies, with small-farm agriculture playing a relatively important role. While manufac-turing jobs were scarce, the service industries that depended on the concentration of population in Quebec and Ontario retained their ability to pro-vide some measure of employment. In Quebec, the small-scale subsistence agriculture that had charac-terized the province since early settlement retained its prominence.

The Prairie Provinces—Manitoba, Saskatchewan, and Alberta—were the hardest hit by the Depression because of their reliance on agriculture, the market for which experienced a major decline. Canada's farmers in these areas had adapted to the world trade in agriculture, especially the demand for wheat in the period after World War I, for which the vast, flat fields of this part of Canada were ideally suited. During the 1920's, production had ex-panded substantially in this area as farmers bought advanced agricultural machinery well suited to the plains; in doing so, they had gone into debt. Then, the collapse of world trade that followed the stock market crash in the United States and elsewhere in the developed world meant that Canada's wheat farmers had to sell in a market in which the supply vastly exceeded the demand. During the late 1920's, wheat sold for more than one dollar per bushel; dur-ing the 1930's the price dropped to thirty-eight cents, the lowest for wheat in modern history. Pro-duction fell, propelled downward by drought in these semiarid areas, and the farmers of these prov-inces often could not support their families, let alone pay off the debt many had accumulated dur-ing the late 1920's.

British Columbia had little viable agricultural land but had vast forests with exceptionally large trees. A large logging and lumbering business had developed that supplied lumber to the United States, particularly for the construction of houses. This business fell into a deep depression, which led companies to lay off loggers and sawmill workers, for whom there was little alternative employment.

Government Response to the Loss of Wages and Sal-aries As in the United States, Canadian workers turned to the government for help. However, Can-ada's large geographic area and its thin population in most parts, plus its political structure, made the creation of a system of unemployment relief diffi-cult. Attempts by the Dominion government were generally ruled unconstitutional by the top constitu-tional authority, the British Privy Council. Although Great Britain had given Canada Dominion status, es-sentially self-government, in 1931, it had kept the fi-nal constitutional power in Britain, vested in its Privy Council. Because of the council's decision, the cen-tral Canadian government turned to the provinces and asked them to provide relief to desperate citi-zens. However, the national government did extend "loans" to the provinces to help them pay for the un-employed; the provinces passed the tasks on to the municipalities. Over time, this resulted in the Do-minion government paying about 40 percent of the costs of relief.

There was one basic restriction: Relief was pro-vided for families but not for individuals. As a result, many cities had large collections of unemployed workers who did not have families. During the first years of the Depression, this system worked ade-quately, at least in the cities of the central manufac-turing provinces. However, as the Depression per-sisted, unemployed singles became more of a problem, and attempts were made to group them to-gether in work camps to engage in infrastructure jobs such as road building. By the mid-1930's, the supply of infrastructure jobs began to run out, and unrest among these men arose. Socialist theory spread widely in the Prairie Provinces, and in 1936, a march of the unemployed was organized, starting in Vancouver. The march reached Regina, Saskatchewan, where these men were met by a cadre of troopers from the Royal Canadian Mounted Police, which forced the march to disband. The following year, the new Liberal government under William Lyon Mackenzie King disbanded the work camps.

The Decline of Wages Across Canada The loss of income by Canadians resulted from a combination of layoffs from manufacturing and mining jobs and the disappearance of profitable employment in the agricultural field. Many farmers who had assumed large debts during the 1920's simply abandoned their holdings and migrated to the cities, where they could secure some relief for their families. Farmers' cash income fell by 94 percent between 1929 and 1933. During that same period, world trade declined by 50 percent, and Canada was heavily impacted by the decline in demand for its raw materials, which were the basis of Canadian prosperity during the 1920's.

The Canadian economy experienced a slow recovery in the latter half of the 1930's. Those few industries that served mainly the consumer market, notably textiles, did best. Elsewhere, recovery was slow except in one industry: gold mining. Canada produced about 90 percent of the world's gold and exported almost all it produced. Unemployment, which had peaked at 20 percent in 1933, gradually declined; however, it still amounted to about 10 percent at the outbreak of World War II, the fall of 1939.

As in the United States, military production put an end to unemployment. Those individuals who were not called up for military service found work in the industries called on to replenish Britain's military supplies.

The Shift to Services When the Depression hit, Canada had already begun the transition from wage work to services. Those who were employed in services experienced less unemployment than those in manufacturing, and if these workers had an annual income of about twelve hundred dollars, they survived reasonably well. Those who were employed in manufacturing became more sympathetic to unionization. The auto industry, which was largely an offshoot of the U.S. industry, experienced dramatic growth in unionization, resulting in a major strike in Oshawa, Ontario, the center of the Canadian auto industry, in 1936 and 1937. The provincial government intervened to force a settlement that in effect acknowledged the legitimacy of the union. However, for the most part, unions did not fare well. A strike organized by the Roman Catholic unions in Quebec against the textile operations of a large firm had to be settled by the intervention of the Catholic cardinal Jean-Marie-Rodrigue Villeneuve.

By the late 1930's, the distribution of income in Canada had reverted to late 1920's levels. Wages and salaries constituted 62 to 64 percent of income, investment income amounted to about 20 percent, and the rest was produced either by farmers or by small businesses. However, the psychological impact of the loss of employment, particularly on the part of individuals who had no relief entitlement, was substantial.

Impact The loss of income, most particularly among farmers, led to a drop in population in the Prairie Provinces. Other workers, such as fishermen and loggers, reverted to subsistence production. The great surge into the prairies, opened to settlement just prior to World War I, was reversed, and many individuals who had claimed land there under the preemption system created by the government to encourage population growth left the land they had claimed; some were moved out of the most drought-stricken areas by the government. Immigration was strictly controlled, and during the early 1930's, about ten thousand immigrants were deported, chiefly because they were linked to union activities that the authorities suspected were inspired by communist beliefs.

Although prices dropped during this period, the uncertainty of employment for wage workers was difficult to overcome. About one-fifth of the employees in manufacturing were immigrants, and these constituted as much as one-third in such fields as mining and logging. Altogether, the difficulties most workers faced led to a pervasive uncertainty that characterized the decade.

Nancy M. Gordon

Further Reading

Horn, Michiel, ed. *The Dirty Thirties: Canadians in the Great Depression.* Toronto: Copp Clark, 1972. Brings together accounts of the impact on working Canadians during the 1930's.

Peitchinis, Stephen G. *The Economics of Labour: Employment and Wages in Canada.* Toronto: McGraw-Hill, 1965. Studies Canada's employment with its group effects.

Safarian, A. E. *The Canadian Economy in the Great Depression.* Toronto: University of Toronto Press, 1959. A detailed history of Canada's Depression economy based on a wide variety of statistics.

Thompson, John Herd, and Allen Seager. *Canada, 1922-1939: Decades of Discord.* Toronto: McClelland and Stewart, 1985. Economist's survey of Canada during the 1920's and 1930's.

Watkins, M. H., and H. M. Grant, eds. *Canadian Economic History: Classic and Contemporary Approaches.* Ottawa: Carleton University Press, 1993. Contains a variety of articles on twentieth century Canadian economic history.

See also Agriculture in Canada; Bennett, Richard Bedford; Canadian regionalism; Demographics of Canada; Elections, Canadian; Great Depression in Canada; Immigration to Canada; Income and wages in the United States; King, William Lyon Mackenzie; Urbanization in Canada.

The Great Depression caused a drop in income, as many previously employed workers found themselves out of work. In this picture, a Government Printing Office staff member carries a batch of unemployment census cards that, when returned, would give the government a better understanding of the unemployment situation in the country and lead to better assessment of the median income of Americans. (Library of Congress)

■ Income and wages in the United States

Between 1929 and 1933, many Americans experienced large declines in their incomes, bringing painful hardships. Income loss was especially severe for the unemployed and for farmers. The decrease in demand for labor reduced wages. The distress underlay the U.S. political turnover in 1933 and spurred the federal government to create many programs intended to raise wage rates and other types of incomes. Incomes did increase, partly in response to economic recovery and partly in response to government policies.

Between 1929 and 1933, the flow of American spending on goods and services declined by almost one-half. In the absence of significant government income-support programs, private incomes experienced a similar decline. National income in 2010

prices declined from $87 billion in 1929 to $40 billion in 1933. Proportionately, the largest decline involved property incomes. The total of rents, corporate profits, and unincorporated business income was $31 billion in 1929 and only $7 billion in 1933. Retired people found their pensions and rent receipts drastically reduced. Numerous farmers and small-business owners were overwhelmed by debts and were forced into bankruptcy.

Labor incomes declined from $51 billion in 1929 to $30 billion in 1933. The income losses were unevenly distributed. People who lost their jobs lost all their wage incomes. Employment in nonfarm business dropped from 31.3 million in 1929 to 23.7 million in 1933. Many workers who kept their jobs found their work hours reduced. Weekly hours in manufacturing averaged forty-four in 1929 but only thirty-eight in 1933. As the demand for labor declined, most employers were able to reduce the wage rates they were paying. In manufacturing, the average wage declined from $0.56 an hour in 1929 to $0.44 in 1933.

American workers earning average wages and working average hours earned $24.76 a week in 1929 but only $16.65 in 1933, a decline of one-third. However, the decline in the demand for goods and services caused the prices to decline substantially. Consumer prices fell by one-quarter from 1929 to 1933, so the loss of real income was significantly less than the decline in nominal wage income.

Sector Incomes   Farm labor was by far the most poorly paid sector of the economy. Services also paid poorly, particularly "household help": cleaning, cooking, and child care. At the other end of the scale was employment in finance, insurance, and real estate; however, much of the premium vanished after the collapse of the era of "high finance."

All sectors shared in the large decline between 1929 and 1933. However, the private sector experi-enced a sizable rebound from 1933 to 1939. Most sectors remained lower in 1939 than they had been in 1929. Transportation, communications, and public utilities ended the decade higher than they were at the beginning of the 1930's.

Recovery After 1933   The Depression bottomed out in 1933, after which the aggregate demand for goods and services moved upward again, though this was interrupted by a brief but painful recession in 1937-1938. National income increased by 79 percent, rising from $40 billion in 1933 to $73 billion in 1939. Corporate profits and proprietors' incomes showed the largest proportional gain, going from $5 billion in 1933, when corporate profits were negative, to $18 billion in 1939. Labor income increased from $30 billion to $48 billion in 1939, a gain of only 63 percent, as the unemployment rate remained high.

President Herbert Hoover exhorted businesses to maintain employment and refrain from wage reductions but did little to improve the economic situation in the early 1930's. Major government interventions in the labor market began with the National Industrial Recovery Act (NIRA) of 1933. Each participating industry was obligated to include in its "code of fair competition" provisions to maintain a minimum wage and to affirm the rights of workers to organize and bargain collectively. After the U.S. Supreme Court overturned the NIRA in 1935, Congress reenacted comparable labor policies. For example, the National Labor Relations Act of 1935 (also known as the Wagner Act) gave support to organizing and maintaining labor unions. Extensive organizing campaigns widened union membership but at the cost of numerous strikes and other labor-market disruptions. Wage costs were increased slightly by the Social Security wage tax, which began in 1937, and by the minimum wages provided by the Fair Labor Standards Act of 1938. Of more immediate importance were the sizable amounts of wages paid out by such New Deal programs as the Civil Works Administration, the Federal Emergency Relief Adminis-

Average Annual Earnings Per Full-Time Employee by Sector

Sector	1929	1933	1939
Agriculture, forestry, and fisheries	$ 401	$ 232	$ 385
Communications and utilities	1,478	1,351	1,691
Construction	1,674	869	1,268
Finance, insurance, and real estate	2,062	1,555	1,729
Government	1,551	1,328	1,337
Manufacturing	1,543	1,086	1,363
Mining	1,526	990	1,367
Services	1,079	854	952
Trade	1,594	1,183	1,360
Transport	1,643	1,334	1,723

Source: Historical Statistics of the United States: Colonial Times to 1970. Washington, D.C.: U.S. Department of Commerce, Bureau of the Census, 1975, pp. 166-167.

Annual Mean Income for Men, by Education, 1939

Schooling	Income
Eight years or less	$1,036
Nine to eleven years	1,379
High school graduate	1,661
One to three years of college	1,931
College graduate	2,607

Source: Historical Statistics of the United States: Colonial Times to 1970. Washington, D.C.: U.S. Department of Commerce, Bureau of the Census, 1975, p. 381.

Note: Statistics are for men twenty-five years old and older.

tration, the Public Works Administration, and the Works Progress Administration (WPA).

Family, Gender, and Ethnicity During the 1930's, women earned significantly less than men in every category. Nationally, women's earnings were only 61 percent of men's, and similar disparities occurred in each job category. The rank ordering of income differences was the same for men and women, reflecting the differences in education requirements of different kinds of work.

African American and other nonwhite workers averaged much lower incomes than white workers. For men, much of this disparity resulted from the concentration of nonwhite workers in farming and unskilled labor. Women and African Americans were proportionately underrepresented in labor unions. Wage discrimination was widespread.

Income inequality was pronounced during the decade. However, the share of income of top groups declined steadily across the time span. This resulted chiefly from the erosion of income from corporate profits and proprietorships. Reduction in unemployment helped to bolster the incomes of people in the middle brackets.

Important differences in income were associated with age and family status. In 1939, married couples with male heads of household had a median labor income of $1,319, whereas female-headed households had a median income of only $909. Families headed by a man under thirty-five years of age averaged $1,171 in income. Families headed by a man between the ages of thirty-five and forty-four earned

an average of $1,444. Income for families headed by a man between the ages of forty-five and fifty-four earned $1,481. Income for age fifty-five and older was $1,243. Unemployment rates were particularly high for newcomers to the labor force and for the elderly. The Social Security Act of 1935 created a category of means-tested public assistance for needy elderly people.

On average, more schooling tended to be associated with higher incomes. College graduates received incomes of more than twice those of high school dropouts. Part of the difference arose from higher unemployment rates among the less educated.

The New Deal and the Aftermath of the Great Depression When Hoover was president, the federal government did little to directly increase employment and income. Distress arising from loss of income was the major reason for the drastic political change that brought Franklin D. Roosevelt into the presidency in 1933. Direct relief payments to the needy and programs to provide government employment were key aspects of the New Deal. Many of these provisions were temporary and were phased out as the economy improved. The Social Security Act of 1935 laid the groundwork for extensive government income support. However, the payouts had hardly begun by 1939. Because the wage tax began to be collected in 1937, its initial impact was deflationary.

Compared to other industrialized countries, economic recovery in the United States was slow and was interrupted by recession in 1937-1938. Critics accused the federal government of creating an atmosphere of hostility toward business, as manifested in increased tax rates and in the creation of new administrative agencies with extensive, ill-defined powers. Constitutional limits on federal authority and on the powers of the executive branch were severely weakened. The loss of business confidence was demonstrated by the prices of corporate stocks. The Standard and Poor's stock price index reached 26 in 1929, fell to 9 in 1933, but then reached only 15 in 1936-1937 and 12 in 1939.

The National Labor Relations Act of 1935 was particularly damaging to business confidence. It was intended to help increase wages and thus boost consumer purchasing power. However, higher wages increased business costs and thus tended to impede the expansion of employment. The new labor law unleashed a furious campaign to unionize major industries, often accompanied by strikes. The number of work stoppages surged from 841 in 1932 to 4,740 in 1937, a year of a number of bitter sit-down strikes.

Because of the slow increase in aggregate demand for goods and services, national income in 1939 was only $73 billion, less than in 1929 and in 1937. After adjusting for price changes and population increase, real disposable personal income per person in 1939 was about 7 percent lower than in 1929. However, this negative result arose from the persistence of high unemployment. The real earnings of full-time employed workers rose about 10 percent from 1929 to 1939.

Impact   The decline in income levels between 1929 and 1933 severely hampered the ability of Americans to consume goods and services. This tendency was aggravated by the decline in the value of people's wealth, as houses, businesses, and stocks and bonds lost value. Most types of income shared in the decline, and most families experienced reductions in money income. Decline in incomes increased the burden of debts, bringing widespread defaults and bankruptcies. These defaults in turn worsened the extent of bank failures.

Paul B. Trescott

Further Reading

Bernstein, Irving. *A Caring Society: The New Deal, the Workers, and the Great Depression.* Boston: Houghton Mifflin, 1985. Examines in detail major policy innovations of the 1930's, notably relief, Social Security, the WPA, and the Fair Labor Standards Act. Dwells on the hardships resulting from income loss.

Chandler, Lester V. *America's Greatest Depression, 1929-1941.* New York: Harper & Row, 1970. Shows the relationships between income changes and both macroeconomic developments and government policies.

Lebergott, Stanley. *Manpower in Economic Growth: The American Record Since 1800.* New York: McGraw-Hill, 1964. Historical evolution of wages is integrated with all elements of labor supply and demand.

Robertson, Ross M. *History of the American Economy.* 2d ed. New York: Harcourt, Brace and World, 1964. Chapters 23 and 24 of this college text deal with the labor market, income changes, and related government policies.

Shlaes, Amity. *The Forgotten Man: A New History of the Great Depression.* New York: HarperCollins, 2008. Explains the various elements of the New Deal program that hampered the restoration of full employment.

See also   Business and the economy in the United States; Fair Labor Standards Act of 1938; Great Depression in the United States; Gross national product; Labor strikes; National Labor Relations Act of 1935; Social Security Act of 1935; Unemployment in the United States; Unionism.

■ Indian Reorganization Act

The Law   Federal legislation that reversed government policies forcing Native American assimilation

Also known as   Wheeler-Howard Law; Indian New Deal

Date   Enacted on June 18, 1934

The Indian Reorganization Act stopped the practice of dividing Native American tribal lands into individual allotments, encouraged each tribe to establish its own formal government under a written constitution, and introduced other reforms to promote Native American autonomy and protect cultural traditions.

Before the U.S. Congress passed the Indian Reorganization Act in 1934, federal government policy regarding Native Americans was based primarily on the Dawes Severalty Act of 1887. That law had pressured tribes to abolish their communally owned reservations and to adopt individually owned parcels of land. The law's intent was to promote Indian assimilation into mainstream American society, but its primary effect was to reduce the amount of Indian-owned land. According to a 1928 report, the policy of creating individual land parcels was one of the causes of the deplorable conditions on Indian reservations. After President Franklin D. Roosevelt took office in 1933, he endorsed the report and appointed John Collier, an outspoken advocate of reform, to head the Bureau of Indian Affairs (BIA).

As head of the BIA, Collier worked closely with Felix Cohen and other government lawyers to draft a congressional bill to repeal the Dawes Act and increase tribal self-government. Burton Kendall Wheeler, the chairperson of the Senate's Indian Af-

Indian Reorganization Act and Tribal Ownership

Section three of the Indian Reorganization Act, a provision outlining the status of Native American lands, is partially reproduced below.

The Secretary of the Interior, if he shall find it to be in the public interest, is hereby authorized to restore to tribal ownership the remaining surplus lands of any Indian reservation heretofore opened, or authorized to be opened, to sale, or any other form of disposal by Presidential proclamation, or by any of the public land laws of the United States; Provided, however, That valid rights or claims of any persons to any lands so withdrawn existing on the date of the withdrawal shall not be affected by this Act: Provided further, That this section shall not apply to lands within any reclamation project heretofore authorized in any Indian reservation: Provided further, That this section shall not apply to lands within any reclamation project heretofore authorized in any Indian reservation.

fairs Committee, insisted on a number of amendments that weakened the bill, including elimination of a special Native American court. Nevertheless, with Roosevelt's support, Congress enacted the forty-eight-page Indian Reorganization Act, although it included most of Wheeler's amendments, in June, 1934.

All the tribes were covered by the act's stipulation that no additional Native American lands would be divided into individual allotments. Although the law did not affect the ownership rights of Native Americans who had already acquired individual parcels of land, it placed all such land under the jurisdiction of the reservations for purposes of taxation. It also returned unsold surplus lands to tribal control. In addition, the U.S. Department of the Interior was authorized to establish reservations, to purchase land and water rights when needed, and to help reservations consolidate areas of land large enough for ranching and other activities.

The tribes were given two years to accept or reject the portions of the law dealing with governmental organization and economic development. For an individual tribe to opt out of the law, a majority of its members had to vote against participation. In 250 tribal elections throughout the United States, the majority of Native Americans voted against the law. Only 78 of the 250 elections resulted in nonpartici-

pation, but Native Americans were so unenthusiastic about adopting formal constitutions that only ninety-three of the tribes adopted them over the next ten years. Most of these constitutions followed a model provided by the BIA. Because the act did not require a separation of powers similar to that of the federal government, a large number of the tribal constitutions concentrated power in elected councils. Although the law recognized "inherent" powers and expanded prerogatives of self-government, enacting laws and making constitutional amendments required BIA approval.

The complex law also contained a number of other provisions, including federal loans for tribal economic development, procedures for creating tribal business corporations, hiring preferences to permit the BIA to recruit more Native American employees, expanded freedom to engage in religious ceremonies and traditional dances, and educational scholarships and academic programs for Native American studies. After 1934, the various components of the legislation were frequently amended in response to changing conditions and political forces.

Impact The Indian Reorganization Act marked a turning point in federal Indian policy, which became more humane and less coercive. Had the law not been passed, continuation of individual allotments might have eventually resulted in the termination of the reservation system. Under the law, about two million acres of land were added to reservations over the following twenty years. The law was also reasonably successful in providing a mechanism for establishing stable reservation governments, even though it increased Native American dependence on the BIA, thereby actually decreasing tribal autonomy. Its affirmative-action preferences for employment with the BIA benefited particular individuals and helped somewhat to minimize Native Americans' long-standing distrust of the agency. However, the law was not greatly successful in expanding economic development and educational opportunities.

Thomas Tandy Lewis

Further Reading

Collier, John. *From Every Zenith: A Memoir*. Denver, Colo.: Sage Books, 1963. Pro-Indian Reorganization Act analysis from the point of view of the head of the BIA, who was the person most responsible for its enactment and implementation.

Deloria, Vine, Jr. *The Indian Reorganization Act: Congresses and Bills*. Norman: University of Oklahoma Press, 2002. Detailed survey of the records of meetings between tribal leaders and BIA officers held to discuss the law's implementation.

Kelly, Lawrence C. *The Assault on Assimilation: John Collier and the Origins of American Indian Reform*. Albuquerque: University of New Mexico Press, 1983. Although highly sympathetic toward Collier, Kelly emphasizes the failure of the Indian Reorganization Act to achieve Collier's high aspirations.

Prucha, Francis Paul. *The Great Father: The United States Government and the American Indians*. Lincoln: University of Nebraska Press, 1986. Balanced account of the Indian Reorganization Act that is particularly good in regard to the Oklahoma tribes.

Rusco, Elmer. *Fateful Time: The Background and Legislative History of the Indian Reorganization Act*. Lincoln: University of Nebraska Press, 2000. Scholarly analysis of the ideologies, people, and conflicting interests that produced the Indian Reorganization Act.

Taylor, Graham. *The New Deal and American Indian Tribalism: The Administration of the Indian Reorganization Act, 1934-1945*. Lincoln: University of Nebraska Press, 1980. Highly critical analysis of the Indian Reorganization Act, arguing that the BIA put pressure on the tribes to accept a cookie-cutter model for their governments that was often inconsistent with tribal customs.

Wunder, John R. *"Retained by the People": A History of American Indians and the Bill of Rights*. New York: Oxford University Press, 1994. Survey of American Indian policy, including an excellent summary of the Indian Reorganization Act within its historical context.

See also Collier, John; Congress, U.S.; Native Americans; New Deal; Reorganization Act of 1939; Roosevelt, Franklin D.

■ Inflation

From 1929 to 1933, prices in the United States fell by about one-fourth. Many economists considered this price decline to be a major cause of the Great Depression, and many New Deal measures were aimed at increasing prices. One measure was the increase in the price of gold, which did boost prices. Higher prices were also a goal of the National Industrial Recovery Act (NIRA) and the Agricultural Adjustment Act (AAA). As recovery accelerated, the Federal Reserve feared large price increases and made an unfortunate increase in bank reserve requirements in 1936-1937, contributing to the ensuing recession.

During the 1920's, prices of goods and services were relatively stable in the United States but fell rapidly as the economy swept downward beginning in 1929. The Agricultural Marketing Act of 1929 created the Federal Farm Board and provided it with $500 million to lend to farm cooperatives to finance purchases of farm products, chiefly cotton, wheat, and wool, in order to keep them off the market to try to raise their prices.

Farm price declines reflected conditions in export markets, areas that were important to American trade. The primary policy response was the adoption of the Hawley-Smoot Tariff in 1930. This greatly increased restrictions on imports into the United States, worsened deflationary pressure on other countries, and did little to stem farm price declines. Rising defaults on farm debts accelerated bank failures. These led to panic withdrawals of currency and to numerous proposals for policies to increase the money supply.

Aggressive Policies Immediately upon his inauguration, President Franklin D. Roosevelt tried to increase the price level, arguing this was essential for the recovery of business. In April of 1933, he wrote "we must inflate" and terminated the convertibility of dollars into gold at the previous fixed price and temporarily forbade the export of gold. In 1934, the official price of gold was increased from $20.67 an ounce to $35 an ounce, and the Treasury became a large purchaser of gold from other countries. These purchases expanded bank reserves and the money supply.

The sharp decline in farm prices lowered farm income in the same proportion. Raising farm prices was a major goal of the AAA of May, 1933. The program aimed to pay farmers to reduce output, with funds coming from a processing tax on agribusiness industries. The Thomas amendment (also called the Inflation Act) authorized the president to use various methods of increasing the money supply, including raising the price of gold. The AAA was followed by more stringent production-control programs directed at cotton and tobacco.

A parallel measure aimed at nonfarm business was the NIRA of 1933. The law created a National Recovery Administration (NRA), which was charged with helping arrange "codes of fair competition" drawn up by individual industries to prevent "disastrous overproduction." The government would help enforce the codes, which were exempted from antitrust laws. Labor provisions included minimum wages and protection for workers' right to join unions and bargain collectively.

Prices did increase. However, the AAA and NIRA reflected a misunderstanding of the nature of the Depression and appropriate remedies. The decline in prices was a symptom of the great reduction in aggregate demand. The government's measures assumed instead that the problem was an excess of supply. Increasing farm prices was a cruel punishment inflicted on consumers, particularly the unemployed, whose food costs increased. Food prices increased by 10 percent in 1934. In any event, both the original AAA and the NIRA were found to be unconstitutional in 1935 and 1936. Major portions of the NIRA were reenacted into programs for motor and air carriers and bituminous coal. Protection for labor unions was restored in the National Labor Relations Act of May, 1935, and the minimum wage was reenacted in the Fair Labor Standards Act of 1938. Revised programs to raise farm prices were adopted in the Soil Conservation and Domestic Allotment Act of 1936 and the AAA of 1938.

Monetary Policies   The Great Depression resulted from the massive decrease in the aggregate demand for goods and services, as measured by gross national product. Recovery from the Depression came as aggregate demand expanded, beginning in 1933. Government fiscal policy contributed to this rise. However, the large rise in government spending was mostly offset by increases in tax rates. The significant rise in aggregate demand resulted from an increase in the money supply. The public's holdings of currency and bank deposits, which averaged around

$30 billion in 1933, reached $43 billion by the middle of 1936. With unemployment remaining high, prices in general did not increase much. A consumer price index that stood at 39 in 1933 increased to only 42 in 1936. However, some Federal Reserve officials looked with alarm on potential inflation of prices.

This alarm arose from the condition of bank reserves. Increasing the price of gold had led to a large inflow of gold to the United States from the rest of the world. When people sold the gold to the government, they received checks in payment. When those were deposited in banks, bank deposits and bank reserves increased. In 1934-1935, bank reserves increased much more rapidly than the amount banks needed to meet legal reserve requirements. Excess reserves of Federal Reserve member banks reached $3 billion at the end of 1935.

The Banking Act of 1935 had authorized the Federal Reserve to raise or lower reserve requirements on bank deposits. A Federal Reserve memorandum of December, 1935, advocated raising reserve requirements, partly because of the fear of inflation. Soon after, the Federal Reserve increased reserve requirements by one-half, effective in August, 1936. A second increase followed, effective in March, 1937. Many economists believe these increases contributed to the brief but painful recession of 1937. Reserve requirements were quickly brought back down. Consumer prices changed relatively little during the late 1930's. The index of consumer prices was essentially the same in 1939 as in 1936.

Impact   In the sense of a large sustained increase in the price level, inflation was not a problem during the 1930's. Rather, the severe deflation of prices from 1929 to 1933 worsened the downswing, aggravating the debt crisis for millions of home owners, farmers, and business firms. New Deal measures did lead to higher prices of food in 1934. The increase in the price of gold led to devaluation of the dollar internationally and to the large inflow of gold. This caused an increase in the excess reserves in banks. Fearing inflation, Federal Reserve officials raised reserve requirements in 1936-1937, with deflationary consequences.

According to the traditional quantity theory of money, a rapid increase in the money supply should have caused substantial price increases. However, the existence of a close link between money and prices was denied in John Maynard Keynes's *The General Theory of Employment, Interest and Money* (1936). The evidence of the 1930's seemed to support Keynes. The same was true of the experience with inflation during World War II. However, as Depression conditions gave way to prosperity during the 1950's, a closer link between money and prices reemerged.

Paul B. Trescott

Further Reading

Chandler, Lester V. *American's Greatest Depression, 1929-1941.* New York: Harper & Row, 1970. Discussions of the farm debt crises are found in this compact and readable survey.

Keynes, John Maynard. *The General Theory of Employment, Interest, and Money.* New York: Macmillan, 1936. Analyzes the relation between money and prices, among other aspects of the economy.

Meltzer, Allan H. *A History of the Federal Reserve.* Chicago: University of Chicago Press, 2003. Reviews the Federal Reserve's actions in the context of the behavior of money and prices during the Depression.

Tracy, Ronald, and Paul B. Trescott. "Monetary Policy and Inflation in the United States, 1912-1978: Evidence from Monthly Data." In *Inflation Through the Ages*, edited by Nathan Schmukler and Edward Marcus. New York: Brooklyn College Press, 1983.

Warren, George, and Frank Pearson. *Gold and Prices.* New York: John Wiley & Sons, 1935. Warren was an adviser to President Roosevelt and was believed to be responsible for the increase in gold prices. This book lays out his views on the importance of gold to prices.

See also Agricultural Adjustment Acts; Business and the economy in the United States; Federal Reserve Board; Gold Reserve Act of 1934; Great Depression in the United States; National Industrial Recovery Act of 1933.

■ *Informer, The*

Identification American film about the Irish Civil War
Director John Ford
Date Released on May 9, 1935

Although the film The Informer *is set in Dublin in 1922 on the eve of the Irish Civil War, Ford's portrayal of hunger, unemployment, and poverty resonated with American audiences during the midst of the Great Depression. The film was a box-office success and won Academy Awards for direction, screenplay, musical score, and leading actor.*

Director John Ford and screenwriter Dudley Nichols transformed Liam O'Flaherty's novel *The Informer* from a story of squalor and degradation into a romanticized tale of dignity and redemption. Ford creates sympathetic characters who, lacking in complexity, take on symbolic meaning. Religion plays an important role in the film.

Gypo Nolan (Victor McLaglen), the informer of the title, has been expelled from the Irish Republican Army (IRA) for refusing to execute a prisoner. Distrusted by the English, who still occupy Dublin, and by the IRA, who doubt his loyalty, he is unable to find work. His girlfriend, Katie (Margot Grahame),

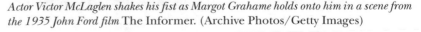
Actor Victor McLaglen shakes his fist as Margot Grahame holds onto him in a scene from the 1935 John Ford film The Informer. *(Archive Photos/Getty Images)*

resorts to streetwalking in an attempt to earn money for food. Driven by forces he can neither control nor understand, Gypo informs on his former comrade-in-arms, Frankie McPhillips (Wallace Ford), who is then killed by the English.

After squandering the reward money he might have used for passage to the United States for himself and Katie, he is summoned to an inquisition by the IRA, at which time he confesses. Like Frankie, he is shot while escaping. In a dramatic closing scene set in a church, Gypo is forgiven by Frankie's mother before he dies beneath the cross.

Impact *The Informer* was an instant classic because of its aesthetic appeal. Ford employs tracking shots, dissolves, double exposures, dramatic camera angles, and shadow and fog; he uses dialogue sparingly at a time when most directors were enamored with the new technology of sound in film. *The Informer* was among the first American films to incorporate elements of German expressionism.

K Edgington

Further Reading

Gilligan, Paula. "'A Monotonous Hell': Space, Violence, and the City in the 1930's Films of Liam O'Flaherty." *Early Popular Visual Culture* 5, no. 3 (November, 2007): 301-316.

Lourdeaux, Lee. *Italian and Irish Filmmakers in America: Ford, Capra, Coppola, and Scorsese.* Philadelphia: Temple University Press, 1990.

Stoehr, Kevin L., and Michael C. Connolly, eds. *John Ford in Focus: Essays on the Filmmaker's Life and Work.* Jefferson, N.C.: McFarland, 2008.

See also Film; Ford, John; Great Depression in the United States; *Stagecoach.*

■ Instant coffee

Definition Nescafé introduced instant coffee to the American consumer market

Instant coffee became an acceptable and much more convenient alternative to regular coffee among consumers during the late 1930's.

The favored stimulant of people around the world, coffee became a major consumer product by the early twentieth century. Instant coffee did not originate during the 1930's. Faust Instant Coffee found a market during World War I among the soldiers in the trenches, who did not have ideal conditions for brewing coffee. Water could be boiled quickly for instant coffee, or coffee could be made with cold water alone for the caffeine boost. However, the poor quality of this instant coffee made for an unappetizing drink.

After the war, people no longer had to consume instant coffee, but the idea of providing consumers with a quick jolt entranced manufactures. In 1938, after eight years of experimentation, the Swiss company Nestlé launched its instant coffee, Nescafé. Nestlé began marketing the product in the United States in 1939. Nescafé did not rely upon the drum method, in which brewed coffee was boiled down to crystals. Instead, Nestlé sprayed the liquid into heated towers, where the droplets turned to powder almost instantly. The company also added an equal amount of carbohydrates, which it believed helped maintain flavor. The taste still paled considerably in relation to regular coffee, but instant coffee was cheaper.

Impact The instant-coffee market grew tremendously during World War II and in the postwar period. Consumers willingly sacrificed quality for convenience, as new instant brands proliferated. An era of high coffee prices also prompted consumers to choose the cheaper alternative. Although soluble coffee required a significant capital outlay for the spraying towers and treatment process, it cost consumers about one penny less per cup than regular coffee. The poor taste meant that it did not matter what kind of beans were used, enabling manufacturers to use cheap ingredients such as African robusta beans. By 1960, instant coffee accounted for about 20 percent of the U.S. market.

Caryn E. Neumann

Further Reading

Pendergrast, Mark. *Uncommon Grounds: The History of Coffee and How It Transformed Our World.* New York: Basic Books, 1999.

Wild, Antony. *Coffee: A Dark History.* New York: W. W. Norton, 2004.

See also Business and the economy in the United States; Food processing; Frozen-food marketing; Great Depression in the United States; Inventions; Supermarkets.

■ Insull Utilities Trusts collapse

The Event   Failure of Chicago's public utilities
    network
Also known as   Insull Trusts scandal
Date   1932
Place   Chicago, Illinois

*A network of public utility companies and electric-powered
interurban railways, the Insull Trusts was originally created through highly leveraged financing. The financial
disruptions of the Great Depression and suspect corporate
governance caused the network to fold. However, the scandal had the salutary effect of calling national attention to
the need for stronger government utilities regulation,
prompting the U.S. Congress to enact legislation designed
to prevent a repetition of the Insull scandal.*

Samuel Insull, the person most responsible for creating the Insull network, began his career working for
the inventor Thomas Edison. In 1889, he rose to the
vice presidency of Edison General Electric Company;
three years later, he became president of the Chicago
Edison Company. During the first decade of the twentieth century he formed Chicago's Commonwealth
Edison Company, which he made the world's biggest
producer of electricity. Along the way, he unified rural electrification projects and won control of financially shaky electric commuter trains to create an integrated electrical conglomerate. He won admiration
for helping to make electric power cheap and abundant. His utilities empire eventually encompassed
more than eighty-five corporations of which he was a
director. He also chaired the boards of sixty-five corporations and was president of eleven. His utility empire reached a value of $4 billion. He achieved this
control through a trust system—a series of holding
companies—that allowed him to organize his companies in a pyramid fashion, with a series of highly leveraged companies owning shares in one another.

Insull's Downfall   After the Great Depression began
in 1929, passenger traffic on the Insull railroads
dropped, and as people lost their jobs, they cut expenses by using less electricity in their homes. Both
developments caused Insull's companies to lose revenue. This decline began in 1929, but the Insull empire's collapse was not triggered until 1932, when
the Chicago Rapid Transit Company went bankrupt,
which was followed by the bankruptcies of many of
its affiliated companies.

After a government investigation into these collapses was made, Insull was indicted for perpetrating
a corporate fraud and cheating investors out of millions of dollars. The seventy-three-year-old Insull
fled the country to avoid prosecution, but a scapegoat was needed, so he was later brought back to face
trial. His indictment for fraud sufficed to convince
unhappy investors that the government was taking
action. In the trial that followed, government prose-
cutors pointed out that while 25 percent of Americans had been out of work in 1931, Insull was receiving a salary of nearly one-half million dollars.
Ultimately, however, Insull was acquitted on all
charges. During the trial, he claimed to have left the
country for fear that if he were tried, his case would
have become a political trial because the state prosecutor was running for reelection.

Impact   The most dramatic result of the collapse of
Insull's empire was investors' loss of millions of dollars. President Franklin D. Roosevelt mentioned
Insull in his pleas to Congress to pass the Securities
Act of 1933, which gave investors greater protection.
Congress also enacted the Public Utilities Holding
Company Act in 1935 to bar the creation of more
investor-owned utility empires. Additional federal
energy regulations followed with Congress's passage
of the Rural Electrification Act in 1936 and its expansion of the Tennessee Valley Authority. Insull himself lived only a few more years, dying in 1938 at the
age of seventy-eight. Although at one time he had
been worth more than $150 million, he died nearly
penniless.

Dale L. Flesher

Further Reading

Busch, Francis X. *Guilty or Not Guilty? An Account of
    the Trials of the Leo Frank Case, the D. C. Stephenson
    Case, the Samuel Insull Case, and the Alger Hiss Case.*
    Buffalo, N.Y.: William S. Hein, 1998.
McDonald, Forrest. *Insull.* Chicago: University of
    Chicago Press, 1962.
Wasik, John F. *The Merchant of Power: Sam Insull,
    Thomas Edison, and the Creation of the Modern Me-
    tropolis.* New York: Palgrave Macmillan, 2006.

See also   Business and the economy in the United
States; Crimes and scandals; Public Utilities Act; Rural Electrification Administration; Securities and Exchange Commission; Tennessee Valley Authority.

■ Inter-American Conference for the Maintenance of Peace

The Event   Conference arranged by the United States at which twenty-one Western Hemisphere nations were represented

Date   December 1-23, 1936

Place   Buenos Aires, Argentina

Four treaties were adopted at the conference, aiming primarily at preventing war and other forms of interference by governments in North and South America in internal affairs of other states. A formal alliance against possible aggression in the region from countries in Europe, a dream of U.S. president Franklin D. Roosevelt, was rejected.

During the mid-1930's, fascist governments ruled Germany and Italy, Spain was engulfed in civil war, and Japan was waging war in Asia. Under these circumstances, President Franklin D. Roosevelt suggested a conference to work toward peace in the Western Hemisphere. Roosevelt wanted to give substance to his Good Neighbor Policy toward Latin America.

Roosevelt hoped to extend the hemispheric Treaty of Non-Aggression and Conciliation of 1933 to the establishment of an antifascist alliance. Because the United States was not a member of the League of Nations, he tried to forge a conceptually similar arrangement in the Americas, but countries south of the U.S. border preferred to use the league.

Latin American governments agreed to a conference, which was to be held at Buenos Aires, Argentina. High on the agenda were the topics of arms limitations, foreign intervention, and neutrality. Roosevelt and Secretary of State Cordell Hull led the American delegation. The official host was Argentine foreign minister Carlos Saavedra Lamas.

The Convention for Maintenance, Preservation, and Reestablishment of Peace provided that governments would consult bilaterally or multilaterally, presumably through foreign ministers conferences, "in the event that an international war outside the United States which might endanger the peace of the American Republics." If diplomacy failed, conciliation based on the 1933 treaty would be attempted. If conciliation failed, either arbitration or adjudication would be sought to resolve the dispute.

Two protocols to the treaty condemned foreign intervention and indicated that signatories to the treaty were expected to convene together in order to urge an end to any foreign intervention by using diplomacy, conciliation, arbitration, or adjudication. Territorial conquest was thereby also prohibited.

A separate Convention to Co-ordinate, Extend and Assure the Fulfillment of the Existing Treaties Between the American States was also adopted. The convention provided that the immediate response to a threat of war in the region should be a six-month cooling-off period while "direct diplomatic negotiation or the alternative procedures of mediation, commissions of inquiry, commissions of conciliation, tribunals of arbitration, and courts of justice" were undertaken to avert hostilities or military action. Meanwhile, noninvolved countries were to remain neutral.

Less important was the Treaty on the Prevention of Controversies. This called upon signatories to set up bilateral commissions, constituted at the request of any government, to study issues that might cause future controversies and to make proposals for dealing with them.

The Inter-American Treaty on Good Offices and Mediation authorized a list of eminent citizens to be drawn up. When a controversy arose between any two countries, they could summon persons from the list to provide good offices or mediation. All four treaties were ratified. Texts were sent to the League of Nations.

Chile's delegation to the conference proposed a human rights treaty to recognize the freedom of life, liberty, and religion. However, the proposal was rejected as contrary to the principle of nonintervention.

Impact   The 1936 conference laid the foundation for the later development of an inter-American system of collective security. Foreign ministers met again at Lima, Peru (1938); Panama City, Panama (1939); Havana, Cuba (1940); and Rio de Janeiro, Brazil (1942). Resolutions adopted at the meetings gradually endorsed the principle of hemispheric solidarity against external aggression, culminating in the Act of Chapultepec (1945) and the Inter-American Treaty of Reciprocal Assistance (1948). Chile's human rights proposal was eventually incorporated into the Universal Declaration of Human Rights (1948).

Michael Haas

Further Reading

Connell-Smith, Gordon. *The United States and Latin America: An Historical Analysis of Inter-American Relations.* London: Heinemann Educational, 1974.

Schoultz, Lars. *Beneath the United States: A History of U.S. Policy Toward Latin America.* Cambridge, Mass.: Harvard University Press, 1998.

See also   Foreign policy of the United States; Good Neighbor Policy; Hull, Cordell; Latin America and the Caribbean; League of Nations; Roosevelt, Franklin D.

■ International trade

International trade of the United States played a significant role in efforts to overcome the devastating effects of the Great Depression. The abrupt change in trade theory and policy that occurred during the middle of the decade also reveals how the United States' view of itself in relation to other countries changed during the 1930's. The reforms in trade policy of the 1930's opened the way for the development of international cooperation and free-trade agreements.

During the 1930's, U.S. trade policy was controlled by two trade acts that were diametrically opposed. From colonial days, the United States had traded almost exclusively with Canada and European countries. In addition, the country had followed a policy that considered trade a matter of domestic economy and had favored protection of its farmers and nascent industries over international cooperation and interdependence. This economic mind-set had resulted in a number of acts that placed high tariffs on imported goods. A pattern of higher and lower tariffs linked to the political party in control of Congress had developed as well. Tariffs were lower under Democratic control, higher under that of the Republican Party; however, tariffs remained relatively high regardless of the political party in control.

At the beginning of the 1930's, the United States was experiencing severe economic problems after the stock market crash of 1929. In an attempt to regain its economic health and stability, the United States moved toward even stronger policies of isolationism and protectionism. World War I had devastated crop production in Europe, causing increased agricultural production in the United States and Canada. Consequently, as European agriculture re-covered after the war, an overproduction of farm products resulted in a significant and steady drop in farm prices during the late 1920's. Many farmers were unable to make their loan payments and lost or were about to lose their farms. The idea of raising the tariff on farm-product imports again entered into American economic thought and political discussion. (The Fordney-McCumber Tariff had already imposed higher tariffs in 1922.) In a short time, many Americans were viewing higher tariffs on imports in general as a means of bringing about economic recovery by limiting or eliminating foreign competition in the manufacturing and agricultural sectors of the economy. Freeing the domestic market of foreign competition would facilitate sales of American-made and -produced goods, improve the severely depressed employment situation, and be beneficial to the United States.

The Hawley-Smoot Tariff Act   On June 17, 1930, Congress passed a tariff bill sponsored by Reed Smoot of Utah and Willis C. Hawley of Oregon. The tariff bill had begun as a means of improving the market situation for farmers but, at the time of its passage, provided for increased tariffs on manufactured goods and farm products. During the period in which the bill was before Congress, there was considerable opposition to its passage from economists and businessmen. A petition signed by more than one thousand economists was presented to President Herbert Hoover urging him to veto the tariff bill. President Hoover, who had included higher tariffs on imports of farm products in his campaign platform, opposed the increases on nonfarm product tariffs. Although Hoover was not a proponent of the bill, he signed it into law and the tariffs on imports to the United States increased to their highest level in the country's history.

The Hawley-Smoot Tariff accomplished its primary purpose. It raised tariff duties to 53 percent of the value of the products or goods imported. The higher tariffs successfully protected American goods, both agricultural and manufactured, from foreign competition. However, on a broader scale, the tariff was detrimental to U.S. international trade and to the country's economic well-being, including that of the farmers and manufacturers it was to protect. The country's trading partners immediately retaliated with reciprocal, higher tariffs on American goods imported into their countries. European countries imposed high tariffs on American goods and also added quotas. Canada imposed new tariffs on sixteen products imported from the United States. The amount of American goods exported declined by 50 percent. Ironically, the tariff did the most harm to the same farmers it was supposed to protect. The foreign market for wheat, cotton, and tobacco virtually disappeared; with the surplus of farm products, prices declined even further and many farmers had no alternative but to default on their mortgages and equipment loans.

The tariff also worsened the economic situation not only in Europe but also globally. From 1930 to 1932, twenty-four other countries followed the American lead and imposed extremely high tariffs on imports. This policy of protectionism and isolationism, which became known as the "beggar-your-neighbor" policy, destroyed confidence and cooperation among countries. The 1932 election, which gave the Democrats control of Congress and made Franklin D. Roosevelt president of the United States, paved the way for an abrupt change in U.S. policies regarding international trade and in the relationship of the United States with other countries throughout the world.

The Role of Cordell Hull In 1933, President Roosevelt selected Cordell Hull as his secretary of state. At the time, Hull was a member of the Senate and a prominent figure in the Democratic Party. He was known for his firm stand on low tariffs and his belief that economic nationalism resulted in wars among countries. There was a certain amount of opposition to the choice of Hull because of his insistence on the importance of economic cooperation among countries and his liberal trade policies. In addition, his

Presidential appointee taking the oath of office as a member of the U.S. Tariff Commission in 1937. U.S. trade with other countries during the 1930's was guided by a string of tariffs that sought to benefit American industries and cut down on overseas' imports. (Library of Congress)

opponents emphasized his lack of experience in foreign affairs and his reputation for working better alone than with a group. In spite of these objections, Roosevelt remained certain that Hull was the best choice for secretary of state.

In June of 1933, Hull represented the United States at the London Economic Conference. In view of the disastrous impact of high tariffs on international trade throughout the world in 1931, President Hoover had initiated plans for a conference to investigate ways of reducing tariffs and revitalizing prices. Attended by representatives of sixty-six countries, the conference addressed issues of debt settlement through write-offs and currency stabilization, as well as tariffs. The conference faltered over the issues of debt settlement and currency stabilization and did not accomplish its goals. Although the London Conference did nothing to improve trade relations among countries, Hull continued his efforts to change U.S. trading policy. In June of 1934, he succeeded in getting the Reciprocal Trade Agreements Act (RTAA) passed by Congress.

The Reciprocal Trade Agreements Act With the passage of the RTAA, Congress relinquished its power to set tariffs and its control of U.S. trading policy to the executive branch. The act provided for negotiation of treaties with individual countries on a bilateral basis and for the equal reduction of tariffs with these trading partners. The act also included the most-favored-nation (MFN) concept, which provided that any and all nations classified as MFNs were to receive the same advantages. The act did not, however, give the president total freedom in negotiating trade agreements. Tariff reduction was limited to 50 percent of the existing tariff.

Under the RTAA, Hull began negotiating bilateral treaties and reciprocally reducing tariffs with the American trading partners. In 1938, the United States signed a new treaty with Canada, its major trading partner, which stipulated significantly lower tariffs. Hull also negotiated trade agreements with reduced tariffs with twenty-one other countries in both Europe and Latin America, including Great Britain, Argentina, and Uruguay. Hull was instrumental in using trade as a means of creating friendly relations between the United States and other countries. However, he also used tariffs and trade agreements as a means of retaliation against aggressive countries during his tenure as secretary of state.

When Germany occupied Czechoslovakia in 1939, he immediately placed an extra duty on German goods imported into the United States as a protest against the German aggression. World War II began in 1939, and international trade suffered a serious interruption.

Impact While considerable disagreement exists among economists as to whether the Hawley-Smoot Tariff Act contributed significantly to the Great Depression or was a reaction to the severe economic conditions of the time, international trade did play an important role in the relationship of the United States with other countries, particularly with Canada and European nations during the 1930's. The trade policy represented by Smoot-Hawley, which sought economic independence from other countries, was a manifestation of the U.S. isolationist and nationalistic attitude at the beginning of the decade.

The RTAA of 1934 reflected the changing American view of international relationships. Cooperation and trust replaced the defensive protectionism of the early 1930's. This meant that the United States no longer relied solely on itself to recover from the economic crisis but worked with its trading partners to effect economic recovery on an international scale. The RTAA became the basis of the General Agreement on Tariffs and Trade, which was signed by twenty-three countries in 1948. From this initial policy of cooperation in trading in 1934, the American national policy has evolved into one of international cooperation on a broad scale, ranging from economic issues to social and environmental ones.

Shawncey Webb

Further Reading

Beaudreau, Bernard C. *Making Sense of Smoot-Hawley: Technology and Tariffs*. Lincoln, Nebr.: iUniverse, 2005. Examines passage of the Hawley-Smoot Tariff in relation to mass production and the disparity between income and production. Attempts to explain reasons for the tariff's passage and its role in the 1930's economy.

Bordo, Michael D., et al., eds. *The Defining Moment: The Great Depression and the American Economy in the Twentieth Century*. Chicago: University of Chicago Press, 1998. Discusses how U.S. economic policy changed as a result of the Great Depression. One article focuses particularly on Hawley-Smoot.

Butler, Michael. *Cautious Visionary: Cordell Hull and Trade Reform, 1933-1937*. Kent, Ohio: Kent State

University Press, 1998. Focuses on Hull's belief that free trade would contribute to a lasting peace among nations as it reduced economic competition. Mentions his role in negotiating bilateral treaties for the United States.

Garside, William Redvers, ed. *Capitalism in Crisis: An International Perspective in the 1930's*. New York: Palgrave Macmillan, 1993. Discusses problems and measures taken to restore the economy in countries trading with the United States. Provides perspectives on the Great Depression from viewpoints other than that of the United States.

Zampetti, Americo Beviglia. *Fairness in the World Economy: U.S. Perspectives on International Trade Relations*. North Hampton, Mass.: Edward Elger, 2006. Discussion of Hull's role in the U.S. conversion from a high-tariff to a free-trade international economic policy. Also examines the role of the United States in developing fairness in trade and the importance of the trade agreements of the 1930's and 1940's.

See also Elections of 1932, U.S.; Export-Import Bank of the United States; Great Depression in the United States; Hawley-Smoot Tariff Act of 1930; Hoover, Herbert; Hull, Cordell; London Economic Conference; Reciprocal Trade Agreements Act of 1936; Roosevelt, Franklin D.

■ Inventions

During the Great Depression of the 1930's, severe economic conditions in North America resulted in high unemployment, bank failures, hunger, homelessness, and despair. However, the decade was also a time of astonishing creativity, research, and technological innovation. Inventions in the areas of science, industry, leisure, transportation, entertainment, and communication transformed the world and improved people's lives.

After the stock market crash of 1929, North America entered the Great Depression, a decade of extreme economic hardship. From 1930 to 1936, the severe dust storms and droughts of the Dust Bowl ruined the prairies of Canada and the United States and brought poverty to thousands of farmers. Increasingly, international events were leading toward another world war. However, at the same time, commercial air travel became more comfortable and commonplace. Between 1936 and 1941, passenger miles traveled in the United States grew by 600 percent. A symbol of the American Dream, automobiles became increasingly popular. The Empire State Building, the world's tallest building at the time, opened, and the San Francisco Bay Bridge was built. Corporations, university research teams, government agencies, and freelance inventors all contributed to changing the world.

Science and Technology The modern jet engine was invented by Sir Frank Whittle, who, in 1930, patented his idea of combining rocket propulsion and gas turbines in a single engine. The first flight occurred in May, 1941. Concurrently, Hans Joachim Pabst Ohain, who had started similar research in 1933, obtained a patent in 1935 and oversaw a first flight in 1939.

In 1931, Massachusetts Institute of Technology engineer Harold E. Edgerton invented ultra-high-speed and stop-action photography, which was the foundation for the modern electronic flash. In 1938, Canadian Alfred J. Gross patented the walkie-talkie, a lightweight, portable, handheld, two-way, high-frequency radio.

German engineers Max Knoll and Ernst Ruska invented the electron microscope in 1931. At the University of Toronto in 1937, Albert Prebus and James Hillier built the first practical electron microscope. Unlike light microscopes, electron microscopes used a particle beam of electrons to magnify objects.

In 1932, Karl G. Jansky, a Bell Laboratories engineer, was the first to detect cosmic radio-frequency waves, when he pointed a directional radio antenna toward the center of Earth's Galaxy. In 1937, in Wheaton, Illinois, engineer Grote Reber built the first radio telescope, which had a parabolically shaped reflector and an antenna system to detect extraterrestrial radio waves.

Although the term "radar" was not used until 1940, German and Allied scientists competed with radio-wave-based detection systems during the second half of the 1930's. Detection was achieved by amplifying radio waves that returned to the site of their emission after they had been reflected by the object. The primary goal was to detect enemy planes and ships. In the United States in 1932, Allen B. DuMont proposed such a ship-locating device to the Army, but he was asked to keep his proposal a secret out of security concerns. Starting in 1934, American

Reflecting radio telescope invented in Wheaton, Illinois, in 1937. (Courtesy, National Science Foundation)

Enrico Fermi of Italy; Otto Hahn, Fritz Strassmann, and Lise Meitner of Germany; and others studied the effects of bombarding uranium atoms with neutrons, resulting in a release of energy and a transformation to barium. Eventually, this was affirmed as nuclear fission, and in 1939, a team of scientists at Columbia University conducted a successful experiment in controlled nuclear fission. During the 1940's, scientists built upon the previous decade's work in nuclear fission in order to initiate fission chain reactions, which made the atomic bomb possible.

Industry There were also many significant industrial inventions. In 1938, Wallace Carothers and his team at the DuPont Company invented nylon, the first completely synthetic or man-made textile fiber. Nylon was dyeable, mildew-resistant, elastic, and strong. DuPont introduced women's stockings made from nylon at the New York World's Fair in 1939. An immediate success, nylon hosiery soon replaced silk stockings. Other uses included automotive parts, carpet, upholstery, machinery, and stretch garments.

In 1938, DuPont chemist Roy J. Plunkett discovered Teflon, a waxy, strong, nonflammable synthetic resin, used as an equipment protector during World War II. Beginning in 1960, Teflon was widely used in nonstick cookware.

In 1938, American physicist Chester F. Carlson invented xerography, the basis of most modern photocopiers. He patented the method, which involved using electrostatic charges, toner, a photoconductive surface, and heat to produce copies of text or graphic material. Haloid Company, which became the Xerox Corporation, introduced the first office photocopier in 1958.

Although the essential prototypes and components of television systems had already been developed during the 1920's, English inventor John Logie Baird, using shortwave transmissions, and

scientist Robert M. Page worked on the first monopulse radar. In England in 1935, Sir Robert Alexander Watson-Watt demonstrated a working system to his government, which immediately prepared to use the invention in the impending war. Similar developments occurred in France, Holland, the Soviet Union, Germany, and Japan. The Allies' successful implementation of radar ultimately helped them achieve victory.

In 1935, Charles Francis Richter of the California Institute of Technology invented the Richter scale for measuring the magnitude of an earthquake. This mathematical device measures an earthquake's magnitude based on the logarithm of the varying amplitude of an earthquake's seismic waves or vibrations as recorded by seismographs.

During the 1930's, European scientists, including

American inventor Philo T. Farnsworth, who invented the first completely electronic system, were instrumental in realizing the potential of developments in electronic image transmission during the 1930's. By the end of the decade, all of the ingredients for the modern television industry were in place.

Everyday Life   In 1930, Richard G. Drew, an engineer at the 3M company in St. Paul, Minnesota, invented the world's first transparent adhesive tape, called the Scotch Brand Cellulose Tape or Scotch tape. Although originally created to seal cellophane wrappers, this waterproof tape became a popular all-purpose adhesive during the Depression years. It was used for holding plaster to walls and ceilings, repairing toys, mending clothing, sealing cracked eggs, and hundreds of other purposes. In 1935, 3M employee John Borden invented the first tape dispenser with a built-in cutting blade.

Michael Cullen opened King Kullen Grocery Company, the world's first supermarket, in Queens, New York in August, 1930. Before then, grocery shopping required frequent trips to specialized neighborhood stores or waiting for grocery wagons in rural areas. By 1939, there were nearly five thousand supermarkets in the United States.

The first marketable electric razor or dry shaver was invented by Jacob Schick, a retired army colonel. After developing the product for years, in 1929, he introduced an unsuccessful two-handed prototype, which consisted of a an electric motor, flexible drive shaft, and separate shaving head. Finally, in 1931, he introduced the successful one-handed dry razor. During the early 1930's, Earle Haas of Denver, Colorado, invented and patented a feminine product, the first tampon with an applicator, which was introduced as Tampax in 1936.

To solve parking problems and relieve traffic congestion in business districts, newspaper editor Carlton C. Magee invented the first parking meter. The first meters were installed in downtown Oklahoma City on July 16, 1935. Then, he and a partner founded the Magee-Hale Park-O-Meter Company (later renamed POM) to manufacture the product.

Entertainment and Leisure   Guitars were popular in jazz and folk music, but were used mostly for accompaniment, because of their low volume. Although engineers seeking to amplify guitars had already created an electrostatic pickup (a kind of contact microphone) during the 1920's, this did not appeal to working musicians. In 1931, George Beauchamp and Adolph Rickenbacker created a different kind of device: an electromagnetic pickup, based on a magnet with wire coiled around it. When connected to an electric current, a vibrating string would generate a magnetic field that could then be carried to a speaker. The enduring popularity of electric guitars with electromagnetic pickups was firmly established by the end of the decade.

In 1932, unemployed Canadian Donald H. Munro invented a tabletop hockey game as a Christmas present for his children. The steel ball (puck) could roll to either end of the board, enabling two people to play. Earlier products had a single slope, permitting only one player at a time. Munro's game was a top-seller throughout Canada, until the Eagle Toy Company of Montreal introduced its National Hockey Game in 1954.

In 1933, New Jersey businessman Richard M. Hollingshead invented the drive-in theater, which combined automobiles with films, both popular during the 1930's. These open-air theaters provided affordable and convenient entertainment for the entire family, and they reached their heyday during the 1950's.

In 1934, Charles B. Darrow invented Monopoly, one of the most successful board games in history; Parker Brothers mass-produced the game in 1935. Based on earlier models, such as the Landlord's Game by Lizzie G. Magie and Finance by Dan Layman, Monopoly consists of a board with rectangles representing real estate properties. The goal is to gain a monopoly of properties and force others out of the game through bankruptcy.

Impact   In spite of dire economic conditions during the 1930's, significant inventions came to fruition throughout the decade. New companies and inventions arose from the research and development of this decade, and many inventions made their inventors wealthy. The work of these inventors and mavericks had significant impacts for following generations. For example, Farnsworth's discoveries helped lay the foundation for the modern electronic age. Gross, who continued to develop products, has been called the father of wireless communication. Drew's adhesive tape, which made a huge fortune for him and 3M, remains one of the most practical and widely used inventions ever. In 1992,

POM introduced the first fully electronic parking meter, and eventually installed meters in foreign languages globally. Cullen's supermarket revolutionized the food industry and empowered the consumer. This first supermarket, King Kullen, eventually established a retail presence on the Internet. Although it took years before any company manufactured the Xerox photocopier, Carlson's invention changed copyright laws and has become standard office equipment in the twenty-first century.

Alice Myers

Further Reading

Brown, David E. *Inventing Modern America: From the Microwave to the Mouse.* Cambridge, Mass.: MIT Press, 2002. Presents accounts of significant modern inventions and their inventors, including Edgerton's stop-action photography and Gross's walkie-talkie. Illustrated with bibliography and index.

Fisher, David E., and Marshall Jon Fisher. *Tube: The Invention of Television.* San Diego: Harcourt Brace, 1997. The crucial developments of the 1930's are covered in this readable history about the inventors of the modern television. Illustrated with bibliography and index.

Flatow, Ira. *They All Laughed: From Light Bulbs to Lasers, the Fascinating Stories Behind the Great Inventions That Have Changed Our Lives.* New York: HarperPerennial, 1993. Entertaining stories about inventions, such as television, Teflon, and the photocopier. Illustrated with bibliography and index.

Haven, Kendall F. *One Hundred Greatest Science Inventions of All Time.* Westport, Conn.: Libraries Unlimited, 2006. Inventions of the 1930's such as radar, nylon, the photocopier, and the jet engine are among the one hundred inventions discussed in this book. Bibliography and index.

Owen, David. *Copies in Seconds: How a Lone Inventor and an Unknown Company Created the Biggest Communication Breakthrough Since Gutenberg: Chester Carlson and the Birth of the Xerox Machine.* New York: Simon & Schuster, 2004. This is a detailed account based on interviews and private and company archives. Illustrated with bibliography and index.

Van Dulken, Stephen. *Inventing the Twentieth Century: One Hundred Inventions That Shaped the World— From the Airplane to the Zipper.* Washington Square: New York University Press, 2000. Arranged by decades, this informative history describes each invention and includes a copy of the original patent. Illustrated with bibliography and index.

See also   Airships; Architecture; Astronomy; Aviation and aeronautics; Bathysphere; Birth control; Car radios; Chemistry; DC-3; Drive-in theaters; Electric razors; Electron microscope; Empire State Building; Freon; Frozen-food marketing; Hearing aids; Heart-lung machine; Instant coffee; Medicine; Monopoly; Muzak; Nuclear fission; Nylon; Parking meters; Photography; Physics; Radar, invention of; Radio astronomy; Refrigerators; Richter scale; Rocketry; Supermarkets; Telephone technology and service; Television technology; Vending machines; Xerography.

■ *Invisible Man, The*

Identification   Film adaptation of a novella by H. G. Wells
Director   James Whale
Date   Released in 1933

The story of a scientist who makes himself invisible and subsequently goes insane, The Invisible Man *was one of the great horror films produced at Universal Studios during the 1930's and one of the top films, both commercially and critically, of 1933.*

Universal acquired the film rights to *The Invisible Man* in 1931. At least nine writers worked on the script, including John Huston; James Whale, the director of *Frankenstein* (1931); R. C. Sherriff, actually listed as the writer in the credits; and Preston Sturges. Three other directors were considered until producer Carl Laemmle chose Whale.

Boris Karloff, who played the monster in *Frankenstein,* was Universal's first choice to play the character of the Invisible Man, but he was disputing his contract with Universal at the time. Colin Clive, who played the title character in *Frankenstein,* turned down the role. Whale had worked with English stage actor Claude Rains a decade earlier in London and recommended him for the role. Rains had previously appeared in only one film, a silent one at that, so he was a risky choice. In one of the oddest starring roles of all time, Rains spent most of his on-screen time covered in bandages and some of it as a disembodied voice. Moreover, the most spectacular scenes used a stunt double. Rains's face is shown clearly for only about twenty seconds at the end.

Featuring state-of-the-art visual effects by John P. Fulton, *The Invisible Man* was one of the top-grossing films of that year. *The New York Times* named it one of the ten best films of 1933, and Whale received a Special Recommendation from the 1934 Venice Film Festival.

Impact   *The Invisible Man* inspired four sequels and many imitations, including *Hollow Man* (2000). The film boosted the film careers of Rains and Fulton. Rains later earned four Academy Award nominations for acting, and Fulton earned five, winning two for visual effects.

Thomas R. Feller

Further Reading

Curtis, James. *James Whale: A New World of Gods and Monsters*. Boston: Faber and Faber, 1998.

Mallory, Michael. *Universal Studios Monsters: A Legacy of Horror.* New York: Universe, 2009.

See also   *Dracula*; *Frankenstein* films; Horror films; Karloff, Boris; *Mr. Smith Goes to Washington*.

■ Isolationism

Definition   Approach to U.S. foreign policy that sought to minimize interaction with the world beyond American borders.

The isolationism that gripped the American people and government alike following World War I endured throughout the 1930's, effectively blocking many of the Roosevelt administration's efforts to undertake proactive foreign policy on behalf of Europe's democracies as the threat of fascist aggression was growing.

Prior to the Cold War that began in the late 1940's, isolationism had been the dominant American approach to foreign policy since the time of President George Washington. In Washington's farewell address in 1796, he advised his young, politically and militarily weak country to have with European states "as little political connection as possible." At different moments in American history, isolationist impulses manifested themselves differently through the long period between 1796 and 1941, when the

Japanese launched a surprise attack on Pearl Harbor, but never more virulently than during the interwar period between World War I and World War II.

Nineteenth century American isolationism was largely unconscious—the product of the country's general disregard of others as it concentrated on fulfilling its own "Manifest Destiny" by expanding its borders from the Atlantic to the Pacific Ocean. In contrast, the isolationist desire became considerably more conscious following the Spanish-American War of 1898, which was ostensibly fought to end the cruelties of Spain's rule over Cuba, only to end with the United States itself becoming an imperial power, with unintended possessions in both the Caribbean and the Pacific Ocean. By the second decade of the twentieth century, the resultant isolationist urge remained so strong that when Europe fell into World War I in 1914, President Woodrow Wilson found it necessary to create a propaganda agency to sell to the American public the need for the country to intervene against the German, Ottoman, and Austro-Hungarian empires "to make the world safe for democracy." The United States eventually entered that war and helped the Western allies to win, only to be disillusioned afterward, when the British and French diplomats at the peace conference focused on carving up the Ottoman Middle East to enlarge their own empires.

The Interwar Period   The ensuing interwar era of isolationism, and especially that of the 1930's, differed from its predecessors in several ways. First, it was not merely conscious but self-conscious isolationism—hardened by public disillusionment with recent forays into international politics and reinforced during the Great Depression by the perceived need for the national government to focus on domestic policies. Secondly, it was out of sync with the country's position in the world. George Washington had recommended tactical isolationism, looking forward to the day when his country would be strong enough to "choose peace or war, as our interest, guided by justice, shall counsel." By the twentieth century, the United States had achieved that status and was one of the world's major powers. Finally, it was a legislated isolationism, with its genesis in the U.S. Senate's refusal to allow the country to join the League of Nations that was created after World War I. Its adolescence developed in the 1921 Washington Conference and the 1930 London Na-

Members of the Stay-Out-of-Europe Legion carry antiwar signs in a demonstration in New York City's Times Square at the start of their campaign to keep the United States out of World War II in October, 1939—a month after Germany's occupation of Poland began. (©Bettmann/CORBIS)

val Treaty, which limited naval shipbuilding. Its maturity arrived in the Neutrality Acts of the 1930's, which were enacted as warfare spread in Europe to prevent the United States from becoming involved.

The isolationists had their critics, to be sure. The film producer Jack Warner, for example, made films during the 1930's to awaken the public to the true nature of German and Italian fascism. President Franklin D. Roosevelt often sought to do likewise, most famously in 1937, when he spoke of the "epidemic" of aggression and the need to "quarantine" the aggressors to prevent the disease from spreading. As a trial balloon, however, his urging crashed, and his hands remained tied throughout the de-

cade. The Neutrality Laws drew no distinction between aggressors and victims in their blanket prohibition against aiding those engaged in war.

Impact   Several schools of thought have arisen concerning the continued American adherence to militant isolationism during the 1930's. None of them is charitable toward the isolationists. The best interpretation is that isolationism merely left the United States ill prepared for war. Less kind critics, such as the former diplomat and historian George Kennan, have argued that had the United States been disposed to help, European leaders might have stood up to the aggression of Germany's Adolf Hitler and

Italy's Benito Mussolini earlier, when the fascists might have been more easily defeated. Most damning, Kennan also argued that when World War II began, it necessarily became a defensive war for the democracies, because by then Germany, Japan, and the Soviet Union had become so powerful that the only way the alliance of any two of the three countries could be defeated was through an alliance with the third. As the aftermath of World War II would later demonstrate, the cost of the Western alliance with the Soviet Union would become Soviet domination over Central and Eastern Europe.

Joseph R. Rudolph, Jr.

Further Reading

Guinsburg, Thomas N. *The Pursuit of Isolationism in the United States Senate from Versailles to Pearl Harbor.* New York: Garland, 1982.

Holsti, Ole R. *Public Opinion and American Foreign Policy.* Ann Arbor: University of Michigan Press, 2004.

Kennan, George. *American Diplomacy.* Rev. ed. Chicago: University of Chicago Press, 1984.

See also Foreign policy of the United States; Germany and U.S. appeasement; Japanese military aggression; League of Nations; London Naval Treaty; Neutrality Acts; Peace movement; Quarantine speech; World War I debts; World War II and the United States.

Actor Clark Gable (left) munches a carrot as Claudette Colbert looks on in a scene from Frank Capra's seminal screwball comedy It Happened One Night. *(Hulton Archive/Getty Images)*

■ It Happened One Night

Identification Comedy film
Director Frank Capra
Date Released in 1934

Often considered one of the first screwball comedies, It Happened One Night *focuses on the growing romance of an unlikely couple set against the background of the Great Depression.*

It Happened One Night centers on the story of a young woman escaping from her wealthy, domineering fa-

ther and a newspaper reporter who has talked himself out of a job. The two meet on a bus trip from Florida to New York. She becomes something more than a spoiled brat, and he becomes something more than an arrogant braggart in the course of their adventures together on the road. The film won five Academy Awards and lasting popularity. In his autobiography, Frank Capra attributed much of the success of the film to the lively off- and on-screen chemistry between the two featured players, Claudette Colbert and Clark Gable, neither of whom wanted to be in the picture. Capra also highlighted the importance of major changes he and his scriptwriter, Robert Riskin, made as they adapted the source story, making the characters more sympathetic and turning the plot into a modern-day version of William Shakespeare's *Taming of the Shrew* (1593-1594, pb. 1623).

Ellie Andrews (Colbert) and Peter Warne (Gable) meet on a bus, as she heads back to a relationship with a foolish suitor and he heads to nowhere in particular. He teaches her to leave behind luxuries and haughty individuality and realize the joys of donuts, coffee in a mug, and, most of all, companionship and sharing. She has a civilizing effect on him, helping him accept her intelligence, liveliness, and deep feelings and learn how to turn his dreams into a real and lasting relationship.

Impact   *It Happened One Night* is primarily a romantic comedy; on a simple level, it is an entertaining and a diverting fantasy of a prickly relationship that ends in a happy marriage. However, it is also a broader fable of readjustment, reconciliation, and recovery, suggesting that society at large needs to learn what Ellie and Peter do: that material goods count for little, that friendship and charity are the basis of love and bind both the couple and the community, and that a spirit of creative playfulness will not only help people endure but also ultimately help overcome the Depression. Some call this sentimental "Capra-corn," but it is also a powerful dramatiza-tion of utopian dreams and practical advice for citizens of an inevitably interconnected society.

Sidney Gottlieb

Further Reading

Gottlieb, Sidney. "From Heroine to Brat: Frank Capra's Adaptation of *Night Bus* (*It Happened One Night*)." *Literature/Film Quarterly* 16, no. 2 (1988): 129-136.

Maltby, Richard. "*It Happened One Night* (1934): Comedy and the Restoration of Order." In *Film Analysis*, edited by Jeffrey Geiger and R. L. Rutsky. New York: W. W. Norton, 2005.

See also   Academy Awards; Capra, Frank; Film; Gable, Clark; Great Depression in the United States; *Mr. Deeds Goes to Town*; *Mr. Smith Goes to Washington*; Newspapers, U.S.; Screwball comedy; Travel.

J

Japanese American Citizens League

Identification   Asian American civil rights advocacy organization
Also known as   JACL
Date   Founded in 1929

The Japanese American Citizens League (JACL) was founded by Nisei, second-generation Japanese immigrants born in the United States. In 1930's, JACL served as an organization to protect civil rights in the light of anti-Japanese sentiment in the United States.

Japanese immigration to the United States began in the late nineteenth century. While more than seventy thousand Japanese settled on the mainland of the United States, by 1910 they had faced racial discriminatory practices in education, housing, and landownership. When Nisei reached adulthood, they started to form many small political groups to cope with the anti-Japanese movement. The American Loyalty League of Fresno, California, founded in 1923, was among them. Similar Nisei leagues were organized in Washington and Oregon during the 1920's. These regional groups in the Pacific Northwest and in California were united in 1929 and became a national Nisei organization called the Japanese American Citizens League. The first JACL national convention took place on August 29, 1930, in Seattle, Washington.

In early 1931, JACL petitioned Congress to amend the Cable Act of 1922, which states that any woman citizen who marries an alien ineligible for citizenship shall cease to be a citizen of the United States. Congress amended the Cable Act in March, 1931, allowing women married to Issei (first-generation Japanese immigrants) to maintain or recover their American citizenship. (The act was repealed in 1936.) In 1935, JACL helped the passage of the Nye-Lea bill, granting citizenship to Issei World War I veterans. After Japan's attack on Pearl Harbor in December, 1941, President Franklin D. Roosevelt signed Executive Order 9066 in February, 1942, which authorized the exclusion of people of Japanese ancestry from the West Coast and southern Arizona. Under this order, about 120,000 people, including JACL members, were removed from their homes and relocated into internment camps.

Impact   Because of JACL long-term efforts to help the recovery of property losses caused by wartime relocation of Japanese Americans, Congress finally passed the Civil Liberties Act of 1988, which granted each surviving internee about twenty thousand dollars in compensation. In the twenty-first century, JACL is the largest Asian American civil rights advocacy organization in the United States.

Fusako Hamao

Further Reading

Hosokawa, Bill. *JACL: In Quest of Justice.* New York: William Morrow, 1982.
Spickard, Paul. *Japanese Americans: The Formation and Transformations of an Ethnic Group.* Rev. ed. New Brunswick, N.J.: Rutgers University Press, 2009.

See also   Asia; Asian Americans; Civil rights and liberties in the United States; Racial discrimination; Roosevelt, Franklin D.; World War II and the United States.

Japanese military aggression

The Event   Japan's territorial expansion in Asia, eventually causing war between Japan and the United States
Date   1931-1939

Beginning with the Mukden incident (also known as the Manchurian incident) in September of 1931, the U.S. government commenced a series of reactions to Japanese acts of violent, military aggression and territorial expansion that continued for the rest of the decade, eventually leading to war between the two countries in the decade that followed.

On September 18, 1931, the Japanese Kwantung Army stationed in Manchuria in northeastern

The Stimson Doctrine

On January 7, 1932, in a letter to the American ambassador to Japan, Secretary of State Henry L. Stimson admonishes the military aggression of Imperial Japan, a maneuver that establishes the U.S. political position in Asia. The letter, later known as the Stimson Doctrine, strained relations between Japan and the United States, a fact that eventually led to military confrontation in World War II.

The American Government deems it to be its duty to notify both the Imperial Japanese Government and the Government of the Chinese Republic that it cannot admit the legality of any situation de facto nor does it intend to recognize any treaty or agreement entered into between those Governments, or agents thereof, which may impair the treaty rights of the United States or its citizens in China, including those which relate to the sovereignty, the independence, or the territorial and administrative integrity of the Republic of China, or to the international policy relative to China, commonly known as the open door policy; and that it does not intend to recognize any situation, treaty or agreement which may be brought about by means contrary to the covenants and obligations of the Pact of Paris of August 27, 1928, to which Treaty both China and Japan, as well as the United States, are parties.

China, acting without the knowledge or consent of its home government in Tokyo, blew up a section of a Japanese-owned railway just north of the city of Mukden (now known as Shenyang). Claiming that the act had been the work of local extremists, the military leadership then used this event in the months that followed as an excuse for assuming control of the region. A puppet regime was established, and in March of 1932, the area was renamed Manchukuo.

In January of 1932, U.S. Secretary of State Henry L. Stimson responded to the events in Manchuria by setting forth what came to be known as the "non-recognition policy" or Stimson Doctrine, stating that the United States refused to recognize territory gained by Japanese aggression. This policy remained the official position of the United States for the remainder of the decade, although no further action was taken against the Japanese at that time.

Additional acts of aggression by the Japanese in China followed. In January of 1932, Japanese planes bombed Shanghai, and the military sent troops into that city. At the same time, the fall of civilian govern-

ments and a series of high-profile political assassinations in Japan contributed further to the growing influence of the military. On March 27, 1933, Japan withdrew from the League of Nations in response to a report issued by the organization condemning Japanese aggression in Manchuria.

In March of 1933, Franklin D. Roosevelt took office as president of the United States, and Cordell Hull replaced Stimson as secretary of state. The Roosevelt administration generally followed the policy of the previous Herbert Hoover administration in its reaction to Japanese aggression and did not take additional actions against the Japanese.

The Japanese military presence in China continued to grow in the years that followed; in July of 1937, full-scale war broke out between the two countries. In October of 1937, although remaining sensitive to the strong isolationist sentiments existing in Congress, President Roosevelt reacted to the actions of both Germany and Japan in his famous "quarantine speech," stating the need to "quarantine" countries involved in acts of international aggression. Again, however, no specific further action regarding the Japanese was taken.

In December of 1937, the Japanese army committed atrocities in the Chinese city of Nanjing, an event that is often referred to as the Rape of Nanjing. Furthermore, controversy ensued between the United States and Japan, resulting from the Panay incident. Although the Japanese government later apologized for the latter event—which involved an attack on a U.S. gunboat patrolling in international waters on the Chang River (also known as the Yangtze River) in southern China—the event led to a further deterioration in U.S.-Japan relations.

The following year, reacting to the events of the previous December, the Roosevelt administration began the first stage of its efforts to place economic sanctions on Japan for its acts of foreign aggression. In July of 1938, the administration urged a "moral embargo" on aircraft and parts shipments to the warring nation, and in July of 1939, it officially notified the Japanese government of its intention to end the 1911 commercial treaty in place between the two countries. War between the United States and Japan seemed to be the inevitable outcome.

Impact The issue of Japanese aggression constituted a major foreign policy concern for the United States throughout the 1930's. Although the matter ebbed and flowed during the course of the decade, the "nonrecognition policy" set forth by U.S. secretary of state Stimson in 1932 remained the basic position of the United States during the period. By the end of the decade, however, the U.S. government had implemented a series of trade embargoes and other economic sanctions against Japan that eventually led the two countries to war two years later.

Scott Wright

Further Reading

Boyle, John Hunter. *Modern Japan: The American Nexus.* Fort Worth, Tex.: Harcourt Brace Jovanovich, 1993.

Herring, George C. *From Colony to Superpower: U.S. Foreign Relations Since 1776.* New York: Oxford University Press, 2008.

LaFeber, Walter. *The Clash: A History of U.S.-Japan Relations.* New York: W. W. Norton, 1997.

McClain, James L. *Japan: A Modern History.* New York: W. W. Norton, 2002.

See also Foreign policy of the United States; Hull, Cordell; Isolationism; League of Nations; Manchuria occupation; *Panay* incident; Quarantine speech; Roosevelt, Franklin D.; Stimson, Henry L.; World War II and the United States.

■ Jews in Canada

Jews in Canada experienced massive unemployment and extreme poverty during the Great Depression. At the same time, anti-Semitic sentiments became heightened and widespread among the Canadian public during the 1930's. Leaders in the Canadian Jewish community mobilized themselves politically to fight for antidiscrimination legislation, but these attempts often failed.

Between 1931 and 1939, the Canadian Jewish community grew 8.3 percent, from 155,766 to approximately 167,000, with a net total of only eighty-three Jewish immigrants, when calculated against the number of foreign-born Jews deported during the Depression. By the outbreak of World War II, Jews represented about 1.5 percent of the total Canadian population.

The Canadian Jewish community was composed almost entirely of Ashkenazi Jews from Western and Eastern Europe. Nonetheless, the community was not homogenous. One-half of the community hailed from Eastern European countries, while the other half of the community were Canadian born. Other differences included social class, professional skill levels, religious dedication, and political affiliation. By 1939, the Jewish community in Canada was concentrated largely in three provinces: Ontario, with a Jewish population of sixty-six thousand; Quebec, with sixty-four thousand; and Manitoba, with twenty thousand. Three-quarters of Canadian Jews lived in three cities: Toronto, with forty-nine thousand; Montreal, with sixty thousand; and Winnipeg, with eighteen thousand.

Anti-Semitism was the one issue that united all Jews in Canada during the 1930's, but it was not the only problem Canadian Jews faced. Other problems included mass unemployment, poverty, malnutrition, and a poor economic future. Anti-Semitism in Canada was one reflection of the general anti-immigrant sentiments and discriminatory practices directed against southern and eastern Europeans, Asians, South Asians, and other "non-natives." The Jewish community in Canada felt largely insecure and powerless, as anti-Semitism swept across Canada in various forms throughout the 1930's.

Nationalist and fascist movements throughout Canada, and particularly in Quebec, espoused the most visible and blatant forms of anti-Semitism through newspaper articles, swastika clubs, political speeches, and sometimes violent acts, such as the Christie Pits riot in Toronto in 1933. Subtler forms of anti-Semitism were embedded in the mainstream society, whereby Jews faced discrimination in education, employment, and housing and were prohibited from assisting family members in Europe in immigrating to Canada in the light of restrictive immigration controls. Signs stating "No Jews Allowed" and "Gentiles Only" were hung in public spaces and private businesses. Jews were not allowed to join certain clubs and organizations.

In response to the vulnerability felt by Canadian Jews, the Canadian Jewish Congress, which had dissipated shortly after it had been established in 1919, reconvened in 1934 as the official political body to represent a national voice for the Canadian Jewish community. The central issue on which the congress focused during the 1930's was lobbying the federal government to lessen the restrictions on Jewish refugees from Nazi Germany and on other Jews trying to immigrate. The group also fought the general anti-Semitism in Canada. However, the pleas of the congress went largely ignored, and Jewish members of parliament found themselves powerless and ineffectual. Congress officials were unwilling to take a militant approach for fear that it would simply reinforce the already existing anti-Semitic sentiments and create even more barriers for Jews in Canada.

Impact   Throughout the 1930's, Canadian society was permeated with anti-Semitism. Although Canadian anti-Semitism constructed barriers and limitations for Jews, it did not pose a direct physical danger of death, as did the anti-Semitism in Germany during this same period. Nonetheless, Canadian Jews felt extremely vulnerable, especially as the Canadian Jewish Congress and Canadian Jewish politicians were rendered powerless. The inability of Canadian Jewish political leaders to lobby for the admission of Jewish refugees from Europe or obtain antidiscrimination laws for Jews in Canada created division and tension within the already fragmented and weak Canadian Jewish community. Not until the 1950's did the Canadian Jewish community gain a sense of confidence, with the birth of the state of Israel and newfound upward social mobility, and could focus on creating a unified voice to fight anti-Semitism.

Kelly Amanda Train

Further Reading

Abella, Irving. *A Coat of Many Colors: Two Centuries of Jewish Life in Canada.* Toronto: Key Porter Books, 1999.

Bialystok, Franklin. *Delayed Impact: The Holocaust and the Canadian Jewish Community.* Montreal: McGill-Queen's University Press, 2000.

Tulchinsky, Gerald. *Canada's Jews: A People's Journey.* Toronto: University of Toronto Press, 2008.

See also   Anti-Semitism; Canadian minority communities; Christie Pits riot; Demographics of Canada; Great Depression in Canada; Jews in the United States; Religion in Canada; Religion in the United States.

■ Jews in the United States

In the decade of the 1930's, descendants of central European Jews and the latter-day Jewish immigrants from eastern Europe began to coalesce into an American Jewish community, united in their goals and dependent on each other for their defense. This happened despite several political and religious issues that tended to divide the Jewish community.

The occupational transformation of the Jewish community that had begun during the 1920's, as second-generation Jews rapidly moved into the middle class and the suburbs, was curtailed by widespread unemployment and poverty resulting from the Great Depression of the 1930's. In addition to these external forces, the Jewish community was split by internal conflicts: The differences among Orthodox, Conservative, and Reform Jewry became institutionalized in this decade, promoting a division over traditional beliefs toward ritual and practice. The ideals of communism, which had strong roots in the countries of origin of many of the Jewish immigrants, were held by almost one-third of Jews in the United States, and the increasing commitment to Zionism provoked conflicts of loyalty.

Jewish Reactions to Economic Hardship   During the 1930's, many Jews accepted government welfare, but they largely preferred to apply to their own Jewish institutions for financial help. Jewish mutual-aid societies and *landsmanschaften* (societies based on towns of origin) struggled to respond to the ever-growing numbers of the needy, and many had to discontinue aid. Jewish federations, which were funded by more affluent contributors, were better equipped to help indigent Jews. New York's Hebrew Free Loan Society offered more than one million dollars to struggling businessmen and destitute families. Yiddish and Anglo-Jewish newspapers provided free advertising for job availability, Jewish employment agencies started to aid the mass of unemployed, and agencies made direct appeals to Jewish businessmen to find work for other Jews. Some relief agencies provided rent money to prevent eviction, some helped professional men get set up with an office, and many of them distributed milk to children of any religion who were facing malnutrition.

Descendants of eastern European Jews were hardest hit during this period because these Jews had not lived in the United States long enough to assimilate into the mainstream culture and did not have the same entrenched economic status of the earlier German Jewish immigrants. Most of them developed an allegiance to the Democratic Party and supported President Franklin D. Roosevelt's New Deal, his attempt to raise the United States from economic depression. Part of Roosevelt's appeal was that he opened government service to Jews and appointed a great number of them to his inner circle of advisers. Critical of Roosevelt's policies, however, was the Workman's Circle, the socialist arm of the Jewish labor movement, which believed the New Deal simply perpetuated the evils of capitalism.

Cultural Impact In the early years of the twentieth century, when many immigrant Jews were living in tenements in New York, a remarkable number of Jewish entertainers emerged, whose careers were prominent in the United States. Although this generation of performers was unmistakably Jewish and defined itself through cultural symbols and references to Yiddish subjects, their early success was through the popularity of acts done in blackface. Entertainers such as Al Jolson, George Jessel, Eddie Cantor, George Burns, Groucho Marx, and Sophie Tucker all had their blackface acts, while Irving

Rabbi Stephan S. Wise (left) and Christian minister Harry A. Atkinson discussing the latter's plan to institute programs to help American Jews fight anti-Semitism. (Library of Congress)

Berlin's first success as a songwriter came from "Alexander's Ragtime Band," written to accompany a blackface act. As their fame grew, these entertainers turned to Jewish themes, and by the early 1930's, they were popular on the American stage. Their spirit persisted in the work of the Marx Brothers, who pushed the conventions of entertainment to the extremes of social satire and antic farce.

The Marx Brothers and other Jewish entertainers were at their prime in the early 1930's, but by the mid-1930's Jewish humor began to fade with the campaign against dialect humor led by Walter Winchell. In the films, veteran actors who had done Jewish roles were unable to find work, and many characters in films and on stage changed their names from conspicuously Jewish ones. However, even in the decade of Adolf Hitler, the disappearance of Jewish characters was not total. A 1934 film made by Jolson, titled *Wonder Bar*, contained snippets of Yiddish, and the Andrews Sisters did a popular English version of "Bei Mir Bistu Shein," which they sometimes sang in Yiddish.

Another important trend during the 1930's was the rise of a group of literary and political writers who came to be called New York intellectuals. The first group that emerged during the 1930's included Philip Rahv, Meyer Schapiro, Paul Goodman, Harold Rosenberg, and Sidney Hook. When these writers first began to appear in the pages of the *Partisan Review* during the 1930's, the immigrant culture from which they sprang played little part in their worldview, which tended toward modernist culture. Jewish influence was felt in the theater also, with such giants as Moss Hart, Lillian Hellman, Irwin Shaw, and, particularly, Clifford Odets writing for the stage.

Impact The 1930's were a difficult time for American Jews. They had to adapt to American culture during a period of economic depression and anti-Semitism. Nonetheless, the ties of Jewish solidarity remained strong; although Jewish relief efforts were not adequate to help all who needed help, they still adhered to the value of Jews helping one another. In popular entertainment and intellectual circles, Jews made advancements that made a lasting impact on American culture.

Sheila Golburgh Johnson

Further Reading

Abzug, Robert H. *America Views the Holocaust, 1933-1945: A Brief Documentary History.* New York: Palgrave Macmillan, 1999. Discusses the reaction of Americans to the Holocaust.

Feldstein, Stanley. *The Land That I Show You: Three Centuries of Jewish Life in America.* New York: Anchor Press/Doubleday, 1979. Chapters 6 and 7 give detailed, anecdotal accounts of the Jews during the 1930's.

Gurock, Jeffrey S. *Orthodox Jews in America.* Bloomington: Indiana University Press, 2009. Traces the history of Orthodox Jews in the United States beginning in the 1600's, charting the development of the culture over the centuries.

Hertzberg, Arthur. *The Jews in America.* New York: Simon and Schuster, 1989. Strong on political and social trends of the period.

Howe, Irving. *World of Our Fathers.* New York: Harcourt Brace Jovanovich, 1976. Chapter 17 provides excellent information on the confluence of American society and Jewish culture during the 1930's.

Kennedy, David. *Freedom from Fear: The American People in Depression and War, 1929-1945.* New York: Oxford University Press, 1999. Detailed and analytical discussion of American attitudes toward immigration.

See also   Anti-Semitism; Coughlin, Charles E.; Jews in Canada; Labor strikes; Miller, Glenn; Socialist parties; Unionism.

■ Jim Crow segregation

Definition   Legal and extralegal limitations on the rights of African Americans, particularly in the American South

Jim Crow laws restricted freedoms for African Americans throughout the South and were a primary target of the Civil Rights movement, especially during the 1930's.

During the 1880's, local and state governments in the American South began passing laws designed to

Sign outside the Halifax, North Carolina, courthouse indicating that the drinking fountain is reserved for "Colored" people—a reflection of the fact that African Americans were not allowed to drink from white-only fountains. Racial segregation was commonplace during the 1930's. (Library of Congress)

restrict the equal rights of African Americans. These laws cleverly skirted the few federal laws protecting African Americans' political and civil rights and so were almost never in direct violation of any federal statute. The 1896 Supreme Court decision *Plessy v. Ferguson* established that public facilities and services could be segregated between African Americans and Caucasians so long as those facilities and services were equal. In many ways, this was the foundation for Jim Crow legislation throughout the first half of the twentieth century.

By the 1930's the legal restrictions on African Americans' civil rights were exacerbated by regular lynchings and violence against African Americans.

In an attempt to limit these activities and in an effort to secure the legal rights ostensibly granted to African Americans by the Reconstruction amendments, organizations such as the National Association for the Advancement of Colored People (NAACP) expanded their legal actions against Jim Crow. During the decade, NAACP head Walter White set in motion a series of court cases aimed at bringing down southern segregation. These cases at all levels of the justice system eventually climaxed in the *Brown v. Board of Education of Topeka* decision in 1954, which found "separate but equal" to be unconstitutional.

Impact   The Jim Crow laws throughout the American South severely limited black rights for decades. In addition, these laws became the target of attempts by the federal government and civil rights organizations to improve rights for African Americans from the 1930's through the 1950's.

Shawn Selby

Further Reading

Brown, Nikki L. M., and Barry M. Stentiford. *The Jim Crow Encyclopedia.* Westport, Conn.: Greenwood Press, 2008.

Litwack, Leon F. *Trouble in Mind: Black Southerners in the Age of Jim Crow.* New York: Alfred A. Knopf, 1998.

Woodward, C. Vann. *The Strange Career of Jim Crow.* New York: Oxford University Press, 1955.

See also   African Americans; Civil rights and liberties in the United States; Lynching; *Missouri ex rel. Gaines v. Canada*; National Association for the Advancement of Colored People; National Negro Congress; Racial discrimination.

■ John Muir Trail

Identification   Trail connecting California's Yosemite and Sequoia National Parks

The trail named for conservationist John Muir provided a pedestrian gateway through the Sierra Nevadas.

Muir arrived in the Sierra Nevadas in California in 1869. He climbed many of the mountains and determined that many of the long valleys, such as Yosemite Valley, had been scoured out by valley glaciers. He published a number of stories about his adventures in books and magazines, which made him famous. He also lectured on the geology and landscapes of this region. Muir became concerned about the destruction of this landscape by people, so his talks and publications were directed toward the conservation

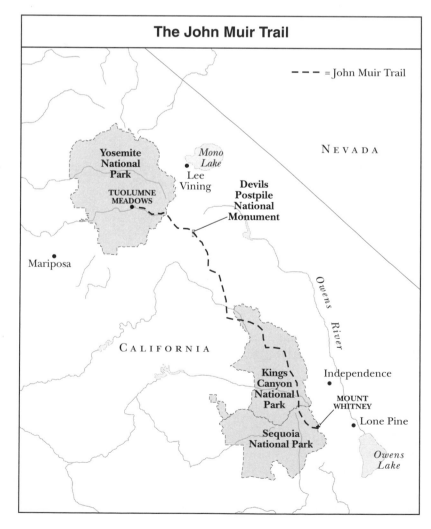

The John Muir Trail

of the area. His efforts helped earn designation as national parks for the Yosemite and Sequoia areas. Muir also cofounded a conservation group called the Sierra Club in 1892. He became friends with President Theodore Roosevelt in 1902 and helped convince him to establish many more national parks and increase the amount of national forests.

In 1915, the California legislature passed a law to develop a trail from Yosemite National Park to Sequoia National Park to be named the John Muir Trail. The construction of many parts of the trail was not easy work, as some portions had to be carved out of steep mountainsides and a number of bridges had to be built. From 1916 to 1930, money continued to be allocated by California to carry out this work, but the trail was not completed during this time. During the Depression, California could not allocate any more money to finish the most difficult portions of the trail. However, the National Park Service and the Forest Service worked together to complete one of these portions in 1932. Finally, the Forest Service completed the last portion in 1938.

Impact   A major trail through some of the most beautiful portions of the Sierra Nevada was developed by the National Park Service and the Forest Service to be enjoyed by many persons. Those interested need only to obtain a permit from the National Forest Service to use the trail.

Robert L. Cullers

Further Reading

Roth, Hal. *Pathway in the Sky.* Berkeley, Calif.: Howell-North Books, 1965.

Wink, Elizabeth, and Kathy Morey. *John Muir Trail.* Berkeley, Calif.: Wilderness Press, 2007.

Witt, Greg. *Ultimate Adventures.* New York: Rough Guides, 2008.

See also   Adams, Ansel; National parks; Natural resources; Wilderness Society.

■ Johnson, Robert

Identification   American musician
Born   May 8, 1911; Hazlehurst, Mississippi
Died   August 16, 1938; Greenwood, Mississippi

A renowned blues musician in the delta region of Mississippi during the 1930's, Johnson crafted a unique performance style and recorded a number of original compositions that influenced his contemporaries and subsequent generations, exerting a lasting impact upon Western popular music.

Robert Johnson was an aspiring blues musician by his late teens but soon developed a reputation in the bourgeoning delta-blues community as an inept performer. When a brief attempt at a stable domestic life ended when his wife died during childbirth, Johnson adopted the transient life of a bluesman, at one point disappearing for several months and returning with a vastly improved musical proficiency that led many of his peers to allege that he had made a pact with the devil—an allegation that Johnson did little to discourage.

Accompanying himself on acoustic guitar, Johnson amassed a body of original songs that were dark and complex even by delta-blues standards. In addition to the themes of loneliness, restlessness, and romantic betrayal common to blues music, his lyrics often incorporated allusions to alcoholism, depression, sexual inadequacy, and spiritual damnation. During two recording sessions conducted in 1936 and 1937, Johnson recorded a total of twenty-nine original songs, twelve of which were released during the 1930's.

During his lifetime Johnson remained an obscure figure who was little known outside the African American communities of the Mississippi Delta. By the time Columbia Records president John Hammond sought Johnson to perform at his 1938 "Spirituals to Swing" concert showcasing African American music, Johnson had died, the victim of an apparent poisoning at the age of twenty-seven.

Impact   The life and music of Johnson exerted an immediate impact upon American blues music and a lasting impact upon Western popular music. Johnson is considered a transitional figure in the progression of American blues from regional folk music to a national institution. The driving rhythms and intricate lead patterns present in his music helped shape the urban-blues, rhythm-and-blues, and rock-and-roll genres that dominated popular music in the postwar era, and his compelling legend inspired generations of musicians and music enthusiasts.

Michael H. Burchett

Further Reading

Graves, Tom. *Crossroads: The Life and Afterlife of Blues Legend Robert Johnson.* Spokane, Wash.: Demers Books, 2008.

Palmer, Robert. *Deep Blues.* New York: Macmillan, 1982.

Ward, Elijah. *Escaping the Delta: Robert Johnson and the Invention of the Blues.* New York: Amistad, 2004.

See also   African Americans; Music: Popular; Recording industry.

■ *Johnson v. Zerbst*

The Case   U.S. Supreme Court ruling on the Sixth Amendment right to counsel in federal criminal proceedings
Date   Decided on May 23, 1938

This case's importance rests on a proposition that was implied, rather than expressly stated, by this ruling: The Sixth Amendment right to counsel compels the appointment of counsel for indigent defendants facing criminal charges in federal court.

The Sixth Amendment provides that "in all criminal prosecutions, the accused shall enjoy the right . . . to have the assistance of counsel for his defense." This clearly allowed people facing criminal charges to hire an attorney. *Johnson v. Zerbst* was an important case in a series of rulings addressing how the law applied to indigent people who could not afford to hire attorneys. The series began six years earlier, when the Court ruled in the famous "Scottsboro Boys" case (*Alabama v. Powell*, 1932) that due process required the appointment of counsel in capital cases.

In *Johnson v. Zerbst*, petitioner John A. Johnson was convicted at trial of passing counterfeit bills and was sentenced to the penitentiary. Johnson sought to overturn his conviction, complaining that he did not

> ## The Sixth Amendment Right to Counsel
>
> *Below is an excerpt from the U.S. Supreme Court's ruling in* Johnson v. Zerbst.
>
> The Sixth Amendment guarantees that, "In all criminal prosecutions, the accused shall enjoy the right . . . to have the Assistance of Counsel for his defence." This is one of the safeguards of the Sixth Amendment deemed necessary to insure fundamental human rights of life and liberty. Omitted from the Constitution as originally adopted, provisions of this and other Amendments were submitted by the first Congress convened under that Constitution as essential barriers against arbitrary or unjust deprivation of human rights. The Sixth Amendment stands as a constant admonition that, if the constitutional safeguards it provides be lost, justice will not "still be done."

have a lawyer at his trial. The U.S. Supreme Court ruled for Johnson. The court was required to go no further to grant Johnson relief, and it did not explicitly address the issue of appointed counsel.

However, just four years later, when considering a related issue in *Betts v. Brady* (1942), the U.S. Supreme Court articulated its ruling in *Johnson v. Zerbst* as requiring "appointment of counsel in all [federal] cases where a defendant is unable to procure the services of an attorney, and where the right has not been intentionally and competently waived." This is the ruling for which *Johnson v. Zerbst* stands.

Impact   *Johnson v. Zerbst* served as the foundation for a string of cases that expanded the right to appointed counsel. The famous case of *Gideon v. Wainwright* (1963) granted the right to appointed counsel in all state felony matters. Later, this right was extended to misdemeanor cases and juvenile proceedings.

Kimberlee Candela

Further Reading

Taylor, John B. *Right to Counsel and Privilege Against Self-Incrimination: Rights and Liberties Under the Law.* Santa Barbara, Calif.: ABC-CLIO, 2004.

Tomkovicz, James L. *The Right to the Assistance of*

Counsel: A Reference Guide to the United States Constitution. Santa Barbara, Calif.: Greenwood Press, 2002.

See also   Black, Hugo L.; Civil rights and liberties in the United States; Scottsboro trials; Supreme Court, U.S.

■ Joliet prison riot

The Event   Illinois prison riot in which inmates hoped to rally outside support for institutional reforms
Date   March 14, 1931
Place   Joliet, Illinois

This was the seventh major prison riot in the United States in two years. The riot highlighted the often dehumanizing conditions present in the U.S. prison system of the time and gave the issue of prisoners' rights a level of legitimacy. Prisoners expressed grievances over a new parole law and prison administration.

Joliet prison sits about thirty miles outside Chicago, Illinois. Unrest leading to the riot reflected inmate displeasure with a 1927 state law that the state's parole board interpreted to mean that many inmates would not be eligible for "good time" or an early parole hearing until they had served at least ten years. Other issues leading to the riot were a lack of inmate jobs in the aftermath of the Depression, overcrowding (built for 800, Joliet housed 1,800 men), and the killing of three prisoners attempting to escape on February 22, 1931. The guards had learned that the three inmates intended to escape. Instead of stopping the escape, the guards let the three inmates get far enough to shoot them. The inmates perceived the act as brutal and avoidable. They referred to the killings as "The Washington Birthday Massacre." After the massacre, prison chaplain Reverend George Whitmeyer resigned. A former convict himself, he had alerted the guards about the planned escape, not expecting that the men would be killed.

Three weeks after the attempted escape, the rioting began at the noon mealtime. Inmates began throwing objects. Captain D. A. Davenport, one of the guards involved in a previous shooting, suffered a broken arm after a prisoner threw a pot at him. One rioter, twenty-three-year-old Albert Yarbeck, was shot to death. Another three, twenty-four-year-

old George Jakowanis, twenty-year-old Joseph Kwoka, and forty-one-year-old Mike Casselli, were wounded. With the exception of Casselli, the victims were shot by Frank Cutchin as they assaulted Davenport. Led by Warden Henry Hill, forty guards attempted to quell the outbursts with gunfire, gas bombs, and fire. On March 18, the inmates at neighboring Stateville, the newer prison nearby, had a related, larger, and more dangerous riot that involved efforts to set that prison ablaze.

Impact   The riot was an effort to garner outside sympathy, especially for ill and dying inmates who had been denied parole. It raised the profile of prisoners' rights.

Camille Gibson

Further Reading
Erickson, Gladys A. *Warden Ragen of Joliet.* New York: E. P. Dutton, 1957.
Useem, Bert, and Peter Kimball. *States of Siege: U.S. Prison Riots, 1971-1986.* New York: Oxford University Press, 1989.

See also   Alcatraz Federal Penitentiary; Great Depression in the United States; Race riots.

■ *Joy of Cooking, The*

Identification   American cookbook
Author   Irma S. Rombauer
Date   Self-published in 1931; published commercially in 1936

The Joy of Cooking *introduced home cooking to a generation of housewives who had no formal training and little time to devote to meal preparation. Its intimate style and innovative recipe format helped make it one of the best-selling cookbooks of all time.*

Irma S. Rombauer, from a prominent German American family, was raised in St. Louis and briefly in Germany while her father served as a diplomat. Finding herself in financial difficulties after the death of her husband, Edgar R. Rombauer, she wrote a cookbook to earn money.

Rombauer was not known as a particularly good cook, but she was intelligent, energetic, and widely experienced as a host. She had a broad network of social contacts. From these contacts and her family she collected and tested twelve hundred recipes, publishing them at the end of 1931 as *The Joy of Cooking: A Compilation of Reliable Recipes with an Occasional Culinary Chat*. This edition was published at her own expense and contained 395 pages of recipes and advice on table settings, entertaining, and handling materials, with silhouette illustrations contributed by her daughter Marion Rombauer Becker. The three thousand copies sold out in about six months.

Encouraged, Rombauer sought a commercial publisher. Bobbs-Merrill Company published an expanded edition in 1936. It too was a success, selling more than fifty-two thousand copies before the second edition came out in 1943. The cookbook satisfied a growing need among middle-class housewives: with little or no training and no longer capable of hiring cooks during the Great Depression, they looked for help in cookbooks. Rombauer's biographer, Anne Mendelson, argues that the amalgam of recipes based on easily attainable ingredients, chatty advice, and forthright opinion in *The Joy of Cooking* was ideal for these readers. Moreover, Rombauer's book had an innovative, readable format for recipes that introduced ingredients step-by-step with the cooking instructions.

Impact   *The Joy of Cooking* came out in four editions during Rombauer's lifetime, and her daughter, who became coauthor in 1953, produced another. Together, they accounted for millions of sales, making it the most prominent American cookbook and the touchstone for household cooks well into the 1960's.

Roger Smith

Further Reading

Mendelson, Anne. *Stand Facing the Stove: The Story of the Women Who Gave America "The Joy of Cooking."* New York: Henry Holt, 1996.

Mindlin, Alex. "The Thirties Were Lean, Even the Recipes." *The New York Times*, February 16, 2009, p. 3.

Rombauer, Irma S., Marion Rombauer Becker, and Ethan Becker. *The Joy of Cooking: Seventy-fifth Anniversary Edition*. New York: Charles Scribner's Sons, 2006.

See also   Agriculture in the United States; Breadlines and soup kitchens; Food processing; Frozen-food marketing; Home furnishings; Instant coffee; Refrigerators; Supermarkets.

K

■ Karloff, Boris

Identification   British-born American film actor
Born   November 23, 1887; London, England
Died   February 2, 1969; Middlehurst, West Sussex,
England

One of the most successful film actors of the 1930's, Karloff became a star after appearing as the monster in James Whale's film adaptation of Frankenstein *(1931). He became identified with horror films and was the most famous horror actor of his time.*

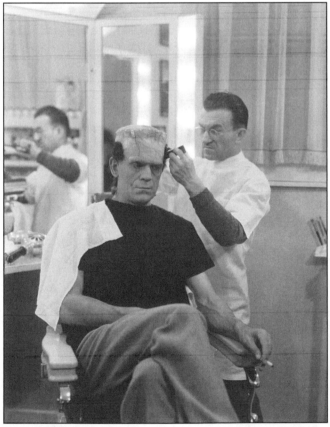

Makeup artist Jack Pierce (right) transforming actor Boris Karloff into the creature for the film Bride of Frankenstein. *(Hulton Archive/ Getty Images)*

Born William Henry Pratt, Boris Karloff began the decade as a relatively anonymous character actor in films such as Howard Hawks's *The Criminal Code* (1931). However, after the success of *Frankenstein*, he became the most celebrated star of horror films since Lon Chaney in the silent era. He followed his success in *Frankenstein* with another horror film from Universal Studios, *The Mummy* (1932), and he also returned to play the Frankenstein monster in two sequels, *Bride of Frankenstein* (1935) and *Son of Frankenstein* (1939). He also teamed up with his greatest rival in the horror genre, Bela Lugosi from Universal's *Dracula* (1931), in several horror films, including *The Black Cat* (1934) and *The Raven* (1935), both somewhat misleadingly named for works by Edgar Allan Poe.

Karloff struggled to maintain respect as an actor in some non-horror films, including *Scarface* (1932), *The Old Dark House* (1932), *The Tower of London* (1939), and, most significantly, John Ford's *The Lost Patrol* (1934). Regardless of the quality of the material, Karloff maintained a reputation for his gentle nature and constant professionalism.

Impact   Karloff became the face and voice of horror in popular culture. His appearance in the *Frankenstein* makeup remains iconic and has been used in sequels, toys, and collectibles. His appearance has also been spoofed in such formats as the 1960's television sitcom *The Munsters* and General Mills' breakfast cereal Frankenberry. One frightening character in the play *Arsenic and Old Lace* (1939) was described as looking like Karloff, and his voice is parodied in the Halloween-themed novelty song "The Monster Mash," performed by Bobby "Boris" Pickett. Karloff used his iconic status late in his life as host of the television horror anthology *Thriller* and in the Peter Bogdanovich film *Targets* (1968), where he plays an aging horror star.

Thomas Gregory Carpenter

Further Reading

Mank, Gregory William. *Bela Lugosi and Boris Karloff: The Expanded Story of a Haunting Collaboration.* Jefferson, N.C.: McFarland, 2009.

Nollen, Scott Allen. *Boris Karloff: A Gentleman's Life.* Baltimore: Midnight Marquee Press, 2005.

See also   Charlie Chan films; *Dracula*; Drive-in theaters; Film; Ford, John; *Frankenstein* films; Gangster films; Horror films; Motion Picture Production Code.

■ Kaufman, George S., and Moss Hart

Identification   American playwriting team

George S. Kaufman

Born   November 16, 1889; Pittsburgh, Pennsylvania

Died   June 2, 1961; New York, New York

Moss Hart

Born   October 24, 1904; Bronx, New York

Died   December 20, 1961; Palm Springs, California

The works written by Hart and Kaufman brought a comic voice to Broadway during the depths of the Great Depression. Some of their most popular plays ran for two years and are considered among the most successful of the decade.

For a decade, George S. Kaufman and Moss Hart were among the most popular of Broadway playwrights. Beginning in 1930 with their first collaboration, the long-running *Once in a Lifetime*, the men produced six plays, one of which garnered a Pulitzer Prize, and two books for musicals, including *I'd Rather Be Right* (1937). Kaufman had previously worked for Washington, D.C., and New York newspapers, including *The New York Times*, for which he became a theater news reporter and drama editor. When he began writing for the stage about 1917, he preferred collaborating with other playwrights, among them established writers such as Marc Connelly (*Dulcy*, 1921; *Merton of the Movies*, 1922), Edna Ferber (*The Royal Family*, 1927), Ring Lardner, and Alexander Woollcott. Reportedly, he liked writing dialogue but largely left plot development to his collaborators. He also produced a small number of solo plays during the 1920's and cowrote the Pulitzer Prize-winning, Depression-era musical *Of Thee I Sing*

(1931). His contemporaries considered him one of the great wits of that era.

Moss Hart, fifteen years younger than his collaborator, became enamored of the theater in childhood and began writing and directing amateur theatricals for summer camps, the Catskill Mountains borscht circuit, and little theater groups. After a disastrous Broadway debut in the early 1920's and a series of unproduced works, he wrote a play on speculation that attracted the interest of Kaufman, with whom he revised it. The result was *Once in a Lifetime*, a satire about Hollywood's transition to talking pictures. Kaufman awarded the rubric of "Forked Lightning" to his ambitious and enthusiastic collaborator, and despite their differences in working styles, they collaborated compatibly. In temperament they were opposite: The laconic and acerbic Kaufman was an inveterate womanizer with a severe germ phobia, and the reportedly closeted bisexual Hart was an exuberant cigar-smoking extrovert.

Continuing Collaboration   The team's second play was *Merrily We Roll Along* (1934), which was somewhat experimental in that the plotline ran chronologically backward from the first act. Although it was not a ringing success, it preceded a play that was, the celebrated Pulitzer Prize-winning farce *You Can't Take It with You* (1936). Made into a 1938 film, it won Oscars for best picture and best director. During the 1930's, the pair also worked separately; Kaufman and other collaborators produced such distinguished works as *Dinner at Eight* (1932) and *Stage Door* (1936). Hart worked on the books of several musicals with top composers such as Irving Berlin, Richard Rodgers and Lorenz Hart, and Cole Porter. The team reunited for another major hit in 1939, *The Man Who Came to Dinner*, supposedly based on the foibles of their friend Woollcott. They had also cowritten the less successful *The Fabulous Invalid* (1938). Their final collaboration came in 1940 with *George Washington Slept Here*. Apparently Hart wished to strike out on his own to prove his success was not solely due to his partnership with Kaufman.

Following their professional breakup, each continued to do distinguished theater work. Hart contributed the "psychological" musical *Lady in the Dark* (1941). As the decades went on, some of his work took on a darker tone, as in the plays *Christopher Blake* (1946) and *The Climate of Eden* (1952). He also wrote several screenplays, among them the Oscar-winning

Gentlemen's Agreement (1947) and the 1954 version of *A Star Is Born*. Both also became noted directors of other people's work. Kaufman was such a significant theater figure that he had a play on Broadway, either as a writer or a director, every season from 1921 to 1958. He was also a noted play "doctor." The accomplishments of Kaufman and Hart were great, alone or with others, but they never quite matched the sublime heights of their collaboration during the 1930's. Hart was posthumously elected to the Theater Hall of Fame in 1972.

Impact The teaming of Kaufman and Hart was one of the most successful in Broadway history, and several of their plays were made into successful films. Their major plays continue to receive numerous amateur and professional revivals. They contained larger-than-life characters, such as the Sycamore family of *You Can't Take It with You* and Sheridan Whiteside in *The Man Who Came to Dinner*. Individually, each contributed to the success of many other Broadway productions.

Roy Liebman

Further Reading

Brown, Jared. *Moss Hart, a Prince of the Theatre: A Biography in Three Acts*. New York: Backstage, 2006. Includes Hart's diary and letters and is considered one of the most reliable sources of information about Hart. Concentrates mainly on his artistic development and professional accomplishments.

Goldstein, Malcolm. *George S. Kaufman: His Life, His Theater*. New York: Oxford University Press, 1979. A competent biography that adds little information to those written by Teichmann and Meredith.

Hart, Moss. *Act One: An Autobiography*. New York: Random House, 1959. Considered one of the greatest theatrical autobiographies ever written, this wildly successful memoir about Hart's early life contains some "enhancements" to his already genuinely colorful life story.

Kaufman, George S. *Kaufman and Co.: Broadway Comedies*. New York: Library of America, 2004. Contains several of Kaufman's most popular plays or books of musicals, including the most successful of those he cowrote with Hart.

Meredith, Scott. *George S. Kaufman and His Friends*. Garden City, N.Y.: Doubleday, 1974. A lengthy biography of more than seven hundred pages.

Teichmann, Howard. *George S. Kaufman: An Intimate Portrait*. New York: Atheneum, 1972. A playwright himself, Teichmann provides an excellent biography, devoting each chapter to a separate facet of Kaufman's life: playwright, wit, family man, and lover.

See also Astor, Mary; Broadway musicals; *I'd Rather Be Right*; *Man Who Came to Dinner, The*; *Since Yesterday*; *You Can't Take It with You*.

■ Kelly, Machine Gun

Identification Notorious criminal
Born July 18, 1897; Memphis, Tennessee
Died July 17, 1954; Fort Leavenworth, Kansas
Also known as George Barnes

A criminal who became synonymous with his weapon of choice, a Thompson submachine gun, Kelly was notorious for kidnapping a wealthy oil tycoon.

Machine Gun Kelly was born George Barnes in Memphis, Tennessee, into a middle-class family. Little is known about Kelly's early life. Federal Bureau of Investigation (FBI) director J. Edgar Hoover reportedly described Kelly as a small-time crook who

Machine Gun Kelly.

had gained notoriety through the influence of his wife. Kathryn Kelly bought her husband his first machine gun, trained him to use it, and gave him his infamous nickname. She also worked to build his reputation by exaggerating his criminal prowess and might have planned a series of bank robberies that he committed. Kelly was reputed to be such a good marksman that he could write his name in bullets with the Thompson submachine gun.

On June 22, 1933, Kelly and an accomplice broke into the Tulsa home of Charles Urschel, a wealthy Oklahoma oilman, and kidnapped him. They demanded a ransom of $200,000. The FBI followed the marked ransom money to Memphis, Tennessee, where they arrested Kelly and his wife on September 26. When Kelly saw the law-enforcement officials, he was reported to have shouted, "Don't shoot, G-men," thus coining a popular slang term for federal agents, or "government men." However, many sources now attribute the phrase to Kathryn, not Kelly. Kelly and Kathryn were convicted on October 12, 1933, and sentenced to life imprisonment. He spent seventeen years at Alcatraz and died at Leavenworth Federal Prison in Kansas in 1954.

Impact The mystery surrounding Kelly's background enabled the legend of Machine Gun Kelly to grow. After he was imprisoned, his reputation as a model prisoner added weight to the suspicions that Kathryn had been the mastermind behind his hardened-criminal persona.

Gerald P. Fisher

Further Reading

Block, Lawrence. "Machine Gun Kelly." In *Gangsters, Swindlers, Killers, and Thieves: The Lives and Crimes of Fifty American Villains.* New York: Oxford University Press, 2004.

Burrough, Bryan. *Public Enemies: America's Greatest Crime Wave and the Birth of the FBI, 1933-34.* New York: Penguin Press, 2004.

Hamilton, Stanley. *Machine Gun Kelly's Last Stand.* Lawrence: University Press of Kansas, 2003.

Toland, John. *The Dillinger Days.* New York: Da Capo Press, 1995

See also Alcatraz Federal Penitentiary; Barker Gang; Barrow, Clyde, and Bonnie Parker; Capone, Al; Crimes and scandals; Floyd, Pretty Boy; Ness, Eliot; Nitti, Frank; Organized crime; Prohibition repeal.

■ King, William Lyon Mackenzie

Identification Canadian prime minister, 1921-1926, 1926-1930, and 1935-1948

Born December 17, 1874; Berlin (now Kitchener), Ontario, Canada

Died July 22, 1950; Kingsmere, Quebec, Canada

King began his third term as prime minister in 1935, and during the next five years, he supported policies that expanded the government's role in society. Between 1936 and 1938, he encouraged appeasement toward Nazi Germany, but in 1939, he was the leading force behind Canada's declaration of war.

The country's most prominent political leader for one-quarter of a century, William Lyon Mackenzie King acquired his name from his maternal grandfather, William Lyon Mackenzie, a Toronto mayor and leader of the 1837 Upper Canada Rebellion. Raised in a wealthy family, the young King was called "Rex" (a play on the Latin for "king" and the popular dog's name) because of his ambition and quick temper. After earning six university degrees, including a law degree and a Harvard doctorate, he held positions as a lawyer, a journalist, a university professor, and a public administrator. An activist member of the Liberal Party, he was first elected to parliament in 1908, and he served as minister of labor from 1908 until defeated in the election of 1911. He then worked as a consultant on labor-management relations for the Rockefeller Foundation. His book *Industry and Humanity: A Study in the Principles Underlying Industrial Reconstruction* (1918) advocated an activist role for government and outlined many of the liberal domestic policies that he pursued for the following thirty years.

In 1919, the Liberal Party selected King as its leader, and two years later, when the Liberals won a plurality of seats in the House of Commons, he became prime minister. The lack of a Liberal majority during King's first term required him to rely on a shaky coalition between the urban-based Liberals and the prairie-based Progressive Party. Because the parties disagreed about tariffs and other issues, King often had to make compromises that he found distasteful. Despite a more stable alliance between the Liberals and Progressive-Conservatives during his term from 1926 to 1930, King remained politically cautious. Probably his most significant legislative accomplishment was the enactment of Canada's first old-age pension act in 1927, which was jointly financed by the federal government and the provinces.

Domestic Policies During the 1930's When the Depression began in 1929, King underestimated its severity, and he emphasized fiscal restraint, pursuing policies that were similar to those of U.S. president Herbert Hoover. One of King's most notable acts was the appointment of the first female member to the Senate in 1930. He was a strong proponent of Canadian sovereignty and independence from Great Britain, and he exercised considerable influence in formulating the principles in the Statute of Westminster of 1931, which gave Canada and other Dominions almost complete autonomy in external relations. Although King was in the opposition when the British parliament enacted the statute, he had earlier made a significant contribution to its provisions in the Imperial Conference of 1926.

During the election of 1930, King stumbled badly when he carelessly stated that he "would not give a five-cent piece" to provincial governments under Tory leadership. The Conservative Party won the election, and Richard Bedford Bennett took over as prime minister. King later viewed defeat in 1930 as a fortunate event, because it attached the label "party of Depression" to the Conservatives. Continuing in parliament as the opposition leader, King skillfully kept the Liberal Party united. Although King did not advocate programs that were different from those of the Conservative Party, he strongly attacked the Conservatives for the growth in unemployment and the deficit. During the election of 1935, the Liberals campaigned on the slogan "King or Chaos," and the voters returned them to power with a comfortable majority.

King's third term as prime minister, from 1935 to 1948, turned out to be one of the most important periods in Canadian history. Despite the continuing hardships of the Depression, King never favored massive employment programs such as those of the New Deal in the United States, and he generally left relief to provincial and lo-

cal governments. One significant reform was enactment of the National Housing Act of 1938. Despite an official policy of a balanced budget, some members of the National Employment Commission were influenced by Keynesian economics, and the budget of 1938 included a small deficit with the goal of stimulating economic growth. Under King's leadership, the parliament established the Canadian Broadcasting Corporation in 1936, the Trans-Canada Airlines (later named Air Canada) in 1937, and the National Film Board of Canada in 1939. The parliament further extended governmental control of the economy when it changed the Bank of Canada from a private corporation into a crown corporation in 1938.

King's Foreign Policy, 1935-1939 A strong proponent of national autonomy, King affirmed time and

William Lyon Mackenzie King, pictured here with his dog, began serving his second stint as the prime minister in 1935. (©Bettmann/CORBIS)

again that the Canadian parliament would decide foreign policy based entirely on Canada's interests. He was slow to recognize the threat posed by Nazi aggression. In 1936, when Adolf Hitler ordered the remilitarization of the Rhineland, King informed the British government that Canada would remain neutral in the event of war. Visiting Germany in 1937, he became the only North American head of state to have a meeting with Hitler. In his journal, King wrote that the führer "truly loves his fellow-men" and that, despite his "cruelty" and "oppression of Jews," he would "rank some day with Joan of Arc among the deliverers of his people." In 1938, during the tense Czechoslovakian crisis that culminated in the Munich Agreement, King strongly supported a policy of appeasement toward Germany, and he informed the British government that if the controversy resulted in war, Canada would remain neutral. In his diary, however, he wrote that if Britain went to war, Canada should provide Britain with "every assistance possible," while "carefully defining in what ways and how far she should participate."

King emphasized the importance of good relations with the United States, and he negotiated trade agreements in 1935 and 1939 that bound the two economies more closely together. King and President Franklin D. Roosevelt were such close friends that he wrote in his diary that "when they met together, they were almost as one." In August, 1938, when Roosevelt publicly declared that the United States would assume the responsibility for protecting the Western Hemisphere, King wrote in his diary that he would have to be careful to show appreciation for the "generous attitude by the president," but at the same time not cause Anglophile Canadians to fear a lack of solidarity with the British Commonwealth.

Like most other countries, Canada under King's leadership refused to increase the number of Jewish immigrants fleeing Nazi persecution. In June, 1939, the Canadian government followed the example of the United States and Cuba in refusing admittance of nine hundred Jewish refugees sailing on the passenger ship *St. Louis.*

By early 1939, King recognized that the policy of appeasement was not moderating Hitler's territorial ambitions. In a speech to parliament on January 16, he quoted an earlier prime minister, Sir Wilfrid Laurier: "If England is at war, we are at war, and liable to attack." By March 15, when Hitler took control of Czechoslovakia, King had accepted the idea that Canada would not be able to maintain neutrality in the event of war, but he was also determined to assert the country's autonomy from Britain. On March 30, he neutralized the opposition to war from French Canadians with a pledge of nonconscription, thereby helping the Liberals to win a provincial election in Quebec. A week before Germany's invasion of Poland, King's cabinet, with his encouragement, agreed that Canada would have to follow Britain's lead in opposing Hitler. On September 8, when King explained the necessity for war to the House of Commons, only a few members expressed disagreement. King then signed a proclamation of war, and as soon as Britain's king, King George VI, signed the proclamation on September 10, Canada officially was at war with Germany.

Under King's cautious guidance, the cabinet had to decide how the country would support Britain and France. On September 18, the cabinet approved a proposal for military spending that increased the budget by almost 50 percent, and it also agreed to dispatch one division of troops overseas as soon as possible, preparing a second division for possible dispatch later. On December 10, the First Canadian Infantry Division sailed for the United Kingdom, and on December 17, following intense negotiations, King announced the British Commonwealth Air Training Plan (BCATP), a mammoth program that would bring thousands of persons from Commonwealth countries to Canada for training as pilots and navigators.

Impact King lacked charisma and had a number of peculiar behaviors, such as communicating with spirits in séances. However, he was also a man who possessed gravitas and inspired confidence. Many historians and political scientists rank him as the most outstanding prime minister in Canadian history, and almost all scholars give him high marks for maintaining national unity throughout the difficult years of World War II, particularly during the 1944 crisis over the controversial issue of conscription. Remaining in office until 1948, King continued to face a number of difficult challenges, and he made important contributions to several of the century's momentous developments, including the defeat of the Axis Powers, the founding of the United Nations, and the beginning of the Cold War.

Thomas Tandy Lewis

Further Reading

Betcherman, Lita-Rose. *Ernest Lapointe: Mackenzie King's Great Quebec Lieutenant.* Toronto: University of Toronto Press, 2002. Study of the French Canadian politician who was the most important and influential member of King's cabinet.

Esberey, Joy E. *Knight of the Holy Spirit: A Study of William Lyon Mackenzie King.* Toronto: University of Toronto Press, 1980. Psychological interpretations of both his public and private lives, emphasizing his séances and other eccentricities.

Goodall, Lian. *William Lyon Mackenzie King: Dreams and Shadows.* Montreal: XYZ, 2003. Short account that provides an introduction to King's life and career.

Granatstein, J. L. *Mackenzie King: His Life and World.* Toronto: McGraw-Hill, 1977. A detailed account by a scholar who has written a number of respected works about King and the period.

Hutchinson, Burce. *The Incredible Canadian: A Candid Portrait of Mackenzie King—His Works, His Times and His Nation.* New York: Longmans, Green, 1952. Despite its age, this book is valuable and dependable, especially for general readers.

Pickersgill, J. W., and D. F. Foster, eds. *The Mackenzie King Record.* 4 vols. Toronto: University of Toronto Press, 1960-1970. Contains large portions of King's diary, which is recognized as one of the most important primary sources of Canadian history.

Reynolds, Louise. *Mackenzie King: Friends and Lovers.* Victoria, B.C.: Trafford, 2005. Concentrates on the private life and possible romances of an enigmatic man.

Stacey, C. P. *1921-1948—The Mackenzie King Era.* Vol. 2 in *Canada and the Age of Conflict.* Toronto: University of Toronto Press, 1981. Contains valuable information, although the work is sometimes verbose and disorganized.

See also   Bennett, Richard Bedford; Canada and Great Britain; Elections, Canadian; Foreign policy of Canada; George VI's North American visit; World War II and Canada.

■ *King Kong*

Identification   Horror film about the discovery of a gigantic ape that is taken to New York and exhibited

Directors   Merian C. Cooper and Ernest B. Schoedsack

Date   Released in 1933

One of the great horror films of the 1930's, King Kong *became the archetype for an entire film genre of "monster movies" and provided a significant contribution to modern mythology by adding to the lexicon of universally recognizable fictional characters.*

King Kong tells a simple story about an ambitious American film director, Carl Denham (Robert Armstrong), who charters a tramp steamer to carry his film crew to an uncharted island in the South Seas where he hopes to find something spectacular to film. Before sailing from New York, Denham invites a beautiful, down-on-her-luck woman, Ann Darrow (Fay Wray), to join his expedition to play the female lead in his film, promising her adventure and thrills. The expedition eventually reaches Skull Island, where its members find a village whose primitive residents are preparing an elaborate ritual to propitiate an unseen creature on the other side of an ancient and gigantic wall. At night, the islanders kidnap Darrow from aboard the anchored steamer and tie her to an altar on the other side of their protective wall.

When Denham's people see Darrow being carried away by Kong—an unimaginably large gorilla—Denham sends a rescue party to go after her. Meanwhile, he organizes preparations for Kong's anticipated return. As Kong carries Darrow to his mountain aerie, it becomes clear that he is charmed by her beauty and is determined to protect, not harm, her. Eventually, most members of Darrow's rescue party are killed, but Darrow is rescued and returned safely. When Kong reaches the village, Denham's people use gas bombs to capture him.

The film then jumps to New York City, where Denham is about to present King Kong as the "Eighth Wonder of the World" to a paying audience in a Broadway theater. Kong's unveiling causes a sensation, and the audience's fright is soon fully justified. When Kong fears that Darrow is being threatened by news photographers' popping flashbulbs, he breaks loose from his chains and goes on a rampage outside the theater. Fortuitously, he sees Darrow through a hotel room window while climbing a building and grabs her. He then carries her to the top of the Empire State Building—which is visually reminiscent of his own island mountaintop—and futilely fights off a squadron of fighter planes peppering him with machine-gun fire. Finally, he falls to his death. The film ends with Denham examining Kong's dead body. When he hears someone say that Kong was killed by the planes, he retorts, "It was beauty killed the beast."

The Production Conceived by Merian C. Cooper and codirected by Cooper and Ernest B. Schoedsack, *King Kong* was to have been scripted by the English thriller writer Edgar Wallace, but he was in-

King Kong terrorizing the human inhabitants of the island they share with him in the 1933 film. (The Granger Collection, New York)

capacitated by what eventually proved to be a fatal illness, and the job was done by James A. Creelman and Ruth Rose, although Delos W. Lovelace wrote the novel that was published in association with the film's release.

The film had a larger budget than most RKO pictures because of its extensive innovative use of the stop-motion animation techniques designed by Willis H. O'Brien and previously used in the 1925 film *The Lost World*. Later refined by O'Brien's protégé Ray Harryhausen, these techniques came into their own in *King Kong* and subsequently became the backbone of a whole genre of "monster movies," which became a staple of "drive-in" films.

The story told by *King Kong* became legendary. Its unique fascination lies in its fairy-tale element. Its exaggeration of the story of "Beauty and the Beast" is not only taken to a grotesque extreme but also given a remarkable tragic flourish in the iconic final scene, in which the hapless Kong stands atop the Empire State Building, fighting a battle against a squadron of tiny fighter aircraft that is just as inevitably hopeless as his bizarre passion for his leading lady. *King Kong* made Wray, incessantly screaming and swooning under the threat of brute masculinity writ large, a household name, although it ruined her reputation as an actor. None of the sequels to or remakes of *King Kong*, in spite of their use of more advanced special effects, had any chance of matching the naive grandeur of the original.

The Film in Its Time *King Kong* was a product of the Depression, not only in the trivial sense that it belonged to a surge of films intended to provide some solace to people caught up in that slow disaster, or merely in the straightforward sense in which Kong, the giant run amok, could be construed as a model of the disaster, but in the subtler sense in which the innocent Kong becomes a victim of callous modernity and buccaneering entrepreneurialism. When Cooper invited the audiences of 1933 to sympathize with Kong in the moment of his destruction, he was mobilizing the public's own self-pity, as people imagined themselves caught up and chewed up by the alien logic of the stock exchange collapse and all its effects.

Impact Since his creation in the 1933 film *King Kong*, Kong has never gone away, and he is likely to live on in the popular imagination for a long time to come, even if no more remakes and sequels are undertaken. The poignant aspects of his tragedy were sharply mirrored in the slew of Japanese monster films made after World War II, which featured several revamped apes and the most influential of Kong's clones, Godzilla, modeling the Japanese people's endeavors to come to terms with the atomic demolition of their aspirant empire. To Americans, Kong is perhaps more memorable than any of the giants of traditional folklore or any of the steel monsters of modern technology.

Brian Stableford

Further Reading

Bellin, Joshua David. *Framing Monsters: Fantasy Film and Social Alienation.* Carbondale: Southern Illinois University Press, 2005. Perceptive sociological study of the role of monster movies in society.

Bergman, Andrew. *We're in the Money: Depression America and Its Films.* New York: New York University Press, 1971. General overview of film and society in the 1930's, with brief but insightful discussions of monster movies, the Marx Brothers, women's roles in film, and other topics.

Erb, Cynthia Marie. *Tracking King Kong: A Hollywood Icon in World Culture.* 2d ed. Detroit: Wayne State University Press, 2009. Scholarly study of the surprisingly broad impact that *King Kong* has had throughout world cultures.

Jewell, Richard B. *The RKO Story.* New York: Crown, 1982. Oversized and filled with photographs, but good for reading as well as for browsing. Covers every film RKO produced year by year and includes useful facts about the costs of productions and the box-office receipts of notable successes, such as *King Kong*, and failures.

Morton, Ray. *King Kong: The History of a Movie Icon from Fay Wray to Peter Jackson.* New York: Applause, 2005. Well-illustrated history of the many sequels and remakes of *King Kong*, through Jackson's lavish 2005 homage to the original film.

See also *Dracula*; Drive-in theaters; Film; *Flash Gordon*; *Frankenstein* films; *Freaks*; Horror films; *Invisible Man, The*; Science fiction; Wray, Fay.

L

■ Labor Day hurricane

The Event   Powerful hurricane that devastated the Florida Keys

Date   August 29, 1935, through September 10, 1935

Place   Florida Keys

The Labor Day hurricane of 1935 was the most intense hurricane to have a U.S. landfall during the twentieth century. In addition to the loss of life and damage it caused in the Florida Keys, it destroyed the scenic Florida Overseas Railroad to Key West, which was the island's only connection with the mainland during the Great Depression.

The Labor Day hurricane originated as a weak tropical storm east of the Bahamas on August 29, 1935. As it approached the Florida Keys, it rapidly intensified to become a hurricane, striking the middle Florida Keys on Monday, September 2, 1935 (Labor Day). The storm destroyed all the weather instruments, but an analysis of the damage indicates the storm had sustained wind speeds of 185 miles per hour, placing it in Category 5 of the Saffir/Simpson Hurricane Scale. The barometric pressure of 892 millibars was the lowest barometric pressure measured in the North Atlantic until 1988.

In 1935, the Overseas Highway to Key West was under construction. This Civilian Conservation Corps (CCC) project was designed to put unemployed World War I veterans to work during the

Great Depression, more than 600 of whom were building bridges on Long Key and Lower Matecumbe Key as the storm approached. A ten-car rescue train

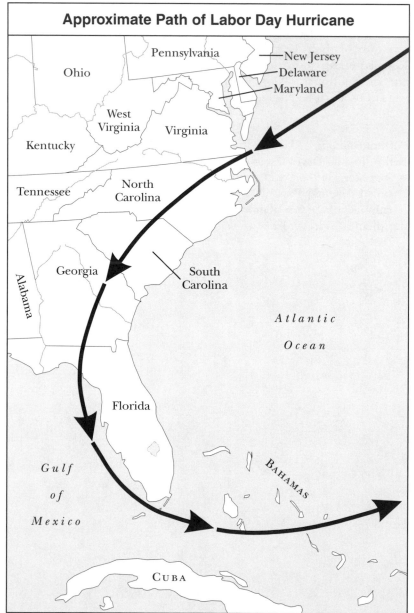

Approximate Path of Labor Day Hurricane

arrived from Miami just as the storm struck, but a twenty-foot-high storm surge washed it off the tracks. More than 425 veterans and residents died. The storm continued up the west coast of Florida, had a second landfall at Cedar Key, crossed the Florida peninsula, and re-entered the Atlantic, where it once more reached hurricane force before finally blowing itself out.

Impact The Labor Day hurricane of 1935 was one of only two Category 5 hurricanes to have a U.S. landfall during the twentieth century. The damage to the Middle Keys was severe, with hundreds of lives lost, almost total destruction of property, and nearly fifty miles of the Overseas Railroad washed out. The storm severed the only link to the mainland for Key West, which lay just ninety miles away. With the Great Depression under way, and tourists unable to get to a city that depended on them for its economic base, Key West faced high unemployment and food shortages for years.

Donald W. Lovejoy

Further Reading

Barnes, Jay. *Florida's Hurricane History.* 2d ed. Chapel Hill: University of North Carolina Press, 2007.

Fitzpatrick, Patrick. *Hurricanes: A Reference Handbook.* Santa Barbara, Calif.: ABC-Clio Press, 2006.

See also Dust Bowl; Great New England hurricane; Heat wave of 1931; Long Beach earthquake; Natural disasters; Ohio River flood.

■ Labor strikes

Definition Work stoppages and protests

The 1930's stand out as a period in which strikes not only increased in frequency and severity but also became more successful in achieving their objectives, one of which was to earn recognition for industrial unions. As a result, unions became increasingly acknowledged formally and were granted unprecedented legal recognition. However, many of the successful strike tactics were outlawed, leading to a decline in labor's militancy.

Strikes and work stoppages are a pervasive aspect of American labor history. The frequency of the use of the strike in all its varieties, but especially the sit-down strike, in which workers refuse to work or to leave their posts, has varied throughout American

history. Historically, strikes and other such actions were declared illegal, and individuals who engaged in labor activity did so outside the law. Nonetheless, in certain periods of history, as labor conditions became intolerable, workers took to the streets in protest.

The Great Depression, the New Deal, and Labor The onset of the Great Depression in 1929 was not an auspicious time for militant labor action. During the course of the 1920's, labor unions declined in number and influence. At the same time, the American Federation of Labor (AFL), the most important labor body at the time, was becoming more conservative in its tactics while remaining reluctant to organize the growing number of unskilled workers. During the early years of the Depression, therefore, there were relatively few strikes or other labor actions, although there were numerous protests to resist eviction from homes and farms.

All of that changed with the ascension of Franklin D. Roosevelt to the presidency and the passage of the National Industrial Recovery Act (NIRA) in 1933. The most controversial, and celebrated, element of the NIRA, section 7a, called for workers to have the right to organize and choose their own representatives for the purpose of collective bargaining, free from management interference and coercion, something that labor organizers quickly leaped upon to build and rebuild independent labor organizations. Many employers, however, refused to abide by, and in some cases actively fought, the provisions of 7a. In response, workers began an unprecedented wave of strikes. In 1933 alone, 1.2 million people went on strike, six times the number in 1930. The following year, 1934, the number of strikes jumped to two thousand and involved 15 million people. From 1933 to 1937, the number of strikes averaged 2,541 per year, reaching a peak of 4,740 in 1937.

Radical Politics and Early Strikes During the 1930's, communist and other leftist organizers played a prominent role in the labor activism and militancy of the period and aided in the creation of a militant alternative to the AFL, through the formation of the Trade Union Unity League (TUUL). The TUUL was instrumental in creating militant, industrially based labor organizations and led a number of strikes. Their radicalism alienated many, preventing more widespread support for the strikes they led, but the efforts of the TUUL and other leftist activists nonetheless played an important role in creating some of the major industrial unions and fomenting some of the most important strikes prior to the formation in 1935 of the Committee for Industrial Organization (CIO), which eventually became the Congress of Industrial Organizations.

Some of the first strikes took place in the Midwest, beginning with the strike against the Auto-Lite plant in Toledo, Ohio, which inspired and created the model for other labor actions that followed. The socialist-led Auto-Lite Strike, which began on February 23, 1934, started with a brief walkout that was ended through the intervention of the AFL and the use of the newly created National Labor Relations Board. On April 13, 1934, the workers regrouped, aided by the Unemployed Councils and other social-

ist activists, and struck again, forming picket lines in defiance of court injunctions. Even when the demonstrations were dispersed, by June 4, enough communal support for the strikers had been generated that the management gave in and signed an agreement, recognizing the union as the sole bargaining agent.

The first of the many actions inspired by the Auto-Lite strike was the Minneapolis Teamsters Strike of 1934. The strike began for two reasons: Workers felt they were forced to work too many hours, and the company had a history of cheating the miners of credit on the coal scales for what they had produced. The strike lasted three days and resulted in union recognition. However, when the manufacturers stalled on key issues during the first contract negotiation, a second strike erupted that lasted for a

Fights break out as police attempt to restrain the masses during the 1934 labor strike at the Electric Auto-Lite plant in Toledo, Ohio. (The Granger Collection, New York)

month. By this time, the strike had gained widespread communal support, which included a rally that swelled to twenty-five thousand people. On the East Coast, a strike wave among textile workers over poor working conditions and speedups began in Alabama in July, 1934, and soon approached the level of a general strike, shutting down production in twenty states and involving forty thousand people. President Roosevelt successfully authorized a mediation board, but the southern textile general strike was a clear indication of labor's growing militancy.

Meanwhile, on the West Coast, the longshoremen's strike began at the port of Los Angeles and grew into one of the largest general strikes in American history. At issue were not only the long hours and poor working conditions of the dockworkers but also the hiring system that placed all control in the hands of the management and left most longshoremen impoverished. The already-formed International Longshoremen's Association (ILA) began the strike on May 9, 1934, under the leadership of the Australian-born Harry Bridges, and within a couple of weeks, ten thousand workers in multiple West Coast cities had gone on strike. Soon, all the western ports except for Los Angeles were closed down. In July, workers succeeded in nearly shutting down the city of San Francisco in a four-day general strike. When shippers attempted to reopen the San Francisco ports, a battle known as "Bloody Thursday" ensued. Widespread public support for the strike led to eventual victory for the strikers, which led to vastly improved conditions and greater ILA control of the hiring process.

The Rise of the CIO and the Passage of the Wagner Act   These strikes and others that took place in 1934 not only achieved their immediate objectives but also inspired the growing number of semiskilled and unskilled workers in the increasingly mechanized heavy industries. They also inspired labor organizers such as John L. Lewis of the United Mine Workers, which increasingly challenged the AFL leadership's unwillingness to organize on an industrial rather than craft basis. When the leader of the carpenters' union publicly objected to Lewis's proposals for industrial organization at a November, 1935, meeting of the AFL leadership, Lewis punched him in the jaw and subsequently convened the Committee for Industrial Organization. When the AFL leadership tried to stamp out the CIO's effects, Lewis and his allies broke away from the AFL and transformed the committee into a alternate federation, the Congress of Industrial Organizations.

The formation of the CIO and the passage of the National Labor Relations Act, or the Wagner Act, of 1935, which for the first time granted the full right of organization, mutually reinforced the growth of industrial unionization. Full legal recognition of the right to organize, however, did not mean that employers were ready to recognize the newly organized unions, and these conditions led to an upsurge in strike activity, with sit-down strikes the tactic of choice. During 1936 and 1937, an unprecedented wave of sit-down strikes occurred, such as the 1936 strike against the Goodyear Tire and Rubber Company, which moved the United Rubber Workers from the AFL to the newly formed CIO.

The Great Flint Sit-Down Strike and Beyond   The most notable of these sit-down strikes was the 1937 United Auto Workers (UAW) strike that began at the Fisher Body plants in Flint, Michigan. The Flint sit-down strike, as it became known, stood out for not only its length of forty-one days but also its transformative effects on the UAW, the CIO, and the American labor movement. The strike began on December 28, 1936, as part of an attempt to prevent the auto companies from breaking the fledgling UAW by moving plant equipment to nonunionized locations. A group of workers of the Fisher Plant 1 began the sit-down in protest over a delayed meeting with the General Motors (GM) management. Two days later, many more workers at the Fisher Body Plants 1 and 2 joined the strike. From the beginning, strike leaders imposed strict discipline on the rank and file, forbidding alcohol and damage to property or equipment, ordering the continued maintenance of the plants and machines, and sending all the women workers away to prevent accusations of impropriety. The women, however, stayed involved through the formation of the Women's Emergency Brigade. In addition to bringing food and supplies and conveying messages, the women also coordinated protests, managed public relations, and helped defend the workers against the January 11, 1937, tear-gas attack on the plant that became known as the "Battle of Running Bulls."

This combination of self-imposed discipline and militancy won the strikers unprecedented public support and, combined with the presence of Michigan's progressive governor Frank L. Murphy, forestalled any state efforts to forcibly remove the strikers. Murphy instead chose to play both sides even as the strike spread to other automobile plants around the Midwest and President Roosevelt pointedly chose not to send the National Guard to break the strike. When GM workers attempted to take over other Fisher plants, however, and used careful ruses to evade both company guards and spies, Murphy attempted to force the strikers out by cutting off the power. In response, UAW leader Walter P. Reuther threatened to light bonfires in the plant to keep the workers warm in the Detroit-area winter. Finally, on February 11, 1937, the management agreed to bargain, and although the settlement was far from total, the symbolic victory for the UAW was incalculable.

Not all of the labor strikes of the 1930's achieved success, and occasionally some ended in tragedy. A key example was the 1937 "Little Steel strike" against a group of the smaller steel corporations in the Midwest, including Bethlehem Steel, Republic Steel, and the Youngstown Sheet and Tube Company that together were known as "Little Steel." In this case, the mill owners sought to break the strike through a combination of legal measures and force, including air-dropping food to the strikebreakers, when the strikers attempted to stop the supply trains. Then, on Memorial Day of 1937, the supporters of the Steelworkers Organizing Committee (SWOC) gathered near the SWOC headquarters for a rally. When they then attempted a march toward the Republic Steel Corporation, they were attacked by the police. Ten people were killed in what became known as the "Memorial Day Massacre." Little Steel refused to recognize the union until 1941.

Impact The strike wave of the 1930's had many effects on American workers and the American labor movement. In the short term, it led to improved working conditions, the full enforcement of the New Deal-era prolabor laws, and the growth and power of the industrial unions and the CIO. In the long term, these advances led to an increased voice and political power for American labor. However, the legal acceptance of the American labor movement was ac-

companied by increased regulation, some of which began the process of checking labor's militancy and, in particular, prohibiting many of the strike practices that had been so successful during the 1930's.

Susan Roth Breitzer

Further Reading

Boyer, Richard, and Herbert M. Morais. *Labor's Untold Story.* Reprint. Pittsburgh: United Electrical, Radio, and Machine Workers of America, 1994. Union publication, providing a radical view of American labor and American history.

Brecher, Jeremy. *Strike.* Rev. ed. Cambridge, Mass.: South End Press, 1997. Sweeping history of the role of mass strikes in American history and their significance in telling labor's story.

Cochrane, Thomas C. *The Great Depression and World War II, 1929-1945.* Glenview, Ill.: Scott, Foresman, 1968. This general history of the Great Depression era highlights the increased labor militancy and relates it to the changes brought about by prolabor, New Deal legislation.

Lens, Sidney. *The Labor Wars: From the Molly Maguires to the Sit-Downs.* Reprint. Chicago: Haymarket Books, 2008. Highlights the often under-recorded incidents in American labor history and attempts to reconnect the protest movements of the 1960's with the militancy of labor's past.

Selvin, David. *A Terrible Anger: The 1934 Waterfront and General Strikes in San Francisco.* Detroit: Wayne State University Press, 1996. A complete account of the dockworkers' and general strikes in San Francisco in 1934 that attempts to reconstruct the events as they happened.

Terkel, Studs. *Hard Times: An Oral History of the Great Depression.* New York: Pantheon Books, 1970. Classic oral history of the Depression that includes firsthand accounts of some of the major labor actions of the era, including the Flint sit-down strike and the failed Little Steel strike.

See also American Federation of Labor; Communism; Congress of Industrial Organizations; Flint sit-down strike; Lewis, John L.; National Industrial Recovery Act of 1933; National Labor Relations Act of 1935; Reuther, Walter P.; Unionism.

■ La Guardia, Fiorello Henry

Identification   New York politician and U.S.
 congressman
Born   December 11, 1882; New York, New York
Died   September 20, 1947; New York, New York

*After a career in the House of Representatives from 1917 to
1933, La Guardia was elected the ninety-ninth mayor of
New York City in 1933. He was a dynamic politician who
shared the belief with Franklin D. Roosevelt that government had a responsibility to help its citizens who were unable to help themselves. La Guardia's progressive congressional ideas helped pave the way for Roosevelt's New Deal
policies of the 1930's.*

When Fiorello Henry La Guardia was in the House
of Representatives, he acted as an independent, although he was officially a Republican. At the beginning of 1930, Congress was suspicious of communist
and socialist propaganda. In 1931, La Guardia negotiated with progressive and conservative politicians to
help liberalize the House rules and protect the rights
of citizens who had been targeted for anti-American
actions. La Guardia's reputation propelled him to lead the Progressive
group during the Seventy-second
Congress.

La Guardia and Senator George W.
Norris of Nebraska sponsored the
Norris-La Guardia Act, also called
the Anti-Injunction Bill, of 1932. The
act allowed employees to join trade
unions without the interference of
their employers; outlawed "yellow
dog" contracts, which are contracts
that force employees not to join a labor union as a condition of employment; and gave employees the right
to strike and picket peacefully in non-
violent labor disputes. Under this law,
federal courts were no longer able to
issue injunctions against laborers.

In 1932, La Guardia campaigned
for his House seat at the same time
that Roosevelt was running for the
presidency. Roosevelt's sweeping win
coincided with the general success
of the Democratic Party across the
United States; because of his affiliation with the Republican Party, La

Guardia lost the election. Even as a "lame duck" congressman, La Guardia continued to fight for programs that benefited all people, including the American Civil Liberties Union, the National Bankruptcy
Act, and the Bill of Rights.

In the spring of 1933, La Guardia returned to
New York City and joined the mayoral race, running
as a Republican from the Central Park East Fifteenth
Assembly District. He ran on a platform of hope and
nonpartisan government. He won the election in
November and was sworn in as mayor on January 1,
1934.

La Guardia was New York City's first Italian mayor,
and although he was able to win the Italian voters, La
Guardia was not a typical Italian New Yorker. He was
born in New York but grew up on military bases in
Arizona. He was Republican and Episcopalian, even
though he had a Roman Catholic father and a Jewish
mother. La Guardia was able to use his background
to help connect diverse groups of New Yorkers during his successful mayoral campaign.

From the first day of his administration, he vowed
to clean up corruption, waste, and excess in the city's

*As a show of commitment to fighting crime and with a sledgehammer poised above
his head, New York City mayor Fiorello La Guardia prepares to smash slot machines
collected after gambling raids. (Archive Photos/Getty Images)*

government in an effort to reform the mistakes of boss politics and Tammany Hall municipal legislation. La Guardia once said, "Municipal government is city housekeeping." He was a tireless worker who often used radio broadcasts to propose his ideas. During a New York City newspaper strike, he even read comic strips, including *Dick Tracy*, over the air so that the children of New York could keep up with their favorite stories.

Although the American Labor Party was connected with the Democratic Party, La Guardia approved of the party in New York and even supported Roosevelt in the presidential campaign of 1936. He helped organize the 1939 New York World's Fair, which opened on the 150th anniversary of George Washington's presidential inauguration in New York City. La Guardia was elected by a huge margin to a second term as mayor in 1937. He later won a third term, serving again from 1941 to 1945. Two years later, La Guardia died of pancreatic cancer.

Impact During the 1930's, La Guardia's administration was responsible for many urban reforms, including expansion of relief and social systems and the overhaul of the parks, construction works, and public-housing systems. His reforms balanced the municipal budget and reduced corruption in civic offices. La Guardia also created transportation infrastructures that helped transform the physical look of New York City. Many of the visionary policies that La Guardia supported became realities under the New Deal of Roosevelt. La Guardia had a strong commitment to the people of New York City and brought hope and optimism to the city after the Depression.

Stephanie A. Amsel

Further Reading

Brodsky, Alyn. *The Great Mayor: Fiorello La Guardia and the Making of the City of New York*. New York: St. Martin's Press, 2003.

Kessner, Thomas. *Fiorello H. La Guardia and the Making of Modern New York*. New York: McGraw-Hill, 1989.

Mann, Arthur. *La Guardia Comes to Power: 1933*. Philadelphia: J. B. Lippincott, 1965.

See also Comic strips; Communism; Congress, U.S.; Fair Labor Standards Act of 1938; House Committee on Un-American Activities; New Deal; Norris-La Guardia Act of 1932; Roosevelt, Franklin D.

■ Landon, Alf

Identification American political figure
Born September 9, 1887; West Middlesex, Pennsylvania
Died October 12, 1987; Topeka, Kansas

As the presidential candidate of the Republican Party in the 1936 election, Landon was trounced by Franklin D. Roosevelt. Landon served successfully as a two-term governor of Kansas and as a leader in the progressive wing of the Republican Party during the 1930's.

Alfred Mossman Landon was born in Pennsylvania and raised in Ohio. When his father moved to Kansas, Alf did also. He graduated from the University of Kansas in 1908 and then began a successful career in the oil business. He married Margaret Flemming in 1916. She died in 1918.

In addition to his business activities, Landon was active in Republican politics, providing behind-the-scenes support for members of its progressive faction. He became chairman of Kansas's Republican Party in 1928 and served as the governor's secretary for two years. In 1930, Landon returned to his career in the oil business. He also married for a second time that year.

Landon won a close, three-way race for governor in 1932. He gained notice for the victory because he was one of the few successful Republican candidates in that year's races. The Depression, along with a devastating drought, hit Kansas hard during the 1930's. As governor, Landon worked successfully to alter the state tax structure, making it more progressive. He was also successful in reducing government expenditures. In addition, he struggled to make certain that Kansas and its citizens received their "fair share" of federal government moneys. Because of these efforts, the state of Kansas was able to balance its budget, while at the same time providing services to its citizens.

Landon won reelection easily in 1934. Because of this he began to draw notice as a potential presidential candidate. His response was to stay in the state, work hard as governor, and write a number of well-publicized letters to notables in the country. In these communications he took a generally progressive stance. He was also able to project an appealing image of a young, decent, small-town man with solid midwestern values.

Landon was not the only person interested in the

1936 Republican nomination. He adopted the strategy of avoiding the primaries (there were only thirteen at the time), while allowing supporters to work behind the scenes. Supporters also worked to write a moderate platform on which he could run. Landon won the nomination on the first ballot. He chose Frank Knox, a newspaper publisher active in progressive Republican circles, as his running mate.

The campaign began with some optimism but was dogged by several problems. For one thing, President Roosevelt was enormously popular. Because of this, many moderate Republican candidates shied away from close connection with Landon, for fear that such an association would hurt their chances of election. Moreover, while Landon was moderate, many forces within the Republican Party were pulling the campaign in a conservative direction. As the campaign progressed, Landon became shriller in his criticism of Roosevelt, charging him with centralizing power too greatly and with spending too much. Democrats portrayed Landon as a spokesperson for the reactionary interests in the United States, who were desperate to defeat Roosevelt.

The Democratic message won easily. Landon was defeated in a landslide. He carried only two states for a total of 8 electoral votes; Roosevelt had 523. Roosevelt received more than 27 million votes, while Landon received fewer than 17 million. A large number of Republican candidates for other offices were also defeated.

Landon never ran for public office again but remained active in Republican politics, seeking to strengthen the moderate wing of the party. He also spoke on public issues and spent his energies in successful business ventures. He died in Topeka, Kansas, shortly after his one hundredth birthday.

Impact   The Republican Party has long contained at least two factions, a conservative, and often isolationist, wing and a progressive, internationalist wing, that have contended for control of the party. Landon was an effective spokesperson for the latter and helped strengthen it during the 1930's and beyond.

David M. Jones

Further Reading
Gould, Lewis L. *Grand Old Party.* New York: Random House, 2003.
McCoy, Donald R. *Landon of Kansas.* Lincoln: University of Nebraska Press, 1966.

Schruben, Francis W. *Kansas in Turmoil, 1930-1936.* Columbia: University of Missouri Press, 1969.

See also   Business and the economy in the United States; Elections of 1936, U.S.; Great Depression in the United States; Hoover, Herbert; Natural Gas Act of 1938; New Deal; Roosevelt, Franklin D.

■ Lange, Dorothea

Identification   American photographer and social activist
Born   May 26, 1895; Hoboken, New Jersey
Died   October 11, 1965; San Francisco, California

Working for the Resettlement Administration (RA) and the Farm Security Administration (FSA), Lange used her camera to document the American people, events, and places of the 1930's. The federal government used her images to publicize social conditions, substantiate the need for federal assistance, and generate increased support for its programs. Lange's Migrant Mother, Nipomo, California *(1936), which she took for the FSA, became the decade's best-known photograph.*

Dorothea Lange was one of two children born to Joan, a librarian, and Henry Nutzhorn, an attorney. She had a difficult childhood: She had few friends, suffered a bout of polio that crippled her right leg, and endured her parents' divorce. After her father's departure, she assumed her mother's maiden name, Lange. Lange often cut school to wander the city and make notes on her observations; she vowed someday to record with a camera. To prepare for her life's work in photography, Dorothea took classes and worked as an apprentice to local photographers. In 1919, she moved to California and established a photography studio, specializing in portraits.

In 1920, Lange wed artist Maynard Dixon. They had two sons—Daniel Rhodes and John Eaglefeather—and lived for a time in Utah, where Lange photographed migrant workers. Lange and the boys moved to San Francisco without Dixon. Though not always appealing, her 1934 photographs recorded the city's true conditions: unemployment, hunger, and despair. She worked with sociologist and economist Paul Schuster Taylor to document these social needs for books, articles, and exhibits and to promote social programs.

Photographer Dorothea Lange. (Library of Congress)

Roy Stryker of the Resettlement Administration (RA) asked Lange to join the organization's photography unit; he later asked her to join a similar unit with the FSA. She accepted the job on September 19, 1935. In December of the same year, she and Taylor were married. Because of budget reductions, Stryker had to terminate an employee. He selected Lange, whom he considered uncooperative at times.

Lange worked out of her California home. She became the most widely published federal photographer of the 1930's. Lange's *Ditched, Stalled, and Stranded, San Joaquin Valley, California* (1935) for the FSA was a character study of an uprooted farmer. In 2002, the U.S. Postal Service selected the photograph for its "Masters of American Photography Series."

In 1936, Lange followed a roadside sign asking for pea pickers. She photographed thirty-two-year-old Native American Florence Neil Owens Thompson with an infant. *Migrant Mother, Nipomo, California* became the best-known image of the decade.

With a 1941 Guggenheim Fellowship, Lange began photographing religious groups. When the United States declared war, however, Lange relinquished the Guggenheim Fellowship and took a job with the War Relocation Authority. Her assignment was to document Japanese aliens and Japanese Americans in relocation camps. The public did not see many of these photographs until after the war.

From 1943 to 1945, Lange worked for the Office of War Information, stopping when she became ill while photographing the United Nations conference. She was unable to work again until 1951. In the 1950's, she worked for *Life* magazine. She continued working after she was diagnosed with cancer in 1964, and she died in 1965.

Impact Dorothea Lange's images for the FSA and the RA provided visual documentation of the economic and social conditions present during the Great Depression. Her *Migrant Mother, Nipomo, California* became the most famous photograph of the 1930's; the United States Postal Service (USPS) issued a stamp bearing that image in 1998. Lange's *Ditched, Stalled, and Stranded, San Joaquin Valley, California* is in the "Masters of American Photography Series" of the USPS. Lange's social activism continued in later years, and her photographic work remains in the Metropolitan Museum of Art and other museums and galleries.

Anita Price Davis

Further Reading

Borhan, Pierre. *Dorothea Lange: The Heart and Mind of a Photographer.* New York: Bulfinch Press, 2002.

Davis, Anita Price. *North Carolina During the Great Depression: A Documentary Portrait of a Decade.* Jefferson, N.C.: McFarland, 2003.

Davis, Anita Price, and Mary Louise Hunt. *Women on U.S. Postage Stamps.* Jefferson, N.C.: McFarland, 2008.

Davis, Anita Price, and Marla J. Selvidge. *Focus on Women*. Huntington Beach, Calif.: Teacher Created Materials, 1995.

Lange, Dorothea, Linda Gordon, and Gary Y. Okihiro. *Impounded: Dorothea Lange and the Censored Images of Japanese American Internment*. New York: W. W. Norton, 2006.

Spirn, Anne Whiston, and Dorothea Lange. *Daring to Look: Dorothea Lange's Photographs and Reports from the Field*. Chicago: University of Chicago Press, 2008.

See also Adams, Ansel; Dust Bowl; Great Depression in the United States; Photography; Postage stamps.

■ Last Mile, The

Identification Play about a Western state prison riot on death row that awakened concern about capital punishment
Author John Wexley
Date Published in 1930

The Last Mile *gained popular and critical attention with its realistic depiction of the final procession of events of a prisoner condemned to die in the electric chair. John Wexley based the drama on prison riots and a published sketch by Robert Blake, a condemned inmate awaiting execution. The play also launched Spencer Tracy's film career; he played the lead when the play was made into a film in 1932.*

To add authenticity, Wexley visited a prison to observe its conditions. The play is set in death-row cells and the death-chamber corridor in an Oklahoma penitentiary. Among seven condemned prisoners are a young man (Walters) to be executed in hours, a poetry-quoting lunatic, a youthful father-to-be (Mayor), and cell-block leader John Mears. The play demonstrates death row's corroding effect on inmates.

In the first act, Walters prepares for electrocution, from the last meal to the final march to the electric chair; the lights dim to indicate electrocution. The other men are anguished by their fellow inmate's suffering. Taking place two weeks later, the second act includes a mutiny. Mayor is set to be executed. Mears takes command by overpowering a guard, freeing the other prisoners, and capturing and locking up four guards and the chaplain. The ri-

oters collect guns. The warden and armed troopers arrive outside. Mears sends an ultimatum to the officials, promising to kill captives hourly until demands are met. In the third act, the warden refuses the prisoners' terms. Mears shoots two guards when deadlines are not reached, and he threatens to kill the priest. The men become discouraged. Realizing the situation is hopeless but that the riot will demonstrate the despair generated by capital punishment, Mears walks out into machine-gun fire. Praised for its emotional impact, the play had a successful run.

Impact The play reflected developing concerns about the death penalty. In the play's preface, Sing Sing Correctional Facility warden Lewis E. Lawes praises it for questioning capital punishment as an effective, humane legal device. Wexley's affecting play became a forerunner of 1930's dramas and films treating prison settings.

Christian H. Moe

Further Reading

Chambers, Jonathan L. *Messiah of the New Technique: John Howard Lawson, Communism, and American Theatre, 1923-1937*. Carbondale: Southern Illinois University Press, 2006.

Salem, James M. *A Guide to Critical Reviews, Part One: American Drama, 1909-1982*. 3d ed. Metuchen, N.J.: Scarecrow Press, 1984.

See also Alcatraz Federal Penitentiary; Federal Theatre Project; Gunther, John; Joliet prison riot; Ohio Penitentiary fire; Tracy, Spencer.

■ Latin America and the Caribbean

During the 1930's, the United States sought to maintain hegemony over Latin America and the Caribbean in a more flexible manner than it had previously. President Franklin D. Roosevelt pursued a policy of winning over allies in the region through economic and diplomatic cooperation, which was particularly important as the United States faced the growing danger of German expansionism in Latin America and localized anti-American nationalism.

The end of Herbert Hoover's presidential administration marked a fresh start in relations between the United States and Latin America. Incoming president Roosevelt faced a host of problems south of the

U.S.-Mexican border, including ending the military occupation of Haiti and Nicaragua, the rise of populist regimes of both left and right, a radical revolution in Cuba, important local communist parties allied to the Soviet Union, growing Latin American fascist groups, and diplomatic and commercial penetration of the region by the Axis Powers of Nazi Germany and fascist Italy.

Roosevelt's response to the activities of Latin America was the Good Neighbor Policy. This meant an end to formal military occupation in favor of collective security, a pledge of nonintervention in the internal affairs of the United States' southern neighbors, and the promotion of trade to further economic growth. However, the United States still remained committed to the principles of the Monroe Doctrine, whereby the American government was responsible for protecting the Western Hemisphere from foreign intervention and domestic disturbances that might invite such intervention.

Mexico and Central America   No country in Latin America was more important for the United States than Mexico, as a trade partner, strategic ally, and bulwark of democracy. However, although U.S.-Mexican relations had been close since the 1920's, the 1930's brought unprecedented challenges to the alliance. President Lázaro Cárdenas was determined to enact some of the more radical measures of the 1917 Mexican constitution, including land reform, mass secular education, and the reclamation of Mexico's vast underground wealth that included copper, silver, and petroleum. All of these measures were loathed by American conservatives and particularly U.S. businesses operating in Mexico.

In 1938, when workers at several American-owned petroleum companies went on strike for higher wages, their union took the case before the Mexican supreme court, which ruled on behalf of labor. The American companies objected to the ruling, and Cárdenas broke the impasse by nationalizing all foreign oil firms in Mexico. Those companies affected by the expropriation pleaded with Roosevelt to impose an economic embargo on Mexican oil. Roosevelt worried that Mexico might sell oil to Germany and Italy instead. Secretary of State Cordell Hull announced that Mexico had the right, under its constitution, to nationalize the oil industry, provided American companies were compensated for their losses, a promise kept by Cárdenas.

The Mexican president also pleased his U.S. counterpart by cracking down on both the Mexican Communist Party and pro-German fifth-columnists— potential collaborators with the Nazi regime.

Central America showcased the contradictions and paradoxes of the Good Neighbor Policy even more than Mexico. Roosevelt fulfilled the promise made by his predecessor to withdraw all U.S. Marines from Nicaragua; Marines had been stationed there since 1912. However, Nicaragua was deemed too vital to the defense of the Panama Canal to let its internal affairs be run democratically. The departing Marines placed Anastasio Somoza García in charge of the national guard, which was the real seat of power in the country. Somoza used the guard to build up his own political power, seizing the presidency for himself in 1937; he was dictatorial but staunchly pro-American.

In 1932 in El Salvador, the infamous La Matanza (the massacre) occurred. The Salvadoran army slaughtered an estimated thirty thousand peasants, workers, and intellectuals after foiling an uprising led by the Communist Party of El Salvador. The United States threw its support behind Salvadoran general Maximiliano Hernández Martínez, to whom the Roosevelt administration granted diplomatic recognition in 1934. Guatemala, the richest of the five Central American republics because of its banana plantations, enjoyed excellent relations with the United States under the local dictator, Jorge Ubico Casteñeda, though Roosevelt pressed him to expropriate German-owned coffee farms in the country. In Panama, where the United States owned both the canal and the Panama Canal Zone to its north and south, no local despot was necessary to protect American economic interests, and the country lived under democratic rule, a rarity in Central America. In 1939, the U.S. Senate ratified a treaty allowing for the deployment of American troops outside the Panama Canal Zone, subject to Panamanian approval.

The Caribbean and South America   U.S. policy toward the Caribbean nations reflected the efforts of the Roosevelt administration to move away from the "big stick" diplomacy of military intervention that had started under Theodore Roosevelt and instead move in the direction of promoting local allies. The 1933 revolution in Cuba in which President Gustavo Machado was overthrown created political chaos.

American ambassador to Cuba Sumner Welles distrusted the president installed by the revolution, Ramón Grau San Martín, as too left-leaning and counseled Roosevelt not to grant the new government diplomatic recognition. Instead, the United States threw its support behind the rising star of Cuban politics, army colonel Fulgencio Batista y Zaldívar; Grau's regime quickly fell from power, and with Welles's blessing, Batista became the kingmaker of Cuban politics, attaining the presidency in 1940. However, Roosevelt did have the wisdom to cancel the hated Platt amendment to the Cuban constitution; since approval by the U.S. Senate in 1902, it had granted the United States the unilateral right of military intervention in Cuba.

Next door to Cuba, on the island of Hispaniola, shared by Haiti and the Dominican Republic, the United States faced a different set of challenges. Rafael Trujillo, dictator of the Dominican Republic, had been installed in power by the U.S. Marines who occupied the country from 1916 until 1924. Trujillo made himself president of the country in 1930, and his unwavering pro-American foreign policy made him a Washington favorite in Latin America; what portion of the U.S. imports of sugar that was not assigned to Cuba by quota went to the Dominican Republic.

A sour point in relations between the two countries occurred in 1937, when Trujillo ordered the massacre of thousands of Haitian sugar-cane cutters on the border between the two countries, an atrocity that received negative publicity in the American media. Trujillo mended his fences with Roosevelt by agreeing to a U.S.-sponsored plan to pay a token indemnity to Haiti. In Haiti itself, the last U.S. troops, stationed there since 1915, were withdrawn in 1934. However, the Haitian government was still run under a constitution written by the United States in 1917, and the government carried a huge debt in the form of American loans extended during the occupation.

In South America were Latin America's most strategically placed country, Brazil, and its richest country, Argentina. In Brazil, the United States had to contend with Getúlio Vargas, a civilian president turned dictator. Vargas continued Brazil's traditional alliance with the United States while emulating many of the ideas and practices, such as corporatism, from the European fascist dictatorships. In 1935, Vargas destroyed Brazil's powerful

Communist Party in a ruthless crackdown and crushed a homegrown fascist movement, the Integralist Party, the following year; both actions aided the United States politically. During the 1930's, Argentina was undergoing a political breakdown, with a new president nearly every two years. Nevertheless, the army kept the landed oligarchy firmly in control of the country, and Argentina modified its historically pro-British foreign policy to a position of neutrality between the Axis Powers and the United States and Great Britain.

Impact   During the 1930's, Latin America and the Caribbean were more significant in American foreign policy than at any time since the Spanish-American War of 1898. From the American point of view, by the end of the decade, the Good Neighbor Policy had achieved its chief goals, which included gaining Latin American allies for the upcoming war with Germany, securing military bases in the region, focusing Latin American trade away from Europe and toward the United States, and eliminating the possibility of revolution from either the far left or the far right.

Julio César Pino

Further Reading

Brewer, Stewart. *Borders and Bridges: A History of U.S. Latin American Relations.* Westport, Conn.: Praeger Security International, 2006. Examines how the United States has used the concept of national security to impinge on Latin American sovereignty.

Dominguez, Rafael, and Jorge I. Fernández de Castro. *The United States and Mexico: Between Partnership and Conflict.* New York: Routledge, 2001. Places the stormy relationship between the administrations of Roosevelt and Càrdenas in the broader perspective of three hundred years of U.S.-Mexican ties.

Green, David. *The Containment of Latin America: A History of Myths and Realities of the Good Neighbor Policy.* Chicago: Quadrangle Books, 1971. Argues that the Good Neighbor Policy was not a departure from but a further step in U.S. efforts to dominate Latin America.

Pike, Frederick B. *FDR's Good Neighbor Policy: Sixty Years of Generally Gentle Chaos.* Austin: University of Texas Press, 1995. Examines Roosevelt's personal and political reasons for engendering the Good Neighbor Policy and the controversial legacy of that policy into the twenty-first century.

Roorda, Eric. *The Dictator Next Door: The Good Neighbor Policy and the Trujillo Regime in the Dominican Republic, 1930-1945.* Durham, N.C.: Duke University Press, 1998. Critical look at the Roosevelt administration's relations with the controversial Caribbean dictator Trujillo.

See also Export-Import Bank of the United States; Foreign policy of the United States; Good Neighbor Policy; Haiti occupation; Hoover, Herbert; Hull, Cordell; Inter-American Conference for the Maintenance of Peace; International trade; Mexico; Roosevelt, Franklin D.

■ Latinos

Identification Diverse ethnic group comprising people of Spanish descent and those who trace their ancestry to the nations of Latin America.

Despite representing between only 1 and 2 percent of the U.S. population during the 1930's, Latinos played a crucial role in the country's agricultural and industrial sectors during the decade, making important contributions to labor organizing. The influence of Latinos on U.S. popular culture, sports, and the arts also began to take shape during this period. Latinos were one of the groups hit hardest by the Great Depression, discrimination, and immigration policies of the time.

The 1930 U.S. Census was the first to count a segment of the country's Latino population, recording "1.3 million Mexicans." Ten years later, the census took a slightly broader approach, reporting 1.6 million people of "Spanish mother tongue." Because of the narrow and changing criteria used to count Latinos or Hispanic Americans during this period, it is difficult to point to exact numbers or determine whether this population grew or decreased throughout the decade.

What is known is that most Latinos during the 1930's were of Mexican descent and lived mainly in southwestern states, New York, and Illinois. Mexican immigration had grown thirteenfold from 1900 to 1930, fueled by the Mexican Revolution, the need for workers during World War I, and the immigration quota system (which did not include Mexicans). Cubans, Dominicans, Puerto Ricans, and Central and South Americans made up a much smaller portion of the total mainland Latino population. Many Latinos came to the United States during the 1930's, fleeing repressive regimes, in Nicaragua and El Salvador, for example, and bloody civil wars, in Spain, for example. Others immigrated as a result of harsh economic conditions resulting from the worldwide Great Depression.

Effects of the Great Depression Latinos were among the most impacted by the economic downturn of the Great Depression in the United States. Although more established Hispanic communities had some upper- and middle-class families, most Latinos in the first part of the twentieth century were part of the burgeoning working class. Latinos took part, and often formed the backbone of, a large

Mexican American migrant workers get a brief respite at a filling station after picking cotton in Mississippi in 1939. (Library of Congress)

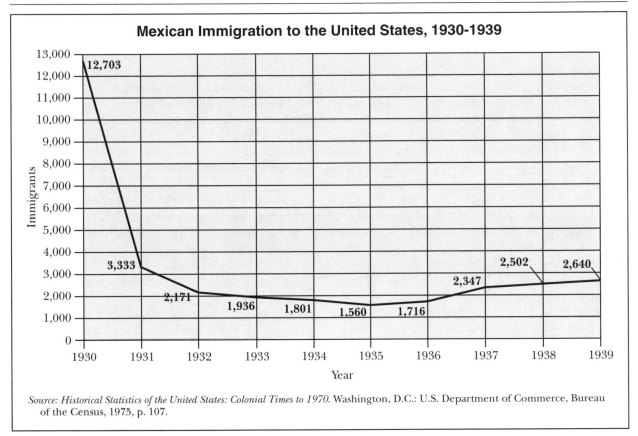

Mexican Immigration to the United States, 1930-1939

Source: *Historical Statistics of the United States: Colonial Times to 1970.* Washington, D.C.: U.S. Department of Commerce, Bureau of the Census, 1975, p. 107.

range of industries, including agriculture, mining, textiles, steel mills, and railroads. Despite their vital contributions to the U.S. economy, Latinos often received less pay than their white counterparts and had little occupational mobility. This, combined with rampant discrimination toward people of color, put Latinos at a great disadvantage during the 1930's.

When the U.S. economy began to deteriorate and jobs were scarce, Latinos became an easy target because they were largely perceived by white Americans as "foreigners" even if they were citizens. In many states, Latinos were the first to be fired, as employers felt obligated to give preference to white workers. In Texas, the number of unemployed Mexican Americans hit 400,000. In Chicago, almost one-third of Mexican Americans and Mexican immigrants were unemployed by 1932. Meanwhile, in Puerto Rico, where the economy depended heavily on a small number of industries, unemployment rates skyrocketed even faster than in the mainland United States, reaching as high as 36 percent. Lati-

nos also found accessing welfare offices and work-relief programs difficult, as many government and charitable organizations adopted a "citizens only" policy, which in practice translated to "whites only."

The Depression also led to the displacement of Latinos. An estimated ten thousand Puerto Ricans returned from the mainland to the island between 1930 and 1934, hoping to find better opportunities at home. In New Mexico and Colorado, workers who had migrated to urban areas during the 1920's returned to rural villages. In California, unemployed agricultural workers poured into the cities, seeking financial assistance. The greatest impact on Latinos during this difficult period resulted from the so-called Mexican Repatriation, which expelled close to half a million people of Mexican origin—both undocumented people and U.S. citizens. Sponsored by the federal government, repatriation was sometimes voluntary. In other cases, however, local governments and self-deputized white citizens took it upon themselves to forcibly remove unwanted populations. Los Angeles County even organized train rides to Mexico, which took some thirteen thousand people "back home" from 1931 to 1934.

Surviving the Crisis Getting through the Depression was hard for those Latinos who remained in the United States. Wages dropped drastically as the economy worsened. Beet workers in Colorado, for example, experienced a shrinkage in their wages from $27 to $12.37 an acre in just three years—so even those families lucky enough to still have an income had to find other ways to make ends meet. The crisis led to changing family and gender dynamics. During this time, Latinas entered the industrial workforce in unprecedented numbers, whether shelling pecans in San Antonio factories or making clothes in New York. Such experiences outside the home contributed to an emerging Latina movement, which matured after World War II.

Despite the fact that Latinos experienced exclusion from many New Deal benefits, some government programs were targeted specifically toward Latino communities, such as the Hispanic arts revival in northern New Mexico and the Puerto Rico Emergency Relief Program. Other broad programs benefited Latinos by default. The Federal Emergency Relief Administration provided financial assistance to Mexican American workers. The Works Progress Administration drew on many experienced Latino construction workers for large-scale infrastructure projects. An estimated 100,000 Mexicans participated in New Deal work programs in the Western states.

Self-help efforts also proliferated during this period. Many Latinos in distress came to rely on traditional ethnic mutual-aid societies, or *mutualistas*, particularly in cities with long-standing middle-class Hispanic populations such as Los Angeles and New York. Some groups, including the Cruz Azul (blue cross), were highly organized, but there were also informal groups, such as women who banded together to sell tamales at low cost to unemployed workers.

Organizing, Politics, and the Forging of an Ethnic Identity Facing discrimination and harsh working conditions, Latinos actively engaged in labor organizing during the 1930's. Latinos constituted the union rank and file in many labor disputes, particularly in the Southwest. Latinos also emerged as prominent labor leaders, helping to organize farmworkers in California, pecan shellers in Texas, and steelworkers in Illinois, to name just a few exam-

ples. Prominent groups organized during this period included the Confederation of Mexican Workers; the League of Latin American Citizens (LULAC); and the National Congress of Spanish-Speaking Peoples, established by Guatemalan American labor leader Luisa Moreno in 1937.

Latinos also fought for civil rights in courts, schools, and places of public accommodation. Latino families protested the unfair ways in which achievement and literacy tests were used to malign their children. For example, they campaigned against a New York State Chamber of Commerce report that claimed Puerto Rican children were "mentally deficient," demanding bilingual education and different assessment methods. George Isidore Sánchez, a prominent Latino educator of the 1930's and 1940's, appeared as an expert witness in many desegregation cases in the Southwest.

Ultimately, the struggles of the 1930's contributed to a more unified sense of ethnic identity among Latinos of different national origins, citizenship statuses, and socioeconomic classes. This emerging sense of communal identity led to greater political mobilization. In 1934, Dennis Chávez became the first Hispanic member of the U.S. Congress, representing New Mexico.

Popular Culture, Arts, and Sports Latinos also came to prominence in various arenas of American arts and culture during the 1930's. Mexican painters such as Diego Rivera and Frida Kahlo toured the country, creating impressive works of art and sometimes stirring controversy because of their radical political views. In Hollywood, actors such as Lupe Velez, César Romero, and newcomer Anthony Quinn left a mark or launched successful careers. Dolores Del Rio became the first Latin American film star to have international appeal, starring in films such as *Bird of Paradise* (1932) and *Madame Du Barry* (1934). Latinos also made inroads in sports during this period. In 1938, Cuban player Miguel Angel González became the first Latino manager in Major League Baseball history, paving the way for Hispanic players and coaches in decades to come.

Impact Latinos played a significant role in labor and civil rights organizing during the Depression era, swelling unions' membership ranks; actively participating in strikes and protests; and, in some cases, leading organized movements that supported farm and industrial workers. Latinos also lent their skills in the construction trades to important New Deal infrastructure programs, even as they were disproportionately impacted by the hardships of the Great Depression and the culture of discrimination and increased nationalist sentiments of the time.

Mauricio Espinoza-Quesada

Further Reading

Balderrama, Francisco E., and Raymond Rodríguez. *Decade of Betrayal: Mexican Repatriation in the 1930's.* Rev. ed. Albuquerque: University of New Mexico Press, 2006. Comprehensive study of the Mexican repatriation episode and its impact on the Latino community.

Forrest, Suzanne. *The Preservation of the Village: New Mexico's Hispanics and the New Deal.* Albuquerque: University of New Mexico Press, 1998. Traces the history of Anglo-Hispanic relations in New Mexico through responses to the New Deal programs.

Guerin-Gonzales, Camille. *Mexican Workers and American Dreams: Immigration, Repatriation, and California Farm Labor, 1900-1939.* New Brunswick, N.J.: Rutgers University Press, 1994. Recounts the history of Mexican workers in California, participation in organized labor, and the effects of immigration policies.

Sánchez, George J. *Becoming Mexican American: Ethnicity, Culture, and Identity in Chicano Los Angeles, 1900-1945.* New York: Oxford University Press, 1993. An analysis of identity formation and the "Americanization" of Mexican Americans.

Thatcher, Mary Anne. *Immigrants and the 1930's: Ethnicity and Alienage in Depression and On-Coming War.* New York: Garland, 1990. Traces the history, culture, and conditions of immigrants during the 1930's.

See also   Civil rights and liberties in the United States; Demographics of the United States; Federal Emergency Relief Administration; Great Depression in the United States; Immigration to the United States; Latin America and the Caribbean; Mexico; Migrations, domestic; Racial discrimination; Unionism.

■ Laurel and Hardy

Identification   American comedy film acting team

Stan Laurel
Born June 16, 1890; Ulverston, Lancashire, England
Died February 23, 1965; Santa Monica, California

Oliver Hardy
Born January 18, 1892; Harlem, Georgia
Died August 7, 1957; North Hollywood, California

After formally joining forces in 1927, Laurel and Hardy went on to become the first significant comedy team of the silver screen. While enjoying a highly successful film career from the late 1920's through the 1940's, the duo also performed on stage across America and Europe.

The first time Stan Laurel and Oliver Hardy were on screen together was in the short 1921 comedy *Lucky Dog.* However, they did not perform as a team, and five years would pass before they appeared together again. In 1926, they filmed thirteen silent "All-Star Comedies" for Hal Roach Studios before officially becoming a team in 1927. The pair quickly became the studio's most recognizable and profitable stars. In 1929, the Boys, as they were popularly known, successfully made the transition from silent to sound films with the short *Unaccustomed as We Are.* Their popularity continued to grow.

Success   During the early 1930's, Laurel and Hardy shorts were commonly billed over feature presentations at theaters around the United States. The stars' tremendous success allowed them artistic freedom with Hal Roach as they moved to feature-length films. The pair's first full-length feature, *Pardon Us,* was released in 1931. The next year, they were rewarded with the first Academy Award for a live-action short film for *The Music Box,* in which they played two dimwits delivering a heavy piano to a house at the top of a seemingly endless set of stairs.

As double features and cartoons became more popular in theaters in the 1930's, Roach canceled the production of many of his short comedy productions, including those of Laurel and Hardy, who made their last short for him in 1935. However, Roach had no intention of canceling the production of the team's feature films, which included *Sons of the Desert* (1933), *Bonnie Scotland* (1935), *The Bohemian*

In their typical fashion, Stan Laurel (left) exhibits remorse as his partner, Oliver Hardy, registers frustration in a scene from the 1932 film Pack Up Your Troubles. (Hulton Archive/Getty Images)

Girl (1936), and *Block-Heads* (1938). For their 1937 film *Way Out West*, Laurel and Hardy sang "The Trail of the Lonesome Pine," which became the number two song in England.

Moving On By 1936, the artistic freedom that Roach had once offered Laurel and Hardy was beginning to wane. Laurel, the primary force behind the team, was growing frustrated with Roach's demands. Roach believed that all feature-length comedies should include musical numbers or some other break in the comedy, fearing the audience would get bored otherwise. Laurel disagreed, and throughout the latter part of the decade, he and Roach often were at odds. At times, Roach threatened to partner Hardy with another actor; the producer always had

kept Laurel and Hardy under separate contracts, minimizing their bargaining power.

Throughout the decade, Laurel typically earned twice as much as Hardy, as he did twice the work. Laurel did much of the writing for the act, while Hardy was primarily a performer. In 1938, in a dispute over salaries, the pair split from Roach. Hardy, however, was still under contract and was obligated to perform when Roach carried out his threat to cast Hardy alongside another performer. In 1939, Roach released *Zenobia* and cast Harry Langdon as Hardy's new partner. Laurel fought back, and it was announced that he had signed with Roach's rival, Sennett Pictures Corporation, for several comedy features. The dispute with Roach resolved quickly, however, and Laurel did not make any films for

Sennett. Laurel and Hardy produced two more features for Roach Studios in 1940, *A Chump at Oxford* and *Saps at Sea*.

The new agreement with Roach was not exclusive, and in 1939 Laurel and Hardy starred in the feature film *The Flying Deuces*, produced and released by RKO Radio Pictures. This marked their first work as a team away from Roach Studios.

Throughout the decade, Laurel and Hardy also continued to give live performances, including a show at the 1939 World's Fair in San Francisco. There they performed Laurel's skit *The Driver's License*, in which Hardy plays a man who is unable to write but applies for a license with the aid of his assistant (Laurel), who cannot read. The two toured the nation with the skit from 1940 to 1942.

Seeking more freedom, Laurel and Hardy left Roach Studios in 1941 and signed with Twentieth Century-Fox and Metro-Goldwyn-Mayer (MGM). Although their films were financially successful, the Boys did not receive the artistic freedom they had sought and were not pleased with the films being produced. In 1945, they released their last American film, *The Bullfighters*. In 1951, while in France, they filmed their last feature, *Utopia*.

Impact Relying heavily on well-choreographed slapstick and witty dialogue, Laurel and Hardy made the transition from silent film to talkies appear effortless. Much of their comedy revolved around one situation that provided the opportunity for numerous missteps and nonsense, often leading the story in unexpected directions. Laurel and Hardy not only were the first successful comedy team on film, they also were two of the biggest film stars of their day.

Michael D. Cummings, Jr.

Further Reading

Everson, William K. *The Complete Films of Laurel and Hardy*. 7th ed. New York: Citadel, 2000. Collection of chronologically arranged articles on all ninety-nine Laurel and Hardy comedies, from their early silent shorts to their features. Fully documented with cast lists, film credits, plot summaries, and more than four hundred images from the films.

Guiles, Fred Lawrence. *Stan: The Life of Stan Laurel*. New York: Stein and Day, 1980. Sympathetic biography of the English actor who became one of the most brilliant American film comedians.

Harness, Kyp. *The Art of Laurel and Hardy: Graceful Calamity in the Films*. Jefferson, N.C.: McFarland,

2006. One of the fullest biographies of Laurel and Hardy, with close attention to how the two worked together as an acting team.

Louvish, Simon. *Stan and Ollie: The Roots of Comedy—The Double Life of Laurel and Hardy*. New York: St. Martin's Press, 2001. Affectionate yet objective dual biography offering one of the deepest looks into the lives of Laurel and Hardy.

Mitchell, Glenn. *The Laurel and Hardy Encyclopedia*. 2d ed. Richmond, England: Reynolds & Hearn, 2008. Comprehensive reference work with more than six hundred entries on all aspects of the actors' lives, films, and nonfilm work. Well illustrated.

Skretvedt, Randy. *Laurel and Hardy: The Magic Behind the Movies*. 2d ed. Beverly Hills, Calif.: Past Times, 1994. Meticulously researched and often revealing joint biography that explores how Laurel and Hardy made their films and offers insights into general comedy filmmaking. Lavishly illustrated, with complete filmography.

See also Academy Awards; Chaplin, Charles; Film; Screwball comedy.

■ Leadbelly

Identification American folk singer
Also known as Huddie Ledbetter
Born January 29, 1885; Mooringsport, Louisiana
Died December 6, 1949; New York, New York

Leadbelly was an influential African American songwriter and folk musician during the 1930's and 1940's. Known for his explosive guitar-playing style, lyrical and melodic gifts, and charismatic showmanship, Leadbelly became a well-known blues musician and one of the most important figures in the twentieth century U.S. folk movement.

Though born in Louisiana, Leadbelly spent his childhood in Leigh, Texas, where he learned to play the accordion, violin, mandolin, piano, and twelve-string guitar, his preferred instrument. By his early 1920's, he had achieved regional fame for his musical talents. Leadbelly's unique vocal and guitar-playing style blended both the gospel traditions he inherited from his family and the percussive, driving music favored in the bars and dance halls of the red-light district of Shreveport, Louisiana. He also began to write autobiographical and politically in-

Folk musician Leadbelly (left), in suit and bow tie, poses with his wife, Martha Promise Ledbetter, in Connecticut in 1935. (Library of Congress)

released early, on August 1, 1934. Following his time in Angola, Leadbelly assisted Lomax as a driver during the musicologist's song-gathering expeditions throughout the southeastern United States.

Leadbelly's commercial recording career began in 1935 with the ARC label, a division of Columbia Records that promoted African American artists. Under his ARC contract, Leadbelly recorded blues songs, rather than the folk songs that later earned him fame. In February of that year, he collaborated with Lomax on the book *Negro Folk Songs as Sung by Leadbelly* (1936). The volume contained transcriptions of Leadbelly's songs and personal interviews with the artist. The subsequent book tour and financial failure of the project created tension between Lomax and Leadbelly; their working relationship soon ended bitterly because of financial disputes.

In 1936, Leadbelly relocated to New York, hoping to further his solo music career. Among his most important appearances were concerts at the Apollo Theater in Harlem. However, these events secured him neither an audience nor commercial success. In 1937, *Time* magazine released an article about Leadbelly entitled "Lead Belly: Bad Nigger Makes Good Minstrel," which sensationalized the singer's violent past and reflected the racial politics of the late 1930's in the United States. After stabbing a man in a fight in New York City, Leadbelly was returned to prison in 1939. After he was released from prison in 1941, he appeared regularly on Alan Lomax's nationally broadcast Columbia Broadcasting System (CBS) radio show *Back Where I Come From*. In 1944, he moved to California, where he recorded with RCA and Capitol Records. Leadbelly continued his work in radio with his own radio program in New York in 1949 on WNYC. He died December 6, 1949, of amyotrophic lateral sclerosis, commonly known as Lou Gehrig's disease.

Impact Leadbelly emerged during the 1930's as an important voice in the blues and folk-music movement. His partnership with the Lomax family not only presented his music to a wide audience but also promoted academic interest in roots music. Lead-

spired songs during this early period, a practice that continued throughout his life.

Leadbelly's bad temper was as well known as his music. By the early 1930's, he had been incarcerated three times for crimes including illegal gun possession, assault with a knife, and murder. While serving a prison sentence in the Angola, Louisiana, state penitentiary, he met musicologist John Lomax and his son, Alan. The Lomaxes were touring the region collecting and recording folk music and befriended Leadbelly. Eventually, they recorded hundreds of his songs, including folk ballads such as "John Hardy" and "The *Titanic*."

Leadbelly's song repertoire was remarkable in its topical variety. He sang about failed relationships with women, frustrations about race relations, the lives of sailors and cowboys, life in prison, religious faith, and pop-cultural figures and politicians. He often used his body as an accompanying percussion instrument by clapping his hands, slapping his knees, or stomping his feet while playing and singing. Certain of Leadbelly's cultural and musical significance, John Lomax petitioned the authorities to release the singer from his sentence by sending the Louisiana governor a copy of "Goodnight, Irene," a tune that became Leadbelly's most popular composition. While Lomax's influence is debatable, Leadbelly was belly's musical success was not limited to the United States. During the 1940's, he became the first African American blues musicians to enjoy European success. With a large and stylistically varied body of original songs and significant recordings made with RCA Records, Capitol Records, and the Library of Congress, Leadbelly influenced some of the twentieth century's most popular musicians.

Margaret R. Jackson

Further Reading

Jess, Tyehimba. *Leadbelly.* Seattle: Wave Books, 2005.

Lomax, John. *Negro Folk Songs as Sung by Lead Belly.* New York: Macmillan, 1936.

Wolfe, Charles, and Kip Lornell. *The Life and Legend of Leadbelly.* New York: HarperCollins, 1992.

See also   African Americans; Guthrie, Woody; Johnson, Robert; Music: Popular; Racial discrimination; Recording industry.

■ League of Nations

Identification   International collective-security organization that was the predecessor of the United Nations

Date   Established on January 10, 1920

The United States' refusal to join the League of Nations contributed to the organization's toothlessness in the 1930's, when its lackluster response to military aggression emboldened fascism in Europe and Asia. American isolationism might have played a significant role in the buildup to World War II.

The League of Nations was an international collective-security organization provided for by the 1918 Versailles Treaty, which formally ended World War I. President Woodrow Wilson proposed the formation of the league as part of his Fourteen Points for Peace, which provided the framework for the treaty. The league's purpose was to provide security for member nations, which agreed to defend fellow members against aggression. Because of the United States' power and prestige, the country's membership was expected to substantially enhance the league's prospects of success. However, the U.S. Senate refused to ratify the league's covenant, and thus a weakened league was inaugurated early in 1920.

Although isolationism is often blamed for the Senate's refusal to ratify the league's covenant, other factors also were involved. A referendum held on league membership in 1919 almost surely would have passed. Moreover, had the president and his Senate supporters accepted reservations proposed to safeguard U.S. sovereignty, the covenant would have been ratified.

American isolationist attitudes grew during the 1920's, reaching a peak during the 1930's as Americans came to regard entering World War I as a mistake. Many thought that arms merchants and other special interests had misled the nation into entering a European war in which the United States had little to gain.

Canada and the League of Nations During the 1930's   Before World War I, as a dominion of the British Empire, Canada had almost no experience in international life. The nation's membership in the League of Nations was part of a growing national desire for autonomy from Great Britain and a role in international affairs. Canada's concern for its autonomy led to its attempt to limit the league's authority over members.

During the 1932 World Disarmament Conference, attended by league members, the United States, and the Soviet Union, Canada supported the view that peace could best be achieved by conflict prevention rather than by punishing aggressors. This policy preserved Canadian autonomy by ruling out mandatory punitive action and preventing the league from becoming a "super-state." Canada also opposed the internationalization of civil aviation, which would have compromised its national autonomy. However, it willingly accepted sanctions applied by the league to Italy in 1935, including oil sanctions that Canadian representatives had suggested. Canada also played an integral role in league affairs throughout the 1930's; it was represented by its prime minister in 1934 and 1936 at the league's headquarters in Geneva, Switzerland.

Growth of American Hostility to Participation in Foreign Wars   American attitudes toward the league during the 1930's were affected by growing isolationist sentiment, which became an organized political position. Americans' hostility to participation in foreign wars intensified just as the league's prestige was declining over its ineffectual attempts to deal with a series of issues, beginning with Japan's occupation of Manchuria in 1931. Other issues included

Germany's shredding of the Versailles Treaty and gradual rearmament after 1933 (secretly begun during the 1920's). The league also was unable to take effective action in 1935 when fascist Italy invaded Ethiopia, which appealed for assistance.

When ardent internationalist Franklin D. Roosevelt assumed office in 1933, anything more than nominal American cooperation with the league was politically infeasible. The Neutrality Acts of 1935 and afterward were designed to tie the president's hands, preventing him from involving the nation in foreign conflicts.

This did not mean, however, that Americans were entirely indifferent to international affairs. There was much concern over Japan's invasion of China in 1937 and the Nazi regime's aggressive behavior, especially its treatment of the Jews and its forcible annexation of Austria and occupation of Czech Sudetenland in 1938. By then, however, the league had become irrelevant.

Impact The United States' absence from the League of Nations mainly resulted in the deepening of isolationist sentiment during the 1930's. American internationalists' view that this absence was harmful to the nation and to world peace strengthened their determination to create a substitute international organization after World War II. The impact of America's refusal to join the league on the course of history might have been monumental. Had the United States provided leadership effectively opposing Japanese and German aggression, a destructive war might have been averted.

Charles F. Bahmueller

Further Reading

Callan, Jim. *America in the 1930's.* New York: Facts On File, 2005. Readable, young-adult-level account of the decade, setting the domestic context for American attitudes toward international affairs and the League of Nations.

Johnson, Paul. "The Myth of American Isolationism—Reinterpreting the Past." *Foreign Affairs* 74, no. 3 (May/June, 1995). Reassesses American isolationism, arguing that the period between the world wars was an aberration for an otherwise internationally engaged nation.

Kennedy, David M. *Freedom from Fear: The American People in Depression and War, 1929-1945.* New York: Oxford University Press, 2001. Places American attitudes to the League of Nations in the context of the nation's social, economic, and political history.

Keuhl, Warren F., and Lynne K. Dunn. *Keeping the Covenant: American Internationalists and the League of Nations, 1920-1939.* Kent, Ohio: Kent State University Press, 1997. Detailed account of how internationalists began a campaign to preserve their ideals through political struggle after their defeat in the U.S. Senate.

"League of Nations." In *The Oxford Companion to United States History,* edited by Paul S. Boyer. New York: Oxford University Press, 2001. Concise account of the relations between the United States and the league and the relationship's consequences.

Soward, F. H. "League of Nations." In *The Encyclopedia of Canada,* edited by W. Stewart Wallace. Vol. 4. Toronto: University Associates of Canada, 1948. Concise history of Canada's membership in the league.

Veatch, Richard. *Canada and the League of Nations.* Toronto: University of Toronto Press, 1975. Describes how Canada's membership in the league revealed its impulses toward autonomy and involvement in international affairs.

See also Canada and Great Britain; Foreign policy of Canada; Foreign policy of the United States; Geneva Disarmament Conference; Isolationism; Japanese military aggression; Manchuria occupation; Neutrality Acts; Nye Committee; Roosevelt, Franklin D.

■ Lee, Gypsy Rose

Identification American striptease dancer, stage and film star, and writer
Born January 9, 1914; Seattle, Washington
Died April 26, 1970; Los Angeles, California

Incorporating humor in her striptease act, Lee became the best-known and the most-photographed burlesque entertainer of the 1930's. She appeared in a few late 1930's Hollywood films. Her interest in writing emerged during this decade. Her autobiographical book Gypsy *(1957), which inspired a musical of the same name, describes her rise and her turbulent relationship with her infamous stage mother.*

Gypsy Rose Lee's career began in American vaudeville during the 1910's and 1920's. Her mother managed Lee's talented younger sister June Hovick (later, June Havoc) while Lee, born Rose Louise Hovick, assumed minor roles. When June married at age thirteen, she left vaudeville. Lee became responsible for supporting herself and her mother through her own act with the "Hollywood Blondes"; however, vaudeville was dying. By 1930, Lee was performing in a Kansas City, Missouri, burlesque theater. Reluctantly, she replaced a stripper in the comedic skits, but eventually she reinvented herself as a striptease entertainer. Rather than emphasizing singing, dancing, or jerky, bump-and-grind stripping techniques, Lee's act featured her ability to engage the audience through comedic dialogue with them and to perform a drawn-out seductive striptease.

Lee's success started with her debut at the Gaiety Theater in Toledo, Ohio, and was extended through her lengthy run at Minsky's Republic Theatre in New York. Her comedic techniques included dropping the names of highbrow luminaries, mentioning academic trivia, reciting and singing bawdy poetry and songs, dropping straight pins into the bell of a tuba, whirling her hand on bald men's heads, and spinning into the stage curtains. Lee's costumes were tasteful, often elegant, and specifically designed for her act. She tended to strip down to lingerie and silk stockings—she believed that going this far was more arousing than revealing her nude body. Her desire to be taken seriously as a performer led her to join Florenz Ziegfeld's production *Hot Cha!* (1932) and assume minor roles in musical theater. By 1935, she was performing at Irving Palace in New York. Charmed by Lee, syndicated gossip columnist Walter Winchell encouraged her writing career.

Just before the Great Depression, burlesque theaters were closing. Lee left Minsky's to become the first stripper to star in a Ziegfeld production, the 1936-1937 *Follies*. She fortified her friendship with sister June and befriended Fanny Brice, whom she credited for influencing her attitude toward show business, her stage appearance, and liberal politics. Lee's film career followed and included *You Can't Have Everything* (1937); *Ali Baba Goes to Town* (1937); *Sally, Irene, and Mary* (1938); *Battle of Broadway* (1938); and *My Lucky Star* (1938). Modest success in films led her back to the stage; however, she later appeared in the popular films *Stage Door Canteen* (1943) and *Belle of the Yukon* (1944). Lee's murder mystery novels, *The G-String Murders* (1941) and *Mother Finds a Body* (1942), received praise from literary critics and from successful writers such as Craig Rice and Truman Capote.

Impact   Lee created an entirely new type of performance art that combined casual stripping with comedy. During the 1930's, she broke down the stereotype of the stripper as a mindless, disreputable, and immoral performer. Lee's influence in the world of burlesque as both entertainer and writer remains strong. She also showed the mainstream that the striptease was capable of incorporating art, beauty, appreciation of the human body, and intelligence.

Melissa Ursula Dawn Goldsmith

Burlesque performer Gypsy Rose Lee during the late 1930's. (Archive Photos/Getty Images)

Further Reading

Frankel, Noralee. *Stripping Gypsy: The Life of Gypsy Rose Lee.* New York: Oxford University Press, 2009.

Lee, Gypsy Rose. *Gypsy: A Memoir.* New York: Harper, 1957.

Preminger, Erik Lee. *Gypsy and Me: At Home and on the Road.* Boston: Little, Brown, 1984.

See also　Dance; Film; Rand, Sally; Theater in the United States.

■ Let Us Now Praise Famous Men

Identification　Book combining photographs and text to document the lives of sharecroppers
Author　James Agee
Photographer　Walker Evans
Date　Published in 1941

In Let Us Now Praise Famous Men, James Agee and Walker Evans document the lives of three tenant farmers. With photographs and complex prose, this work combines realism with a compassionate portrayal of the poverty and hardship experienced by many Americans during and after the Great Depression of the 1930's.

Let Us Now Praise Famous Men grew out of a commission to write an article for *Fortune* magazine. In 1936, Agee and Evans spent the summer living with and studying the lives of three tenant families, identified by the pseudonyms Rickets, Woods, and Gudgers. However, Evans's photographs preserved in the Library of Congress collection identify them respectively as Tengles, Fields, and Burroughs. The book is titled for a passage from the apocryphal book Ecclesiasticus quoted in Agee's conclusion.

Agee and Evans found that their work grew beyond the confines of the original commission, and they restructured their work into book form. They intended to create a three-volume work entitled *Three Tenant Families*, but only *Let Us Now Praise Famous Men* was published. The book opens with Evans's sixty-four photographs, featuring the family members, the exteriors and interiors of their houses, and ordinary objects. The subjects gaze unflinchingly and seriously into the camera. The photographs document both the extreme poverty of the subjects and their innate dignity. The style of Agee's prose is complex, alternating among traditional narrative, detailed description of the people and their surroundings, poetry, quotations, and stream-of-consciousness passages. Agee included himself as a main character, and his internal conflict over his dual role of participant in these families' lives and, at the same time, an outsider to their lives as a journalistic observer shapes the narrative.

Impact　Since the time of its publication, this work has been acclaimed for its nuanced approach to social issues. Its intricate prose and its haunting photographs have become representative of the widespread suffering during the 1930's, particularly in rural areas of the United States.

Joanna R. Smolko

Further Reading

Davis, Hugh. *The Making of James Agee.* Knoxville: University of Tennessee Press, 2008.

Lowe, James. *The Creative Process of James Agee.* Baton Rouge: Louisiana State University Press, 1994.

Maharidge, Dale, and Michael Williamson. *And Their Children After Them: The Legacy of "Let Us Now Praise Famous Men"—James Agee, Walker Evans, and the Rise and Fall of Cotton in the South.* New York: Pantheon Books, 1989.

Mellow, James R. *Walker Evans.* New York: Basic Books, 1999.

See also　Agriculture in the United States; Art movements; Great Depression in the United States; Lange, Dorothea; Literature in the United States; Magazines; Photography.

■ Lewis, John L.

Identification　American labor leader
Born　February 12, 1880; Lucas, Iowa
Died　June 11, 1969; Alexandria, Virginia

Lewis was one of the most powerful and charismatic American labor leaders of the 1930's. He created the Congress of Industrial Organizations (CIO) with the primary purpose of unionizing unskilled, mass-production workers for the first time in American history.

John L. Lewis was born into a mining family, worked as a coal miner, and was a member of the United Mine Workers of America (UMWA). By 1911, he was working for the American Federation of Labor (AFL), a coalition of craft unions. From 1920 to

1960, Lewis served as president of the UMWA, which was the largest and most powerful union in the nation by the 1930's. As its leader, Lewis worked hard to improve mining safety standards and increase wages. By the 1930's, he was also advocating the organization and collective-bargaining rights of other unskilled, mass-production workers, including those in the automobile, glass, rubber, and steel industries. In contrast, the AFL did not want to organize unskilled laborers because it believed that the skills its members possessed gave the AFL the leverage they needed to negotiate union contracts.

On November 9, 1936, Lewis created the CIO—originally named the Committee of Industrial Organizations and started as a faction of the AFL—in order to organize industrial unions. By the end of 1937, the CIO had nearly four million members. With Lewis's leadership, the CIO successfully organized and brought collective-bargaining agreements to numerous groups of U.S. industrial workers, including the United Steel Workers of America and the United Electrical, Radio and Machine Workers of America.

Labor leader John L. Lewis making an oratorial point at a U.S. Senate committee hearing during the lae 1930's. (Library of Congress)

Impact As the founder of the CIO, Lewis believed that all workers deserved fair labor standards and wages through union representation. His success at unionizing industrial workers continues to have a positive impact on the working conditions and competitive wages of millions of American laborers.

Bernadette Zbicki Heiney

Further Reading

Alinsky, Saul. *John L. Lewis: An Unauthorized Biography.* Whitefish, Mont.: Kessinger, 2008.

Dubofsky, Melvyn, and Warren R. Van Tine. *John L. Lewis: A Biography.* New York: Quadrangle/New York Times Books, 1977.

Ziegler, Robert H. *John L. Lewis: Labor Leader.* Boston: Twayne, 1988.

See also American Federation of Labor; Automobiles and auto manufacturing; Congress of Industrial Organizations; Great Depression in the United States; National Industrial Recovery Act of 1933; New Deal; Roosevelt, Franklin D.; Unionism.

■ Lewis, Sinclair

Identification Nobel Prize-winning American novelist

Born February 7, 1885; Sauk Centre, Minnesota

Died January 10, 1951; Rome, Italy

American novelist Lewis is best known for his satirical writings depicting American life. In 1930, he became the first American to win the Nobel Prize in Literature.

Sinclair Lewis, born Harry Sinclair Lewis, had a writing career spanning several decades. His greatest period of writing was during the 1920's. When Lewis received the Nobel Prize, he had many critics. Some argued that he had received the award from a European agency for his negative depiction of American life. Others questioned his acceptance of the award after he had previously turned down the Pulitzer Prize because he felt awards of this type affected the integrity of an author. After he received the Nobel

Prize, much attention was paid to Lewis's work and the expectations were high. Three years later, he published *Ann Vickers*.

Unfortunately for Lewis, *Ann Vickers* signaled the beginning of a decline in his work. Many felt his novels no longer presented the same creative energy as his previous works, seemingly rehashing familiar themes. However, Lewis pushed forward, trying new genres and acting. In 1934, he helped create dramatizations of his 1929 novel *Dodsworth* and a new play, *Jayhawker* (1935). In 1935, *It Can't Happen Here*, his best-received work of the decade, was released.

In 1936, Lewis was awarded an honorary degree from Yale. While continuing to publish and lecture throughout the later part of the decade, he expanded his craft into the theater as a playwright, pro-

ducer, and director. He took his love for the stage on the road in 1938, as he toured as the lead in his play *Angela Is Twenty-two*. Lewis continued to write up to his death in 1951.

Impact   Lewis was the first American to win the Nobel Prize in Literature. His satirical writings captured both the shortcomings and the virtues of American life.

Michael D. Cummings, Jr.

Further Reading

Lingeman, Richard. *Sinclair Lewis: Rebel from Main Street*. New York: Random House, 2002.

Lundquist, James. *Sinclair Lewis*. New York: Frederick Ungar, 1973.

O'Connor, Richard. *Sinclair Lewis*. New York: McGraw-Hill, 1971.

Schorer, Mark. *Sinclair Lewis: An American Life*. New York: McGraw-Hill, 1961.

See also   Faulkner, William; Fitzgerald, F. Scott; Hemingway, Ernest; Literature in the United States; Nobel Prizes; West, Nathanael.

Works Progress Administration poster for a Federal Theatre production of Sinclair Lewis's It Can't Happen Here, *a satirical novel that addresses the rise of fascism during the decade.* (Library of Congress)

■ *Life Begins at Forty*

Identification   Self-help book
Author   Walter Boughton Pitkin
Date   Published in 1932

Although life expectancy for the average American during the 1930's had greatly increased as the result of improvements in medicine and sanitation, individuals older than thirty were increasingly portrayed as "old-fashioned" and "dated," an attitude that Walter Boughton Pitkin decided should be challenged.

An American psychologist and philosopher, Pitkin noticed a growing trend of depression in middle-aged Americans. During the 1920's, a youth movement had begun in which a person's adolescence was celebrated as the most productive and vibrant time of life. Liberated from parental control by the invention of the automobile and encouraged by a technology-driven mode of life to leave the family home in search of independence, the young were the new heroes and heroines of stage and screen.

In response, Pitkin published his self-help book *Life Begins at Forty* to question this youth-oriented perspective on life and living. In his opinion, American middle-aged citizens needed to redefine their age group as vibrant and their station in life as rewarding. Pitkin used Herbert Hoover and Henry David Thoreau as examples of the kind of wise, active men who lived their most vital years in their forties and beyond. Their lives were held up as examples of what mature Americans should strive to achieve. The most gratifying part of the increasingly long life that Americans enjoyed, Pitkin declared, was that living into one's forties was no longer accompanied by a slow descent into feebleness. Rather, he declared, the wisdom of one's middle years were accompanied by health and well-being. The United States was changing, Pitkin declared, and the American view of youth and age needed to change as well.

Impact Although Pitkin has been attributed with coining the phrase "life begins at forty," he simply popularized it. The phrase became the title of a film, directed by George Marshall in 1935, and a song written by Jack Yellen and Ted Shapiro, which was recorded by Sophie Tucker in 1937. It symbolized America's increasing appreciation of the greater health and vitality of its older citizens as well as the awareness of the value of a long life well spent.

Julia M. Meyers

Cover of the first issue of Life *magazine, dated November 23, 1936, featuring Montana's Fort Peck Dam.* (Time & Life Pictures/Getty Images)

Further Reading

Henrickson, Wilma Wood. *Detroit Perspectives: Crossroads and Turning Points.* Detroit: Wayne State University Press, 1991.

Pitkin, Walter B. *Life Begins at Forty.* New York: McGraw-Hill, 1932.

See also Education; Hobbies; Hoover, Herbert; Literature in the United States; Recreation.

■ *Life* magazine

Identification First major photojournalistic magazine in the United States

Date First issue dated November 23, 1936

Life was the first major American magazine to contain mostly pictures, with minimal writing. Many of its stories during the 1930's documented people's problems during the Depression, whether the subjects were poor or rich. Most stories were newsworthy.

In 1936, Henry R. Luce started *Life* as a weekly magazine that cost ten cents a copy. The magazine lasted until 1972 but was revived as a monthly magazine from 1978 to 2000. About 380,000 copies were printed at first, but the circulation jumped to more than one million copies shortly after that. The first issue of *Life* had a cover picture, taken by Margaret Bourke-White, and an eleven-page story about Fort Peck Dam in Montana. The pictures were mostly of workers' living conditions in the desert rather than of the dam. Each picture had a short caption, which became a typical practice of the magazine.

During the 1930's, pictures featured in *Life* were black and white, but they were printed clearly and on good paper. Many famous photographers were employed by the magazine, including Bourke-White, Robert Capa, Alfred Eisenstaedt, and W. Eugene Smith. Bourke-White traveled extensively to take pictures for *Life*. She estimated that she had traveled at least one million miles and exposed more than 250,000 pictures by the time she finished with the magazine. She was a good writer, often writing captions for her photographs. Capa specialized in war photographs. In 1936, he went to Spain to photograph the Spanish Civil War, and he later photographed World War II. Eventually, he was killed photographing a battle. Eisenstaedt used small, 35-millimeter Leica cameras so that he could take pictures quickly and unobtrusively. He had more than thirteen hundred assignments while working for *Life*. Smith worked for *Life* from the late 1930's to 1954, and he produced some outstanding photo stories, such as one about Albert Schweitzer and another about life in a Spanish village.

Typically, each issue of *Life* had about fifty pages of pictures on a variety of subjects. For instance, the May 31, 1937, issue had articles about falling horseback riders, censorship, Henry Ford, Ford workers and unions, the Memphis Cotton Festival, the Golden Gate Bridge opening, the film of the week, and King George VI's coronation. There were also sections of news pictures of some famous and not-so-famous persons and events; the Kent School rowing team; the bombing of Bilbao, Spain; the high school prom in Antigo, Wisconsin; and pictures by readers sent to the editor.

Advertisements in the magazine were mostly in black and white, though a few liquor and car ads were in vivid color. Some of the companies whose products were advertised remain familiar, such as Chevrolet, General Electric, Elgin watches, Schick razors, and Van de Camp's. Other products are no longer familiar, such as Sal Hepatica, Kremel Hair Tonic, the Tumbler auto beauty process, Oralgene chewing gum, the New Haven passenger train, and Mavis face powder.

Impact   *Life* magazine was the first major photojournalism magazine featuring photo stories of important news events as well as everyday, commonplace occurrences. The few photographs featured in newspapers had poor resolution, so they were difficult to see. Thus, *Life* magazine was an important medium for seeing news events. Once television began in the early 1950's, the circulation of *Life* began to drop. Nevertheless, *Life* had a major place in photojournalism during the peak of the magazine's popularity.

Robert L. Cullers

Further Reading

Doss, Erika Lee. *Looking at "Life" Magazine.* Washington, D.C.: Smithsonian Institution Press, 2001.

The Great Life Photographers. London: Thames and Hudson, 2004.

See also   *Fortune* magazine; *Look* magazine; Luce, Henry; Magazines; Photography.

■ *L'il Abner*

Identification   Syndicated comic strip
Cartoonist   Al Capp
Date   First published on August 13, 1934

A comic strip about a young hillbilly, his family, and his friends in the bizarre community of Dogpatch, L'il Abner *provided entertainment for millions during the Depression, with a viewpoint that mocked while it sympathized with the poor and marginalized members of American society. Al Capp's drawing skills, flair for characterization, and absurd situations made his work popular.*

When *L'il Abner* first appeared on August 13, 1934, Capp was already a veteran of the fiercely competitive comic-strip world. His first venture into hillbilly humor appeared in the *Joe Palooka* strip; he worked as an assistant to *Palooka* creator Ham Fisher in 1933. A native of New Haven, Connecticut, Capp had no direct connection to the Appalachia he ruthlessly mocked. After a falling out with Fisher in 1934, Capp sold *L'il Abner* to syndication giant United Features.

The strip's central character was the lazy and stupid but good-hearted and patriotic hillbilly Abner Yokum. Other characters inhabiting the fictional community of Dogpatch in *L'il Abner*'s early years included his formidable mother, Pansy Yokum, known as "Mammy," and his overmatched father, Pappy Yokum. There were also attractive young girls who demonstrated the exuberant physicality that was a hallmark of Capp's art. These women were often competing for Abner's favors, but his true love was the buxom blond Daisy Mae. Abner's rival for Daisy's affections was massive wrestler Earthquake McGoon. A master caricaturist, Capp relished drawing both ugly and pretty women. Dogpatch denizen Sadie Hawkins was too ugly to find a husband, so her father organized an event in which single women chased down the town's bachelors with the object of matrimony. Sadie Hawkins Day first appeared in the November 15, 1937, strip. Always occurring in November, Sadie Hawkins Day inspired events at hundreds of American colleges in the following few years, when in a mild gender reversal, girls asked out boys. Despite his mockery of Dogpatch and its citizens, Capp took their side against outsiders, including greedy capitalists.

Impact   *L'il Abner* is one of the classic comic strips of the twentieth century. In addition to its licensing success, it was adapted to films and the Broadway stage and was featured on a postage stamp. Capp's work helped shape American views of Appalachia and its denizens and contributed numerous words and concepts to the cultural vocabulary, such as "druthers," Dogpatch, and Sadie Hawkins Day. It ran until November 13, 1977.

William E. Burns

Further Reading

Theroux, Alexander. *The Enigma of Al Capp.* Seattle: Fantagraphics Books, 1999.

Walker, Brian. *The Comics Before 1945.* New York: Harry N. Abrams, 2004.

See also   *Apple Mary; Blondie* comic strip; Comic strips; *Dick Tracy;* Fads; *L'il Abner, Little Orphan Annie;* Newspapers, Canadian; Newspapers, U.S.; Travel.

■ Lincoln Continental Mark I

Definition   American luxury automobile

Introduced in 1939, the Lincoln Continental became a symbol of American emergence from the Great Depression and a profound influence on American automobile design during the mid-twentieth century.

During the late 1930's, the Ford Motor Company was recovering from the effects of the Great Depression. Its Lincoln division, known as a producer of luxury automobiles, had responded to the economic downturn by introducing the Zephyr, a more affordable model, during the mid-1930's.

In 1938, company president Edsel Ford and chief designer Eugene T. Gregorie, inspired by the design of European automobiles, modified the design of the Zephyr by streamlining its profile and adding several distinctive features, including a shortened trunk with a push-button latch and an externally mounted spare tire. The result was the Continental, known retrospectively as the Mark I. Initial production runs were limited, numbering in the hundreds of vehicles. The cars were composed of many hand-crafted parts. The vehicles sold for around $2,800, well above the average price of $850 for an American automobile but accessible to affluent, upwardly mobile households and established socialites whose wealth had been diminished by the Great Depression. Production increased to more than twelve hundred vehicles in 1941, as machinery was added to the assembly lines, and to more than sixty-five hundred in 1942. Production ceased in 1942 because of World War II.

Impact   The introduction of the Lincoln Continental signaled the reemergence of the American luxury car in the aftermath of the most severe stages of the Great Depression. In contrast to the luxury cars of the 1920's and 1930's, the Continental Mark I, although expensive, was sufficiently affordable to attract buyers from the growing American middle class. Its streamlined, futuristic design attracted the attention of contemporary arbiters of style, such as Frank Lloyd Wright, and its combination of luxury with relative affordability provided a model for American automobile production in the postwar era. The automobile remained a symbol of American economic affluence and industrial dominance throughout the latter half of the twentieth century.

Michael H. Burchett

Further Reading

Dominguez, Henry L. *Edsel Ford and E. T. Gregorie: The Remarkable Design Team and Their Classic Fords of the 1930's and 1940's.* Warrendale, Pa.: SAE International, 1999.

Howley, Tim. *The Lincoln Continental Story: From Zephyr to Mark II.* Hudson, Wis.: Iconongraphix, 2005.

Lamm, Michael. *A Century of Automotive Style: One Hundred Years of American Car Design.* Stockton, Calif.: Lamm-Morada, 1996.

See also   Automobiles and auto manufacturing; Business and the economy in the United States; Ford, Henry; Great Depression in the United States; Wright, Frank Lloyd.

■ Lindbergh, Anne Morrow

Identification Aviator, writer, wife of pilot Charles
    A. Lindbergh, and daughter of Ambassador and
    Senator Dwight Morrow
Born June 22, 1906; Englewood, New Jersey
Died February 7, 2001; Passumpsic, Vermont

*Lindbergh's role in aviation and partnership with her hus-
band throughout the 1930's helped to familiarize the public
with flying, while her books detailing her air travels and aerial impressions enjoyed popular success. The kidnapping
and death of her first son received overwhelming publicity
and resulted in changes to the law.*

Anne Morrow Lindbergh married Charles A. Lindbergh on May 27, 1929, and soon after adopted a
passion of her own for flying. In 1930, she became
the first American woman to acquire a glider pilot's
license. Over the following decade, she worked
alongside her husband as copilot, navigator, and radio operator. The pair set a transcontinental record
in speed for their Los Angeles to New York City flight
of fourteen hours and forty-five minutes in 1930. A
year later, they journeyed for three months, survey-
ing air routes over Canada and Alaska to East Asia.
Lindbergh's first book, *North to the Orient* (1935),
chronicled the couple's trip for an eager reading
public. *Listen! The Wind* (1938) detailed their survey
of transatlantic air routes in 1933-1934. Her reputation as a writer was strengthened by her second
book, even as her adventures sparked national interest in flying and made the public more open to the
possibilities of aviation.

Lindbergh gave birth to her first child, Charles,
Jr., in June of 1930. Less than two years later, the baby
was abducted and held for ransom. The "Lindbergh
baby" kidnapping became one of the most famous
crimes of the decade and, perhaps, the century.
Most Americans were seeking security in a difficult,
tumultuous economic era, and the child's disappearance was additional evidence of the unsettling
times. After a high-profile investigation, the baby's
body was discovered about two months later. Police
arrested Bruno Richard Hauptmann as a suspect.
He was later tried, convicted, and executed for
the crime. Eventually, the first federal abduction
statute, commonly called "the Lindbergh Law,"
was passed, making kidnapping a capital offense.

To respond to threats made against their second child and to create some privacy for themselves, the Lindbergh family moved to England
in 1935. They remained in Europe until just before World War II. There, Charles A. Lindbergh
began touting an isolationist stance, which
Anne Lindbergh feared was causing him to lose
public support. Her next book, *The Wave of the
Future, a Confession of Faith* (1940), attempted to
explain the couple's political stance to an increasingly critical public.

Lindbergh's later works reinstated her popularity. They include a novel, *The Steep Ascent*
(1944), *The Unicorn, and Other Poems, 1935-1955*
(1956), and her journals covering the years
1922 to 1944: *Bring Me a Unicorn* (1972), *Hour of
Gold, Hour of Lead* (1973), *Locked Rooms and Open
Doors* (1974), *The Flower and the Nettle* (1976), and
War Within and Without (1980). In her lifetime
she was awarded honors from the National Geographic Society, the U.S. Flag Association, and
Women in Aerospace as well as honorary degrees from several educational institutions.

*Aviator and writer Anne Morrow Lindbergh smiles while seated next to
an airplane in Chicago.* (Archive Photos/Getty Images)

Impact Lindbergh's descriptions and love of flying during the 1930's helped ease the way for later commercial aviation and opened the door for other women pilots. The 1930's case and trial of her son's suspected killer resulted in significant changes to U.S. federal law. She received acclaim for her books, particularly her 1955 book, *Gift from the Sea*, which consisted of contemplative essays exploring the struggle of individuals, especially women, to find balance and peace in life.

Rhea Davison-Edwards

Further Reading

Hertog, Susan. *Anne Morrow Lindbergh: Her Life.* New York: Anchor Books, 1999.

Milton, Joyce. *Loss of Eden: A Biography of Charles and Anne Morrow Lindbergh.* New York: HarperCollins, 1993.

Winters, Kathleen C. *Anne Morrow Lindbergh: First Lady of the Air.* New York: Palgrave Macmillan, 2006.

See also Aviation and aeronautics; Germany and U.S. appeasement; Lindbergh baby kidnapping; Literature in the United States; Recreation.

■ Lindbergh baby kidnapping

The Event Abduction for ransom of the two-year-old son of celebrated aviator Charles A. Lindbergh

Date Child abducted on March 1, 1932

Charles A. Lindbergh, Jr., the infant son of famous aviator Charles A. Lindbergh, was kidnapped from his crib for ransom and killed, to the outrage of the nation. Bruno Richard Hauptmann was convicted and executed for committing what was dubbed the "crime of the century."

The kidnapping of baby Lindbergh was labeled the crime of the century because of the fame of the child's parents, the audacity of the crime, and the heartlessness of the kidnapper. In 1927, Lindbergh had successfully completed the first nonstop, solo air flight across the Atlantic. Showered with wealth and fame, he married Anne Morrow Lindbergh in 1927, and they had their first child, Charles Lindbergh, Jr., in 1930. In 1932, the Lindbergh family was spending weekends in their newly built mansion in Hopewell, New Jersey. At about 9:30 P.M. on March 1, 1932, twenty-month-old Charles Lindbergh, Jr., was surreptitiously kidnapped from his second-floor nursery. Shortly thereafter, the baby's empty crib was discovered by the baby's nurse, along with a ransom note and a homemade ladder used by the kidnapper.

The Ransom and Manhunt The ransom note demanded fifty thousand dollars. On March 9, John Condon, a Bronx resident who had offered his services as intermediary in a local newspaper, was contacted by the kidnapper, who arranged for a meeting in the Woodlawn cemetery in the Bronx. Using the pseudonym "Jafsie," Condon met with the kidnapper twice, the second time on April 2, 1932, with Lindbergh in the distance, to pay fifty thousand dollars in gold certificate currency in exchange for directions to the baby's whereabouts. However, the Lindbergh baby was not located. In fact, the kidnapper had murdered the baby on the night of the crime, disposing of the body in nearby woods, where it was found on May 12, 1932, by a passerby.

A massive manhunt was launched for the murderer, aided by passage of the "Lindbergh Law" on June 22, 1932, making kidnapping a federal crime. The search met with little success except that by executive order of President Franklin D. Roosevelt, all gold certificate currency was required to be exchanged by May 1, 1933. Thus, the ransomed gold certificates became conspicuous, and by their prerecorded serial numbers, the police were able to trace their expenditures to a radius of the Lexington Avenue subway running through the Bronx. The big break in the case came on September 15, 1934, when a gas-station attendant recorded the automobile license number of a man who paid with a ransomed gold certificate. The automobile was registered to Hauptmann, a Bronx carpenter, who was arrested four days later. The police found nearly fifteen thousand dollars in ransomed gold certificates concealed in Hauptmann's garage.

The Trial of Hauptmann Hauptmann's trial began on January 2, 1935, in the Flemington, New Jersey, courthouse. The trial was covered by newspaper, teletype, radio, and film, with media stars reporting from the courthouse, which attracted worldwide publicity. The trial lasted thirty-two days, during which 162 witnesses presented more than one million words of testimony. The weight of the evidence against Hauptmann at the trial was incontrovertible.

He was found in possession of the ransom money. The homemade ladder used in the kidnapping was linked to him: A sketch of the ladder was found in his notebook, and wood expert Arthur Koehler demonstrated that unique marks on the ladder were made by Hauptmann's carpentry tools and that "rail sixteen" of the ladder had actually been made from a missing floorboard in Hauptmann's attic. Eight of the world's leading handwriting experts testified that Hauptmann wrote the ransom notes. In his native Germany, Hauptmann had been convicted of numerous crimes, including burglarizing the house of a mayor with a two-story ladder. He did not work on the day of the kidnapping. The contact information for Jafsie was hidden in Hauptmann's closet. After Jafsie handed over the ransom money to the man in the cemetery, Hauptmann stopped working altogether, to live a life of ease as a Wall Street speculator. Hauptmann's account books showed that he spent thirty-five thousand dollars over the course of two years, the amount of the missing ransom money. Finally, Hauptmann was identified at trial by Condon and Lindbergh as the man in the cemetery and by other eyewitnesses to various events relating to the crime.

On February 13, 1935, Hauptmann was convicted of murder. After his appeals to various New Jersey and federal courts and to New Jersey governor Harold G. Hoffman were exhausted, Hauptmann was executed on April 3, 1936. In the meantime, the Lindberghs, traumatized by the tragedy and publicity, relocated to Europe.

Impact The crime of the century riveted the entire nation and world. It resulted in legislation to make kidnapping a federal offense, under the jurisdiction of the Federal Bureau of Investigation (FBI). With circumstantial evidence meticulously assembled by the New Jersey State Police, and the central role of handwriting, nail, and wood experts in proving Hauptmann's guilt, the trial demonstrated the reliability and importance of modern forensic techniques and evidence.

Howard Bromberg

Further Reading

Berg, Scott. *Lindbergh*. New York: Berkeley, 1999. Pulitzer Prize-winning biography, with extensive treatment of the kidnapping.

Fensch, Thomas, ed. *Files on the Lindbergh Baby Kidnapping*. Woodlands, Tex.: New Century Books:

2001. Publication of early FBI files and reports on the case as well as New Jersey State Police photographs and an annotated bibliography.

Fisher, Jim. *The Ghosts of Hopewell: Setting the Record Straight in the Lindbergh Case*. Carbondale: Southern Illinois University Press, 1999. An authority on the case refutes efforts to exonerate Hauptmann.

_____. *The Lindbergh Case*. New Brunswick, N.J.: Rutgers University Press, 1998. Straightforward, compelling account that demonstrates Hauptmann's guilt beyond question.

Gardner, Lloyd. *The Case That Never Dies: The Lindbergh Kidnapping*. New Brunswick, N.J.: Rutgers University Press, 2004. A neutral retelling of the kidnapping, arrest, and trial, emphasizing the significance of the case in American history.

Kennedy, Ludovic. *The Airman and the Carpenter: The Lindbergh Kidnapping and the Framing of Richard Hauptmann*. New York: Viking Press, 1985. By the narrator of a 1982 pro-Hauptmann television documentary; blames Hauptmann's conviction on a conspiracy by law-enforcement personnel.

Scaduto, Anthony. *Scapegoat: The Lonesome Death of Bruno Hauptmann*. New York: G. P. Putnam's Sons, 1976. The first of several modern books that claim Hauptmann's innocence, theorizing that the prosecution evidence was perjured and the physical evidence fabricated.

See also Crimes and scandals; Lindbergh, Anne Morrow; Newspapers, U.S.; Organized crime.

■ Literature in Canada

During the 1930's, the Great Depression stimulated the growth of modernism and realism in Canadian literature in English. In French Canada, some writers struck blows at ecclesiastical-political control, laying groundwork for the later Quiet Revolution.

Canadian poetry and prose in both English and French developed significantly during the 1930's. At a time when Canada was asserting its political independence from Great Britain, a national literature was coalescing.

Canadian Poetry in English Modernism and its auxiliary movements, such as surrealism and formalism, came belatedly and intermittently to Canada. Since the late nineteenth century, Canadian poetry had been characterized by descriptions of traditional, picturesque landscapes. Fitting subject matter for poetry was limited to patriotism, spirituality, and Canadian life and landscapes.

Development of modernism in Canadian poetry was accelerated during the 1920's and 1930's by a collection of poets known as the Montreal group, composed of A. J. M. Smith, Frank Scott, and A. M. Klein. Modernism is a literary genre that breaks with conventionalism; thus, these poets freed themselves from the constraints of rhyme and traditional meters and the romantic worldview of the nineteenth century. The group encouraged poets to imitate realistic themes, metaphysical intricacy, and techniques of British and American poets. Along with E. J. Pratt and Robert Finch, the Montreal group produced *New Provinces* (1936), an anthology demonstrating advances in early Canadian modernism regarding subjects, technique, poetic perspective, and use of unadorned language of everyday speech.

Canadian modernism continued to develop as poets learned from the expressionists, imagists, modernists, experimenters in free verse, and British and American poets who had a social orientation. The resulting modernism in Canadian poetry was a fascinating amalgamation of Victorian, Romantic, and modernist practices.

Of the modern Canadian poets, Pratt is one of the most original and vivacious. He displayed an inclination toward fantasy and an Elizabethan enjoyment in the effervescent splendor of words. He possessed a sense of the poet's prophetic role, as did his poetic forbears, both British and Canadian.

Pratt's poetry reflects his fascination with science and the sea. He believed science was not incompatible with the principles of his Christian faith, which he infused into epic narratives. His famous epic *The Titanic* (1935) is a long mythic poem, depicting the calamity of that ship's sinking, including a portrayal of the band playing on in the face of death. Filled with the technical nuance of archaisms, mythological allusion, and scientific terms, it produces a sense of historical opera. In *The Titanic*, Pratt pictures the human-sized heroic action up against whatever problems individuals regarded as insurmountable. His writing celebrated courageous action and the efficacy of personal and public decision.

Although Pratt is associated with the emergence of modernism in Canadian poetry, he did not abandon all poetic tradition. His proclivity to create myth ties him to the preceding century, but his brutal realism is partially what distinguishes his verse as modern.

Smith composed compelling representations of the Canadian landscape that demonstrated metaphysical complexity and careful craftsmanship. In "The Lonely Land" (1936), he united a nationalist character with a modernist aesthetic that together ensured its standing as an emblematic modern Canadian poem.

Scott was skillful in satiric verse. He also published a number of imagist poems, but he moved rapidly into social verse during the 1930's.

Klein was steeped in Jewish tradition. He wrote with profound understanding of Jewish culture and other minority groups. His psalms and prophetic poems run from social satire to political protest.

Annie Dalton was a great Canadian female poet. Her most renowned published work is *Lilies and Leopards* (1935). Her poems are exceptionally varied and packed with thought. She was skillful in both conventional meters and free-form poetry.

Dorothy Livesay, another female poet, wrote and published verse on a wide range of topics, including social protest, but her most robust work was from the imagist movement. Her work juxtaposes personal experience with social causes and uses a wide range of styles: lyrical, narrative, dramatic, reflective, documentary, and memoir.

Canadian Prose in English   The Great Depression strengthened the tendency of writers to be critical of Canadian values and institutions and to increase expressions of social protest. Realistic novels emerged; these sought to reconstruct societal norms by challenging the prudence of the status quo. As psychological constructs of the twentieth century influenced Canadian writing, psychological realism began to develop. As humanity emerged, nature receded, yet the strong sense of place on which Canadian fiction is founded continued to dominate.

The move toward realism impacted subjects as well as settings. Characteristic themes of the 1930's involved the lives of ordinary individuals, factory laborers, and immigrants and the violent life of the urban street.

Frederick Philip Grove, founder of the realist tradition in Canadian fiction, penned some of Canada's best-known novels of the time. European-born, he moved to the Manitoba prairie and wrote about the lives of pioneer immigrants arriving in the wilderness and struggling against uncleared land and a hostile environment.

The Yoke of Life (1930), *Fruits of the Earth* (1933), and *Two Generations* (1939) are three of Grove's "realistic" farm novels, telling of stress and failure, particularly the failure to overcome self-centeredness. Len Sterner in *The Yoke of Life* commits suicide when the world does not meet his expectations; Abe Spalding in *Fruits of the Earth* estranges his wife and daughter as he forces himself to power. One of the first writers of sociological novels, Grove also analyzed the Canadian economic class structure.

Urban realism was solidly established by Morley Callaghan's novels. His fiction depicts crime and poverty in Canadian cities but also looks to the Roman Catholic faith as a sustaining force. Callaghan wrote in a simple and economical style. A fresh exemplar for Canadian prose was established by Callaghan's plain style. In his early novels, including *It's Never Over* (1930) and *A Broken Journey* (1932), characters are victimized by forces that seem to be beyond their control.

In his next three novels, Callaghan moved to a more Christian outlook. He describes with compassion the experiences of those who are different and those who are morally disoriented in urban society. In *Such Is My Beloved* (1934), he depicts a priest's attempt to save two prostitutes, a venture that, according to the authorities, brings his reputation and that of the church into question. In *They Shall Inherit the Earth* (1935), a father and son clash during the Great Depression. In *More Joy in Heaven* (1937), a reformed bank robber is misunderstood by society. In each of these novels, a saintly hero stands against society.

Some novelists sought to chronicle the disillusionment of the era. A powerful examination of social protest during the Great Depression is Irene Baird's *Waste Heritage* (1939), a documentary novel about labor discord and class conflict in Vancouver in 1938.

The most popular Canadian novelist of the time was Mazo de la Roche. She blended the genres of the early twentieth century regional idylls with nineteenth century historical romances. De la Roche wrote the Jana series, a recounting of the Whiteoak family and of their Ontario estate, the longest series in Canadian fiction, comprising sixteen volumes. De la Roche published other novels as well as children's and animal stories.

Travel and adventure in the undeveloped parts of Canada proved to be popular themes in Canadian literature. Travel literature during the 1930's included *Arctic Trader* (1934), an account by fur trader P. H. Godsell; *My Seventy Years* (1938), an autobiography by Martha Louise Black, who trekked the thirty-three miles of the Chilkoot Trail into the Yukon while pregnant; *Outcasts of Canada* (1932) by E. F. G. Fripp, a story of farming in the Okanagan and work as a salesman in Vancouver; and G. H. Westbury's *Misadventures of a Working Hobo in Canada* (1930), a dreary trek through a world of trains and rooming houses.

Nature writing is a preeminent literary genre in Canada. *The Fur Trade in Canada* (1930), by Harold Adams Innis, recounts the beaver fur trade from the sixteenth century to the early twentieth century. The book begins with a natural history of the beaver and attests that the fur trade created economic dependence among immigrants and had devastating effects on aboriginal peoples.

Charles G. D. Roberts and Ernest Thompson Seton originated the animal story, another form of nature writing and the sole art form native to Canada. They each created anthropomorphic animal characters and imaginatively adapted Darwinian scientific method.

Grey Owl, famous for his nature stories, was a noted naturalist and conservationist who boasted about his Apache ancestry in his books about "beaver lodge" set on Lake Ajawaan, Saskatchewan. Grey Owl lived with a moose and his "beaver people" deep in a pine, aspen, and spruce forest, taking on the role of a modern Hiawatha, a selfless "Messiah of the Wilderness" and advocate for nature. In his books, he bewailed the loss of a past in harmony with uncontaminated nature and exalted the gentleness of his humanlike companions. Grey Owl's autobiographical *Pilgrims of the Wild* was published in 1935. At his death in 1938, it was disclosed that he was actually English-born Archie Belany.

In the science-fiction genre, A. E. van Vogt published "Black Destroyer" (1939), a short story influenced by Charles Darwin's *On the Origin of Species*. It portrayed a ferocious man-eating alien that hunted the crew of a spaceship. The story became an immediate classic and eventually inspired a number of science-fiction films.

The experiences of immigrants continued to be an important theme in Canadian literature during the 1930's. Frederick John Niven, in the three-volume narrative that began with *The Flying Years* (1935), traced the historical development of the prairies from the 1920's to the 1950's. The protagonist of the story becomes a representative immigrant who experiences a profound existential isolation, which cuts him off from the community. Hans Harder, in *In Wologdas Weissen Wäldern* (1934), describes the ordeal of displacement from Russia and migration to Canada. Icelandic Canadian writer Laura Goodman Salverson, in her autobiography, *Confessions of an Immigrant's Daughter* (1939), explores the problems faced by an immigrant family.

Canadian Writing in French During the 1930's in Canada, anglophone writing was different from francophone writing. Canadian literature in French centered mainly on Canadian history, religion, and patriotism. The historical novel was a favored art form. Writers of historical novels spotlighted the insidious nature of Anglo-Saxon characters and the moral virtue of French Canadian ones. In spite of the redeeming characteristics of a few Anglo-Saxon characters, the characters seldom, if ever, prevailed over their French-Canadian counterparts.

Rural novels were also popular. Gonzalve Desaulniers's *Les Bois qui chantent* (1930) is a representative anthology of legends and poetic songs, in which nature's voice stimulates in the reader an acknowledgment of the divine. In Maurice Constantin-Weyer's *La Foret* (1935), the immigrant settlers are doomed because they did not live in concert with nature. A conflict between living in the country and living in the city gave rise to a number of novels with the theme of desertion, such as *Le Déserteur et autres récits de la terre* (1934) by Claude-Henri Grignon, in which a homesteader who moves to the city is declared to be a deserter.

The apex of the rural novel genre was reached in 1938 with *Trente Arpents* by Ringuet. In the novel, the land, which in the nineteenth century had been regarded as society's salvation, ceased supporting its lord. During this economic crisis, industrialization was taking place and country people were lured to the city.

With the migration to urban areas and the economic crisis of the 1930's, the French Canadian novel modified its perspective and highlighted the city and the individual. French Canadian writers became more innovative, realistic, and introspective. The psychological novel gradually evolved as character development increased in works such as Grignon's *Un Homme et son péché* (1933; *The Woman and the Miser,* 1978). Rex Desmarchais further deepened character analysis in *L'initiatrice* (1932) and *Le feu intérieur* (1933).

Natural and creative French Canadian writing was held back by isolationism, strict Roman Catholicism, and a small reader market. Only morality tales and conformist novels won the acceptance of the church and the political establishment.

During the 1930's, some writers struck blows at the ecclesiastical-political control. Quebec Catholic tradition already had been strongly exposed in Albert Laberge's *La Scouine* (1918). The Catholic Church was further criticized by Grignon in *Un Homme et son péché,* Jean-Charles Harvey in *Les Demi-Civilisés* (1934; *Sackcloth for Barner,* 1938), and Ringuet in *Trente Arpents.* These writers laid the groundwork for the Quiet Revolution, a period in Quebec during the 1960's in which many institutions controlled by the Catholic Church were rapidly secularized. However, throughout the 1930's, despite these isolated voices, Quebecois fiction writers largely continued to be loyal to the ecclesiastical and political establishment.

Impact Canadian literature continued to develop during the 1930's in spite of—and also because of—the Great Depression. Canadian writers moved into the domain of modernism and realism. Multiple languages and multiculturalism spurred by immigration allowed Canadians to produce a wide variety of literature.

Chrissa Shamberger

Further Reading

Atwood, Margaret. *Survival: A Thematic Guide to Canadian Literature.* Toronto: Anansi, 1972. One of Canada's leading writers argues that most patterns found in Canadian literature are related to the theme of survival.

Hammill, Faye. *Canadian Literature.* Edinburgh, Scotland: Edinburgh University Press, 2007. Combines historical and thematic approaches to texts by important writers, with excellent introduction and historical synopsis. Includes chronology, glossary, list of student resources, and bibliography.

Keith, W. J. *Canadian Literature in English.* New York: Longman, 1985. Sections on fiction and on poetry show how these branches of literature developed during the 1930's. Useful chronology, brief notes on individual authors, bibliography, and index.

Klinck, Carl F. *Literary History of Canada.* Toronto: University of Toronto Press, 1965. Older but useful survey of Canadian literary history.

New, William H. *A History of Canadian Literature.* 2d ed. Montreal: McGill-Queen's University Press, 2003. Indispensable history of the development of Canadian literature from First Nations myths through the early years of the twenty-first century. Chronology and bibliography.

See also Great Depression in Canada; Immigration to Canada; Jews in Canada; Literature in the United States; Native Americans; Science fiction; Urbanization in Canada.

■ Literature in the United States

Literature during the 1930's contained energy and purpose and helped Americans deal with the multiple crises of the Great Depression. It documented the problems of poverty, unemployment, and hunger across the country, while giving readers glimpses of the courage and camaraderie to help them pull through tough economic times.

The decade of the 1930's is set off by the economic crash of 1929 and the beginning U.S. involvement in World War II in 1941. Its bookends, the boom years of the Jazz Age and the tense war and postwar years—help to highlight the significant differences between the literatures of the disparate eras. The poetry, fiction, and drama of the 1930's reflected the issues of the Great Depression with a focus on social, economic, and political issues.

The Activist Commitment The novelists who created innovative styles in the 1920's, such as Ernest Hemingway, F. Scott Fitzgerald, and William Faulkner, continued to publish during the 1930's, but their work either reflected the changes in the atmosphere of the Depression or appeared less important. Fitzgerald never matched the success of *The Great Gatsby* (1925), and he died just as the 1930's ended. He was never satisfied with *Tender Is the Night* (1934), which critic Edmund Wilson reedited after

his death, and *The Last Tycoon* (1941) was left unfinished but revealed a departure in subject matter, focusing on the power structure of Hollywood. Hemingway's best novel of the period was *For Whom the Bell Tolls* (1940), a romantic story of the Spanish Civil War that revealed the increasing literary interest during this period in the international rise of fascism. Of major American writers who started during the 1920's, only Faulkner did his best work during the 1930's; novels he wrote in the decade included *Light in August* (1932) and *Absalom, Absalom!* (1936), but his fiction seemed out of touch with the main issues of American fiction. By 1944, Faulkner was out of print in the United States, and he reemerged only when he won the Nobel Prize in Literature in 1950. Like Nathanael West, who wrote *Miss Lonelyhearts* (1933) and *The Day of the Locust* (1939), Faulkner was one of the writers of the 1930's who had to wait for a different cultural climate in which to be rediscovered.

Reflected across the literary spectrum, from poetry and theater to fiction and nonfiction, the dominant mood of the 1930's was an awareness of pressing social and economic issues and a political commitment to address these massive problems in the United States. The enormity of the Great Depression struck many writers at once: In 1932, when one of four American workers was unemployed, fifty-two leading writers and intellectuals—including Malcolm Cowley, John Dos Passos, Langston Hughes, Lincoln Steffens, and Wilson—signed an open letter supporting the Communist Party USA candidate for president of the United States. From the perspective of these writers, American capitalism was near collapse, and they found solutions in the ideas of the political and literary left. One of those ideas was that writers should address the social and economic problems of the United States, and in numerous articles and editorials, not only in the Marxist *New Masses* but also in liberal magazines such as *The Nation* and *The New Republic,* reviewers and critics urged novelists and poets to examine and write about the multiple problems of the United States.

The literary result of this focus was a newfound interest in social and economic subjects. Writers such as Wilson, who wrote *The American Jitters: A Year of the Slump* (1932), and Sherwood Anderson, who wrote *Puzzled America* (1935), traveled back and forth across the country, documenting how Americans were surviving or not during the early years of the Depression. This documentary journalism led writers to enlist photographers to help illustrate the multiple problems: Erskine Caldwell joined with photographer Margaret Bourke-White in *You Have Seen Their Faces* (1937), Archibald MacLeish wrote a prose-poem that accompanied Farm Security Administration photographs in *Land of the Free* (1938), Paul Schuster Taylor and Dorothea Lange teamed up in *An American Exodus: A Record of Human Erosion in the Thirties* (1939), and James Agee and Walker Evans published the classic of this genre in *Let Us Now Praise Famous Men* (1941), a study of three Alabama tenant-farm families. This documentary impulse can be seen in the dozens of books the Federal Writers' Project produced, such as *These Are Our Lives*

(1939)—a collection of interviews of residents in North Carolina, Tennessee, and Georgia—or the American Guide series to the forty-eight states.

This energy spilled over into poetry and theater during the 1930's as well. Modernist Anglo-American writers of the poetic renaissance of 1910 to 1930 continued to work through the 1930's, but they seemed to be increasingly irrelevant to what was happening in the United States; this was especially true of T. S. Eliot and Ezra Pound, who lived permanently in Europe. Popular older poets included Robert Frost (*A Further Range* [1937]) and Carl Sandburg (*The People, Yes,* [1936]), whose roughened voices seemed closer to the tone of the 1930's. Closer still to the spirit of the decade were poets such as Joseph Kalar, Kenneth Patchen, Muriel Rukeyser, Kenneth

Author Ernest Hemingway (right), while serving as a reporter during the Spanish Civil War, conversing with a commander of the American Brigade, which fought for the Loyalists. (AP/Wide World Photos)

Fearing, and Alfred Hayes, who rejected many of the modernist assumptions about poetry to face more directly the crises of the period. Langston Hughes's poem "Goodbye Christ" (1932), for example, ends with the line, "Goodbye Christ, good morning Revolution!" Genevieve Taggard's "Mill Town" (1936) concerns the death of a child by hunger, Kay Boyle's "A Communication to Nancy Cunard" (1937) focuses on the famous Scottsboro case, and Mac-Leish's *Frescoes for Mr. Rockefeller's City* (1933) celebrates American history.

The same trend was true in drama. While the giant of the American theater, Eugene O'Neill, continued to produce his dark plays, for example *Mourning Becomes Electra* (1931), a newer generation of playwrights emerged who dealt with the political and economic issues of the day. These included Clifford Odets, who wrote *Waiting for Lefty* (1935) about a labor strike; Marc Blitzstein, who wrote a labor "opera," *The Cradle Will Rock* (1937); and Lillian Hellman, who wrote *The Little Foxes* (1939), about avarice and other evils. Collective ensembles, such as The Group Theatre, which produced works by Odets, Paul Green, and others, or the Federal Theatre Project, which put on hundreds of performances of plays, classic and modern, to eager audiences across the country, also played major roles in the 1930's theater scene.

As in any period, other literary themes emerged as well. Like the screwball comedies Hollywood produced during the 1930's, some American literature included escapist themes. The novel that led the best-seller lists in both 1936 and 1937 was Margaret Mitchell's historical romance, *Gone with the Wind* (1936). One popular genre that emerged during the 1930's and left a lasting mark was the hard-boiled detective novel, particularly as practiced by Dashiell Hammett, who wrote *The Maltese Falcon* (1930) and *The Thin Man* (1932), and Raymond Chandler, who wrote *The Big Sleep* (1939) and *Farewell, My Lovely* (1940). In many ways, the "tough guy" tone of the detective novel fit perfectly into the harsh economic times of the Depression.

Proletarian Literature In addition to actual economic conditions, the main catalyst for the social protest literature of the 1930's was the Marxist literary criticism that emerged in the *New Masses, Partisan Review,* and other radical journals but increasingly in liberal journals such as *The Nation* and *The New Republic* as well. *New Masses* editor Mike Gold's attack on popular novelist Thornton Wilder in *The New Republic* in 1930 represented dozens of articles and reviews he wrote in the first half of the decade that attacked bourgeois writers and called for a working-class literature. The literary criticism he espoused was refined and articulated in less strident tones by critics such as Granville Hicks and Joseph Freeman, whose *An American Testament* (1936) is also a first-rate memoir. By the mid-1930's, a milder form of Marxist literary criticism was regularly written by left-leaning critics such as Cowley, Wilson, Newton Arvin, and others.

The call for proletarian literature resulted in a wealth of firsthand reports on actual social and economic conditions in the United States in the first years of the Depression. These included the 1932 *Harlan Miners Speak: A Report on Terrorism in the Kentucky Coal Fields* by a National Committee for the Defense of Political Prisoners that included Theodore Dreiser, Anderson, and Dos Passos. By 1934, a distinctive genre of "proletarian reportage" could be identified in the decade's journalism: John L. Spivak's "A Letter to President Franklin D. Roosevelt," from a fifteen year-old girl working in the cotton fields in California's Imperial Valley; Joseph North's "Taxi Strike"; Tillie Olsen's "The Strike"; and Meridel Le Sueur's "I Was Marching." The landmark 1935 collection *Proletarian Literature in the United States: An Anthology,* edited by Hicks, Gold, and others, had a reportage section that included the pieces that appeared in the *New Masses* by Le Sueur, North, and Spivak and a literary-criticism section with essays by Gold, Cowley, Hicks, and others. The fiction in the anthology included selections from Gold, Dos Passos, and Lerner, while the poetry was written by Fearing, Gold, Hayes, Hughes, Kalar, Patchen, Rukeyser, Taggard, and Richard Wright.

The most distinctive literary movement of the 1930's was the "proletarian novel," a form that emerged in the early 1930's in response to the calls by critics and editors for work covering the multiple social and economic problems of the Depression from working-class perspectives. If documentary reportage could look at these problems, leftist critics argued, fiction should as well. As just one example of this movement, six novels were written centering on a single 1929 textile-mill strike in Gastonia, North Carolina, including Anderson's *Beyond Desire* (1932), Fielding Burke's *Call Home the Heart* (1932), and

Grace Lumpkin's *To Make My Bread* (1932), all of which were published in 1932. Perhaps the best proletarian novel of this subgenre was Robert Cantwell's *The Land of Plenty* (1934), about a strike in a coastal Washington wood-veneer factory. So many proletarian novels appeared in the early 1930's, in fact, that literary historians have developed separate categories to describe them: in addition to strike novels, "bottom dog" novels were identified. Jack Conroy's *The Disinherited* (1933) and Nelson Algren's *Somebody in Boots* (1935) are probably the best examples of this subgenre about down-and-out victims of the Depression.

Two of the best proletarian novels of the decade appeared early: Gold's *Jews Without Money* was published in 1930 and told the story of a young man growing up on the lower East Side of Manhattan. Henry Roth's *Call It Sleep* (1935) was a similar story of a lower East Side childhood and had a far more complex and subtle structure and style than Gold's. Perhaps the most lasting proletarian work of the early 1930's was James T. Farrell's *Studs Lonigan* trilogy, produced between 1932 and 1935, that included *Young Lonigan* (1932), *The Young Manhood of Studs Lonigan* (1934), and *Judgment Day* (1935). These books followed a young Irish American growing up in lower-class Chicago to his premature death at twenty-nine. Another noteworthy proletarian trilogy in the decade was written by Josephine Herbst. *Pity Is Not Enough* (1933), *The Executioner Waits* (1934), and *Rope of Gold* (1939) traced the lives of the Trexler family from the mid-nineteenth century up to the sit-down strikes of 1937.

The Social Realist Energy of 1930's Fiction The proletarian impulse can be seen in other fictional works of the 1930's. Dos Passos's trilogy *U.S.A.*—*The Forty-second Parallel* (1930), *1919* (1932), and *The Big Money* (1936)—constitutes a historical examination of social and economic forces in conflict, including unions and capitalists, in the first decades of the twentieth century. John Steinbeck's *In Dubious Battle* (1936) was a strike novel set in the San Joaquin Valley; his classic *The Grapes of Wrath* (1939)—which showed the migration of the Joad family from their Oklahoma farm, from which they had been evicted, to their struggles in California's farmland—clearly revealed the influence of the earlier proletarian novel. Wright, the most important African American writer of the 1930's, wrote *Uncle Tom's Children*

John Dos Passos, a leading member of the 1930's literary scene. (©Bettmann/CORBIS)

(1938), which contained four novellas detailing the difficulties of poor African Americans in the rural South, and *Native Son* (1940), which showed the brutal conditions under which they lived in northern industrial cities such as Chicago. None of these later works was strictly "proletarian," but they showed the influence of this literary movement. Like the social realist art of Ben Shahn, Jack Levine, Jacob Lawrence, and other painters, this fiction revealed a deeper social commitment than had been seen in American art and literature since the nineteenth century. Increasingly in the second half of the 1930's, as conditions worsened in Europe with the rise of fascism, writers turned their attention from domestic to international subjects. Hemingway's *For Whom the Bell Tolls* (1940) is only the best-known example of this impulse to examine issues in Europe. Others included Dalton Trumbo's antiwar *Johnny Got His Gun* (1939) and Hellman's antifascist *The Watch on the Rhine* (1941).

Impact The literature of the 1930's showed how fruitful and energizing the clash of literature and society could be for both writers and their work. In contrast to the often sterile and academic art and literature of the following two decades, the literary work of the 1930's demonstrated just how valuable the confrontation with social and economic issues could be. The novels of Dos Passos, Steinbeck, and Wright and the plays of Odets and Hellman are filled with anger, compassion, and frustration, but they often reveal the United States in ways it had not been portrayed before.

The 1930's was the first decade in which a significant amount of literature by women, black, and working-class writers appeared. The decade called for these "minority" voices, at the same time as it energized scores of others. Steinbeck, Odets, Wright, Farrell, and Dos Passos, among many artists, never again achieved the same level of success they did during the Great Depression. As a sign of the deep sense of concern and commitment of the decade, American writers got together, in a series of American Writers' Congresses, beginning in 1935, to discuss literary and social issues of mutual interest; the 1930's was the only decade in which this happened.

This positive spirit of the decade ended abruptly, however. World War II immediately absorbed most American energy, and after the war the Cold War culture began, in which the literary works of the 1930's were denigrated and investigated as communist. The anticommunist hysteria of the 1950's, in particular, questioned the whole decade of the 1930's. Not until the 1960's and after did the writers of the 1930's began to emerge from the shadows, and critics and historians could honestly evaluate their accomplishments and recognize the true literary contributions.

David Peck

Further Reading

Conn, Peter. *The American 1930s: A Literary History.* New York: Cambridge University Press, 2009. Focuses on the complexity and heterogeneity of the decade; examines the theme of the search for a meaningful American past in historical novels, biography and memoir, and southern literature.

Denning, Michael. *The Cultural Front: The Laboring of American Culture in the Twentieth Century.* New York: Verso, 1996. Exhaustive survey of the literature of the 1930's that recognizes the continuing influence of the left. Includes analyses of proletarian literature, Dos Passos, Steinbeck, Orson Welles, and the decade's music and film.

Dickstein, Morris. *Dancing in the Dark: A Cultural History of the Great Depression.* New York: Norton, 2009. Encyclopedic panorama of 1930's culture, providing analyses of literary works, screwball comedies, popular music, films, and musicals; shows how the arts helped Americans cope with the difficulties of the Depression.

Foley, Barbara. *Radical Representations: Politics and Form in the U.S. Proletarian Fiction, 1929-1941.* Durham, N.C.: Duke University Press, 1994. Emphasizes the value and vitality of 1930's leftist culture as shown in a range of proletarian forms.

Mullen, Bill, and Sherry Lee Linkon, eds. *Radical Revisions: Reading 1930s Culture.* Urbana: University of Illinois Press, 1996. Reading of the contributions of a broad spectrum of left-wing poets, playwrights, and authors.

Shulman, Robert. *The Power of Political Art: The 1930s Literary Left Reconsidered.* Chapel Hill: University of North Carolina Press, 2000. An important answer to earlier Cold War critical views; recognizes the avant-garde quality of leftist writers Le Sueur, Herbst, Wright, Rukeyser, and Hughes.

See also Faulkner, William; Federal Trade Commission; Federal Writers' Project; *Grapes of Wrath, The*; Group Theatre; Hemingway, Ernest; Odets, Clifford; Steinbeck, John; Theater in the United States; *U.S.A.* trilogy.

■ *Little Caesar*

Identification Early gangster film
Director Mervyn LeRoy
Date 1931

Although Little Caesar *was not the first gangster film, it set the standard for the genre and has been imitated many times. Based on the 1928 novel of the same name by W. R. Burnett,* Little Caesar *launched the career of Edward G. Robinson, who played the title character.*

Little Caesar's title character, Rico Bandello (Robinson), was not based on gangster Al Capone, as has been widely reported, but rather on Salvatore "Sam" Cardinella, another Roaring Twenties Chicago gangster. Pete Montana (Ralph Ince) was modeled on "Big Jim" Colosimo, known as the "King of the

Edward G. Robinson as Rico in the seminal gangster film Little Caesar *(1931).* (Archive Photos/Getty Images)

Douglas Fairbanks, Sr., a superstar during the silent-film era, and became a star in his own right. Zanuck became head of Twentieth Century-Fox. Wallis produced thirty additional films, including the Academy Award-winning *Casablanca* (1942). LeRoy produced or directed thirty more films and also served as head of production at both Metro-Goldwyn-Mayer and Warner Bros.

Thomas R. Feller

Further Reading

Gansberg, Alan J. *Little Caesar: A Biography of Edward G. Robinson.* Lanham, Md.: Scarecrow Press, 2004.

Peary, Danny. *Alternate Oscars.* New York: Dell, 1993.

Roddick, Nick, ed. *Encyclopedia of Great Movies.* London: Octopus Books, 1985.

See also   Academy Awards; Capone, Al; Film; Gangster films; Robinson, Edward G.

Pimps," and the "Big Boy" (Sidney Blackmer) was based upon corrupt Chicago mayor William H. "Big Bill" Thompson.

Little Caesar is technically primitive, has a linear and simple story, and does not feature graphic violence. However, its authenticity still attracts audiences, and its low-budget sets and sleazy atmosphere actually add to the film's effectiveness.

The film was a major commercial success and was nominated for an Academy Award for the screenplay by Robert N. Lee and Francis Edwards Faragoh. It was selected for the National Film Registry in 2000.

Impact   This film advanced the careers of Robinson; Douglas Fairbanks, Jr., a member of the cast; Darryl F. Zanuck, head of production at Warner Bros.; Hal Wallis, the producer; and Mervyn LeRoy, the director. Robinson starred in additional gangster films and went on to appear in more than eighty motion pictures. Some critics consider him to be the best film actor never nominated for an Academy Award. Fairbanks escaped the shadow of his father,

■ Little Orphan Annie

Identification   Comic strip
Cartoonist   Harold Gray
Date   Launched on August 5, 1924

One of the most popular comic strips of the 1930's, Little Orphan Annie *spawned a long-running juvenile radio drama and two motion pictures during its heyday. The strip traced the adventures of a girl and a dog traveling across the United States.*

The creation of cartoonist Harold Gray, *Little Orphan Annie* debuted in 1924 in the *Chicago Tribune* syndicated newspapers. The inspiration for the strip was James Whitcomb Riley's poem "Little Orphant Annie." As originally conceived, the comic was to feature an orphan named Otto, but because other strips starring boys were already in production, Gray made the main character a girl. Despite her circumstances, ten-year-old Annie—born February 29, so she aged slowly over time—was typically cheerful, honest, and self-reliant, and persevered through hard work and pluck.

At first, red-haired, blank-eyed Annie, an escapee from a cruel orphanage, traveled with a doll, later replaced with her constant companion, a dog named Sandy. In the second year of her adventures, she met wealthy, bald capitalist Oliver Warbucks, a surrogate father she called "Daddy," who served as her sporadic benefactor. Other major characters introduced during the 1930's included Warbucks's associates Punjab, a giant, turbaned Indian, and the mysterious black-clad Asp. Warbucks, Punjab, and the Asp appeared periodically at crucial moments to assist beleaguered Annie.

Initially a humorous strip intended for young readers, by the beginning of the 1930's, *Little Orphan Annie* had evolved into an adventure story with political undertones and included murderers, mobsters, spies, and other nasty villains with names such as Bill McBribe and Claude Claptrap because adults enjoyed the comic as much as children did. To accommodate the tastes of grown-ups, Gray subtly changed the look of the series, using areas of solid black to produce a more somber tone that replicated black-and-white crime films of the time. He also incorporated his own thoughts about private enterprise, government, crime and punishment, morality, and other similar subjects, often putting long orations into large speech balloons attributed to various characters. Such statements occasionally aroused controversy and caused a few publishers to temporarily withdraw the strip from their newspapers.

In 1930, a radio serial based on *Little Orphan Annie* was first broadcast from Chicago, and the following year, it went national on the National Broadcasting Company (NBC) Blue Network, featuring its own theme song. The first drama intended for juvenile audiences, it was sponsored for most of its run by chocolate-drink maker Ovaltine and became the first show to offer premiums such as secret decoder rings, toys, games, watches, and other items to faithful listeners. The hugely popular show ran until 1942. Youthful Shirley Bell played the title role for most of the fifteen-minute episodes; Annie lifted spirits in the United States throughout the Great Depression and into the beginning of World War II. Like her newspaper counterpart, the radio Annie provided a shining example of determination and youthful spunk as she battled all manner of evildoers on a global scale. To further capitalize on the complementary popularity of the comic strip and radio program, two films entitled *Little Orphan Annie* were produced. A 1932 version starred Mitzi Green, and a 1938 version starred Ann Gillis.

Impact   For more than forty years, Gray enthralled millions of readers with his dramatic, warmhearted, and uplifting *Little Orphan Annie* comic strip. After

his death in 1968, the strip continued for a decade with different artists and writers but was decidedly inferior to the original. The 1977 comic-inspired Broadway musical *Annie*, which ran for 2,377 performances, won seven Tony Awards, spun off a 1982 film, and helped revive the strip. In late 1979, the venerable serial, retitled *Annie* and updated to reflect the sensibilities of modern audiences, was introduced. In 1995, the strip was commemorated on a U.S. postage stamp.

Jack Ewing

Further Reading

Gray, Harold. *Arf! The Life and Hard Times of Little Orphan Annie, 1935-1945.* New Rochelle, N.Y.: Arlington House, 1970.

Marshall, Richard. *America's Great Comic-Strip Artists.* New York: Stewart, Tabori & Chang, 2007.

Walkerdine, Valerie. *Daddy's Girl: Young Girls and Popular Culture.* Cambridge, Mass.: Harvard University Press, 1998.

Young, William H., and Nancy K. Young. *The Great Depression in America: A Cultural Encyclopedia.* Westport, Conn.: Greenwood Press, 2007.

See also   Advertising in the United States; Comic strips; Film; Great Depression in the United States; Newspapers, U.S.; Radio in the United States; Unemployment in the United States.

■ Lobotomy

Definition   Psychosurgery severing nerve fibers connecting the thalamus and frontal lobes of the cortex

U.S. psychiatric hospitals of the 1930's were overcrowded, housing approximately ten thousand patients. From the 1930's to the 1960's, forty thousand people in the United States had lobotomies, and approximately 75 percent were deinstitutionalized.

In 1935, Portuguese neurologist Egas Moniz developed the frontal leucotomy. Surgeons drilled a hole in the cranium and injected the brain with alcohol to kill brain tissue. Later, surgeons used a picklike leucotome to cut neural connections between the frontal lobes and the thalamus. Moniz believed cutting these nerve fibers stopped schizophrenic obsessions. Patients became calmer and more manageable, and often left the hospital.

In the United States, Walter Jackson Freeman and James W. Watts believed that people with mental illness had too much imagination. In 1935, in order to remove imagination, Freeman and Watts performed the lobotomy, a modified leucotomy. Surgeons drilled holes from both sides of the top of the forehead, using the leucotome to sever neural connections. Electroconvulsive therapy (ECT) temporarily rendered the patient unconscious during the lobotomy. Freeman thought ECT quieted pathological thinking, and lobotomy prevented pathological thinking from reoccurring. Mood and anxiety levels improved.

While lobotomy was used in extreme cases, with disabled and suicidal patients, overcrowded institutions used it to manage unruly residents. Many lobotomy patients left institutions relieved of emotional distress, but with frontal-lobe deficit: they were unmotivated, had trouble concentrating, and were hypersexual. Proponents of lobotomy believed the mental illness was worse than the surgery's side effects.

Impact Freeman created the transorbital lobotomy. He hammered an ice pick into the brain over the eye and under the eye socket, moving the pick to destroy brain tissue. Freeman performed the operation in asylums nationwide, earning him the name "the traveling lobotomist." In 1941, he performed a lobotomy on Rosemary Kennedy, daughter of Joseph P. and Rose Fitzgerald Kennedy, possibly as a treatment for mental retardation. Moniz won the 1946 Nobel Prize in Physiology or Medicine for the frontal leucotomy. By the 1950's, medication replaced lobotomy to treat mental illness.

Elizabeth M. McGhee Nelson

Further Reading

Getz, Marshall J. "The Ice Pick of Oblivion: Moniz, Freeman and the Development of Psychosurgery." *TRAMES: A Journal of the Humanities and Social Sciences* 13, no. 2 (2009): 129-152.

Wallace, Irving. "The Operation of Last Resort." *The Saturday Evening Post* (October, 1951): 24-95.

Whitaker, Robert. *Mad in America: Bad Science, Bad Medicine, and the Enduring Mistreatment of the Mentally Ill.* New York: Basic Books, 2003.

See also Health care; Medicine; Nobel Prizes; Psychology and psychiatry.

■ London Economic Conference

The Event International economic conference focusing on monetary stabilization, reduction of tariffs, and Allied war debts from World War I

Dates June 12 to July 27, 1933

Place Geological Museum, London, England

International agreement on monetary solutions to combat the Depression could not be reached at the London conference, giving rise to nationalistic policies. Each nation wanted to protect its own economy, as evidenced by President Franklin D. Roosevelt's denunciation of currency stabilization and his refusal to cancel war debts.

The London Economic Conference was called to relieve European nations and their former Allies of the burden of debts stemming from World War I. The agenda had been established by a preliminary meeting of six nations in Geneva in 1932. The goal was for the international community to work together to revive the world economy through reviving trade, eliminating tariff barriers, and forgiving debts. However, the United States, suffering from the Great Depression, was reluctant to forgive, reduce, or postpone payment of the war debts owed by Europeans. American unemployment, hunger, and despair had dictated this resolve.

While desiring to restore world trade by international adjustment of tariff barriers, Roosevelt had to respond to the emergency within the United States first, taking the country off the gold standard. He pursued monetary inflation by issuing additional paper currency and making money cheaper through devaluation. On the other hand, European countries wanted to stabilize the dollar against their currencies and fix it at a high value to stimulate foreign trade and regularize the balance of payments in their favor.

Secretary of State Cordell Hull led the American delegation to the London conference and initially entered into currency stabilization discussions with Clement Moret of the Bank of France, Montagu Norman of the Bank of England, and other gold-bloc nations. However this initial internationalism was replaced by a nationalistic stance when Roosevelt, fearing that the dollar's rise against foreign currencies would further depress U.S. exports, issued a statement to the conference in the form of a radio message sent from a cruiser in the North Atlantic. He criticized the conference's attempts at currency stabilization when broader economic problems existed. He instructed Hull to reject all currency stabilization proposals, however tentative, that were made at the conference. Roosevelt believed economic recovery should begin in the United States, and he did not wish to jeopardize the slight economic gains already made through devaluation. He had little confidence in European central bankers and believed the United States had nothing to gain by linking itself to a potentially hazardous international agreement. European countries noted this assertion of economic independence. The United States was lambasted for its policies, and the London Economic Conference failed to achieve significant agreement on any of the targeted issues.

Impact The London Economic Conference was futile and dealt a temporary blow to international camaraderie and cooperation between countries against the Depression. This result was a drifting toward isolationism and extreme nationalism, as exhibited by Germany's withdrawal from the League of Nations and the Geneva Disarmament Conference. France had defaulted on its war debts in 1932, and Italy and Great Britain made only token payments in 1933. The Johnson Act of 1934 made it illegal for U.S. citizens and corporations to loan money to governments in default to the United States, and former war debts had to be paid in full so as not to be considered in default. Only Finland fully repaid its Allied war debts, with all other Allies formally defaulting on June 15, 1934. The plight of the Depression had taken its toll worldwide and sabotaged international economic cooperation.

However, by 1934, Roosevelt supported Hull's enthusiasm for reciprocal trade agreements as a means of alleviating internal economic problems, and the Reciprocal Trade Agreements Act of 1934 became law. Negotiated by Roosevelt without the consent of Congress, free trade agreements and relatively low tariffs "primed the pump" and stimulated the economy. Hull negotiated eighteen reciprocity treaties within the next four years, effectively halting further decline in the world economy. Several target issues of the London Economic Conference were finally resolved, such as the reduction of tariffs to stimulate international trade.

Barbara Bennett Peterson

Further Reading
Hinton, Harold B. *Cordell Hull, A Biography.* New York: Hinton Press, 2008.

Hull, Cordell. *The Memoirs of Cordell Hull.* 2 vols. New York: Macmillan, 1948.
Pratt, Julius W. *Cordell Hull, 1933-1944.* New York: Cooper Square, 1964.

See also Credit and debt; Export-Import Bank of the United States; Good Neighbor Policy; Great Depression in the United States; Hawley-Smoot Tariff Act of 1930; Hull, Cordell; International trade; Roosevelt, Franklin D.; World War I debts.

■ London Naval Treaty

The Treaty Pact among the United States, Great Britain, Japan, France, and Italy to regulate submarine fleets and limit warship building
Date Signed on April 22, 1930; took effect October 27, 1930

Continuing the efforts started in the 1922 Washington Naval Treaty, the London Naval Treaty tried to lower international tensions by reducing the size of the major navies of the world. Its terms did limit the size of the major navies, but contentious elements of the treaty later helped to fuel the outbreak of World War II.

In the aftermath of World War I, nations strove to cut their military forces to save money and prevent future conflicts. In 1922, the United States, Great Britain, Japan, France, and Italy agreed to the Washington Naval Treaty, which limited the size and number of battleships and aircraft carriers a nation could possess. The United States and Great Britain received the largest authorization, Japan receiving a smaller authorization, and France and Italy were permitted only small numbers of capital ships. Because the Washington treaty did not address all types of warships, the five nations continued discussions on naval disarmament, talks that culminated in the 1930 London treaty. France and Italy opted not to sign the treaty.

The main participants in the naval talks, the United States, Great Britain, and Japan, generally agreed on limitations on the size and number of destroyers and submarines. The treaty permitted the United States and Great Britain to each construct up to 150,000 tons of destroyers, while Japan could build 105,500 tons. Individual destroyers could not exceed 1,850 tons displacement, nor have a gun armament greater than 5-inch caliber. This prevented the signatories from building larger ships but disguising their capability by labeling them as destroyers. The treaty authorized an equal tonnage in submarines to all nations of 52,700 tons. The agreement limited submarine displacement to 2,000 tons and armament to 5-inch caliber.

The three nations disagreed on definitions and limitations on cruiser construction. Smaller than battleships but bigger than destroyers, cruisers were effective, multipurpose ships with heavy armament and long range. The three navies differed on how they used cruisers and, therefore, disagreed on how many cruisers to authorize and how the ships were to be armed. The United States employed cruisers as scouts and escorts for its main battle fleet, so it wanted a relatively small number of heavily armed ships. The British used cruisers to police their global empire, so they favored a larger number of lightly armed ships. Because the Washington treaty granted them fewer battleships, the Japanese wanted a large number of heavily armed ships to support their battleships in a fleet engagement. The solution was to divide cruisers into two distinct categories that permitted the respective nations to construct limited numbers of the types they wanted.

The London treaty grouped cruisers as "heavy," ships larger than 1,850 tons but less than 10,000 tons and gun armament greater than 6-inch caliber, or "light," ships larger than 1,850 tons but less than 10,000 tons and gun armament limited to a maximum of 6-inch caliber categories. The treaty permitted the United States to construct 180,000 tons worth of heavy cruisers to escort the battle fleet and 143,500 tons of light cruisers to serve as scouts. The British navy, however, could construct 146,800 tons of heavy cruisers but 192,200 tons of light cruisers to provide enough ships to patrol their empire. As with the Washington treaty, the Japanese received a smaller authorization than the United States and British of 108,400 tons of heavy cruisers and 100,450 tons of light cruisers to augment their battle fleet.

Impact The London Naval Treaty was the last successful naval disarmament treaty of the interwar period, but its success was short-lived. Japan, unhappy with its second-class status relative to the United States and Great Britain, refused to extend the terms of the Washington and London treaties, and the subsequent naval arms race helped to trigger World War II.

Steven J. Ramold

Further Reading

Goldman, Emily O. *Sunken Treaties: Naval Arms Control Between the Wars*. University Park: Pennsylvania State University, 1994.

Hammond, James W. *The Treaty Navy: The Story of the US Naval Service Between the World Wars*. Bloomington, Ind.: Trafford, 2006.

Morley, James William. *Japan Erupts: The London Naval Conference and the Manchurian Incident, 1928-1932*. New York: Columbia University Press, 1984.

See also Aviation and aeronautics; Foreign policy of the United States; Japanese military aggression; Naval forces; *Panay* incident; *Ranger*, USS.

■ Long, Huey

Identification Governor of Louisiana and U.S. senator

Born August 30, 1893; near Winnfield, Louisiana

Died September 10, 1935; Baton Rouge, Louisiana

Long was a charismatic southern populist leader with national ambitions who championed economic policies to feed and house the poorest Americans while limiting the incomes of the wealthiest. His policies as governor of Louisiana highlighted education reform and road improvements while providing jobs in one of the poorest states in the country, but his attempts to direct state politics after entering the U.S. Senate won him powerful enemies.

While serving as governor of Louisiana and later as U.S. senator during the early years of the Great Depression, Huey Long attracted national attention by promoting economic policies that helped revitalize Louisiana's economy while offering possible solutions to national economic problems. Elected Louisiana's governor in 1928, he promoted extensive and rapidly constructed public-works building projects designed to increase trade and travel throughout the sparsely populated, hilly, agrarian, northern parts of his state and its swampy, bayou-filled, southern parts. During his single term as governor, he aggressively pushed state legislators to fund the construction of dozens of bridges over the state's many rivers and bayous and paved many muddy and gravel roads that had been prone to washing out during the rainy season, while also building thousands of miles of entirely new paved roads. Long also supported educational improvements and enhanced his popularity among Louisiana's poor by providing nearly one-half million schoolchildren with textbooks that many of them had previously been unable to afford.

Long's move from the Louisiana statehouse to the U.S. Senate came about through an unusual gamble on his part. After suffering several legislative setbacks, he announced he would challenge one of Louisiana's incumbent senators in the 1930 Democratic primary election to prove his popularity among voters. Moreover, he promised to resign his governorship if he lost. He won the primary by a wide margin and swept the November election virtually unopposed. He became eligible to enter the U.S. Senate in January, 1931, but instead announced his intention to finish out his term as governor. He thus left his Senate seat vacant until he finally joined that body in January, 1932.

As a member of the U.S. Senate, Long gained not only a national platform on which to champion his economic policies but also the opportunity to channel additional federal funds to Louisiana. Meanwhile, he remained involved in Louisiana state politics by working closely with his chosen successor, Governor Oscar K. Allen, who was virtually his puppet. Using newly available federal funds from New Deal programs, Long ensured the continuation of Louisiana's road-improvement projects and job programs during the Depression years of high unemployment.

Long's experience of growing up poor in rural Winnfield in northern Louisiana left a lasting imprint on his political views. After Long achieved power, he focused his social and economic policies on the needs of the poor in Louisiana—a state with few industries and job opportunities beyond farming and fishing. His 1933 book, *Every Man a King*, described how he would ensure that poor people suffering through the Great Depression would be given additional funding from the government. He also organized a national group called Share Our Wealth, which advocated capping the income of the wealthiest citizens of the United States and dispersing the additional money to the poor.

Long supported for fellow Democrat Franklin D. Roosevelt in the 1932 presidential campaign but later parted ways with him because he thought Roosevelt's New Deal programs moved too slowly. He eventually planned to help get Roosevelt defeated by a Republican or third-party candidate in 1936 so that he himself could be elected president in 1940.

Consequently, he became a thorn in Roosevelt's side.

While Long toured other states to increase his name recognition among voters throughout the nation, he remained heavily involved with Louisiana state politics. He told his successor when to summon sessions of the state legislature, wrote many bills himself, and personally lobbied for their passage, often using high-handed methods to get what he wanted. As a U.S. senator with no official role in state politics, he made many enemies with his strong-arm tactics, his support of the interests of the poor, and his outspoken criticisms of the Roosevelt administration. In 1935, some of his Louisiana opponents began organizing, and a climate of impending violence developed.

In early September, 1935, Long was in Baton Rouge, Louisiana,

Louisiana governor Huey Long, a ubiquitous political figure of the 1930's, addressing students at Louisiana State University. (AP/Wide World Photos)

working every day of the week while the state legislature was in session. On September 8, he was shot within the state capitol building by a young doctor, Carl Weiss, who was quickly killed by Long's bodyguards. Long himself died two days later. Apparently not involved in any kind of organized plot, Weiss seems to have killed Long for his own personal and political reasons.

Impact　Long left a mixed legacy. On one hand, he was recognized as a true champion of the poor during the worst economic downturn in American history. The success of some of his economic programs in Louisiana and his populist ideas helped increase national support for the progressive programs of Roosevelt's New Deal. On the other hand, however, Long was reviled for transforming his state's legislature into his personal tool and his state's government into an extension of the Long political machine. His defenders have argued that he was driven to these tactics by the political opposition that he faced. During his career, he was passionately loved and hated; he was called both a fascist and a friend of the common man. His life and career remain an American enigma.

Bonnye Busbice Good and the Editors

Further Reading

Hair, William Ivy. *The Kingfish and His Realm: The Life and Times of Huey P. Long.* Baton Rouge: Louisiana State University Press, 1997. Biography of Long that looks at the range of his power.

LeVert, Suzanne. *Huey P. Long: The Kingfish of Louisiana.* New York: Facts On File, 1995. Useful biography of Long that puts his life in a broad political perspective.

Long, Huey P. *Every Man a King.* 1933. Reprint. Chicago: Quadrangle Books, 1964. Reprint of Long's 1933 autobiography edited with an excellent introduction by T. Harry Williams. Although the book's autobiographical section may seem lean on hard facts and naturally stops with Long in midcareer, it nevertheless offers a fascinating glimpse of Long's energetic personality.

Huey Long, President

In 1935, looking forward to the next presidential election, Huey Long published My First Days in the White House. *Never short on chutzpah, Long predicted his own victory over President Franklin D. Roosevelt and proposed a cabinet to include Roosevelt, Herbert Hoover, and Idaho senator William E. Borah, a controversial isolationist. (Reportedly, Roosevelt was worried that Long might actually defeat him.) The book opens with Long's imagined inauguration.*

IT HAD happened. The people had endorsed my plan for the redistribution of wealth and I was President of the United States. I had just sworn upon the Bible from which my father read to us as children to uphold the Constitution and to defend my country against all enemies, foreign and domestic. Yet standing there on the flag-draped platform erected above the East portico of the Capitol, delivering my inaugural address, it all seemed unreal. I felt that I was dreaming. The great campaign which was destined to save America from Communism and Fascism was history. Other politicians had promised to re-make America; I had promised to sustain it.

The campaign had been bitter. I was cartooned and caricatured unmercifully in some of the newspapers. . . .

As my eyes swept the throng before me, I paused in my inaugural address and looked into the face of the retiring president. He seemed worn and tired. He wore the same expression of resigned fatigue that I had observed in the face of President Hoover on Inauguration Day in 1933 when Mr. Roosevelt declared so confidently that: "The only thing we have to fear is fear itself."

And with all humility, fully conscious of the solemnity of the promise I was making, I laid aside my prepared speech and closed my inaugural address extemporaneously with these words:

"I promise life to the guaranties of our immortal document, the Declaration of Independence, which has decreed that all shall be born equal, and by this I mean that children shall not come into this life burdened with debt, but on the contrary, shall inherit the right to life, liberty and such education and training as qualifies them and equips them to take their proper rank in the pursuance of the occupation and vocation wherein they are worth most to themselves and to this country. And now I must be about my work."

White, Richard D., Jr. *Kingfish: The Reign of Huey P. Long.* New York: Random House, 2006. Well-researched and readable biography recounting the details of Long's life and political career.

Williams, T. Harry. *Huey Long.* New York: Alfred A. Knopf, 1969. Perhaps the definitive biography of Long. Williams worked extensively with contemporaries of Long, including many members of the Long organization, who spoke remarkably freely. Excellently researched and extremely well written—a classic of modern American biography.

See also Business and the economy in the United States; Education; Elections of 1932, U.S.; Great Depression in the United States; National Recovery Administration; New Deal; Newspapers, U.S.; Roosevelt, Franklin D.; Unemployment in the United States; Works Progress Administration.

■ Long Beach earthquake

The Event A 6.4-magnitude earthquake occurring along the Newport-Inglewood fault zone
Date March 10, 1933
Place Long Beach, California

The Long Beach earthquake of 1933 ranks as one of the most destructive in the history of North America. In its aftermath, construction laws were changed to protect buildings in seismically active areas.

At 5:47 P.M. on Friday, March 10, 1933, an earthquake measuring 6.4 on the Richter scale occurred along the Newport-Inglewood fault zone. Its epicenter was 3.4 miles offshore of Newport Beach at an estimated depth of 5.3 miles. Though this earthquake was not as intense as the 1906 one in San Francisco, and only slightly more intense than the 1925 Santa Barbara quake, it occurred in a densely populated area, resulting in considerable damage.

After the quake, numerous fires spread in the city, partly because the central fire station was destroyed. Medical efforts were impeded because of partial destruction of the Seaside Hospital. Fortunately for residents, at the time of the earthquake, nearly one hundred U.S. Navy vessels were anchored offshore.

Within two hours, more than three thousand sailors and Marines were deployed to emergency-aid stations. Destruction from the earthquake stretched northward into Los Angeles and east into Orange County.

While Corona del Mar and Laguna Beach were relatively near geographically to the quake's epicenter, they suffered less damage than other areas because of their geology; they are both situated close to bedrock. Long Beach and nearby Compton suffered greater destruction because they are situated on unstable alluvium. As a result of the earthquake, twenty-one hundred homes were damaged beyond habitation, fifteen of Long Beach's thirty-five schools were completely destroyed, and nearly 30 percent of other buildings suffered structural damage. In Los Angeles, forty-one schools were rendered unsafe for occupancy. The estimate of the damage was $40 million, which would have equaled about $670 million in 2010 dollars. The quake resulted in 120 deaths, 52 of which occurred in Long Beach. If the quake had happened during school hours, the number of casualties would have been much higher.

Impact The most significant outcomes of the Long Beach earthquake were the changes made to California's construction laws. As a result of the destruction to Long Beach and Los Angeles schools, the California legislature passed the Field Act, empowering the state to approve school-building plans, and the Riley Act, ensuring earthquake-resistant construction. These acts were the first step in the establishment of modern seismic safety standards in California.

Randall L. Milstein

Further Reading
Geschwind, Carl-Henry. *California Earthquakes: Science, Risk and the Politics of Hazard Mitigation.* Baltimore: Johns Hopkins University Press, 2001.
Yeats, Robert S. *Living with Earthquakes in California: A Survivors Guide.* Corvallis: Oregon State University Press, 2001.

See also Great New England hurricane; Labor Day hurricane; Natural disasters; Ohio River flood; San Francisco Bay bridges.

■ *Look* magazine

Identification Weekly photojournalism magazine
Date First published in February, 1937

Look *was a biweekly magazine that contained many pictures documenting famous and not-so-famous events and persons from 1937 to 1971.* Look *began shortly after another similar but more popular magazine,* Life, *started.*

Gardner "Mike" Cowles, Jr., started *Look* magazine, selling it for ten cents a copy. The first issue of *Look* sold more than 700,000 copies, and sales rapidly increased to several million copies per issue, reaching a peak of more than seven million copies per issue in 1969. During the 1930's, most pictures in *Look* were black and white and of good quality. Each issue had a color cover and around two hundred photographs, each with a caption.

The first issue of *Look* had stories about a bullfighter, geishas of Japan, the hats of Queen Mary I of England, a trained goldfish, Joan Crawford, gypsies, and a film. There were stories about science and medicine that touched on the use of X rays; reviving stopped hearts, specifically about a dog used in experiments to revive the dead; and sex-change operations. Some photographs were sensationalist, such as a series of photographs of a woman hit and killed by a car. After World War II, *Look* had fewer sensationalist stories, and it had more features about sports, fashion, and food. The magazine continued to publish articles about people, especially celebrities; medicine and science; and social issues.

The photographers and writers working for *Look* either earned regular salaries or worked on commission. Several of the well-known photographers working for *Look* were Paul Fusco, Bob Lerner, and Douglas Kirkland. Fusco usually worked on stories about social issues, including one on miners working in bad conditions. Lerner covered sports, social problems, and celebrities. Kirkland photographed well-known celebrities and films. Published and unpublished photographs from *Look* are located in the Library of Congress. Along with *Life* magazine, *Look* elevated the quality of the popular American periodical.

Impact During the late 1930's, *Look* magazine provided high-quality photojournalism that covered subjects that were not easily found elsewhere. Newspapers generally had poor-quality pictures.

Robert L. Cullers

Further Reading

Albrecht, Donald, and Thomas Mellins. *Only in New York: Photographs from Look Magazine.* New York: Monacelli Press, 2009.

Cowles, Gardner. *Mike Looks Back: The Memoirs of Gardner Cowles, Founder of "Look" Magazine.* New York: G. Cowles, 1985.

Preston, Edward A. *Our Land, Our People: People in Pictures from "Look" Magazine.* Upper Saddle River, N.J.: Prentice-Hall, 1958.

See also *Fortune* magazine; *Life* magazine; Magazines; Newspapers, U.S.; Photography.

■ Louis, Joe

Identification American heavyweight boxing champion
Born May 13, 1914; near Lafayette, Alabama
Died April 12, 1981; Las Vegas, Nevada

Louis dominated professional boxing's heavyweight division during the late 1930's, holding the title for a record twelve years. He emerged as the first African American sports icon because of not only his finesse and sheer power but also his low-key charisma, his scrupulous moral public persona, and his patriotic sentiment on the cusp on World War II.

When Joe Louis made his professional debut in Chicago on July 4, 1934, boxing had spiraled into a sharp decline since its heyday a decade earlier. Rapacious promoters, a long run of lackluster champions, gambling scandals involving organized crime, and accusations of fixed fights had cost the sport much of its national following. However, in three years of amateur fighting, Louis had emerged as a fighter to watch, not only for his impressive record, which included fifty wins and only four losses, but also for his singular style, his natural sense of power punching, and his ability to work the ring. Louis dominated his opponents and in his first year of professional fighting earned more than $300,000. His most notable fight among his record thirteen bouts in 1935 was his domination of Italian Primo Carnera; the fight took on significant symbolism because it occurred during Benito Mussolini's occupation of Ethiopia.

Rise to the Championship Promoters were reluctant to give Louis a championship bout after the controversial career of Jack Johnson, an African American heavyweight champion who a generation earlier had alienated white American audiences with his flamboyant lifestyle and his incendiary attitudes about race. Louis's handlers, keen to Johnson's legacy, encouraged Louis to keep a low profile, live an exemplary private life, maintain his focus on the ring, and, when interviewed, appear deferential and low key. The advice paid off. His fights were covered live on radio, and his wins were celebrated in the streets. The press dubbed Louis "the Brown Bomber," and when Louis knocked out former titleholder Max Baer in just four rounds in September, 1935, aficionados of the sport clamored to give Louis a title shot. At the time the title was held by James J. Braddock, the "Cinderella Man."

Heavyweight boxing champion Joe Louis in 1938. (Popperfoto/ Getty Images)

Most felt that former heavyweight champion Max Schmeling was the next logical bout for Louis, so promoters agreed that the winner of a Schmeling/ Louis match would face Braddock. The fight was set for Yankee Stadium on June 19, 1936. Louis did little preparation for the fight, and Schmeling stunned the sports world by knocking out Louis in the twelfth round. However, growing anti-Nazi sentiment made a Schmeling-Braddock bout risky; therefore, promoters arranged for Louis to fight Braddock. Louis knocked out the champ in the eighth round.

Heavyweight Champion Louis's ascent to the heavyweight championship resonated most profoundly in the African American community, which was reeling in the Depression and struggling against intransigent racism. Louis became the first African American sports icon embraced by the mainstream media. However, he knew he had to fight Schmeling again to prove his worth. The anti-Nazi fervor in the United States, coupled with Adolf Hitler's celebration of Schmeling as the embodiment of Aryan power, gave the rematch a hype that boxing had never known. The entire country seemingly wanted Louis to single-handedly defeat German aggression and swagger. Franklin D. Roosevelt hailed the boxer and told him privately what a victory would mean for the country. This time, Louis dedicated himself to preparation; at the rematch on June 22, 1938, at Yankee Stadium, in one of the twentieth century's landmark fights, Louis mercilessly pummeled Schmeling before his managers threw in the towel, stopping the fight. The bout had lasted only 124 seconds. Over the following two years, Louis defended his title thirteen times, a pace that has never been equaled. He held the title for twelve years until he retired.

Impact Joe Louis was primarily a master fighter. He delivered fearsome body punches along with explosive hooks and furious combinations; he was known for strategy, sizing up an opponent's vulnerability, whatever the body size, and delivering blows designed for maximum effect with machinelike accuracy. He could fight hurt, shook off opponents' blows, and maintained his edge in long bouts with remarkable stamina. As such, Louis became the embodiment of American power and of a resurging nation coming out of the Depression and gearing itself to confront the challenge of Nazi aggression. Louis secured his position as a defining cultural icon whose reach far exceeded his sport.

Joseph Dewey

Further Reading

Bak, Richard. *Joe Louis: The Great Black Hope.* Cambridge, Mass.: Da Capo, 1998. Defines Louis and the African American community; positions Louis as a harbinger of later African American heroic athletes.

Hietala, Thomas R. *The Fight of the Century: Jack Johnson, Joe Louis, and the Struggle for Racial Equality.* Armonk, N.Y.: M. E. Sharpe, 2004. Highly readable account of the history of boxing and race that compares Louis to the controversial Johnson.

Margolick, David. *Beyond Glory: Joe Louis vs. Max Schmeling, and a World on the Brink.* Vintage, 2006. Engaging history of the rivalry that takes significant issue with the depiction of Schmeling as a Nazi hero and offers insight into how Schmeling initially beat Louis.

Mead, Chris. *Joe Louis: Black Champion in White America.* Mineola, N.Y.: Dover, 2010. Definitive biography focused on Louis's emergence in the Depression and what he meant to African Americans.

Myler, Patrick. *Ring of Hate: Joe Louis vs. Max Schmeling—The Fight of the Century.* New York: Arcade, 2006. Reviews the cultural importance of the rivalry, with special focus on the second fight. Handsomely illustrated.

See also Boxing; Braddock, James J.; Fascism in the United States; Gambling; Jim Crow segregation; National Negro Congress; Newspapers, U.S.; Racial discrimination; Roosevelt, Franklin D.

■ *Lovell v. City of Griffin*

The Case U.S. Supreme Court ruling on freedom of the press
Date March 28, 1938

Lovell v. City of Griffin was the first case that dealt directly with a city-created prior restraint for the distribution of handbills and the first that applied the First Amendment against such city ordinances.

Lovell v. City of Griffin dealt with the Jehovah's Witnesses, but it was decided on the grounds of freedom of the press and speech, not freedom of religion. The city of Griffin, Georgia, had adopted an ordinance holding that no one could distribute handbills without prior consent and approval. The Supreme Court held that the ordinance was too broad, as it covered all manner of publications. Time, place, and manner restrictions have generally been allowed, but not overall bans. The ordinance was also problematic because it required that all materials be approved, not just those considered obscene or indecent. Griffin officials argued that the First Amendment protected only certain types of publications, such as those that had existed when the amendment was written. Nonetheless, the Supreme Court struck down the law, stating that all publications were part of the public marketplace of ideas and therefore subject to First Amendment protections.

Impact Because the Jehovah's Witnesses were probably targeted on a religious basis, this case was one of the first to combine freedom of religion with freedom of the press. The occasion also marked one of the many times the Jehovah's Witnesses appealed a case to the Supreme Court. The group has appeared before the Court more than almost any other religion. Additionally, this case continued a line of rulings striking down prior restraints on publishing. Colonial Americans had resisted the licensing and prior restraints employed by the British Empire before the American Revolution, and *Lovell v. City of Griffin* was one of many cases seen by the Court as involving practices largely forbidden under the First Amendment.

Scott A. Merriman

Further Reading

Chryssides, George D. *Historical Dictionary of Jehovah's Witnesses.* Lanham, Md.: Scarecrow Press, 2008.

Lewis, Anthony. *Freedom for the Thought That We Hate: A Biography of the First Amendment.* New York: Basic Books, 2010.

Ross, William G. *The Chief Justiceship of Charles Evans Hughes, 1930-1941.* Columbia: University of South Carolina Press, 2007.

See also Civil rights and liberties in the United States; *Grosjean v. American Press Co.*; Hughes, Charles Evans; *Near v. Minnesota*; Religion in the United States; *Stromberg v. California*; Supreme Court, U.S.; *United States v. Carolene Products Co.*

■ Luce, Henry

Identification   American publisher
Born   April 3, 1898; Tengchow (now Penglai),
    China
Died   February 28, 1967; Phoenix, Arizona

Luce radically changed journalism in the United States by creating the modern news magazine, popularizing photojournalism, and founding the first popular business magazine.

Henry Luce created the modern news magazine when he founded *Time* in 1923. *Time*'s format was groundbreaking. Rather than reporting news stories in minute detail, the magazine encapsulated the week's events for its readers by synthesizing reports from newspapers around the country. Under the direction of Luce and cofounder Briton Hadden, *Time* quickly grew into one of the country's largest and most profitable publications.

Luce's empire continued to grow throughout the 1930's. *Fortune* magazine, which began publishing in 1930, was the first popular magazine to cover business as a discrete subject. Luce's next publication was *Architectural Forum*, which was a small trade magazine when he purchased it in 1932. He turned it into the largest architectural magazine in the country. The most popular magazine in Luce's empire was *Life*, which was founded in 1936. *Life* popularized photojournalism by publishing awe-inspiring and sometimes gaudy images, whose subjects ran the gamut of content from politicians, to natural vistas, to police fighting with striking workers. Luce also promoted his material over the radio by serializing *Time* magazine content in *The March of Time*, a radio show that ran from 1928 until 1943.

Luce was a Republican and a dedicated anticommunist, a friend of business and foe of labor unions, and he did not shy away from expressing these sympathies in his publications. He rejected the convention of journalistic objectivity, which he often asserted was a fallacy.

Impact   Luce was a visionary who predicted the desire for news magazines that could provide readers with a single source of information. As his company grew throughout the politically tumultuous 1930's, he used his amplified voice to promote conservative causes, his belief in a Christian God, and American exceptionalism. By the time Luce retired in 1964, his magazines had a total circulation of thirteen million, making him one of the most influential and wealthiest figures in the history of journalism.

Colin Asher

Further Reading

Baughman, James. *Henry R. Luce and the Rise of the American News Media.* Baltimore: Johns Hopkins University Press, 2001.

Herzstein, Robert. *Henry R. Luce, "Time," and the American Crusade in Asia.* New York: Cambridge University Press, 2005.

See also   Communism; *Fortune* magazine; *Life* magazine; Magazines; Radio in the United States.

■ Luciano, Lucky

Identification   Italian American gangster who
    helped reinvent the Mafia
Born   November 24, 1897; Lercara Friddi, Sicily,
    Italy
Died   January 26, 1962; Naples, Italy

Luciano was one of the best-known Italian American gangsters of the 1930's. He "organized" organized crime via a corporate structure, with a board of directors and systematic infiltration of legitimate enterprise. The syndicate controlled bakeries, the garment trade, the waterfront, the union, politics and law, prostitution, and narcotics.

In 1906, Charles "Lucky" Luciano, born Salvatore Lucania, emigrated from Sicily to New York City with his family. He was nine years old, and by 1907, when he turned ten, he was already involved in criminal activity, including shoplifting and delivering drugs. While in elementary school, he began his first racket, offering to protect students for a fee. This crime led to one of the most important relationships of his life. Meyer Lansky was a Jewish child who would not pay up and ended up becoming a close friend and partner in crime.

Because of his brushes with the law, Lucania changed his name to Charles Luciano. At the age of eighteen, he spent six months in a reformatory. He continued to deal narcotics upon his release and by 1916 was one of the leading members of the Five Points Gang. By 1920, he and Lansky were involved in more serious crimes.

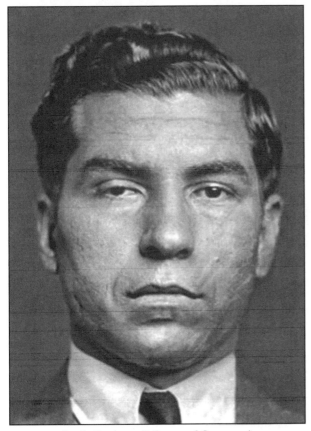

Lucky Luciano. (Library of Congress)

During the 1920's, the two largest Mafia families were embroiled in a long blood war. Luciano thought the war was disruptive to business, so he and Lansky planned to eliminate the two rival Sicilian mob bosses, Giuseppe Masseria and Salvatore Maranzano. Luciano found out that his own boss attempted to have him killed in 1929. Even though he survived, and thus obtained the nickname "Lucky," Luciano offered to end the violence by ensuring his boss, Masseria, was executed first.

In 1931, Masseria was dead, but Maranzano wanted sole power. He decided to have Luciano killed. Before Maranzano could accomplish this goal, Luciano was cunning enough to have his friends, Lansky and Bugsy Siegel, kill Maranzano. With both bosses dead, Luciano officially became the boss of all bosses in 1934. In 1935, New York City special prosecutor Thomas E. Dewey, who had been appointed to crack down on racketeering, tried Luciano on sixty-two counts of compulsory prostitution. In June, 1936, Luciano was sentenced to thirty to fifty years in prison. While incarcerated, he still managed to run the business (via Lansky and other associates). In 1946, Luciano was released from prison—ironically by Dewey, who had become New York governor—by using his influence to convince the dockworkers and fishermen to offer information to naval intelligence, which led to the seizure of explosives, maps, and blueprints for sabotage by German spies along the waterfront.

In exchange for his assistance, Luciano was released from prison and immediately deported to Rome in February, 1946, where he lived for a year. Though he still conducted business in the United States through Lansky, he was not happy with the state of affairs. Thus, he resurfaced in Cuba a few months later. By February, 1947, the U.S. Federal Bureau of Narcotics learned of his behavior and again deported him to Italy. On January 26, 1962, he was going to meet a Hollywood producer who wanted to write the story of his life. As Luciano went to shake hands with the producer, he had a fatal heart attack.

Impact   Luciano will always be known for his creative business tactics and his personal style. He was successful, powerful, and innovative. Luciano created an arbitration system called the commission, where differences were aired through a board. He added the *consigliere* position to the criminal family structure and created a national crime syndicate with nonmember associates who were not Italian. He never lost his position as the crime boss.

Gina Robertiello

Further Reading

Feder, Sid, and Joachim Joesten. *The Luciano Story.* New York: David McKay, 1954.

Gosch, Martin A., and Richard Hammer. *Last Testament of Lucky Luciano.* New York: Dell, 1981.

Jamieson, Alison. "Mafia and Political Power 1943-1989." *International Relations* 10 (1990): 13-30.

Klerks, Cat. *Lucky Luciano: The Father of Organized Crime.* Canmore, Alta.: Altitude, 2005.

Poulsen, Ellen. *The Case Against Lucky Luciano: New York's Most Sensational Vice Trial.* New York: Clinton Cook, 2007.

Powell, Hickman. *Lucky Luciano: The Man Who Organized Crime in America.* Rev. ed. New York: Barricade Books, 2000.

Turkus, Burton B., and Sid Feder. *Murder Inc.: The Story of the Syndicate.* Cambridge, Mass.: Da Capo Press, 2003.

See also Anti-Racketeering Act of 1934; Capone, Al; Crimes and scandals; Gambling; Organized crime; Schultz, Dutch.

■ Ludlow amendment

The Law Failed constitutional amendment that would have required a public vote on going to war

Date Introduced in Congress multiple times between 1935 and 1940

This proposed amendment, which almost made it to the floor of the House of Representatives, signified the deep public opposition to war and to U.S. involvement with the world. While the amendment did not pass, the level of support exhibited for it indicated that the United States, as of 1938, was generally not ready to be involved with foreign affairs.

During the 1910's and 1920's, the amendment was introduced in a number of different forms, but it got its greatest support during the 1930's because of antiwar and isolationist sentiment. Congressman Louis Ludlow introduced the 1930's version; thus, it was named for him. The amendment would have required a public vote on whether or not to go to war; some thought that this amendment might lead to an end to war around the world, similar to how people felt about the Kellogg-Briand Pact of the 1920's. The Ludlow amendment was widely opposed by President Franklin D. Roosevelt and others who considered it to be either weak or impractical, but many people favored it. The closest that it got to passage was a vote that, if approved, would have allowed congressional debate on the measure; that vote failed by about twenty votes in the House of Representatives.

Impact The proposed Ludlow amendment reinforced popular sentiment that the United States should not go to war and showed that Congress was listening to the American populace. It was similar to the Oxford Pledge in England and demonstrated that much of the world was not ready to fight, regardless of the reason. Those opinions changed in Great Britain by 1939 and in the United States by 1941, but a strong antiwar sentiment persisted during the 1930's.

Scott A. Merriman

Further Reading

Doenecke, Justus D., and Mark A. Stoler. *Debating Franklin D. Roosevelt's Foreign Policies, 1933-1945.* Lanham, Md.: Rowman & Littlefield, 2005.

Dubofsky, Melvyn, and Stephen Burwood, eds. *American Foreign Policy in the 1930's: Selected Articles on the Depression, the New Deal, and Foreign Relations.* New York: Garland, 1990.

Herring, George C. *From Colony to Superpower: U.S. Foreign Relations Since 1776.* New York: Oxford University Press, 2008.

See also Congress, U.S.; Foreign policy of the United States; Isolationism; Neutrality Acts; Peace movement; Quarantine speech; World War II and the United States.

■ Lynching

Definition Mob killing, often by hanging and usually motivated by racism

During the 1930's, an increase in the lynching of African Americans occurred. This was accompanied by efforts from individuals, groups, and government to eradicate lynching. There were attempts to enact a federal law against lynchings. The newspapers of the South played a significant role in white attitudes toward lynching; some decried the practice, and others incited the act.

Tuskegee Institute records indicate that between the years 1880 and 1951, 3,437 African Americans and 1,293 Caucasians were lynched. Some of the Caucasians were accused of criminal acts, while others tried to help prevent a lynching or were against lynching as a practice. Most lynchings occurred in the South in the Cotton Belt states of Alabama, Georgia, Louisiana, Mississippi, and Texas. Beginning in the 1910's and continuing through the 1920's, the number of lynchings dropped steadily. However, in the first half of the 1930's, instances of lynching increased; they declined after 1935. The downward trend continued through the 1960's.

Resistance to Lynching Resistance to lynching was carried out in many ways via plays, songs, poetry,

An African American youth hanging from a tree after being lynched by a group of fifty men for allegedly gunning down a state highway worker. (©Bettmann/ CORBIS)

films, and newspapers. In 1937, Abel Meeropol wrote "Strange Fruit," a song that protested the practice of lynching and was made most famous by Billie Holiday.

Some believed the best way to combat lynching was to use town newspapers to influence Caucasians against the practice. Newspapers were ambivalent in their coverage of lynchings; some campaigned against lynching, while others advocated its use. Many Caucasians believed lynching was necessary to control African Americans. Others rejected this idea and considered the phenomenon of lynching to be a societal issue. Integrated groups of African Americans and Caucasians organized against lynching, lobbied Congress, and engaged in other forms of resistance and education. The National Association for the Advancement of Colored People (NAACP)

had the support of black and white Americans as it campaigned against lynching. The Association of Southern Women for the Prevention of Lynching was active in raising funds to support antilynching efforts, writing letters and petitions, and demonstrations against lynching. The organization often targeted newspaper editors and sheriffs to highlight the issue, praising them when they went against lynching.

The 1918 Dyer Anti-Lynching Bill was the first of its kind introduced to the U.S. Congress. However, its passage was blocked by white southern Democrats. During the 1930's, the Costigan-Wagner bill, influenced by the Dyer bill, would have punished local sheriffs who did not protect their prisoners from lynch mobs. Sometimes, sheriffs participated in lynchings. While the Costigan-Wagner bill was supported by many members of Congress, President Franklin D. Roosevelt did not support it out of his belief that he would lose the 1936 presidential election if he did so. The bill was defeated by the southern opposition. However, the Costigan-Wagner bill made more Americans aware of lynching.

Impact   Eventually, lynching became a felony in the first degree in all of the United States. The practice is considered one of the most brutal symbols of the legacy of racism in the history of U.S. society.

Judy Porter

Further Reading

Allen, James, et al. *Without Sanctuary: Lynching Photography in America.* Santa Fe, N.Mex.: Twin Palms, 2000. Documentary focused on photographs of lynchings taken around the country.

Howard, Walter T. *Lynchings: Extralegal Violence in Florida During the 1930s.* New York: Authors Choice Press, 2005. History of lynchings in Florida during the 1930's.

Jonas, Gilbert S. *Freedom's Sword: The NAACP and the Struggle Against Racism in America, 1909-1969.* New York: Routledge, 2005. Provides a good commentary about the emergence of the NAACP and its efforts to eliminate lynching.

Markovitz, Jonathan. *Legacies of Lynching: Racial Violence and Memory.* Minneapolis: University of Minnesota Press, 2004. Provides an examination of the evolution of lynching and its role as an ongoing symbol of racism.

Perloff, Richard M. "The Press and Lynchings of African Americans." *Journal of Black Studies* (January, 2000): 315-330. Gives a good account of the press coverage of lynchings and the role editors and news coverage played in both provoking and abolishing the practice.

Pfeifer, Michael J. *Rough Justice: Lynching and American Society, 1874-1947.* Urbana: University of Illinois Press, 2004. Explores the relationships among lynching, white supremacy, and the law in the postbellum United States. Lynchings were symbolic of the conflicts between lower- and middle-class Caucasians as they sought a balance between rough justice and due process.

Wright, George C. *Racial Violence in Kentucky 1865-1940.* Baton Rouge: Louisiana State University Press, 1990. Provides an excellent history of racial strife in Kentucky.

Zangrando, Robert. *The NAACP Crusade Against Lynching, 1909-1950.* Philadelphia: Temple University Press, 1980. Gives a history of the NAACP's attempt to bring the practice of lynching to an end.

See also   African Americans; Civil rights and liberties in the United States; Holiday, Billie; Jim Crow segregation; Race riots; Racial discrimination.

M

■ MacArthur, Douglas

Identification   Chief of staff of the U.S. Army,
    1930-1935
Born   January 26, 1880; Little Rock, Arkansas
Died   April 3, 1964; Washington, D.C.

*MacArthur's behavior during the 1930's was controversial
and contradicted his reputation as a great American military leader.*

Douglas MacArthur was the son of General Arthur
MacArthur, the U.S. Army's highest-ranking officer
from 1906 to 1909. As a boy, MacArthur lived on
frontier army posts before entering the U.S. Military
Academy at West Point and graduating at the head of
his class in 1903. Thereafter, he served as an engineering officer in the United States, the Philippines,
Panama, and Japan. From 1913 to 1917, MacArthur
worked on the U.S. Army General Staff. Following
U.S. entry into World War I in April, 1917, he fought
in a series of military operations in France. From
1919 to 1922, Brigadier General MacArthur enacted
reforms as superintendent at West Point before serving two command tours in the Philippines. Appointment as U.S. Army chief of staff came in August,
1930.

American isolationism and the Great Depression
combined to make MacArthur's time as chief miser-
able, as he could not prevent budget reductions.
Then, in July, 1932, when World War I veterans demanding bonuses refused to vacate U.S. government property and clashed with police, MacArthur
implemented orders to evict them. With tank support, he led two thousand combat troops with fixed
bayonets in an assault that injured many protesters.
MacArthur believed communists were behind the
Bonus Army March, which was "animated with the
essence of revolution." In March, 1933, he met with
President Franklin D. Roosevelt in a failed effort to
avoid cuts in defense spending. Thereafter, he su-
pervised the Civilian Conservation Corps, improved
officer training, and activated a centralized air command. In November, 1934, Roosevelt extended Mac-

Arthur's term to use his influence in Congress to expand military funding.

MacArthur returned to the Philippines in October, 1935, as head of a U.S. military mission for the
Philippine Commonwealth, arranging to receive secret compensation of $250,000 to build a defense
force. Presented in April, 1936, his plan provided for
a huge reserve of citizen soldiers under a regular
army, a flotilla of torpedo boats, and an air force.
The Philippine legislature lacked the funding to pay
for trainers, facilities, weapons, and salaries. As important, U.S. military leaders believed that the islands were indefensible and withheld military aid.
Expecting termination of his mission in 1937, Mac-
Arthur accepted appointment as field marshal of
the Philippine army and retired from the U.S. Army
in December. His unilateral actions in 1938 alienated President Manuel Quezon, who began assuming more power over the military. Anticipating
dismissal, MacArthur made desperate efforts to
gain appointment as U.S. high commissioner but
failed.

In July, 1941, the U.S. Army recalled MacArthur
to service. After Japan attacked Pearl Harbor in December, he became commander of Allied forces in
the southwest Pacific, following a strategy to retake
the Philippines after Japan's easy defeat of the hollow force he had built. In September, 1945, MacArthur presided over Japan's surrender and then was
supreme commander for the Allied Powers in super-
vising the occupation of Japan. Governing as a be-
nevolent despot, he enacted a series of reforms and
lobbied for prompt restoration of sovereignty. After
the Korean War began in June, 1950, MacArthur
commanded the United Nations forces that halted
the invasion. His famous landing at Inchon made
possible an assault into North Korea that provoked
Chinese intervention and inflicted a humiliating defeat on MacArthur. His public criticism of U.S. refusal to extend the war into China forced President
Harry S. Truman to recall the general in April, 1951.
MacArthur spent his remaining years quietly, living
in New York City.

Impact During the 1930's, MacArthur's actions exposed serious flaws in his character, including egotism, melodrama, paranoia, and self-promotion. World War II saved his career and reputation.

James I. Matray

Further Reading

Manchester, William. *American Caesar: Douglas MacArthur, 1880-1964.* Boston: Little, Brown, 1978. Generally favorable biography of MacArthur.

Perrett, Geoffrey. *Old Soldiers Never Die: The Life of Douglas MacArthur.* New York: Random House, 1996. Thorough biography revealing that MacArthur learned early in his career how to manipulate reporters with great effect.

Schaller, Michael. *Douglas MacArthur: The Far Eastern General.* New York: Oxford University Press, 1989. Damning critique of MacArthur that presents evidence exposing his numerous personal flaws and exaggerations of his military abilities.

Weintraub, Stanley. *Five Stars: Eisenhower, MacArthur, Marshall—Three Generals Who Saved the American Century.* New York: Free Press, 2007.

See also Asia; Bonus Army March; Foreign policy of the United States; Great Depression in the United States; Hoover, Herbert; Isolationism; Japanese military aggression; Philippine Independence Act of 1934; Philippine Islands; Roosevelt, Franklin D.

McCormack Act of 1938. See **Foreign Agents Registration Act of 1938**

■ McDaniel, Hattie

Identification African American actor
Born June 10, 1895; Wichita, Kansas
Died October 26, 1952; Woodland Hills, California

McDaniel excelled as a singer, actor, and performer during the 1930's, a time when African Americans did not always receive acceptance. Often ignored in film credits, she appeared in almost two hundred films. As "Mammy" in Gone with the Wind *(1939), McDaniel became the first African American to receive an Academy Award nomination, to win an Oscar, and to attend the Academy Awards ceremony as a guest—not a servant.*

Hattie McDaniel was born to Susan Holbert McDaniel and former slave Henry McDaniel in Wichita, Kansas. She grew up in Denver, Colorado. Accompanied by his sons Sam and Otis, her minister father often toured. He never allowed young McDaniel to travel with them. At sixteen, McDaniel won the Women's Christian Temperance Union's recitation contest. With this encouragement, she left school and began traveling with vaudeville companies, minstrel shows, and musical ensembles. During the 1920's, she began singing with the Morrison Orchestra.

McDaniel moved to Hollywood in 1931 and began to secure film roles. She appeared in more than one hundred films for which she received no screen credit; in more than ninety, however, her name appears in the listings. Her performances included a duet with Will Rogers in *Judge Priest* (1934), a role in *The Little Colonel* (1935) with Shirley Temple and Lionel Barrymore, performances with Katharine Hepburn and Jean Harlow, and a part in *Show Boat* (1936). Although McDaniel's four marriages were unsuccessful, her screen career was.

McDaniel secured the role of "Mammy" in *Gone with the Wind.* Hers was one of eight Oscars awarded to the film. McDaniel also appeared in *Song of the South* (1946). She sang "Sooner or Later" in the film and appears on the sound track.

From 1947 to 1951, McDaniel had her own radio show, *Beulah.* She began a television series of the same name in 1951. After only three episodes, however, she was diagnosed with breast cancer. McDaniel died on October 26, 1952, in Woodland Hills, California.

McDaniel wanted to be buried in Hollywood, but the racism of the era prevented this. Eventually, her wish came true, when she received a pink-and-gray granite monument in Hollywood Forever Cemetery. In 2006, the U.S. Postal Service issued its "Black Heritage Series" and recognized McDaniel. One of the stamps in this series is a multicolored image of McDaniel in the dress she wore when she received her Academy Award.

Impact McDaniel was a multitalented woman. She was a singer, film actor, and radio and television performer. As "Mammy" in *Gone with the Wind,* she became the first African American to win an Oscar. Her achievements made advancements easier for other African Americans in Hollywood.

Anita Price Davis

Hattie McDaniel (right) tying Vivien Leigh's corset in Gone with the Wind. *(Archive Photos/Getty Images)*

Further Reading

Davis, Anita P. *Georgia During the Great Depression.* Jefferson, N.C.: McFarland, 2008.

_____. *Margaret Mitchell: A Link to Atlanta and the World.* Atlanta: Atlanta Historical Society, 2006.

Davis, Anita Price, and Mary Louise Hunt. *Women on U.S. Postage Stamps.* Jefferson, N.C.: McFarland, 2008.

Watts, Jill. *Hattie McDaniel: Black Ambition, White Hollywood.* New York: Amistad Press, 2007.

See also Academy Awards; Civil rights and liberties in the United States; *Gone with the Wind*; Great Depression in the United States; Literature in the United States; Postage stamps.

Mackenzie King, William Lyon. See **King, William Lyon Mackenzie**

■ MacLeish, Archibald

Identification American poet, playwright, essayist, teacher, and public servant

Born May 7, 1892; Glencoe, Illinois

Died April 20, 1982; Conway, Massachusetts

During the 1930's, MacLeish evolved from a largely apolitical poet to an increasingly engaged anticommunist and antifascist poet, playwright, and essayist.

In 1915, newly graduated from Yale, Archibald MacLeish entered the Harvard Law School. He married the next year, and in 1917, he enlisted in the Army and served in France as an artillery officer. He graduated from law school in 1919 and joined a Boston law firm. However, he found that he preferred writing poetry to practicing law, and in 1923, he and his young family left Boston for Paris, joining the émigré community while he established himself as a poet. In 1928, the MacLeishes returned to the United States, buying a farm in the foothills of Massachusetts's Berkshires. The next year, MacLeish joined the staff of *Fortune* magazine, a position he held until 1938. His experience writing for *Fortune* and other publications on the social, business, and economic issues of the 1930's helped to foster his blossoming patriotism and his increasing opposition to the doctrinaire ideologies that threatened American democracy from the political left and right.

At the beginning of the 1930's, MacLeish believed that poetry should be private—that is, personal and reflective. In 1930, he published *New Found Land*, including the later widely anthologized "You, Andrew Marvell," which depicts night rising in the east and advancing inexorably across the globe toward the poet—and his readers—in the United States, and "American Letter," which looks back nostalgically to his expatriate days.

Several years in its gestation, *Conquistador* (1932) was a long poem based on the journals of Bernal Diaz del Castillo, a soldier in Spaniard Hernán Cortés's expedition to find new lands, adventure, and gold in Mexico. The poem alternates between episodes of violence and episodes of almost idyllic harmony between Spaniards and Aztecs. The harmony is lost in violence, and the outcome is bitter for the common soldier. *Conquistador* earned MacLeish the first of his three Pulitzer Prizes.

Even before *Conquistador*, MacLeish was beginning to find his stance against political expression in poetry limiting. In 1931, he first articulated a goal for poetry—to create for Americans, and for humankind, a challenging and inspirational self-image. In poems such as "Invocation to the Social Muse" (1933), this search for a persuasive image of humankind became political as MacLeish responded to criticism from the Left and attacked the facile hypocrisy of communists. In *Public Speech* (1936), he made his rejection of the extreme egalitarianism of the Left clear in "Speech to Those Who Say Comrade." He made clear his rejection of fascist militarism in the satirical "The German Girls! The German Girls!" He attempted to articulate the vision

driving New Deal democracy in poems such as the 1936 "Speech to a Crowd" and *America Was Promises* (1939).

Between 1935 and 1939, MacLeish experimented with three verse dramas: *Panic* (1935), *The Fall of the City* (1937), and *Air Raid* (1939); the latter were pioneering radio dramas. With its antiappeasement theme, *The Fall of the City* earned MacLeish a reputation for prescience; the poem came shortly before the Anschluss.

In 1938, MacLeish left *Fortune* to become curator of the Nieman Foundation for Journalism at Harvard. The next year, he accepted an appointment as librarian of Congress. During World War II, he served in the Roosevelt administration as a public information officer and a propagandist. During the mid-1940's, he served significantly as a diplomat. Subsequently, he taught for more than a decade at Harvard and Amherst and resumed his writing, winning two more Pulitzer Prizes for his *Collected Poems* (1952) and his play *J.B.* (1958).

Impact During the 1930's, MacLeish moved beyond his earlier vision of the poet as one who offers personal reflections on the human experience to a vision of the poet as one also accepting public responsibilities for leadership in current events. At the end of the decade, his acceptance of public responsibility carried him even further, into government service and teaching. At the time of MacLeish's death, the poet Richard Wilber paid him this tribute: "Not all good poets are good men, but Archie was always both."

David W. Cole

Further Reading

Donaldson, Scott. *Archibald MacLeish: An American Life*. Boston: Houghton Mifflin, 1992.

Falk, Signi Lenea. *Archibald MacLeish*. New York: Twayne, 1965.

See also Communism; *Fortune* magazine; Germany and U.S. appeasement; Literature in the United States; New Deal; World War II and the United States.

■ Magazines

The decade of the 1930's was a heyday for the magazine industry in the United States. Though magazines had been publishing for decades, their availability, reasonable cost, and role as a means of escapism made them one of the few ways the average American could learn about the nation and the world and be entertained in a decade of few pleasures. The journalistic ethics and business protocols the industry instituted at the time influenced how the mass media operated for several subsequent decades.

Magazines have been published in the United States since 1741. The earliest ones were addressed to a limited readership since literacy was not widespread during the early years of the nation. For many years, most magazines were general interest publications meant to appeal to any age, sex, or proclivity. By the 1930's, however, the reading public had increased and its interests had become both varied and specialized. Magazine publishers, seeking ways to attract more readers and increase revenue, modified their publications accordingly.

Magazines from Earlier Decades Some magazines founded during the late nineteenth and early twentieth centuries continued to be published during the 1930's: *The Saturday Evening Post* was founded in 1821, *Harper's Magazine* in 1850, *Atlantic Monthly* in 1857, *Ladies Home Journal* in 1883, *Good Housekeeping* in 1885, *Collier's* and *National Geographic* in 1888, *Vogue* in 1892, *Billboard* in 1894, *Reader's Digest* in 1922, and *Time* in 1923. All these and others continued publication into, through, and after the era of the Great Depression. These magazines showed the industry's commitment to increased diversity of focus and the change from general interest to "niche" readership. Ranging in content from serious essays and literary fiction to muckraker articles, urbane humor pieces, and news commentary and analysis, these magazines were models for what came during the 1930's.

The Diversity of 1930's Magazines In spite of, or perhaps because of, the economic downturn following the stock market crash in 1929, Americans were eager for ways to forget, if only briefly, the ongoing woes of the nation. One of the cheapest, most accessible ways was the inexpensive magazines whose contents provided momentary escape from daily problems. Publishers quickly caught on to the advantages, and financial gain, of catering to the more specific interests of readers.

While many long-running publications simply revamped their contents, formats, and styles, other publications were founded to meet the needs of the public. In 1933, *Esquire* magazine was launched as the first men's magazine. An oversized journal, it had a slick, sophisticated style and quickly became famous for its drawings of beautiful young women in skin-baring outfits. Also in 1933, *Newsweek* began publication, competing with the other news magazine, *Time*. Founded in 1935, *The New Yorker* focused on events in New York and on concerns of the city's residents but also appealed to readers all across the country. By the end of the decade, there were magazines specifically produced for women, men, children, sports fans, news buffs, popular-culture and self-improvement enthusiasts, and people with practically any other interest one could imagine.

Henry Luce and Condé Montrose Nast Two men, Henry Luce and Condé Montrose Nast, were important figures in magazine publishing. According to some sources, Luce created the modern news magazine. Beginning with *Time* in 1923, he went on to publish such trendsetters as the photojournalistic *Life* (1936) and business-focused *Fortune* (1930). *Time* sought to abridge news so readers got a condensed version of what was happening in the nation and the world. *Life*'s purpose was "to see life . . . [and] the world; to eyewitness great events; [and] to watch the faces of the poor and the gestures of the proud." It sometimes used startling photos of, for example, statesmen caught off guard or actual battlefield combat with soldiers fighting and dying. It showed babies being born, policemen beating strikers with their billy clubs, everyday people, and even nearly nude models.

Luce wanted his *Fortune* magazine to exemplify that "business is obviously the greatest single denominator of interest" to leading American citizens. To that end, he produced a luxurious looking periodical printed on thick matte paper using expensive inks. It had high-quality color illustrations and photographs enclosed in ruled frames. It cost one dollar a copy, a high price compared to other magazines. During its first year of publication, its articles were critical of large corporations, such as U.S. Steel Corporation. Eventually, its focus changed to reportage and included stories on technological changes and insights into how executives operated. *Fortune* was considered the best and most influential American magazine of the 1930's.

Around 1936, Luce set up the Time-Life group, which later produced such periodicals as *Sports Illustrated, Money,* and *People.* He is credited with restyling pictorial reporting, developing group journalism, creating the concept of covering business, and even creating a writing style that employed free use of adjectives.

Nast founded his magazine publishing company in 1907. He is considered the creator of a magazine marketing strategy used widely throughout the industry. The strategy was to publish magazines that focused on specific social classes, income levels, or common interests, creating what became known as "lifestyle" magazines. Although the Great Depression nearly ruined Nast's business, his company survived, and many of his earliest magazines continue to be published.

Some of Nast's magazines started before the 1930's and continued into later decades. The fashion and lifestyle monthly *Vogue* began as a weekly in 1892 and was taken over by Nast in 1909, becoming a biweekly. *Cosmopolitan,* originally a family magazine called *The Cosmopolitan,* became a literary magazine and then a women's magazine, with a circulation of 1.7 million and an advertising income of $5 million during the 1930's. Two long-lasting magazines that started during the 1920's are *The New Yorker*—a weekly filled with commentary, fiction, satire, poetry, essays, reportage, and cartoons—and *Architectural Digest*—an interior-design monthly that critiqued trends in architectural interiors and furnishings. *Vanity Fair* was started in 1913 and contained stories on fashion, popular culture, and, occasionally, politics. *Glamour,* a women's fashion-and-lifestyle magazine, was started in 1939.

Popular but Short-Lived 1930's Magazines Several magazines that were popular during the decade lost advertising revenue or failed to attract enough new readers to continue publication against the competition of films and radio. One of the most popular publications was *Liberty,* begun in 1924 by Bernarr Macfadden (also known as Bernard McFadden) as a weekly general-interest magazine. Its popularity reached a peak during the 1930's with stories and

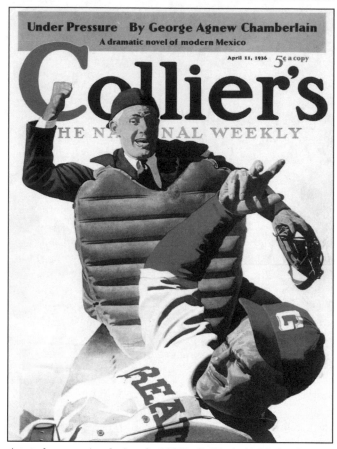

A popular magazine during the 1930's, Collier's *highlights the opening of the 1936 baseball season on its cover.* (Getty Images)

articles by such famous contributors as Amelia Earhart, Mae West, F. Scott Fitzgerald, and Leon Trotsky. It contained cartoons, articles about Hollywood and movie stars, news about crime, and film reviews. An unusual feature it introduced was attaching to each article the amount of time the reader should allot for reading and comprehending the article. This original idea set *Liberty* apart.

Collier's was founded in 1888. By the 1930's, it was competing for readers with *The Saturday Evening Post,* which was selling three million copies each week. A general interest magazine, *Collier's* attracted significant contributors such as Zane Grey, Ring Lardner, Sinclair Lewis, Willa Cather, and even Winston Churchill, a regular article contributor until he became a minister of the British government. It serialized novels, published cartoons by outstanding cartoonists, and contributed stories and serials for broadcast on its National Broadcasting Company

(NBC) radio station program, *The Collier Hour Magazine of the Air.*

A number of pulp magazines, so called because they were printed on cheap, wood-pulp paper, reached their height of popularity during the 1930's. Costing about ten cents a copy, they continued the tradition of the penny dreadful and the dime novel of the nineteenth century. Full of sensationalistic, exploitative stories and lurid cover art, the best-selling pulp magazines were *Black Mask, Flying Aces, Marvel Tales, Adventure, Weird Tales,* and *Argosy,* which, founded in 1882, is considered the first American pulp magazine and lasted until 1978.

Impact By the middle of the decade, there were more than sixty-five hundred monthly and weekly magazines published in the United States, including pulp fiction and comic books. The industry developed journalistic ethics and business protocols that continued to govern subsequent decades of mass media, giving American mass media its distinctive character. As a purveyor of American popular culture in all its aspects, the magazine industry was instrumental in standardizing, centralizing, and, in some respects, nationalizing Americans' tastes.

Jane L. Ball

Further Reading

Alexander, Charles C. *Nationalism in American Thought, 1930-1945.* Chicago: Rand McNally, 1969. Chapter 4 discusses how American thought and tastes were nationalized during the 1930's.

Augspurger, Michael. *An Economy of Abundant Beauty: "Fortune" Magazine and Depression America.* Ithaca, N.Y.: Cornell University Press, 2004. Looks at what made *Fortune* unique and how it survived during a time of economic depression.

Best, Gary D. *The Nickel and Dime Decade: American Popular Culture During the 1930's.* Westport, Conn.: Praeger, 1993. Includes discussions of 1930's magazines, comics, and popular literature.

Janello, Amy, and Brennon Jones. *The American Magazine.* New York: Harry N. Abrams, 1991. Lavishly illustrated source that describes the founders of major magazines.

Nourie, Alan, and Barbara Nourie. *American Mass Market Magazines.* Westport, Conn.: Greenwood Press, 1990. Profiles of the one hundred most significant general magazines with circulations of more than 100,000, arranged alphabetically by title.

See also Advertising in the United States; Earhart, Amelia; Fashions and clothing; Fitzgerald, F. Scott; *Fortune* magazine; Great Depression in the United States; Lewis, Sinclair; *Life* magazine; Luce, Henry; West, Mae.

■ Man Who Came to Dinner, The

Identification Play about a pompous radio broadcaster who takes over a family's home after injuring himself in a fall
Authors George S. Kaufman and Moss Hart
Date Premiered on October 16, 1939

The play was a smash hit and enjoyed a long run on Broadway. It became a film in 1941, starring Monty Woolley from the stage version, with Bette Davis and Ann Sheridan.

In the small town of Mesalia, Ohio, the famous critic Sheridan Whiteside is guest lecturing for six weeks before Christmas of 1930. At the home of Ernest W. Stanley, a wealthy factory owner, Whiteside slips on icy steps, breaks his hip, and is confined to a wheelchair in the Stanley home for his recuperation.

Before *The Man Who Came to Dinner,* George S. Kaufman and Moss Hart had already had two smash hits with their stage comedies *Once in a Lifetime* (1930) and *You Can't Take It with You* (1936). The inspiration for the title character, Sheridan Whiteside, was the American critic and commentator Alexander Woollcott, known for his acerbic wit and thorny personality as a member of the Algonquin Round Table.

Orson Welles played the title role in a 1972 television production that received mixed reviews. The play was revived in 2000, first as the Kaufman and Hart stage play, starring Nathan Lane, then as a televised broadcast on October 7, 2000, of the Roundabout Theatre production. It continues to enjoy regular productions at regional and community theaters around the United States.

Impact *The Man Who Came to Dinner* contributed to the evolution of the talk shows of the radio personalities of the 1930's, who played key roles in setting the nation's tastes and styles. As critics, men similar to the character of Sheridan Whiteside were able to make or break careers overnight. Woollcott, for example, contributed indispensably to the career of the Marx Brothers.

Richard J. Rundell

Further Reading

Brown, Jared, and Moss Hart. *Moss Hart: A Prince of the Theatre—A Biography in Three Acts.* New York: Back Stage Books, 2006.

Drennan, Robert E. *The Algonquin Wits.* Bridgewater, N.J.: Replica Books, 1999.

Goldstein, Malcolm. *George S. Kaufman: His Life, His Theater.* New York: Oxford University Press, 1979.

Meredith, Scott. *George S. Kaufman and the Algonquin Round Table.* Winchester, Mass.: Unwin Hyman, 1977.

See also Kaufman, George S., and Moss Hart; Screwball comedy; Theater in the United States; *You Can't Take It with You.*

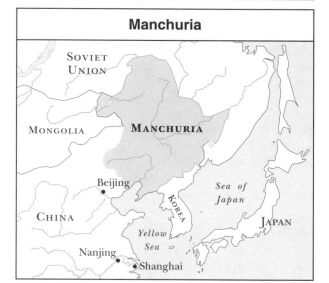

Manchuria

■ Manchuria occupation

The Event Japanese invasion of northeastern China's Manchuria provinces, which began a thirteen-year occupation

Dates 1932-1945

The Japanese takeover of Manchuria created a Sino-Japanese impasse and a challenge to U.S. decision makers. The aggression eventually led to a full-scale war between China and Japan and contributed to the outbreak of the U.S.-Japan conflict in World War II.

Manchuria is the northeastern territory of China, where Japan started its imperialist expansion in the late nineteenth century. Through the Sino-Japanese War of 1894-1895 and the Russo-Japanese War of 1904-1905, Japan seized extensive economic and political interests in the region, which Japan protected with troops stationed at strategic points. In the late 1920's, as Chinese Nationalists campaigned to unify China, Japan maneuvered to maintain its dominant position in Manchuria. In June, 1928, Japanese militarists assassinated Zhang Zuolin, the Chinese warlord based in the region who had shown signs of resistance to Japanese demands. In reaction, Zhang Xueliang, son of Zhang Zuolin, declared allegiance to the newly established Nationalist government of China.

On September 18, 1931, officers of the Japanese Kwantung Army staged an explosion on the Japanese-controlled Manchurian railroad outside the city of Shenyang (Mukden). Using the incident as a pretext, Japanese forces attacked Chinese authorities and troops in Manchuria. By the beginning of 1932, Japan had brought the whole Manchurian region under its control.

Soon after Japan launched attacks in Manchuria, China appealed to the international community for intervention. The League of Nations, pressed by Japan and lacking serious support from the major world powers, could not take meaningful actions to stop Japanese aggression. The United States had no intention of confronting Japan. The Herbert Hoover administration chose simply to register disapproval of the events in Manchuria. In a note sent to both Japan and China in January, 1932, Secretary of State Henry L. Stimson declared that the U.S. government would not recognize the legality of any changes and arrangements that were brought about by aggression and that might impair U.S. treaty rights and violate the open-door policy. This constituted what came to be known as the Stimson Doctrine.

In October, 1932, the Lytton Commission, which the League of Nations had set up to investigate the conflict in Manchuria and was headed by the second earl of Lytton of Great Britain, put forward its discoveries. Among these findings was the conclusion that Japanese military operations in Manchuria could not be viewed as self-defense. In response, Japan withdrew from the League of Nations.

In the meantime, in an attempt to legitimize its actions, Japan created a puppet Manchurian state. To serve as the head of the newly established Manchukuo, Japan installed Puyi, the last emperor of the Qing Dynasty, the Manchu dynasty that had ruled China until its overthrow in the Chinese republican revolution of 1911.

Impact The Japanese seizure of China's northeastern territory caused a national awakening in China. Chinese Communists and Chinese Nationalists, who had been fighting in a civil war, moved to form a united front against Japanese aggression, an initiative that became reality after 1937, when Japan invaded China proper and started a full-scale Sino-Japanese war. The U.S. policy of nonrecognition of Japanese military conquests continued under President Franklin D. Roosevelt. The outbreak of war in Europe in 1939 and Japan's alliance with Germany and Italy deepened U.S. concerns over Japan's position on the Asian continent. In November, 1941, in a communication to Japan, Secretary of State Cordell Hull called for the unconditional withdrawal of Japanese troops from China, a demand that Japan found unacceptable.

Jing Li

Further Reading

Borg, Dorothy. *The United States and the Far Eastern Crisis of 1933-1938: From the Manchurian Incident Through the Initial Stage of the Undeclared Sino-Japanese War.* Boston: Harvard University Press, 1968.

Howard, Harry Paxton. *America's Role in Asia.* Reprint. Roselle, N.J.: Howard Press, 2007.

Liang, Ching-chun. *The Sinister Face of the Mukden Incident.* New York: St. John's University Press, 1969.

The Verdict of the League: China and Japan in Manchuria, the Official Documents with Notes and an Introduction by Manley O. Hudson. Boston: World Peace Foundation, 1933.

See also Asia; Foreign policy of the United States; Hull, Cordell; Japanese military aggression; League of Nations; Stimson, Henry L.

■ Marathon dancing

Definition Depression-era dance competitions

Most fads have a life expectancy of less than a year, but the dance-marathon craze lasted throughout the 1930's. The fad illustrated the lengths to which people were willing to go to make some money during the Great Depression. About twenty thousand contestants and supporting personnel participated in these sport and entertainment events. Audiences, mostly women, are estimated to have numbered in the millions.

Dance marathons emerged out of the 1920's passion for bizarre record-breaking activities. They began as a craze but soon evolved into a money-making, show-business venture. Couples, each consisting of a man and a woman, competed against each other. Contestants came from every part of the country and every

Marathon dancers cling to their partners in hour nine hundred of an exhausting competition in New York City's Bronx borough in 1932. (NY Daily News via Getty Images)

ethnicity, including Native Americans. Brothers and sisters, fathers and daughters, and mothers and sons participated. The contestants tended to be younger because of the physical demands of the fad, although some older people danced.

The marathons were not pleasant for the participants. Dancers were housed in one building for the duration of the show, which might last from six weeks to many months. During this time, couples were required to follow a strict regimen. Once on the dance floor, teams were required to remain in motion, forty-five minutes of every hour, day and night. Additional physical demands were made upon contestants in the form of a variety of foot races. The team that lasted the longest won first prize, although there were many other ways of earning money during the course of the contest. Few of the dance endurance contests were run honestly, with "ringers" often participating.

By the mid-1930's, one-half of the states had enacted legislation to ban dance marathons. Many cities used local ordinances to prohibit the events. The craze, however, continued into the 1950's.

Impact The marathon dance craze was essentially a predecessor to the reality shows that dominate twenty-first century entertainment. An exploitative form of mass entertainment, the marathons took advantage of financially desperate Americans.

Caryn E. Neumann

Further Reading

Calabria, Frank M. *Dance of the Sleepwalkers: The Dance Marathon Fad.* Bowling Green, Ohio: Bowling Green State University Popular Press, 1993.

Martin, Carol. *Dance Marathons: Performing American Culture in the 1920s and 1930s.* Oxford: University Press of Mississippi, 1994.

See also Dance; Fads; Recreation; Unemployment in the United States.

■ Marble, Alice

Identification American tennis player
Born September 28, 1913; Beckwourth, California
Died December 13, 1990; Palm Springs, California

Marble dominated women's tennis from 1936 to 1940 with eighteen majors titles, including four U.S. singles, one Wimbledon singles, four U.S. doubles, four U.S. mixed-doubles, two Wimbledon doubles, and three Wimbledon mixed-doubles crowns.

Alice Marble grew up in San Francisco, California, and graduated from Polytechnic High School in 1931. She learned to play tennis at Golden Gate Park, developing a powerful serve and becoming the first female player to popularize the technique of rushing the net. In 1932, Eleanor Tennant became Marble's teacher and mentor.

Marble's tennis career suffered two major setbacks. In 1933, Marble played both the singles and doubles semifinals and finals in a Long Island, New York, tennis tournament the same day. She won both semifinals matches but then lost both finals contests. After playing 108 games spanning eleven sets that day, she collapsed from dehydration, sunstroke, and anemia.

Marble traveled to France with a women's team in 1934 and fainted during her initial match. Doctors diagnosed her with tuberculosis and put her in a sanatorium for several months. Tennant formulated an exercise and diet program to restore Marble's health.

In 1936, Marble captured her first major championships, taking both the U.S. singles and the mixed-doubles crowns with Gene Mako. Marble took U.S. singles titles from 1938 to 1940, the U.S. doubles crowns from 1937 to 1940 with Sarah Palfrey, and the U.S. mixed-doubles championships with Don Budge in 1938, Harry Hopman in 1939, and Bobby Riggs in 1940. Her victories in three consecutive singles, doubles, and mixed doubles between 1938 and 1940 matched the all-time records of Hazel Wightman and Mary Kendall Browne.

At Wimbledon, Marble won the 1939 singles title and teamed with Palfrey to take the 1938 and 1939 doubles crowns. She combined with Budge to take the 1937 and 1938 mixed-doubles titles and with Bobby Riggs to capture the 1939 mixed-doubles crown. The Associated Press named Marble female athlete of the year in 1939 and 1940.

Marble performed tennis exhibitions, lectured, sang, designed women's clothing, contributed to *American Lawn Tennis* magazine, and taught tennis at Palm Desert Country Club in California. In 1964, the International Tennis Hall of Fame enshrined her.

Impact   During her time, Marble had the most powerful serve in women's tennis, an aggressive full-court game, speed, and agility. She inspired Doris Hart to achieve championship potential and persuaded tennis officials to let African American Althea Gibson enter tournaments.

David L. Porter

Further Reading

Marble, Alice. *The Road to Wimbledon*. New York: Charles Scribner's Sons, 1947.

Marble, Alice, with Dale Leatherman. *Courting Danger*. New York: St. Martin's Press, 1991.

Morrish, Elizabeth C. E. "Alice Marble." In *Great Athletes: Golf and Tennis*. Pasadena, Calif.: Salem Press, 2010.

See also   Budge, Don; Moody, Helen Wills; Riggs, Bobby; Sports in Canada; Sports in the United States; Tennis; Tilden, Bill.

■ March of Dimes

Identification   Charitable organization
Date   Established January 3, 1938
Also known as   National Foundation for Infantile Paralysis

The March of Dimes was the name of the fund-raising activity of the National Foundation for Infantile Paralysis. It became one of the most successful fund-raising campaigns of the first half of the twentieth century and directly led to the development of effective polio vaccines in 1955 and the eventual eradication of polio from the United States in 1979.

In 1921, thirty-year-old Franklin D. Roosevelt was stricken with polio. Later in the decade, Roosevelt and his law partner, Basil O'Connor, purchased a resort in Warm Springs, Georgia, and converted it into a facility to provide therapy and care for polio patients. O'Connor and Roosevelt eventually turned the resort into a nonprofit foundation, the Georgia Warm Springs Foundation. In 1938, President Roosevelt formed the National Foundation for Infantile Paralysis to replace the Georgia Warm Springs Foundation. The mission of the foundation was to care for polio patients and to find an effective treatment, cure, and vaccine.

The Depression had a severe impact on the fund-raising activities of the Georgia Warm Springs Foundation, reducing the money that potential donors had for charitable giving. Therefore, in 1933, the foundation hired Carl Robert Byoir, a public-relations pioneer, to run its advertising and fund-raising campaigns. The first venture was a nationwide birthday fund-raiser campaign for President Roosevelt. More than six thousand parties were held on January 29, 1934, and more than one million dollars was raised.

Hollywood celebrity Eddie Cantor was a strong supporter of the foundation and referred to its fund-raising campaign as the March of Dimes after the newsreel *The March of Time*. Cantor used his radio program to launch the fund-raising effort by asking everyone to send a dime to the White House to help fight the disease. Soon many other Hollywood, theater, sports, and political celebrities joined Cantor's campaign. For several years, the primary fund-raising activities were the annual parties and balls held on or for President Roosevelt's birthday. At each year's event, a child was chosen to symbolize polio survivors. The child's photograph was placed on a poster promoting the March of Dimes campaign. The aggressive and visible March of Dimes campaign revolutionized fund-raising.

In 1938, the National Foundation for Infantile Paralysis formed a committee on scientific research. Priorities were reordered to focus on the basic biology of the polio virus. Later, the foundation distributed moneys to various vaccine research programs, which eventually led to the development of the Jonas Salk and Albert Bruce Sabin vaccines and the later eradication of polio from the United States. Foundation moneys were also expended to develop and distribute the tank respirator, also known as the iron lung, a machine that aided the breathing of polio victims whose respiratory muscles were affected. Mass distribution of the iron lung began in 1939.

Rather than end its fund-raising efforts after the development of the polio vaccines, in 1958, the March of Dimes refocused its attention on the prevention of premature births, birth defects, and in-

Jack Benny (left) playfully inserting his cigar into the mouth of dummy Charlie McCarthy while ventriloquist Edgar Bergen (right) feigns concern at a March of Dimes benefit radio broadcast in 1938. (AP/Wide World Photos)

fant mortality. The name of the foundation was officially changed to the March of Dimes in 1979.

Impact Polio was one of the most devastating and feared diseases to affect the United States in the first half of the twentieth century, when more than one-half million people, primarily children, were stricken. The National Foundation for Infantile Paralysis's March of Dimes campaign revolutionized fund-raising and directly led to the development of effective vaccines in the mid-1950's.

Charles L. Vigue

Further Reading

Oshinsky, David M. *Polio, an American Story.* New York: Oxford University Press, 2005.

Silver, Julie K., and Daniel Wilson. *Polio Voices: An Oral History from the American Polio Epidemics and Worldwide Eradication Efforts.* Westport, Conn.: Praeger, 2007.

Wilson, Daniel J. *Polio.* Santa Barbara, Calif.: Greenwood Press/ABC-CLIO, 2009.

See also Health care; Medicine; Polio; Roosevelt, Franklin D.

■ Marihuana Tax Act of 1937

The Law Federal law that imposed a tax on anyone who dealt in marijuana commercially
Also known as Marijuana Tax Act of 1937
Date Introduced August 2, 1937

The act shaped U.S. domestic and international drug policies and served as a precursor to the war on drugs that was ushered in during the Ronald Reagan and George H. W. Bush presidential administrations.

The Marihuana Tax Act probably never would have been written and passed if not for the efforts of

Harry J. Anslinger, who served as the first director of the Federal Bureau of Narcotics (FBN), established by the U.S. Treasury in 1930.

Recreational use of marijuana was not evident in the United States until the first decade of the twentieth century. Marijuana appeared first in the United States along the Mexican border, brought into the country by migrant laborers. Coupled with the passage of the Eighteenth Amendment, which made the sale, manufacture, or transportation of alcohol illegal, the use and popularity of marijuana mushroomed as it spread across the land.

When Anslinger became the director of the FBN, marijuana was not even known by that name; it was referred to as hemp or cannabis. Anslinger may have borrowed the term marijuana, the Spanish Mexican word for cannabis, in order to give cannabis an association with Mexicans, tapping into the racial prejudice of the people in the United States to gain public support for laws against the drug. In addition, by using the term "marihuana" in the language of the bill, the plant's legitimate uses in medicine may have been diminished, in which it was commonly known as cannabis, and in the fiber industry, in which it was referred to as hemp.

Because drugs could not be outlawed at the federal level, federal taxes became the mechanism to control the use, possession, and sale of marijuana. If they were not taxed, they represented a loss of revenue for the government. Thereafter, those who failed to comply with the law found themselves in trouble with the U.S. Treasury.

By most accounts, Anslinger passed the Marihuana Tax Act of 1937 by rather questionable means, using yellow journalism, which involved sensationalized and distorted stories to stimulate public opinion. Anslinger's efforts were supported by William Randolph Hearst, who owned a chain of newspapers and had a number of self-serving interests for making marijuana illegal. Besides Hearst's interests, the FBN seems to have used propaganda to demonize marijuana in order to protect government and private investment in the wood-pulp industry. Therefore, the prohibition of marijuana did not occur because of a true problem with the drug: The FBN did not produce any evidence of a crisis with marijuana, but relied instead on Anslinger's "Gore File," which consisted mainly of exaggerated claims of murder and mayhem taken from articles in Hearst-owned newspapers.

Impact   Seemingly, Anslinger and Hearst were motivated by money and prejudice. The end result was that the hemp (the fiber from the cannabis plant) industry one completely unrelated to narcotics production, was wiped out within a few years, as the act rendered hemp almost worthless because it was taxed out of existence.

Paul Finnicum

Further Reading

Abel, Ernest. *Marihuana: The First Twelve Thousand Years.* New York: Plenum Press, 1980.

Bonnie, Richard J., and Charles H. Whitebread II. *The Marihuana Conviction: A History of Marihuana Prohibition in the United States.* Charlottesville: University of Virginia Press, 1974.

Booth, Martin. *Cannabis: A History.* New York: Thomas Dunne Books/St. Martin's Press, 2004.

Gray, Michael. *Drug Crazy: How We Got into This Mess and How We Can Get Out.* New York: Random House, 1998.

Grinspoon, L. *Marijuana Reconsidered.* 3d ed. Oakland, Calif.: Quick American Archives, 1994.

Herer, Jack. *Hemp and the Marihuana Conspiracy: The Emperor Wears No Clothes.* Van Nuys, Calif.: Hemp, 1991.

Inciardi, James A. *The War on Drugs: Heroin, Cocaine, Crime, and Public Policy.* Palo Alto, Calif.: Mayfield, 1986.

Slaughter, James B. "Marijuana Prohibition in the United States: History and Analysis of a Failed Policy." *Columbia Journal of Law and Social Problems* 21, no. 4 (1988): 417-474.

See also   Agriculture in the United States; Business and the economy in the United States; Prohibition repeal; Revenue Acts.

■ Marquand, John P.

Identification   American writer
Born   November 10, 1893; Wilmington, Delaware
Died   July 16, 1960; Newburyport, Massachusetts

Marquand began the 1930's as a writer of magazine fiction and continued in this genre with the creation of the Mr. Moto spy thriller series, but he also established himself as a serious writer at the end of the decade with The Late George Apley *(1937), a novel satirizing the Boston elite.*

As the 1930's began, John Phillips Marquand was already a popular writer of short stories and serialized novels, most of which appeared in mass circulation magazines such as the *The Saturday Evening Post.* The stories tended to be formulaic fictions about pirates and thieves, with romantic, boy-meets-girl plots, but Marquand tended to infuse even this commercial fiction with some deeply felt themes about social snobbery. He also became adept at creating compelling historical backgrounds focused on New England. At the beginning of the decade, he published two works of fiction set in New England, the novel *Warning Hill* (1930) and the collection of stories *Haven's End* (1933).

In 1934, *The Saturday Evening Post* sent Marquand to China and Japan, hoping he would acquire enough understanding of Asia to write adventure stories set in the Far East to fill the void caused by the death of the creator of the Charlie Chan detective stories, Earl Derr Biggers. Marquand was much taken with what he found and produced an adventure story set in China, *Ming Yellow* (1935), which is notable for its evocation of the Asian setting. After this, he wrote a series of spy thrillers featuring the Japanese agent Mr. Moto, beginning with *No Hero* (1935) and continuing with four more Mr. Moto adventures over the next six years. These novels not only were successful on their own but also were turned into a series of popular films between 1937 and 1939, starring Peter Lorre.

At the same time that Marquand was inventing Mr. Moto, he began work on a more serious novel, *The Late George Apley* (1937), a satire of life among the elite of Boston. Cast in the form of a biography, the novel explores the oppressive weight of convention and conformity while poking gentle fun at foolish and stuffy, "proper" Bostonians. Despite the qualms of his agent, who feared he would alienate his regular readership, and the fears that no one outside Boston would understand the novel and those inside Boston would be offended, the novel was a great success, eventually selling more than Marquand's more commercial fiction and winning him the Pulitzer Prize in 1938.

Marquand followed up this success with another novel satirizing the Boston elite, *Wickford Point*

(1939), and completed what became known as his Boston trilogy with *H. M. Pulham, Esquire* (1941). For the following two decades, he was one of the most popular and successful novelists in the United States and was featured in profiles in *Time, Newsweek, Life,* and *The New Yorker* magazines. His books sold millions of copies during this time, but after his death, he faded into obscurity.

Impact   At a time when some writers, such as William Faulkner, were experimenting with innovative forms and others were producing novels of protest against the conditions of the Great Depression, Marquand produced traditional narratives that avoided the social and political issues of the day. Perhaps as a result, or perhaps because he began as a magazine writer, he received little attention from academic critics. Edmund Wilson dismissed him as a journalist, and even those who praised him sometimes focused on his ability to depict the higher reaches of American society, as if he were more a sociologist than a fiction writer.

Thus, some commentators considered it only natural that Marquand should fall into obscurity, saying that his main accomplishment was to depict the old-fashioned, genteel society of upper-class Boston, which had more or less disappeared by the time of his death. Others, though, say he deserves to be reconsidered because he had deeper things to say about the human condition, success and failure, disappointment, the passage of time, and the erosion of values.

Sheldon Goldfarb

Further Reading

Auchincloss, Louis. "John P. Marquand." In *Writers and Personality.* Columbia: University of South Carolina Press, 2005.

Bell, Millicent. *Marquand: An American Life.* Boston: Little, Brown, 1979.

Gross, John J. *John P. Marquand.* New York: Twayne, 1963.

See also   Asia; Charlie Chan films; Faulkner, William; Magazines; Mr. Moto films.

■ Marx Brothers

Identification   American film and Broadway stars

The chaos of the Marx Brothers' films, which poked fun at wealth, pomposity, and established institutions, helped dispel Depression-era gloom.

The phenomenal popularity of the Marx Brothers during the 1930's began in late 1929 with their first feature film, *The Cocoanuts*. Any musical show transferred that year from Broadway theater was likely to succeed, as the film industry made the transition from silent films to talkies, and the Marx Brothers' words brought wit, audacity, incongruity, literalism, and excruciating puns to the screen.

The Cocoanuts was followed by eight films during the 1930's. The best of them combined the talents of some of the greatest playwrights and comic writers of the time, including George S. Kaufman, Morrie Ryskind, and S. J. Perelman, with the unique characters of the Marx Brothers, which, perfected since 1912 in live theater, were fully formed by the start of their transition to film.

The mute character of Harpo was no less popular than those of his wisecracking brothers, Groucho and Chico. His facial expressions ranged from adorable to lecherous. He might change quickly to an angelic harpist after chasing a screaming girl around the set. One of his most memorable scenes, the mirror scene in *Duck Soup*, was reprised on 1950's televi-

Typical Marx Brothers chaos develops within the cramped confines of a ship's cabin in this famous scene from the 1935 film A Night at the Opera. *Groucho (second from left) pins a smiling woman against the wall; Chico (center, looking toward the camera) holds back the group of people; Harpo sleeps horizontally on top of Chico's shoulders; Zeppo, with his head only partly visible, peers over Harpo and Chico.* (The Granger Collection, New York)

sion when Harpo became the reflection of his impersonator Lucille Ball.

Chico Marx portrayed an Italian immigrant, usually the pal and straight man to Harpo and master antagonist to Groucho. Chico supplied incomparable, often incomprehensible, piano interludes.

Groucho was equally skilled as a comedian or straight man, nearly always losing any encounter with his brothers. Despite that, Groucho was the central character, no less responsible for any mayhem that ensued and as irritating to the dowager characters, usually played by Margaret Dumont, as his brothers alternatively were to him. Groucho could have been consistent in his proclamations of love and devotion to Dumont, but he could not resist following a sweet sentiment with an insult, usually to his detriment. This was the real Groucho, to a considerable degree, and this persona served him well throughout his long career, particularly later as host of *You Bet Your Life*, his long-running radio and television quiz program.

Zeppo appeared in five films without eccentric character traits, though his brothers considered him the funniest of all offstage. Gummo was not in films but served as Groucho's agent for many years.

According to various accounts, Groucho (whose given name was Julius) got his nickname from the "grouch bag" around his neck (for protecting valuables while traveling in vaudeville) or else from appearing grouchy. Chico (given name Leonard) liked the girls, or "chicks." Harpo (given name Adolph) played the harp. Zeppo (given name Herbert) was perhaps named after a zeppelin, or perhaps not, and Gummo (given name Milton) wore gumshoes.

The film *Animal Crackers* (1930), like *The Cocoanuts*, was adapted from Broadway. *Animal Crackers* set the brothers loose amid a high-society weekend party at the grand home of Mrs. Rittenhouse (played by Dumont). As a famous African explorer, Groucho sang what became his theme song: "Hooray for Captain Spaulding."

Monkey Business (1931), written for the screen, took place on an ocean liner. The four brothers are stowaways who spend the entire filming trying to avoid capture.

In *Horse Feathers* (1932), Groucho is welcomed as the dean of a college, an ideal setup for chaos. He competes with his "son" Zeppo for the love of the "college widow," Thelma Todd. The four brothers

make a mockery of higher education, satirizing the conventions of college life.

To some, *Duck Soup* (1933) is the best of the five films the Marx Brothers did for Paramount, while others prefer the two that preceded it. In *Duck Soup*, Groucho's diplomacy leads a mythical country into war.

A Night at the Opera (1935) was the Marx Brothers' first film for Metro-Goldwyn-Mayer (MGM) and the first without Zeppo. Producer Irving Thalberg insisted on a "serious" story for romantic leads. Nevertheless, it contains some of the best Marx Brothers ensemble work, which they perfected in front of live audiences before filming. *A Day at the Races* (1937) is an MGM epic and again features some of the best Marx Brothers portrayals, such as Chico's ice cream seller or Groucho's great lover. These two MGM films are generally considered the pinnacle of the brothers' career. The death of Thalberg left them without a champion at that studio.

Room Service (1938) was adapted from a play, rather than created as a Marx Brothers vehicle. Lucille Ball played the female lead. Back at MGM for *At The Circus* (1939), the brothers continued to make entertaining films, though never approaching the perfection of earlier efforts.

Impact The brothers' careers together declined during the 1940's. Groucho went on to greater fame on radio and television, becoming a living legend to younger audiences as the films were revived. The Marx Brothers have since attained entertainment immortality, providing a link from the 1930's to each subsequent generation.

Richard Simonton

Further Reading

Adamson, Joe. *Groucho, Harpo, Chico, and Sometimes Zeppo.* New York: Simon & Schuster, 1983. Perhaps the quintessential biography of the Marx Brothers. Includes extensive documentation, historical information, and excerpts from the films.

Marx, Groucho. *Groucho and Me.* New York: Bernard Geis, 1959. Rambling, autobiographical reminiscence replete with anecdotes, wisecracks, and some valuable observations on the Marx Brothers' rise from vaudeville to Hollywood stardom.

Marx, Harpo. *Harpo Speaks.* New York: Limelight Editions, 2004. Describes his role in the comedy team and charts his life story, including his interactions with numerous celebrities of the day.

Mitchell, Glenn. *The Marx Brothers Encyclopedia*. Rev. ed. London: Reynolds & Hearn, 2008. Comprehensive look at every possible aspect of the Marx Brothers' lives and careers.

See also   Anti-Semitism; Broadway musicals; Fields, W. C.; Film; Great Depression in the United States; Kaufman, George S., and Moss Hart; Screwball comedy; Theater in the United States.

■ Massie trial

The Event   Celebrated murder trial in Hawaii
Dates   April 4-29, 1932
Place   Honolulu, Hawaii

The Massie trial highlighted the relationship in the Hawaii Territory between U.S. personnel stationed there, the island's native residents, and other foreigners. The trial also marks the final appearance of Clarence Darrow in a highly publicized trial.

Shortly after sixteen-year-old Thalia Fortescue married U.S. naval officer Thomas Massie, they settled in Hawaii, where Thomas was stationed. Thomas was an up-and-coming naval officer, and his advancement depended on both performance at sea and performance in Navy social circles. Thalia, whose parents were among the social elite of Washington, D.C. (her mother was the niece of Alexander Graham Bell, and her father was a military hero who had served with Theodore Roosevelt's Rough Riders during the Spanish-American War in 1898), could benefit his career.

However, the marriage was troubled by Thalia's impetuous and often indiscreet behavior. On September 12, 1931, the couple attended a Navy event at a nightclub. During the evening, Thalia left the party, alone. Thomas later called home and spoke with his wife, who told Thomas "something terrible has happened"—she had been assaulted and raped, she said, by several Hawaiian men.

Police took Thalia's statement, but she provided few details. A physical examination at a hospital confirmed that Thalia had suffered a broken jaw but not rape. At police headquarters, Thalia remembered the license number of the car her assailants had been driving and the fact that the men were "locals." The police arrested Horace Ida, the owner of the car, who denied assaulting Thalia, as did the four men who were with him. Thaila stated, however, that one of those men, Joseph Kahahawai, had broken her jaw. Thalia's story started to unravel when it became clear that she had learned of the car's license number through police and when it was established that Ida and his friends were across town when the alleged rape occurred.

After a mistrial, Thalia's mother, Grace Hubbard Fortescue (who had traveled to Hawaii after hearing from Thomas of the assault), Thomas Massie, and two Navy friends kidnapped Kahahawai. They tried to beat a confession out of him, intent on saving Thalia's (and the family's) reputation, and one of the group shot him. They were in an automobile, on the way to dump the body, when a police motorcyclist, whose suspicion was aroused by the car's lowered shades, pulled them to the side of the road. All were arrested for murder.

After family and friends raised money for a defense, celebrated defense attorney Darrow was hired to act on behalf of the accused, but all the defendants were eventually convicted of manslaughter. Nevertheless, the territorial governor commuted Grace's ten-year sentence to a single hour in his office. This incredibly light "sentence" reflected the biases of the time, which were underscored by newspaper headlines that touted the murder as an "honor killing." Charges against the four remaining defendants were dropped. Later, the group departed Hawaii via ship. Thalia and Thomas were divorced in 1934; she committed suicide in 1963. Grace lived until 1979.

Impact   Thalia's accusations, the media's response to the ensuing trial, and the white outcry against the sentences handed down for the murder cast light on the anti-native sentiment among Caucasians in the islands. The commuted sentences announce the prejudice of the time: There was no question that the perpetrators were guilty; the majority of the white population, particularly among the Navy, felt that the beatings and murder were justified. In fact, Rear Admiral Yates Stirling, the commandant of the Hawaiian naval district, was outraged that the four criminals were not acquitted. The sensational response in the press—which looked on the native Hawaiians as criminals and rationalized the murder as deserved in the name of defending white women's honor—provides an example of the extreme racism of the time.

Ski Hunter

Further Reading

Packer, Robert, and Bob Thomas. *The Massie Case.* New York: Bantam Books, 1966.

Stannard, David. *Honor Killing: How the Infamous "Massie Affair" Transformed Hawaii.* New York: Viking, 2005.

See also Cleveland "torso" murders; Crimes and scandals; Racial discrimination; Scottsboro trials.

■ Medicine

In the 1930's, the U.S. government became increasingly involved in the study of infectious diseases. Private foundations, such as the National Foundation for Infantile Paralysis, and private industry continued to carry out much of the research into control and prevention of diseases. The increase in the prevalence of venereal diseases and the disaster associated with the marketing of sulfanilamide resulted in increasing government intervention in matters of public health.

In the post-World War I years of the 1920's, moral restraints were lifted, and the incidence of sexually transmitted diseases significantly increased. At the same time, scientific discoveries, including antibiotics, in the first decades of the twentieth century began to be applied in the fight against diseases.

Antibiotic Discoveries Some success was achieved by the 1930's in the search for a broad-spectrum treatment for bacterial infections. Arguably the primary impetus in the search for antimicrobials was the increasing prevalence of sexually transmitted diseases, usually referred to as venereal diseases, and in particular the spread of syphilis. Only a single drug was known for treatment of the disease, salvarsan, developed by German scientist Paul Ehrlich early in the century. An arsenic derivative, salvarsan was effective only against this one disease and produced significant side effects. However, its effectiveness illustrated that other drugs might also be developed for treatment of syphilis and deadly diseases caused by *Staphylococcus* and the streptococci.

The first of these remedies was an azo-dye derivative known as sulfanilamide. Initially developed by German physician Gerhard Domagk in the late 1920's, sulfanilamide was the first of a class of antibiotics known as sulfa drugs. Working with the German industrial giant I. G. Farbenindustrie, Domagk tested derivatives of dyes for any antibacterial activity. Unexpectedly, Domagk observed that sulfur derivatives from azo dyes were effective in killing streptococci. In 1932, more extensive testing in mice demonstrated the efficacy of the drug, known as prontosil, in protecting animals against streptococcal infections; the drug was shown to be less effective in treating staphylococcal infections. Prontosil was subsequently shown to be equally effective in the treatment of streptococcal infections in humans, including in the deadly puerperal fever among women in the postpartum weeks and in the venereal disease gonorrhea. However, it had little efficacy in the treatment of other sexually transmitted diseases such as syphilis.

The unregulated development and use of sulfanilamide had tragic consequences. In 1937, a series of deaths occurred among children in Oklahoma who had been using a marketed form of the drug, elixir sulfanilamide. In order to solubilize the drug to distribute it as a syrup, sulfanilamide had been dissolved in ethylene glycol, or antifreeze. Eventually sixty-seven deaths were confirmed. As a result, the Food and Drug Administration was enlarged and given broader powers for enforcement of drug regulations.

Following the success of sulfanilamide, additional sulfur derivatives were developed and tested for their effectiveness in treating bacterial infections. The British company May and Baker prepared a variation of the sulfa drug, which they named sulfapyridine, more commonly called simply M&B 693. The drug proved effective in treatment of pneumococcal pneumonia, a disease that regularly killed hundreds of thousands people, primarily the elderly.

The discovery of penicillin was more fortuitous than that of sulfanilamide. Though evidence of antibacterial properties of molds dated to the 1870's, the actual discovery is generally credited to British scientist Alexander Fleming. In 1928, Fleming observed the ability of a mold contaminant of the genus *Penicillium* to kill cultures of bacteria in laboratory dishes. The work was published a year later, but the significance of the discovery was overlooked by Fleming. In 1931, a physician at the Royal Infirmary in Sheffield, England, Cecil Paine, used a crude penicillin broth to treat several eye infections and a case of gonorrhea. However, difficulty in growing cultures of the mold limited any testing for its clinical application. Scientists Howard Walter Florey, Norman Heatley, and Ernst Boris Chain worked on finding a solution to both the problem of culturing the mold and purifying sufficient quantities of the antibiotic to warrant large-scale clinical trials.

Vaccine Development The ability to isolate and grow in laboratories etiological agents of disease quickly found its application in development of vaccines against those agents. Ernest Goodpasture and the husband and wife team of Alice and Eugene Woodruff developed a means to culture in the laboratory the *Rickettsia* agent that caused typhus, leading to a vaccine against the microbe by the end of the decade. Goodpasture also developed an early version of a mumps vaccine; the inability to grow the mumps virus in the laboratory limited its usefulness.

The discovery of a less virulent strain of the yellow-fever virus, known as 17-D, was tested by Rockefeller Institute scientist Max Theiler and found to provide protection against the wild strain of the virus. In 1951, Theiler was awarded the Nobel Prize in Physiology or Medicine for his work.

The election of Franklin D. Roosevelt to the presidency in 1932 was a watershed event in the struggle against another viral disease, poliomyelitis. The incidence of polio during the 1930's was relatively low as infectious diseases went, averaging approximately five to ten thousand cases per year. Nor were all cases severe. However, Roosevelt had contracted polio in 1921, and though much of the public was unaware of the severity of his case, the president had permanently lost the use of his legs. In 1927, Roosevelt founded a hospital in Warm Springs, Georgia, for polio patients, but the cost of maintaining the facility was beyond his means. He proposed an annual fund-raising event on his birthday in January as a means to support the hospital; the first such event was held on January 29, 1934. Though more than one million dollars was raised that year, political controversies resulting from the balls and the effects of the Depression on charitable contributions reduced their usefulness. In 1938, Roosevelt announced the formation of the National Foundation for Infantile Paralysis (NFIP), an organization that funded research into development of a safe, effective vaccine. Fund-raising events became known as the March of Dimes.

Scientists remained doubtful as to how quickly a vaccine could be developed; the search had al-

ready proven disastrous. In 1934, Canadian researcher Maurice Brody had attempted to produce a formalin-killed polio vaccine. The sloppy production of the vaccine and poorly designed field trials resulted in the vaccine actually causing the disease in children. Similar results happened with an attenuated vaccine developed by Philadelphia physician John Kolmer; the vaccine caused polio, killing at least nine children.

The Social Security Act, signed into law by President Roosevelt in August, 1935, was noted primarily for establishing an insurance program for the elderly. Title VI of the act also appropriated $2 million for the Public Health Service for the study of sanitation and disease, including the disbursement of funds for equivalent state agencies. The law represented one of the first examples of government funding of medical research.

Pharmaceuticals In 1931, Miles Laboratories of Elkhart, Indiana, a company then known as Miles Medical, introduced one of the first effective antacid/analgesics to the market. Known as Alka-Seltzer, the agent was noted for its fizzing and bubbling when dropped into water. The following year, Smith, Kline and French Laboratories of Philadelphia introduced the Benzedrine inhaler. The active ingredient, an amphetamine, dilated bronchial sacs and proved useful in treating asthma. However, before long the presence of amphetamines resulted in abuse of the medication.

In 1936, Abbott Laboratories chemists Ernest H. Volwiler and Donalee L. Tabern developed Pentothal, a barbiturate that could be administered before surgery as a means to relax patients or could be used in place of ether prior to minor surgical procedures. The ability of the drug to depress the nervous system and relax the patient led to its later application as a "truth serum."

Impact The 1930's provided the first practical evidence that a "magic bullet" could be developed in the fight against infectious disease. The sulfa drugs represented only the first of a long line of antibiotics that were discovered and developed during the ensuing decades. Furthermore, the discovery of "natural" antimicrobials such as penicillin provided the impetus for screening common soil organisms as sources for such drugs. During the war years, increasingly effective antibiotics, in particular penicillin, were developed and applied in treatment of life-threatening infections.

The disaster associated with the elixir sulfanil-amide resulted in pressure on President Roosevelt to improve the oversight of drugs allowed on the market. The decade did not start off well in this respect, as the U.S. Supreme Court ruled in *Federal Trade Commission v. Raladam* that while advertising of the efficacy of drugs may be misleading to the public, it is not the role of the Federal Trade Commission to protect consumers from deception. However, the Food, Drug, and Cosmetic Act signed into law by Roosevelt in 1938 strengthened the ability of the Food and Drug Administration to monitor the safety of products brought to the market. Federal agencies were further strengthened when the Wheeler-Lea Act (1938) amended the law to promote enforcement by the FTC to prevent misleading advertising. The laws were not perfect but did produce the first major overhaul of such agencies since the early part of the twentieth century.

The incidence of polio continued to rise on a yearly basis, eventually producing more than fifty thousand cases per year by the 1950's. However, funding of research through the NFIP eventually resulted in a safe and effective inactivated vaccine developed by Jonas Salk in the mid-1950's and, subsequently, an equally effective attenuated vaccine by Albert Bruce Sabin. By the end of the twentieth century, polio had nearly been eradicated.

The application of sulfanilamide in treatment or prevention of puerperal fever and in improved training of physicians resulted in a significant reduction in maternal mortality during the decade, an improvement in health care that continued through the following decades as more antibiotics were discovered.

Richard Adler

Further Reading

Grob, Gerald. *The Deadly Truth: A History of Disease in America*. Cambridge, Mass.: Harvard University Press, 2002. A history of disease and evolving health care in the United States.

Hager, Thomas. *The Demon Under the Microscope*. New York: Harmony Books, 2006. The story of sulfanil-amide, the first of the broad-spectrum antibiotics. Includes information on its accidental discovery, the arguments over who owned the patent, and the tragedies arising from its marketing.

Oshinsky, David. *Polio: An American Story*. New York: Oxford University Press, 2005. The beginning of an organized fight against polio occurred during the decade, which included the establishment of the March of Dimes.

Sheehan, John. *The Enchanted Ring: The Untold Story of Penicillin*. Cambridge, Mass.: MIT Press, 1982. Story behind the discovery, development, and application of penicillin from 1928 to its widespread application during and after World War II.

See also Birth control; Blood banks; Cancer; Elixir sulfanilamide scandal; Health care; Hearing aids; Heart-lung machine; March of Dimes; Polio; Sexually transmitted diseases; Typhus immunization.

■ Memorial Day Massacre

The Event Chicago police attacked a crowd gathered in support of striking workers
Date May 30, 1937
Place Chicago, Illinois

Images of the Memorial Day Massacre were captured on film by Indianapolis 500 filmmaker Otto Lippert (later edited by Paramount News) and by the cameras of the Associated Press and World Wide Photos. The pictures were broadly disseminated as evidence of corporate America's ruthless opposition to organized labor.

In early 1936, the Steel Workers Organizing Committee (SWOC) used the media and a multiracial, multiethnic appeal to build its union. The efforts worked, and a year later the committee attempted to engage "Little Steel" corporations in collective bargaining. Little Steel, organized under the leadership of Republic Steel president Thomas Girdler, would not negotiate. He responded by getting some workers to advance a back-to-work campaign, terminated strikers, and used tear gas on demonstrators. He also hired Hill and Knowlton as Little Steel's public-relations firm.

According to historian Carol Quike, Girdler believed that SWOC was weak and thus provoked it into the May 26, 1937, strike at Republic Steel's Chicago plant. The strike went national by May 28, with eight thousand on strike from plants in different locations. The police began arresting protesters in south Chicago. A couple of days later, the Chicago strikers numbered more than one thousand. By Memorial Day, they were joined by University of Chicago students, professionals, social workers from Hull House, church groups, and many women and children. The atmosphere was described as festive, and the weather was sunny and warm. There were singing and speeches, followed by a march to the gates of the south Chicago Republic Steel Corporation plant. As the crowd approached, police captain James Mooney commanded them to disperse; however, when an object (possibly a tree branch) was thrown toward the police contingent of more than two hundred officers, the latter responded with gunfire, tear gas, and clubs. Some eyewitnesses described the protesters as stunned that the police were firing shots at them. The brutal attack left four dead on the spot; six died later. Thirty others, including a baby and an eleven-year-old boy, were wounded.

Initially, major newspapers such as the *Chicago Tribune* and *The New York Times* framed the event as Republic Steel and the police reported it, claiming that the police were justified in efforts against an unruly mob. Conservatives had long deemed union efforts to be part of a communist agenda. The *San Francisco Chronicle*, the *Chicago Daily News*, *Time*, and *Newsweek* published the other side of the story, including images of police subduing the crowd and descriptions of conspiracies to murder workers, in addition to images of the day's shock and horror. President Franklin D. Roosevelt expressed discontentment with the actions of both parties in the dispute. This was much to the disappointment of the labor movement, which had contributed nearly one million dollars to Roosevelt's 1936 election campaign.

Thereafter, the union presented Mayor Edward Kelly with a petition for Police Commissioner James P. Allman and Captain Mooney to resign and for the prosecution of officers who fired upon the protesters. The funeral of those who died during the protest was attended by about seven thousand. Not until 1942 did the "Little Steel" companies make their first contract with the union.

Impact   The event brought to the forefront of the American psyche the savagery of antilabor efforts. Unlike previous disputed stories, photographs presented evidence of extreme efforts to stop organized labor in the United States.

Camille Gibson

Further Reading

Dennis, Michael. *The Memorial Day Massacre and the Movement for Industrial Democracy*. New York: Palgrave Macmillan, 2010.

Quirke, Carol. "Reframing Chicago's Memorial Day Massacre, May 30, 1937." *American Quarterly* 60, no. 1 (2008): 129-157.

Turrini, Joseph M. "The Newton Steel Strike: A Watershed in the CIO's Failure to Organize." *Labor History* 38, nos. 2/3 (1997): 229-265.

See also   Congress of Industrial Organizations; Income and wages in the United States; Labor strikes; National Labor Relations Act of 1935; *National Labor Relations Board v. Jones and Laughlin Steel Corp.*; Unemployment in the United States; Unionism.

■ Mencken, H. L.

Identification   American author and editor
Born   September 12, 1880; Baltimore, Maryland
Died   January 29, 1956; Baltimore, Maryland

Mencken was a sharp critic of the politics and culture of his day. As a newspaperman and book reviewer, his targets included the New Deal and Franklin D. Roosevelt.

Henry Louis Mencken had only a high school education, which emphasized practical topics at his parents' insistence. A self-taught journalist, he wrote for *The Baltimore Sun* newspaper for more than forty years. He also edited *The American Mercury* magazine until 1933. He was known for his wit and acerbic style, which he used expertly in his criticism of politicians. He was widely read and enjoyed Mark Twain and Joseph Conrad. Frequently described as a conservative, he was the author of many quotable barbs directed at major issues of his day, such as Prohibition and censorship.

Mencken lived all his life in Baltimore, where he married Sara Powell Haardt, a college professor. When she died in 1935, he devoted his remaining years to his writing.

During the 1930's, Mencken was a sharp critic of Roosevelt and an arch opponent of the New Deal. He used his deadly wit and widespread readership to launch attacks on those leaders and programs that he felt constituted an affront to American values and freedoms. He was unable to allow the people in power he felt were hypocritical to go unchallenged.

Journalist H. L. Mencken. (Archive Photos/Getty Images)

Mencken lost popularity as World War II approached and stopped writing for *The Baltimore Sun*. He focused instead on his memoirs and personal projects. He lived out his years with the aftereffects of a stroke suffered in 1948.

Impact Mencken's works produced both supporters and critics. His writings attacked ignorance and intolerance through wit and sarcasm. Although he has been described as racist for his views on religion and ethnicity, he is often cited as a clear thinker who saw through pomposity and deceit and exposed society's faults with his clever writings.

Dolores Amidon D'Angelo

Further Reading

Hobson, Fred. *Mencken: A Life*. New York: Random House, 1994.

Rodgers, Marion Elizabeth. *Mencken: The American Iconoclast*. New York: Oxford University Press, 2005.

See also Literature in the United States; New Deal; Newspapers, U.S.; Prohibition repeal; Roosevelt, Franklin D.

■ *Merry Widow, The*

Identification Musical film
Director Ernst Lubitsch
Date Released on November 2, 1934

During the economically bleak 1930's, the Depression-era audiences sought escape into films portraying an imaginarily lavish world populated by glamorous characters. The Merry Widow met this need perfectly. The story dealt with the romance between a beautiful, wealthy widow and a charming philanderer and was set in a tiny, fictional Balkan state near the close of the nineteenth century.

Franz Lehár's operetta *Die lustige Witwe* (*The Merry Widow*), with a libretto by Viktor Léon and Leo Stein, was a great success upon its appearance in 1905 and has remained so into the twenty-first century. *The Merry Widow* has been adapted as a motion picture on four occasions. The first was a silent two-reeler in 1912. The second silent version was released in 1925 and featured several fabled Hollywood names. Eric von Stroheim, known for the expensive opulence of his films, directed. The principal roles were played by Mae Murray and John Gilbert, the foremost romantic leading man of the 1920's. Lacking music, these earliest adaptations relied upon the entertainment value of the comic premise and plot.

The 1934 musical version (also released under the title *The Lady Dances*) features Maurice Chevalier as Count Danilo and Jeanette MacDonald as Sonia, the rich widow. The picture was filmed simultaneously in French under the title *La veuve joyeuse* for the European market. Metro-Goldwyn-Mayer (MGM) had planned a sound version for 1930, but legal complications with Stroheim and his coauthor delayed production for several years. Critical consensus holds that a 1952 remake with Lana Turner and Fernando Lamas playing the leads, though shot in color, failed to measure up to the 1934 film.

The plot is simple and appealing. The widow Sonia represents most of the wealth of Marshovia, a tiny, backward, and otherwise impoverished European country, where sheep and cows impede the marching of the Marshovian army and where the king measures public opinion by the comments of the shepherd in the street. Count Danilo, who has apparently romanced every young woman in Marshovia—including the queen—is fascinated by Sonia but has never seen the face behind her widow's veil. Sonia is attracted to Danilo, despite his reputation, and to flee this troubling emotion she travels to Paris. King Achmed fears that she will not return, thus bankrupting the kingdom and costing him his crown. He sends Danilo to effect her return by wooing and marrying her.

The two subsequently meet at Maxim's, the capital of Parisian night life. Sonia assumes the guise of Fifi, one of the bar girls, all of whom have been Danilo's lovers in the past. Fifi and Danilo fall in love, prompting him to defy the royal command to marry the widow. At a grand ball at the Marshovian embassy, beautifully choreographed and photographed, Danilo learns Fifi's true identity, and she learns of Danilo's mission. Assuming that his interest in her is purely pecuniary, she rejects him. He is arrested on charges of treason, meaning failure. At his Marshovian trial, he pleads guilty to the foolhardiness of falling in love with just one woman in a world full of women. Sonia visits Danilo in prison and, assisted by the manipulation of Achmed and Ambassador Popoff, played by veteran character actors George Barbier and Edward Everett Horton, the lovers reconcile, marry, and kiss at the fade-out.

The term the "Lubitsch touch" is a tribute to the director's mastery of the witty, light-comedy genre. MacDonald had been a supporting actress at Paramount Studios; *The Merry Widow* established her as the star of MGM's 1930's musicals. She was frequently teamed with tenor Nelson Eddy. Several other familiar faces from the period appear in minor roles. Lane Chandler, a cowboy star of the 1920's and early 1930's, plays a Marshovian soldier. Akim Tamiroff, at an early point in his four-decades-long career, plays the manager of Maxim's in the English-language version and a Turk in the French. Among the popular melodies in the film are "Girls, Girls, Girls" and "I'm Going to Maxim's," sung by Chevalier, and "Vilia," "Tonight Will Teach Me to Forget," and the lilting signature number, "the Merry Widow Waltz," sung by MacDonald.

Impact   *The Merry Widow* is set in 1885, during an idealized era of peace, plenty, and gaiety before World War I and the Great Depression. It rejected the drabness of the 1930's by offering an artistic escape for Depression-era audiences.

Patrick Adcock

Further Reading
Paul, William. *Ernst Lubitsch's American Comedy.* New York: Columbia University Press, 1983.
Powrie, Phil, and Robynn Stilwell, eds. *Changing Tunes: The Use of Pre-existing Music in Film.* Burlington, Vt.: Ashgate, 2006.
Thomas, Lawrence B. *The MGM Years.* New York: Columbia House, 1971.

See also   Academy Awards; Film; Music: Popular; Theater in the United States.

■ Mexico

Mexico and the United States share a border of nearly two thousand miles. The two countries had a complicated historical relationship, but during the 1930's, the relationship stabilized, though brief periods of tension followed in the subsequent decades. Also during this period, Mexico achieved political, social, and economic stability after the difficult years of the revolution.

Following the trauma of the Mexican Revolution, which lasted from 1910 to 1920, and the difficult task of consolidating the government during the 1920's, Mexico began its ascent into the group of politically stable, industrialized, Latin American countries. The political, cultural, and social relations among Mexico, the United States, and Canada underwent great modifications, leaning toward a more peaceful and economically profitable interaction. Moments of tension among the countries were fewer than in the previous decades and were negotiated with the goal of achieving fruitful relationships. During the 1930's, Mexico became a favorite destiny for North American tourists, artists, anthropologists, and archaeologists. The political, social, and cultural changes that took place in Mexico during the 1930's became the focus of interest for many.

A New Political System   The beginning of the 1930's marked a new era for the Mexican political system. The ruling party that originated in 1924, the Partido Nacional Revolucionario (PNR, or National Revolutionary Party), held the reins of government

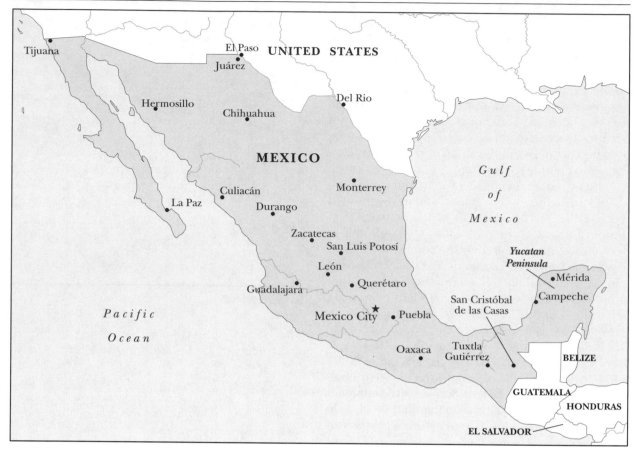

and economic power. The founder and leader of the PNR, Plutarco Elías Calles, frequently called the "maximum chief" of the revolution, was president of Mexico from 1924 to 1928 but remained the de facto leader until 1934, in which year he handpicked his protégé, Lázaro Cárdenas, for the presidency. Cárdenas quickly realized that he needed to shake off Calles's influence to be able to put in place the reforms that he had envisioned for his government. Therefore, in 1936, after political maneuvering, he managed to exile Calles to the United States.

During his government, Cárdenas developed a series of measures that involved large sectors of the Mexican population. The president encouraged the formation of national workers' unions and pushed for an agrarian reform that called for the massive redistribution of lands to peasants. He made active use of new means of mass communication to engage in conversation with the Mexican population. His inauguration speech was broadcast throughout Mexico, the United States, and Latin America, and he had a

Sunday radio show in which he addressed issues that concerned the general population; he also constantly toured the nation.

Cárdenas's foreign policy was centered on keeping a cordial relationship with the United States; during this period, the U.S. government repatriated hundreds of thousands of Mexicans because of the Great Depression. Many of the Mexican people who lived in the United States had crossed the border during the revolution searching for peace, work, and better wages. However, many more were Americans of Mexican descent. This forceful push produced political tensions, but Mexican officials were aware that their country was in great need of a stable relationship with the United States, so they did not push for measures that might cause a diplomatic crisis. This was also a period of economic nationalism, which implied that for Mexico to become a stable, industrialized country, it needed to establish economic independence from North America and Europe.

The Oil Conflict   The 1917 Mexican constitution featured Article 27, which asserted that all Mexican territory, including what could be found underground, belonged to the nation. This article referred particularly to oil and minerals, which had been exploited by foreign companies, many of them American. Between 1917 and 1934, the conflicts produced by Article 27 remained mostly dormant, with the occasional debate between Mexican officials and American companies concerning taxes and different interpretations of what constituted private property in Mexico. The main source of controversy, however, arose during Cárdenas's period, when the president supported the creation of a national union of oil workers.

The foreign companies, which until then had dealt with small and divided groups, were faced with a national labor force that demanded collective contracts and had the support of the Mexican government. In 1937, the national oil workers' union went on strike. The government intervened to complete a financial analysis to determine the amount that oil companies could afford to pay their employees in wages and benefits. Despite the arduous negotiations, an agreement could not be reached. On March 18, 1938, Cárdenas announced through the radio his determination to seize all foreign oil holdings in Mexico.

One of the most salient aspects of the 1938 oil expropriation was the quiet response it produced from U.S. president Franklin D. Roosevelt and U.S. ambassador Josephus Daniels. Despite the American oil companies' pressure for governmental intervention, Roosevelt maintained his Good Neighbor Policy. Roosevelt's decision may have been made with the possibility of a war with Europe in mind; he might have wanted to ensure Mexico's unconditional help in case the United States needed it. Also, Roosevelt recognized the importance of stopping Mexico from supplying oil to war enemies. Cárdenas understood Roosevelt's position even before expropriation, and he took advantage of the world political situation to negotiate with the United States.

Mexican Art in the United States   The artistic movements that originated from the Mexican Revolution focused on the construction of a national identity. This identity was based on Mexico's central characteristics: the existence of great pre-Hispanic civilizations and the presence of a racially mixed population. Mestizos, people of mixed European and indigenous blood, constituted the biggest part of the Mexican population and came to symbolize the nation. Ideologically, the main national project was to recognize the mestizo traditions. Historians engaged in studies on the pre-Hispanic cultures, and a great deal of money went into the exploration of archaeological sites. The indigenous culture became an element of pride and an essential component of nationality. Consequently, the 1930's were characterized by an active search for a "true" Mexican identity through a combination of indigenous elements, including symbols and aesthetic techniques, that coordinated with the ideal of industrialized modernity.

Throughout the 1930's, cultural relations between Mexico and United States were mostly based on the arts. American intellectuals and artists were attracted to this aspect of postrevolutionary Mexico and its people. In turn, Mexican artists admired the ongoing industrialization of U.S. cities. During this period, the "*tres grandes*," muralists Diego Rivera, José Clemente Orozco, and David Alfaro Siqueiros, lived and worked in the United States, where they created a few of their most famous and controversial works. Mexican painting of the 1930's not only was marked by the novelty of using murals as a secular, educational, artistic form but also created a new idea of public art, which combined elements of social realism with a national project of revolutionary justice and the democratization of public institutions. In the context of a newfound peaceful relationship between Mexico and the United States, "art diplomacy" became pivotal for the Mexican postrevolutionary state.

Impact   The 1930's marked the first stable phase of economic growth in Mexico since 1910, despite the negative effects of the Great Depression. Between 1930 and 1940, the Mexican state defined itself as the arbiter of the different elements of industrial production and as the conductor of the main economic and social forces. During the 1930's and 1940's, Mexico built a national agenda that was followed until the 1970's. In the 1930's, Mexico redefined itself on the world stage, using a combination of traditional culture and modern politics and economics. During the worst period of the 1930's Depression in the United States, when the Roosevelt administration embarked on a policy of state-funded initiatives to alleviate hardship, supporters of the Federal Art Project looked to the Mexican mural movement as a model for a democratic, radical art. Mexican art was not supposed to be intellectual, academic, or pretentious; the painters wanted to create beautiful and intense art that revealed the sentiments of the people. In sum, the 1930's were a time of fruitful, active exchange between Mexico and the United States and Canada that marked the beginning of a new type of diplomacy benefiting the three countries.

Julia del Palacio Langer

Further Reading

Bethell, Leslie, ed. *Mexico Since Independence.* New York: Cambridge University Press, 1991. General survey of Mexican history from 1821 to 1970.

Brown, Jonathan, and Alan Knight, eds. *The Mexican Petroleum Industry in the Twentieth Century.* Austin: University of Texas Press, 1993. Group of essays that offers economic, political, and social perspectives related to the Mexican oil industry.

Kirkwood, Burton. *The History of Mexico.* Westport, Conn.: Greenwood Press, 2000. Brief survey of Mexican history.

Sánchez, George J. *Becoming Mexican American: Ethnicity, Culture and Identity in Chicano Los Angeles, 1900-1945.* New York: Oxford University Press, 1994. Explores the processes of cultural adaptation and ethnic identity among Mexican migrants in the United States.

See also   Business and the economy in the United States; Communism; Foreign policy of Canada; Foreign policy of the United States; Good Neighbor Policy; Great Depression in the United States; Latin America and the Caribbean; Rockefeller Center Rivera mural; Soviet Union.

■ Micheaux, Oscar

Identification   African American novelist and filmmaker
Born   January 2, 1884; Metropolis, Illinois
Died   March 26, 1951; Charlotte, North Carolina

Micheaux was the most successful black filmmaker of his era. He was a writer, director, producer, and promoter of approximately forty films. These include The Homesteader *(1919), the first feature-length silent film made by an African American, and* The Exile *(1931), the first full-length "talkie" produced and directed by an African American. Often combining elements of melodrama and romance, he offered an African American perspective on racism, lynching, domestic violence, rape, "passing," and miscegenation.*

A son of former slaves, Oscar Micheaux grew up on a farm in southern Illinois. As a young man, he worked in Chicago and then as a Pullman porter. Returning to a more rural life in 1905, he became a homesteader in South Dakota, where he was a rarity among an overwhelmingly white population. This experience, which included a difficult and short marriage and the failure of the farm, led to a new career as a writer. His first book, an autobiographical novel of his Dakota experience called *The Conquest* (1913), provided material that he revisited over the years in both novels and film, most immediately in his third novel, *The Homesteader* (1917). Successfully going from town to town to promote his books, Micheaux was approached in 1918 by the Lincoln Motion Picture Company—producers of "race pictures," films for and, largely, by African Americans—about filming *The Homesteader.* When the deal fell through, Micheaux chose to make the film himself. A true self-promoter, talented and self-taught, he made at least eighteen more films by the end of the 1920's.

Moving to Sound   By 1930, Micheaux had shown the cost and tragic inhumanity of racial violence in films such as *Within Our Gates* (1920) and *The Symbol of the Unconquered* (1920), given Paul Robeson his screen debut in *Body and Soul* (1925), given a vision to his version of "racial uplift," and established a market for films meant for African Americans. He had married, moved to Harlem, and found in Alice B. Russell a partner who played a significant role in his productions. He had also fought with censors, created controversy by portraying unflattering aspects of black life, worked consistently with insufficient financing, and declared bankruptcy just months after *The Jazz Singer* (1927) signaled the end of the silent film era. Micheaux became the only producer of "race films" to make the jump to sound.

With new partners, Micheaux set out to make all-talking pictures. *The Exile* (1931) was the first "race talkie" directed by an African American. Another reworking of Micheaux's own homesteading story, it involves themes of prejudice, intermarriage, and "passing" joined with an underworld subplot of murder, gambling, nightclubs, and vice. With the club as a backdrop, Micheaux was able to feature musicians and other entertainers to attract audiences. With the largest and most secure budget of his career, he was able to increase production values as never before. The film was a success, opening to large crowds and excellent reviews from the black press. A historic achievement, it was ignored by the white press.

More Success and Failure   Between 1930 and 1940, Micheaux made fifteen films—all sound, all African American. Several were remakes of earlier silent films with new titles. Despite this less costly method of producing films, money was a problem; Micheaux never had a large budget like that of *The Exile* again. In late 1932, he was sued by his partners. However, by 1935, he was able to start again, this time with backing from a Texas company that planned to show his films in the Southwest. *Len Hawkins' Confession* (1935) drew on Micheaux's 1921 silent *The Gunsaulus Mystery* and was a reworking of the 1913 trial of Leo Frank, a Jewish factory owner accused of murder in Atlanta and convicted on the testimony of a black worker. Renamed *Murder in Harlem* when playing beyond the East Coast, this film was the first of Micheaux's to be shown in Los Angeles.

With Hollywood making more films to attract African American audiences and a dwindling number of theaters showing "race films," continued success and survival of these films were now beyond hope. Still, in 1938, Micheaux made three films, most notably *God's Stepchildren* (1938), a powerful film about "passing." Despite protests from African American communists in Harlem who called for either the film's withdrawal or its alteration, *God's Stepchildren* remained one of Micheaux's most popular films and was regarded as his most accomplished until his death.

Filmmaker Oscar Micheaux. (AP/Wide World Photos)

Impact   Micheaux was largely forgotten for nearly twenty years after his death. Many of his films were lost. Only three of his approximately twenty-five silent films are known to exist, while twelve of his sound pictures are available. Resurgent interest in Micheaux started to develop following publication of a 1969 article by Thomas Cripps that offered high praise. Subsequent critical scholarship has burgeoned, assuring a lasting place of value for Micheaux. Black filmmakers, including Spike Lee, often cite his influence. In 1986, the Directors Guild of America awarded high honors to three directors—Akira Kurosawa, Federico Fellini, and Micheaux.

Marc D. Brodsky

Further Reading
Bowser, Pearl, Jane Gaines, and Charles Musser, eds. *Oscar Micheaux and His Circle.* Bloomington: Indi-

ana University Press, 2001. Essays by many prominent Micheaux scholars.

Bowser, Pearl, and Louise Spence. *Writing Himself into History: Oscar Micheaux, His Silent Films, and His Audiences.* New Brunswick, N.J.: Rutgers University Press, 2000. Examination of Micheaux that focuses on his silent films and the relation of his films to his novels.

Green, J. Ronald. *Straight Lick: The Cinema of Oscar Micheaux.* Bloomington: Indiana University Press, 2000. A critical look at the films and career of Micheaux.

McGilligan, Patrick. *The Great and Only Oscar Micheaux.* New York: HarperCollins, 2007. Detailed biography of Micheaux with an annotated filmography.

Robinson, Cedric J. *Forgeries of Memory and Meaning: Blacks and the Regimes of Race in American Theater and Film Before World War II.* Chapel Hill: University of North Carolina Press, 2007. Offers an understanding of race in the United States via analysis of the theater and film industries of the early twentieth century; includes analysis of Micheaux's films.

See also African Americans; *Children's Hour, The*; Film; Gangster films; Harlem Renaissance; *Imitation of Life*; Jim Crow segregation; Robeson, Paul.

■ Mickey Mouse

Identification Cartoon character and corporate icon
Creators Walt Disney and Ub Iwerks
Date Debuted May 15, 1928

Mickey Mouse, the two-dimensional mouse in red velvet pants, became an immediate multimedia success, and his creators parlayed that success to make the mouse the representative of the first international entertainment conglomerate. Mickey also proved to be an important economic engine during the Depression.

Mickey Mouse came to be because Walt Disney lost control of his rabbit. Walt Disney's animation studio was a tiny shop, among many that worked for filmmaking giant Universal Studios. Disney's studio had garnered attention from the studio heads with the success of a character Disney had created, Oswald the Lucky Rabbit. When Disney went to ne-gotiate a new contract with Universal for more Oswald films, he discovered that Universal had taken control of the character and of many of Disney's employees.

Disney, along with Ub Iwerks, the only one of his animators who did not jump ship and leave with Universal, decided to come up with a replacement character that could not be stolen from them. After a number of late-night work sessions, Disney got the idea to make the Mickey Mouse character, based on a pet mouse he once owned, during a sleepless five-day train trip. The mouse was originally to be named "Mortimer," but clearer thinking prevailed, and the world was introduced to Mickey Mouse on May 15, 1928, in the unsuccessful film *Plane Crazy*.

The moviegoing public did not begin to show interest in Mickey until November 18, 1928, with the release of the third Mickey Mouse short film, "Steamboat Willie," which had a synchronized sound track added in postproduction. In 1929's "Karnival Kid," Mickey spoke his first words, "Hot dog!" on the silver screen. In his early days, Mickey was more the impish trickster than the symbol of childish innocence that he came to represent by the 1930's.

Mickey became so popular that theater managers displayed as many posters advertising the Mickey Mouse cartoons as they did advertising the feature films with which the shorts were playing. In 1932, the film industry took notice as Walt Disney won a Special Oscar for his role in the creation of Mickey Mouse. During the 1930's, the mouse became a superstar; Disney Studios made eighty-seven Mickey Mouse shorts in which he played a range of characters, including a giant killer, a detective, and a football hero. These short films relied on wordplay and slapstick for their humor; since Mickey was so popular with children, he always displayed solid character traits and a proper morality.

Despite the Depression, a veritable industry grew up around Mickey. His short films were commercial successes, and the marketing that they spawned proved to be a commercial phenomenon. His adventures were chronicled in books and comic strips. His image was licensed and plastered, worldwide, on products ranging from soap and phonographs to hot-water bottles and the ubiquitous Mickey Mouse watch. Mickey also served as a pitchman for a variety of products. Mickey's commercial impact was so prominent that it is credited with single-handedly saving both the Ingersoll-Waterbury Clock Company and Lionel Trains from bankruptcy.

In September of 1929, a theater manager named Harry Woodin proposed the Mickey Mouse Club to Walt Disney. By 1932, club membership topped one million. By 1935, the number of clubs meeting in theaters worldwide had grown so large that Disney had to phase them out. Even without the clubs, by the end of the 1930's, Mickey Mouse had gone from a series of sketches to become an economic engine and the most recognizable corporate icon in the country.

Impact The Disney Corporation claims that Mickey Mouse, as a character, is recognized by upwards of 98 percent of the world's children aged three to eleven, and his image is the most reproduced icon in the world. During the 1930's, the success of Mickey Mouse not only had a strong positive effect on the American economy but also created the first worldwide entertainment corporation. The Mickey Mouse shorts also paved the way for Disney's groundbreaking full-length animated films, beginning with *Snow White and the Seven Dwarfs* in 1937. These films changed the way the world looked at animation and filmmaking.

B. Keith Murphy

Flanked by oversized versions of Mickey Mouse (left) and Minnie Mouse, Walt Disney sketches on a drawing board balanced on his lap. (©Condé Nast Archive/CORBIS)

Further Reading

Gabler, Neal. *Walt Disney: The Triumph of the American Imagination.* New York: Random House, 2006.

Heide, Robert, and John Gilman. *Mickey Mouse: The Evolution, the Legend.* New York: Disney Editions, 2003.

Tieman, Robert. *Mickey Mouse Treasures.* New York: Disney Editions, 2007.

See also Advertising in the United States; Comic strips; Film; *Snow White and the Seven Dwarfs.*

Midterm elections. See **Elections of 1930, 1934, and 1938, U.S.**

■ Migrations, domestic

Domestic migrations during the 1930's changed the demographics and economic foundations of the United States and altered the balance between the rural and the urban in the country. The United States that emerged after the Depression and World War II was fundamentally different from the country that had existed before 1930.

The Great Depression created or intensified most twentieth century migratory patterns, except in at least one major case. Between 1915 and 1960, some five million African Americans made the journey north from southern states, in search of jobs and better social conditions. During the 1920's, for example, some 800,000 black southerners moved north, usually to cities, and to work mostly in factories. During the 1930's, however, and because of the economic collapse, jobs were scarcer, and that number was cut by more than one-half; only 398,000 African Americans made the move north. Not until World War II did the flow of southern African Americans to the north increase again.

Agriculture and Migration   African Americans were not the only group on the move during the 1930's. Caucasians also migrated north to cities such as Detroit, searching for jobs in the auto industry. At the same time, the population of the South was shifting from farm to town. The transformation of agriculture in the twentieth century from family or tenant farming to the larger "farm factory" or agribusiness meant that millions of farmers were forced to migrate from rural to urban settings across the country, from farm work to industrial work. Between 1930 and 1935, for example, nearly one out of every five farms in the South, Midwest, and Great Plains states went into foreclosure. Those numbers translate into millions of Americans on the move, often just to the nearest town or city but sometimes to cities hundreds or thousands of miles away. Historian Carey McWilliams documented the agricultural changes in *Factories in the Field: The Story of Migratory Farm Labor in California* (1935), while *American Exodus: A*

With dirty feet and clothes, a migrant mother and her three children rest on a soiled mattress in a ramshackle shelter in Weslaco, Texas. (Library of Congress)

The children of migrant workers, waiting to go wherever their parents can find agricultural employment. (Library of Congress)

Record of Human Erosion in the Thirties (1939) documented this human migration with text by Paul Schuster Taylor and photographs by his wife, Dorothea Lange.

The Dust Bowl　The symbol of this transformation of the American landscape was the Dust Bowl. Brought on by decades of destructive farming that exhausted the land and years of drought, dust storms in the first half of the 1930's created huge clouds that traveled as far as New York City. Affecting more than nine million acres across the Great Plains states, dust storms left hundreds of thousands homeless and created the largest migration in American history. The African American Great Migration from the South to urban cities eventually involved more than five million people, but it took place over four decades. The Dust Bowl affected more than one-half that number in a decade. Almost one million people from the Great Plains states left farms in the first half of the decade, and by 1940, 2.5 million

people had been dislocated because of the Dust Bowl, which included areas of Oklahoma, Arkansas, Kansas, Texas, Colorado, and New Mexico. Oklahoma lost more than 440,000 people, or nearly 20 percent of its 1930 population, during the early years of the Depression; Kansas lost 227,000. More than 450,000 people moved to the Pacific Northwest, to jobs in the lumber industry and construction of the Bonneville and Grand Coulee Dams. Over the course of the 1930's, 1.1 million migrants moved to California, an almost 20 percent increase from the state's 1930 population. In addition to finding farming work, many migrants eventually found work in the burgeoning aircraft industries. The dislocations caused by the Dust Bowl and the farming crisis in the United States were epic.

The Dust Bowl is also the most visible symbol of the Great Depression because it was documented in some of the landmark works of art of the 1930's: Pare Lorentz's documentary film *The Plow That Broke the Plains*, which included a musical score by Virgil

Thomson; the photography of Lange, Arnold Rothstein, Walker Evans, and other artists working to document the disaster for the Farm Security Administration and its director Roy Stryker; the songs of Woody Guthrie; and the most famous novel to come out of the Depression, John Steinbeck's *The Grapes of Wrath* (1939). Traveling across the country from eastern Oklahoma to the promise of the fertile fields of California, the members of Steinbeck's Joad family were actually not victims of the Dust Bowl but of the transformation of American farmland into agribusiness. However, they became symbols of the Dust Bowl and the accompanying migration westward, especially after an Academy Award-winning film adaptation of the novel was released in 1940.

Other Migratory Groups   Other migrations of the dislocated took place during the 1930's. The Okies and others who poured into California during the 1930's displaced hundreds of thousands of Mexicans, who constituted the largest minority in California and the backbone of the farm labor force. As a result of losing jobs to Dust Bowl refugees, hundreds of thousands of Mexicans returned to Mexico. More than 82,000 were voluntarily deported to Mexico under a program started by the Bureau of Immigration in 1930, and more than 300,000 others, many of them American citizens by birth, were forced to leave because of the loss of jobs or relief payments. The Mexican-born population in both Texas and Los Angeles fell by one-third. In the same period that Americans were leaving farms and heading to cities for jobs, however, a reverse migration was also occurring. As urban employment peaked during the 1930's, there was a movement back to the land, and by 1935, there were more people on farms than ever before in American history, especially in New England and in small farming areas around major cities.

The most vulnerable migrants during the 1930's were children. In the hard times of the Depression, many children simply left home in search of a better life, many of them "riding the rails" to some vague but hopeful future. Their numbers are difficult to gauge, since they rarely appear on public records as adults do, but evidence indicates that as much as 25 percent of the migratory population of the 1930's were under twenty-one years old. Newspapers across the country noted this alarming trend, and director William Wellman's film *Wild Boys of the Road* (1933) captured their plight. One of the most sensational

trials of the 1930's centered on the Scottsboro Boys, nine black youths ages thirteen to nineteen who were accused of raping two white women while they were all riding a freight train in Alabama in 1933. The Scottsboro trial went on for years, and the young men served between six and nineteen years in prison.

Impact   The domestic migrations of the 1930's changed the American landscape. By the time the Depression had ended, millions of Americans had relocated, often thousands of miles away; agriculture had been transformed; and the rural United States had become urban. A decade of disillusion and dislocation had also changed the ways Americans acted and thought about themselves and had given them new understanding of their capacity for deprivation and hard work, which they carried through the difficult years of World War II.

David Peck

Further Reading

Egan, Timothy. *The Worst Hard Time: The Untold Story of Those Who Survived the Great American Dust Bowl.* Boston: Houghton Mifflin, 2006. Discusses the High Plains disaster that drove so many people West; includes portraits of families and interviews with survivors.

Gregory, James N. *American Exodus: The Dust Bowl Migration and Okie Culture in California.* New York: Oxford University Press, 1989. Account of the more than one million Dust Bowl migrants who settled in California during the 1930's and their subsequent lives.

Kirby, Jack Temple. *Rural Worlds Lost: The American South, 1920-1960.* Baton Rouge: Louisiana State University Press, 1987. Comprehensive social-scientific study of the transformation of the South in the twentieth century.

Thompson, Warren Simpson. *Research Memorandum in Internal Migration in the Depression.* New York: Arno Press, 1972. Contains primary research on migration during the 1930's.

Trotter, Joe William, Jr., ed. *The Great Migration in Historical Perspective: New Dimensions of Race, Class, and Gender.* Bloomington: Indiana University Press, 1991. A collection of essays focusing on black migration, including detailed studies of Virginia, West Virginia, Pittsburgh, and Chicago.

Webb, John H., and Malcolm Brown. *Migrant Families.* Reprint. New York: Da Capo Press, 1971. First produced in 1938 as a monograph under the WPA Division of Social Research, this volume contains a great amount of valuable primary documentation on migrants.

Worster, Donald. *Dust Bowl: The Southern Plains in the 1930's.* New York: Oxford University Press, 1979. One of the best studies of the disaster includes a long chapter titled "Okies and Exodusters."

See also   African Americans; Agriculture in the United States; Demographics of the United States; Dust Bowl; *Grapes of Wrath, The*; Guthrie, Woody; Immigration to the United States; Lange, Dorothea; Latinos; Steinbeck, John.

■ Migratory Bird Hunting and Conservation Stamp Act of 1934

The Law   Federal legislation creating a source of revenue for buying and conserving wetlands
Also known as   Duck Stamp Act of 1934
Date   Signed into law March 16, 1934

During the 1930's, the United States began an era of environmental conservation, partly because of the degradation caused by the Dust Bowl. The Migratory Bird Hunting and Conservation Stamp Act of 1934 became an important step in preserving American wetlands.

In the late 1920's, conservationists noticed a dramatic decrease in the populations of wild ducks and geese in the United States. They attributed this to an extended drought in the center of the country, which dried up wetlands; the draining of wetlands for development; and over-hunting. In 1929, Congress passed the Migratory Bird Conservation Act, which authorized the federal government to purchase and set aside wetlands. However, the law did not provide funding, and as the effects of the Depression were felt, it did not seem prudent to designate money from the federal budget for this purpose. In 1934, the Migratory Bird Hunting and Conservation Stamp Act created the so-called duck stamp, initially bearing an illustration of two ducks, to raise funds.

Although commonly called the Duck Stamp Program, the act actually protects and conserves waterfowl of all kinds. All waterfowl hunters aged sixteen and older are required to purchase a stamp each year, and profits from the sale of the stamps are used to purchase and conserve wetland habitat. In addition to purchase by hunters, the stamps are bought by collectors and by other citizens who wish to contribute to waterfowl conservation.

Impact   By 2010, sales of Federal Duck Stamps had generated revenues in excess of $750 million, which has been used to expand the National Wildlife Refuge System by more than 5.3 million acres. The duck stamp contest, the only art competition sponsored by the federal government, attracts entries from more than two thousand artists each year.

Cynthia A. Bily

Further Reading

Fischman, Robert. *The National Wildlife Refuges: Coordinating a Conservation System Through Law.* Washington, D.C.: Island Press, 2003.
Swope, Kurtis J., Daniel K. Benjamin, and Terry Lee Anderson. "Bucks for Ducks or Money for Nothin'? The Political Economy of the Federal Duck Stamp Program." *In Political Environmentalism: Going Behind the Green Curtain*, edited by Terry Lee Anderson. Stanford, Calif.: Hoover Institution Press, 2000.
U.S. Fish and Wildlife Service. *The Federal Duck Stamp Seventy-fifth Anniversary Field Guide.* Washington, D.C.: Author, 2008.

See also   Congress, U.S.; Dust Bowl; Great Depression in the United States; Hoover, Herbert; Roosevelt, Franklin D.

■ Miller, Glenn

Identification   American swing-era big band leader
Born   March 1, 1904; Clarinda, Iowa
Died   December 15, 1944; English Channel

With a band that featured a clarinet lead within the saxophone section, Miller created a distinctive sound among swing-era big bands. His uniquely orchestrated arrangements and superb performances set high standards among the dance bands of the 1930's.

Before organizing his first band in 1937, Glenn Miller was a freelance trombonist for Broadway shows and with bandleaders Ben Pollack, Red Nichols, and Tommy and Jimmy Dorsey. In 1935,

Trombonist and bandleader Glenn Miller demonstrating his slide technique in 1937. (Archive Photos/Getty Images)

ments included on-location radio programs, which further publicized the band. By the end of the decade, the Miller band was the most popular swing band in the United States.

Impact   The 1930's was the swing era. Big bands performed primarily for dancers and emphasized ensemble over improvisation. Miller understood what pleased the public, and he gave it to them. His band played danceable arrangements with rehearsed perfection, absolute precision, and an unusual instrumental blend of clarinet and saxophones. Countless hit songs of the 1930's ultimately became nostalgic standards during the World War II years that followed. Within just a few years, the Miller band had become the sentimental favorite in the United States.

Douglas D. Skinner

Further Reading

Grudens, Richard. *Chattanooga Choo Choo: The Life and Times of the World Famous Glenn Miller Orchestra.* New York: Celebrity Profiles, 2004.

_____. *Stardust: The Big Band Bible.* New York: Celebrity Profiles, 2008.

See also   Dorsey, Tommy; Ellington, Duke; Goodman, Benny; Music: Jazz; Recording industry; Shaw, Artie.

while working with Ray Noble, Miller experimented with using a lead clarinet supported by four saxophones, a technique that later proved highly successful with his own bands.

Because of intense competition among the numerous existing swing bands, the ability to survive depended on developing a characteristic sound that could be recognized by fans and be unique. Miller's first band was unsuccessful because it lacked an identity.

In 1938, Miller's second attempt at leading a band was marginally successful. The primary melody was assigned to the clarinet and a tenor saxophone, while the other three saxophones provided supporting harmonies within an octave range. The blend produced a distinctive and easily recognizable sound. Miller even published an orchestration textbook that included this method of arranging.

In 1939, the Miller band was hired at the prestigious Glen Island Casino in New York and Meadowbrook Supper Club in New Jersey. Both engage-

■ Missouri ex rel. Gaines v. Canada

The Case   U.S. Supreme Court decision to overturn a Missouri law mandating racial segregation in state law schools

Date   Decided on December 12, 1938

While not directly ruling on the question of segregated education, the Supreme Court determined an out-of-state legal education was not equivalent to the in-state opportunities afforded Caucasians.

In 1935, after Lloyd Gaines was denied admission to the University of Missouri School of Law, based solely on state law requiring segregated education, he commenced litigation, assisted by attorneys for the National Association for the Advancement of Colored People. The case shaped the context of racial discrimination during the 1930's.

At a time of Caucasians-only primary elections, the absence of African Americans on juries, and segregated public facilities predicated on the "separate but equal" test of *Plessy v. Ferguson* (1896), the Missouri education system was typical. Nonetheless, the state offered a comparatively progressive option: African Americans who wanted to study law would have their tuition paid at an out-of-state school.

Gaines believed this policy violated his Fourteenth Amendment rights to equal protection of the law, arguing an out-of-state education was not equivalent to attending the state university, especially because he intended to live and practice law in Missouri. In 1938, the U.S. Supreme Court, overturning Missouri's state supreme court, agreed with Gaines. Because no law school for African Americans existed in the state, the Supreme Court ordered Gaines to be admitted to the University of Missouri, despite the segregation policies in place. Missouri attempted to dodge the ruling by hastily setting up a black law school as an acceptable in-state alternative, an action Gaines's attorneys planned to challenge as inadequate. However, on March 19, 1939, Gaines vanished in Chicago, and the mystery of his disappearance was never solved. The University of Missouri School of Law did not accept its first black students until the early 1950's.

Impact The case opened a dialogue on what the "equal" in separate but equal really meant. Eventually, it became clear that separation itself is inherently unequal, as the U.S. Supreme Court decreed in *Brown v. Board of Education* (1954).

Francine S. Romero

Further Reading

Kelleher, Daniel T. "The Case of Lloyd Lionel Gaines: The Demise of the Separate but Equal Doctrine." *The Journal of Negro History* 56, no. 4 (1971): 262-271.

Klarman, Michael. *From Jim Crow to Civil Rights*. New York: Oxford University Press, 2004.

See also African Americans; Civil rights and liberties in the United States; Jim Crow segregation; National Association for the Advancement of Colored People; Racial discrimination.

■ Modern Corporation and Private Property, The

Identification Book about corporate management
Authors Adolph A. Berle, Jr., and Gardiner C. Means
Date Published in 1933

Influential treatise by key players in the creation of the New Deal arguing that modern corporations consisted of managers and directors who often did not act in the best interests of the real owners of corporations: the stockholders. The authors also proposed a broader social role for the corporation beyond the mere pursuit of profits. This book was the impetus for laws and regulations that govern corporations.

The Modern Corporation and Private Property is the most influential book in the field of corporate governance. This important book was written by Adolph A. Berle, Jr., a professor of corporate law at Columbia who also worked for President Franklin D. Roosevelt, focusing on the New Deal. His coauthor was Gardiner C. Means, an economist at Harvard University.

The book analyzed how corporations had evolved from the nineteenth century, when they were primarily small operations owned and operated by an identifiable number of individuals, often family members. By the early 1930's, average corporations had grown considerably; they were large and powerful enterprises with enormous numbers of shareholders who bought and sold their shares on stock exchanges. Typically, no one shareholder owned more than a tiny fraction of the shares of the company.

Berle and Means introduced the concept of the separation of ownership and management in describing the modern corporation. They stated that the real power lay in the hands of managers and boards of directors who typically owned only small amounts of stock in the company. The small number of insiders (managers and directors) had greater knowledge and incentives that differed from those of the large number of outsiders (the shareholders) and could operate the company for their own benefit, potentially harming the shareholders and the corporation itself.

The book argued for increased voting rights for shareholders, increased disclosures by management, and other controls for the benefit of the shareholders. The authors also proposed a broader social role for the corporation as a key institution in the modern economy and society.

Impact   *The Modern Corporation and Private Property* changed the way businesses, investors, lawyers, and government regulators looked at corporations. It also led to the creation of much of the modern regulation of corporations, their managers, and corporate directors. It remains one of the most cited and relied on texts for experts in corporate management and law.

Spencer Weber Waller

Further Reading

Kaysen, Carl, ed. *The American Corporation Today.* New York: Oxford University Press, 1996.

Mason, Edward, ed. *The Corporation in Modern Society.* College ed. New York: Atheneum, 1980.

Miner, John B. *Organizational Behavior: Foundations, Theories, and Analyses.* New York: Oxford University Press, 2002.

See also   Brains Trust; Business and the economy in the United States; *Functions of the Executive, The*; *General Theory of Employment, Interest and Money, The*; Great Depression in the United States; Roosevelt, Franklin D.; Securities and Exchange Commission.

■ *Modern Times*

Identification   Film about the dehumanizing effects of industrial labor
Director   Charles Chaplin
Date   Released on February 6, 1936

Aptly described by film critic Charles Maland as "a cultural artifact of the mid-Depression year," Modern Times contains some of Charles Chaplin's most inventive comic sequences in the service of a distinctly humane vision of individuals struggling amid a ruthless social system.

Chaplin ventured into the era of synchronous sound films in 1936 with the somewhat sardonically titled *Modern Times.* The opening shot of shorn sheep herded in a chute juxtaposed with men entering an industrial complex establishes strikingly the primary theme of machines figuratively consuming the men who are operating them. Characteristically, Chaplin located his iconic protagonist—the "little chap" or "tramp," who represents the average human—in a daunting environment: the modern in-

dustrial assembly line. He is employed in a factory that embodies corporate indifference, epitomized by a chief executive officer with access to a closed-circuit network permitting him to watch every moment of the workers' lives.

As the assembly line accelerates its pace, Chaplin is gradually and comically driven out of his mind and is eventually sucked into the elaborate mechanism in a shot that has become world famous. When he emerges, his wild anarchic reaction to the entire corporate arrangement is a satisfying and hilarious counterstrike against an upper management that is not interested in distinguishing between a human and a productive device. Not surprisingly, he is subdued and confined following his liberating spree and diagnosed as mentally unstable after his determined assertion of individuality. In the middle of the Depression, with more than one-quarter of American workers unemployed, this kind of resistance was extremely unlikely but gratifying for viewers who felt exploited and misused in jobs they could not afford to lose.

These unforgettable factory sequences are the most memorable sections of the film, which shifts its focus in an extended romantic interlude in which Chaplin's character joins a woman described as the "gamin," a description that indicates her free-spirited, unconvential approach to life. Paulette Goddard, who played this part, was chosen by Chaplin because her physical presence evoked the mood of innocent exuberance and energetic defiance that Chaplin's factory worker exhibited in his encounters with the machine-dominated world.

During a world tour to promote *City Lights* (1931), Chaplin often commented on the financial crisis of the Western nations, to which Albert Einstein, in Germany, remarked, "You are not a comedian, Charlie, but an economist." The relationship between the factory worker and the gamin is constructed as a sympathetic exploration of the condition of citizens affected by the Depression. Establishing a pattern of incarceration and escape, Chaplin's character is arrested as the accidental leader of a communist protest march when he picks up a red flag in a parade. The gamin avoids institutional restriction when juvenile authorities take custody of her sisters following her father's death. Chaplin's character actually attempts, successfully, to get back into jail when the couple cannot find sufficient food to survive; this is followed by another es-

In one of the most famous scenes in cinematic history, Charles Chaplin gets trapped in a massive set of gears in the film Modern Times. (Archive Photos/Getty Images)

cape. A sequence in a department store results in another arrest, and after Chaplin's character returns to the factory, he is arrested again. The couple then find temporary employment in a café, before their final release to a life on the road at the film's conclusion.

Chaplin was particularly sensitive to a critique of his career by political activists who felt that his comic style ought to include what they called "social realism." In spite of the fortune that his films earned, Chaplin's background as the child of two struggling London music-hall performers left him acutely conscious of economic realities. The first working title for the film was the suggestive *Commonwealth*. Chaplin also considered *The Masses*, referencing the name of the radical journal *New Masses*, while the film was in production prior to its release as *Modern Times*. The sequence in which Chaplin's character and the

gamin dream of a comfortable, conventional, middle-class life is both an acknowledgment of many viewers' basic desires and a biting portrayal of many people's realities as the couple are actually residing in a collapsing hovel. The last shot of the couple on the road, perhaps heading toward a better life, both offers encouragement and implies ongoing obstacles to their survival.

Impact   In 1989, *Modern Times* was included among the twenty-five films selected by the National Film Preservation Board for the National Film Registry. It appears on many lists as a top film of the twentieth century, and its iconic image of Chaplin entangled in the gears and pistons of a huge machine has become an emblem of the dominance of machinery over human endeavor.

Leon Lewis

Further Reading

Lynn, Kenneth. *Charlie Chaplin and His Times.* New York: Simon & Schuster, 1997.

Maland, Charles J. "Modern Times (1936), Charlie Chaplin." In *Film Analysis: A Norton Reader,* edited by Jeffrey Geiger and R. L. Rutsky. New York: W. W. Norton, 2005.

Steward, Garrett. "Modern Hard Times: Chaplin and the Cinema of Self-References." *Critical Inquiry* 3 (1976): 295-315.

See also Business and the economy in the United States; Chaplin, Charles; Fair Labor Standards Act of 1938; Film; Great Depression in the United States; National Labor Relations Act of 1935.

■ Monopoly

Identification Board game in which players buy, sell, and trade properties
Inventor Elizabeth Magie
Date Created in 1903; published by Parker Brothers in 1935

In 1935, when 20 percent of the American population was unemployed, Monopoly offered a welcome escape into a world in which players could get rich quickly and forget the reality of economic privation. Though the game was released during the Depression, more than one million copies were sold between 1935 and 1936.

Monopoly gained popularity during the Depression, but it had been patented in 1903 as the Landlord's Game, created by Elizabeth Magie. It was designed to demonstrate the evils of property taxes and promote a single-tax system. Magie attempted to get it published twice: in 1909, with Parker Brothers, and in 1923, with Milton Bradley. Both companies rejected the game, finding it too complicated. Although neither company published her game, homemade copies of the game circulated around college campuses, and versions of the game were used as educational tools in college classrooms.

In 1932, one of the homemade versions was introduced to Charles B. Darrow, an unemployed repairman in Pennsylvania. The game that Darrow played was similar to the one eventually published by Parker Brothers. It featured Atlantic City street names, rectangular spaces, and Chance and Community Chest cards. Darrow soon created copies of the game himself, which he sold successfully to friends, relatives, and local residents. Darrow even included a Community Chest card that reflected Depression-era politics. Franklin D. Roosevelt's Executive Order 6102, signed in 1933, became the card "We're off the Gold Standard, Collect $50.00." Darrow copyrighted his version in 1933, protecting the rules, layout, and appearance of the game. In 1934, he presented it to Parker Brothers, who rejected it. Darrow then ordered five hundred copies printed, which he sold himself at Wanamaker's Department Store. The game was a huge success, and other department stores began to place orders with Darrow, including the high-profile toy store FAO Schwartz.

Robert Barton, head of Parker Brothers, watched the success of Darrow's game in early 1935. During the Depression, Parker Brothers experienced a drastic drop in sales and had to fire many employees. In the hope that this game would revitalize the company, Barton met with Darrow in March, 1935, to gain the rights to the game. Barton was successful. Darrow signed a standard inventor's contract, which stated that he was the sole creator of the game. However, when Barton sought to patent his game, his application was denied. The U.S. Patent Office uncovered Magie's 1903 and 1924 patents for the Landlord's Game, which was too similar to Monopoly, and therefore the latter could not be patented. Barton subsequently bought the patents from Magie for five hundred dollars. Parker Brothers began to distribute the game in 1935, selling one-quarter of a million copies. The company sold more than one million more the following year. The game was featured in magazines, on the radio, and in film.

Monopoly has not changed significantly since its publication in 1935. Players roll dice to move around the board and can buy property on which they land. If another player lands on a property that is already owned, she or he must pay the owner rent. If a player acquires all of the properties in a color group, she or he has a monopoly, which increases the value of the property and raises the rent. The goal of the game is to bankrupt the other players.

Impact Monopoly remains a popular board game; it has sold more than 250 million copies worldwide. Throughout its history, it has also been more than a game. During World War II, it was used to sneak maps, money, and supplies to Allied prisoners of war.

After Monopoly was displayed as part of the American National Exposition in Moscow in 1959, the Soviet Union banned the game, claiming it was capitalistic propaganda. During the 1970's, Monopoly was at the center of a landmark case, *Anti-Monopoly, Inc. v. General Mills Fun Group.* Parker Brothers claimed Ralph Anspach, creator of Anti-Monopoly, infringed upon the trademark for Monopoly. Citing a consumer poll, Anspach argued that "monopoly" was a generic word, not a brand name, because people did not associate it with the company. In 1985, the two parties settled in the Ninth Circuit Court of Appeals. Parker Brothers maintained control over Monopoly and Anti-Monopoly. This case set a precedent for the protection of other companies' brand names, even if their identity was not associated with their product.

Alexandra Carter

Further Reading

Anspach, Ralph. *Monopolygate: During a David and Goliath Battle, the Inventor of the Anti-Monopoly® Game Uncovers the Secret History of Monopoly®.* Philadelphia: Xlibris, 2007.

Orbanes, Philip. *Monopoly: The World's Most Famous Game—And How It Got That Way.* Cambridge, Mass.: Da Capo Press, 2006.

See also Fads; Gold Reserve Act of 1934; Great Depression in the United States; Recreation; Roosevelt, Franklin D.; Unemployment in the United States; World War II and the United States.

Practicing her backhand, Helen Wills Moody prepares for the 1935 Wimbledon tennis tournament in London. (AP/Wide World Photos)

■ Moody, Helen Wills

Identification   American tennis player
Born   October 6, 1905; Centerville (now Fremont), California
Died   January 1, 1998; Carmel, California

Moody was the first American female athlete known internationally. She won thirty-one Grand Slam tennis titles during her career. Wills was undefeated from 1927 until 1932. During this time, she did not lose a set until the Wimbledon final in 1933.

Helen Wills Moody began playing tennis at the age of fourteen and won the national girls' championships in 1921. She began competing in the women's division at sixteen, winning the national doubles title and finishing second in singles. As a girl, Wills was known for her long pigtails and white visor. She won gold medals in singles and doubles at the 1924 Paris Olympics; tennis was not included again in the Olympics until 1988.

Wills showed little emotion while on the court, ignoring both her opponent and the crowd, and reporters quickly nicknamed her "Little Miss Poker Face." Wills made no apologies for her attitude on court, saying that her only thought was getting the ball over the net. Over the course of her tennis career, from 1921 to 1938, Wills won twelve doubles titles and nineteen singles titles, including eight Wimbledons, seven U.S. Championships, and four French Championships. Her most famous match was played in 1926, against Suzanne Lenglen, who was ranked number one in the world at the time. Wills lost the only match the two ever played by a score of 3-6, 6-8. Wills married Fred Moody in 1929 and was known as both Helen Wills and Helen Wills Moody. She graduated from the University of California in 1927. Wills was also well known as a published author and artist.

Impact Wills divorced Moody in 1937 and married Aidan Roark two years later. She retired from tennis in 1938 but continued to play into her eighties. Wills was inducted into the International Tennis Hall of Fame in 1959. In her will, she donated $10 million to the University of California to found a neuroscience institute. Her white visor, referred to as a "Wills eyeshade," later became popular among other players. Wills was considered scandalous for not wearing long stockings with her knee-length pleated skirt during a match in 1927. Her divergence from ankle-length skirts and stockings eventually paved the way for the short skirts and shorts of the modern game.

Jennifer L. Campbell

Further Reading

Davenport, Joanna. "Helen Wills Moody." In *Great Athletes: Golf and Tennis*. Pasadena, Calif.: Salem Press, 2010.

Englemann, Larry. *The Goddess and the American Girl*. New York: Oxford University Press, 1988.

King, Billie Jean. *We Have Come a Long Way*. New York: McGraw-Hill, 1988.

Wills, Helen. *Fifteen-Thirty*. New York: Charles Scribner's Sons, 1937.

See also Marble, Alice; Riggs, Bobby; Sports in the United States; Tennis; Tilden, Bill.

■ Morgenthau, Henry T., Jr.

Identification U.S. secretary of the Treasury
Born May 11, 1891; New York, New York
Died February 5, 1967; Poughkeepsie, New York

As secretary of the Treasury during the era of the New Deal, Morgenthau helped shape the goals of President Franklin D. Roosevelt's administration while attempting to adhere to sound economic and financial principles. He was especially critical in the framing of the Social Security Act.

Henry T. Morgenthau, Jr., was a member of a prominent New York City Jewish family. His father, Henry, Sr., was a real estate tycoon. His mother was Josephine Sykes. His son, Robert, became district attorney for the county of New York. Morgenthau graduated from Cornell University in agriculture and architecture and later was an editor of the journal *American Agriculturist*. He met Roosevelt and his wife, Eleanor, in 1914 and was their neighbor in Hyde Park, New York. As governor of New York, Roosevelt appointed Morgenthau conservation commissioner and to an agricultural committee.

Morgenthau worked on Roosevelt's campaigns for governor (1928) and president (1932). Roosevelt appointed him as secretary of the Treasury in 1933, a position he held until Roosevelt died in 1945. Morgenthau's personal financial policy was to maintain a balanced budget, but because of his loyalty to Roosevelt, he managed the Keynesian deficit policy of the New Deal. Therefore, he was in charge of $370 billion of expenditures, three times the amount spent by all previous Treasury secretaries combined.

Morgenthau supported the idea of a special budget for New Deal projects in order to keep regular government spending under control. He opposed some programs but sponsored others. However, he believed the programs should end when the country recovered from the Depression. He succeeded in his desire to establish a special-account Social Security, instead of financing coming from the general fund.

In 1937, Morgenthau broke publicly with Roosevelt over continued deficit spending. Conservative bankers did not believe him and blamed him along with the president for the Keynesian policies.

Impact Morgenthau helped change economic matters in the U.S. federal government and in the lives of individual Americans. Although he was a fiscal conservative, he helped make Keynesian deficit-spending policies an instrument of national economic practice.

Frederick B. Chary

Further Reading

Blum, John Morton. *Roosevelt and Morgenthau*. Boston: Houghton Mifflin, 1970.

Shlaes, Amity. *The Forgotten Man: A New History of the Great Depression*. New York: HarperCollins, 2007.

See also Elections of 1932, U.S.; Great Depression in the United States; National debt; New Deal; Roosevelt, Franklin D.; Social Security Act of 1935; Unemployment in the United States; Works Progress Administration.

■ *Morro Castle* **disaster**

The Event   Cruise ship fire
Date   September 8, 1934
Place   Atlantic coast off Asbury Park, New Jersey

The Morro Castle *tragedy called public and governmental attention to the fire hazards of passenger ships, especially those that have combustible interior finishes and large undivided spaces such as ballrooms. The crew's failure both to assist passengers and to launch more than a few of the lifeboats demonstrated a need for improved training and routine inspection of lifesaving gear.*

In September, 1934, a fire aboard the cruise ship *Morro Castle* killed 137 persons returning to New York from Havana, Cuba. A fire that may have begun in a storage locker in a public area on B deck was discovered at 3:10 A.M. By 3:30 A.M., it had spread through the entire ship, burning through the electrical and hydraulic systems and cutting off both power and steering. The untrained crew gathered in the forecastle, leaving passengers to find their own way to the stern, where they found no assistance in evacuating the ship. The confusion was compounded by the sudden death of the ship's captain from a heart attack only a few hours before and by an Atlantic storm that fanned the flames and hindered rescue efforts.

The interim captain and radio crew were slow to send radio distress calls, and other ships and onshore authorities failed to realize the gravity of the situation until bodies began washing up on the Jersey shore at dawn. The inebriated condition of many of the passengers was a factor as well; cruise ships had continued to find a market during the early years of the Depression, in part because the consumption of alcohol at sea was legal and inexpensive even during the years of Prohibition.

Impact   The international standard for ship safety, called Safety of Life at Sea (SOLAS), had been revised in 1929 and was revised again during the 1940's to reflect the painful lessons learned from the fire on the *Morro Castle*. National governments began requiring fire-resistant electrical and hydraulic systems and incombustible interior finishes in ships, a development that proved timely as these measures saved many sailors' lives during World War II.

Rachel Maines

Further Reading

Burton, Hal. *The Morro Castle*. New York: Viking Press, 1973.
Gallagher, Thomas Michael. *Fire at Sea: The Story of the Morro Castle*. Reprint. Guilford, Conn.: Lyons Press, 2003.
Hicks, Brian. *When the Dancing Stopped: The Real Story of the Morro Castle Disaster and Its Deadly Wake*. New York: Free Press, 2006.
Thomas, Gordon, and Max Morgan Witts. *Shipwreck: The Strange Fate of the Morro Castle*. New York: Stein and Day, 1972.

See also   Business and the economy in the United States; Great Depression in the United States; Prohibition repeal; Recreation.

■ Motion Picture Production Code

Identification   Ethics code for motion pictures adopted by the Hollywood studios
Dates   Adopted on March 31, 1930; enforced July 1, 1934; replaced by a ratings classification on November 1, 1968
Also known as   Hays Code; Production Code

The Motion Picture Production Code defined what was and was not acceptable content in films. It placated the general public's concern about immorality in films, forestalled pro-censorship pressure groups, and prevented federal censorship of films.

After a series of scandals during the 1920's, Hollywood formed the Motion Picture Producers and Distributors Association (MPPDA) in 1922, installing former U.S. postmaster general Will Hays as its head. Trying to ward off federal censorship, he concocted a list published by the MPPDA in 1927 of "don'ts" and "be carefuls" concerning censorable items. The 1927 publication listed the things that were never to be in a motion picture, no matter how they were treated. These included profanity, nudity, illegal drug trafficking, sexual perversions, white slavery, miscegenation, scenes of childbirth, scenes of children's sex organs, and "ridicule of the clergy." Other topics to be treated with restraint included murder techniques, robberies, hangings, electrocutions, and rape. This list of taboo subjects had no attendant rationale. It became an important part of the 1930 Motion Picture Production Code, which was based on a list of regulations drafted by Daniel A. Lord, a Roman Catholic priest and professor of English and dramatic literature at St. Louis University.

With no real threat of enforcement, Hollywood ignored the 1930 code. Several forces, however, congealed to threaten censorship against Hollywood: The Roman Catholic Church formed the Legion of Decency in 1933, which denounced Hollywood and threatened to boycott films; a best seller, *Our Movie-Made Children* (1934), summarized the disturbing results of a study by the Motion Picture Research Council; politicians proposed bills concerning film censorship; and the Depression caused a slump at the box office in 1933.

In 1934, an amendment to the Motion Picture Production Code allowed Joseph Breen, the head of the Production Code Administration (PCA), to strictly enforce the code. After 1934, films were subject to review and were expected to display a symbol of approval if they passed the PCA's review. Throughout the code's existence, however, the PCA lacked serious punitive measures to enforce compliance. In essence, the code was the motion-picture industry's attempt at self-regulation as a way to prevent censorship by federal, state, or local government censorship boards. Nonetheless, until the mid-1950's, studios were afraid to release films without the PCA seal of approval.

Breen's strictness in adhering to the code influenced many pictures, such as *Tarzan and His Mate* (1934), *Casablanca* (1942), *Double Indemnity* (1944), and *Crossfire* (1947). In the latter film, the subject of the novel, homosexuality, could not even be mentioned at all, so the topic was changed to anti-Semitism in the film version.

Hays retired in 1945; Breen did so in 1954. The Hays Code lingered, but with many challenges. Films such as *The Moon Is Blue* (1953), *The Man with the Golden Arm* (1955), *Some Like It Hot* (1959), *Blow-up* (1966; originally titled *Blowup* in the United Kingdom), and *Who's Afraid of Virginia Woolf?* (1966) either were released to commercial success without a seal of approval or defied the code concerning sexuality, drug use, or "vulgar" language and were reluctantly granted a seal. Several factors signaled the end of the code: the decline in the influence of the Legion of Decency; the 1951 Supreme Court decision to allow films as "artistic expression" to be covered under the First Amendment, which made censorship more difficult; the influx of foreign films, independent films, and exploitation films after the 1948 Supreme Court decision to no longer allow studio control over theater distributors; and the general change in cultural mores. The Hays Code was scrapped as

---

From the Motion Picture Production Code (1930)

Section II. Sex

The sanctity of the institution of marriage and the home shall be upheld. Pictures shall not infer that low forms of sex relationship are the accepted or common thing.

1. Adultery, sometimes necessary plot material, must not be explicitly treated, or justified, or presented attractively.
2. Scenes of Passion
   a. They should not be introduced when not essential to the plot.
   b. Excessive and lustful kissing, lustful embraces, suggestive postures and gestures, are not to be shown.
   c. In general passion should so be treated that these scenes do not stimulate the lower and baser element.
3. Seduction or Rape
   a. They should never be more than suggested, and only when essential for the plot, and even then never shown by explicit method.
   b. They are never the proper subject for comedy.
4. Sex perversion or any inference to it is forbidden.
5. White slavery shall not be treated.
6. Miscegenation (sex relationships between the white and black races) is forbidden.
7. Sex hygiene and venereal diseases are not subjects for motion pictures.
8. Scenes of actual child birth, in fact or in silhouette, are never to be presented.
9. Children's sex organs are never to be exposed.

unenforceable, and by 1968, a new ratings code was substituted, simply labeling the film content rather than prescribing it.

Impact The Golden Age of Hollywood was strongly shaped by the Motion Picture Production Code, which dictated the stories, themes, types of characters, dialogue, and specific scenes of the films that audiences could see. The code also served as a model for subsequent self-regulatory codes in other industries, such as television and comic books. Furthermore, it prevented the discussion of some significant topics until a decade or two after World War II—perhaps one reason that the code eventually was discarded as something out of touch with contemporary society.

Joseph Francavilla and Shawn Selby

The giant bust of George Washington emerges as workers shape the rocky face of Mount Rushmore into designer Gutzom Borglum's vision of four U.S. presidents in 1933. (AP/Wide World Photos)

Further Reading

Cook, David A. *A History of Narrative Films.* 4th ed. New York: W. W. Norton, 2004.

Doherty, Thomas. *Pre-Code Hollywood: Sex, Immorality, and Insurrection in American Cinema, 1930-1934.* New York: Columbia University Press, 1999.

Muscio, Giuliana. *Hollywood's New Deal.* Philadelphia: Temple University Press, 1996.

Pollard, Tom. *Sex and Violence: The Hollywood Censorship Wars.* Boulder, Colo.: Paradigm, 2009.

See also *Ecstasy*; Film; Gangster films; National Film Act of 1939 (Canada); West, Mae.

■ Mount Rushmore National Memorial

Identification Massive sculpture memorializing U.S. presidents George Washington, Thomas Jefferson, Abraham Lincoln, and Theodore Roosevelt

Place Black Hills of southwestern South Dakota

The Mount Rushmore sculpture is significant in part because of its imposing size and the amount of work involved to create it. Work on the memorial supported many laborers during the Great Depression of the 1930's.

In the mid-1920's the idea for a mountain-sized sculpture in the Black Hills of South Dakota was initiated by the head of the South Dakota historical society and supported by a South Dakota senator. These two obtained financial support and engaged a prominent international sculptor, Gutzon Borglum, to conceive of the monument and to plan the work. The first thoughts had been to include some regional heroes; however, Borglum wanted to do something of national significance, so four major national figures were chosen as subjects of the sculpture.

The first issue was to find a mountain suitable for carving. Borglum made several trips to South Dakota before finding Mount Rushmore, which he deemed to be perfect. Funding efforts were difficult until Calvin Coolidge visited the area in the late 1920's and was persuaded to dedicate the project.

Borglum spent fourteen years, including the entire decade of the 1930's, on the sculpture. The project employed almost four hundred local workers and for many, provided the food and subsistence they needed during the Depression. At first, the work was simply a way for the men to be fed and clothed, but as the project developed, the workers became part of the "dream" that was to be realized by the completion of this project.

Borglum was concerned that future generations of people seeing Mount Rushmore would not understand the effort involved in the project. In 1938, he began excavating a vault behind and within the mountain in which records would be preserved of the building process and the history of the Western world's pursuit of liberty. Borglum died in 1941, postponing the completion of this hall of records, but it was eventually opened, on a smaller scale than Borglum envisioned, by the National Park Service.

Impact   Mount Rushmore is a major tourist attraction, bringing many to the Black Hills of South Dakota. It is an engineering and artistic marvel and was one of the major art projects of the 1930's. Coolidge called it a "national shrine."

Mary C. Ware

Further Reading

Griffith, T. D. *America's Shrine of Democracy: A Pictorial History.* Rapid City, S.Dak.: Mount Rushmore National Memorial Society, 1990.

Slott, Roger. *Carved High: A Pictorial Essay of Mount Rushmore National Memorial.* Rapid City, S.Dak.: Mount Rushmore National Memorial Society, 2008.

See also   Architecture; Boulder Dam; Rockefeller Center.

In a scene from the 1936 film Mr. Deeds Goes to Town, *actor Raymond Walburn (left) helps Gary Cooper put on his shoes.* (Hulton Archive/Getty Images)

■ Mr. Deeds Goes to Town

Identification   Film about a small-town innocent in the big city
Director   Frank Capra
Date   Released on April 12, 1936

At a time when economic pressures affected most people, Frank Capra's film showed that virtues exist apart from money. Celebrating the "common man," Capra set a pattern in his movies of showing that populism and goodness can triumph against adversity and power. Considered the first film in his "social problem" trilogy (with Mr. Smith Goes to Washington *in 1939 and* Meet John Doe *in 1941), the film foreshadowed themes in other Capra works, such as* It's a Wonderful Life *(1946).*

In *Mr. Deeds Goes to Town*, Gary Cooper plays small-town businessman and aspiring poet Longfellow Deeds, who inherits $20 million. When he travels to New York to deal with legalities, he is swept up in several misadventures involving the clash between his rural values and the attitude of city snobs.

In her first featured role, Jean Arthur costars as Louise "Babe" Bennett, an urban reporter who poses as a jobless woman to secretly observe Deeds. Her intention is to mock him in her newspaper stories. Babe appeals to Deed's romantic side. In turn, she falls in love with him. However, when he discovers her ruse, he is heartbroken. When he is confronted by an unemployed man, he decides to give away his wealth to the needy. When unscrupulous relatives challenge his mental competence, he is despondent. Eventually, Babe convinces Deeds her feelings are genuine, and he is inspired to successfully defend himself. Skeptics are warmed, and idealism is restored.

Based on the story "Opera Hut" by Clarence Budington Kelland, *Mr. Deeds Goes to Town* was nominated for five Academy Awards, and Capra won the Oscar for best director, his second. Frequent Capra collaborator Robert Riskin wrote the screenplay. The cast also features familiar 1930's character actors Lionel Stander and George Bancroft. In 2002, the film was remade and starred Adam Sandler and Winona Ryder.

Impact   Capra had made other popular films, such as *Platinum Blonde* (1931) and *It Happened One Night* (1934), but soon after the latter film, he became ill; he said he was visited by a stranger who scolded him for making likable escapist films, so he decided to make films with a message. Occasionally criticized for making sentimental cinema, dubbed "Capra-corn," Capra won his third best director Oscar in 1938 for *You Can't Take It with You*, another nostalgic gem about regular people coping with the rich and powerful and earning redemption.

Bill Knight

Further Reading

Capra, Frank. *The Name Above the Title: An Autobiography.* New York: Belvedere, 1982.

Ehrlich, Matthew. *Journalism in the Movies.* Urbana: University of Illinois Press, 2004.

McBride, Joseph. *Frank Capra: The Catastrophe of Success.* New York: Simon & Schuster, 1992.

Saltzman, Joe. *Frank Capra and the Image of the Journalist in American Film.* Los Angeles: Norman Lear Center, 2002.

See also   Academy Awards; Capra, Frank; Film; *It Happened One Night*; *Mr. Smith Goes to Washington*.

■ Mr. Moto films

Identification   Series of Hollywood films about a fictional Japanese sleuth
Date   Released 1937-1939

American audiences quickly grew to like the fast-paced, action-oriented "Mr. Moto" detective film series, often set in exotic Asian locations. The protagonist, Kentaro Moto, played by Peter Lorre, remained mysterious and independent from the various American and European "good guys" he supported. American concern over Japanese aggression against China led to cancellation of the series in 1939.

In 1936, the great success of its Charlie Chan films persuaded Twentieth Century-Fox to launch another film series with an Asian detective. It chose the character of Mr. Moto, which had been created by John P. Marquand in a serial novel for *The Saturday Evening Post* in 1935. On January 11, 1937, the studio signed a contract for Marquand's Mr. Moto stories,

and the right to use the character thereafter, for an initial eight thousand dollars.

Norman Foster directed the first film, and did so for six of the eight films. Reflecting the general prejudices of the American film audience of the time, the studio chose Hungarian Lorre to play Moto, instead of an Asian American actor. Lorre was a Jewish refugee from Nazi Germany famous for his portrayal of a child murderer in Fritz Lang's *M* (1931). Foster was impressed by Lorre's trademark sad, protruding eyes and his reputation for mysterious characters.

For the first film, *Think Fast, Mr. Moto* (1937), the makeup department made Lorre look more stereotypically "Japanese," blackening and slicking back his hair and giving him round, steel-rimmed glasses; they did not outfit him with buck teeth, a stereotypical accoutrement for Asian character types. To set him apart from Charlie Chan, Foster made Mr. Moto an action hero. Mr. Moto displayed mastery of jujitsu and quickly and effectively dispatched his enemies. Stuntman Harvey Perry performed these actions for the overweight Lorre.

Like the seven other "Mr. Moto" films that followed, *Think Fast, Mr. Moto* was a thriller set in an exotic locale. To get at smugglers in Shanghai, Mr. Moto goes on a double-date with the naive American protagonist. Mr. Moto's girlfriend is Lela Liu, played by Japanese American and Hawaiian native Lotus Long (born Lotus Pearl Shibata). She gets killed in the action, setting up a happy ending for Mr. Moto and his American love interest.

The film's great success led to a quick sequel, *Thank You, Mr. Moto,* which opened on December 24, 1937. Mr. Moto helps another American and his girl escape trouble in Beijing. However, he destroys an Asian treasure map rather than give it to them.

The third film in the series, *Mr. Moto's Gamble* (1938), actually started as a Charlie Chan film. Because its intended lead, Warner Oland, fell ill and died that year, the studio turned it into a "Mr. Moto" film. It kept Chinese American actor Keye Luke in a supporting role.

Long reappeared next to Lorre in the fifth film, *Mysterious Mr. Moto* (1938), even though she is credited as Karen Sorrell. The only time Mr. Moto was played by a Japanese American actor, Teru Shimada, was as Mr. Moto's short-lived double in *Mr. Moto's Last Warning* (1939). American concern over Japan's aggression against China during the 1930's led to American antipathy toward Japan. In June, 1939, the studio phased out the Mr. Moto series. *Mr. Moto Takes a Vacation* (1939) was its last.

Impact Over a three-year period, the eight "Mr. Moto" films were popular with American audiences. The series character became a household name. Lorre gently spoofed his character in four radio shows in 1938 and 1939, with one final radio satire each in 1943 and 1944. In 1951, the National Broadcasting Company featured twenty-three radio episodes of James Monk as I. A. Moto fighting communists. A 1965 British film, *The Return of Mr. Moto*, with actor Henry Silva in the title role, was a failure.

Perhaps because of Lorre's acting skills or perhaps because of Mr. Moto's generally active and nonsubservient role toward American characters, as well as his relative independence as a Japanese international policeman, the character of Mr. Moto met considerably less hostile criticism by those American academics, writers, and critics who found much fault in the Charlie Chan character. While clearly a stereotype, Mr. Moto was always an independent American ally. The films gave rare supporting roles to Asian American actors.

R. C. Lutz

Further Reading

Berlin, Howard. *The Complete Mr. Moto Film Phile: A Casebook.* Rockville, Md.: Wildside Press, 2005.

Wires, Richard. *John P. Marquand and Mr. Moto: Spy Adventures and Detective Films.* Muncie, Ind.: Ball State University Press, 1990.

Youngkin, Stephen. *The Lost One: The Life of Peter Lorre.* Lexington: University of Kentucky Press, 2005.

See also Asian Americans; Charlie Chan films; Film; Film serials; Japanese military aggression; Marquand, John P.; Racial discrimination.

■ *Mr. Smith Goes to Washington*

Identification Film about a junior senator battling graft among American legislators
Director Frank Capra
Date Released on October 17, 1939

As the Great Depression persisted and World War II broke out abroad, Mr. Smith Goes to Washington *offered timely reassurance in democracy. Highlighting a derailed but redeemable American political system, the film voiced national anxieties, applauded individual integrity, and asserted faith in basic democratic principles. It was nominated for eleven Academy Awards and won the Oscar for best original story of 1939.*

Based on a tale by Lewis R. Foster, *Mr. Smith Goes to Washington* depicts a humble youth leader who becomes a greed-fighting statesman. Fledgling senator Jefferson Smith, played by James Stewart, believes in the United States defined by Abraham Lincoln and the Declaration of Independence; cynical politicians and journalists think him a gullible stooge. Aided by Congress-savvy secretary Clarissa Saunders, played by Jean Arthur, Smith writes legislation establishing a national boy's camp for future leaders. He soon learns, however, that land for the camp has been slated for a dam in a dishonest moneymaking scheme devised by Senator Jim Taylor, played by Ed Arnold, and corrupt legislators. Smith's bill exposes their graft and threatens political careers.

Against the advice of his tainted mentor, Senator Joseph Harrison Paine, played by Claude Rains, Smith defends his bill, speaks out against congressional wrongdoing, and thwarts efforts to discredit and silence him. After a lengthy, one-man filibuster with a landmark speech on liberty, Smith manages to reclaim hearts and votes: Democracy triumphs, the film purports, when leaders put common good before personal gain.

Impact Among political films of the 1930's, *Mr. Smith Goes to Washington* was uniquely set in the hub of American politics, featuring the process of national lawmaking. Popular audiences liked the plainspoken statesman. Although it became a classic, Capra's film incited controversy in 1939: Washington insiders resented its unflattering portrayal of Congress; others said the motion picture hurt the United States' image. For championing democracy

In a pivotal scene from the 1939 Frank Capra film Mr. Smith Goes to Washington, *Senator Jefferson Smith, played by actor James Stewart, clutches handfuls of letters from citizens demanding his resignation, as actor Claude Rains watches.* (Hulton Archive/Getty Images)

and resistance, the film was banned by Nazis and fascists in Germany, occupied France, and Spain.

Wendy Alison Lamb

Further Reading

Coyne, Michael. *Hollywood Goes to Washington: American Politics on Screen.* London: Reaktion Books, 2008.

Flinn, Denny Martin. *Ready for My Close-Up! Great Movie Speeches.* New York: Limelight Editions, 2007.

Young, William H., and Nancy K. Young. *The Great Depression in America: A Cultural Encyclopedia.* Westport, Conn.: Greenwood Press, 2007.

See also   Capra, Frank; Congress, U.S.; Film; *It Happened One Night*; Motion Picture Production Code; *Mr. Deeds Goes to Town*.

■ Muni, Paul

Identification   American actor
Born   September 22, 1895; Lemberg, Galicia, Austro-Hungarian Empire (now Lviv, Ukraine)
Died   August 25, 1967; Montecito, California

One of the greatest character actors of his generation, Muni established his reputation on the stage, in films, and on radio. His professional example, while grounded on the early twentieth century stage, was a powerful influence on actors during the 1930's and later.

Paul Muni, born Muni Weisenfreund, came to the United States with his family as a young actor in the Yiddish theater, which constituted his livelihood from 1907 until 1926. His emergence on the English-speaking stage during the 1920's was partially a response to the passing of the golden age of Second Avenue, an area of Manhattan once referred to as the Yiddish Broadway, but it was also the result of the recognition of his brilliance in widely varied roles, which he had learned as a hardworking and conscientious "actor's actor."

While continuing to work on the stage in New York during the 1930's—in productions including *Counsellor-at-Law* (1931), *The Eternal Road* (1936), and *Key Largo* (1939)—Muni established his reputation in Hollywood in such films as *Scarface* (1932); *I Am a Fugitive from a Chain Gang* (1932); *The Story of Louis Pasteur* (1936), for which he won the Oscar for best actor; *The Good Earth* (1937); *The Life of Emile Zola* (1937); and *Juarez* (1939). He was especially known for biographical roles that challenged the viewer politically. He set an example for other actors with his work ethic, which compelled him to immerse himself in historical background, social and visual context, and even speech patterns of characters from other cultures in preparation for every role.

Muni's connection to his Jewish heritage did not diminish even when he left the Yiddish theater for the English-speaking stage and screen. He demonstrated this enduring tie in both his choice of roles and his loyalty to professional associates, from his marriage to Bella Finkel, who was a niece of the Yiddish theater actor and producer Boris Thomashefsky, to his enduring work with the Adler, Bernardi, and Schildkraut families, who also made the transition from the Yiddish theater to the New York stage and Hollywood. Muni also visited Palestine in 1938, an experience that influenced his later support of the establishment of the state of Israel.

The height of Muni's professional career was during the 1930's. He demonstrated the relevance of American film during the early years of the sound era while continuing his work in other acting media.

Impact Muni's professional methodology influenced actors as diverse as Joseph Schildkraut, Yul Brynner, and Marlon Brando. While he cannot be said to have established a "school" of acting comparable to those of Konstantin Stanislavsky or Michael Chekhov, his insistence on realism, based on understanding of subject matter, in every performance is considered his greatest contribution to the profession.

Susan M. Filler

Further Reading

Cohen, Sarah Blacher, ed. *From Hester Street to Hollywood: The Jewish-American Stage and Screen.* Bloomington: Indiana University Press, 1983.

Kanfer, Stefan. *Stardust Lost: The Triumph, Tragedy and Mishugas of the Yiddish Theater in America.* New York: Knopf, 2006.

Lawrence, Jerome. *Actor: The Life and Times of Paul Muni.* New York: Putnam, 1974.

See also   Anti-Semitism; Broadway musicals; Film; Gangster films; Jews in the United States; Theater in the United States.

■ Music: Classical

Definition   Music derived from European tradition, encompassing forms such as chamber and symphonic music and ballet and opera

The 1930's marked the American symphonic coming-of-age. Orchestras continued to grow, proliferate, and present the public with access to the established classical canon. Unprecedented activity by composers, conductors, and various musical organizations focused attention on American artists. Nationalistic efforts combined with burgeoning media and mass migrations to the United States established the country as a center for classical-music activity.

Myriad factors impacted the development and distribution of classical music throughout the 1930's. Jazz, folk, and popular music styles regularly found their way into serious compositions intended for the concert hall; the newly discovered music of Charles Ives and serial techniques of Arnold Schoenberg inspired a generation of ultramodernists; and American composers and conductors, such as Henry Cowell and Serge Koussevitzky, took leading roles in the promotion, performance, and publication of modern classical music. New works by American composers appeared regularly in concerts and music festivals across the nation and around the world.

Emerging technologies and the growing influence of the media presented musicians with a paradox: Amplification, radio broadcasts, films, and television supplied musicians with broader audiences and job opportunities, but technology also introduced competition, as recorded media offered a cheap alternative to live musicians. The rise of fascism in Europe caused many classical artists, such as

An important figure in both classical music and African American history, William Grant Still, shown here in 1939, was the first African American to conduct a top-level American orchestra, doing so in 1936 with the Los Angeles Philharmonic. (The Granger Collection, New York)

Otto Klemperer and Schoenberg, to seek asylum in the United States. American universities and conservatories, such as the Institute of Musical Arts (Juilliard) and the University of California, Los Angeles, benefited greatly from the influx of talent and became viable alternatives to European conservatories for the study of music.

Black American musicians such as William Grant Still and Todd Duncan fought institutionalized racism by breaking color barriers in the concert halls, and female composers such as Ruth Crawford, Johanna Beyer, and Marion Bauer struggled to make their marks. Responding to unemployment rates that were estimated by the American Federation of Musicians to be nearly 70 percent in 1935, the Works Progress Administration launched a Federal Music Project (FMP) with former Cleveland Symphony Orchestra conductor Nikolai Sokoloff at its helm to provide work for some ten thousand musicians.

American Compositional Styles American composers turned to a wide variety of techniques and resources, frequently cross-pollinating styles. Ives, whose complicated cross-rhythmic, multitempi programmatic works with dissonant paraphrases of popular tunes and hymns, as in works such as *Three Places in New England*, helped fuel continued interest in ultramodern techniques and fresh sounds. Cowell, for example, composed a concerto, *Rhythmicon*, which employed an electronic instrument he created with Russian inventor Léon Theremin. Edgard Varèse composed *Ionisation* entirely for percussion ensembles; the piece featured such unusual instrumentation as siren, bongos, and sleigh bells. George Gershwin continued his integration of jazz into the concert hall with his *Second Rhapsody* for piano and orchestra, and his pioneering folk-opera *Porgy and Bess*. Like many of his contemporaries, Adolph Weiss also included elements of jazz, as in his freely dissonant work *American Life*.

Composers such as William Schuman, Roy Harris, and Cowell increasingly turned to American sources for inspiration throughout the decade. For example, Schuman produced an *American Festival Overture*, Harris wrote *Chorale* for strings based on early American church hymns, and Cowell included banjo in *Old American Country Set*, a work inspired by musical styles he had heard as a child in the Midwest. Virgil Thomson's score for *The Plow That Broke the Plains* (1936) included quotations of cowboy songs such as "I Ride an Old Paint" and "Streets of Laredo" along with jazzy saxophone and clarinet melodies. Aaron Copland embraced an international perspective of Americana with his orchestral work *El Salón México*, examined Western legend Billy the Kid in his ballet named for the outlaw, and took on the U.S. judicial system in another ballet, *Hear Ye! Hear Ye!* Also on the political front, Marc Blitzstein employed elements of blues, jazz, vernacular speech, and quotations of Johann Sebastian Bach and Ludwig van Beethoven for his scathing look at big money corruption in the banned Brechtian musical drama *The Cradle Will Rock*. George Antheil included a thinly veiled attack on J. P. Morgan and political influence in his machine-age opera *Transatlantic*.

Media Radio transmissions provided a broader audience for orchestras and helped acculturate the general public to classical music in the comfort of their homes. Starting in 1930, the Columbia Broadcasting System (CBS) began airing weekly New York Philharmonic concerts from Carnegie Hall on Sunday afternoons. In 1932, Leopold Stokowski took the Philadelphia Orchestra on the air with works by American composers; pieces performed included *Abraham Lincoln* by Robert Russell Bennett, *The Pleasure-Dome of Kubla Khan* by Charles Tomlinson Griffes, *Suite* by Walter Piston, and *Virginia Reel* by John Powell, as well as works by Louis Gruenberg, Arcady Dubensky, Copland, and Cowell.

With guidance from esteemed New York music critic Deems Taylor, the CBS Symphony Orchestra under Harold Barlow commissioned works from six American composers specifically for radio broadcast. Among these were *Music for Radio* by Copland and the ballet *Lenox Avenue* by Still. Still had previously distinguished himself as the first black American to conduct a white radio orchestra in New York for Willard Robison's *Deep River Hour.*

Corporate sponsors such as General Motors subsidized classical programs on the National Broadcasting Company (NBC) networks throughout the 1930's, and in 1937, NBC established its own radio orchestra to perform weekly classical broadcasts with famous conductors such as Arturo Toscanini and Frank Black. In 1939, Black conducted the world premiere of Harold Morris's *Violin Concerto*, with Philip Frank as soloist, while on the air. Record companies such as Columbia and RCA Victor provided unprecedented access to historically significant works by revered masters such as Wolfgang Amadeus Mozart by producing record albums with performances by American orchestras such as the Chicago Symphony Orchestra.

The film industry regularly blended serious and popular music in film, and Universal Pictures opened the decade with *King of Jazz* (1930). Directed by John Murray Anderson and featuring Paul Whiteman's Orchestra in a performance of George Gershwin's *Rhapsody in Blue*, this all-star musical also contained performances by John Boles, Joe Venuti, and Bing Crosby with the Rhythm Boys. Virgil Thomson became one of the first classical composers to write scores for film when he penned folk-based, nondiegetic themes for Pare Lorentz's documentaries *The Plow That Broke the Plains* and *The River.* By the end of the decade, Deems Taylor, Leopold Stokowski, and the Philadelphia Orchestra were in the studio working on the sound track for Walt Disney's animated feature *Fantasia.*

American Activism from the Page to the Stage American composers' organizations, such as the League of Composers and Cowell's New Music Society, published scores by composers in their respective journals, *Modern Music* and *New Music Quarterly.* Scores by Ives, Cowell, Carl Ruggles, Crawford, Bauer, Antheil, Henry Brant, and Vivian Fine appeared in print for the first time. Works by American classical composers provided the foundation for annual musical festivals at Yaddo, in Saratoga Springs, New York; Tanglewood, in Lenox and Stockbridge, Massachusetts; the MacDowell Colony in Peterborough, New Hampshire; Howard Hanson's American Composers Orchestral Concerts; and concert series sponsored by the New Music Society and the Pan American Association of Composers (PAAC). Under the leadership of eminent musicologist Nicolas Slonimsky, the PAAC carried the works of Americans such as Copland, Cowell, Gershwin, Harris, Ives, and Varèse to major cities around the world. Established orchestras such as the New York Philharmonic Society, the Philadelphia Orchestra, the Chicago Symphony Orchestra, and the Los Angeles Philharmonic regularly premiered and featured works by American composers. In 1931, the Rochester Philharmonic Orchestra, for example, premiered Still's *Afro-American Symphony*, the first symphonic work by a black American to be performed by a major orchestra. Another first came when Paul Whiteman presented Still's work *A Deserted Plantation* at the Metropolitan Opera House in New York for the "Sixth Experiment in American Music."

As musical director of the Boston Symphony Orchestra (BSO), Koussevitzky stands out as one of the most ardent advocates of modern music during the 1930's. To celebrate the fiftieth anniversary of the BSO during the 1930-1931 season, Koussevitzky commissioned many works from both established and emerging composers, including Symphony in G Minor by Albert Roussel; *Metamorphoseon, Modi XII* by Ottorino Respighi; Symphony No. 4 by Sergei Prokofiev; Symphony No. 2 by Hanson; Symphony of Psalms by Igor Stravinsky; and Symphony by Arthur Honegger. Despite economic hardships during the 1930's, many classical performance groups were formed, some of which are still in existence. These include the National Symphony Orchestra (1931), the North Carolina Symphony (1932), the Vermont Symphony Orchestra (1934), the Charleston Symphony Orchestra (1936), the Black Hills Symphony

Orchestra (1937), the Louisville Orchestra (1937), the San Antonio Symphony (1939), and the West Virginia Symphony Orchestra (1939). Classical music had increasing competition from popular music, and the 1939 New York World's Fair marked the end of an era when organizers canceled classical music performances for more popular and low-priced entertainment.

The Federal Music Project   In addition to establishing performance groups such as the Illinois Symphony and venues for music such as the Composers' Forum-Laboratory in New York, the FMP supported music-copying projects devoted to producing sets of classical works for orchestral performances. The largest of the copying projects operated at the Free Library of Philadelphia between 1935 and 1943. With support from pioneering orchestral music collector and philanthropist Edwin Adler Fleisher, the library wrote to more than 350 American composers in search of unpublished symphonic manuscripts. In the spirit of the Good Neighbor Policy, the Philadelphia music-copying project expanded in 1938 to include Latin American composers from Central and South America in its quest to create performance sets for lending. Over the course of the project, as many as one hundred professional music copyists produced thousands of conductors' scores and complete sets of parts from the manuscript scores of hundreds of pan-American composers. More than one thousand scores of American composers were lent by the library to orchestras around the world, securing the Fleisher Collection's legacy as the largest repository of American orchestral works in the world available for lending to performance organizations.

Impact   The 1930's provided an unparalleled environment for growth of classical music in the United States. In addition to acculturating the country to the traditional European canon, American orchestras actively promoted new classical music from composers throughout the world. Unprecedented activity by and attention to American classical musicians and composers brought some of most enduring classical icons of the United States to prominence in this decade, as classical music entered its American age.

Gary Galván

Further Reading

Bindas, Kenneth J. *All This Music Belongs to the Nation: The WPA's Federal Music Project and American Society, 1935-1939.* Knoxville: University of Tennessee Press, 1995. Provides a broad overview of the formation of the WPA music projects and selected social aspects.

Cowell, Henry, ed. *American Composers on American Music: A Symposium.* Reprint. New York: Ungar, 1962. Contains American composers' essays on their peers; includes entries on and by Carlos Chávez, Copland, Gershwin, Ives, Piston, Dane Rudhyar, Roger Sessions, Slonimsky, and Edgard Varèse, among others.

The Edwin A. Fleisher Music Collection. Philadelphia: Innes & Sons, 1945. Documents orchestral works acquired under the WPA Music Copying Project at the Free Library of Philadelphia. Entries for each work include biographical data for the composers, orchestration, premiere dates, and other details for nearly three thousand compositions by pan-American composers.

Galván, Gary. "The ABCs of the WPA Music Copying Project and the Fleisher Collection." *American Music* 26, no. 4 (2008): 514-538. Examines the largest and most enduring manifestation of the Federal Music Project through primary source documents and with attention to the project's dedication to American composers.

Geiringer, Karl. "A Relief Scheme for Music in America." *The Musical Times* 81 (January, 1940): 11-12. Noted musicologist Karl Geiringer provides a contemporaneous examination of the Federal Music Project.

See also   Federal Emergency Relief Administration; Gershwin, George; Harlem Renaissance; Music: Jazz; Music: Popular; *Porgy and Bess*; Radio in the United States; Recording industry; Works Progress Administration.

■ Music: Jazz

Definition   American musical style emphasizing syncopation, swing, and improvisation that is most commonly associated with instrumental music and dancing

During the 1930's, jazz was a popular type of dance music and was becoming the most popular musical style in the United States. Although it was originally associated with African Americans, its audience expanded to include other people, particularly college students and members of upper-class society.

The decade of the 1930's has been called the swing era—a reference to the tremendous influence of its dominant jazz style. Swing jazz differed from earlier jazz primarily in terms of the rhythm section and its approach to playing. The string bass replaced the tuba as the low-end instrument of choice. The tuba bass line tended toward an "oom-pah" sound, playing every other beat and giving those beats a weighty feeling. String basses in the swing era played every beat, which lightened the rhythms. In addition, drummers focused more on the high-hat cymbals, which could be opened and closed to create different accents. These changes, as well as refined techniques by the guitarists and pianists, led to a bouncier, more focused rhythm section that gave the music the characteristic drive known as swing.

The Depression and the Rise of Radio   The worldwide Great Depression that dominated the early 1930's had numerous impacts on jazz; most significant was the fact that Americans had less money to spend on entertainment such as the theater and recorded and live music. As a result, families tended to stay at home and get their entertainment from radio broadcasts. Radio stations usually based musical programming around live performances, and many jazz performers became staples of this programming. The Duke Ellington Orchestra's performances at the Cotton Club in Harlem were broadcast live starting in 1927, the Benny Goodman Orchestra was a regular guest on NBC's *Let's Dance* program starting in 1934, and numerous other bands received airtime on various broadcasts. These broadcasts provided several benefits for the bands. They made the music available during a time when the record industry was struggling and made the bandleaders household names, making some quite wealthy and giving them star power and appeal. Because the broadcasts were regional or even national in scope, they provided exposure to a wider audience, not just those who frequented the nightclubs and dance halls where these bands worked.

Changing Audiences   A radical shift in the jazz audience occurred during the 1930's. Previously, jazz was popular primarily among African Americans in lower to lower-middle classes, but with the popularity of the radio broadcasts on which they appeared, some bands began to develop a following among white middle- and upper-class audiences. One group that was particularly significant in the spread and popularity of jazz was college students, some of whom developed a fanatical interest in their favorite bands, following them as they might their favorite sports teams. With this audience came new opportunities for jazz bands and their leaders. Some of these groups began to be invited to perform more frequently at society functions.

Making "a Lady out of Jazz"   The popularity of swing jazz was partly the result of the increasing influence of classical music. As early as 1924, bandleaders such as Paul Whiteman consciously attempted to water down some of the more experimental elements of jazz and make it more appealing to white listeners, or as he put it "to make a lady out of jazz." This classical influence is evidenced in part by the dominance of large ensembles, usually referred to as "big bands" or even "swing orchestras." These groups typically consisted of four or five reed players, who could be called on to play either saxophone or clarinet; two or three trombonists; three or four trumpeters; a piano player; a string bass player; a drummer; and, occasionally, a guitarist. These larger groups allowed for a lusher and more orchestral sound than the preceding small groups and led to the second major change in jazz—the dominance of written arrangements.

With more musicians in these larger ensembles, bandleaders felt the need to establish control over what each one played. The leader credited with establishing the standard for swing arrangements was Fletcher Henderson, who, along with saxophonist Don Redman, created arrangements based around alternating sections for the reed and brass instruments and limited improvised solos. With these arrangements, jazz began to move toward a written tradition rather than an oral one.

Hot Versus Sweet Jazz   One of the biggest distinctions among bands during the swing era was between "hot" bands and "sweet" bands. The hot bands maintained the most ties to traditional jazz, played arrangements based on or influenced by the blues, featured a considerable amount of improvisation, and tended to be composed of African American musicians. The sweet bands tended to play arrangements based on popular song, had limited improvisation, and tended to be composed of white musicians. The sweet bands were far more commercially successful than the hot bands primarily because their style of jazz was similar to the music that the predominantly white mainstream audience was used to. Some fans of hot jazz referred to these sweet bands derogatorily as "Mickey Mouse" bands. The prime example of the sweet bands was the Glenn Miller Orchestra, which featured bouncy dance numbers such as "In the Mood" and lush ballads such as "Moonlight Serenade." The most successful hot bands, led by people such as Benny Goodman and Duke Ellington, included more commercial "sweet" songs in their performances to attract fans of sweet jazz. Those hot bands that did not make commercial compromises like that, such as those led by Benny Carter and Henderson, struggled to survive.

Kansas City   Unlike the jazz of the 1920's, jazz during the 1930's did not really have a geographic center, though most bands tended to work in and around the major cities of the East Coast. One area that developed a significant jazz culture was Kansas City. While Kansas City may at first glance seem like an unlikely place for jazz to take hold and flourish, there were factors that contributed to its role as a major jazz hub. Most notably, it was controlled politi-

Glenn Miller (center) leading the six-piece horn section of his orchestra in 1938. (Michael Ochs Archives/Getty Images)

DownBeat Magazine's Readers Poll, 1936-1939

1936
- Sweet band: Ray Noble
- Bass: Pops Foster
- Drums: Gene Krupa
- Guitar: Eddie Lang
- Piano: Teddy Wilson
- Swing band: Benny Goodman
- Trombone: Tommy Dorsey
- Trumpet: Bix Beiderbecke

1937
- Alto saxophone: Jimmy Dorsey
- Bass: Bob Haggart
- Drums: Gene Krupa
- Guitar: Carmen Mastren
- Piano: Teddy Wilson
- Record: "Sing, Sing, Sing" (Benny Goodman)
- Soloist: Benny Goodman

- Sweet band: Hal Kemp
- Swing band: Benny Goodman
- Tenor saxophone: Chu Berry
- Trombone: Tommy Dorsey
- Trumpet: Harry James
- Vocalist: Ella Fitzgerald

1938
- Alto saxophone: Jimmy Dorsey
- Bass: Bob Haggart
- Clarinet: Benny Goodman
- Drums: Gene Krupa
- Guitar: Benny Heller
- Piano: Bob Zurke
- Recording: "Sing, Sing, Sing" (Benny Goodman)
- Soloist: Benny Goodman
- Sweet band: Casa Loma
- Swing band: Artie Shaw

- Tenor saxophone: Bud Freeman
- Trombone: Tommy Dorsey
- Trumpet: Harry James
- Vocalist: Ella Fitzgerald

1939
- Alto saxophone: Jimmy Dorsey
- Bass: Bob Haggart
- Clarinet: Benny Goodman
- Drums: Gene Krupa
- Guitar: Charlie Christian
- Male singer: Bing Crosby
- Piano: Jess Stacy
- Sweet band: Tommy Dorsey
- Swing band: Benny Goodman
- Tenor saxophone: Coleman Hawkins
- Trombone: Tommy Dorsey
- Trumpet: Harry James

Source: DownBeat magazine online archives.

cally during the late 1920's and early 1930's by Thomas Joseph Pendergast, a gangster with an interest in developing a strong nightlife. While nightclubs around the country struggled to draw customers during Prohibition, those in Kansas City thrived because of the lack of liquor enforcement under Pendergast, making Kansas City an entertainment hub.

The jazz that came out of Kansas City was different from that of the East Coast bands. Rather than being based on popular song and singable melodies, Kansas City jazz was based around the blues and short, repeated melodic figures known as riffs. Some of the better known bands to come out of Kansas City were Andy Kirk and His Twelve Clouds of Joy, which featured pianist and arranger Mary Lou Williams; the Jay McShann Orchestra, which featured some of the earliest recorded playing of alto saxophonist Charlie Parker; and the Bennie Moten Orchestra. Until his death in 1935, Moten was the biggest name in Kansas City jazz. After his death, many of the members of his orchestra left the group to follow the group's pianist William "Count" Basie. The Count

Basie Orchestra became the group that later audiences considered synonymous with Kansas City jazz.

Singers, Soloists, and Small Groups Many bands hired singers in order to connect with fans of popular songs. Some of these songs had been instrumental standards, but bandleaders found that people preferred to hear the words as well as the melodies. The singers were generally young and attractive and sat on the stage throughout the show, then were brought to the front to sing a couple of songs, usually ballads or novelty songs. They seem to have been reluctant additions to many bands, as their leaders typically treated them like an unnecessary ornament and rarely rehearsed their numbers. Despite this, many of these vocalists soon became more popular than the band that hired them and went on to legendary solo careers. Vocalists who launched their careers with swing bands include Frank Sinatra, Peggy Lee, Ella Fitzgerald, Sarah Vaughan, Lena Horne, Rosemary Clooney, and Billie Holiday.

While the big bands receive most of the attention during the 1930's, there were still some small groups and solo performers who made a name for themselves. By the mid-1930's, Fifty-second Street in New York was home to several small "basement" clubs where audiences gathered to listen to performers such as tenor saxophonist Coleman Hawkins. Small clubs in Kansas City were the venues for informal jam sessions where soloists were pitted against each other and were challenged to innovate in their improvisations. Those jam sessions also provided an opportunity for soloists to exchange ideas and served as a rite of passage for aspiring musicians.

One of the great soloists to come out of the 1930's was pianist Art Tatum. He blended classical piano styles with the Harlem stride-piano style, which was popular among swing-era pianists, and added some of the florid runs and hornlike articulations of Earl "Fatha" Hines's piano style to create a distinctive sound that intimidated other performers. Stories abound of musicians who at least considered giving up their music careers after hearing Tatum play. His virtuosic playing, along with his tendency to change the harmonies of the pieces he played, was tremendously influential in the development of bebop.

Small groups also became popular in these clubs. The groups usually consisted of two or three soloists and a rhythm section. Some of them were newly created out of the collaborations of the musicians already working there, and others were born out of the big bands. Members of groups led by Ellington, Goodman, Basie, and others formed small groups of three to seven members to perform in the smaller venues. Recordings by some small groups, such as the Benny Goodman Trio and Count Basie's Kansas City Seven, have become jazz classics.

Jazz in Europe   Jazz was not restricted to the United States. In 1934, Belgian-born guitarist Django Reinhardt and French violinist Stéphane Grappelli formed the Quintette du Hot Club de France (Quintet of the Hot Club of France) in Paris. Reinhardt eventually toured the United States with Ellington and recorded with Hawkins, Rex Stewart, and Carter. He is credited with changing the way jazz guitar was played in the same ways that Tatum changed jazz piano. American musicians also frequented Europe during the early and mid-1930's. Hawkins

spent several years in France, as did clarinetist Sidney Bechet.

Impact   Jazz of the swing era played a pivotal role in the development of American popular music during the mid-twentieth century. The dance music created by the big bands spawned dance styles that defined the era. The solo and small-group jazz laid the foundations for bebop and other modern jazz styles that focused on improvisation and collaborative composition. Many of the singers whose careers were launched singing with the big bands not only entertained audiences into the rock-and-roll era but also served as the models and inspirations for many of the most successful vocalists of later generations.

Eric S. Strother

Further Reading

Driggs, Frank, and Chuck Haddix. *Kansas City Jazz: From Ragtime to Bebop—History.* New York: Oxford University Press, 2005. History of jazz in Kansas City from its earliest stages.

Erenberg, Lewis A. *Swingin' the Dream: Big Band Jazz and the Rebirth of American Culture.* Chicago: University of Chicago Press, 1999. Examines the mingling of jazz and popular culture during the 1930's and 1940's.

Gottlieb, William. *The Golden Age of Jazz.* New York: Simon and Schuster, 1979. A history of jazz during the 1920's and 1930's. Includes classic jazz pictures.

Shaw, Arnold, and Bill Willard. *Let's Dance: Popular Music in the 1930s.* New York: Oxford University Press, 1998. A history of popular music during the 1930's. Includes biographies of significant big band leaders.

Stowe, David W. *Swing Changes: Big Band Jazz in New Deal America.* Cambridge, Mass.: Harvard University Press, 1996. Chronicles jazz in the swing era in terms of the New Deal.

See also   Armstrong, Louis; Basie, Count; Dance; Dorsey, Tommy; Ellington, Duke; Fitzgerald, Ella; Gershwin, George; Goodman, Benny; Holiday, Billie; Miller, Glenn; Shaw, Artie; Smith, Bessie.

■ Music: Popular

Definition   Fashionable forms of music outside the classical and jazz genres

During the 1930's, technological advances helped music shift toward distinctly popular genres. Radio, in particular, became the medium of choice, and people listened to music on both their automobile and home radios. As a result, Americans were introduced to a growing number of musical styles that reflected the diversity of their culture.

Like nearly every aspect of society during the 1930's, music in the United States reflected the sociocultural effects of the Great Depression. Despite the economic conditions of the era, the musical styles of the day were often a reflection of hope, as evidenced by the energetic, distinct genres that emerged.

One of the most profound changes to the dissemination of music was the technological innovation of radio. By the middle of the decade, radios were in more than 20 million homes and were becoming increasingly popular in automobiles as well. Though radios had become commonplace in the preceding decade, not until the 1930's did the medium became more than a vehicle for entertainment and newscasts. During this golden age of radio, it also became a means of escape from the economic hardships of the day. Various dance-music genres were popular, and noted musicians often performed live broadcasts, as ongoing royalty disputes precluded many records from dissemination over the airwaves. Artists including Louis Armstrong, Cab Calloway, Tommy Dorsey, Duke Ellington, Benny Goodman, and Artie Shaw were frequent performers, and George Gershwin even hosted his own radio show entitled "Music by Gershwin," which was broadcast on NBC's Blue Network. The repeal of Prohibition early in the decade also helped juke joints promote new musical styles to which their patrons wanted to dance.

Phonographs were also fashionable, and were another means of featuring the music of diverse regional genres. As a result, music helped Americans develop a popular culture that transcended economic, ethnic, and geographic boundaries. Another effect of this transcendence was that it opened performance doors for both professional and semiprofessional musicians. Even classical music composers, including Aaron Copland and Gershwin, sought to incorporate the nation's vernacular music into their works. Copland's "Prairie Journal," composed for radio broadcast, was one of his earliest forays into what later became his signature Western American sound. As a result, technology had a direct influence on spreading vernacular American music and in instilling a sense of unification and hope.

Musical Styles   The extravagant styles of the popular 1920's Broadway musicals seemed to disappear with the onset of the Great Depression. Instead, diverse regional styles became widespread among Americans of all walks of society.

Hillbilly, or Western, music had gained popular-

Gene Autry, pictured with his horse, Champion, was one of the leaders of the country music scene that expanded in popularity during the 1930's. (Time & Life Pictures/Getty Images)

ity in the 1920's, and by the 1930's, several distinct variations of the genre emerged. One approach, exemplified by the Carter family, had a distinct Southeast and Appalachian style that was best represented by Maybelle Carter's particular guitar method. Dubbed "Carter scratch" or "Carter style," it is credited as a precursor to bluegrass music. Another technique was likely the result of a convergence of the primarily rural style's influx into urban areas. The romanticized image of the Western cowboy influenced the musical artistry of the day, as represented by Gene Autry, Roy Rogers and the Sons of the Pioneers, and Tex Ritter, who had several of his own radio shows. Instrumentation—particularly the addition of electric guitars and drums—produced subgenres of the style, including honky-tonk, Western swing, and hillbilly boogie. In subsequent decades, bluegrass, rockabilly, and country rock emerged from hillbilly roots.

Though the decade was primarily characterized by upbeat, hopeful music and lyrics, the blues style of previous decades remained a representative of the hardships of the Great Depression. Characterized by a more electrified feel that was likely the result of urbanization, the American blues in the 1930's influenced subgenres such as boogie-woogie and the regional Delta blues and Memphis blues. Likewise, folk music was epitomized by the soulful sounds of Woody Guthrie, "the Oklahoma cowboy" whose lyrics reflected the plight of the layperson and eventually paved the way to the protest songs that emerged later.

Largely influenced by Thomas A. Dorsey, "the father of gospel music," gospel music was a unique genre characterized by the amalgamation of Christian lyrics with jazz and blues melodies and rhythms. Dorsey, a former blues pianist dubbed "Georgia Tom," had a successful career as a jazz and blues composer before he began experimenting with what was to become gospel music; one of his most famous hits as a jazz and blues composer was the provocative "It's Tight Like That." For a time, Dorsey composed in both the jazz-and-blues and gospel styles simultaneously, before eventually abandoning the former altogether. "Take My Hand, Precious Lord," one of his most famous gospel songs, has been recorded by numerous artists from Elvis Presley to Aretha Franklin and is a prime example of distinctly personal lyrics that are characteristic of the jazz and blues styles from which he drew.

Swing The Jazz Age that immediately preceded the 1930's was an era characterized by a shift from conservative to liberal values. As a result, jazz was often deemed licentious by those who thought that the style promoted the sociocultural values of the Roaring Twenties. The stock market crash and the subsequent effects of the Great Depression led to a decline in the jazz style that was once so popular. As a result, a distinct style of jazz called "swing" developed and eventually came to epitomize the music of the era.

Dubbed "sweet," the jazz style of the 1920's that spilled into the following decade was characterized by four-beat, syncopated rhythms accompanied by the dulcet, simple melodies of a string orchestra or vocal soloist. Bandleaders such as trombonist and trumpeter Tommy Dorsey; his older brother, clarinetist and saxophonist Jimmy Dorsey; violinist Guy Lombardo; and trombonist and arranger Glenn Miller, epitomized the "sweet" sounds of a less improvised swing style. By contrast, the "hot" style that began to develop relied less on the string orchestra as it did on band instrumentation—particularly woodwinds and brass instruments—and was characterized by highly improvised melodies by various soloists. Two of the most prominent composers and bandleaders of this subgenre were pianists Count Basie and Duke Ellington. Despite the various monikers, proponents of both styles also occasionally performed in the other style. Further, clarinetist Benny Goodman was also known for leading one of the first racially mixed bands, which had a historic performance in Carnegie Hall featuring Basie and some members of the Duke Ellington Orchestra. Swing music became so popular that, in addition to well-known jazz singers such as Ella Fitzgerald and Billie Holiday, legendary vocalists of other genres such as Bing Crosby and Frank Sinatra also appeared with the big bands of Basie, Ellington, and Goodman.

Swing music swept the nation, offering upbeat rhythms and tunes that became immensely popular both on live radio broadcasts and in dance halls such as New York City's Savoy and Roseland Ballrooms and Los Angeles's Palomar Ballroom. In addition to the evolution of jazz instrumentation and notation, the technological advances in microphone manufacturing also allowed performers greater range of instrumental and vocal nuances.

Though dance bands and dance music had existed prior to the 1930's, the swing music of the decade differed from its musical predecessors in several ways. The style was immensely popular with all the people of what was still a largely racially segregated nation. Further, the style moved away from the string-orchestra instrumentation that characterized earlier incarnations of the dance band. In doing so, the genre began to rely more on brass and woodwind instrumentation with a pronounced percussion section with rhythmic nuances that were both innovative and unique. Also during this period, the piano began to be recognized as a solo instrument. Furthermore, jazz vocalists began to thrive. A growing reliance on improvisation also meant that the performers were of a higher caliber than those of amateur ensembles. Musicians had not only to read music but also to perform equally well as both a member of a tightly knit, larger unit and a sensational soloist. These characteristics were part of what contributed to the call-and-response style of swing music.

Despite the improvisation that characterized swing style, bandleaders often relied on well-arranged numbers that were actually used both to foster improvisation and to assist in maintaining unity during improvised solo sections. The level and amount of improvisation could vary drastically among different bands and bandleaders—especially if they were strong proponents of either the contrasting "sweet" or "hot" style. Swing music was met by resistance by those who believed the rhythms, occasionally risqué lyrics or themes, and African American associations were unacceptable. Swing music was also heavily tied to various dance forms of the day, including the lindy hop, shag, and jitterbug. Depending on the type of swing style that was performed, the different dances could produce a ballroom full of frenzied men and women dancing quickly and closely together in what many felt was reflective of a primitive and uncivilized culture. Nevertheless, swing music not only survived but also thrived in the United States and abroad.

Impact Popular music during the 1930's experienced rapid growth and development. Though the country was in the throes of the Great Depression, Americans found solace, respite, and escape in music. Technology—particularly phonographs and radios—helped to expose the country to various genres that influenced a distinct American popular culture. From hillbilly to folk, gospel, blues, jazz, and swing, American music during the 1930's was characterized by the vernacular influences of its diverse people and provided hope during a devastating period of economic hardship. Further, the styles that developed during the decade not only grew to influence subsequent musical genres and styles but also remain a fixture with subsequent music lovers in both their original forms and their adaptations.

Anastasia Pike

Further Reading

Crawford, Richard. *America's Musical Life: A History.* New York: W. W. Norton, 2001. Provides an account of American musical development within the relative historical context.

Garrett, Charles Hiroshi. *Struggling to Define a Nation: American Music and the Twentieth Century.* Berkeley: University of California Press, 2008. Examines the political and cultural implications of musical development in the United States.

Gourse, Leslie, ed. *The Billie Holiday Companion: Seven Decades of Commentary.* New York: Schirmer Books, 1995. Compendium of articles, essays, and reviews.

Starr, Larry, and Christopher Waterman. *American Popular Music: From Minstrelsy to MTV.* New York: Oxford University Press, 2003. Views the development of American popular music through the greater sociocultural and historical lens.

Sudhalter, Richard M. *Lost Chords: White Musicians and Their Contributions to Jazz, 1915-1945.* New York: Oxford University Press, 1999. Emphasizes the contributions of Caucasian musicians such as Goodman and the Dorsey brothers to the jazz genre.

Young, William H., and Nancy K. Young. *Music of the Great Depression.* Westport, Conn.: Greenwood Press, 2005. Provides a history of American popular music during the 1930's.

See also Basie, Count; Carter family; Dorsey, Tommy; Ellington, Duke; Goodman, Benny; Guthrie, Woody; Miller, Glenn; Music: Jazz; Radio in the United States; Sons of the Pioneers.

Musicals. See **Broadway musicals**

■ *Mutiny on the Bounty*

Identification Film about Great Britain's Royal
    Navy in the late eighteenth century
Director Frank Lloyd
Date Released on November 8, 1935

The first American cinematographic version of the 1789 incident aboard the British Royal Navy ship HMS Bounty, *the film* Mutiny on the Bounty *was a box-office blockbuster. The film was nominated for seven Academy Awards but received only one, for best picture. It was the first film in which all three main actors were nominated for the best-actor Oscar.*

Starring Charles Laughton, Clark Gable, and Franchot Tone and produced by Irving Thalberg for Metro-Goldwyn-Mayer, *Mutiny on the Bounty* is based on the first two books in a trilogy of novels written by Charles Nordhoff and James Norman Hall. Because the film was shot at seas, it was plagued by problems, including stars' seasickness. The most serious incident involved the accidental death of a cameraman.

The film recounts how the crew of the *Bounty*, under the leadership of Fletcher Christian, played by Gable, start a mutiny against their captain, William Bligh, played by Laughton, because of the many abuses he has inflicted upon them. Christian imprisons Bligh and gets control of the ship with the support of part of the crew. Eventually, he decides not to kill Bligh but leave him and those who support him in a boat adrift at sea. The film also recounts the subsequent trials.

The film is marred by a few historical inaccuracies, especially concerning the character of Bligh, who is presented as a cruel and vicious captain, so as to justify his crew's rebellion. Most of these mistakes,

In the historical drama Mutiny on the Bounty, *Fletcher Christian (Clark Gable, at left) confronts Captain William Bligh (Charles Laughton) on the deck of the HMS* Bounty. (Archive Photos/Getty Images)

however, are attributable to the fact that the film was not based on the historical events themselves but on the series of novels inspired by the events. Further changes were done by the scriptwriter to adapt the original characters to the characteristics of the actors playing them.

Impact   *Mutiny on the Bounty* has been remade twice—with the same title in 1962 and as *Bounty* in 1984. John Boyne's novel *Mutiny on the Bounty* (2008) recounts the same events from the point of view of Captain Bligh. The mutiny on the *Bounty* incident has also been the subject of a parody in the episode "The Wettest Stories Ever Told" of the animated television comedy *The Simpsons*.

M. Carmen Gomez-Galisteo

Further Reading

Alexander, Caroline. *The Bounty: The True Story of the Mutiny on the Bounty.* New York: HarperPerennial, 2004.

Bret, David. *Clark Gable: Tormented Star.* Cambridge, Mass.: Da Capo Press, 2008.

See also   Academy Awards; Film; Gable, Clark; Motion Picture Production Code; Thalberg, Irving.

■ Muzak

Definition   Company that provides background music services
Date   Established 1934

Muzak changed the way music was implemented in the daily lives of Americans. It was used to program mood, and its creation meant that most public spaces were filled with canned music.

The Telharmonium distributed music by telephone wires to New York City clients in 1906, and a music service over power lines was offered in Cleveland in 1929. Both were limited by available technology; however, music via phone line became practical in 1934, and Muzak Holdings LLC led the way.

The name Muzak was inspired by trademarks such as Kodak and Kleenex, though eventually it became viewed as a derogatory term, implying canned music and elevator music. During the 1930's, however, Muzak was considered to be a prestige service with little competition. Muzak was heard and generally welcomed in high-quality restaurants, shops, and offices. Fine dining meant a printed program of the evening's Muzak proudly displayed on each table.

Muzak was not random. It was programmed by psychological content for the time of day and was to be heard but not listened to, an unobtrusive aid to productivity. There was music for daytime shopping and business, for evening dining and dancing, and up-tempo selections to keep factory workers alert in the predawn hours.

Commercial recordings were never used. Instead, a dual-purpose record library was created. The Associated Recorded Program Service offered music of all types to radio stations, while appropriate selections doubled for use as Muzak, many of which fall into a forgotten classification known as "hotel music." The library's list of big-name performers of the 1930's includes the Dorsey Brothers, Victor Young, Andre Kostelanetz, Ray Noble, Morton Gould, Ben Selvin, Ozzie Nelson, Xavier Cugat, and Fats Waller, though most were not known outside New York, except perhaps on radio.

Muzak used a high-quality Western Electric recording process, developed from the Vitaphone motion-picture sound system of the 1920's. The 12- and 16-inch cherry-red vinyl discs played at 33-$\frac{1}{3}$ revolutions per minute, and the vertically modulated groove was traced by a sapphire stylus. Despite superior disc quality, the sound was compressed and bandwidth-limited when distributed as background music over leased telephone lines.

Impact   Muzak was successfully franchised beyond New York in 1939 and became international. Some complained that it replaced live musicians. Others considered the slow extinction of supper club orchestras as inevitable. Muzak's legacy includes fascinating and forgotten musical styles of the 1930's, preserved in its library.

Richard Simonton

Further Reading

Bellamy, Edward. *Looking Backward.* New York: Dover, 1996.

Lanza, Joseph. *Elevator Music: A Surreal History of Muzak, Easy-Listening, and Other Moodsong.* Rev. and expanded ed. Ann Arbor: University of Michigan Press, 2004.

See also   Dorsey, Tommy; Music: Popular; Radio in the United States; Recording industry.

N

NAACP. See **National Association for the Advancement of Colored People**

■ Nancy Drew novels

Identification   Series of mystery novels for young
readers
Date   Launched in 1930
Author   Carolyn Keene (pseudonym used by
different authors)

*Nancy Drew is the most enduring of the sleuthing heroes of
young-adult series books. She has been celebrated by the feminist movement as a role model. Although accurate sales figures for the early volumes of the series are incomplete, publishers claim the books, which have appeared in twenty-five
languages, have sold more copies worldwide than the mysteries of Agatha Christie.*

Nancy Drew was the brainchild of Edward Stratemeyer, founder of the Stratemeyer Syndicate, which
packaged series books for young people, written to
formula by a number of ghostwriters. Stratemeyer's
Hardy Boys books, from 1927, had been so successful
that he planned a similar series for girls. "Nan Drew"
was a name he initially proposed, but his publishers,
Grosset & Dunlap, settled on "Nancy Drew." Stratemeyer wrote plot outlines and devised titles for the
volumes.

Mildred Benson wrote the first four volumes to
Stratemeyer's specifications. They were published in
1930, under the name Carolyn Keene. Of the sixteen
volumes published during the decade, Benson
wrote all but three; Walter Karig became Carolyn
Keene for volumes eight through ten. Benson, who
received $125 per book, put much of her own per-
sonality into the vivacious, outspoken Nancy. Benson was an energetic midwestern journalist who piloted her own plane. Architectural interests took her
to Mayan ruins and canoe trips in Mexico.

From the first published volume, *The Secret of the
Old Clock* (1930), to the last volume of the decade,
The Clue of the Tapping Heels (1939), Nancy Drew lives
a charmed life. She is sixteen years old, relieved of
school attendance and parental oversight. Her single parent, Carson Drew, is a busy attorney, preoccupied with his own mysteries, which Nancy sometimes
has to solve for him. The housekeeper, Hannah
Gruen, provides domestic comforts when Nancy
rests from her escapades at the Drew home in midwestern River Heights, an idyllic town untouched by
the Depression. Nancy travels backcountry roads in
her blue roadster and, when danger threatens, carries her father's revolver. She never lacks for money,
wears beautiful clothes, and snacks in picturesque
tearooms. Police sometimes ask her for help, and
adults generally defer to her. Though she has little
interest in romance, her devoted boyfriend is Ned
Nickerson, a college athlete. Always ready to lend
their support in her perilous exploits are her best
girlfriends: Helen Corning, Bess Marvin, and George
Fayne. None of Nancy's friends resents her beauty,
privilege, and facility with horses, boats, the French
language, Morse Code, and anything else that comes
her way. Most of all, Nancy is skilled at sleuthing.
Though she finds herself frequently caught in underground passages; bound up in deserted cottages;
and threatened by vicious dogs, poisonous insects,
and an array of desperate criminals, she is never at
a loss. Every mystery is solved by the end of each
book, along with a teaser promoting the next series
volume.

The illustrations of the early books, by Russell H.
Tandy, a commercial fashion artist, added much to
their appeal and made the original volumes collector's items. Nancy has bobbed hair and wears cloche
hats, pearls, and shoes with high heels that are sharp
enough to tap out messages when she is held captive.
She comes equipped with gloves, handbags, and Art
Deco coats. The dust jackets invariably capture
Nancy in a dramatic moment, climbing the stairs in a
hidden passage or peeping in the broken window of
a deserted bungalow.

Impact   The early Nancy Drew volumes have been
attacked for their ethnic stereotypes of Jews, Eastern

Europeans, and African Americans. Later editions attempted to correct these problems, while making Nancy more conventional, if less interesting. Collectors prefer the original volumes. Nancy's adventures in River Heights helped readers escape the deprivations of the Depression and rumors of war. The fact that teachers and librarians found the books objectionable only added to their popularity. Nancy enabled young girls to believe they too could lead lives of achievement and adventure. Among the many accomplished women who have acknowledged the early influence of Nancy Drew are politician Hillary Clinton, opera singer Beverly Sills, television journalist Barbara Walters, former First Lady Laura Bush, and the first three women appointed to the U.S. Supreme Court.

Allene Phy-Olsen

Further Reading

Mason, Bobbie Ann. *The Girl Sleuth: A Feminist Guide.* Old Westbury, N.Y.: The Feminist Press, 1975.

Plunkett-Powell, Karen. *The Nancy Drew Scrapbook.* New York: St. Martin's Press, 1993.

Rehak, Melanie. *Girl Sleuth: Nancy Drew and the Women Who Created Her.* New York: Harcourt, 2005.

See also African Americans; Anti-Semitism; Great Depression in the United States; Literature in the United States; Recreation.

■ Nation of Islam

Identification American-based Muslim religious organization
Date Founded in July, 1930
Place Detroit, Michigan

Established during a period of African American migration out of the South and growing economic disparities between the races, worsened by the Great Depression, the Nation of Islam represents an important strain of African American nationalism. It served the religious and political needs of many African Americans during the 1930's by espousing freedom and justice for black people, and it would become one of the most important African American institutions in later decades as well.

The exact beginnings of the Nation of Islam (adherents call themselves Muslims) are not clearly recorded. The founder, Wallace Dodd Fard (also

known as Wallace Fard Muhammad), spread word of his variant of Islam through door-to-door sales in Detroit among dispossessed blacks, beginning in July, 1930. Fard initially used the Bible to teach about Islam as the religion of black people in Asia and Africa, and eventually he introduced followers to the Qur'ān, the holy book of Islam. At its inception, the Nation of Islam held religious meetings in private homes. Within three years, as a result of the religion's rapid growth, Fard was holding temple meetings in a hall and had established Muslim schools for children in Detroit.

Mainstream Muslims regard the Nation of Islam as a separatist Islamic sect. Fard's religious doctrines were heavily infused with racial ideologies (though the exact racial lineage of Fard himself remains debated and unknown). Among its tenets, the Nation of Islam teaches that black people are the original humans and Caucasians the result of the workings of a mad scientist named Yakub. Likened to "devils," white people, the Nation of Islam argued, were inferior to black people. Shortly after its founding, the Nation of Islam attracted controversy for some of its more inflammatory racial teachings. Fard taught his followers that one could be ensured salvation through Mecca by sacrificing (murdering) four "white devils." In 1932 and 1933, the Nation of Islam attracted much attention from the Detroit police over this tenet, and rumors of at least one sacrifice persist to this day, though the tenet is omitted from modern teachings.

Fard disappeared from the organization sometime during 1933 or 1934. Speculation arose that he had been murdered. Historians have deemed this unlikely, but stories have circulated about his subsequent whereabouts for decades. Since 1931, Fard had been grooming a convert, Elijah Poole (who later was given a Muslim name, Elijah Muhammad), for ministry in the Nation of Islam. After Fard's disappearance, Muhammad continued to preach throughout the United States, predominantly in the North and in Washington, D.C., proselytizing according to the doctrine he had learned from Fard. These messages were passed down in written form in *The Supreme Wisdom* (1957) and included the belief in one god (Allah), the holy Qur'ān, and the Bible. The Nation of Islam experienced internal fractures during this time and was threatened by outside attempts to weaken the organization, including efforts from the Communist Party USA and the Japanese.

Who Was Wallace D. Fard?

The first prophet of the Nation of Islam is shrouded in mystery: His national origins, his real name, and the circumstances of his 1934 disappearance are not fully known, but an FBI memorandum from Special Agent Edwin O. Raudsep, dated March 8, 1965 (approximately three decades after Fard's death), rehearses the known facts about Fard at that time.

[Wallace] Dodd arrived in the United States from New Zealand in 1913, settled briefly in Portland, Oregon. He married but abandoned his wife and infant son. He lingered in the Seattle Area as Fred Dodd for a few months, then moved to Los Angeles and opened a restaurant at 803 W. Third Street as Wallace D. Ford. He was arrested for bootlegging in January, 1926; served a brief jail sentence (also as Wallace D. Ford)—identified on record as white.

On June 12, 1926, also as Ford, was sentenced to San Quentin for sale of narcotics at his restaurant; got 6-months to 6-years sentence—released from San Quentin May 27, 1929. Prison record lists him as Caucasian.

After release, went to Chicago, then to Detroit as a silk peddler. His customers were mostly Negro and he himself posed as a Negro. He prided himself as a biblical authority and mathematician.

When Elijah Muhammad (Poole) met him, he was passing himself off as a savior and claiming that he was born in Mecca and had arrived in the U.S. on July 4, 1930.

In 1933 there was a scandal revolving about the sect involving a "human sacrifice" which may or may not have been trumped up. At any rate, the leader was arrested May 25, 1933, under the name Fard with 8 other listed aliases (W. D. Farrad, Wallace Farad, Walt Farrad, Prof. Ford, etc.). The official report says Dodd admitted that his teachings were "strictly a racket" and he was "getting all the money out of it he could." He was ordered out of Detroit.

[In a] newspaper article which appeared in the *San Francisco Examiner* and the *Los Angeles Examiner* on July 28, 1963, reporter Ed Montgomery... claimed to have contacted Dodd's former common law wife.... According to this account, Dodd went to Chicago after leaving Detroit and became a traveling suit salesman for a mail order tailer [*sic*]. In this position he worked himself across the midwest and ultimately arrived in Los Angeles in the spring of 1934 in a new car and wearing flowing white robes. He tried to work out a reconciliation with the woman, but she would not agree to one.... He stayed in Los Angeles for two weeks, frequently visiting his son. Then he sold his car and boarded a ship bound for New Zealand where he said he would visit relatives.

On Sunday, February 28, 1965, Ed Montgomery wrote a rehash of the above in which he said the Muslims claim "police and San Quentin Prison records dating back to the early 1920's had been altered and that fingerprints identifying Farad as Dodd had been doctored." Elijah Mohummad [*sic*] said he would have posted $100,000 reward "for any person who could prove Farad and Dodd were one and the same person." Ten days later Muhammad's office in Chicago was advised Farad's common law wife and a blood relative were prepared to establish the truth of Farad's identity. The $100,000 never was placed in escrow and the matter was dropped forthwith.

In 1942, Muhammad headquartered the Nation of Islam in Chicago and started the arduous task of rebuilding the membership, which had begun to dwindle during the latter half of the 1930's. In the 1950's, the organization gained public attention once again when Malcolm X took a position as its national spokesman, until he broke with the Nation of Islam in 1964. Elijah Muhammad retained control of the organization until his death in 1975.

Impact During a time of great economic and racial difficulty for northern blacks, many of whom had found their prospects for economic and social equality little improved after migrating north from the South, the Nation of Islam proved to be an important religious and political vehicle within the African American community. Initial memberships spread quickly after an ambiguous start in urban Detroit. A uniquely American version of Islam, the Nation of Islam had special resonance for racially and economically dispossessed African Americans in the 1930's. The message of hope and equality espoused by the Nation of Islam became an important vein of African American nationalism throughout 1950's and 1960's.

Sadie Pendaz

Further Reading

Lee, Martha F. *The Nation of Islam: An American Millenarian Movement.* New York: Syracuse University Press, 1996.

Lincoln, C. Eric. *The Black Muslims in America.* Grand Rapids, Mich.: Wm. B. Eerdmans, 1994.

Muhammad, Elija. *The Supreme Wisdom.* 2 vols. Atlanta, Ga.: Messenger Elijah Muhammad Propagation Society, 1957.

Walker, Dennis. *Islam and the Search for African-American Nationhood: Elijah Muhammad, Louis Farrakhan, and the Nation of Islam.* Atlanta, Ga.: Clarity Press, 2005.

See also African Americans; Great Depression in the United States; Jim Crow segregation; Migrations, domestic; Religion in the United States.

■ National Association for the Advancement of Colored People

Identification Civil rights advocacy organization
Date Founded on February 12, 1909

The National Association for the Advancement of Colored People (NAACP) began as a grassroots organization in response to increased violence against African Americans. Throughout its existence, the NAACP has worked primarily through the U.S. legal system in its campaign to help African Americans gain equal civil rights.

The 1930's were a turbulent time for race relations in the United States. The increased presence of African Americans in southern cities resulted in heightened tension between the African Americans and Caucasians. As more and more African Americans moved north, these tensions increased in northern cities as well. The NAACP's principal objective was to ensure the political, educational, social, and economic equality of all citizens of the United States, regardless of race. The organization used the democratic processes of lobbying and litigation in an effort to remove what it considered to be the three major evils of discrimination against African Americans—school segregation, lynching, and Jim Crow laws that legalized segregation in the South.

Fighting Discrimination Through the Courts and Congress In 1930, with meager resources and personnel, the NAACP launched its first successful protest, challenging President Herbert Hoover's nomination for the U.S. Supreme Court. The NAACP opposed the nomination of U.S. Circuit Court judge John J. Parker of North Carolina because he supported laws that discriminated against African Americans. When President Hoover refused to withdraw Parker's name, the NAACP launched a massive six-week campaign to prevent his confirmation by the U.S. Senate. Senators received numerous wires, letters, and telephone calls from NAACP branches across the country and received pressure from African American newspapers, important segments of the white press, and organized labor. As a result of the NAACP's efforts, Judge Parker failed to receive Senate confirmation by a vote of 41-39.

The NAACP staged a coordinated strategy of legal battles in its campaign to end racial segregation in the nation's schools. It took states and counties to court to force them to abide by the Supreme Court's decision in *Plessy v. Ferguson* (1896), which ruled that segregation was permissible only if the separate facilities for African Americans were equal to those for Caucasians. This legal strategy forced states, counties, and municipalities either to abandon segregation or to incur the costs of providing truly equal facilities, a practically impossible undertaking during the Depression.

For its early litigation efforts, the NAACP relied on lawyers who volunteered their services. However, by the 1930's, it was able to hire its own legal team, which consisted of Charles Hamilton Houston, the dean of Howard University School of Law, and Thurgood Marshall, who argued many cases before the U.S. Supreme Court. In 1967, he became the first African American Supreme Court associate justice. The NAACP's legal strategy worked. In 1936, the NAACP won a lawsuit that resulted in the desegregation of the University of Maryland School of Law, and in 01938, another NAACP lawsuit caused the Supreme Court to order the admission of an African American student to the University of Missouri School of Law.

Fighting to End Lynching and to Protect Voting Rights

While lynchings peaked during the 1890's, an upsurge in lynchings of African Americans occurred during the 1930's, perhaps because of frustrations unleashed by the Depression. The NAACP had concentrated its attention on the lynching epidemic sweeping the nation in the first two decades of the twentieth century but renewed its efforts for a federal antilynching law after a series of highly publicized lynchings in Ala-

The National Association for the Advancement of Colored People fought to end the racial segregation—represented by this "white-only" restaurant sign in Lancaster, Ohio—prevalent in most parts of the United States. (Library of Congress)

bama, Maryland, Indiana, and California. The Communist Party USA launched its own antilynching campaign. However, opposition from southern Democrats blocked the passage of such a law. The U.S. House of Representatives had passed the bill despite the opposition of all but one southern member. The U.S. Senate, however, carried out a six-week-long filibuster that resulted in the withdrawal of the bill in February, 1938. Although unsuccessful in its efforts to encourage a federal law to be passed, the NAACP brought public attention to the brutality of lynching and helped to significantly reduce its occurrence, and states began to pass their own antilynching laws.

The NAACP also was devoted to ending racial discrimination at the voting booth. Even though African American males were guaranteed the right to vote by the Fifteenth Amendment, which had been ratified in 1870 shortly after the end of the Civil War, states and local municipalities continued to use various elaborate tactics to prevent African Americans from voting. All-white state, county, and local police forces routinely intimidated, harassed, and even arrested African American voters. Throughout the South, African Americans faced losing their homes or their jobs if they tried to exercise their constitutional right to vote. If intimidation and economic pressure did not work, white mobs turned to vio-

lence that included cross burnings, church burnings, arson of African American businesses and homes, and even murder and lynchings. The NAACP lobbied for laws that would not only outlaw these discriminatory tactics but also ban the use of poll taxes and literacy tests to deny African Americans their voting rights. The NAACP suffered a setback in its bid for equal voting rights when in 1937 a unanimous U.S. Supreme Court upheld as constitutional state poll-tax laws. Because many African Americans could not afford to pay poll taxes, they were effectively denied the right to vote. The NAACP continued its voting rights campaign throughout the 1930's, but another thirty years passed before southern states were forced to abandon these discriminatory tactics.

Fighting Discrimination During the Depression

The Great Depression of the 1930's created havoc inside and outside the NAACP. While all Americans suffered during the Depression, the economic situation was particularly disastrous for African Americans. The Harlem Renaissance and the exuberance of the Roaring Twenties were over. In addition to its other civil rights activities, the NAACP had to focus on ways to win jobs for African Americans and end discriminatory hiring practices. With white middle-class income drastically reduced, almost one-half million African American women who worked cleaning white families' homes found themselves without jobs. In the South, hungry Caucasians began to take jobs that had been traditionally held by African Americans. Bellhops and other African American workers were fired so that Caucasians could have their jobs.

At the peak of the Depression, a majority of African American workers were on government relief. The Works Progress Administration (renamed the Works Projects Administration in 1939) and other government agencies created by the New Deal to help U.S. citizens affected by the Depression often discriminated against African Americans. Private charities—even some religious organizations—also found ways of favoring needy Caucasians over needy African Americans and some soup kitchens and breadlines turned away African American families.

Despite a sharp decline in its membership as a result of the Depression, the NAACP still managed to continue its civil-rights mission. It successfully opposed southern plans to close down relief projects in order to force African Americans into picking cotton for considerably low wages. NAACP executive secretary Walter White, who was a friend and adviser to First Lady Eleanor Roosevelt, met with her often in attempts to persuade President Franklin D. Roosevelt to outlaw job discrimination in the armed forces, defense industries, and the agencies spawned by Roosevelt's New Deal legislation. Roosevelt did not publicly support civil rights for African Americans, and his administration was silent on the issue until the late 1930's, when Eleanor Roosevelt began to speak up on behalf of African Americans.

The NAACP's other activities ranged from supporting a student strike at Fisk University in Nashville, Tennessee, to challenging the exclusion of African Americans from juries. The NAACP represented African Americans accused of crimes, which included its help with the defense of nine African American boys, aged fourteen to twenty, later known as the "Scottsboro Boys," who were charged with raping two white women on a freight train in Scottsboro, Alabama. The NAACP also fought against Jim Crow-segregated cars on railroads and street railways and segregated neighborhoods and for the right for African Americans to belong to trade unions. The NAACP also opposed vigorously the unequal salaries paid to African American public school teachers. The association was successful in preventing the exclusion of African American Boy Scouts from the 1937 Scout Jamboree held in Washington, D.C. In 1939, the Daughters of the American Revolution refused permission for famous opera singer Marian Anderson to sing to an integrated audience in Constitution Hall in Washington, D.C., because it did not allow African Americans to perform there. The NAACP, with the aid of the Roosevelts, was able to arrange an open-air concert for her on the steps of the Lincoln Memorial. On Easter Sunday in 1939, Anderson performed to a crowd of more than seventy-five thousand people of all colors and to a radio audience of millions.

Throughout the 1930's the NAACP mounted scores of investigations and court actions that challenged efforts to deny African Americans the civil rights that were guaranteed to all U.S. citizens under the Thirteenth, Fourteenth, and Fifteenth Amendments to the U.S. Constitution. The NAACP during the 1930's was relentless in keeping the issues of race discrimination in the public eye. By the end of the decade, the NAACP had begun to realize the fruit of its labor with important legal victories and its increasing influence nationally and internationally.

Impact   The NAACP's forceful and persistent litigation and civil rights activism during the 1930's ultimately resulted in the U.S. Supreme Court overthrowing its "separate but equal" doctrine for public schools with its 1954 landmark ruling in *Brown v. the Board of the Education*. The NAACP's lobbying efforts and legal challenges continued throughout the Civil Rights movement of the 1950's and 1960's and resulted in the eventual passage of a number of laws designed to stop racial inequality in the areas of civil rights, voting rights, and housing.

Eddith A. Dashiell

Further Reading

Jones, Gilbert. *Freedom's Sword: The NAACP and the Struggle Against Racism, 1909-1969*. New York: Routledge, 2005.

Rhym, Darren. *The NAACP.* Philadelphia: Chelsea House, 2002.

Santella, Andrew. *The NAACP: An Organization Working to End Discrimination.* Chanhassen, Minn.: Child's World, 2004.

Sullivan, Patricia. *Lift Every Voice: The NAACP and the Making of the Civil Rights Movement.* New York: New Press, 2009.

Tushnet, Mark V. *The NAACP's Legal Strategy Against*

Segregating Education, 1925-1950. Chapel Hill: University of North Carolina Press, 2005.

Zangrando, Robert L. *The NAACP Crusade Against Lynching, 1909-1950.* Philadelphia: Temple University Press, 1980.

See also Anderson, Marian; Bethune, Mary McLeod; *Breedlove v. Suttles*; Civil rights and liberties in the United States; Du Bois, W. E. B.; Jim Crow segregation; Lynching; *Missouri ex rel. Gaines v. Canada*; Race riots; Racial discrimination; Scottsboro trials; Supreme Court, U.S.; Voting rights.

■ National Association of Manufacturers

Identification Business interest group formed to promote the growth of American industry

Date Established in 1895

The National Association of Manufacturers (NAM) has been one of the most powerful and important business interest groups in the United States. During the economic turmoil of the 1930's the organization undertook a massive public-relations campaign highlighting the strengths of American business.

Since its late nineteenth century founding in Cincinnati, Ohio, the NAM has consistently been one of the most powerful broad-based business interest groups in the United States. The NAM was originally conceived as an umbrella interest organization for manufacturers during the recessionary 1890's. Following the prosperous 1920's, the NAM was forced to return to its roots as an advocate for a befallen industrial base. During the 1930's, Franklin D. Roosevelt's New Deal expanded the federal government to cope with the shrinking U.S. economy and, in the following decade, the heavy demands of World War II. This increased government activity took the form of bureaucratic hiring and spending and expanded regulation and oversight of business not seen since the Progressive Era.

American manufacturing concerns, which had enjoyed a position of societal leadership in the preceding decades and would during the postwar boom of the 1950's, were threatened and entrenched during the 1930's. This collective anxiety prompted the NAM to spend the decade in a defensive posture. The group's strategy was to launch a massive, multi-million-dollar public-relations campaign not selling particular products, such as laundry soap or small appliances, but selling the broadly conceived idea of American business. The group transformed into a public-relations firm for what it called at the time "the American way of life," a euphemism for positioning business at the vanguard of U.S. society.

The NAM aimed for private-sector businesses and not the Roosevelt administration to hold the controlling interest in the United States. Actions by the NAM during the 1930's solidified the bond between conservative political ideology and the corporate lobby. For example, the NAM sponsored conservative radio commentators in most major media markets. It even launched its own radio program, called *The American Family Robinson*, that highlighted the regulatory misdeeds of what the NAM considered to be the overactive Roosevelt administration. Specifically, the NAM took issue with pro-labor collective-bargaining policies, a shortened workday, and increases in the minimum rate of pay.

Impact In NAM-produced short films and newspaper ads, interventionist government policies were painted as enemies of the common working man. At first blush, the NAM could have been seen as an elite organization composed of capital-driven organizations, but the group did not present itself that way while making its policy points. It was a strong advocate for business leaders but also relayed the message of solidarity with everyday working Americans.

R. Matthew Beverlin

Further Reading

Fones-Wolf, Elizabeth. "Creating a Favorable Business Climate: Corporations and Radio Broadcasting, 1934 to 1954." *Business History Review* 73 (Summer, 1999): 221-255.

Soffer, Jonathan. "The National Association of Manufacturers and the Militarization of American Conservatism." *Business History Review* 75 (Winter, 2001): 775-805.

Tedlow, Richard S. "The National Association of Manufacturers and Public Relations During the New Deal." *Business History Review* 50, no. 1 (1976): 25-45.

See also Advertising in the United States; Business and the economy in the United States; Great Depression in the United States; New Deal; Recession of 1937-1938; Unemployment in the United States.

■ National Baseball Hall of Fame

The Event The National Baseball Hall of Fame
and Museum was created to preserve the history
of Major League Baseball

Date Opened to the public on June 12, 1939

*The National Baseball Hall of Fame and Museum was es-
tablished to showcase legends of baseball and to display
baseball memorabilia.*

The National Baseball Hall of Fame and Museum
was inaugurated in 1939 to commemorate the one
hundredth anniversary of baseball's invention in
Cooperstown, New York. The myth that Abner
Doubleday invented baseball in Cooperstown, New
York, was perpetuated by Albert Goodwill Spalding,
sporting goods magnate, in 1905.

To commemorate baseball as the national game
of the United States, Alexander Cleland spear-
headed the creation of a hall of fame and museum
devoted to baseball. As a result of the Work Relief
Program, a dilapidated baseball field named Doubleday Field was renovated in Cooperstown. Opened
on September 6, 1920, to memorialize the site where
baseball was originally played, the field reopened on
August 3, 1934. In October, 1934, Cleland was appointed by the trustees of Cooperstown to promote
the development of a baseball shrine next to
Doubleday Field. Cooperstown officials realized the
potential of making Cooperstown a tourist destination for baseball fans.

Cleland appealed to the governing bodies of the
National and American Leagues to support the construction of a baseball shrine next to Doubleday

*Members of the National Baseball Hall of Fame posing at New York City's Polo Grounds in 1939. Clockwise from the top left: Harry
Hooper, Eddie Collins, Roger Bresnahan, Connie Mack, Bill Klem, Nap Lajoie, George Sisler, Tris Speaker, Walter Johnson, Babe Ruth,
Frankie Frisch, and Honus Wagner. (Getty Images)*

Field. Officials of Major League Baseball supported the concept as a means to address the dwindling attendance that baseball was experiencing as a result of the Depression.

As part of the baseball shrine, Cleland persuaded the Baseball Writers Association of America to come up with names of baseball greats to induct into the hall of fame. In 1936, the first five players were elected: Ty Cobb, Babe Ruth, Honus Wagner, Christy Mathewson, and Walter Johnson. By 1939, a total of twenty-five inductees had been selected.

Impact The National Baseball Hall of Fame and Museum became one of the premier sport shrines in the world and a pilgrimage for multiple generations of baseball fans. Approximately 350,000 visitors enter the museum each year.

Alar Lipping

Further Reading

Chafets, Ze'ev. *Cooperstown Confidential: Heroes, Rogues, and the Inside Story of the Baseball Hall of Fame.* New York: Bloomsbury, 2009.

Reisler, Jim. *A Great Day in Cooperstown: The Improbable Birth of Baseball's Hall of Fame.* New York: Carroll & Graf, 2006.

Vlasich, James A. *A Legend for the Legendary: The Origin of the Baseball Hall of Fame.* Bowling Green, Ohio: Bowling Green State University Popular Press, 1990.

See also Baseball; Gehrig, Lou; Negro Leagues; Ruth, Babe; Sports in the United States.

■ National Council of Negro Women

Identification Organization promoting African American women's rights, interests, and success as leaders
Date Established on December 5, 1935

The National Council of Negro Women (NCNW) brought together leaders of major black women's groups to work on issues affecting them during the Depression and afterward. Cooperating with the National Association for the Advancement of Colored People and the National Urban League, which had mostly male leadership, the NCNW addressed the combined problems of sexism and racism that distinctly affected black women.

During the 1930's, African American women built upon a strong legacy of activism against racism and segregation. To expand their influence during the 1890's, black women had formed the National Federation of Afro-American Women and the National League of Colored Women. These groups combined in 1896 as the National Association for Colored Women (NACW), which had more than 100,000 members by the mid-1920's. The Depression weakened the NACW financially, reducing the organization's effectiveness. To build more powerful leadership for black women, Mary McLeod Bethune, who was the NACW president from 1924 to 1928, began in 1930 to consult with directors of more than two dozen organizations for black women (including the NACW) and promote a forum for their work. The result was the establishment of the National Council for Negro Women with Bethune as its first president and Washington, D.C., as its home.

The pursuit of direct power for black women in American society was a hallmark of NCNW activism throughout the 1930's. Bethune strongly supported President Franklin D. Roosevelt's administration and guided the NCNW toward a prominent role in the federal government. The organization hosted a national conference in April of 1938 to focus on improving the government's attention to black women and children. More than sixty black women leaders met with members of the Roosevelt administration, lobbying for increased involvement for black women regarding New Deal programs that affected African Americans.

Impact The NCNW grew steadily under Bethune, who retired as president in 1949. Subsequent leaders, especially Dorothy Height, who was president from 1957 to 1998, guided the organization to prominence as a well-funded, widely honored network, uniting approximately forty groups with more than 240 active sections. It has actively promoted the civil rights, education, employment, and historical memorialization of African American women since its inception and continues such work in the twenty-first century in selected African nations and in the United States.

Beth Kraig

Further Reading

Giddings, Paula. *Where and When I Enter: The Impact of Black Women on Race and Sex in America.* New York: Morrow, 1984.

Height, Dorothy. *Open Wide the Freedom Gates: A Memoir.* New York: PublicAffairs, 2005.

See also African Americans; Bethune, Mary McLeod; Jim Crow segregation; National Association for the Advancement of Colored People; Racial discrimination; Voting rights.

■ National debt

Definition All bonds and other debt securities issued by the U.S. Treasury to finance government deficits

Reluctance by U.S. government leaders to increase the national debt led to a conviction that taxes should be raised to cover prospective increases in expenditure. This conviction, which persisted until the late 1930's, conflicted with the goal of using federal fiscal policies to stimulate increase in aggregate demand.

At the beginning of 1930, the national debt of the United States amounted to $16.3 billion. This was from the government's bond issues to finance World War I. During the 1920's, federal tax rates were set high enough to generate annual surpluses that steadily reduced the national debt. With the onset of the Great Depression, government revenues declined. Revenue from taxes on incomes and profits fell from $2.4 billion in fiscal year 1930 to only $746 million in fiscal year 1933. Some debt reduction occurred in 1930, but then the debt began to rise, particularly because the pressure for increased government expenditure was strong. Alarmed by the rising debt, President Herbert Hoover approved the largest peacetime tax increase in American history in 1932.

During his successful campaign for the presidency in 1932, Franklin D. Roosevelt condemned the deficit spending and increased debt occurring under Hoover. Initially after taking office, Roosevelt reduced federal spending, but this was soon reversed. Federal spending in 1935 was almost double what it had been in 1933.

Even though federal tax rates increased almost every year after 1933, deficits persisted. The national debt increased from approximately $21 billion at the end of 1932 to $42 billion by the end of 1939.

In general, the most immediate burden of the national debt is the interest that must be paid. In fiscal year 1930, the government spent $659 million on interest. Because of the great decline in interest rates during the Depression, interest costs rose to only $941 in fiscal year 1939. Most of the national debt in 1930 was in long-term marketable bonds. As these matured, new issues were made to replace them. Because short-term interest rates declined more than long-term rates during the 1930's, the Treasury relied heavily on short-term securities in its refunding operations. Treasury bills, introduced in 1929 with maturities as short as thirty days, were sold at a discount from the round-number redemption value. The discount represented the interest paid. By June, 1935, about one-half of the national debt had maturities of five years or less. In 1935, the government introduced nonmarketable U.S. savings bonds.

Because of the low risk of default, interest rates on Treasury securities have generally been lower than other notes and bonds. The persistence of economic

Leaders of the Social Security Advisory Council meet in Washington, D.C., in 1937, to discuss potential alterations to the Social Security Act. Reducing the national debt was an integral function of the act. From left to right: Gerard Swope, president of General Electric Company; Philip Murray, head of the Congress of Industrial Organizations; and E. R. Stettin, head of U.S. Steel Corporation. (Library of Congress)

depression and unemployment led to low rates on Treasury issues. Yields on Treasury bonds remained between 3 and 4 percent in the turbulent early 1930's, then declined steadily to 2.4 percent in 1939. From mid-1933 through 1939, Treasury bills yielded less than 1 percent per year.

The Social Security Act of 1935 provided for the collection of a wage tax to finance the payment of retirement pensions. Fiscal conservatism led to the arrangement in which the tax revenues came in first and pension payments began later. The revenue surplus was to be invested in a special issue of government bonds, paying interest into a trust fund, and redeemable as needed to pay pensions. By the end of 1939, trust-fund assets totaled $1.7 billion.

Impact The negative attitude toward increasing the national debt contributed to the overly conservative tone of New Deal fiscal policy. In combination, Keynesian economics and the recession of 1937-1938 persuaded Roosevelt and his advisers that large deficits were appropriate to stimulate aggregate demand and reduce unemployment—as they did from 1939 to 1944.

While government securities are a liability to the government (and the taxpayers), they are an asset to the investors who hold them. Because of their safety and liquidity, they have become standard investments for many financial institutions. They are the medium through which the Federal Reserve conducts open-market operations. By the end of 1939, the Fed held $2.5 billion of Treasury securities. The savings bonds introduced during the 1930's became a major financial resource during World War II.

Paul B. Trescott

Further Reading

Homer, Sidney, and Richard Sylla. *A History of Interest Rates.* 4th ed. New York: John Wiley & Sons, 2005.

Kimmel, Louis H. *Federal Budget and Fiscal Policy.* Washington, D.C.: Brookings Institution, 1959.

Markham, Jerry W. *A Financial History of the United States.* Armonk, N.Y.: M. E. Sharpe, 2002.

Stein, Herbert. *The Fiscal Revolution in America.* Chicago: University of Chicago Press, 1969.

Villard, Henry H. *Deficit Spending and the National Income.* New York: Farrar and Rinehart, 1941.

See also Credit and debt; Great Depression in the United States; Hoover, Herbert; New Deal; Roosevelt, Franklin D.

■ National Film Act of 1939 (Canada)

The Law Legislation designed to initiate and promote the production and distribution of films in the national interest of Canada

Date May 2, 1939

The National Film Act of 1939 created the National Film Board of Canada, which promoted wartime propaganda films in its early years. It remains a leading force in film production of Canadian cultural and social themes.

In 1938, Canadian high commissioner to London Vincent Massey and his secretary, Ross McLean, identified the need to improve the quality of Canadian films produced by the Canadian Government Motion Picture Bureau. In June, 1938, after British filmmaker John Grierson was commissioned to survey the film industry, a report was released recommending both legislation and a central body for the film industry. On May 2, 1939, the National Film Board was established through the National Film Act. This act was designed to "initiate and promote the production and distribution of films in the national interest" of Canada as well as promote a positive image of Canada internationally. Grierson was appointed the first government film commissioner.

By the end of the 1930's, the National Film Board moved away from its initial mission of coordinating film-related activities within government departments and promoting strong Canadian identity in film to producing and promoting patriotic films in support of war efforts. It also expanded its focus from traditional film production to include the creation of animated filmstrips.

Impact The National Film Act of 1939 expanded and adjusted its mission throughout the years and underwent major revisions in 1950, 1970, and 1985 to address the need for inclusion of French-language works, female-originated projects, and television programming. Films produced by the National Film Board have garnered more than forty-five hundred awards and more than sixty-nine Academy Award nominations. Although its impact has waned over the years, it was once one of the largest and most influential government-controlled film producers in the world.

Tom Smith

Further Reading

Evans, Gary. *In the National Interest: A Chronicle of the National Film Board of Canada from 1949-1989.* Toronto: University of Toronto Press, 1991.

Khouri, Malek. *Filming Politics: Communism and the Portrayal of the Working Class at the National Film Board of Canada, 1939-1946.* Calgary, Alta.: University of Calgary Press, 2007.

Waugh, Thomas, Michael B. Baker, and Ezra Winton. *Challenge for Change: Activist Documentary at the National Film Board of Canada.* Montreal: McGill-Queen's University Press, 2010.

See also Academy Awards; Film; Great Depression in Canada; World War II and Canada.

■ National Firearms Act of 1934

The Law Federal law imposing a tax and a registration requirement on certain types of guns
Date Became law June 26, 1934
Also known as NFA

The first major federal gun-control law, the National Firearms Act (NFA) imposed what was at the time a heavy tax of two hundred dollars on machine guns and some other weapons. The tax burden significantly slowed, but did not eliminate, acquisition of such weapons by Americans.

Alcohol prohibition in the 1920's and early 1930's had resulted in a proliferation of organized crime. The bootlegging gangsters sometimes shot one another, most spectacularly with Thompson submachine guns—a portable automatic rifle. Many famous bank robberies occurred during the 1930's, including some by Machine Gun Kelly and John Dillinger, who used Thompsons.

Accordingly, the Franklin D. Roosevelt presidential administration proposed the NFA, which required the owners and future acquirers of certain weapons to pay a federal tax and to federally register their guns. Attorney General Homer S. Cummings told the House Ways and Means Committee that the administration had chosen to use tax power because an outright ban would violate the Second Amendment.

As originally proposed, the NFA also applied to handguns. At the request of the National Rifle Association (NRA), handguns were removed from the bill, and with NRA consent, the revised NFA was adopted with little controversy. The NFA has been amended over the years.

Impact The NFA was constitutionally tested and upheld by a unanimous Supreme Court during the 1939 case of *United States v. Miller.* Following a line of state constitutional law cases from the twentieth century, *Miller* held that not all firearms are necessarily protected by the Second Amendment.

The NFA tactic of using the federal tax power to assert federal control over intrastate activity was copied by the Marihuana Tax Act of 1937, the Federal Firearms Act (FFA) of 1938, and by many subsequent laws. After the NFA settled the machine-gun issue, and the FFA imposed some restrictions on licensed dealers, the gun-control issue lay mostly dormant until the 1960's.

David B. Kopel

Further Reading

Carter, Gregg Lee. *Guns in American Society: An Encyclopedia of History, Politics, Culture, and the Law.* Santa Barbara, Calif.: ABC-Clio, 2002.

Frye, Brian. "The Peculiar Story of *United States v. Miller.*" *NYU Journal of Law and Liberty* 3, no. 1 (2008): 48-82.

See also Civil rights and liberties in the United States; Dillinger, John; Kelly, Machine Gun; Marihuana Tax Act of 1937; Organized crime; Roosevelt, Franklin D.; Supreme Court, U.S.

National Foundation for Infantile Paralysis.
See **March of Dimes**

■ National Industrial Recovery Act of 1933

The Law Federal legislation that created the National Recovery Administration to negotiate codes of fair competition with individual industries
Also known as NIRA
Date June 16, 1933

From a businessperson's perspective, the Great Depression resulted from excess supply of goods and unfair competition and price-cutting. The NIRA codes were intended to permit firms to join together to reduce competition.

The NIRA came in three parts. Title I contained the law's special features. It created a National Recovery Administration (NRA) with the responsibility of convening representatives of individual industries and working with each to develop a code of fair competition. Once a code was approved, it had the force of law and was exempted from the antitrust laws. Each code was required to contain provisions establishing minimum wages and maximum hours for labor. Section 7a established the right of workers to join unions and bargain collectively.

Title II provided for a program of public-works expenditures of $3.3 billion, to be financed by taxes on capital stock and "excess profits" provided in Title III. The expenditures were a sensible way to increase aggregate demand. However, their potentially expansionary effect was largely offset by the tax increases.

The NRA began with an intense publicity blitz. Its symbol was the blue eagle; its motto was "we do our part." General Hugh S. Johnson was appointed the first administrator of the NRA. According to President Franklin D. Roosevelt, the intention of the NIRA was to ensure a shortened workweek and competitive wages for workers to "prevent unfair competition and disastrous overproduction."

Trade associations and labor unions were actively involved in developing the codes. The first approved was for the cotton textile industry. Over its lifetime, the NRA approved 557 basic and 189 supplementary industry codes, covering about 95 percent of industrial employers.

The code negotiations were dominated by the largest firms, but there were often bitter disagreements on details. Labor unions were quick to press for the enlargement of their membership and influence. However, many employers evaded the spirit of section 7a by developing company unions that could be dominated by the employer. By the spring of 1934, one-fourth of all industrial workers worked in plants where there was a company union. Section 7a inspired greater militancy by labor unions. The number of workers involved in labor disputes increased sharply, rising from 324,000 in 1932 to 1.2 million in 1933.

A major goal of the codes was to prevent further price reductions and, if possible, to gain increased product prices. Some codes achieved this by prescribing "standard costs" on which firms were supposed to base their selling prices. Some codes provided that each firm's prices be publicized. Other codes limited the number of hours of plant operation—the pioneer cotton-textile code restricted machinery operation to two, forty-hour shifts a week. Some codes assigned production quotas to individual firms.

Wholesale prices of nonfarm products rose sharply after March, 1933, rising about 10 percent by October of the same year. Business expectations of price increases led many firms to add to their inventories. Industrial production experienced a sharp rise from March, 1933, but gave way to a renewed slump later that year. The NRA program did little to expand aggregate demand for goods and services.

In May, 1935, the NIRA was declared unconstitutional by the U.S. Supreme Court. However, important elements of it were reenacted. Labor's right to organize and bargain collectively was firmly established by the National Labor Relations Act (Wagner Act) of 1935. Provisions for minimum-wage rates and maximum work hours were permanently created by the Fair Labor Standards Act of 1938. The quasi-monopolistic elements of the NRA codes were reestablished in individual programs for motor and air transportation, bituminous coal, and petroleum extraction and in the Miller-Tydings Act of 1937, permitting resale price maintenance.

Impact   In the short term, adoption and administration of the NIRA stimulated a brief boom in business inventory buildup. The NRA codes themselves tended to cause increases in product prices but were widely evaded. The program reflected the misconception that the Great Depression was a problem of excess supply of goods and services, instead of primarily a great fall in aggregate demand. Most economists were relieved when the program was terminated.

Paul B. Trescott

Further Reading

Brand, Donald R. *Corporatism and the Rule of Law: A Study of the National Recovery Administration.* Ithaca, N.Y.: Cornell University Press, 1988.

Johnson, Hugh S. *The Blue Eagle from Egg to Earth.* Garden City, N.Y.: Doubleday Doran, 1935.

Ohl, John Kennedy. *Hugh S. Johnson and the New Deal.* DeKalb: Northern Illinois University Press, 1985.

Rosen, Elliott A. *Roosevelt, the Great Depression, and the Economics of Recovery.* Charlottesville: University of Virginia Press, 2007.

See also Business and the economy in the United States; Great Depression in the United States; National Labor Relations Act of 1935; National Recovery Administration; Unionism.

■ National Labor Relations Act of 1935

The Law Federal law establishing the right of employees to organize and establishing the National Labor Relations Board
Also known as Wagner Act; NLRA
Date July 8, 1935

The National Labor Relations Act (NLRA), also known as the Wagner Act, was a landmark piece of legislation that enshrined into law labor's right to organize and bargain collectively, creating an unprecedented relationship between the American labor movement and the federal government.

From the late nineteenth century through the early twentieth century, the right of American workers to organize for mutual protection was severely limited by laws and customs that favored employers and emphasized individual rights. As a result, the nascent American labor movement operated largely outside the law, fighting the legal system not to be defined as "conspiracies in restraint of trade," which finally happened with the passage of the Clayton Act of 1914, as labor unions were exempt from the antitrust laws set forth by the act. Even then, the American legal climate remained so unfavorable to organized labor that the American Federation of Labor, the most successful labor organization to arise during this period, rejected reliance on governmental protection of labor as less reliable than protections achieved through union contracts. The craft orientation and other exclusionary practices of the AFL, however, drove the majority of American workers to seek legislative protection. The role of the government in protecting the rights of workers and the right of labor to organize dramatically increased during the 1930's.

The New Deal and the American Labor Movement The federal government's role in protecting and expanding labor's rights both coincided with and inspired the rise of the industrial union movement that culminated with the founding of the Congress of Industrial Organizations (CIO). The increased governmental involvement in labor-management regulations was also part of a larger pattern of New Deal efforts to regulate industry. For that reason, the NLRA was both an outgrowth of the earlier regulatory efforts of the National Industrial Recovery Act (NIRA) of 1933 and a turning point from a governmental focus on shoring up business to one focused on aiding people. Nonetheless, there was an important thread of continuity when it came to labor-management relations. Section 7a of the NIRA granted workers the right to organize and collectively bargain and required em-

In 1938, Senator Robert Wagner testifies before the Senate Education and Labor Subcommittee, imploring the committee to create a provision to force recipients of federal government contracts to uphold the collective bargaining bylaws that are part of the National Labor Relations Act. (Library of Congress)

ployers to bargain in good faith with their employees' chosen representatives. Additionally, it set up the National Labor Board (NLB) to mediate disputes. However, the NLB proved ineffectual, and the voluntary nature of the codes undercut their effectiveness. Even with these limitations, the CIO took advantaged of section 7a to rapidly advance the organization of unskilled workers.

Meanwhile, mixed reaction existed to the possibility of greater labor organization among industrialists. While many industrial leaders were sharply opposed to any infringements on their right to manage, others, whose industries had experience with regulatory unionism, appreciated the role that the relatively conservative unions could play in maintaining industrial peace and, hence, productivity. These industrialists therefore cautiously favored these kinds of regulations, as long as their competitors were required to adhere to them as well. The kind and scope of regulation, however, remained controversial, leading the Supreme Court to invalidate the NIRA on May 27, 1935.

The passage of the NLRA also resulted from an unprecedented labor and working-class influence on the American political environment during President Franklin D. Roosevelt's second term. The act was introduced by the progressive New York senator Robert F. Wagner, on February 28, 1934. The passage of the NLRA in July, 1935, was aided by the support of Secretary of Labor Frances Perkins and eventually of President Roosevelt, along with the rising political power of industrial union movement and the cautious support of industry. Hailed as "labor's Magna Carta," the NLRA legally required employers

---

National Labor Relations Act

A significant portion of the National Labor Relations Act is reproduced below.

The inequality of bargaining power between employees who do not possess full freedom of association or actual liberty of contract, and employers who are organized in the corporate or other forms of ownership association substantially burdens and affects the flow of commerce, and tends to aggravate recurrent business depressions, by depressing wage rates and the purchasing power of wage earners in industry and by preventing the stabilization of competitive wage rates and working conditions within and between industries.

Experience has proved that protection by law of the right of employees to organize and bargain collectively safeguards commerce from injury, impairment, or interruption, and promotes the flow of commerce by removing certain recognized sources of industrial strife and unrest, by encouraging practices fundamental to the friendly adjustment of industrial disputes arising out of differences as to wages, hours, or other working conditions, and by restoring equality of bargaining power between employers and employees.

Experience has further demonstrated that certain practices by some labor organizations, their officers, and members have the intent or the necessary effect of burdening or obstructing commerce by preventing the free flow of goods in such commerce through strikes and other forms of industrial unrest or through concerted activities which impair the interest of the public in the free flow of such commerce. The elimination of such practices is a necessary condition to the assurance of the rights herein guaranteed.

It is hereby declared to be the policy of the United States to eliminate the causes of certain substantial obstructions to the free flow of commerce and to mitigate and eliminate these obstructions when they have occurred by encouraging the practice and procedure of collective bargaining and by protecting the exercise by workers of full freedom of association, self-organization, and designation of representatives of their own choosing, for the purpose of negotiating the terms and conditions of their employment or other mutual aid or protection.

---

to bargain with their employees' chosen independent bargaining representatives. It also banned company unions, allowed for closed shops, and forbade numerous employer efforts to thwart unionization as unfair labor practices. Finally, it created the

National Labor Relations Board (NLRB) to mediate labor disputes in private industry.

Impact The NLRA had profound, immediate effects on the American labor movement. It further energized the CIO and helped shore up the industrial union movement, especially important because organization began to falter by the late 1930's and public opinion began to turn against organized labor over the continued strikes against companies that refused to abide by the NLRA's provisions. The NLRA survived its first constitutional test with the case of *National Labor Relations Board v. Jones and Laughlin Steel Corp.*, settling a lawsuit over discrimination against union members in labor's favor. It made the labor movement fully "legal" but also made it subject to government regulation. In turn, this closer relationship between labor and the government made the American labor movement vulnerable to both subsequent legislation that was less prolabor and NLRB rulings that have not always been favorable to the labor movement. The enforcement of the act's prolabor provisions have been weakened, showing how the NLRA fulfilled both labor's greatest hopes and worst fears about full legal recognition by the federal government.

Susan Roth Breitzer

Further Reading

Babson, Steve. *The Unfinished Struggle: Turning Points in American Labor, 1877-Present.* Lanham, Md.: Rowman & Littlefield, 1999. Study of the major watershed periods in American labor history, highlighting the 1930's as a significant period of the expansion of labor's rights.

Folsom, Burt, Jr. *New Deal or Raw Deal? How FDR's Legacy Has Damaged America.* New York: Threshold Editions, 2008. Revisionist account of the New Deal that argues that the New Deal lengthened the Great Depression and created problems that lasted well beyond it.

Gordon, Colin. *New Deals: Business, Labor, and Politics in America, 1920-1935.* New York: Cambridge University Press, 1994. Groundbreaking interpretation of the New Deal that demonstrates the essentially pro-big-business focus of the economic reforms of the New Deal.

Lichtenstein, Nelson. *State of the Union: A Century of American Labor.* Princeton, N.J.: Princeton University Press, 2002. Study of the rising and then declining role of the labor movement as a democra-

tizing force in the American workplace and American life.

National Labor Relations Board. *Legislative History of the National Labor Relations Act.* 2 vols. Washington, D.C.: Government Printing Office, 1985. Commemorative documentary history of the NLRA published in honor of the fiftieth anniversary of its passage.

See also American Federation of Labor; Business and the economy in the United States; Congress of Industrial Organizations; Income and wages in the United States; Labor strikes; National Industrial Recovery Act of 1933; *National Labor Relations Board v. Jones and Laughlin Steel Corp.*; New Deal; Unionism.

■ National Labor Relations Board v. Jones and Laughlin Steel Corp.

The Case U.S. Supreme Court upheld the constitutionality of the National Labor Relations Act of 1935

Date Decided on April 12, 1937

The Jones and Laughlin *case brought to an end the Supreme Court's supervision of the economy, rejected commerce-clause decisions that had declared major New Deal legislation unconstitutional, and initiated the Court's deference to congressional economic legislation.*

The National Labor Relations Act (NLRA) of 1935, also known as the Wagner Act, gave labor the right to organize and to bargain with management over wages, hours, and working conditions and created the National Labor Relations Board (NLRB) to hear unfair labor practice claims. Jones and Laughlin Steel fired workers for attempting to organize a union. The NLRB decided that the company had committed an unfair labor practice and ordered the workers reinstated. The court of appeals refused to enforce the board's order, holding that the NLRA was unconstitutional.

In a 5-4 decision, the Supreme Court rejected its *Schechter Poultry Corp. v. United States* (1935) and *Carter v. Carter Coal Co.* (1936) decisions, in which its conservative members, known as the Four Horsemen, had persuaded the Court to overturn major New Deal legislation and prohibit Congress from regulating business and labor relations because the activities were local and had only an indirect effect on interstate commerce.

Then, the Court held that the NLRA did not violate the commerce clause because Congress had the power to regulate labor relations in businesses that substantially affected commerce. Jones and Laughlin manufactured steel at only its Pennsylvania plant, but the company depended on the interstate marketplace to acquire its raw materials and sell its finished products. The Court concluded that the effect of a strike by the company's workers would create a burden on interstate commerce that Congress had the constitutional authority to prohibit.

Impact   The *Jones and Laughlin* case upheld the right of labor to organize and bargain with management. Along with the *West Coast Hotel Co. v. Parrish* (1937) decision and Justice Willis Van Devanter's retirement in June, 1937, the decision in the *Jones and Laughlin* case contributed to the demise of President Franklin D. Roosevelt's court-packing legislation pending in Congress. Subsequent Supreme Court decisions by liberal Roosevelt appointees extended the reach of the NLRA and upheld the Social Security Act and the Agricultural Adjustment Act of 1938. Together with the Court's decisions in *United States v. Darby Lumber* (1941) and *Wikard v. Filburn* (1942), the *Jones and Laughlin* decision established foundations of the Supreme Court's interpretation of the commerce clause.

William Crawford Green

Further Reading

Cortner, Richard C. *The Jones and Laughlin Case.* New York: Alfred A. Knopf, 1970.

Lewis, Thomas T., ed. *U.S. Supreme Court.* Pasadena, Calif.: Salem Press, 2007.

Rose, Gary L. *The Shaping of a Nation: Twenty-five Supreme Court Cases That Changed the United States.* Bethesda, Md.: Academica Press, 2010.

See also   *Carter v. Carter Coal Co.*; Four Horsemen vs. Three Musketeers; National Labor Relations Act of 1935; New Deal; Roosevelt, Franklin D.; Roosevelt's court-packing plan; *Schechter Poultry Corp. v. United States*; Supreme Court, U.S.; Wagner, Robert F.; *West Coast Hotel Co. v. Parrish.*

■ National Negro Congress

Identification   Civil rights advocacy organization
Date   Begun on February 14, 1936

The National Negro Congress brought together an alliance of leaders in the labor and union movements with activist clergy and businesspeople within the American black community. Its domestic political goals centered on opposing restrictive and unequal legal discrimination such as the Jim Crow laws.

The origin of the National Negro Congress dates to May, 1935, when a conference on the economic status of the black community was held at Howard University. At the conference, evidence was presented on continuing racial discrimination in New Deal programs. John P. Davis, secretary of the Joint Committee for National Recovery, and Ralph Bunche, chair of Howard's department of political science, invited a group of community leaders to Bunche's home following the meetings, where they agreed that better coordination of organizational activities was needed for effective movement toward racial justice. Davis wrote a pamphlet entitled *Let Us Build a National Negro Congress*, whose printing ran to fifty thousand copies.

The inaugural meeting of the congress was held in Chicago on February 14, 1936. The 817 delegates represented a hugely diverse range of organizations, from fraternal societies to political parties of all shades of opinion, religious groups, unions, and civic bodies. Despite this, there was substantial agreement that the intent of the nonpartisan congress was not to formulate another platform or ideology but to serve as a vehicle for the creation of a unified effort to promote progress for the black community from within its own ranks. Veteran activist A. Philip Randolph was elected president of the congress, although much of the administrative work was handled by Davis.

Fifty councils of the congress were established in nineteen states. Between 1936 and 1938, they focused on activism on local issues of discrimination in sectors as varied as housing and rent control, employment and professional training, textbooks with stereotyped images of African Americans, and police brutality. After 1938, the grassroots nature of the congress shifted to a more national political orientation, working to promote legislation banning lynching and promoting better working conditions. A major project in the latter area was to support directly the efforts of the Congress of Industrial Organizations to unionize the American steel industry, a position rooted in the congress's prolabor orientation. While local National Negro Congresses worked successfully to aid in significant progress for their members within steel unions, and in many other unionized industrial professions, the degree of partisanship that was evident in 1938 and 1939 severely undermined the organization's claim to neutrality. Another complicating factor was the association of the congress with the Communist Party USA, which had endorsed many of its objectives.

Impact   In the last years of the 1930's, the National Negro Congress moved away from the mainstream politics of the United States and was on record as frequently supporting the antifascist actions taken by the Soviet Union. This attempt at introducing international political issues into an already explosive domestic civil rights environment alienated many who had initially supported the congress.

Robert Ridinger

Further Reading

Horne, Gerald. "National Negro Congress." In *Encyclopedia of African American Culture and History.* New York: Macmillan Library Reference, 1996.

Teal, Orion A. " National Negro Congress." In *Encyclopedia of African American History, 1896 to the Present.* Vol. 3. New York: Oxford University Press, 2009.

Wittner, Lawrence S. "The National Negro Congress: A Reassessment." *American Quarterly* 22, no. 4 (1970): 883-901.

See also   African Americans; Communism; National Association for the Advancement of Colored People.

■ National parks

The 1930's was a decade of profound change within the U.S. National Park Service (NPS). The agency's mission expanded to include historic preservation and interpretation. Passage of the Reorganization Act in 1933 transferred sixty-three natural and historic sites from other federal agencies to the NPS. At the same time, programs that evolved through President Franklin D. Roosevelt's New Deal provided labor and financial support for developing new park units.

When the NPS was established in 1916 some of its proponents argued that the agency should also have responsibility for several natural and historic sites managed by other U.S. federal agencies. At the urging of NPS director Horace M. Albright, President Roosevelt signed the Reorganization Act in 1933 transferring national memorials, historic sites, national monuments, and military parks from the Department of Agriculture and Department of War to the Department of the Interior and the NPS. Roosevelt's support of the act was, in part, an effort to engender greater government efficiency through the consolidation of land management responsibilities. Among areas transferred were Gettysburg National Battlefield from the Department of War and Cedar Breaks National Monument from the Department of Agriculture. The act also placed Washington, D.C., sites such as the Ford Theater, the Custis-Lee Mansion in Arlington National Cemetery, and the Lincoln Memorial under administrative control of the NPS.

Park Visitation and New Types of Park Units   The 1930's was also a period of growth in park visitation. To encourage travel, advertising campaigns such as "1934 A National Parks Year" promoted park tourism as a means of supporting businesses struggling as a result of the economic downturn. Promotional efforts proved extremely successful. Between 1929 and 1939 national park visitation increased from 2.7 million visits to nearly 16 million visits. During the same time period several additional types of park units were added to the system. In 1933, the first U.S. national historic park was created in Morristown, New Jersey, to preserve the location of General George Washington's winter camp in 1777 and 1779. Several other historic sites were added later, including Richmond National Battlefield Park (1936),

Salem Maritime National Historic Site (1938), and Saratoga National Historic Park (1938).

Other new types of units were created to address growing interest in and demand for outdoor recreation. In 1936, a partnership between the NPS and the Bureau of Reclamation created Boulder Dam National Recreation Area (now Lake Mead National Recreation Area). In 1937, Cape Hatteras National Seashore was designated to provide public access to a section of scenic coastline in North Carolina. Extending along a corridor of the Appalachian Mountains in North Carolina and Tennessee, the Blue Ridge Parkway became one of four scenic highways designated as national parkways in 1936. During the 1930's the NPS also experimented with units created on submarginal lands that had been retired from farming. Of forty-five National Demonstration Areas (NDAs) all but two were eventually returned to their respective states: Catoctin Mountain NDA (now Catoctin Mountain Park in Maryland) and Prince William NDA (now Prince William Forest Park in Virginia).

New Deal Recovery Programs and Administrative Changes Before its reorganization in 1933 the NPS was a relatively small and close-knit organization. NPS rangers and other employees were sometimes identified with their first director, Stephen Mather, as part of the "Mather family." This situation changed between 1933 and 1935, when the agency expanded in size from about one thousand employees to more than thirteen thousand. Many of the new employees had been hired on a temporary basis through funds provided by the Public Works Administration, the Works Progress Administration, the Federal Emergency Relief Administration, and the Civilian Conservation Corps. The abundant supply of labor and funding provided by the New Deal helped in the construction of buildings, roads, and hundreds of other park facilities.

Teepees frame the foreground of a view of Logan Pass on Mount Reynolds in Montana's Glacier National Park. (National Park Service)

As the NPS grew, it became increasingly difficult for the Washington-based administrative staff to communicate with and oversee dozens of widely scattered parks. During the 1920's, field offices had been established in Denver, Portland, Los Angeles, San Francisco, and Yellowstone National Park to provide technical assistance for specific topical areas such as landscape architecture and sanitation. However, these offices had no supervisory authority or control over park units. At the urging of park superintendents four regional offices were created in 1937 to improve support and coordination of field units.

In 1931, the Washington, D.C., office of the NPS was organized into four branches; each was led by an assistant director. As the NPS adapted to its expanded responsibilities involving historic preservation, the agency realized it needed a separate division staffed by professional historians. Passed by Congress in 1935, the Historic Sites Act led to the formation of the Historic Sites and Building branch within the NPS. In addition to oversight of education and historical research programs, the branch had responsibility for maintaining records associated with historic and archaeological sites and buildings. By 1939, the NPS had ten branches, including operations, planning, recreation and land planning, and engineering.

Impact During the 1930's the National Park System expanded its long-standing mission of protecting sites of scenic geological significance to include the preservation and interpretation of sites important to the country's history and development as a nation. In addition to doubling the number of units managed by the NPS, the agency reorganization required the service to adapt to new and unfamiliar responsibilities. National historic sites are the most numerous type of unit managed by the NPS. Taking advantage of New Deal recovery funds, the NPS also expanded services during the 1930's through units intended for mass recreation, such as parkways, seashores, and recreation areas.

Thomas A. Wikle

Further Reading

Albright, Horace M. *The Birth of the National Park Service: The Founding Years, 1913-33.* Salt Lake City, Utah: Howe Brothers, 1985. Account of the foundation and early years of the NPS by one of the most important participants in the events.

Everhart, William C. *The National Park Service.* Boulder, Colo.: Westview Press, 1983. Begins with a history of the establishment of the agency and continues through the early 1980's. The author served as adviser to two directors of the NPS.

Foresta, Ronald A. *America's National Parks and Their Keepers.* Washington, D.C.: Resources for the Future, 1984. Analysis of modern park policies and issues, informed by a sense of history.

Lowry, William R. *The Capacity for Wonder: Preserving National Parks.* Washington, D.C.: Brookings Institution, 1994. Discusses how the political compromises that have shaped the structure of the NPS from the beginning have dictated its ability to meet the modern problems of overcrowding, crime, inadequate infrastructure, and environmental pollution.

Mackintosh, Barry. *The National Park Service Administrative History: A Guide.* Washington, D.C.: National Park Service, 1991. Bibliographic guide contains annotated entries on the administrative and topical histories of the national parks, books contained in the park service's history collection, and records on the parks held in the National Archives. Invaluable resource for anyone researching any U.S. national park or the history of the service.

Runte, Alfred. *National Parks: The American Experience.* 4th ed. Lanham, Md.: Taylor Trade, 2010. Interpretive history of the national parks and what they mean to Americans. Argues that park creation and maintenance have had more to do with nationalism and commercialism than with environmentalism. Includes maps, illustrations, and index.

See also Civilian Conservation Corps; New Deal; Recreation; Roosevelt, Franklin D.; Works Progress Administration.

■ National Recovery Administration

Identification   Regulatory administration
  overseeing business practices
Date   Established on June 16, 1933

The National Recovery Administration (NRA) was set up under the National Industrial Recovery Act of 1933 to regulate business practices. In particular, it was designed to keep wages and prices up and working hours low in order to encourage recovery.

The National Industrial Recovery Act started out as a Senate bill, proposed by Hugo L. Black, to bar from interstate commerce factories whose employees worked more than thirty hours per week. President Franklin D. Roosevelt doubted this would be constitutional or wise, but labor unions favored it, so his administration designed a modified version, which he sent to Congress on May 17, 1933. Part one formed the NRA to regulate business practices, especially work hours and wages. Part two formed the Public Works Administration, intended to reduce unemployment. The law passed a month later and was authorized for two years.

Starting the NRA   Roosevelt appointed General Hugh S. Johnson, an associate of wealthy social reformer Bernard Mannes Baruch, to run the NRA, with antibusiness progressive Donald Randall Richberg as general counsel. The Special Industrial Recovery Board provided nominal oversight; the board was replaced December 6, 1933, by the National Emergency Council. Johnson started organizing even before the bill passed, helped by longtime friend Alexander Sachs of Lehman Brothers. Inspired by his service with the War Industries Board in 1918, Johnson wanted to replace unrestrained competition with cooperation and class struggle with a balanced economy, providing economic opportunity for laborers to restore consumption, and thereby bringing about economic recovery.

Johnson and Sachs organized a series of boards to oversee the regulatory codes. The Industrial Advisory Board was appointed by Secretary of Commerce Daniel C. Roper and chaired by Walter Clark Teagle of Standard Oil of New Jersey. The Labor Advisory Board was chaired and appointed by Secretary of Labor Frances Perkins. The Consumers' Advisory Board was chaired and appointed by Mary

Rumsey, older sister of diplomat Averell Harriman—this board had little influence.

Johnson set about energetically organizing the codes to be practiced by the various industries; eventually there were at least 550. These were created in cooperation with major businesses, such as automakers General Motors and Chrysler. As soon as the codes were developed by the industries, they were reviewed by the Code Analysis Division—to verify that the codes included the labor provisions mandated by section 7 of the NIRA, such as mimimum wages, maximum hours, and a ban on child labor—and the advisory boards. After a formal public hearing advertised in advance, Johnson took them to Roosevelt for approval. He issued the first, for cotton textiles, on July 9, 1933. With other industries initally slow to act, he set up a basic blanket code for businesses to sign and follow; these companies displayed a blue eagle as a symbol of their support.

Within three months, businesses in the ten largest industries joined. There were also codes for minor industries, such as shoulder-pad makers, burlesque theaters, and dog-food makers. Johnson launched a massive publicity campaign to encourage businesses to participate and consumers to pledge to patronize only businesses displaying the blue eagle; the campaign was highlighted by a massive parade down Fifth Avenue in New York. Johnson had also hoped to use public works contracts to encourage participation, but the administrative separation of the Public Works Administration from the NRA, coupled with the slow progress of the former, prevented this for all sectors but shipbuilding.

Inevitably, some businesses refused to cooperate, and Johnson had fourteen hundred enforcers in fifty-four branch offices scattered throughout the country to deal with them. The enforcers were empowered to punish recalcitrant businesspeople with fines up to five hundred dollars and imprisonment for up to six months for trivial violations. Johnson preferred voluntary cooperation, but while membership was voluntary, obedience to the individual codes was mandatory.

Developing Problems   Although initially popular, the NRA had its critics from the start. Many—including the Special Industrial Recovery Board, which was overseen by Roosevelt—disliked Johnson's publicity campaign and its symbol, which reminded them of fascism. In fact, the idea of state-business-labor cooperation came from Italian fascism, but few noticed or cared. Radical progressives believed the codes encouraged corporatism and monopoly, a claim supported by a 1934 study of the NRA chaired by Clarence Darrow.

Consumers opposed higher prices and production restrictions, which also worked against recovery. Some industrialists, notably Henry Ford, never accepted the NRA. Labor unions also were unhappy with the codes, which permitted but did not mandate unions and did not ban company unions. Although Johnson hoped the NRA would generate labor peace, many major strikes occurred during this period. Initially supportive, small businesses disliked the domination of the code-making by large businesses, and many found obeying the codes and staying in business virtually impossible. In one spectacular case, dry cleaner Jacob Maged of Jersey City, New Jersey, was jailed and fined for charging thirty-five cents instead of forty to press a suit, as mandated by the NRA.

Johnson saw himself as an impartial arbiter forcing business, labor, and consumers to compromise. Under fire for these problems and unhappy for personal reasons, Johnson resigned in September, 1934; that led to a reorganization by a September, 27, executive order. The National Emergency Council, chaired by Richberg, who was considered ambitious and untrustworthy by many of his old progressive allies, set policy, while a National Industrial Recovery Board executed it. This failed to stem the tide of hostility as Roosevelt sought the NRA's renewal. Many considered it a relief when the Supreme Court finally struck down the NRA. Some parts were soon restored by new laws, such as the Wagner Act, codifying labor law, and the Guffey Act, codifying the NRA's bituminous coal code; the latter was later overturned by the Supreme Court.

From the start, the NRA was unlikely to bring recovery even aside from its production limits. Whatever their value as reforms, the many business regulations discouraged hiring. In particular, the bipartisan notion that high wages and prices could end a depression resulting from deflation was dubious. Johnson argued that modern man could transcend supply and demand just as he did other natural laws.

Constitutional Difficulties Many employers were tried for code violations, and three cases reached the Supreme Court. *United States v. Belcher* was a test of the lumber codes, and the administration hoped to use it as a test case for the NRA's general authority. However, the Court dismissed the case before it was actually argued.

The first case argued was *Panama Refining Co. v. Ryan*, concerning oil-industry codes. One problem, discovered right before the case was argued, was that the penalty codes had never been written—though people had been tried and punished. The Court was also concerned with the unlimited executive authority to regulate, with only vague standards in place to use as guidelines. In January, 1935, the Court overturned the codes, with only Benjamin N. Cardozo dissenting.

The most important case was *Schechter Poultry Corp. v. United States.* This involved a small poultry dealer in Brooklyn convicted of selling an unfit chicken, allowing buyers to select individual chickens, and selling to unlicensed dealers. None of these was deemed a matter of interstate commerce, which was sufficient in itself to reverse the company's conviction. However, Chief Justice Charles Evans Hughes was also concerned about the excessive delegation of legislative authority. The administration argued that the NRA was a cooperative effort, but the Court disagreed because the regulations were binding on all employers. On May 27, 1935, the Court unanimously voted to overturn section 3 of the NIRA, effectively eliminating the NRA.

Impact The NRA had a major effect on the economy during its brief existence. However, for a variety of reasons, it ultimately did far more to retard recovery than to promote it; only World War II finally ended the Great Depression.

Timothy Lane

Further Reading

Davis, Kenneth S. *FDR: The New Deal Years 1933-1937.* New York: Random House, 1986. Detailed history of Roosevelt's first term from a progressive viewpoint, including extensive coverage of the NRA.

Flynn, John T. *The Roosevelt Myth.* Reprint. San Francisco: Fox & Wilkes, 1998. Moderately progressive critique of Roosevelt as unethical and of the New Deal, including the NRA, as corporatist and inspired by fascism.

Johnson, Hugh S. *The Blue Eagle from Egg to Earth.* New York: Garden City, 1935. Personal memoir focusing on service with the NRA, explaining its purpose and denying all accusations against it, while admitting to personal errors.

Leuchtenberg, William E. *Franklin D. Roosevelt and the New Deal, 1932-1940.* New York: Harper & Row, 1963. Sympathetic study of the subject from a liberal viewpoint, including the NRA and Roosevelt's attitude toward it.

Powell, Jim. *FDR's Folly.* New York: Three Rivers Press, 2003. Topical libertarian critique of the New Deal, including a full chapter on the NRA and another on the key court cases.

Shlaes, Amity. *The Forgotten Man.* New York: HarperCollins, 2007. Generally critical, but fair, conservative history of the New Deal, including the NRA.

See also   Business and the economy in the United States; Great Depression in the United States; Hughes, Charles Evans; Income and wages in the United States; National Industrial Recovery Act of 1933; New Deal; Perkins, Frances; *Schecter Poultry Corp. v. United States*; Supreme Court, U.S.; Unemployment in the United States.

■ National Wildlife Federation

Identification   Wildlife conservation, advocacy, and educational organization
Also known as   General Wildlife Federation
Date   Established February 3-7, 1936

The National Wildlife Federation (NWF) brought together a variety of individuals, from bird-watchers to hunters, in an attempt to lobby for the protection of American wildlife, solutions to environmental problems, and the education of people to become responsible stewards of nature. The NWF has become the largest grassroots, wildlife-conservation organization in the United States.

The genesis of nature conservancy in the United States dates to the public-trust doctrine, a concept established in the 1872 Supreme Court case *Martin v. Wadell,* which held that wildlife belongs to the people. Despite this precedent, no move toward conservancy occurred until overhunting and overfishing began threatening game species with extinction during the late nineteenth century. As a result, states began to pass the first wildlife conservation laws.

Matters got worse during the 1930's, when poor agricultural practices, promoted by the federal gov-

ernment, turned the nation's bread basket into a dust bowl. In March of 1934, Iowa political cartoonist Jay "Ding" Darling's cartoons came to the attention of President Franklin D. Roosevelt, and he was appointed the chief of the U.S. Biological Survey. In 1936, Darling urged President Roosevelt to convene a meeting of some two thousand persons who had a stake in the conservation of American wildlife.

During Darling's North American Wildlife Conference, held February 3-7, 1936, the General Wildlife Fund (GWF) was formed. The GWF's goals were to unite the seemingly disparate individuals and groups into a united voice of advocacy for conservancy. At the conclusion of the first conference, the participants were sent home to form branch offices in their home states to create a nationwide network of advocacy.

The GWF became the National Wildlife Federation (NWF) in 1938. The NWF's main goals remain the same as they were during the 1930's: to connect people to nature and to protect and restore habitat.

Impact   During the 1930's, the NWF began its legacy of educating the American public about the importance of nature conservancy. Through the organization's advocacy, beginning with the 1937 Federal Aid in Wildlife Restoration Act, the NWF has been able to bring the fiscal and enforcement strength of the U.S. federal government to bear on conservancy issues.

B. Keith Murphy

Further Reading

Allen, Thomas B. *Guardian of the Wild: The Story of the National Wildlife Federation.* Bloomington: Indiana University Press, 1987.

Krech, Shepard, John Robert McNeill, and Carolyn Merchant. *Encyclopedia of World Environmental History.* New York: Routledge, 2004.

Lendt, David L. *Ding: The Life of Jay Norwood Darling.* Ames: Iowa State University Press, 1979.

Nash, Roderick Frazier. *Wilderness and the American Mind.* 4th ed. New Haven, Conn.: Yale University Press, 2001.

See also   Dust Bowl; Migratory Bird Hunting and Conservation Stamp Act of 1934; Natural resources; Roosevelt, Franklin D.; Wilderness Society.

■ National Youth Administration

Identification   Federal government agency
   supporting the development of American youth
Date   Established on June 26, 1935

*The National Youth Administration (NYA) provided
young Americans greater access to education, employment,
and vocational training. During its eight-year existence,
from 1935 to 1943, the NYA provided practical work experience and training to several million American young people who were underserved by other New Deal programs.*

The onset of the Great Depression resulted in the
unemployment of millions of Americans. Young
adults, ages eighteen to thirty, were significantly affected by the economic downturn. During the early
1930's, nearly five million young adults were both
out of school and unemployed. President Franklin
D. Roosevelt's early New Deal programs, such as the
Civilian Conservation Corps and the Federal Emergency Relief Administration, employed thousands
of American youth, but millions more still needed
work.

On June 26, 1935, Roosevelt signed an executive
order creating the NYA. The programs of the NYA
targeted Americans between the ages of sixteen and
twenty-five who were enrolled students, unemployed, or from families on relief. The NYA offered
these young people training, education, and employment. Headed by social activist Aubrey W. Williams, the new agency was part of the Works Progress
Administration (WPA), the most expansive New
Deal agency. Williams wanted to strengthen the
democratic character of American youth through
the NYA's educational programs.

Williams began his work with a budget of $50 mil-
lion. Similar in structure to other New Deal agencies, the NYA established an office in each of the
forty-eight states and hired a director for each office.
The NYA created training centers in various cities,
towns, and counties to help reach its target audience. The agency also established training camps for
young women.

Similar to other New Deal agencies, the NYA recognized the need to improve the lives of young African Americans. In 1935, three out of five African
American youths were unemployed,
compared to one of five white youths.
That year, the NYA appointed noted African American educator Mary Mc-
Leod Bethune to direct the agency's Division of Negro Affairs.

The NYA reached college and high
school students by offering them part-
time work to help pay for their education. The organization also helped unemployed young Americans not in
school by placing them in full-time jobs
or providing them with relevant training. Nearly one-half of the youth in the
NYA's programs had not previously
held a job.

Initially, the agency focused on public-works projects, such as the construction of schools, playgrounds, roads,
bridges, libraries, and parks. NYA employees helped complete thousands of
public buildings and hundreds of new
infrastructure projects. The NYA also
found students permanent jobs and
provided vocational training and ap-
prenticeships. Many NYA participants
gained experience for clerical, factory,

*National Youth Administration worker sawing boards during the construction of
a defense housing project in Colorado.* (Library of Congress)

and professional careers. At the end of the decade, the agency helped employ young Americans in defense-related positions. In 1939, Roosevelt placed the NYA within the new Federal Security Agency, which separated the NYA from the WPA.

Impact During the Great Depression, the NYA provided millions of young Americans educational, career, and vocational opportunities not previously available to them. Unlike other New Deal programs, the NYA offered American youth specialized skills and incentives to remain in school. New Deal opponents charged that the agency meddled in education, race relations, and local government. Despite support from Congressman Lyndon B. Johnson and Senator Harry S. Truman, public criticism and the changing needs of wartime led to the end of the NYA in 1943. The NYA proved to be an important and unique New Deal program that reached out to millions of unemployed American youth. The NYA served as a model for later government programs designed to transition young Americans from the classroom to the workplace.

Aaron D. Purcell

Further Reading

Lindley, Betty, and Ernest K. Lindley. *A New Deal for Youth: The Story of the National Youth Administration.* New York: Viking Press, 1938.

Reiman, Richard A. *The New Deal and American Youth: Ideas and Ideals in a Depression Decade.* Athens: University of Georgia Press, 1992.

Salmond, John. *A Southern Rebel: The Life and Times of Aubrey Willis Williams, 1890-1965.* Chapel Hill: University of North Carolina Press, 1983.

See also African Americans; Bethune, Mary McLeod; Civilian Conservation Corps; Education; Federal Emergency Relief Administration; Great Depression in the United States; New Deal; Unemployment in the United States; Works Progress Administration.

■ Native Americans

Identification Members of the aboriginal societies of North America and their descendants
Also known as American Indians

The Indian Reorganization Act (IRA), passed by the U.S. Congress in 1934, altered the nature of Native American life during the 1930's. Changing the policies of the Allotment Act of 1887 (often called the Dawes Act), the IRA reversed nearly fifty years of reservation land loss and a failed attempt to assimilate Native Americans into American culture through Native American schools.

However well intended the policies of the Dawes Act had been, their practical result was to make Native Americans wards of the state, both financially and psychologically. The reservation system was, in essence, an attempt to confine Native Americans to large tracts of land that white settlers did not want. Most Native American tribes in the West had developed lifestyles, religious practices, and self-governance while roaming freely over large tracts of land. The reservation system confined these tribes to limited space and pushed them into becoming farmers, an occupation to which most tribes were not acculturated. Though the U.S. government did promise to provide food and resources to help tribes make the transition in lifestyle, these promises were often broken through a combination of poor management of the Bureau of Indian Affairs (BIA) and corruption. Most important, the reservation system essentially destroyed the core parts of tribal life.

The idea behind the Dawes Act was to remedy the failures of the reservation system, to "Kill the Indian and save the man." Each Native American family would be granted an allotment of 160 acres of land to farm and would be given American citizenship. The remaining reservation land would be available for public use or sale. Furthermore, the children of the "new citizens" were to be educated into American life by attending "Indian Schools," boarding schools away from the reservations designed to teach Native American children the ways of white people, including the Christian religion. A concerted effort was made on the part of this educational enterprise to acculturate Native American children into American life in such a way that they would forget tribal customs and tribal religious practices.

The practical result of the Dawes Act was disastrous on every level. Not only did tribes lose large

parcels of reservation land to greedy land speculators, but also the attempt to acculturate Native
American children created a generation of Native
Americans who were alienated from their own tribes
and families as well as from American society. Widespread questioning of these policies and many other
aspects of American society began after World War I.
The uneasy end of World War I tore away at the pat
assumptions that most Americans had about every
facet of American life, even the way in which the government had treated the original inhabitants of the
land the country occupied. It was in this environment that John Collier began to advocate for better
treatment of Native American tribes.

John Collier and the Indian New Deal   John Collier,
who had been a journalist, an educator, and a social
worker, was passionate about Native American culture. Despite his romanticism, his commitment to
Native American causes enabled him to become a
formidable advocate for Native American rights. In
1923, he founded the American Indian Defense Association, an organization that moved against the
grain of the Dawes Act by actively supporting Native
American rights, not by pushing Native Americans
into becoming Americans, but by preserving their
cultures. This organization directly challenged the
BIA and its commissioner, Charles Burke, on various
high-profile issues, such as the right of native people
to practice traditional ceremonies that the BIA
found objectionable or their right to control and
market the products of their own land. The bad publicity that the BIA continued to get through the
1920's, plus frequent conflicts with Congress over
BIA inefficiency, eventually caused Interior Secretary Lewis Meriam to propose an investigation. The

*Chief Kolchavteewah holds Franklin D. Roosevelt's hand as part of a blessing, an act that surprised the president as he departed from a
summit meeting with southwestern Native American officials at the White House in 1936.* (AP/Wide World Photos)

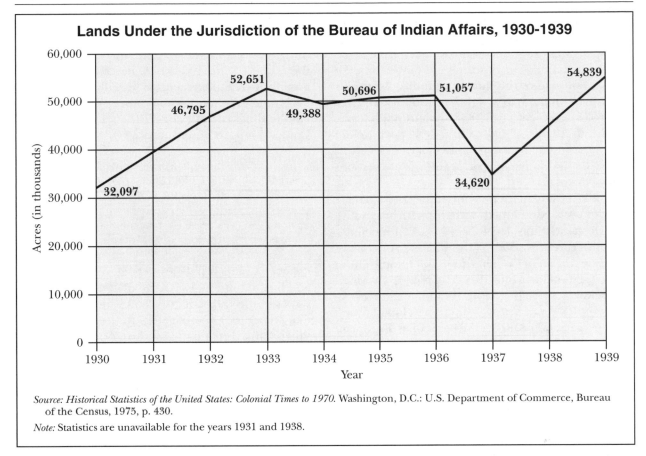

Lands Under the Jurisdiction of the Bureau of Indian Affairs, 1930-1939

Source: Historical Statistics of the United States: Colonial Times to 1970. Washington, D.C.: U.S. Department of Commerce, Bureau of the Census, 1975, p. 430.

Note: Statistics are unavailable for the years 1931 and 1938.

result was the *Problem of Indian Administration* (1928), a report that concluded that Native Americans had been largely abandoned by the government to poverty and destitution. Moreover, the education that Native Americans were receiving in Indian schools was woefully inadequate in preparing them to make a living. A year later, when the stock market crashed and even white Americans began to find themselves without work or money, Native Americans became the poorest of the poor.

The election of Franklin D. Roosevelt in 1932 created an environment in which Collier could be a powerbroker for Native Americans, as the new administration was actively seeking ways to address a nation of poor people. Collier became commissioner of the Bureau of Indian Affairs in 1934. In his classic book *The Indians of the Americas* (1947), Collier devotes an entire chapter to the "Indian New Deal," describing in detail the rationale behind his legislative agenda. Actually, however, what was referred to as the "Indian New Deal" consisted of sev-

eral important legislative initiatives that carried forward into the first half of the 1940's. All were in large part brought about by the work of Collier and reformers of his type. The Johnson-O'Malley Act of April, 1934, allowed tribes to contract directly with the secretary of the Department of the Interior through their state or territory for medical or educational services that had been provided by the Bureau of Indian Affairs.

The Indian Reorganization Act (IRA), passed in June of 1934, was the central component of Collier's policies. It reversed the Dawes Act, bringing an end to the allotment policy and seeking to reverse the damage these policies caused. The federal government set forth a program to restore tribal lands that had been deemed surplus and to spend up to two million dollars per year to purchase additional land for Native American communities. The federal government also encouraged tribes to develop constitutions and loaned money to them for economic development. This program was actually an attempt to enable tribes to act as corporate entities and thereby to manage their own resources and assets. One model for this program was the Klamath tribe in Oregon, who, after years of seeing the timber on their reservation sold by the Bureau of Indian Affairs for virtually nothing, had sought and won the right to control and thereby profit from their own resources. Finally, in August of 1935, the federal government set up the Indian Arts and Crafts Board in an effort to encourage Native American cultural expressions and works of art.

Unlike government policies of the past, Collier's policies were developed with input from Native Americans. He traveled to various tribal meetings, listening carefully to ideas from Native Americans. However, for all of Collier's good intentions, within the legislation was a fatal flaw: The policies provided a bureaucratic, homogenous solution to an incredibly complex set of issues that had developed over a long period of time. From the beginning, European settlers had assumed that all aborigines of the New World were the same. The very name "Indian" underscores that point: Christopher Columbus called the first Native Americans "Indians" because he thought he was in India. Despite his obvious error, subsequent settlers continued to use the name, thus embedding in the English language a misnomer. Moreover, because of the effects of hundreds of years of European colonization, many of the tribes were at various stages of adapting and responding to American culture. For example, tribes such as the Cherokee and the Crow had been banished from their homeland in the southeast to Oklahoma and had been forced to adapt to the environment around them. They had largely assimilated. They had no strong tribal organization left. Some Native Americans had retained the allotments they received during the time of the Dawes Act and had no intention of moving back to communal ownership of land. Perhaps influenced by the Red Scare of the 1920's, other Native Americans saw what Collier wanted to do as socialistic. Thus, though Collier took his proposals to the Native American people whom he sought to help, he did not get the universal support for which he had hoped. Out of 258 tribes, 181 voted to support and participate in the program.

Nonetheless, Collier's accomplishments are noteworthy and transformed Native American life during the 1930's. Collier was the first director of the Bureau of Indian Affairs to last eleven years, and he was actually able to reverse the loss of native lands, something that had not been done since the creation of the United States. Native American landholdings grew from 47 million acres to 51 million during Collier's time in office. Perhaps more important, those landholdings lasted. In his *The Indians of the Americas*, Collier points to other successes:

> We have seen the Indian prove himself to be the best credit risk in the United States: of more than $10.3 million loaned across the years, only $69,000 is today delinquent. We have seen the Indian beef-cattle holdings . . . increase 105 percent in number of animals and 2,300 percent in yield of animal products.

Impact Collier's policies were never fully funded, and by the time he left office in 1945, the political forces in the U.S. Congress had reverted the policy that recognized an obligation to the land's original inhabitants. Termination and relocation, the policies that were voted in during the 1940's, repudiated all the "Indian New Deal" had brought into being. Native Americans were offered free fare to the city, where they were placed in jobs and acculturated into American urban life. The system did not work to bring prosperity or security to Native Americans, despite the fact that many Native Americans served admirably in World War II. Native Americans remain one of the most impoverished segments of American society.

H. William Rice

Further Reading

Ballantine, Betty, and Ian Ballantine. *Native Americans: An Illustrated History*. Atlanta: Turner, 1992. Two chapters of this illustrated text explore Native American life during the 1930's and 1940's. One focuses upon the so-called New Deal for Indians and the other on termination.

Collier, John. *The Indians of the Americas*. New York: Norton, 1947. Provides a complete history of Native Americans. One chapter focuses on Collier's work as commissioner of the Bureau of Indian Affairs.

Limerick, Patricia Nelson. *Legacy of Conquest: The Unbroken Past of the American West*. New York: W. W. Norton, 1987. Seminal text on the complex history of westward expansion; discusses the contradictory policies of the U.S. government toward the Native American people.

Wilson, James. *The Earth Shall Weep: A History of Native America.* New York: Grove, 1999. A complete history of native people in the United States; readable for the nonscholar. The last chapters explore the political policies of the 1930's and the 1940's.

See also   Collier, John; Great Depression in Canada; New Deal.

■ Natural disasters

Definition   Catastrophic natural and weather-related events with significant impacts on human communities

The natural disasters of the 1930's ranged from hurricanes to floods, earthquakes, dust storms, and heat waves. Individually and collectively, the natural disasters of the decade only added to the widespread misery caused by the Great Depression.

During the 1930's, severe, drought-inspired heat waves took thousands of lives. A freakishly intense cold spell claimed the unprotected and unprepared. Hurricanes and tropical storms lashed Atlantic and Pacific shorelines. Sudden torrential downpours caused floods that swept away property and people. Tornadoes zeroed in on towns and leveled them. In terms of duration, geographic area, and the number of people affected, the North American drought of 1930-1940 was the greatest natural catastrophe of the decade. In fact, in sheer impact, it was the worst continental disaster of the twentieth century. The drought was oppressive and continual, with peaks in 1930-1931, 1934-1936, and 1939-1940.

Through much of the decade, parched, dry conditions seared vast areas, from the wheat fields of North Dakota to the cotton fields of Texas, the valleys of California, and the rolling hills of Pennsylvania. Incorporating millions of acres of Great Plains farms and ranches, the middle portion of the United States felt the drought the most. Fields that had been relentlessly plowed free of native grasses, which could have retained water and checked erosion, dried out, cracked, and crumbled. Crops withered and died, and their desiccated roots could not hold onto precious topsoil. Winds sprang up, carrying away millions of tons of grain in fierce storms that rained fine dust on East Coast cities. Malnourished livestock fell dead in blistering heat, their lungs clogged with grit. Vulnerable humans—the young, the elderly, and the infirm—sickened and died from what was called "dust pneumonia." The Bread Belt, the pride of American agriculture, turned to a sterile dust bowl that seemed to spawn extremes of weather across the entire country.

Major Disasters, 1930-1935   Despite the stock market crash of 1929, prospects for agriculture seemed bright at the dawn of the 1930's. Abundant early rains made for bumper wheat crops in the heartland of the United States. Meanwhile, the eastern seaboard sweltered: In July, 1930, temperatures hit 110 degrees Fahrenheit in Delaware. The winter of 1930-1931 was dry in the nation's center, and in the following year, summer temperatures soared. In 1931, a heat wave started in April and stayed into November, setting many all-time high temperatures in communities throughout Arizona, Minnesota, Wisconsin, North Dakota, Florida, Kentucky, and elsewhere.

On March 10, 1933, the first significant earthquake to be recorded at the new seismological lab at the California Institute of Technology in Pasadena rattled the environs of Long Beach, California. Estimated at a magnitude of 6.4, the quake and its aftershocks wrecked homes and toppled schools that were empty at the time. In office buildings, windows shattered and ornamental facades broke off to fall on the heads of terrified citizens as they dashed outside. The Long Beach earthquake caused the death of some 120 people, hundreds of injuries, and $50 million worth of property damage.

In 1935, two devastating hurricanes struck Florida. The first was called the Labor Day hurricane. The event was Category 5, one of the strongest storms ever to hit the United States. On September 2, it roared ashore in the Upper Keys, blowing 185-mile-per-hour winds and generating a murderous storm surge. Winds ripped apart buildings, bridges, roads, and railways in Islamorada, Craig Key, Long Key, and Matecumbe Key. Twenty-foot-high waves washed away the unwary, including many World War I veterans constructing a highway for the Works Progress Administration (WPA). More than four hundred people died, and for months afterward, bloated corpses were found in the mangrove swamps—an image immortalized in the 1948 film *Key Largo.* The second storm, a late-season blow dubbed "The Yankee Hurricane" because it slammed

Massive waves crashing against a seawall during the 1938 Great New England Hurricane. (NOAA)

into Miami from the north instead of from a normal southerly direction, was tame by comparison but still killed nineteen people and caused millions of dollars in property damage.

Major Disasters, 1936-1939 The year 1936 was hard, particularly for those in the middle and eastern parts of the United States. January and February produced some of the lowest temperatures on record in Iowa, North Dakota, South Dakota, and Minnesota, where hundreds suffered the effects of frostbite and hypothermia while enduring wind chills of −100 degrees. Snowfalls were heavy in the East, which experienced an early thaw. On St. Patrick's Day, rain and meltwater swelled the three rivers converging in Pittsburgh, Pennsylvania—the Allegheny, Monongahela, and Susquehanna—to thirty feet above flood stage. More than sixty people drowned, hundreds were injured, and the city's downtown was submerged.

On April 5-6, 1936, a series of tornadoes swirled across the Southeast. One flattened Tupelo, Mississippi, killing 216 citizens, and the other took out Gainesville, Georgia, where 203 people died. A heat wave that summer—particularly oppressive in Ohio,

Michigan, and Pennsylvania—killed more than five thousand individuals from heat stroke.

In the Midwest, the following year began ominously, with days of heavy snowfalls mixed with rain and sleet. In late January and early February, the Ohio River swelled beyond its banks to cause flooding across six states. Water levels reached historic heights in Louisville, Kentucky; Cincinnati, Ohio; and elsewhere. Nearly four hundred people drowned, five hundred dollars worth of property was damaged, and one million individuals from Pittsburgh to Cairo, Illinois, were left homeless.

In 1938, another significant flood occurred, this time in Los Angeles, where February storms dropped an unusual amount of rain across Southern California. Swollen rivers swept away bridges, roads, homes, and people. More than one hundred people died, and water or mudslides caused more than $50 million in damages. That fall, New England was the victim of the first major hurricane in nearly seventy years to strike the region. Labeled "the Long Island Express," the unusually fast-moving Category 5 storm pounded Long Island, New York; Connecticut; Rhode Island; Massachusetts; New Hampshire; and Vermont. One of the most destructive hurricanes in U.S. history, it killed eight hundred people and caused more than $300 million in damages— equivalent to $4.5 billion in the twenty-first century.

The decade of the 1930's closed with a last, unusual disaster: the only tropical storm to hit California in the twentieth century. Coming ashore at San Pedro with force 11 winds and copious amounts of rain, it killed forty-five people on land and an equal number at sea.

Impact Natural disasters are harsh learning experiences. Those who survive make provisions where possible to prevent future disasters from inflicting the same level of destruction. Many measures, including the Soil Conservation Service (now known as the Natural Resources Conservation Service), were established during the Depression to educate farmers about avoiding practices that led to the Dust Bowl. Following the Long Beach earthquake, California passed legislation governing building codes, which saved countless lives. After the devastating floods of the 1930's, many communities erected or improved levies and dikes to ameliorate the effect of recurrences. Areas prone to hurricanes and tornadoes have established evacuation routes or standardized protective procedures to lessen destruction.

Jack Ewing

Further Reading

Castro, James E. *The Great Ohio River Flood of 1937.* Mount Pleasant, S.C.: Arcadia, 2009. Illustrated work about one of worst floods in U.S. history; discusses the measures taken afterward to prevent future disasters.

Knowles, Thomas Neil. *Category Five: The 1935 Labor Day Hurricane.* Gainesville: University Press of Florida, 2009. Incorporating official records, personal accounts of survivors, and interviews with the family members of victims, this book presents a vivid picture of the devastation caused by an intense localized hurricane.

Meyer, William B. *Americans and Their Weather.* New York: Oxford University Press, 2000. Exploration of how weather has caused adaptations in American culture since the founding of the United States.

Scotti, R. A. *Sudden Sea: The Great Hurricane of 1938.* New York: Back Bay Books, 2004. Includes published recollections and personal interviews of the unusually fast-moving hurricane that ripped across New England.

Steinberg, Theodore. *Acts of God: The Unnatural History of Natural Disaster in America.* New York: Oxford University Press, 2006. Detailed examination of the economic effects of the worst natural disasters in U.S. history, emphasizing how many postdisaster changes excluded consideration of those who needed the most help.

Worster, Donald. *Dust Bowl: The Southern Plains in the 1930's.* New York: Oxford University Press, 2004. Part social history, part environmental study, this book focuses on the far-ranging causes and effects of the Dust Bowl.

See also Agriculture in the United States; Black Monday; Dust Bowl; *Grapes of Wrath, The;* Great New England hurricane; Heat wave of 1931; Labor Day hurricane; Long Beach earthquake; Ohio River flood; Soil Conservation Service.

■ Natural Gas Act of 1938

The Law   Federal law giving the Federal Power Commission the authority to regulate interstate natural-gas sales

Date   June 21, 1938

With the Natural Gas Act of 1938, the federal government asserted its authority to regulate interstate energy prices, limiting the ability of producers and distributors to profit from abusive monopolies. It expanded the authority of the Federal Power Commission, created originally to regulate only hydroelectric power.

During the 1910's and 1920's, new technologies made possible the transportation of natural gas over long distances through pipelines. As companies producing and distributing natural gas expanded during the 1930's, concern grew that they were overcharging customers for what was seen as an essential commodity. Through the 1920's, various states attempted to regulate the pipelines, but the U.S. Supreme Court concluded that states did not have the authority to regulate interstate pipelines.

In 1935, the Federal Trade Commission issued a report that concluded that prices for natural gas and electricity were unreasonable and favored certain customers over others. The Natural Gas Act of 1938 expanded the authority of the Federal Power Commission, which regulated how much companies could charge for the gas in exchange for allowing them exclusive use of the pipelines in their region. Under the regulations, companies could pass along to their consumers the legitimate expenses incurred in building and maintaining the pipelines.

Impact   The Natural Gas Act of 1938 was the first federal law regulating the interstate energy supply. With other energy regulations from the 1930's, it established the principle that utility companies could charge amounts based on the cost of generating and delivering their product, plus what was considered a fair profit, rather than charging whatever the market would bear. These principles determined natural gas pricing until 1978, when an energy shortage led to the National Energy Act, which took steps toward achieving a better balance between supply and demand.

Cynthia A. Bily

Further Reading

Busby, Rebecca L. *Natural Gas in Nontechnical Language.* Tulsa, Okla.: PennWell Books, 1999.

MacAvoy, Paul W. *The Natural Gas Market: Sixty Years of Regulation and Deregulation.* New Haven, Conn.: Yale University Press, 2000.

Tomain, Joseph P. *Energy Law.* St. Paul, Minn.: West, 1981.

See also   Business and the economy in the United States; Federal Power Commission; Public Utilities Act; Supreme Court, U.S.

■ Natural resources

The exploitation of natural resources such as coal, oil, water, timber, and land continued to fuel American economic development during the 1930's. Some of the long-term costs of this process were not yet noticeable, but others, such as soil erosion, were starting to become problems. Most Americans still thought that natural resources were inexhaustible.

The use of natural resources has driven American economic growth throughout the history of the United States. The cornucopian philosophy that natural resources are inexhaustible and therefore should be used unsustainably for pure economic gain has been the underlying justification for the process of resource utilization. This philosophy considers only the present rather than the consequences of extracting natural resources or the possibility that the resource could someday be exhausted. It also does not count the environmental costs of resource extraction or use. The impact of the Depression further diminished environmental concerns, as business and government turned their attention to economic recovery.

By the 1930's, the United States had a mature industrial economy that needed extensive natural resources in order to foster economic growth. Soil and water usage were important drivers of agricultural production, for both food and crops such as cotton. American forests continued to provide building material for homes and industry. Coal was the country's major energy source, although oil was beginning to be used in increasing amounts and water power was still important in some areas. Metallic ores such as iron, copper, and nickel were at the core of indus-

trial production, while gold and silver were important for both industry and luxury consumption. Many Americans drew their incomes from extractive industries, and agriculture and industrial workers depended on these products in the workplace.

Agriculture, Water Use, and Timber   Agricultural and timber production had long been important American industries. By the 1930's, farmers had increased production of both food crops and market crops, most notably cotton. Overproduction was considered a problem, and one New Deal program, the Agricultural Adjustment Act (enacted in 1933), tried to deal with overproduction by taking land out of use. Many crops such as cotton can exhaust the soil if they are planted every year. By the 1930's, soil exhaustion had become an issue in many parts of the cotton-producing South. As farmers tried to increase their incomes by raising more cotton, often with little use of fertilizer, they exhausted the soil; thus, by the 1930's, some southern farms were no longer suitable for growing any crops.

In some cases massive erosion occurred so that fields were covered with gullies as the remaining topsoil washed away. Farmers had also tried to increase production on the Great Plains by planting row crops, such as wheat, that were unsuitable for the arid climate of the region. Starting during the 1920's, a succession of dry years made growing anything impossible on many farms in Western states such as Kansas, Oklahoma, Colorado, South Dakota, and North Dakota. In this case the topsoil blew away once there was no vegetation to hold it in place. Even more than southern soil erosion, the problems of the Dust Bowl illustrated the dangers of poor agricultural practices that did not take environmental conditions into account.

By 1930, many areas in the eastern United States had been deforested by logging. Logging continued in the southern Appalachians, but some areas were turned into national parks and forests. Logging continued in the upper Midwest and the Pacific Northwest, as timber companies continued to seek out old-growth timber to obtain better quality lumber. A few timber companies started programs to replant timber, but many continued the policy of moving on to new forests, leaving devastation behind. Areas that had been clear-cut still contained scrap timber and were often subject to forest fires. Fires and the erosion that resulted from rain on hillsides that no longer had tree cover caused floods and degraded land quality in many areas. Some timber companies eyed federal and state forests with interest as they logged off their own land. Some conservation groups such as the Wilderness Society tried to limit the impact of logging but often were unsuccessful, as wood products continued to be in high demand. Federal programs such as the Civilian Conservation Corps did engage in tree planting in some areas during the late 1930's.

Erosion that was caused by poor agricultural practices and logging also had a negative impact on another important natural resource: water. Americans had long taken the availability of water for granted. Water is necessary for human consumption but also is an important energy source and recreation outlet and is used for irrigation. During the 1930's, the federal government and electric-power companies worked to harness water energy and to prevent flooding. Dams large and small were built. Some such as Boulder Dam (later Hoover Dam), which dammed the Colorado River, and the dams of the Tennessee Valley Authority were designed to provide jobs and to provide electric power. Power companies also constructed dams, such as Bagnell Dam built by Union Electric Company on the Osage River in Missouri. The lakes created by these dams provided recreational outlets as well as jobs, marinas, and restaurants. Some of these lakes, however, flooded productive farmland and displaced residents.

The lack of rainfall in the Great Plains region led to the Dust Bowl and created havoc with agriculture elsewhere. In the Central Valley of California, farmers had already turned to irrigation, but they were often in conflict with cities such as Los Angeles that needed the water. Water appeared to most Americans to be a resource to be exploited without regard to the consequences.

Coal and Oil Coal continued to power much of American industry, railroads, and homes during the 1930's. Most of the coal mined in the United States during the 1930's came from underground mines in the eastern and midwestern parts of the country. Underground mining was less harmful to the environment than surface mining, but it presented high human costs. Underground mining was dangerous and led to long-term health problems such as black lung disease. Underground mining was somewhat

wasteful as miners had to leave pillars of coal behind to shore up tunnels.

The negative impact of burning coal was not yet evident, although air pollution generated by coal smoke had become a problem in some areas such as Pittsburgh. During the early stages of the Depression, surface mining sprang up in some areas of Kentucky and West Virginia as individuals tried to eke out a living by mining readily available coal. Underground mining required large amounts of timber to shore up tunnels, and in some areas, forests were harvested to service the coal industry. Mine run-off often contained heavy metals and acids and so created water pollution problems for nearby residents.

The automobile was already becoming a major consumer of oil products during the 1930's, and some industries also used oil for energy. The chemical industry used oil as a feedstock for many chemical products. However, coal continued to be the major source of energy for American railroads, although a few lines used electric power, and some diesel engines were introduced by the end of the decade. Oil production continued to be concentrated in Oklahoma, Texas, Louisiana, and California. Almost all oil wells were shallow, as no technology existed for drilling deep wells. During the decade some oil companies also began to drill for oil in the shallow water of the Gulf of Mexico. Oil drillers had often been wasteful, failing to cap wells, so that large amounts of oil blew out onto the ground or caught fire and burned. Such waste was generally considered a normal part of production, and few considered that oil deposits might be limited. By the end of the 1920's, this approach was beginning to change; with developments in oil refining and the impact of the economic downturn, there was a glut in oil production for part of the 1930's. Several small oil companies either went bankrupt or were taken over by the larger firms. Various efforts were made to control production, most notably by the Railroad Commission of Texas, which assumed nearly defacto control over oil production by requiring producers to limit production.

Minerals and Metals The steel industry continued to be the major American industry during the 1930's. Steel-making required large amounts of coal for energy and iron ore to be turned into steel. Much of the iron mined in the United States came from the Mesabi Range in northern Minnesota. Copper production also was an important aspect of American industry; most copper was mined in the West, especially in Arizona and Montana. The vast, open-pit copper mine on the edge of Butte, Montana, crept steadily closer to the town during the decade. Copper smelting, generally done near the mines, generated large amounts of sulfuric acid as well as acid deposition. For example, much of the countryside around the copper smelters of Copper Hill, Tennessee, was totally denuded of vegetation during the 1930's by the sulfur dioxide produced by the copper smelters; the countryside remained wasted into the 1980's, long after the smelters had closed. Gold and silver production also generated acid-treated wastes that could harm nearby water supplies. These by-products of mining and smelting were regarded as an acceptable cost of doing business throughout the decade even though they caused short-term health and long-term environmental degradation.

Resource extraction and consumption during the 1930's continued in the wasteful fashion that had been followed in earlier years. Few people were aware of the long-term costs of resource extraction and use, although some commentators pointed to short-term issues such as "killer smog" or the health problems of miners. The need to overcome the Depression also dampened any reservations that people had about resource exploitation. Only in agriculture were people becoming aware of the long-term problems of poor practices. The erosion caused by what some scholars have labeled "soil mining" by cotton farmers was evident during the 1930's. In 1935, the Soil Conservation Service went so far as to introduce the Japanese plant kudzu as a means of providing ground cover for soil that was unable to grow any other plants. However, kudzu has no natural enemies in the United States and became a problem plant in many areas of the Southeast.

Impact   Driven by a perceived economic need and an unawareness of any environmental problems, the United States continued its unabated efforts at extracting and consuming natural resources during the 1930's. Aside from agriculture, most of the costs of this extraction and consumption would be paid by later generations.

John M. Theilmann

Further Reading
Caudill, Harry M. *Night Comes to the Cumberlands.* Boston: Little, Brown, 1963. Essential treatment of the impact of coal mining in eastern Kentucky.

Lynch, Martin. *Mining in World History.* London: Reaktion Books, 2004. Good historical overview of mining.

Maugeri, Leonardo. *The Age of Oil.* Guilford, Conn.: Lyons Press, 2006. Places American oil production in a world perspective.

Merchant, Carolyn. *American Environmental History: An Introduction.* New York: Columbia University Press, 2007. Deals with several long-term aspects of natural resource exploitation and contains a useful bibliography.

Powell, James Lawrence. *Dead Pool.* Berkeley: University of California Press, 2008. Describes the building of Boulder Dam and the resulting environmental and legal issues surrounding Lake Powell.

Williams, Michael. *Americans and Their Forests.* New York: Cambridge University Press, 1989. Although much of the focus is pre-1930, contains important insights about forests in the United States during the 1930's.

Worster, Donald. *Dust Bowl.* Rev. ed. New York: Oxford University Press, 2004. Classic treatment of the impact of the Dust Bowl.

See also   Agriculture in the United States; Boulder Dam; Dust Bowl; Great Depression in the United States; Soil Conservation Service; Tennessee Valley Authority.

■ Naval forces

In the age before intercontinental air travel, control of the sea was the primary assurance of national defense. Nations relied upon their navies to protect their soil; however, navies were expensive organizations, and the major powers tried to limit naval armaments to reduce costs and lower the threat of naval competition that might trigger another world war.

Naval forces during the 1930's faced a number of challenges stemming from international treaties intended to limit naval armament and prevent future wars. In 1922, the United States, Great Britain, Japan, France, and Italy agreed to the Washington Naval Treaty, which limited the size and number of battleships and aircraft carriers each country could possess. In 1930, the nations agreed to the London Naval Treaty, which limited the number of cruisers, destroyers, and submarines that each fleet could

Commissioned in 1934, the aircraft carrier USS Ranger *roved the Atlantic Ocean during World War II.* (NARA)

possess. Together, the two treaties imposed strict limits on size, firepower, and capability of each ship type, forcing navies to innovate and compromise on ship design.

Battleships, long the centerpiece of naval power, were a particular problem. The Washington Treaty imposed a ten-year "battleship holiday," meaning treaty signers agreed not to construct any battleships for ten years; this agreement was renewed in 1930. As battleships aged, navies had to reconstruct and rebuild their battleships to ensure their effectiveness. Older battleships received a variety of improvements throughout the 1930's. Coal-fueled ships were converted to oil-fueled ships, side "bulges" was added to absorb torpedo hits, and deck armor to counter air-dropped bombs was added. Battleships also received new equipment during the 1930's,

such as improved fire-control systems and antiaircraft guns to deal with the aerial threat.

Aircraft carriers, also limited by the Washington Treaty, became a more prominent part of the world navies, first as reconnaissance platforms and then as attack weapons. The first aircraft carriers in the U.S. Navy were converted battle-cruiser hulls, but the first purpose-built aircraft carriers appeared during the 1930's, starting with USS *Ranger* in 1934. Allowed only a limited tonnage of aircraft carriers, the U.S. Navy debated whether more small carriers or fewer larger carriers were preferable. *Ranger*, at fifteen thousand tons, represented the small-carrier theory. The ship was too cramped for effective service, however, and the next class of aircraft carriers, the *Yorktown* class, began service in 1937 at a displacement of twenty thousand tons.

The same debate on tonnage distribution also affected submarine construction after the United States signed the London Treaty. As it had with aircraft carriers, the U.S. Navy opted to build a smaller number of large submarines with operations in the Pacific Ocean in mind. The U.S. Navy viewed Japan as its most likely adversary in a future war, so it needed large submarines with long range to patrol the vast expanse of the Pacific. The *Salmon* class submarines of 1937, for example, displaced nearly three thousand tons and had a range of more than eleven thousand miles.

Size was also an issue for American destroyers. Some strategists in the U.S. Navy wanted small destroyers as battle-fleet escorts, requiring only guns and depth charges to ward off enemy destroyers and submarines. However, other officers wanted large destroyers with a heavy torpedo armament so destroyers could act as fast-attack forces on their own. Eventually, the heavy destroyer won out, as demonstrated by the 1936 *Benham*-class destroyers armed with four 5-inch guns and eight 21-inch torpedo tubes on a displacement of twenty-four hundred tons.

The allocation of cruiser tonnage, however, was the most contentious debate, because cruisers could do so many things. Various strategists wanted cruisers to escort the battle fleet, while others viewed them as advanced battle-fleet scouts; others still perceived cruisers as a separate offensive wing of the fleet. Again, the debate between "heavy" cruisers armed with relatively few 8-inch guns versus "light" cruisers armed with more 6-inch guns emerged. In the immediate aftermath of the London Treaty, the U.S. Navy opted for heavy cruisers, such as the 1933 *Portland* class, with nine 8-inch guns. In 1935, however, the Japanese navy commissioned the first *Mogami* class light cruiser with a massive armament of fifteen 6-inch guns. In reply, the U.S. Navy began construction of similar vessels: the *Brooklyn* class, which entered service in 1937, with an armament similar to the *Mogami* class ships. The U.S. Navy concentrated on light-cruiser construction thereafter.

During the late 1930's, weight requirements ceased to matter. Unhappy with the treaty tonnage allocations that placed its navy behind those of the United States and Great Britain, in 1936 Japan announced that it was no longer abiding by the agreements. That, in turn, freed the other treaty signers to increase the size of their ships and fleets. The United States responded by authorizing the *North Carolina*- and *South Dakota*-class battleships—thirty-six thousand tons and thirty-five thousand tons, respectively—and the heavy *Essex*- and light *Independence*-class aircraft carriers—thirty-six thousand tons and eleven thousand tons, respectively. Other ship types during the late 1930's also grew in displacement, such as the *Cleveland*-class light cruisers, at fourteen thousand tons; the *Fletcher*-class destroyers, at twenty-five hundred tons; and the *Tambor*-class submarines, at twenty-four hundred tons.

In addition to warship construction, naval forces during the 1930's introduced other technological and tactical innovations. Aircraft carriers came into their own during the 1930's. At first, navies centered on battleships considered the aircraft to be simply a launch platform for scout planes to locate the enemy for the battleships to engage. Improvements in aircraft, however, meant that aircraft carriers became offensive weapons in their own right. Besides fighter aircraft to defend the fleet, aircraft carriers could attack enemy ships with their torpedo bombers or dive bombers. First developed during the 1920's, torpedo bombers flew in at low levels to launch their torpedoes at an enemy ship. A tactic introduced in the 1930's, however, was dive-bombing, where an aircraft swooped down from high altitude to low altitude in a steep dive, literally flying the bomb directly into the target before pulling out of the dive and flying away. The U.S. Navy in particular favored dive bombing as more accurate than torpedo attacks, acquiring its first specialized dive bomber, the Curtiss F8C Helldiver, in 1929.

Although often perceived as an element of World War II, the first electronic equipment began to appear on naval ships during the 1930's. In 1935, the U.S. Navy introduced the MK 37 Gun Fire Control System, a complex electromechanical aiming system for medium-caliber guns on destroyers and cruisers. The MK 37 provided central aiming data for antiaircraft guns shooting at fast-moving enemy aircraft, data that the gun crews themselves could not calculate. Submarines also received an electromechanical aiming device for its torpedoes, the Torpedo Data Computer, developed during the late 1930's and first deployed in 1940. The Torpedo Data Computer calculated a variety of variables, such as the speed of the submarine and the speed and distance of the target, to calculate firing solutions against enemy targets at high angles of deflection. For navigation, ships received radio direction finders to reference their position relative to fixed radio emitters on shore. In 1931, the U.S. Navy introduced its first submarine-detecting sonar system, code-named the "QB," which emitted a supersonic sound wave into the water from a hydrophone array under the bow of the ship.

Impact The treaties that limited naval armament during the early 1930's ultimately failed, and the ships designed and introduced during the late 1930's became the cornerstone of the massive fleets that battled in World War II. The weaponry and ships of the era shaped how the fleets of the world fought the battles of the 1940's. Battleships still played a role but were surpassed by the aircraft carrier as the primary fleet weapon, as their torpedo planes and dive bombers could dominate a naval battle at ranges far beyond those of a battleship's guns. The early electronic devices of the 1930's also expanded into full-blown electronic warfare during the 1940's.

Steven J. Ramold

Further Reading

Felker, Craig C. *Testing American Sea Power: U.S. Navy Strategic Exercises, 1923-1940.* College Station: Texas A&M University Press, 2007. Faced with the limits of existing naval treaties, the U.S. Navy used naval exercises to test its capabilities with its limited number of ships.

Goldman, Emily O. *Sunken Treaties: Naval Arms Control Between the Wars.* University Park: Pennsylvania State University Press, 1994. Discussion of the failure of the Washington, D.C., and London treaties by placing the agreements in the context of diplomatic and nationalistic goals.

Kuehn, John T. *Agents of Innovation: The General Board and the Design of the Fleet That Defeated the Japanese Navy.* Annapolis, Md.: Naval Institute Press, 2008. Institutional study of the General Board of the United States Navy, an organization that shaped requirements, designs, and construction of ships in the interwar period.

Marriott, Leo. *Treaty Cruisers: The First International Warship Building Competition.* London: Pen and Sword, 2005. A discussion of how the major navies accommodated, and sometimes cheated on, the London Treaty in their 1930's cruiser construction programs.

Murray, Williamson R. *Military Innovation in the Interwar Period.* New York: Cambridge University Press, 1998. Although the book also depicts land and air innovations, most of the pages are devoted to the creative means by which navies accommodated the restrictive treaties.

See also *Akron* disaster; Aviation and aeronautics; Foreign policy of the United States; Geneva Disarmament Conference; London Naval Treaty; *Panay* incident; *Ranger,* USS; *Squalus* sinking.

Nazi Germany. See **Germany and U.S. appeasement**

■ *Near v. Minnesota*

The Case U.S. Supreme Court ruling on freedom of the press
Date Decided on June 1, 1931

In this case the U.S. Supreme Court ruled that a state law violated freedom of the press and held, for the first time, that injunctions on the press to prevent publication are presumptively unconstitutional "prior restraints" and that the parties seeking them have a heavy burden to overcome; however, it also suggested that prior restraints could be acceptable under certain circumstances.

The case of *Near v. Minnesota* originated when a Minnesota man, Jay Near, publisher of *The Saturday Press,* was charged with violating a state law prohibiting publication of "malicious, scandalous and defamatory" articles. From 1919 through 1933, the manufacture, sale, or importation of intoxicating liquor was prohibited in the United States. Bootlegging and associated illegal activities attempted to circumvent such prohibitions. In 1927, Near's newspaper published articles claiming that a Jewish gangster controlled gambling and bootlegging in Minneapolis and that local officials—including the city's chief of police, the county attorney, and the mayor—failed to perform their duties and were complicit with the criminals. The articles leveled serious allegations against these public officials. Minnesota officials obtained a gag order enjoining continued publication of the newspaper. The injunction could be lifted only by the judge who issued it, and that judge would have to be convinced that Near's publication would not be objectionable in the future.

When Near's challenge to the Minnesota law reached the U.S. Supreme Court in 1931, the Court voted five to four to invalidate the law. Writing for the majority, Chief Justice Charles Evans Hughes observed that there was no doubt that freedom of the press was a liberty protected by the Fourteenth Amendment's due process clause. The law allowed public authorities to bring a publisher before a judge and to obtain an order suppressing further publication. This, Hughes said, constituted censorship. Reviewing the historical record, Hughes concluded that a chief purpose of liberty of the press is to prevent previous restraints on publication. He also wrote that public officers objecting to press characterizations of their conduct could take action under libel laws, but not by restraining publication before the fact. Subsequent punishment for false accusations was the appropriate remedy. The fact that press liberty may be abused by "miscreant purveyors of scandal" did not justify prior restraint upon publication.

Impact Since the *Near v. Minnesota* ruling, the Supreme Court has upheld the doctrine against prior restraints on the media. With only narrow exceptions, governmental restraints on publication before the fact have been regarded as constitutionally impermissible.

Joseph A. Melusky

Further Reading

Edelman, Rob, ed. *Freedom of the Press.* San Diego: Greenhaven Press, 2007.

Hebert, David L., ed. *Freedom of the Press.* Detroit: Greenhaven Press, 2005.

Kersch, Ken I. *Freedom of Speech: Rights and Liberties Under the Law.* Santa Barbara, Calif.: ABC-Clio, 2003.

See also Civil rights and liberties in the United States; *Grosjean v. American Press Co.*; Newspapers, U.S.; Supreme Court, U.S.

■ Nebbia v. New York

The Case U.S. Supreme Court ruling on constitutionality of New York price controls
Date Decided on March 5, 1934

Deferring to legislative findings on the condition of New York's milk industry, the Supreme Court held that reasonable regulation of the economy by the government cannot be overturned by the courts.

In 1932, the price of milk in New York declined to below the cost of its production. In response, the New York legislature established a Milk Control Board in 1933 to regulate milk prices. Leo Nebbia, a Rochester grocer, sold two quarts of milk below the minimum price of nine cents a quart set by the board. He was arrested and fined five dollars; his conviction was affirmed by a county court and the highest New York court. In 1934, the U.S. Supreme Court decided his appeal on the question of whether price regulation violated the due process clause of the Fourteenth Amendment of the U.S. Constitution.

In the historic case of *Lochner v. New York,* 198 U.S. 45 (1905), the Supreme Court had invalidated previous employment regulation as violating the liberty right to contract—what became known as "substantive due process." In his opinion in *Nebbia v. New York* (1934), Justice Owen J. Roberts did not explicitly overturn *Lochner.* He did, however, defer to the extensive empirical evidence compiled by the legislature as to conditions of the milk industry to find that regulation of milk prices was a legitimate exercise of New York's authority to legislate in the public interest. Over the dissent of the justices known as the "Four Horsemen," Roberts stated that neither property nor contract rights are absolute and cannot be used by courts to invalidate reasonable regulations of the economy.

Impact Reflecting a turn away from judicial hostility to government intervention, the *Nebbia* decision was cited by the historic case of *West Coast Hotel Co. v. Parrish* (1937) to uphold regulation of the use of private property and the making of private contracts, if neither arbitrary nor discriminatory, thereby protecting New Deal-era government regulation from judicial review.

Howard Bromberg

Further Reading

Hall, Kermit, and Peter Karsten. *The Magic Mirror: Law in American History.* 2d ed. New York: Oxford University Press, 2008.

Kahn, Paul. *Legitimacy and History. Self-Government in American Constitutional Theory.* New Haven, Conn.: Yale University Press, 1993.

Philips, Michael. *The Lochner Court, Myth and Reality: Substantive Due Process from the 1890s to the 1930s.* Westport, Conn.: Praeger, 2001.

See also   Business and the economy in the United States; Four Horsemen vs. Three Musketeers; Great Depression in the United States; Nonpartisan League; Roberts, Owen J.; *Schechter Poultry Corp. v. United States*; Supreme Court, U.S.; *United States v. Carolene Products Co.*; *West Coast Hotel Co. v. Parrish.*

■ Nebraska unicameral legislature

The Event   Nebraska state government's conversion from a two-chamber to a one-chamber legislature

Date   Authorized in November, 1934; first session of revised legislature on January 5, 1937

In an experiment intended to make government more transparent and efficient, Nebraska's legislature eliminated one of the traditional legislative chambers and required candidates to run for office as nonpartisan candidates. The new legislative form was also more economical, an important consideration during the Great Depression. Since the 1930's, Nebraska has remained the only U.S. state with a unicameral legislature.

In 1934, reeling from the Great Depression and angry at the political system considered responsible for the poor economic condition of the country, voters in Nebraska approved an amendment to the state constitution that revised their state legislature. Instead of the traditional two houses, the Senate and the House of Representatives, Nebraskans created a smaller body known simply as the state legislature. Several factors drove the change. Antigovernment attitudes ran high because of the seeming inability of the government to alleviate the suffering of the Great Depression, and a smaller state government seemed to be a means of limiting its power. Reducing the size of the government would also lead to

lower government costs and a reduced tax burden. Supporters of the measure claimed that having only one house would prevent legislative bickering and facilitate the movement of legislative bills, as would a provision requiring candidates to run for office without stating their political party allegiance.

In November, 1934, a state constitutional amendment effecting the change passed easily and became law despite several legal challenges. In January, 1937, the new legislature opened its first session. The new body was much smaller, reflecting the desire for simpler government. Whereas the last session with the two-chamber legislature had a combined 133 members, the new unicameral legislature had only 30; later, the legislature expanded to 49 seats. Even with the expansion of seats, Nebraska still maintains the smallest state legislature in the country.

Impact   Although the unicameral legislature was held up as a promising new form of government, no other state adopted the system; however, a single-chamber legislature does exist in nonstate entities such as the District of Columbia, the Virgin Islands, and Guam. While not a widespread form of government, the unicameral system has functioned well for Nebraska.

Steven J. Ramold

Further Reading

Berens, Charlyne. *One House: The Unicameral's Progressive Vision for Nebraska.* Lincoln: University of Nebraska Press, 2005.

Todd, Tom. *Nebraska's Unicameral Legislature.* St. Paul: Minnesota House of Representatives, 1998.

See also   Congress, U.S.; Great Depression in the United States; New Deal; Voting rights.

■ Negro Leagues

Definition   Professional baseball leagues for African American players

The Negro Leagues provided black players a venue to play professional baseball. During the 1930's and 1940's, the leagues attracted vast crowds and were among the largest black-owned businesses in the United States.

As professional baseball grew in popularity during the last half of the nineteenth century, an attempt was made to organize the various clubs around the country. In 1858, the National Association of Base Ball Players (NABBP) was formed to govern teams and establish rules of play. The NABBP's constitution of 1867 specifically prohibited black players, refusing to allow teams that included even one nonwhite player. Although political pressure eventually led to the removal of the clause from the constitution, by 1887, many Major League Baseball team owners entered into "gentleman's agreements" that barred African Americans and Caucasians from playing baseball together. When the season began in 1890, there were no black players on any minor or major league teams.

The First Leagues   Hotel owners in Florida and New York formed the first paid, all-black teams during the 1880's. The teams featured hotel employees who played for the entertainment of guests. One of the teams, the Cuban Giants, played a number of exhibition games against major and minor league clubs—a practice often called "barnstorming"—and was financially successful. A number of other barn-

storming teams arose during the late nineteenth and early twentieth centuries and followed the same model as the Giants.

Several attempts were made to create independent, all-black leagues from the 1880's into the twentieth century. However, organizations such as the League of Colored Baseball Clubs and the Iron and Oil League failed, usually because of a lack of financial backing.

The First and Second Negro National Leagues   In 1920, Rube Foster, a former pitcher for the Cuban Giants, actively pursued the creation of a league of all-black teams. The Negro National League was created in 1920 by owners of eight midwestern, all-black baseball clubs. With the exception of the Kansas City Monarchs, all Negro National League teams had black owners. The rival Eastern Colored League soon followed in 1922, and the two leagues agreed to an annual Negro League World Series. Increasing black populations in urban areas and the support of black-owned newspapers made the teams successful

Newark Eagles, a top Negro League team. Monte Irvin is at the far left in the second row. (Getty Images)

throughout the 1920's, but the leagues did not last long. Facing the tough economic climate of the Great Depression of the late 1920's and early 1930's, both leagues were out of business by 1932.

Gus Greenlee, owner of the Pittsburgh Crawfords, founded a second Negro National League in 1934, organizing seven existing all-black clubs under the National Organization of Professional Baseball Clubs. Greenlee's league improved on the model of the first Negro National League by adding fan promotions and banking on its star players. The second Negro National League boasted a number of celebrity players, and future National Baseball Hall of Fame inductees, including Satchel Paige, Josh Gibson, Willard Brown, and Cool Papa Bell.

A second league created in 1937, the Negro American League, added to the Negro Leagues' success. The existence of two leagues meant that both a World Series and, for the first time, an all-star game could be staged. The East-West All-Star Game was held annually at Chicago's Comiskey Park. Fans selected players by newspaper ballots, and the contests were wildly successful. A series of exhibition games against major league all-stars followed.

The End of the Negro Leagues   As the 1930's ended, many groups were calling for black players to be integrated into major league teams. Numerous politicians, sportswriters, and labor unions believed that integrating baseball would lead to the end of segregation in other areas.

In 1945, Brooklyn Dodgers owner Branch Rickey founded the United States Negro Baseball League with sole purpose of recruiting players to sign with Major League Baseball teams. Rickey eventually chose Jackie Robinson in 1946, signing him to the minor league Montreal Royals. Robinson was chosen for his talent, discipline, and because Ricky felt he could handle the pressure of becoming the first black player on a Major League Baseball team in the twentieth century. Robinson played one year with the Royals and was called up to the majors in 1947, playing the full season with the Dodgers.

The Negro National League merged with the Negro American League in 1948 and continued

through the 1950's. After Robinson signed with the Dodgers and more teams eventually featured black players, the Negro Leagues failed to attract the press and fans it once had.

Impact   Negro League teams were the first to feature such innovations as feet-first slides, night games, and the hit-and-run, and a number of players were later inducted in the National Baseball Hall of Fame. Many baseball scholars agree that the level of talent seen on black teams rivaled that of white teams. After Robinson broke the color barrier in 1947, other major league teams followed. The Boston Red Sox were the last team to hire a black player, finally signing Pumpsie Green to a contract in 1959. The Negro Leagues went a long way in the struggle to end segregation. Many civil rights leaders during the 1960's pointed to the eventual integration of baseball as the harbinger of later civil rights successes.

Bethany E. Pierce

Further Reading

Heaphy, Leslie A. *The Negro Leagues: 1869-1960.* Jefferson, N.C.: McFarland, 2003. Covers the Negro Leagues from the establishment of separate, racially defined baseball associations to the demise of the leagues, which was a result of integration in Major League Baseball.

Lanctot, Neil. *Negro League Baseball: The Rise and Ruin of a Black Institution.* Philadelphia: University of Philadelphia Press, 2004. History of the Negro Leagues that includes interviews with former players and extensive research into the development and management of the leagues.

Peterson, Robert. *Only the Ball Was White: A History of Legendary Black Players and All-Black Professional Teams.* Englewood Cliffs, N.J.: Prentice-Hall, 1970. Seminal text on the history of the Negro Leagues that focuses on its central irony: its very existence was made possible by exclusion.

See also   African Americans; Baseball; National Baseball Hall of Fame; Racial discrimination; Recreation; Sports in the United States.

■ Ness, Eliot

Identification   Federal Treasury Department
  agent
Born   April 19, 1903; Chicago, Illinois
Died   May 16, 1957; Coudersport, Pennsylvania

Ness was a Prohibition agent who was famous for battling organized crime and bringing down the infamous Al Capone. He led a group of law-enforcement officers who were known as "The Untouchables" because of their refusal to take bribes.

Born in Chicago in 1903, Eliot Ness was the youngest of five children of Norwegian immigrants. He graduated from the University of Chicago in 1925 with a degree in business and law and took a job with the Retail Credit Company in Atlanta, Georgia. Ness's brother-in-law, a federal government agent, encouraged Ness to get involved with law enforcement. He felt that the young man's skills could be put to use in a Prohibition unit being formed under the U.S. Treasury Department. Ness enrolled in criminology courses in early 1926 and eventually earned a master's degree in the field.

Ness was hired by the Treasury Department in 1927 and went to work in his hometown, Chicago. His familiarity with the city and its people was viewed as a benefit by his superiors. Ness worked for two years with the Prohibition unit in Chicago and in 1929 was assigned the task of bringing down Al Capone. Capone was the most powerful criminal in the Chicago underworld, known for ruthless retaliation against anyone who crossed him. Capone built his criminal enterprise by bootlegging alcohol from Canada and other sources during Prohibition; by the late 1920's, he had become the sole supplier of alcohol to the greater Chicago area.

Ness, at age twenty-six, was tasked with bringing to justice the most powerful, ruthless, and heavily armed man in Chicago. Capone also had bribed police officers and other law-enforcement officials throughout Chicago; Ness's original unit, comprising nearly sixty men, was no different. Ness weeded out those he suspected of taking bribes and eventually settled on a tight-knit group of nine to eleven men. Because Ness's men considered themselves immune to criminal influence, they were dubbed "The Untouchables."

Ness spent several years raiding Capone's breweries and safe houses. While he never was able to try Capone for murder or any other violent crime, Ness disrupted his business and documented many Prohibition violations. In 1931, Capone went on trial for multiple counts of tax evasion. That October, he was sentenced to eleven years in prison.

Ness continued to work within the federal government until 1935, when he was hired as the safety director for the city of Cleveland, Ohio. He oversaw all emergency response personnel, and vowed to reduce crime and restore order to the streets. He was successful in many ways, but his popularity waned as he developed a reputation for arrogance—perhaps fueled by his success in Chicago—and was accused of overstepping his authority. He was divorced twice and was suspected of drunken driving.

Most damaging, however, was Ness's failure to solve a series of gruesome killings that were dubbed the Cleveland Torso Murders. Although Ness claimed to know the killer's identity, he had no physical evidence to prove it. Fearing a lawsuit from the suspect's wealthy family, Ness never identified the person he believed to be the killer.

Eliot Ness at his desk during the early 1930's. (Hulton Archive/ Getty Images)

In 1942, Ness returned to Washington, D.C., and a position with the federal government. He spent the next few years investigating low-level prostitution and drug offenses. In the mid-1940's, he took a position with the security firm Diebold. After an unsuccessful campaign for mayor of Cleveland in 1947, Ness fell into obscurity. He died of a heart attack in 1957.

Impact The Prohibition-era underworld became a subject of fascination for subsequent generations, and Ness and Capone became cultural icons. The Untouchables were lionized as symbols of honesty and bravery amid a corrupt and crime-ridden city. Ness's autobiography, *The Untouchables* (1957), was published just one month after his death. Several years later, Ness's crime-fighting career was dramatized in a popular television series of the same title, in which actor Robert Stack played Ness. The success of the series made Ness a household name during the 1960's and led to a feature film, also titled *The Untouchables* (1987), in which Kevin Costner played Ness.

Keith J. Bell

Further Reading

Heimel, Paul. *Eliot Ness: The Real Story.* Nashville, Tenn.: Cumberland House, 2001.

Ness, Eliot, and Oscar Fraley. *The Untouchables.* 1957. Reprint. New York: Barnes & Noble Books, 1996.

Nickel, Steven. *Torso: The Story of Eliot Ness and the Search for a Psychopathic Killer.* Winston-Salem, N.C.: J. F. Blair, 2001.

Tucker, Kenneth. *Eliot Ness and the Untouchables: The Historical Reality and the Film and Television Depictions.* Jefferson, N.C.: McFarland, 2000.

See also Capone, Al; Crimes and scandals; Floyd, Pretty Boy; Gangster films; Nitti, Frank; Organized crime; Prohibition repeal; Revenue Acts.

■ Neutrality Acts

The Law U.S. laws designed to prevent participation in a foreign war

Also known as Neutrality Legislation; Neutrality Statutes

Dates Enacted 1935-1941

Attempting to prevent U.S. involvement in a foreign war, Congress passed four neutrality laws that limited the ability of the United States to provide assistance to countries that were at war with Germany and Japan.

Throughout the decade of the 1930's, the desire to stay out of foreign wars was extremely strong in the United States, particularly in the midwestern states. Adding support to isolationist sentiments, Senator Gerald Prentice Nye's committee held well-publicized hearings between 1934 and 1936, alleging that bankers and arms dealers had orchestrated U.S. entrance into World War I for reasons of profit. Several best-selling books reinforced the accusation. As threats of war began to appear in Europe and Asia, several pro-isolationist members of Congress believed that any such intervention in the future might be prevented by laws mandating neutrality.

Although President Franklin D. Roosevelt believed that neutrality legislation was imprudent, he recognized that such legislation enjoyed widespread support in public opinion, and he feared that a veto fight might interfere with the New Deal agenda. In 1934, he acquiesced in signing the Johnson Act, which prohibited loans to governments that were in default on their debts to the U.S. Treasury. In 1935, when Congress debated proposals for a neutrality act, officials in the Roosevelt administration attempted to persuade Congress that the president should have the discretion to decide when to apply a trade embargo. However, Senator Key Pittman, chair of the Foreign Relations Committee, told the president that he would be "licked as sure as hell" if he insisted on the right to support a particular belligerent in a foreign war.

First Neutrality Act Congress passed the Neutrality Act of 1935 with almost no debate, and President Roosevelt reluctantly signed it on August 31. The act prohibited U.S. companies from selling arms and war materials to any warring country during the following six months, and it established the National Munitions Control Board for the purpose of licensing all imports and exports of arms. The act also authorized the president to warn American citizens that if they traveled on ships of belligerent countries, they did so at their own risk. When Italy invaded Ethiopia in October of that year, Roosevelt announced American neutrality toward the conflict, prohibiting the sale of war goods to either side. The embargo did not apply to nonwar goods such as oil and steel, which were easily converted to military use. Because Italy was purchasing large amounts of

nonwar goods from U.S. companies, Roosevelt called for a "moral embargo" against Italy, which had little effect. Italy formally annexed Ethiopia on May 9, 1936.

Second Neutrality Act   Not long after the 1935 statute expired, Congress passed the Neutrality Act of 1936. In addition to continuing the provisions of the earlier statute for another fourteen months, the second Neutrality Act forbade credits and loans to warring countries. The act, however, did not apply to civil wars, and when the Spanish Civil War broke out, most members of Congress opposed any U.S. involvement, despite concern about the support that Nazi Germany and fascist Italy gave to the rebel forces of Francisco Franco. During the 1936 U.S. elections, both parties strongly advocated neutrality. Roosevelt declared, "I hate war," and if faced with "the choice of profits or peace, the nation will answer— must answer 'we choose peace.'" On January 6, 1937, Congress passed a joint resolution prohibiting the sale of munitions to either the loyalists or the pro-fascist rebels in Spain. Although Roosevelt disagreed with the resolution, he strictly enforced the embargo, which generally worked to the disadvantage of the loyalist government.

Third Neutrality Act   The Neutrality Act of 1937, enacted on May 1, required belligerent countries to pay cash for all nonwar materials and to transport them in their own ships. The act continued the ban on war materials and prohibited Americans from traveling on ships of belligerents. One provision authorized the president to decide when nations were at war and which materials were classified as war materials. In pubic opinion polls more than 68

Borah Argues Against European Involvement

The following is an excerpt from a radio address titled "Retain the Arms Embargo: It Helps Keep Us out of War," delivered by Senator William E. Borah on September 14, 1939. Borah argued strongly against a revision of the Neutrality Act of 1937 that would end the arms embargo.

We are met on the threshold of all debate, of all consideration, of this subject of neutrality with the statement often delivered and with an air of finality that we cannot be neutral, that Europe is now so near to the United States, owing to modern inventions and the mingling of business affairs, that neutrality is impracticable if not impossible.

This seems to me a spineless doctrine. It is not the doctrine inherited from our forebears. If true, we would be the most ill-fated nation on the earth instead of being, as we had long supposed, the most favorably circumstanced of any, or all, nations. . . .

But we have no alternative, it is in effect declared, after these 150 years of self-government, we must go in some way or other into all these controversies, broils and wars of Europe. It is useless, we are told, to try to avoid this fate. . . .

Although our people have sought peace and now seek peace, still we must make war because European governments maintain an eternal saturnalia of human sacrifices. Though the law of our land banishes racial and religious persecution from our common country, still, because Europe is "near," we must join in the racial and religious conflicts and sacrifice our people over conditions which our forebears long since rejected.

Though we seek no people's territory, nevertheless, because Europe is "near," we must sacrifice the savings of our people and the sons of our mothers in this endless imperialistic strife. Though we would take no part of the loot which was divided up at the close of the World War, we are now called upon to make sure the title to a vast amount of this loot. What a fateful doctrine to propose! Let us renounce it and make the effort at least to establish freedom from the European system.

percent of respondents said that they approved of the act and wanted it to be strictly enforced. In July, when Japanese troops invaded the Chinese mainland, Roosevelt wanted to help China and initially declined to designate the conflict as a war. Nevertheless, on September 14, he forbade the transportation of materials to either China or Japan in government vessels, and he notified private companies that any shipments would be at their own risk. On October 5, he called for an international quarantine on "bandit nations" guilty of aggression. Faced with overwhelming opposition, however, he quickly backed away from the suggestion. During the Munich crisis of 1938, he encouraged compromise with Hitler and made clear to Great Britain and France that the United States would not provide assistance in the event of war.

Fourth Neutrality Act On September 21, 1939, three weeks after Nazi Germany invaded Poland, Roosevelt called Congress into special session and requested that the cash-and-carry provision of the last neutrality act be amended to allow for the exports of war materials to belligerent countries. Although neutral in appearance, the proposal was clearly designed to help Britain and France, because the British Royal Navy prevented German ships from reaching American ports. Despite the fierce opposition of isolationists, Congress passed the Neutrality Act of 1939, which included Roosevelt's recommendation. Without the arms and supplies purchased under the act, the British would have almost certainly not been able continue their struggle. On December 21, 1940, the German government denounced U.S. assistance to Britain as "moral aggression."

Impact Most modern historians are critical of the first three of the Neutrality Acts because they provided no distinctions among aggressive countries and victims. By insisting on no assistance to any belligerent country, the isolationists responsible for the acts refused to make a choice in favor of the lesser of two evils. The Neutrality Act of 1939, with its cash-and-carry provisions, constituted a major departure from a policy of strict neutrality, and it meant that a future war with Nazi Germany was likely, but perhaps not inevitable.

Responding to Roosevelt's state of the union address that included an appeal for Congress to repeal the cash-and-carry requirements in the 1939 act, Congress passed the Lend-Lease Act, which allowed the president to transfer, sell, or lease war goods to any country that he considered vital to the defense of the United States. Within a few months, the Lend-Lease Act resulted in an undeclared naval war with Germany. On November 13, four days after a German submarine sank the U.S. destroyer *Reuben James*, Congress repealed all significant restrictions still remaining in the Neutrality Acts, allowing merchant vessels to arm themselves and to carry cargoes to belligerent ports.

Thomas Tandy Lewis

Further Reading

Cole, Wayne S. *Roosevelt and the Isolationists, 1932-1945*. Lincoln: University of Nebraska Press, 1983. Standard work by a historian devoted to the study of isolationism before World War II.

Dallek, Robert. *Franklin D. Roosevelt's Foreign Policy, 1932-1945*. New York: Oxford University Press, 1979. A scholarly and balanced account of Roosevelt's policies and his disagreements with the isolationists.

Divine, Robert. *The Reluctant Belligerent: American Entry into World War II*. Malabar, Fla.: Robert E. Krieger, 1976. Detailed examination of U.S. diplomacy, arguing that the delay in entering the war probably increased its destructiveness.

Guinsburg, Thomas. *The Pursuit of Isolationism in the United States Senate from Versailles to Pearl Harbor*. New York: Garland, 1982. Presents a sympathetic analysis of isolationist senators even though the author considers them to have been mistaken.

Ross, Stewart H. *How Roosevelt Failed America in World War II*. Jefferson, N.C.: McFarland, 2006. Defends the Neutrality Acts and argues that Roosevelt's interventionist policies were contrary to U.S. interests.

U.S. Department of State. *Peace and War: United States Foreign Policy, 1931-1941*. Washington, D.C.: Government Printing Office, 1943. Texts of the four Neutrality Acts are found of pages 494-505.

See also Foreign policy of the United States; Germany and U.S. appeasement; Isolationism; Peace movement; Quarantine speech; Spanish Civil War; World War II and the United States.

■ Neutron star theory

Definition   Theory explaining the massive
    collapsed stars found in nature

*The recognition of the possibility that collapsed stars might
be made entirely of neutrons explained for the first time the
final step of massive star evolution.*

The idea of a star consisting only of neutrons followed the discovery by James Chadwick in 1932 of
neutrons, which are particles similar in mass to protons, but without charge. The idea was developed by
several physicists and astronomers, including Walter
Baade and Fritz Zwicky in 1934 and J. Robert Oppenheimer and George Michael Volkoff in 1939. Scientists recognized that stars like the sun collapsed to
what were known as white dwarf stars when their nuclear fuel was exhausted. However, the known white
dwarfs had masses of only about 1.4 solar masses or
less. This fact confirmed a prediction made by
Subrahmanyan Chandrasekhar in 1931 that more
massive white dwarfs would not be formed. Thus scientists wondered what happens when a more massive star collapses.

The discovery of the neutron suggested a possible
solution. Scientists showed that, given a sufficiently
high pressure, matter could exist in the form of a
densely packed sea of neutrons. Baade and Zwicky's
idea was that the collapse of a massive star to form
a neutron star might be the explanation of the supernovas (objects that briefly flared up to incredible luminosity) that had been detected in galaxies.
However, Oppenheimer and Volkoff's calculations
indicated that neutron stars were not massive
enough to be formed from massive stars, and the
idea was almost forgotten for the following twenty
years.

During the 1960's, physical models showed that
when nuclear forces were taken into account stars
made up of neutrons could have greater masses than
white dwarfs and might, after all, result from massive
star collapse. With the discovery of the pulsar in the
Crab nebula, a remnant of a supernova, the evidence indicated that Baade and Zwicky's hypothesis
was correct: Neutron stars can be formed when stars

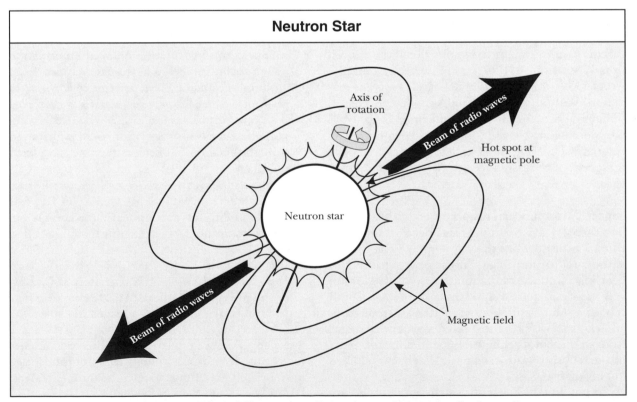

Neutron Star

Axis of rotation

Beam of radio waves

Hot spot at magnetic pole

Neutron star

Magnetic field

Beam of radio waves

A neutron star's strong magnetic field generates radiation that can be detected on Earth as radio waves.

blow up as supernovas, leaving their cores in the form of neutron stars.

Impact Neutron star theory ultimately explained pulsars and other superdense stars. These were not discovered in nature until decades after the 1930's.

Paul Hodge

Further Reading

Becker, Werner. *Neutron Stars and Pulsars*. New York: Springer, 2008.

Irvine, J. M. *Neutron Stars*. Oxford, Oxfordshire, England: Clarendon Press, 1978.

See also Astronomy; Black hole theory; Physics.

■ New Deal

Identification Domestic policies and programs designed to combat Depression-era problems

Dates 1933-1938

The New Deal encompassed a wide variety of programs designed to promote economic and political reforms, recovery, and relief during the Great Depression. As such, three distinct goals have been attributed to the New Deal: economic relief to the unemployed, recovery of the American economy, and economic reform of business and banking. Stuart Chase, the popular economist who had infamously predicted a "continuing boom" in 1929, coined the term "new deal." Coincidentally or not, President Franklin D. Roosevelt promised a "new deal for America" in his acceptance speech at the 1932 Democratic National Convention.

Historians divide the New Deal into two periods, a first New Deal in 1933 and a second New Deal from 1934 to 1936. One major piece of New Deal legislation was enacted after 1936, the Fair Labor Standards Act (FLSA), which outlawed child labor and established a national minimum wage and overtime pay for hours worked above forty hours a week.

The year 1937 is often considered the end of the New Deal for two reasons. First, Roosevelt's unpopular and unsuccessful attempt to increase the size of the U.S. Supreme Court, an event known as the court-packing plan, greatly weakened his popularity among both the American people and Democrats. Second, resenting opposition to his court-packing plan from conservative Democrats, primarily in the South, in 1938, Roosevelt campaigned against these members, supporting Democratic challengers who were more supportive of the New Deal. However, all but one conservative Democrat was reelected, and in the 1938 election, the Democratic Party lost seven seats in the Senate and seventy-one in the House of Representatives. Roosevelt's campaign against members of his own party poisoned his relations with conservative Democrats, who joined with Republicans to oppose Roosevelt and any additional New Deal programs.

The First One Hundred Days: Banking and the Economy The New Deal redefined and changed the roles of the U.S. government and the public's expectations about the obligations and duties of government. Under the New Deal, the U.S. government impacted the lives of the American people more than it ever had before. The New Deal authorized the government to intervene in such areas of the economy as agriculture, business, banking, welfare, and public infrastructure. The role of the president was also transformed by the New Deal. The era of congressional dominance in American politics was over, and the executive branch became more powerful. Because of Roosevelt's political philosophy and promotion of the New Deal, the American people came to regard the federal government as obligated to either provide for or at least protect the people's needs.

When Roosevelt was inaugurated as president on March 4, 1933, the American economy was in deep crisis. Industrial production had declined almost 50 percent, the nation's gross domestic product had been halved, and one-third of the banks had collapsed. Roosevelt had inherited an economy in crisis that showed no sign of improvement, and he recognized the need for bold action. Roosevelt implemented the first New Deal during the first one hundred days of his presidency. He called a special session of Congress, resulting in a flurry of legislation passed by Congress and signed into law by Roosevelt. The fact that this legislation was initiated by the president signaled a major shift in the role of the executive branch and the relationship between the president and the legislative branch. No president before Roosevelt had played such a direct and visible role in American politics, particularly in the lawmaking process.

During his first hundred days in office, Roosevelt acted decisively to deal with the Great Depression. His tremendous popularity and a largely cooperative, if not subservient, Congress made his task eas-

Political cartoon satirizing the proliferation of President Franklin D. Roosevelt's New Deal legislation in 1934. (Library of Congress)

ier. One of Roosevelt's first objectives was rescuing the collapsing banking system. Per the Trading with the Enemies Act of 1917, the president ordered the closure of all the banks in the United States for four days until federal legislation could be passed to permanently close insolvent banks—actions the previous president, Herbert Hoover, had asked for but failed to receive. On March 9, 1933, the Emergency Banking Relief Act of 1933 was passed with the assistance of officials from the Hoover administration, particularly former secretary of the Treasury Ogden Livingston Mills, who worked with his successor, William Woodin. Reflective of the urgency of the situation, at 1:00 P.M. on March 9, the House debated the bill for about forty minutes. The debate was interrupted only by cries of "vote, vote!" The bill was approved and signed into law that evening. The Emergency Banking Relief Act closed more than one thousand, or 5 percent, of the banks and gave the remaining banks a federal certificate of soundness. This and the commitment by the Federal Reserve to loan money to any reopened bank meant that the U.S. government would insure all the banks. The Emergency Banking Relief Act was the first, and probably the most important and successful, New Deal

measure because it restored confidence in the U.S. banking sector and helped avert any further collapse of the banking system.

Rescuing the banks was only one of Roosevelt's priorities. On March 10, Roosevelt urged Congress to cut federal spending by $500 million, including a 50 percent cut in payments to veterans, which then accounted for almost one-quarter of the $3.6 billion in the federal budget. Despite objections among many liberal members of the House, particularly in the wake of the Bonus Army March disaster under President Hoover, the Economy Act bill passed the House and was quickly approved in the Senate, right after a vote to legalize alcohol sales in the United States. On March 20, 1933, the president signed into law the Economy Act and also a bill to legalize the sale of liquor once the Eighteenth Amendment to the U.S. Constitution was repealed. On December 3, 1933, the Twenty-First Amendment legally repealed the Eighteenth Amendment, ending Prohibition.

The First One Hundred Days: Agriculture, Unemployment, and Public Power   On May 12, 1933, Roosevelt addressed the crisis among American farmers by signing into law the Agricultural Adjustment Act (AAA). Farmers' incomes had dropped by 60 percent over the previous four years, and by 1933, banks were foreclosing on twenty thousand farms a month. The AAA sought to increase the income of farmers. The central idea behind the AAA was to reduce deliberately the supply of crops in the market by paying farmers to reduce their planting of certain crops voluntarily, thereby increasing the income of farmers. In other words, farm prices would be raised by government subsidization of a decrease in the supply of crops. Along with the AAA, the Emergency Farm Mortgage Act was passed to offer relief to farmers by providing mortgages at lower interest rates. It was signed into law the same day as the AAA.

The AAA was modestly successful in its first years. However, the long-term effects of the AAA will never be known because in 1936, in the case of the *United States v. Butler,* the Supreme Court declared the AAA unconstitutional because it exceeded the power of the federal government. According to the Court, by regulating and controlling agricultural production, the AAA violated the rights reserved to the states by the Tenth Amendment to the U.S. Constitution. Furthermore the provision to pay farmers to reduce their production of crops was not in fact voluntary since the refusal to comply was the loss of benefits and this, ruled the Court, amounted to coercion by economic pressure. In June, 1934, a year after the AAA was passed, Congress amended existing bankruptcy laws by passing the Frazier-Lemke Farm Bankruptcy Act to restrict the ability of creditors to repossess farms by delaying for five years the ability of a creditor to foreclose on a bankrupt farmer's property. However, in the 1935 case of *Louisville Joint Stock Land Bank v. Radford,* the U.S. Supreme Court declared that the Frazier-Lemke Act deprived creditors of their right to property under the Fifth Amendment to the U.S. Constitution. That same year, Congress responded to this decision by revising the Frazier-Lemke Act, passing the Farm Mortgage Moratorium Act. Added to the act were provisions safeguarding the creditor's rights; this was upheld by the Supreme Court in 1937.

Another urgent problem addressed by President Roosevelt was the estimated thirty million Americans without regular incomes. The Civil Works Administration (CWA) was created in December, 1933, to provide temporary employment until a longer-term program could be created. The CWA was disbanded in 1934 over allegations of graft and corruption and was replaced by the Public Works Administration (PWA). Roosevelt chose Harry Hopkins to oversee the CWA, which employed approximately four million people. In March, 1933, the president asked Congress to create the position of federal relief administrator to oversee federal-aid grants to states for public assistance. Congress initially appropriated $500 million dollars to the Federal Emergency Relief Administration (FERA). Hopkins became the federal relief administrator.

Meanwhile, President Roosevelt chose Secretary of the Interior Harold Ickes to run the PWA. The PWA was created per Title II of the National Industrial Recovery Act to provide employment and stimulate the economy by expanding the number of federally funded public-works projects. In 1933 and 1934, $3.3 billion was appropriated to the PWA to build thirty thousand projects and became a major part of the New Deal's efforts to reduce unemployment and spur economic growth. Congress ended the WPA during World War II.

Roosevelt decided to use the New Deal to accomplish two other goals: conservation and development of public power. As governor of New York, he had hired 100,000 unemployed men to work on a reforestation program, and as president, he sought to duplicate this program for the United States, creating the Civilian Conservation Corps (CCC). The CCC was created on March 21, 1933, and employed more than two million people; Congress disbanded it in 1942. The CCC's legacy was restoring forests, beaches, rivers, and parks and providing flood control and disaster relief. Roosevelt also sought to increase the availability and accessibility of public power, particularly electricity. The centerpiece of Roosevelt's public power project was the Tennessee Valley Authority (TVA), created in May, 1933. This ultimately led to the creation of numerous hydroelectric dams along the Tennessee River, producing flood control and providing electricity to rural parts of the South. The TVA continues as a government-run corporation.

The National Industrial Recovery Act   To address the depressed state of industry, Congress passed the National Industrial Recovery Act (NIRA) in June, 1933. Roosevelt had not proposed the creation of an industrial reform bill; however, Congress had begun work on such a bill. Because Roosevelt was unwilling to veto a bill that enjoyed major Democratic support and because he also was desirous of influencing such a bill, he worked with Congress to draft it. The National Recovery Administration sought to do to industry and business what the AAA had done to farmers: raise the income of businesses by encouraging them to cooperate, and even collude, with one another on "fair codes of competition"—including wages, prices, and working conditions—that would be exempt from federal antitrust laws.

In a radio address to the American people, Roosevelt characterized the NIRA as promoting "a partnership in planning" between business and government based on the idea that this was superior to laissez-faire business practices. Roosevelt and many Democrats regarded capitalism as chaotic and unstable because it emphasized competition over planning and cooperation. Roosevelt believed that planning and cooperation between businesses and between business and government would promote employment and prosperity. Essentially, the NIRA constituted government-approved collusion and price-fixing among businesses. In return, the government expected businesses to accept long-sought labor reforms, such as allowing workers to unionize, the establishment of minimum-wage and maximum-working-hours provisions, improved working conditions, and the elimination of child labor.

Most businesses resisted these reforms and focused instead on increasing their profits, thereby making the NIRA unpopular among unions and many workers. In addition, authorizing cooperation among businesses created collusion naturally; the NIRA benefited large businesses because their size enabled them to dictate terms at the expense of small businesses. Consequently, small businesses came to dislike the NIRA as did Republicans and conservative Democrats, charging that it interfered with property rights and the free market and promoted cooperation between government and business, which resembled Italian fascism under Benito Mussolini. In addition to all the different groups that opposed the NIRA, perhaps the main reason it failed to promote economic recovery was that it ran counter to the American economy, which was based on free enterprise, such that government was powerless to directly regulate prices and wages.

Roosevelt concluded that admitting publicly that the NIRA had failed was politically risky, so he called for a two-year extension of the NIRA in February, 1935, claiming that failure to do so would create chaos for industry and labor. Whether Congress would have reauthorized the NIRA cannot be known because on May 25, 1935, the Supreme Court declared the NIRA unconstitutional. In the case of *Schechter Poultry Corp. v. the United States,* a unanimous Supreme Court ruled that the NIRA violated the principle of separation of powers by granting legislative power to the president that exceeded Congress's authority under the commerce clause. In its decision, the Supreme Court may have unintentionally rescued Roosevelt from a continued defense of the program.

Other New Deal Acts   By Roosevelt's inauguration, home foreclosures had reached a rate of one thousand per day, primarily affecting the middle class. In June, 1933, Roosevelt tackled the mortgage crisis by signing into law the Home Owners Refinancing Act, which created the Home Owners' Loan Corporation (HOLC) to assist people facing mortgage foreclosure and to prevent additional foreclosures. The HOLC provided refinancing at lower interest rates and ultimately became involved in 20 percent of all urban home mortgages. In 1951, Congress ended the HOLC.

In May, 1933, to address lax regulations on Wall Street and discourage fraud, Roosevelt signed into law the Securities Act, which made all companies selling stock legally responsible and liable for accurately reporting on the company's finances and allowed investors who could prove fraud to recover monetary damages. The following month, Congress passed the Glass-Steagall Act (also known as the Banking Act of 1933), which created the Federal Deposit Insurance Corporation (FDIC) to ensure bank deposits in the event of bank failures, thus preventing a repeat of the stock market crash of 1929. The FDIC is one of the most successful New Deal programs and remains in existence. Since the FDIC was created, no depositor has lost a cent of insured deposits. Building on the Securities Act of 1933, as part of the second New Deal, Roosevelt signed into law the Securities Exchange Act of 1934, which created the Securities Exchange Commission to protect investors and punish fraud on Wall Street. Like the FDIC, the SEC remains in existence and is an important legacy of the New Deal.

In 1935, Roosevelt passed the Social Security Act, also part of the second New Deal, which provided a government-backed system of old-age pension, unemployment insurance, and welfare benefits for the poor, blind, and disabled. With people's savings wiped out, Roosevelt envisioned Social Security as a means to provide assistance to the poor, disabled, and the elderly during the Great Depression. Social Security remains the most visible legacy of the New Deal and accounts for the largest expenditure by the U.S. government. That same year, Roosevelt signed into law the National Labor Relations Act (NLRA; also known as the Wagner Act), which legalized the rights of Americans to unionize and bargain with their employers over wages and working conditions and also outlawed a series of unfair labor practices. To enforce this act, the National Labor Relations Board (NLRB) was created and remains in existence. Following passage of the Wagner Act, union membership in the United States increased dramatically and marked the culmination of decades of attempts by workers to unionize.

Impact   The legacy of the New Deal is disputed. Although it did not end the Great Depression, it provided much-needed assistance and relief to millions of people, particularly in the form of public works programs such as the CCC, the PWA, and Social Security. However, other parts of the New Deal, such as the AAA and the National Industrial Recovery Act, were less successful or failed altogether, as was the case with the latter. Liberals and Democrats have tended to exaggerate the success of the New Deal, claiming that without it the U.S. economy might have collapsed; conservatives and Republicans often understate its successes, some of whom claim it prolonged the Great Depression. It can be argued that much of the New Deal was but a continuation—and probably an improvement—of President Hoover's policies. In fact, one of Roosevelt's advisers, Rexford Guy Tugwell, admitted as much in 1974. However, Roosevelt was far more popular and persuasive than Hoover, and this may explain the success that Roosevelt and the New Deal had in comparison to Hoover's programs.

Stefan Brooks

Further Reading

Atler, Jonathan. *The Defining Moment: FDR's Hundred Days and the Triumph of Hope.* New York: Simon & Schuster, 2006. Covers Roosevelt's policies during the first one hundred days in office, which restored people's hope in the U.S. government's ability to deal with the Great Depression.

Flynn, Kathryn. *The New Deal: A Seventy-fifth Anniversary Celebration.* Layton, Utah: Gibbs Smith, 2008. Detailed account of the major New Deal programs.

Leuchtenburg, William E. *Franklin Roosevelt and the New Deal, 1933-1940.* New York: Harper & Row, 2009. Comprehensive account of Roosevelt and the New Deal.

Shlaes, Amity. *The Forgotten Man: A New History of the Great Depression.* New York: HarperCollins, 2007. Conservative view that argues the New Deal failed and actually prolonged the Great Depression.

Smith, Jean Edward. *FDR.* New York: Random House, 2008. An inclusive view of Roosevelt and his presidency.

See also   Brains Trust; Civilian Conservation Corps; Federal Theatre Project; Federal Writers' Project; Great Depression in the United States; Roosevelt, Franklin D.; Roosevelt's first one hundred days; Tennessee Valley Authority; Works Progress Administration.

■ *New State Ice Co. v. Liebmann*

The Case   U.S. Supreme Court ruling striking down regulation of ice producers and suggesting that substantive due process prevented such regulations

Date   March 21, 1932

This case outlawed regulation of many businesses, holding that only laws applied to businesses considered "public interests," and thus different from average businesses, were allowed. It put into question some of the early efforts at government supervision during the Great Depression.

New State Ice Co. v. Liebmann dealt with controls on ice production. One of the regulations in question was the limit set on the number of ice companies allowed to do business. The Supreme Court, in an opinion by Justice George Sutherland, struck down the statute, holding that this type of business was not of as much public interest as those previously allowed to be covered by governmental decrees. The court held that allowing this legislation would destroy the right to have a legal business, as it removed one's liberty and property without due process. Louis D. Brandeis's dissent held that the regulation was justified and that states and the federal government should have within their power the right to make rules such as these.

Impact   The decision in *New State Ice Co. v. Liebmann* was a temporary victory of substantive due process; it argued that regulations such as this could not be adopted in the first place because they destroyed people's liberty. Sutherland allowed for decrees, but only in cases in which the industry was "clothed with a public interest," and such areas were few and far between. As the Great Depression continued, many wanted industry to be controlled; Sutherland's view of liberty, and his use of substantive due process to support it, did not bode well for regulation. Brandeis's view did prevail in the end, though, with increased government regulations that were permitted by the Court.

Scott A. Merriman

Further Reading

Arkes, Hadley. *The Return of George Sutherland: Restoring a Jurisprudence of Natural Rights.* Princeton, N.J.: Princeton University Press, 1994.

Parrish, Michael E. *The Hughes Court: Justices, Rulings, and Legacy.* Santa Barbara, Calif.: ABC-Clio, 2002.

Urofsky, Melvin I. *Louis D. Brandeis: A Life.* New York: Pantheon Books, 2009.

See also Brandeis, Louis D.; Four Horsemen vs. Three Musketeers; *Home Building and Loan Association v. Blaisdell; Nebbia v. New York;* New Deal; *Schechter Poultry Corp. v. United States;* Supreme Court, U.S.; *West Coast Hotel Co. v. Parrish.*

■ New York World's Fair

The Event New York City's public exhibition featuring pavilions from nations around the world and developments in architecture and consumer products

Dates April 30-October 29, 1939; May 11-October 27, 1940

Place New York, New York

The New York World's Fair attracted visitors from around the United States and the world to experience the "world of tomorrow." One of the main purposes of the fair was to allow Americans to move past the struggles they had faced during the Great Depression and envision a modern lifestyle of prosperity.

The first world's fair took place in London in 1851 as an economic development strategy to show off international manufactured goods and to promote tourism. Every few years thereafter, a major global city hosted a world's fair, which provided many social and economic benefits. For example, fair attendees often provided a boost to the local economy by shopping in stores and eating in restaurants. In 1934, business leaders and government officials began advocating for a world's fair in New York with the hopes that it would help to lift the spirits of Americans who had been suffering through the Great Depression.

High Hopes for the Fair In the early stages of the fair's development, the fair's planning committee formed the World's Fair Corporation to oversee the fair and elected former New York City police chief Gerald Whalen as its head. The committee began generating funding for the event through the sales of bonds to millionaires, trade unions, major corporations, and the general public. The committee determined that 40 percent of the proceeds from the fair would be used to repay these original investors. The fair also received funding from the city and state of New York, the U.S. federal government, and each of the countries who had a pavilion at the fair. However, the fair generated less revenue than it took in from these investors and was thereby declared an economic failure. Even local business owners were disappointed that the fair did not generate as many customers as planners had originally estimated.

Opening day was set for April 30, 1939, the 150th anniversary of George Washington's inauguration as U.S. president. In part, this day was selected to emphasize the United States' past accomplishments and to provide hope that the United States would once again become a prosperous nation. Because one of the main priorities for the fair was to lift the country and the world out of depression, the predominant theme of the fair was "Building the World of Tomorrow." The selection of the fairgrounds site on a former ash dump in Flushing, Queens, contributed to the notion that urban renewal and redevelopment could lead to the future prosperity of the United States. In particular, the fair both celebrated and catered to the emerging middle class, whom politicians and social reformers hoped would form the backbone of American society.

Architecture, Zones, and Pavilions at the Fair The New York World's Fair was the first major world exhibition that departed from a focus on trade in favor of imagining a future utopian society in which the material conditions of the average American would dramatically improve. The fair emphasized cultural achievements in architecture and design more than previous exhibitions of its kind had. In particular, the fair served as a showcase for the Art Deco and Bauhaus styles, and many pavilions housed priceless artwork by renowned artists such as Rembrandt, Leonardo da Vinci, Michelangelo, and Caravaggio. Artists of the 1930's, such as Alexander Calder and Salvador Dalí, constructed artworks for the fair. Creators of the Westinghouse time capsule also hoped to preserve some of the culture of the 1930's for future generations. They hoped that people in the future would enjoy artifacts such as a Gillette safety razor, messages to the future from Albert Einstein, a Mickey Mouse cup, a copy of *Gone with the Wind*, and a picture of Jesse Owens winning a gold medal in the 1936 Olympics in Berlin.

As fairs in the past had done, the New York World's Fair served as a showcase for the latest technologies, but the focus was on the consumption of goods, rather than their production. Various zones on the fairground represented the major industries that were trying to establish themselves as the foundation of the American economy in the era after the Depression. The Transportation Zone, which housed pavilions by General Motors, Ford, and Chrysler, promoted the concept of the automobile as the future of transportation for the middle class. The Ford pavilion featured a "road of tomorrow," where fair visitors could ride in sample cars onto the roof to overlook the fair from several different viewpoints. General Motors' Futurama ride carried passengers through a diorama of a projected 1960's roadway, featuring seven-lane highways, model homes, and cities that were free from blight. As passengers progressed through the ride, the dioramas gradually increased in size until they were finally life-sized. Other areas of the fair included the Communications and Business Systems Zone, which highlighted American Telephone and Telegraph's (AT&T's) advancements in telephone technology and exposed many members of the general public to television for the first time. The Food Zone demonstrated how advancements in agricultural technology and transportation could deliver mass-produced, low-cost foods to the American public, which was particularly important for morale after a decade in which many Americans went hungry. A "Town of Tomorrow" provided a model community comprising single-family homes, which featured the latest electronic appliances from General Electric.

Entertainment was another luxury that Americans were expected to enjoy after the Depression. Thus, one of the most popular zones at the fair was the Amusement Area. This area of the fair stayed open until 2 A.M. every night, long past the 10 P.M. closing time of the international pavilions. Large fluorescent bulbs illuminated the nightlife activities and exposed Americans to the latest innovation in

A poster promoting the 1939 New York World's Fair featuring the architecturally innovative Trylon and Perisphere. (The Granger Collection, New York)

lighting. The most popular pavilion in the Amusement Area, and in the fair as a whole, was the Aquacade, a water show featuring professional swimmers, divers, dancers, and singers. Another highly successful attraction in the Amusement Area was the parachute drop, which was later moved to Coney Island and continues to serve as the iconic "Eiffel Tower of Brooklyn."

The Fair and the Pending World War As in past world exhibitions, a major emphasis of the fair was to allow visitors to experience a simulation of international tourism and thus to promote a sense of unity among the nations of the world. This goal was particularly difficult in 1939, when Americans felt uneasy about the communist and fascist dictatorships emerging in Europe. Many pavilions glossed over the international conflicts that were threatening the stability of the world's most powerful nations and presented idealized cultural models of the nations they represented. Germany's absence from the fair was glaring, and in 1940, the Soviet Union and several smaller nations were no longer represented at the fair. The central theme of the fair shifted from the utopian "Building the World of Tomorrow" to the more pertinent "For Peace and Freedom." Nevertheless, warring nations such as France and Great Britain built weaponry displays into their pavilions for the second year of the fair. The Polish pavilion featured photographs from the war, and the Czech pavilion showed the film *The Rape of Czechoslovakia* (1939), which showed the hardships of life under German occupation. The shift in focus turned the fair from a lighthearted event into a relatively somber experience.

Impact   The New York World's Fair had a profound effect on the consumer consciousness of the post-Depression era, especially among the 45 million fair attendees. The fair achieved its primary goal of bringing the consumption of mass-produced, modern goods to the forefront of American society. If anything, critics say that one of the downsides of the fair was that it was overcommercialized, which took away from its artistry and its ability to promote world harmony. Nevertheless, most fair attendees genuinely enjoyed the consumer presentations at the fair, which left them with an optimistic vision of the future. In many cases, this presentation of the future world became reality, particularly in the case of the development of the American suburban landscape to easily accommodate automobile travel. The secondary goal of promoting "peace and freedom" was less successful, as many of the world's countries became involved in World War II. Nevertheless, the presence of pavilions from war-torn European nations brought the realities of the war to the American people, who later rallied around the Allied cause.

Jill Eshelman

Further Reading

Duranti, Marco. "Utopia, Nostalgia, and World War at the 1939-1940 New York World's Fair." *Journal of Contemporary History* 41, no. 4 (2006): 663-683. Looks at the shift in focus from the first half of the fair to the second, as the emphasis of consumerism changed to the theme of peace and freedom.

Gelenter, David. *1939: The Lost World of the Fair.* New York: Free Press, 1995. Examines the unique chronological state of the fair, bookended by the Great Depression and World War II.

Kuznick, Peter J. "Losing the World of Tomorrow: The Battle over the Presentation of Science at the 1939 New York World's Fair." *American Quarterly* 46, no. 3 (1994): 341-373. Discusses the shift from the emphasis on science and technology in previous fairs to consumerism in the New York fair.

Wurts, Richard. *The New York World's Fair 1939/1940 in 155 Photographs.* New York: Dover, 1977. Detailed photographic exploration of the fair.

See also   Architecture; Automobiles and auto manufacturing; Chicago World's Fair; La Guardia, Fiorello Henry; World War II and the United States.

■ Newspapers, Canadian

During the 1930's, Canadian newspapers scrambled to keep up with rapid economic, technological, and cultural changes that were taking place in the world. The processes of newspaper production, news gathering, and distribution, as well as the basic content of the papers, changed rapidly. Amid this upheaval, competition began among the largest daily newspapers in the nation, and a "national" media was born.

In the first two decades of the twentieth century, the daily newspaper gained acceptance as a valuable cultural institution, giving rural and urban citizens a window on the world and creating a sense of national connectedness, even in a nation as vast and diverse as Canada. Papers provided news of local, state, and national events and also were the main source of entertainment, culture, and correspondence with their puzzles, comics, contests, poems, sports reporting, advice columns, and editorial commentary. Whether readers were catching up on the day's events, following their favorite sports team, or finding amusement in the comics, they were being exposed to a source of cultural power.

During the culturally and technologically explosive 1930's, reporters gained the ability to gather news faster and more efficiently. The automobile, train, airplane, telegraph, and telephone became weapons of press warfare. The aim always was to be the first to print an exclusive story and to produce such blanket coverage as to make rival reporting seem meager.

The teletype (a marriage of the telegraph and the typewriter) was introduced into Canadian newsrooms in the late 1920's. It sped up the dissemination of news, enabled easier pooling of news-gathering resources, and contributed to a considerable increase in the national and international content of Canada's news pages.

Canadian journalists also discovered new ways to circulate newspapers during the first decades of the twentieth century. To such nineteenth century agents of distribution as trains, mail delivery, and general stores were added trucks and airplanes. These technological innovations were expensive, but they also fueled readership, which in turn generated revenue. The connections among circulation, technology, and revenue drove relentless competition. The newspapers that survived often did so by absorbing or merging with competitors, creating dominant amalgams such as *The Globe and Mail, The Recorder and Times*, and *The Sentinel-Review*. The 1930's were a time of centralization and consolidation for Canadian newspapers, and the result was that many multinewspaper cities became single-newspaper cities.

Even the large and powerful papers created by consolidation were challenged by the emerging technology of radio. Universally, radio grabbed precious advertising revenue and threatened to render print trades obsolete during the 1930's. Radio's ability to transmit news instantly across the country left newspapers struggling to get a scoop, and its live reporting made the dailies seem stale.

Impact By the early 1930's, Canadian newspapers were reaching more citizens than ever before, thanks to technological improvements to the production and distribution processes and the centralization of press power created by the consolidation of newspapers into urban areas. Even so, a burgeoning technology—radio—challenged the newspapers' dominance of the news and entertainment markets. Editors and publishers spent the rest of the decade revamping their content and formats to keep pace with the changing media landscape.

Cynthia Gwynne Yaudes

Further Reading

Bassam, Bertha. *The First Printers and Newspapers in Canada*. Toronto: University of Toronto Press, 1968. Examines and explains the development of the press in Canada, comparing it to the development of the press in the United States.

Bonavia, George, ed. *Ethnic Publications in Canada*. Ottawa: Department of the Secretary of State of Canada, 1987. Provides the histories of many smaller, native-language newspapers in Canada.

Fetherling, George. *The Rise of the Canadian Newspaper*. Toronto: Oxford University Press, 1990. Chronicles the development of Canada's largest newspapers from the late 1880's through the 1990's.

Fiamengo, Janice Anne. *The Women's Page: Journalism and Rhetoric in Early Canada*. Toronto: University of Toronto Press, 2008. Examines the development of culturally significant sections of Canadian newspapers—specifically the pages devoted to women's issues.

Sotiron, Minko. *From Politics to Profit: The Commercialization of Canadian Daily Newspapers, 1890-1920*. Montreal: McGill-Queen's University Press, 1997. Thorough look at the technological and cultural changes in Canadian newspapers at the beginning of the twentieth century.

See also Business and the economy in Canada; Great Depression in Canada; Income and wages in Canada; Literature in Canada; Urbanization in Canada.

■ Newspapers, U.S.

In the 1930's, mainstream print culture expanded. Newspapers, in particular, began to reach wider audiences than before and took on an increasingly national tone through the expansion of press associations, increased use of wire services, and the consolidation of newspaper ownership. Even so, the Great Depression, coupled with the rise of radio, ate away at the economic health of the print trades, and by the end of the decade, newspaper circulation numbers had fallen substantially.

Through the first two decades of the twentieth century, the American daily newspaper was accepted as a valuable cultural institution, giving rural and urban citizens a view of the wider world and engendering a sense of national identity. The newspaper industry's power both to inform and to direct peaked just before the stock market crash under the leadership of some of the country's most influential men.

William Randolph Hearst was the country's most powerful publisher during the late 1920's, running a journalistic empire that encompassed twenty-eight dailies and seventeen Sunday papers, including the *Los Angeles Examiner,* the *Boston American,* the *Atlanta Georgian,* the *Chicago Examiner,* the *Detroit Times,* the *Seattle Post-Intelligencer,* the *Washington Times,* the *Washington Herald,* the *New York Daily Mirror,* and his flagship, the *San Francisco Examiner.* His financial backing and his reputation allowed him to acquire the best equipment and the most talented cartoonists and writers. Hearst directed the tone of his papers toward conservatism, focusing on maintaining American distance from "foreignness" and railing against the government's inability to enforce law and order in the uproarious 1920's.

Joseph Medill Patterson was known more for his association with a certain journalistic style than for a vast newspaper empire. His *New York Daily News* was a tabloid filled with large headlines, short stories, and many sensational photographs. The daily tabloid had first appeared in the United States after World War I, and by the late 1920's, tabloid mania was at its peak. At that time, the *New York Daily News* had a daily circulation of approximately 1.7 million; its Sunday edition circulation topped three million. Unlike Hearst, Patterson used his publication to identify with and uplift the common person. He frequented subways, spent nights in flophouses, and wandered about Coney Island to get a sense of the public's mind. Such a social conscience made him an exception within the publishing fraternity and also paid big dividends.

Printer working for the Philadelphia Evening Public Ledger *adjusts a mechanism on a R. Hoe & Company web press.* (Archive Photos/Getty Images)

Robert McCormick had built the *Chicago Tribune* into the leading newspaper of the Midwest by the late 1920's by adding advice columns, homegrown comic strips, and story-line crusades. As a sensationalistic tabloid like the *New York Daily News*, the *Chicago Tribune* had earned the ignominious title of the "most irresponsible of the American newspapers" for its alleged lack of dedication to truth and accuracy in reporting. The label did nothing to diminish the paper's popularity; during the late 1920's its circulation was more than one million. As an unwavering advocate of individualism, hard work, and limited government, the proud McCormick saw that number as validation of the *Tribune*'s role as a reflector of true public opinion in the American heartland.

Press Associations and the Zenith of the Press
Hearst, McCormick, and Patterson had become wealthy and powerful men in pursuit of their respective and individual newspaper enterprises. Nevertheless, during the first decades of the twentieth century, they recognized that to cover the enormous volume of news required the pooling of news-gathering resources among the nation's newspapers. Under the burgeoning press-association plan, local editors continued to develop their own spot news but depended on an association of their peers to collect the news from around the nation and the world. By 1930, three primary press associations—the Associated Press, the United Press, and the International News Service—competed for news content and distribution power among American papers.

Public trust in newspapers was never as high as it was during the late 1920's. Home delivery brought newspapers into the homes of most Americans on a daily basis. Most morning and evening metropolitan papers seemed to have editions around the clock, using every possible pretext for extra editions.

Even newsgathering techniques and professional standards for reporters, editorial writers, and columnists were at their peak during the period. Hard-boiled city reporters became popular folk heroes. Whether at large metropolitan dailies or quaint rural "rags," their work and their reputations sold advertising space and newspapers. Soaring revenues delighted editors and owners: 1928 aggregate national daily circulation reached a record high of 36 million as advertising revenues reached $775 million.

Effect of the Great Depression The quality of American newspapers did not deteriorate markedly during the dark days of the Great Depression, but some of the youthful spirit did go out of them during those years. Great newspapers continued to shine after 1929, and the majority of well-run papers lost none of their luster. Every failure, however, enhanced the growing sense of doom that accompanied economic collapse. The sudden death of the legendary *New York World* in 1931 persuaded publishers that the Depression was real. Other smaller "disappearing dailies" left many cities with few, if any, competing newspapers.

Overall, national newspaper circulation fell by 12 percent; consequently, staff wages were cut by up to 40 percent and staff numbers were reduced by layoffs and attrition. The 1933 National Recovery Administration (NRA) was the New Deal's primary engine for industrial recovery. Under its auspices, representatives from each sector of the economy drew up codes of conduct that set prices, minimum wages, maximum hours, and production standards. The NRA also guaranteed labor's right to organize, and during the 1930's, that spirit influenced professional journalism. Economic distress troubled both reporters and publishers. Spurred by layoffs and reduced paychecks, journalists sought better wages and working conditions. Some banded together to establish their first labor organization.

In 1933, the American Newspaper Guild was founded with the goal of "organizing" the low-paid newspaper reporter. Affiliated with the American Federation of Labor and the Congress of Industrial Organizations, the organization defied publishers' visions of journalism as a romantic profession that attracted individualistic, hardworking idealists. Instead, it focused on remedying the inequities of low pay, inadequate vacations, and irregular hiring and firing practices. By the end of the 1930's, the guild's membership stood at twenty thousand members—more than one-half of eligible press employees.

Effect of Radio For newspapers, the rise of radio compounded the pain created by the Great Depression. The new audio medium grabbed precious advertising revenue and threatened to render print trades obsolete. Radio's ability to transmit news instantly across the country made getting a "scoop" difficult for newspapers, and its live reportage made the dailies seem stale. One *Fortune* magazine survey noted that the radio news reporter was "closer to being a national newspaper than any paper has ever attempted to be."

By the end of the 1930's, radio had matured from a communications craze for a mechanical minority to an industry with about 200,000 employees serving as much as one-third of the population. A range of audio programming, including drama, literature, popular entertainment, professional sports, and news, catered to a growing audience and competed with newspapers for Americans' attention. Radio had claimed a space in American living rooms and in the daily culture. From 1930 to 1935, radio revenues rose by $83.5 million and radio's share of advertising placed in the major media increased from 2 percent to 10 percent, much of which was taken from newspapers. Advances in communication technology also often allowed radio broadcasters to beat newspapers with the first information on stories.

Impact   By the start of the 1930's, American newspapers were reaching more citizens than ever before, thanks to the consolidation of newspaper ownership under the direction of a few men and the creation of press associations to efficiently and rapidly disseminate information via wire service. Average national newspaper circulations reached their highest historical point just before the stock market crash. Editors and publishers spent the remainder of the decade not only recovering from the brink of economic disaster but also reprogramming their media to keep pace with the content and form of information offered by radio.

Cynthia Gwynne Yaudes

Further Reading

Danky, James P., and Wayne A. Wiegand, eds. *Print Culture in a Diverse America.* Urbana: University of Illinois Press, 1998. Interdisciplinary essays that examine the many ways print culture functions within different groups. Essays link gender, class, and ethnicity to the uses and goals of a wide variety of publications and explore the role print materials play in constructing certain historical events.

Douglas, George H. *The Golden Age of the Newspaper.* Westport, Conn.: Greenwood Press, 1999. Details the development of the bond between newspapers and American citizens and examines how newspapers molded themselves into a distinctly American character to become an intimate part of everyday life.

Emery, Michael, and Edwin Emery. *The Press and America: An Interpretive History of the Mass Media.* Englewood Cliffs, N.J.: Prentice-Hall, 1988. Traces how major events in U.S. history were covered by reporters, editors, and broadcasters and how other writers, advertisers, and advocates influenced events in the United States.

Mott, Frank Luther. *American Journalism: A History of Newspapers in the United States Through 250 Years, 1650-1940.* New York: Macmillan, 1941. Thorough and detailed history of American papers and press practices by a Pulitzer Prize-winning author.

Nord, David Paul. *Communities of Journalism: A History of American Newspapers and Their Readers.* Urbana: University of Illinois Press, 2007. Reveals how newspapers have intersected with religion, politics, reform, and urban life over nearly three centuries in a lively and wide-ranging discussion that shows journalism to be a vital component of the community.

Teel, Leonard Ray. *The Public Press, 1900-1945: The History of American Journalism.* Westport, Conn.: Praeger, 2006. Considers the nature of American journalism between 1900 and 1945 and traces the movement of mainstream commercial journalism toward the vision of professionalism and public responsibility articulated by Joseph Pulitzer in 1904.

See also   Great Depression in the United States; Magazines; Newspapers, Canadian; Radio in the United States; Urbanization in the United States.

NIRA. See **National Industrial Recovery Act of 1933**

■ Nitti, Frank

Identification   Well-known criminal
Born   January 27, 1881 or 1888; Angri, Salerno, Campania, Italy
Died   March 19, 1943; North Riverside, Illinois

Nitti was one of the top henchmen of Al Capone during the early 1930's and later became the leader of the Chicago Outfit, the organized crime syndicate that Johnny Torrio and Capone had created.

Frank Nitti was born Francesco Raffaele Nitto. His mother, Rosina, and his stepfather, Francesco Dolendo, immigrated to the United States in 1890. Three years later, Nitti joined his parents in Brooklyn, New York. Nitti quit school after the seventh grade and helped support his family with a number of odd jobs, working as a factory worker, a pinsetter in a bowling alley, and a barber.

In 1913, Nitti moved to an Italian neighborhood on the Westside of Chicago, where he worked as a barber. He met the local gangsters and soon began committing crimes himself, stealing jewelry, smuggling liquor, and fencing stolen goods. Through his gang contacts, Nitti was introduced to Capone and Torrio and joined their criminal enterprise. In recognition of Nitti's business acumen and leadership skills, Capone promoted Nitti to a high-ranking position in the Outfit.

In 1931, Nitti and Capone were convicted of income tax evasion. While Capone received an eleven-year sentence, Nitti received eighteen months and was released in 1932. Upon his return to Chicago, Nitti took control of the city's leaderless criminal underworld. He was surrounded by a cadre of powerful and experienced gangsters: Paul "The Waiter" Ricca, Tony "Big Tuna" Accardo, Murray "The Camel" Humphreys, and Jake "Greasy Thumb" Guzik. During Nitti's tenure, the Outfit expanded into other criminal activities to fill the void left by the repeal of Prohibition. Gambling, extortion, and labor racketeering became mainstays of Mob operations.

On December 19, 1932, a team of Chicago police, headed by Detective Sergeants Harry Lang and Harry Miller, raided Nitti's office. Lang shot Nitti in the back and neck, then shot himself to make it appear that he had shot Nitti in self-defense. It was ru-

Frank Nitti (center) being arrested in Chicago in 1930. (Gamma-Keystone via Getty Images)

mored that the attempt on Nitti's life had been ordered by Chicago mayor Anton Cermak. Cermak likely had hoped to shift power from the Chicago Outfit to gangsters who were loyal to him, notably Teddy Newberry. Newberry was killed by Accardo three weeks after the Nitti shooting. Nitti survived and was acquitted of attempted murder and all other charges stemming from the incident, while Lang was dismissed from the police force.

On February 15, 1933, Cermak was shot and killed by Giuseppe Zangara, an Italian immigrant, while Cermak was talking to President-elect Franklin D. Roosevelt on a podium in Bayfront Park in Miami, Florida. There is considerable historical speculation about Zangara's motive for the shooting; some assume that he meant to assassinate Roosevelt, while others believe the Outfit had hired him to kill Cermak.

With Newberry and Cermak gone, the Outfit again ruled the Chicago underworld. Nitti and his deputies began using their influence with labor unions to extort money from major Hollywood film studios, including Columbia Pictures, Metro-Goldwyn-Mayer (MGM), Paramount Pictures, RKO Pictures, and Twentieth Century-Fox. On March 18, 1943, the federal government indicted Nitti, Ricca, and several others for extortion after their dealings with the studios were exposed. The next day, Nitti took a walk along the Illinois Central Railroad tracks near his North Riverside home, drew a gun from his waistband, and fatally shot himself in the head. The remaining defendants in the trial were each sentenced to ten years in prison.

Impact　Nitti led the Chicago Outfit in the wake of two major setbacks: the imprisonment of Capone and the end of Prohibition, which put an end to the bootlegging business. With Nitti at the helm, the Outfit turned its attention to gambling, extortion, and labor racketeering. He encouraged the Mob to invest in legitimate businesses and to stay heavily involved in politics through the bribery and election of public officials complicit in the Outfit's activities. Nitti also took the organization back underground, a marked change from the leadership of the flashy, high-living Capone.

Arthur J. Lurigio

Further Reading

Binder, John J. *The Chicago Outfit*. Charleston, S.C.: Arcadia, 2003.

Eghigian, Mars. *After Capone: The Life and World of Chicago Mob Boss Frank "The Enforcer" Nitti.* Nashville, Tenn.: Cumberland House, 2006.

Humble, Ronald D. *Frank Nitti: The True Story of Chicago's Notorious Enforcer.* Fort Lee, N.J.: Barricade Books, 2007.

Tucker, Kenneth. "The Real Al Capone and Frank Nitti." In *Eliot Ness and the Untouchables: The Historical Reality and the Film and Television Depictions.* Jefferson, N.C.: McFarland, 2000.

See also　Barker Gang; Barrow, Clyde, and Bonnie Parker; Capone, Al; Dillinger, John; Floyd, Pretty Boy; Ness, Eliot; Organized crime; Prohibition repeal; Roosevelt assassination attempt.

■ *Nixon v. Condon*

The Case　U.S. Supreme Court ruling on whites-only primary elections

Date　Decided on May 2, 1932

Texas state laws did not allow African Americans to vote in primaries, thus disenfranchising the group and effectively enforcing the status quo of institutionalized racism.

From the end of the Civil War to the early 1930's, the Democratic Party dominated Texas politics. A Democratic primary victory was essentially a win in the general election. State laws barred African Americans from participating in primaries. In 1927, in *Nixon v. Herndon*, the Supreme Court held that a Texas statute prohibiting African Americans from voting in the state's primaries denied the group Fourteenth Amendment protection. Texas responded by granting state party executive committees the power to determine voter qualifications. The state Democratic Party committee then limited primary participation to Caucasians only. L. A. Nixon, an African American, was denied his right to vote in the primary. He sued the Democratic Party committee, alleging that it had acted under the authority of the state statute and violated his Fourteenth Amendment rights. The Supreme Court ruled five to four that the party's executive committee was in effect a creation of the state legislature, and therefore, that the prohibition of black voters was unconstitutional.

Impact　This case highlighted the state of racism during the 1930's. The response of Texas and the

Democratic committee is illustrative. The majority opinion's legal reasoning rested on the fact that the Texas Democratic committee's authority to decide on party membership was granted by a state statute. After this ruling, Texas repealed all primary election statutes, thus allowing state party conventions to exclude African Americans. The Texas Democratic Party then passed a resolution limiting participation in primaries to Caucasians only. In *Grovey v. Townsend* (1935), the Supreme Court upheld Texas's whites-only primary. This form of black disenfranchisement was permitted until 1944, when such schemes were declared unconstitutional.

Eric T. Bellone

Further Reading

Epps, Garrett. *Democracy Reborn: The Fourteenth Amendment and the Fight for Equal Rights in Post-Civil War America.* New York: Henry Holt, 2006.

Goldman, Robert M. *Reconstruction and Black Suffrage.* Lawrence: University Press of Kansas, 2001.

Zelden, Charles L. *The Battle for the Black Ballot: Smith V. Allwright and the Defeat of the Texas All-White Primary.* Lawrence: University Press of Kansas, 2004.

See also   African Americans; Civil rights and liberties in the United States; *Grovey v. Townsend*; Jim Crow segregation; National Association for the Advancement of Colored People; Racial discrimination; Supreme Court, U.S.; Voting rights.

■ Nobel Prizes

Definition   Prestigious international awards given annually in the fields of chemistry, physics, medicine, peace, and literature

Of the forty-six Nobel Prizes awarded from 1930 to 1939, eleven were won outright or shared by fourteen Americans. Americans won at least one award in each of the five prize categories and also won at least one award during every year but 1935. Some of the awards received by Americans have been subjects of controversy, but the contributions made by the science winners were not.

The Nobel Prizes are awarded annually by the Nobel Prize Committee in Stockholm, Sweden, for international discoveries that should "confer the greatest benefit on mankind." The Nobel Foundation coordinates the judging, public award ceremony in Stockholm, the accompanying Nobel Symposia, and the conveying of both a gold medal and a considerable cash award to each winner. Except during the two world wars, the prizes have been awarded every year since 1901.

Between 1930 and 1939, a total of forty-six Nobel Prizes were awarded for achievements in literature, peace, chemistry, physics, and "physiology or medicine," as that award has been officially called. Potential awardees were nominated by various designated organizations and persons, and then a Nobel Prize Committee, appointed by the Royal Swedish Academy of Sciences, evaluated the work of each of the hundreds of nominees within each field. Eleven awards (including shared awards) went to Americans; eleven to British subjects; nine to Germans; five to Austrians; four to French subjects; two each to Italian, Swedish, and Swiss recipients; and one each to an Argentine, a Belgian, a Finn, a Hungarian, an Indian, a Netherlander, a Russian, and a Yugoslavian. No awards were made to Canadians.

The statutes of the Nobel Foundation state that awards should not be granted if the achievements being considered do not rise to the level of making the most important discoveries, inventions, or contributions within their fields. Consequently, some awards have not been made in every year. During the 1930's, no awards were made in chemistry in 1933, in physics in 1931 and 1934, in peace in 1932 and 1939, and in literature in 1935. (Awards for economics were not made until 1969.)

Prize money not paid out in years when no awards are made is reserved and added to the following year's awards. Because German chancellor Adolf Hitler forbade German laureates from accepting their Nobel Prizes, Richard Kuhn (1938) and Adolf Butenandt (1939) in chemistry and Gerhard Domagk (1939) in physics never received their prize money. However, when World War II ended, they did receive their Nobel Prize diplomas and medals.

Chemistry Prizes   The 1930's awards in chemistry spanned a wide range of research, from identification of naturally occurring substances and compounds to those synthesized or artificially created. The decade was a seminal period in chemistry that saw the chemical structures of many compounds elucidated, thanks to increasing theoretical understandings and insights, as well as the creation of more precise technological tools and techniques.

The German scientist Hans Fischer synthesized hemin, a naturally occurring pigment known as a pyrrole, in 1929 and was awarded the 1930 prize. Germany's Friedrich Bergius and Carl Bosch shared the prize the following year for their invention and development of chemical high-pressure methods involving fossil fuels, ammonia, and methanol.

The American chemist Irving Langmuir won in 1932 for his discoveries and investigations in surface chemistry. In 1934, another American, Harold C. Urey, was recognized for his discovery of heavy hydrogen. That discovery would later lead to heavy water used to moderate nuclear fission reactions and, when fused with tritium, would become the fuel for thermonuclear reactions in hydrogen bombs. In 1935, the French husband-and-wife team, Frédéric Joliot and Irène Joliot-Curie, shared the chemistry prize for their work in creating new radioactive chemical elements. Along with her mother, Marie Curie, Joliot-Curie was one of only four women to win a chemistry prize through the year 2010. Other chemistry awards were given for work on molecular structures by Peter J. W. Debye in 1936, on vitamins by Walter Norman Haworth and Paul Karrer in 1937 and Kuhn in 1938, on sex hormones by Butenandt in 1939, and on inorganic compounds found in the oils of plants and ketones by Leopold Stephen Ružička in 1939.

Physics Prizes   The achievements of physics Nobelists during the 1930's ranged from the pioneering work on light scattering by the Indian scientist Chandrasekhar Venkata Raman in 1930 to major advances in atomic theory made by Great Britain's Paul A. M. Dirac and Germany's Erwin Schrödinger in 1933. Also highlighted was the strange world of quantum mechanics, in which observations at the atomic level disturb and alter what is observed, by Werner Karl Heisenberg from Germany in 1932.

The Nobel Committee recognized fundamental discoveries of atomic particles, including the work on neutrons by James Chadwick of Britain in 1935 and the work on the antiparticle of the electron, christened the positron, by the American Carl David Anderson in 1936. Also honored was the work on diffraction of electrons by crystals by the American Clinton Joseph Davisson and George Paget Thomson of Britain in 1937. Many of these discoveries overturned previous scientific dogma and opened new vistas of matter to the world's scientists with profound implications for all fields of science and many fields of technology and engineering.

The Austrian Victor Franz Hess was recognized in 1936 for his discovery of cosmic radiation. The brilliant Italian theoretician and experimenter Enrico Fermi won in 1938, and his colleague, the equally agile American experimentalist Ernest Orlando Lawrence, in 1939. Both were honored for their fundamental achievements related to radioactive elements and controlled nuclear reactions. Fermi would later construct the world's first nuclear reactor in Chicago and oversee the construction of the first nuclear weapons, and Lawrence's cyclotron invention would be used to help produce the required uranium.

Physiology or Medicine Prizes   Medical breakthroughs honored in the 1930's included the discoveries of human blood groups by Austria's Karl

Nobel Prize-winning physicists Ernest Orlando Lawrence (left) and Enrico Fermi during the 1930's. (©Bettmann/CORBIS)

American Nobel Prize Winners During the 1930's

Year	Field	Recipient
1930	Literature	Sinclair Lewis
1931	Peace	Jane Addams Nicholas Murray Butler
1932	Chemistry	Irving Langmuir
1933	Physiology or Medicine	Thomas Hunt Morgan
1934	Chemistry	Harold C. Urey
	Physiology or Medicine	George Richards Minot William Parry Murphy George Hoyt Whipple
1936	Literature	Eugene O'Neill
	Physics	Carl David Anderson
1937	Physics	Clinton Joseph Davisson
1938	Literature	Pearl S. Buck
1939	Physics	Ernest Orlando Lawrence

make sense of the organizer effect in embryonic development. The Hungarian physician Albert Szent-Györgyi was honored in 1937 for his discoveries relating to biological combustion processes, with special reference to vitamin C and the catalysis of fumaric acid, a powerful stimulus to the understanding that the human body itself is a massively complex chemical factory synthesizing thousands of substances—many via pathways still not fully understood in the early twenty-first century.

The role that the sinus and aortic mechanisms play in regulating respiration was the pioneering work of the Belgian Corneille Jean François Heymans, who mapped out how the entire system operated and received the 1938 award. The German Domagk discovered prontosil, the first of the so-called sulfa drugs that are produced naturally by microorganisms. His work, honored by the 1939 prize, gave medicine vital new drugs to fight infections and diseases such as pneumonia, meningitis, and gonorrhea and would save many lives when World War II engulfed the entire globe.

Peace Prizes Traditionally the most controversial of the Nobel Prizes are those awarded in the field of peace. In contrast to awards made in other categories, peace prizes have generally been made to people and organizations whose contributions to world peace and brotherhood have been very recent. The emphasis on recent contributions makes it difficult to judge how the acts being honored will stand up over time, and the 1930's was a particularly tumultuous period in which to make such judgments. Most of the awards made during the 1930's honored efforts to promote peace through international conferences and mediation of international conflicts. Given that the bloodiest and most far-reaching military conflict in world history was soon to erupt, many of the peace awards made during the 1930's would appear to have been inappropriate. Unsurprisingly, perhaps, no award at all was made in 1939, the year in which World War II began in Europe.

In 1930, the decade's first Nobel Peace Prize went to the archbishop of Uppsala, Sweden, Nathan

Landsteiner (1930), respiratory enzymes by the German Otto Heinrich Warburg (1931), the functions of neurons by Britain's Baron Edgar Douglas Adrian and Charles Scott Sherrington (1932), the chemical transmission of nerve impulses by Britain's Henry Hallett Dale and Germany's Otto Loewi (1936), and the role of chromosomes in heredity by the American Thomas Hunt Morgan (1933). These discoveries alone would radically alter medicine, basic biological understanding, and the understanding of tempo and mode in evolution.

A trio of Americans demonstrated for the world how fundamental work in science could lead to practical application. George Hoyt Whipple lowered hemoglobin in dogs to induce long-term anemia so it could be better understood. He experimentally determined that liver stimulated hemoglobin production. George Richards Minot and William Parry Murphy applied his findings to humans and saw remarkable responses from anemic patients to liver and liver extract. All three Americans shared the 1934 prize.

In 1935, Hans Spemann from Germany was recognized for his painstaking work to identify and

Söderblom. He was one of the principal promoters of the Universal Christian Conference on Life and Work, a Christian ecumenical movement striving to promote international understanding. The 1931 award was shared by two Americans. Jane Addams, perhaps most famous as the founder of Chicago's Hull House, was honored for her work as the president of the Women's International League for Peace and Freedom. Nicholas Murray Butler, the president of Columbia University, shared the award, primarily for having helped to promote the Kellogg-Briand Pact of 1928, an international agreement designed to prevent future wars.

The next two awards went to British subjects who played principal roles in peace conferences. Sir Norman Angell won in 1933 for his work on the executive committee of the League of Nations and of the National Peace Council. In 1934, former British foreign secretary Arthur Henderson won for his service as president of the 1932 Disarmament Conference. Argentina's foreign minister, Carlos Saavedra Lamas, was honored in 1936 for helping to mediate an end to the Chaco War between Bolivia and Paraguay.

The 1937 award went to the British diplomat Robert Cecil (Viscount Cecil of Chelwood), the founder and president of the International Peace Campaign. The 1938 award went to a Swiss-based organization, the Nansen International Office for Refugees, an international relief organization that the Norwegian explorer Fridtjof Nansen had founded during the early 1920's.

Literature Prizes   During the 1930's, Nobel Prizes in Literature were awarded to a single writer in every year except 1935. Until 1930, no American had ever received this honor, but during the decade three awards went to Americans: novelist Sinclair Lewis in 1930, playwright Eugene O'Neill in 1936, and novelist Pearl S. Buck—the first American woman writer to win—in 1938. The decade's other recipients included Swedish poet Erik Axel Karlfeldt (1931), the first writer to receive an award posthumously. British novelist and playwright John Galsworthy, perhaps best known for *The Forsythe Saga*, won in 1932, and Russian author Ivan Bunin won in 1933. The prolific Italian author of short stories, novels, and plays Luigi Pirandello won in 1934, and French novelist Roger Martin du Gard won in 1937. Finnish novelist Frans Eemil Sillanpää, who was noted for his depictions of peasant life, won in 1939.

To many observers, the literature awards made during the 1930's represented a serious regression in quality over those made in earlier decades. European politics overshadowed both the era and, apparently, many of the academy's decisions. However, two recipients were outstanding exceptions—Pirandello and O'Neill, both playwrights without whose work twentieth century Western drama would have been greatly diminished. Critical opinions about the award given to American novelist Lewis have been roughly evenly split between defenders and detractors. However, both sides have tended to agree that whether Lewis deserved his award or not, he was not the best American writer eligible for it the moment when the academy was finally ready to give its first literature award to an American writer. Most critics would have preferred to see Theodore Dreiser, best known for his novels *Sister Carrie* (1900) and *An American Tragedy* (1925), get the award. Dreiser may have been handicapped by not publishing any significant works during the 1930's. He would live to 1945 without receiving an award.

Among the other award recipients during the 1930's generally deemed unworthy of Nobel Prizes two stand out: Galsworthy and Buck, who has the dubious distinction of being perhaps the worst choice ever in the view of many critics within and outside the academy. Her fame during the 1930's rested largely on her 1931 novel *The Good Earth*, a powerful depiction of the daily lives of ordinary Chinese peasants. She would live until 1973 and publish many more books, but none of them vindicated her Nobel award. Among the many worthier candidates not receiving awards during the decade, the name of only one other American stands out: T. S. Eliot, the Missouri-born poet who had become a British subject in 1927. He, however, would receive the award in 1948.

Impact   While many of the Nobel Prizes in Peace and Literature awarded during the 1930's may have been controversial, those awarded in the science categories generally were not. The science prizes honored scientific achievements that would prove seminal to the advancement of chemistry, physics, physiology, medicine, and the life sciences throughout the twentieth century and beyond. Fundamental theories, insights, and inventions pioneered and/or recognized in the 1930's laid the foundation for whole new sciences and far-reaching spinoffs that no one in the 1930's could possibly have predicted, including nuclear weapons just a few years later and the peaceful uses of nuclear energy and nuclear medicine. World War II caused many of these prizewinners and fellow scientists to flee their home countries. Nine of the science laureates not only relocated but also ultimately became citizens of their new homelands; many became citizens of the United States. This transition brought about by war provided the impetus for American scientific and technological prowess in subsequent decades, accelerated the growth and prestige of American research universities, and established the United States as a dominant producer of subsequent Nobel Prizes in the sciences.

Dennis W. Cheek and the Editors

Further Reading

Hargittai, Istvan. *The Road to Stockholm: Nobel Prizes, Science, and Scientists.* New York: Oxford University Press, 2003. Comprehensive history of the creation and awarding of the Nobel Prizes with particular attention to common characteristics among winners, controversies regarding the awards, and the subsequent impact of the awards on the winners and on science more broadly.

Kurian, George Thomas. *The Nobel Scientists: A Biographical Encyclopedia.* Amherst, N.Y.: Prometheus Books, 2002. Succinct set of short biographical entries for all 466 winners of the Nobel Prize in the sciences from their inception through 2000, including a short bibliography of their most important publications and key works about them by others.

Leroy, Francis, ed. *A Century of Nobel Prize Recipients: Chemistry, Physics, and Medicine.* New York: Marcel Dekker, 2003. Following an opening chapter on Alfred Nobel, this book traces the discoveries and assesses the contributions of nearly five hundred scientists who have received the Nobel Prize in the fields of chemistry, physics, and medicine. Features chronological tables of recipients.

Riggan, William. "The Nobel Prize in Literature: History and Overview." In *The Nobel Prize Winners: Literature,* edited by Frank N. Magill. Vol. 1. Pasadena, Calif.: Salem Press, 1987. Informative essay provides background on the influences involved in decision making regarding the Nobel Prize in Literature.

Sherby, Louise S. *The Who's Who of Nobel Prize Winners, 1901-2000.* 4th ed. Westport, Conn.: Oryx, 2002.

Contains detailed information on prizewinners through 2000, organized chronologically by prize, as well as a brief history of the prizes. Entries include biographical details about recipients and lists of their relevant publications as well as summaries of their achievements. Four indexes.

Worek, Michael, ed. *Nobel: A Century of Prize Winners.* Richmond Hill, Ont.: Firefly Books, 2008. Extended look at two hundred of the most famous Nobelists by prize and year with a good description of the key work that led to receipt of the award.

See also   Addams, Jane; Buck, Pearl S.; Chemistry; Cyclotron; Germany and U.S. appeasement; League of Nations; Lewis, Sinclair; Literature in the United States; Medicine; Nuclear fission; O'Neill, Eugene; Physics; Positron discovery.

■ Nonpartisan League

Identification   Political organization formed to advocate for farmers
Also known as   NPL; Non-partisan League; Farmers' Nonpartisan League
Date   Established in February, 1915

The Nonpartisan League (NPL) was one of the most influential political organizations in the northern plains, particularly in North Dakota and Minnesota. It is best known for gaining control of the state government of North Dakota during the late 1910's and enacting various state programs to alleviate conditions for farmers, including the creation of a state bank and a state mill and grain elevator.

The NPL was an organization affiliated primarily with the Republican Party in North Dakota and was founded at Fred Wood's farm in northwestern North Dakota in February of 1915. The idea for the organization came several weeks prior to the founding, as farmers in North Dakota faced hardships, including property foreclosures and adverse weather. The main person behind the NPL was Arthur C. Townley, a former state Socialist Party organizer who was using the party to draw members to the concept that eventually became the NPL. Because of Townley's ability to organize and recruit, the NPL swept the 1916 primary elections in North Dakota. In the 1916 general election, the party won a majority of the House seats and almost all executive positions in the state, including the governorship.

The NPL quickly attempted to realize its platform of state-controlled industries and entities and was successful to a degree, establishing a state bank, a state mill and grain elevator, and a state hail insurance program. While the NPL was asserting its elected power in North Dakota, it was spreading in other midwestern states, claiming more than 200,000 members in thirteen states in 1916. However, accusations that the group was socialist quickly surfaced, as the NPL attempted to amend North Dakota's constitution to bring about more of its program. In addition, the U.S. entry into World War I, coupled with Townley's perceived anti-American remarks regarding the wealthy and the war, began to hurt the NPL, though it continued to win elections in North Dakota in 1918 and 1920. In 1921, the NPL suffered major setbacks when Townley was jailed for his remarks and Lynn Frazier, the NPL governor of North Dakota, and several other officials were recalled. These actions ended the NPL for a number of years.

By the 1930's, the NPL was in its third incarnation; a few politicians had attempted, unsuccessfully, to revive it during the 1920's. The NPL of the 1930's was firmly within the Republican Party and was most associated with William "Wild Bill" Langer, who was elected governor of North Dakota twice in the decade. The conditions in the state allowed for the resurgence of the NPL, as North Dakota was hit hard with drought and the Dust Bowl. The Langer administration was popular among North Dakotans, even though Langer spent a brief period of time in prison. The 1930's represented one of the last great periods for the NPL, as it declined with World War II and the postwar boom. It eventually joined the Democratic Party in 1956.

Impact   The NPL represented a significant victory for populist-based politics in the Great Plains. Farmers and, to a lesser extent, laborers tired of being controlled by groups that did not have their concerns at heart, took matters into their own hands. Though commonly associated with the 1910's, the NPL experienced a brief resurgence during the 1930's because of the hard conditions of the Great Depression and the Dust Bowl. The Nonpartisan League represents one of the last great agrarian political movements in American history.

Daniel Sauerwein

Further Reading

Morlan, Robert. *Political Prairie Fire: The Nonpartisan League, 1915-1922*. St. Paul: Minnesota Historical Society Press, 1955.

Robinson, Elwyn B. *History of North Dakota*. Lincoln: University of Nebraska Press, 1966.

See also   Agriculture in the United States; Dust Bowl; Elections of 1932, U.S.; Elections of 1936, U.S.; Great Depression in the United States; Socialist parties; Unemployment in the United States.

■ Norris-La Guardia Act of 1932

The Law   Federal law that effectively reduced the use of court injunctions to restrict labor union activities

Date   March 23, 1932

Since the passage of the Sherman Antitrust Act in 1890, labor unions had been vulnerable to prosecution for actions in restraint of trade. The Clayton Act of 1914 contained passages limiting the scope for such prosecutions, but court decisions during the 1920's continued to allow firms to obtain injunctions against strikes, picketing, or boycotts.

The Norris-La Guardia Act enumerated nine specific, peaceable union activities against which federal courts might not issue injunctions. These included ceasing or refusing to work, joining a union, paying strike benefits, publicizing facts in a labor dispute, and advising or persuading others regarding the listed items. So-called yellow-dog contracts, in which a worker, as a condition of employment, agreed not to join a union, were explicitly held to be unenforceable. The law also severely restricted applying the concepts of conspiracy or shared liability for engaging in the enumerated actions.

The constitutionality of the Norris-La Guardia Act was upheld in the case of *Lauf v. E. G. Shinner & Co.* (1938). Significant cases in which injunctive relief was refused were *Apex Hosiery Co. v. Leader* (1939) and *United States v. Hutcheson* (1941). However, the law was largely superseded by other major federal labor legislation. The National Industrial Recovery Act of 1933 and the National Labor Relations Act (Wagner Act) of 1935 established a national policy that workers had the right to organize unions and bargain collectively. The Wagner Act prohibited various unfair labor practices by employers and created the National Labor Relations Board to protect these.

Impact Norris-La Guardia contributed to the general climate of opinion legitimizing the formation and activities of labor unions, reacting to worker distress from the Depression. While emphasis shifted to other policies, under which union membership increased rapidly, both the *Apex* and *Hutcheson* cases involved union activities with strongly antisocial elements such as secondary boycotts. The Taft-Hartley Act of 1947 restricted these and other harmful union activities.

Paul B. Trescott

Further Reading

Daugherty, Carroll R. *Labor Problems in American Industry.* 5th ed. Boston: Houghton Mifflin, 1941.

Gregory, Charles O. *Labor and the Law.* New York: W. W. Norton, 1949.

Lehman, Jeffrey, and Shirelle Phelps, eds. *West's Encyclopedia of American Law.* Detroit: Thompson/Gale, 2005.

Norris, George W. *Fighting Liberal.* New York: Collier Books, 1961.

See also Business and the economy in the United States; Labor strikes; La Guardia, Fiorello Henry; National Industrial Recovery Act of 1933; National Labor Relations Act of 1935; Unionism.

The architects of the Norris-La Guardia Act, George W. Norris (left) and Fiorello La Guardia, confer with each other in the former's office in Washington, D.C., in 1938. (Library of Congress)

■ Northrop, John Howard

Identification American biochemist
Born July 5, 1891; Yonkers, New York
Died May 27, 1987; Wickenberg, Arizona

Northrop's research resulted in the development of a method for isolating and crystallizing enzymes in their purest form. This allowed biochemists to determine the chemical nature of enzymes, proteins, and viruses. His work confirmed that enzymes obeyed the laws of normal chemical reactions and were not "vital processes" outside the normal laws of chemistry, as previously hypothesized.

John Howard Northrop entered Columbia University in 1908 to study zoology and chemistry. He received a bachelor of science degree in 1912 and a master of arts in 1913. He completed the Ph.D. in chemistry in 1915. Northrop's then spent a year studying under Jacques Loeb at the Rockefeller Institute. Northrop's initial research interest dealt with fermentation processes and environmental factors related to the heredity and life span of fruit flies. During this phase of his career, he successfully cultivated the flies aseptically, totally free of any contaminants. This work helped to demonstrate that environmental conditions helped to determine the duration of life.

During World War I, Northrop served as a captain in the U.S. Army Chemical Warfare Service. At this time, he developed a method for producing acetone and ethanol from the fermentation of potatoes.

Northrop became a member of the Rockefeller Institute in 1924 and spent the majority of his career there. At the institute, he continued to study enzymes, viruses, and antibodies. Enzymes had been studied for years but were poorly understood. Northrop developed a method to isolate and crystallize enzymes in the pure state. This allowed scientists to develop a clear understanding of what they consisted of, rather than merely studying their effects.

Northrop's work with enzymes related to digestive processes and respiration resulted in the isolation and crystallization of pepsin, an enzyme produced in the stomach lining that degrades protein. Pepsin had been known as an effective treatment for stomach disorders, but the chemical properties of the enzyme were not understood. Only with Northrop's crystallization of pepsin in 1930 did it become apparent that pepsin was actually a protein, thus confirming James Batcheller Sumner's earlier work, which had ignited a violent debate among chemists. Northrop demonstrated that enzymes actually acted as catalysts in chemical reactions that were not qualitatively different from other chemical reactions.

Northrop's primary interest was in understanding the nature of the chemical substances that control reactions in living cells and the rate of those reactions, especially in self-duplicating systems. This led to his interest in viruses. The actual chemical nature of viruses was not understood prior to the investigations by Northrop and Wendell Meredith Stanley, with whom he shared the Nobel Prize in Chemistry in 1946. Northrop and Stanley identified the precise chemical structure of viruses. Northrop discovered that nucleic acid was present in viruses and that acid was encased in a protein that protected the DNA of the transforming agent. This protein shell allowed the DNA of the virus to be introduced into the susceptible cell of the target. With the proof that viruses contain protein, developing methods to control viruses became possible. In 1938, Northrop succeeded in isolating and crystallizing bacteriophage, a virus that attacks bacteria. He demonstrated that the bacteriophage activity was due to the presence of nucleic acid.

In recognition of his work, Northrop was awarded the Stevens Prize in 1931, the Chandler Medal in 1936, and the Daniel Giraud Elliot Medal in 1939; he shared the Nobel Prize in Chemistry in 1946. Northrop also published numerous technical articles and served as the editor of the *Journal of General Physiology*. In 1939, he published *Crystalline Enzymes*, the seminal work in the field. In addition to his work at the Rockefeller Institute, he served as a professor of bacteriology at the University of California, Berkeley, from 1949 to 1958.

Impact Northrop's groundbreaking work in isolating and crystallizing enzymes and viruses had a far-reaching impact in the field of biochemistry. He disproved many of the previously held hypotheses regarding the nature of enzymes. His discovery that enzymes were proteins and followed the normal laws of science allowed development of antitoxins and various medical treatments to progress rapidly. This work allowed him to crystallize diphtheria antitoxin in 1940. His work resulted in the development of methods and technologies still in use.

Ronald J. Ferrara

Further Reading

Farber, Edward, ed. *Nobel Prize Winners in Chemistry, 1901-1950*. New York: Abelard-Schuman, 1953.

Northrop, John H., M. Kunitz, and R. M. Herriot. *Crystalline Enzymes*. 2d ed. New York: Columbia University Press, 1948.

Shampo, M. A., and R. A. Kyle. "John Northrop: Definitive Study of Enzymes." *Mayo Clinic Proceedings* 75, no. 3 (March, 2000): 254.

See also Chemistry; Medicine; Nobel Prizes; Typhus immunization.

NRA. See **National Recovery Administration**

■ Nuclear fission

Definition Splitting of atomic nuclei to release large amounts of energy

Desirable and undesirable practical applications of science are rooted in attempts to understand and control nature. Although nuclear fission was discovered accidentally, during investigations whose purpose was to create transuranium elements, it was at once recognized as a reaction by which a large amount of energy could be released.

Leading to the development of atomic bombs and nuclear reactors, the 1939 discovery of nuclear fission was mostly the result of an international effort. It was preceded by the 1932 discovery of neutrons by James Chadwick in England and the 1933 discovery of artificial radioactivity by Irène Joliot-Curie and Frédéric Joliot in France. In 1934, when uranium was the last known element in the periodic chart, a team of Italian scientists headed by Enrico Fermi started bombarding uranium with neutrons. They wanted to produce artificially elements "beyond uranium."

German chemists Otto Hahn, Lise Meitner, and Fritz Strassmann also bombarded uranium with neutrons for several years, investigating properties of reaction products. At first, they suspected these products were radium, actinium, and thorium. However, in a January, 1939, paper, published without the coauthorship of an exiled Meitner, they wrote that these products might be barium, lanthanum, and cerium. This was not a definite statement, however; the authors hesitated because they had no idea how such elements could be produced.

Credit for understanding the mechanism reactions belongs to Meitner, who was in Sweden when the paper was published. She was the first to realize that an atomic nucleus could split into two large fragments. Meitner coined the term "nuclear fission" and subsequently published a paper in which the amount of energy released in fission was calculated on the basis of Albert Einstein's $E = mc^2$ formula. Two scientists, Otto Robert Frisch in Denmark and Joliot in France, provided experimental evidence for the magnitude of released energy. This was at once confirmed in early nuclear fission experiments in the United States.

Another important discovery, made in 1939 by Joliot and his collaborators Hans von Halban, from Austria, and Lew Kowarski, from Russia, was the emission of several energetic neutrons during each fission event. This was a clear indication of the possibility of an explosive chain reaction. Basic principles of future applications of nuclear energy were already known when World War II started. However, technical details leading to practical applications were not clear. Fearing that Nazi Germany was planning to develop nuclear weapons, Leo Szilard, one of many refugees from Europe, persuaded Einstein to write a letter to President Franklin D. Roosevelt. The large-scale U.S. nuclear bomb project (1942-1945) can be traced to that letter.

Prior to the discovery of fission, early American nuclear-science efforts focused on accelerators, such as the Columbia University cyclotron built by John Dunning. The first American nuclear fission experiments were conducted using this accelerator in January and February of 1939. Fermi, by then one of many European refugees, joined Dunning's team. After confirming the high energy of fission fragments and the possibility of a chain reaction, the team showed that only a rare uranium isotope, uranium 235, and not the common uranium 238, was responsible for fission fragments. This important American discovery opened the path toward both military and peaceful applications of nuclear energy.

Reacting to Einstein's letter, President Roosevelt asked the director of the National Bureau of Standards to organize a secret Advisory Committee on Uranium. The first meeting of that body took place on October 21, 1939. A modest sum of six thousand dollars was at once budgeted to support basic chain-reaction research. The United States was still a neutral country at that time. The Manhattan Project, whose purpose was to develop atomic bombs, was created in August, 1942, and the enrichment of uranium with uranium 235 became its high-priority task.

Impact The first atomic bomb was exploded in Alamogordo, New Mexico, in July, 1945. One month

---

Albert Einstein on Nuclear Weapons

On August 2, 1939, Einstein wrote a letter to President Franklin D. Roosevelt outlining the discovery of nuclear fission and its possible military implications.

In the course of the last four months it has been made probable—through the work of Joliot in France as well as Fermi and Szilard in America—that it may become possible to set up a nuclear chain reaction in a large mass of uranium, by which vast amounts of power and large quantities of new radium-like elements would be generated. Now it appears almost certain that this could be achieved in the immediate future.

This new phenomenon would also lead to the construction of bombs, and it is conceivable—though much less certain—that extremely powerful bombs of a new type may thus be constructed. A single bomb of this type, carried by boat and exploded in a port, might very well destroy the whole port together with some of the surrounding territory.

later, two atomic bombs were dropped on Hiroshima and Nagasaki, Japan, killing or injuring several hundred thousand people. The bombs prompted Japan to surrender unconditionally to the Allies, thereby ending World War II. The obvious value of nuclear weapons in combat prompted an international arms race during the ensuing Cold War. However, the possibility of mutual annihilation in an all-out nuclear war helped prevent the use of such weapons.

Ludwik Kowalski

Further Reading

Bird, Kai, and Martin J. Sherwin. *American Prometheus: The Triumph and Tragedy of J. Robert Oppenheimer.* New York: A. A. Knopf, 2005.

Dahl, Per F., ed. *From Nuclear Transmutation to Nuclear Fission, 1932-1939.* London: Taylor & Francis, 2002.

Graetzer, Hans G., and David L. Anderson. *The Discovery of Nuclear Fission.* New York: Van Nostrand Reinhold, 1971.

Sime, Ruth. *Lise Meitner: A Life in Physics.* Berkeley: University of California Press, 1996.

See also Cyclotron; Einstein, Albert; Electron microscope; Inventions; Nobel Prizes.

■ Nye Committee

Identification U.S. Senate committee formed to investigate the reasons for U.S. involvement in World War I

Also known as Special Committee Investigating the Munitions Industry

Dates Formed on April 12, 1934; submitted final report on June 19, 1936

The Nye Committee investigated the origins of American involvement in World War I, and helped popularize the conviction that the United States had intervened in that conflict at the behest of powerful bankers and arms manufacturers, the so-called merchants of death. The committee's operations represented one of the high points of American isolationism during the 1930's.

The failure of the United States to ratify the 1919 Treaty of Versailles and enter the League of Nations challenged the idealism that had sanctioned American participation in World War I. Greater knowledge about the human toll of the war, and the disorder that it had left across the world, led many to question whether American victory had been worth the cost. In the postwar years, revisionist historians raised doubts about the moral and political premises that had guided American policy makers as they made the decision for intervention. One of the most politically corrosive lines of revisionist criticism asserted that the American decision for war had been driven by the interests of big American businesses hoping to profit from the war. Implicated groups included Wall Street banks that had made loans to the Allies and companies producing munitions and weapons. The Great Depression created an antibusiness mood that made such claims both more believable and politically attractive. In 1934, H. C. Engelbrecht and F. C. Hanighen's muckraking tract *The Merchants of Death* found a wide audience.

Peace activists had long wanted a congressional investigation into the munitions industry. In December, 1933, Dorothy Detzer, executive secretary of the Women's International League for Peace and Freedom, approached Senator George W. Norris. He sympathized but considered himself too old for such investigative work. Norris suggested that Senator Gerald Prentice Nye take the lead. Nye was a progressive Republican from North Dakota. As an heir to the tradition of midwestern agrarian radicalism, he distrusted big business and had supported much of President Franklin D. Roosevelt's New Deal. With Norris's support, Nye agreed to submit a resolution for a munitions investigation. On April 12, 1934, Senate Resolution 206 was adopted without dissent.

The Senate Munitions Committee consisted of four Democrats and three Republicans. The Democrats were James P. Pope of Idaho, Homer T. Bone of Washington, Bennett Champ Clark of Missouri, and Walter F. George of Georgia. The Republicans were Nye, Arthur Hendrick Vandenberg of Michigan, and W. Warren Barbour of New Jersey. The members of the committee promptly elected Nye as chairman. Stephen Raushenbush was appointed secretary and chief investigator. John T. Flynn, a writer from the *New Republic*, served as an adviser. Alger Hiss, on loan from the Agricultural Adjustment Administration, acted as the committee's general counsel.

Between 1934 and 1936, the Senate Munitions Committee held ninety-three hearings and questioned more than two hundred witnesses. Among the witnesses called before the committee were J. P. Morgan and members of the Du Pont family. The testimony at these hearings filled thirty-nine volumes. The committee explored the munitions industry, the shipbuilding industry, war profits, and the American entry into War World I. It submitted seven reports, making recommendations on such topics as taking the profits out of war, the government manufacture of munitions, and neutrality legislation. Nye took advantage of the visibility provided by his investigations to speak frequently on the radio and undertake lecture tours around the country. Though the committee never found hard evidence of a business conspiracy to embroil the United States in World War I, Nye firmly believed that the desire for profits on the part of bankers and arms manufacturers had pushed the nation into war. He argued that unless Congress took action, greed might lead to another war. The Senate cut funding for the committee after Nye asserted that President Woodrow Wilson had falsely denied knowledge of secret treaties among the Allies during the war. He had documentary evidence for this in an unreleased British memorandum. Nevertheless, his unflattering statement about a former president led to an uproar that ended support for the committee.

Impact The Nye Committee proved nothing about the "merchants of death," but by shining an unflattering light on the actions of American businessmen and statesmen, its highly publicized hearings did persuade many that American belligerence in 1917 had been a mistake. The Nye Committee played a major role in justifying American isolationism during the 1930's. Its investigations encouraged the passage of the Neutrality Acts of 1935, 1936, and 1937.

Daniel P. Murphy

Further Reading

Black, Conrad. *Franklin Delano Roosevelt: Champion of Freedom.* New York: PublicAffairs, 2003.

Cole, Wayne S. *Senator Gerald P. Nye and American Foreign Relations.* Minneapolis: University of Minnesota Press, 1962.

Rhodes, Benjamin D. *United States Foreign Policy in the Interwar Period, 1918-1941: The Golden Age of American Diplomatic and Military Complacency.* Westport, Conn.: Praeger, 2001.

Wiltz, John E. *In Search of Peace: The Senate Munitions Inquiry, 1934-1936.* Baton Rouge: Louisiana State University Press, 1963.

See also Congress, U.S.; Foreign policy of the United States; Isolationism; Neutrality Acts; Peace movement.

■ Nylon

Definition Generic term for a family of the first completely synthetic fibers

Dates First produced on February 28, 1935; publicly announced on October 27, 1938

Place DuPont Central Laboratories, Wilmington, Delaware

An indispensable, ubiquitous polymer, nylon initiated an eagerly embraced revolution in which numerous tailor-made synthetic materials, many with properties superior to those of natural materials, were developed and applied to various consumer products.

The development of nylon was the result of a long-term commitment to basic or fundamental research by Charles M. A. Stine, director of the Chemicals Department of E. I. du Pont de Nemours, and was a daring gamble and radical departure from U.S. industrial practice at the time. Stine sought unsuccessfully to staff his fundamental research program with eminent academics. University of Illinois organic chemistry professor Roger Adams recommended Wallace Hume Carothers—a young, unknown former student—who, after considerable vacillation, accepted the position in 1928.

Carothers made major contributions to theoretical organic chemistry and helped define the field of polymer chemistry, of which he became the foremost U.S. researcher. He convinced skeptics of Hermann Staudinger's view that polymers are not aggregates of small molecules connected by undefined forces but are giant molecules, macromolecules, linked by ordinary covalent bonds, enabling the German chemist to earn the 1953 Nobel Prize in Chemistry. In attempting to resolve the controversy, Carothers subjected well-known compounds to standard chemical reactions so that they formed long-chain molecules with structures that were unequivocally established.

By April, 1930, Carothers and his team discovered

that monovinyl acetylene reacted with hydrogen chloride to produce chloroprene, which polymerized spontaneously to yield neoprene, the first commercially successful synthetic rubber made in the United States. In July, 1930, Carothers produced the forerunner of nylon and filed a patent for linear-condensation polymers on July 3, 1931. His molecular still eliminated the water by-product more efficiently than others, allowing the polymerization to proceed to a greater extent.

Carothers's colleague Julian W. Hill found that filaments of superpolyesters, formed from glycols and dicarboxylic acids, could be pulled like taffy into fibers, which made them more pliable, elastic, flexible, and tough. However, they were unsuitable because they had low melting points, were only moderately stable in water, and were soluble in solvents.

Carothers substituted diamines for glycols and obtained higher-melting, more inert superpolyamides, linked by the bonds that hold together proteins such as natural silk.

Nylon, produced from hexamethylenediamine and adipic acid, was first marketed as "Exton" toothbrush bristles in July, 1938. Nylon stockings were first marketed in 1940. Nylon arrived on the market just in time to replace the supply of natural silk from Asia, which had been cut off during World War II. In February, 1942, the U.S. War Production Board commandeered all nylon production for military uses and thousands of prewar nylon stockings were donated to make parachute cloth, towropes, tire cords, fabric, and other items vital to the war effort.

In 1936, Carothers became the first industrial organic chemist elected to the U.S. National Academy

On the road to developing nylon, scientists from DuPont pour a liquid concoction into a machine, experimenting to discover the exact chemical combination necessary to create the synthetic polymer. (The Granger Collection, New York)

of Sciences. Unfortunately for Carothers, who is revered as the founder of American polymer chemistry, he endured a tormented personal life that contrasted sharply with his success as a scientist. Suffering from depression since his youth, he did not play a significant role in the development of nylon after 1935 because of his mental illness. Convinced that he was a failure as a scientist, he committed suicide by drinking lemon juice laced with potassium cyanide on April 29, 1937, at the age of forty-one. He was posthumously inducted into the National Inventors Hall of Fame in April, 1984.

Impact   Nylon, a symbol of modern American industrial achievement, is the prototypical example of basic research that begins with no practical end use in mind but that results in an almost endless array of products. Nylon has spread to all segments of society throughout the world.

George B. Kauffman

Further Reading

Aharoni, Shaul M. *N-Nylons: Their Synthesis, Structure, and Properties.* New York: Academic Press, 1997.

Gratzer, Walter. *Giant Molecules: From Nylon to Nanotubes.* New York: Oxford University Press, 2009.

Handley, Susannah. *Nylon: The Manmade Fashion Revolution.* Baltimore: Johns Hopkins University Press, 1999.

Hermes, Matthew E. *Enough for One Lifetime: Wallace Carothers, Inventor of Nylon.* Washington, D.C.: American Chemical Society, 1996.

Kauffman, George B. "Wallace Hume Carothers and Nylon, the First Completely Synthetic Fiber." *Journal of Chemical Education* 65, no. 9 (1988): 803-808.

MacIntyre, J. E., ed. *Synthetic Fibres: Nylon, Polyester, Acrylic, Polyolefins.* Cambridge, Cambridgeshire, England: Woodhead, 2004.

See also   Chemistry; Fashions and clothing; Inventions.

O

■ Odets, Clifford

Identification   American playwright
Born   July 18, 1906; Philadelphia, Pennsylvania
Died   August 14, 1963; Los Angeles, California

*Odets is considered by many scholars to be the most impor-
tant proletarian playwright of the 1930's. He was inti-
mately involved with the influential Group Theatre, and
six of his plays were produced by that organization during
the 1930's; five of them dealt with matters directly related to
the Great Depression. At the end of the decade, the six plays
he wrote during the 1930's were published in* Six Plays of
Clifford Odets *(1939).*

During the early 1930's, Clifford Odets played minor roles in a number of Theatre Guild productions
but left the group in 1931 to join the fledgling Group
Theatre established by Cheryl Crawford, Lee Strasberg, and Harold Clurman, Odets's close friend and
mentor. Seeking to produce socially relevant plays
that examined and commented on current social issues, this organization rejected the star system in favor of producing plays with seven or eight essentially
equal characters.

Members of the organization became surrogate
family to many of the alienated actors and playwrights who were drawn to the Group Theatre. They
lived together and were involved with one another
in every aspect of play production, often acting in a
production one week and serving as stagehands the
next. Between 1931 and 1935, Odets acted regularly
in the group's productions and worked on writing
plays but did not experience substantial success until late 1935, with the production *Waiting for Lefty*, a
short play that Odets wrote in three days.

This play focuses on a disparate group of taxicab
drivers protesting their working conditions. They
have been forced by the pressures of the Great Depression into driving taxis. They are in a union hall
awaiting the arrival of Lefty, a labor organizer who
will never appear because he has been killed. The
play plants its actors in the audience among the people watching the play, whose simple set makes it possible to perform almost anywhere.

Waiting for Lefty won Odets the George Pierce
Baker Cup awarded by Yale University, and the play
won the New Theatre-New Masses Contest as well.
Producers wanted to bring the play to Broadway, but
it was too short to constitute a full evening's entertainment, so Odets paired it with a short play about
the rise of Nazism, *Till the Day I Die* (1935), which he
had written earlier but not finished. Soon afterward,
he revised *Awake and Sing!* (1935), on which he had
been working, to be presented as a double bill with
Waiting for Lefty. By April of 1935, he had also
brought to Broadway *Paradise Lost*, of which he had a
working draft before *Waiting for Lefty* brought him
the incredible recognition that created a public de-

Playwright Clifford Odets in 1935. (©Bettmann/CORBIS)

Odets and the Group Theatre

Out of the work of the Group Theatre came one of the most important American playwrights of the twentieth century, Clifford Odets, whose major works of drama are listed below. The Group Theatre produced all of Odets's plays through Night Music *in 1940.*

- *Waiting for Lefty* (pr., pb. 1935)
- *Till the Day I Die* (pr., pb. 1935)
- *Awake and Sing!* (pr., pb. 1935)
- *Paradise Lost* (pr. 1935, pb. 1936)
- *I Can't Sleep* (pr. 1935, pb. 1936)
- *Golden Boy* (pr., pb. 1937)
- *Rocket to the Moon* (pr. 1938, pb. 1939)
- *Night Music* (pr., pb. 1940)
- *Clash by Night* (pr. 1941, pb. 1942)
- *The Russian People* (pr. 1942, pb. 1946; adaptation of Konstantin Simonov's play The Russians)
- *The Big Knife* (pr., pb. 1949)
- *The Country Girl* (pr. 1950, pb. 1951)
- *The Flowering Peach* (pr., pb. 1954)

mand for his plays. In the first third of 1935, Odets had four plays on Broadway, all produced by the Group Theatre.

Each of these plays, except *Till the Day I Die*, dealt directly with the social consequences of the Great Depression, as did *Golden Boy*, which was produced in 1937. Odet's final play during the 1930's, *Rocket to the Moon* (1938), deals with the love life of a dentist and is a marked departure from the social commentary of his earlier plays.

Impact Odets's impact upon theater during the 1930's was profound, affecting not only theater audiences but also society at large. When the Depression was at its peak, Odets railed against the social inequalities that accompanied it and against "life printed on dollar bills." Captured in his rich dialogue, Odets's social commentary was most strident during the 1930's; however, as the Great Depression began to fade with an improving economy and employment situation, the social problems he had dwelt on during the mid-1930's diminished substantially.

R. Baird Shuman

Further Reading

Brenman-Gibson, Margaret. *Clifford Odets: American Playwright—The Years from 1906-1940.* Vol. 1. New York: Atheneum, 1981.

Cantor, Harold. *Clifford Odets: Playwright-Poet.* 2d ed. Lanham, Md.: Scarecrow Press, 2000.

Herr, Christopher J. *Clifford Odets and American Political Theatre.* Westport, Conn.: Praeger, 2003.

Weales, Gerald. *Clifford Odets: Playwright.* New York: Pegasus, 1971.

See also Anti-Semitism; *Awake and Sing!*; Federal Theatre Project; Great Depression in the United States; Group Theatre; Jews in the United States; New Deal; Theater in the United States.

■ Ohio Penitentiary fire

The Event Fire that killed 320 state prisoners and injured 133 others
Date April 21, 1930
Place Columbus, Ohio

The most fatal in the history of U.S. correctional facilities, this fire called national attention to the dangers of antiquated, overcrowded prisons full of combustible materials, in which staff were not trained in fire evacuation and rescue.

In the late afternoon of April 21, 1930, prisoners were repairing the wooden roof of cell blocks I and K. Work ended at 4:00 P.M., and prisoners in the old wing, G and H cell blocks, had returned to their cells and been locked in for the night. About ninety minutes later, several prisoners and a guard reported a fire on the roof, and a passerby on the street outside the prison turned in the first alarm at 5:39 P.M. The fire department eventually called in four alarms.

Prison staff did not fight the fire, instead concentrating their attention on controlling, rather than evacuating, the prisoners. A guard in G and H block was overwhelmed by smoke before he could unlock the cells in these units, where the largest loss of life occurred. Chester Himes's *Yesterday Will Make You Cry* (1998), a fictionalized autobiography of one of the four thousand prisoners in the massively overcrowded Ohio Penitentiary during this period, depicts this scene graphically. African Americans were significantly overrepresented among the dead and injured.

Impact The Ohio Penitentiary fire initiated the development of fire-safety codes for correctional facilities nationwide. It also had consequences for the state of Ohio, which repealed mandatory sentencing in 1931, relieving prison overcrowding. Because of the fire safety measures instituted in the wake of the disaster, the number of fires in prisons and jails has fallen steadily since 1930. In 1980, for example, there were only four fires in U.S. prisons and jails, and there was only one in 2002.

Rachel Maines

Further Reading

Ahrens, Marty. *Selections from U.S. Fires in Selected Occupancies: Prisons and Jails.* Quincy, Mass.: National Fire Protection Association, 2006.

Carson, Wayne G. "Detention and Correctional Facilities." In *Fire Protection Handbook.* 20th ed. Boston: National Fire Protection Association, 2008.

Himes, Chester B. *Yesterday Will Make You Cry.* New York: Norton, 1998.

Sellers, T. B. *Report on the Ohio State Penitentiary Fire, Columbus, Ohio, April 21, 1930.* Columbus: Ohio Inspection Bureau, 1930.

See also African Americans; Joliet prison riot; Racial discrimination.

■ Ohio River flood

The Event Natural deluge that devastated the Ohio River floodplain

Dates January 5 to early February, 1937

Places Ohio River Valley, which includes Pennsylvania, West Virginia, Kentucky, Indiana, Ohio, and Illinois

The Ohio River flows some fifteen hundred miles from Pittsburgh, Pennsylvania, to Cairo, Illinois. Every city along the fifteen-hundred-mile stretch of the river experienced some form of flooding during the Ohio River flood of 1937, which was one of the deadliest and most costly natural disasters of the Great Depression era. Several cities were entirely engulfed by the overflowing banks of the Ohio River.

In late December of 1936 and early January of 1937, after years of dust storms resulting from drought and overfarming on the plains of the United States, rain fell on the snow-covered midwestern cities of Evansville, Paducah, Dayton, Cincinnati, and Hunt-

ington across several states. On January 5, 1937, water began to rise because of poor vegetation during the winter months, snow-covered streets, and chunks of ice adrift in the river. By the following week, flood warnings were posted across six states. By January 16, seventeen cities had already experienced record rainfalls, and by January 18, the flooding had begun. For many regions of Indiana, Ohio, and Kentucky, rain fell for nineteen consecutive days, and by January 24, martial law was in order for many southern Indiana cities, including Evansville.

By January 26, 1937, Cincinnati had experienced record rainfall, and the Ohio River had breached its banks at nearly eighty feet, the highest-recorded water level in the city's history, flooding the city. Cities such as Louisville, Kentucky, and Huntington, West Virginia, experienced similar situations on January 27. Some reports estimated more than 70 percent of Louisville was under water. In Cincinnati alone, estimates indicated nearly fifty thousand people were homeless. Areas north of Cincinnati, such as Wheeling, West Virginia, and Pittsburgh, Pennsylvania, recorded levels twelve feet above flood stage.

By February 5, 1937, much of the water had begun to fall around the hardest hit areas of the Ohio River and damage totals and death tolls began to rise. Most areas along the banks of the Ohio had rain for twenty-three of the thirty-one days of January, and many cities were recovering from floodwaters more than thirty feet above flood stage. The aftermath of the flood brought even more devastating news. Many towns were completely destroyed, and damage totals were estimated to be between five hundred and seven hundred million dollars. The death toll for the storm was a reported 385 people; however, many historians estimate the count to be significantly higher because of the large homeless population at this time. Missing citizens were presumed dead, and many bodies were never discovered. In some cities, such as Louisville, it was estimated that more than 170,000 citizens were homeless or displaced.

Impact The seriousness of the flood gained national attention, as the U.S. government vowed to control the flooding problems plaguing the areas along the Ohio River and its tributaries. Over the following decade, the Army Corps of Engineers, as well as many towns along the banks of the Ohio River, built flood and retaining walls along many low-lying areas of the river and created storage reservoirs and effective drainage for the cities. After the flood, the dam construction from Pennsylvania to Illinois increased, bringing a feeling of safety to the hardest hit areas as well as jobs and revenue for areas damaged from the flood and the years of the Great Depression. The residents of the Ohio River Valley did not experience flooding again for another sixty years.

Keith J. Bell

Further Reading

Castro, James E. *Great Ohio River Flood of 1937.* Charleston, S.C.: Arcadia, 2009.

Kleber, J. *The Encyclopedia of Louisville.* Lexington: University Press of Kentucky, 2001.

Stradling, D. *Cincinnati: From River City to Highway Metropolis.* Charleston, S.C.: Arcadia, 2003.

See also   Civilian Conservation Corps; Dust Bowl; Federal Emergency Relief Administration; Great Depression in the United States.

■ Oklahoma Welfare Act of 1936

The Law   Federal legislation offering an alternative to the Indian Reorganization Act of 1934
Also known as   Oklahoma Indian Welfare Act; Thomas-Rogers Act
Dates   Introduced February 27, 1935; enacted on June 26, 1936

The Oklahoma Welfare Act was designed to improve the livelihood of Native Americans residing in Oklahoma. It allowed for the reorganization of many tribes in Oklahoma that had been negatively impacted by the Oklahoma Land Run. The act enhanced the ability of tribes to create independent tribal governments.

Oklahoma politicians did not believe the Indian Reorganization Act of 1934 best represented the interests of the state's Native American population. Senator Elmer Thomas of Oklahoma argued that removing Native Americans residing in Oklahoma from their allotted land and forcing them to reservations would overturn the progress made between Caucasians and Native Americans. Thomas led a political delegation that wrote a bill better suited to the needs of the state's Native American population.

The original draft had eighteen sections that focused on a variety of issues ranging from the taxation of mineral rights, the incorporation of Native Americans into mainstream culture, and restrictions of Native Americans selling their land. There was much opposition to this draft. The most vocal opposition came from representatives of Osage County who disagreed with the idea of taking probate control of Native American money and property away from the Oklahoma courts.

Impact   The revised draft of this law centered on empowering Native Americans without forcing them onto reservations. This legislation outlined how tribes could construct and implement new constitutions. It also addressed how Native Americans could acquire land and establish credit. The legislation did not remove probate decisions from the state courts. Furthermore, section 8 of the act stipulated that Osage County was exempt from all parts of this legislation.

Jay Gilliam

Further Reading

Cornell, Stephen, and Joseph P. Kalt. "Sovereignty and Nation-Building: The Development Challenge in Indian Country Today." *American Indian Culture and Research Journal* 22, no. 1 (1998): 187-214.

Cowan, Klint A. "International Responsibility for Human Rights Violations by American Indian Tribes." *Yale Human Rights and Development Law Journal* 9, no. 1 (2006): 1-41.

Kalt, Joseph P., and Joseph W. Singer. *Myths and Realities of Tribal Sovereignty: The Law and Economics of Indian Self-Rule.* Cambridge, Mass.: Harvard Project on American Indian Economic Development, 2004.

See also   Civil rights and liberties in the United States; Congress, U.S.; Indian Reorganization Act; Native Americans; New Deal; Reorganization Act of 1939.

■ Olympic Games of 1932 (Summer)

The Event International multisport event held every four years

Date July 30-August 14, 1932

Place Los Angeles, California

The 1932 Summer Olympic Games were hosted by the United States. Despite the Great Depression, the Olympics were successful both financially and competitively. Economic challenges and location reduced participation, but the athletes who attended set numerous world and Olympic records.

The 1932 Summer Olympics were held in Los Angeles, California. Of the previous nine Olympic Games, only the 1904 Games in St. Louis had been

Canadian high-jumper Duncan McNaughton attempting to clear the bar on his way to the gold medal at the 1932 Olympic Games in Los Angeles. (Popperfoto/Getty Images)

held outside Europe. Because of the Great Depression, the cost involved in traveling to Los Angeles left many nations and athletes unable to attend the Games. Almost half as many athletes attended the 1932 Games as had attended the 1928 Games held in Amsterdam. The number of countries competing fell from forty-nine to thirty-seven. Despite the drop in attendance, however, the Games were considered a great success. More than one million spectators attended the events, and the Los Angeles Olympic Organizing Committee made a profit of more than one million dollars, the first significant profit generated during the modern Olympic era.

New Traditions The Olympic Coliseum in Los Angeles was built in 1924 when the city was bidding for that year's Summer Olympics. The city was not awarded the Games in 1924 or 1928 but finally won the right to host the Summer Olympics in 1932. The Olympic Coliseum was far superior in quality and scale to any other stadium that previously had been used for the Olympic Games, and the opening ceremony drew a record crowd of 100,000 people.

One reason for Los Angeles's success in securing the Olympics involved the organizing committee promising transportation, food, and housing subsidies for all the competitors. These ideas gave rise to one of the most important innovations in Olympic history: the building of the first Olympic Village. The village housed male athletes in 550 cottages on a 250-acre plot of land in a Los Angeles suburb. Female athletes were housed in a hotel. Despite many problems, such as complaints of political and racial disturbances and fears that training secrets would be stolen, the Olympic Village proved popular, and the concept continued in subsequent Olympics.

Traditionally, the head of the host nation's government attended the Olympic Games, but U.S. president Herbert Hoover made no appearance. In another break with tradition, the Los Angeles Olympics lasted only sixteen days. Starting in 1900 with the second modern Olympic Games, the festivities previously had stretched at least seventy-nine days. Before the 1932 Games, medals were presented with little fanfare; the victory podium on which the gold, silver, and bronze medalists received their awards made its debut in Los Angeles. China participated in the

Olympics for the first time in 1932, sending a single competitor.

The 1932 Games also were the first to use stopwatches, which enabled officials to time competitions to the nearest tenth of a second. An important innovative feature of the watches was the split-seconds function, which made it possible to record both the total elapsed time and intermediate (lap) times posted by each competitor.

The Stars The United States dominated the competition, winning forty-one gold medals; the nation with the next highest total was Italy with twelve. Leading the way for the United States was sprinter Eddie Tolan, who won gold in the 100 and 200 meters and the 4-by-100-meter relay. Sixteen world and Olympic records fell in men's track and field alone. Diving also was a strong suit for the U.S. team, which won all twelve medals in the sport. The American women dominated swimming, winning five of six events. Swimmer Buster Crabbe, who won a gold medal in the 400-meter freestyle, went on to become an actor and star in more than one hundred films. He was best known for playing Tarzan and Flash Gordon in popular serials in the late 1930's.

Babe Didrikson Zaharias emerged as the first female star of the Olympics. Zaharias threw the javelin 143 feet, 4 inches, to set an Olympic and world record. She won the 80-meter hurdles in world-record time and later competed in the high jump. She cleared 5 feet, 5¼ inches, but was penalized for diving over the bar instead of jumping feet first and had to settle for a silver medal. The high jump rule was later changed to allow the head-first jumping technique. As of 2010, Zaharias was the only athlete in Olympic history to win individual medals in running, jumping, and throwing. After the Olympics, she became one of the best female golfers in the sport's history and was named the greatest female athlete of the half century.

Stella Walsh also was versatile and durable. Although born in Poland, she lived in the United States and won more than forty American and world titles, competing well into her forties. In the 1932 Summer Games, she competed for Poland and set a world record in the 100 meters. At the age of sixty-nine, Walsh was killed in an armed robbery. Controversy swirled when an autopsy revealed she had ambiguous genitalia and could not easily be classified as biologically male or female.

Medal Count by Country, 1932 Summer Olympics

Country	Gold	Silver	Bronze	Total
United States	41	32	30	103
Italy	12	12	12	36
Finland	5	8	12	25
Sweden	9	5	9	23
Germany	3	12	5	20
France	10	5	4	19
Japan	7	7	4	18
Great Britain	4	7	5	16
Canada	2	5	8	15
Hungary	6	4	5	15
Netherlands	2	5	0	7
Poland	2	1	4	7
Denmark	0	3	3	6
Australia	3	1	1	5
Austria	1	1	3	5
South Africa	2	0	3	5

Source: The International Olympic Committee.

Canada sent 102 athletes, its second largest team to date, to the 1932 Olympics. Canadians won two gold medals, in high jump and bantamweight boxing. Phil Edwards, a black Canadian track star, won three bronze medals; his five total medals (including bronzes from the 1928 and 1936 Games) made him Canada's most decorated Olympian until his feat was matched in the twenty-first century.

Finnish distance runner Paavo Nurmi, one of the biggest stars of the past three Olympics, was notably absent from the 1932 Games. He was ruled ineligible for amateur competition after receiving excessive expense funds during a 1929 trip to Germany.

Impact The 1932 Summer Olympics were considered a great success and a model for future Olympic Games. Los Angeles's Olympic Coliseum set the standard for venues and attendance at the Olympics. Important innovations, such as the Olympic Village and the presentation of medals at the victory podium, became mainstays of the Olympics. The Games also introduced stars such as Zaharias and

Crabbe, who remained public figures for decades after their Olympic successes.

Mark Stanbrough

Further Reading

Cayleff, Susan. *Babe Didrikson: The Greatest All-Sport Athlete.* Champaign: University of Illinois Press, 1995. Describes how Didrikson's athletic prowess and personality made her a celebrity from the 1930's to 1950's. Her achievements redefined the woman athlete and stirred debate by challenging contemporary notions of femininity.

Freedman, Russell. *Babe Didrikson Zaharias: The Making of a Champion.* New York: Clarion, 1999. Biography covering Didrikson's track and field success and later career in basketball and golf.

Gifford, Clive. *Summer Olympics: The Definitive Guide to the World's Greatest Sports Celebration.* Boston: Kingfisher, 2004. Complete survey of and introduction to every Summer Olympics event. Includes information on athletes' training routines and great athletic rivalries throughout history.

Guttmann, Allen. *The Olympics: A History of the Modern Games.* Champaign: University of Illinois Press, 2002. Guttmann analyzes the political and social implications of each of the modern Olympic Games from 1896 to 2000.

Leder, Jane. *Grace and Glory: A Century of Women in the Olympics.* Chicago: Triumph Books, 1996. Describes how women's athletic competition changed along with women's roles in society from 1896 to 1996.

Miller, David. *The Official History of the Olympic Games and the IOC: From Athens to Beijing, 1894-2008.* Edinburgh, U.K.: Mainstream, 2008. Thorough history of the modern Games, covering major competitors and developments.

See also Boxing; Germany and U.S. appeasement; Olympic Games of 1932 (Winter); Olympic Games of 1936 (Summer); Olympic Games of 1936 (Winter); Sports in Canada; Sports in the United States.

■ Olympic Games of 1932 (Winter)

The Event International multisport event held every four years
Date February 4-15, 1932
Place Lake Placid, New York

In 1932, the Winter Olympics were held in the United States for the first time; previously they had been hosted only by European nations. The U.S. Olympic team also won the most medals for the first time at the Winter Games, a feat it did not repeat until the Vancouver Olympics in 2010.

The 1932 Winter Olympics had been scheduled for Big Pines, California, site of what was then the world's largest ski jump. However, poor snow condi-

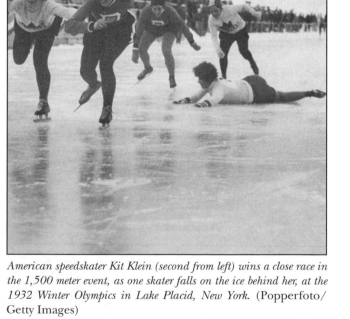

American speedskater Kit Klein (second from left) wins a close race in the 1,500 meter event, as one skater falls on the ice behind her, at the 1932 Winter Olympics in Lake Placid, New York. (Popperfoto/ Getty Images)

tions in California led the Games to be moved to Lake Placid, New York, a resort town in the Adirondack Mountains with a population of less than four thousand. Lake Placid went on to host the 1980 Winter Olympics, becoming the first North American city to host the Winter Games twice.

The Events　New York governor Franklin D. Roosevelt, who would be elected president of the United States later that year, opened the Olympics on February 4. Despite the effects of the Great Depression, the state of New York provided funding to help Lake Placid build sufficient facilities to host the Games. The city soon was home to the first bobsled run in North America, a 60-meter ski jump, and the Winter Olympics' first indoor skating arena.

Seventeen nations competed in the Games, down from the twenty-five that had attended the 1928 Winter Olympics. A total of 252 athletes competed in bobsled, figure skating, skiing, speed skating, and ice hockey.

American Billy Fiske had steered a five-man bobsled team to victory in the 1928 Winter Olympic Games at St. Moritz, Switzerland, when he was only sixteen years old. By 1932, five-man competition had been changed to four-man competition, but the result was the same: Fiske led his team to another gold. Among Fiske's bobsled teammates was Eddie Eagan, who also had won a gold medal in boxing at the 1920 Summer Olympics. As of 2010, Eagan remained the only athlete ever to win gold medals at both the Summer and Winter Games. The 1932 Olympics also marked the debut of the two-man bobsled competition. The United States took gold in that event as well.

Sonja Henie of Norway and the French pair of Andrée and Pierre Brunet, gold medalists at the 1928 Olympics, defended their figure-skating titles in 1932. In Nordic skiing, athletes competed in 18-kilometer and 50-kilometer cross-country skiing races, ski jumping, and Nordic combined, which consists of both cross-country skiing and ski jumping. Because of a lack of snow in the Lake Placid area, snow had to be trucked in to cover the ski jump staging area.

On the Ice　Canada won the gold medal in ice hockey, as it had in the previous two Winter Olympics. However, it faced a serious challenge from the U.S. team, which played the Canadians to a tie in the final. After three overtimes, Canada was declared

Medal Count by Country, 1932 Winter Olympics

Country	Gold	Silver	Bronze	Total
United States	6	4	2	12
Norway	3	4	3	10
Canada	1	1	5	7
Finland	1	1	1	3
Sweden	1	2	0	3
Austria	1	1	0	2
Germany	0	0	2	2
France	1	0	0	1
Hungary	0	0	1	1
Switzerland	0	1	0	1

Source: The International Olympic Committee.

the winner because it had a better goal average throughout the Olympics.

In speed skating, the United States swept the gold medals in all four events. American Irving Jaffee won the 10,000-meter and 5,000-meter races. Jaffee had been close to winning gold at the 1928 Olympics, but after he recorded the fastest time early in the competition, the ice began to thaw and the event was canceled; no official winner was declared. Jack Shea, a native of Lake Placid who had recited the Olympic Oath at the Games' opening ceremony, won the 500-meter and 1,500-meter races.

The 1932 Olympics marked the first time that speed-skating competitors all raced against one another in a mass start. This pack-racing style was common in the United States and differed from the European system, in which skaters raced in two-person timed heats. After 1932, the mass start was abandoned in long-track speed skating, but it returned to popularity sixty years later when short-track speed skating was introduced at the 1992 Olympics.

At the 1932 Games, women competed in speed skating for the first time, but only in demonstration events at 500, 1,000 and 1,500 meters. The Games also featured women's dogsled racing and curling as demonstration sports.

Impact　The 1932 Winter Olympics ended the European monopoly on hosting, and the Games' move to the United States gave North American athletes a clear boost. Although fewer countries sent athletes because of the cost and distance involved, competition was fierce and memorable. The Games helped to introduce winter sports to a wider international audience, and the facilities built in Lake Placid to accommodate the competition turned the city into a world-class winter-sports destination.

Mark Stanbrough

Further Reading

Fry, John. *The Story of Modern Skiing*. Hanover, Md.: University Press of New England, 2006. Covers the history and development of the sport, including the rise of a ski culture and advances in equipment, technique, instruction, and competition.

Hines, James. *Figure Skating: A History*. Champaign: University of Illinois Press, 2006. Hines follows figure skating through its evolution and development into an international sport. Includes profiles of 148 world and Olympic champions.

Ortloff, George Christian, and Stephen C. Ortloff. *Lake Placid, the Olympic Years, 1932-1980: A Portrait of America's Premier Winter Resort*. Lake Placid, N.Y.: Macromedia, 1976. Traces the development of Lake Placid from 1932, when it hosted its first Winter Olympic Games, through its successful bid to host them again in 1980.

Wallechinsky, David, and Jaime Loucky. *The Complete Book of the Winter Olympics*. Toronto: Sport Classic Books, 2009. Useful reference for facts and figures from the Winter Olympics, including illustrations and profiles of major athletes.

Wukovits, John. *The Encyclopedia of the Winter Olympics*. Princeton, N.J.: Franklin Watts, 2002. Includes information on key people and events in the history of the Winter Olympics.

See also Germany and U.S. appeasement; Ice hockey; Olympic Games of 1932 (Summer); Olympic Games of 1936 (Summer); Olympic Games of 1936 (Winter); Sports in Canada; Sports in the United States.

■ Olympic Games of 1936 (Summer)

The Event International multisport event held every four years
Dates August 1-16, 1936
Place Berlin, Germany

In 1931, the International Olympic Committee selected Germany as the host nation for the Winter and Summer Olympic Games of 1936. In 1933, Adolf Hitler became chancellor of Germany. With the transition of Germany from a democracy to a one-party dictatorship, many nations considered boycotting the Olympic Games.

On August 1, 1936, the Games of the XI Olympiad opened officially. Presiding at the Opening Ceremony was Chancellor Hitler. After Hitler came into power in Germany in 1933, considerable worldwide debate about boycotting the 1936 Olympic Games occurred. Avery Brundage, president of the American Olympic Committee, opposed a boycott, and in 1934, he visited German sports facilities, assuring the American public that the United States should send a team to Berlin to participate in the Olympics. On December 8, 1935, the Amateur Athletic Union voted that American Olympians would not boycott the 1936 Games. In the end, forty-nine nations attended the 1936 Olympic Games, including teams from France and Great Britain; Spain boycotted the Games, however.

Innovations Although the Olympic flame was used for the first time in the 1932 Los Angeles Olympic Games, the torch relay was introduced in 1936. Beginning in Olympia, Greece, the torch was carried through seven countries to the Berlin stadium, where 100,000 spectators awaited its arrival during the Opening Ceremony on August 1, 1936. More than four million tickets were sold for the Olympic competitions. To provide an opportunity for a wider audience to view the contests, live television was utilized for the first time; seventy hours of coverage was broadcast to twenty-five viewing centers in Berlin.

Two sports were introduced: field handball and basketball. Both sports were played outdoors. Americans ensured the inclusion of basketball as an Olympic sport after it had been an exhibition sport in the previous Olympics. The game was played on a clay tennis court and included no dribbling. The United States beat Canada for the gold medal by a score of

19 to 8. Two demonstration sports were introduced: gliding and baseball. Two American baseball teams demonstrated the sport on August 12, 1936, at the Olympic Stadium before 100,000 spectators.

The International Olympic Committee commissioned filmmaker Leni Riefenstahl to film the 1936 Olympic Games. Riefenstahl utilized techniques in her documentary that became common in the film documentation of sports. In 1938, her documentary entitled *Olympia* was released.

Medal Standings and Athletic Achievements A total of 3,963 athletes (3,632 men and 331 women) participated in the 1936 Olympic Games. Germany had the largest representation with 348 athletes, and the United States sent the second largest team, consisting of 312 athletes. Germany won the most medals, with a total of eighty-nine: thirty-three gold, twenty-six silver, and thirty bronze. The United States came in second with a total of fifty-six medals: twenty-four gold, twenty silver, and twelve bronze.

Among the American contingent of athletes were eighteen African Americans, sixteen of them men, three times the number that participated in the 1932 Los Angeles Games. African American athletes won fourteen medals, accounting for one-fourth of the total medals won by the United States, and dominated many of the track-and-field events. Cornelius Johnson won gold in the high jump, setting an Olympic record of 6 feet 8 inches. Archie Williams won the gold in the 400-meter event with an Olympic record of 46.5 seconds, and John Woodruff won the gold in the 800-meter event.

The performances of Jesse Owens received the greatest attention during the Berlin Games. Owens won four gold medals. In the 100-meter race he achieved a wind-assisted world record of 10.2 seconds; American Ralph Horace Metcalfe won the silver. In the 200 meters, Owens set an Olympic record of 20.3 seconds, missing the world record of 20.2; Matthew "Mack" Robinson, the brother of Jackie Robinson, won the silver. In the long jump, Owens, who was the world-record holder, set an Olympic record. Also, Owens was on the 400-meter relay team that set an Olympic record. Owens's performance in the 1936 Olympic Games stands out as one of the greatest in Olympic history, and he is considered one of the top athletes of the twentieth century.

Track-and-field events were dominated by athletes from the United States. Of the twenty-two events for

Medal Count by Country, 1936 Summer Olympics

Country	Gold	Silver	Bronze	Total
Germany	33	26	30	89
United States	24	20	12	56
Italy	8	9	5	22
Sweden	6	5	9	20
Finland	7	6	6	19
France	7	6	6	19
Japan	6	4	8	18
Netherlands	6	4	7	17
Hungary	10	1	5	16
Switzerland	1	9	5	15
Great Britain	4	7	3	14
Austria	4	6	3	13
Canada	1	3	5	9
Czechoslovakia	3	5	0	8
Argentina	2	2	3	7
Estonia	2	2	3	7

Source: The International Olympic Committee.

men, American athletes won twelve gold, seven silver, and four bronze. High-jump and decathlon events were swept by American athletes; Glenn Morris won the gold in the latter. Among the six track-and-field events for women, Helen Stephens, an eighteen-year-old from Missouri, won two gold medals.

In swimming and diving, American Jack Medica won the 400-meter freestyle with an Olympic record, and world-record-holder American Adolph Kiefer of Chicago was victorious in the 100-meter breaststroke. However, Rie Mastenbroek of the Netherlands emerged as the dominant swimmer, compiling three gold medals and a silver medal. In diving, American women won both springboard and platform events. Of the six medals in women's diving, athletes from the United States were awarded five medals. At the age of thirteen, Marjorie Gestring won the gold medal in springboard diving; she remains the youngest female gold medalist in the history of the Summer Olympic Games.

Several Olympic feats during the 1936 Olympic Games withstood time. The Egyptian weightlifter

Khadr El Touni set a record that lasted sixty years. Kristjan Palusalu of Estonia won a gold medal in two heavyweight wrestling classes: freestyle and Greco-Roman. This feat has never been duplicated in Olympic competition.

Impact The 1936 Berlin Olympic Games introduced several innovations and extraordinary athletic feats, most notably by Owens. However, the Games will always be remembered as taking place during Hitler's dictatorship. Three years after the Berlin Olympic Games, World War II began. The 1940 Olympic Games, originally scheduled for Tokyo and later moved to Helsinki, and the 1944 Olympic Games, scheduled for London, were canceled. The Olympic Games did not resume until 1948 in London.

Alar Lipping

Further Reading

Eisen, George. "The Voices of Sanity: American Diplomatic Reports from the 1936 Berlin Olympiad." *Journal of Sport History* 11, no. 3 (1984): 56-78. Reviews accounts of American diplomats stationed in Germany prior to the Olympic Games of 1936.

Espy, Richard. *The Politics of the Olympic Games.* Berkeley: University of California Press, 1979. Provides a historical account of the political, economic, social, and philosophical forces that have influenced the conduct of the Olympic Games.

Kass, D. A. "The Issue of Racism at the 1936 Olympics." *Journal of Sport History* 3, no. 3 (1976): 223-235. Presents the arguments for and against an American boycott of the 1936 Olympic Games.

Mandell, Richard D. *The Nazi Olympics.* New York: Macmillan, 1971. Utilizing primary and secondary historical sources, provides a detailed account of the conflict of Olympic ideals and Nazi ideology during the 1936 Olympic Games.

Senin, Alfred E. *Power, Politics, and the Olympic Games.* Champaign, Ill: Human Kinetics, 1999. Chapter 4 is devoted to reviewing the social and political forces that shaped the Berlin Olympics.

Walters, Guy. *Berlin Games: How the Nazis Stole the Olympic Dream.* New York: HarperCollins, 2006. Includes interviews of surviving participants from all over the world.

See also Olympic Games of 1932 (Summer); Olympic Games of 1932 (Winter); Olympic Games of 1936 (Winter); Owens, Jesse; Sports in Canada; Sports in the United States.

■ Olympic Games of 1936 (Winter)

The Event International multisport event held every four years

Date February 6-16, 1936

Place Garmisch-Partenkirchen, Bavaria, Germany

The 1936 Winter Olympic Games were held in Bavaria, Germany, the birthplace of Adolf Hitler's German National Socialist German Workers' (Nazi) Party. The Games were dominated by a political struggle between the International Olympic Committee (IOC) and Hitler, who saw the Olympics as a major propaganda tool.

When Berlin, Germany, was named the host of the 1936 Summer Olympics, Germany also was given the option to host the Winter Olympics. This marked the last time that the same country hosted both the Winter and Summer Olympics in the same year. The resort town of Garmisch-Partenkirchen was chosen because it already had many of the necessary facilities and because Bavaria was home to the Nazi Party. The IOC immediately clashed with Hitler, who sought to suppress any negative reporting on the Nazis. Hitler's administration allowed only German photographers and videographers to cover the

Medal Count by Country, 1936 Winter Olympics

Country	Gold	Silver	Bronze	Total
Norway	7	5	3	15
Sweden	2	2	3	7
Finland	1	2	3	6
Germany	3	3	0	6
Austria	1	1	2	4
United States	1	0	3	4
Great Britain	1	1	1	3
Switzerland	1	2	0	3
Canada	0	1	0	1
France	0	0	1	1
Hungary	0	0	1	1

Source: The International Olympic Committee.

Entry of the American team into the ski stadium during the opening ceremony of the 1936 Winter Olympics held in Germany. (AP/Wide World Photos)

events and screened all images before making them available for international distribution.

The actions of Hitler's Nazi regime also caused international controversy with regard to Olympic participation. Although German officials claimed that there was no discrimination against Jews in the nation's athletic organizations, some American officials were unconvinced. American participation was seen as crucial to the success of the Games, which were in turn crucial to promoting the Nazi Party's prestige. Ultimately, the Amateur Athletic Union narrowly voted against a boycott of the Olympics. In total, twenty-eight nations participated in the 1936 Winter Games.

Alpine skiing was included in the Olympics for the first time in 1936, and although the move was controversial at the time, the downhill and slalom events became popular in future Olympics. The Scandinavian countries had excelled in Nordic skiing at the first three Olympics, but they resisted the alpine events. When the IOC ruled that ski instructors could not compete because they were professionals, Swiss and Austrian skiers boycotted the Olympics.

The biggest upset of the Games occurred when the British ice hockey team defeated the Canadians. Canada had won gold in ice hockey in the previous three Olympic Games. However, controversy surrounded the British team. The country's Ice Hockey Federation had obtained a list of all registered Canadian players who had been born in the British Isles and recruited them to play for Great Britain. The Britons lured eight of the top Canadians to their team.

One of the biggest stars of the Games was speed skater Ivar Ballangrud of Norway, who had medaled at the previous two Winter Olympics. He won the 500, 5,000, and 10,000 meters at the 1936 Games. Ballangrud also took silver in the 1,500 meters, his seventh Olympic medal.

Sonja Henie of Norway won her third consecutive gold medal in figure skating and became a favorite of Hitler. She turned professional after the Olympics and toured the world performing in popular ice shows. Norway was the top medal winner at the 1936 Olympics with fifteen. The United States tied for fourth with four total medals; its only gold came in the two-man bobsled. Canada's silver in ice hockey was its only medal of the Games.

Impact Because of the fraught international political climate, both the 1936 Winter and Summer Olympics loom large in history. Hitler saw the Games as a prime opportunity to bring prestige to his regime and further his political agenda. Although the International Olympic Committee forced some concessions from the suppressive Nazi leadership, the Winter Games set the stage for the historic Berlin Summer Olympics, in which Hitler's heavily militarized nation and its white supremacist beliefs were on full display.

Mark Stanbrough

Further Reading

Hines, James. *Figure Skating: A History.* Champaign: University of Illinois Press, 2006.

Krüger, Arnd, and W. J. Murray, eds. *The Nazi Olympics: Sport, Politics, and Appeasement in the 1930s.* Champaign: University of Illinois Press, 2003.

Large, David Clay. *Nazi Games: The Olympics of 1936.* New York: W. W. Norton, 2007.

Walters, Guy. *Berlin Games: How the Nazis Stole the Olympic Dream.* New York: William Morrow, 2006.

Wukovits, John. *The Encyclopedia of the Winter Olympics.* Princeton, N.J.: Franklin Watts, 2002.

See also Germany and U.S. appeasement; Ice hockey; Olympic Games of 1932 (Summer); Olympic Games of 1932 (Winter); Olympic Games of 1936 (Summer); Sports in Canada; Sports in the United States.

■ *100,000,000 Guinea Pigs*

Identification Nonfiction, consumer-affairs book
Authors Arthur Kallet and Frederick John Schlink
Date Published in 1932

This pioneering book about hidden dangers in everyday foods, drugs, and cosmetics exposed numerous commercial enterprises that placed profit ahead of human values, safety, and health.

During the 1920's and 1930's, there was a large increase in the consumption of canned and processed foods and the use of cosmetics. Manufacturers, advertisers, and marketing professionals could make outlandish claims concerning their products in an effort to boost sales. While the existing Federal Food and Drug Act forbade false labeling of drugs shipped across state lines, if no claims or ingredients were listed on the product label, the act did not apply. The same act prohibited adding poisonous ingredients to foods, but because manufacturers were not required to prove additives were safe, only when consumers suffered severe illness in large numbers did the U.S. government intervene. During the Depression years of the 1930's, the government was often reluctant to act if investigating a product could interfere with business interests and profits.

In 1932, Arthur Kallet and Frederick John Schlink, both of the independent Consumers' Research testing bureau, published *100,000,000 Guinea Pigs.* The book asserts that many foods, drugs, and cosmetics contained toxic chemicals and unhealthy additives and that products were clandestinely tested on an unknowing "guinea pig" American population; the result was an increase in illnesses and deaths. The book further asserts the Food and Drug Administration (FDA), established in 1906, had allowed itself to be unduly influenced into lax supervision by big business interests and untested science.

One Hundred Million Guinea Pigs is essentially a compilation of information from the Consumers' Research testing bureau, with individual chapters dedicated to food, drugs, cosmetics, farm-chemical usage, advertising, and government unresponsiveness to consumer protection. About one-third of the book is information and examples gleaned from past issues of the *Journal of the American Medical Association*, but rather than providing critical analysis of the journal information regarding possible illnesses and deaths attributed to food, drug, and cosmetic additives, the authors tend to use dramatic and sensational language to describe anecdotal evidence in an effort to shock readers. Besides manufacturers and farmers, members of scientific and medical specialties actively criticized *100,000,000 Guinea Pigs* for exploiting and misinterpreting much of the published research cited and for presenting unscientific conclusions. The authors' writing styles also tended to hold farmers, advertisers, drug and cosmetics manufacturers, and government regulators all of equal culpability for perceived health hazards in the marketplace. The reality was that many of the foods and cosmetics were laced with extremely toxic chemicals and residues, including arsenic, lead, radium, strychnine, and thallium, and that many drugs, such as ether and ergot derivatives, were known to be of substandard quality yet marketed to hospitals nonetheless.

One Hundred Million Guinea Pigs had thirteen printings in the first six months of its release, twenty-seven printings in twelve months, and thirty-three printings overall, making it one of the best-selling books of the 1930's. Even though the authors were labeled "guinea-pig muckrakers," their book argued that the common good is best served when consumers force the government to protect citizen rights in the open marketplace. The book spawned the writing of numerous other consumer advocacy books, including *Skin Deep: The Truth About Beauty Aids—Safe and Harmful* (1934); *Paying Through the Teeth* (1935); *Eat, Drink and Be Wary* (1935); *Facts and Frauds in Woman's Hygiene: A Medical Guide Against Misleading Claims and Dangerous Products* (1936); *40,000,000 Guinea Pig Children* (1937); and *Our Master's Voice: Advertising* (1934). These books struck a chord with consumers and spurred them to change national policy, pressuring the FDA to rectify omissions in existing regulations and establish national consumer protections.

Impact The "guinea-pig muckraker" books and the consumer movement they inspired were catalysts in convincing the federal government to increase regulations by passing the 1938 Federal Food, Drug, and Cosmetic Act. *One Hundred Million Guinea Pigs* also helped bring to light and promote the fact that while exposure to small amounts of certain toxic substances may not be harmful in the short term, continual exposure and ingestion of even small amounts of toxins over time

---

A Menace to Health and Life

In the first chapter of their book, titled "The Great American Guinea Pig," Kallet and Schlink set forth in shocking detail the dangers posed by U.S. manufacturers of foods and other consumer goods:

In the magazines, in the newspapers, over the radio, a terrific verbal barrage has been laid down on a hundred million Americans, first, to set in motion a host of fears about their health, their stomachs, their bowels, their teeth, their throats, their looks; second, to persuade them that only by eating, drinking, gargling, brushing, or smearing with Smith's Whole Vitamin Breakfast Food, Jones' Yeast Cubes, Blue Giant Apples, Prussian Salts, Listroboris Mouthwash, Grandpa's Wonder Toothpaste, and a thousand and one other foods, drinks, gargles and pastes, can they either postpone the onset of disease, of social ostracism, of business failure, or recover from ailments, physical or social, already contracted.

If these foods and medicines were—to most of the people who use them—merely worthless; if there were no other charge to be made than that the manufacturers', sales managers', and advertising agents' claims for them were false, this book would not have been written. But many of them, including some of the most widely advertised and sold, are not only worthless, but are actually dangerous. That All-Bran you eat every morning—do you know that it may cause serious and perhaps irreparable intestinal trouble? That big juicy apple you have at lunch—do you know that indifferent Government officials let it come to your table coated with arsenic, one of the deadliest of poisons? The Pebeco Toothpaste with which you brush your teeth twice every day—do you know that a tube of it contains enough poison if eaten, to kill three people? . . .

Source: Arthur Kallet and Frederick John Schlink, *100,000,000 Guinea Pigs: Dangers in Everyday Foods, Drugs, and Cosmetics* (New York: Vanguard Press, 1933).

have a cumulative negative effect and result in catastrophic and often deadly health risks.

Randall L. Milstein

Further Reading

Fuller, John G. *Two Hundred Million Guinea Pigs: New Dangers in Everyday Foods, Drugs, and Cosmetics.* New York: Putnam's Sons, 1972.

Levenstein, Harvey. *Paradox of Plenty: A Social History of Eating in Modern America.* Berkeley: University of California Press, 2003.

Palmer, Rachel Lynn, and Isadore M. Alpher. *Forty Million Guinea Pig Children.* New York: Vanguard Press, 1937.

See also Advertising in the United States; Book publishing; Business and the economy in the United States; Federal Food, Drug, and Cosmetic Act of 1938; Food processing; Frozen-food marketing; Supermarkets.

■ O'Neill, Eugene

Identification Irish American playwright
Born October 16, 1888; New York, New York
Died November 27, 1953; Boston, Massachusetts

O'Neill revolutionized American theater with his existential yet realistic portraits of individuals and families in turmoil. Most of his greatest works were completed and performed to critical acclaim during the 1920's. The 1930's was a decade of isolation and declining health for him. Awarded the Nobel Prize in Literature in 1936, he began writing what were to be his final works: The Iceman Cometh *(1946),* Long Day's Journey into Night *(1956),* A Moon for the Misbegotten *(1947), and* A Touch of the Poet *(1957).*

In 1930, Eugene O'Neill was at the height of his writing abilities and continued to experiment with theatrical forms and expression. After living in France since 1928, he and his third wife, Carlotta Monterey, returned to the United States in May, 1931, so O'Neill could oversee the Broadway production of *Mourning Becomes Electra* (1931). After winning his third Pulitzer Prize, he wrote his only comedy, *Ah, Wilderness!* (1933), and the commercially and critically unsuccessful exploration of Roman Catholicism *Days Without End* (1933). O'Neill retreated from the theater and the public eye with his wife to

their home on Sea Island, Georgia. O'Neill's self-imposed isolation marked his career until 1945.

During his hiatus, O'Neill focused his energies on a grand epic cycle of nine to eleven plays, a story of one American family from the American Revolution to 1900. During the 1930's, he engaged in intense writing, researching, and outlining of his vision of American history. Dealing with the divorce from his second wife, Agnes; his struggles with alcohol; and physical ailments that were the result of a rare nerve disorder were not conducive to completing his envisioned works. Hoping to recover his health and needing a cooler climate, O'Neill and his wife sold their Sea Island home and moved first to Seattle, then traveled to California.

On November 12, 1936, the day he was notified of his Nobel Prize in Literature, O'Neill and his wife were searching for a home near San Francisco. In February, 1937, Swedish representatives of the Nobel Prize Committee presented him with the Nobel medal and award in his hospital room in Oakland, California, where he was recovering from appendicitis. His poor health continued. Bouts of rheumatism, respiratory infections, hand tremors, and kidney and prostate illnesses plagued O'Neill until his death in 1953. In 1937, the O'Neills built the Tao House, in Danville, California, where they lived until 1943. These environs, coupled with winning the Nobel Prize, seemed to have redoubled his efforts to bring his massive play cycle to fruition.

O'Neill's play was initially titled *The Calms of Capricorn*; as the cycle expanded, it was renamed *A Tale of Possessors, Self-Dispossessed* in summer, 1936. He completed *A Touch of the Poet* and *More Stately Mansions*, the third and fourth parts of the cycle, by the spring of 1939, with story lines for the entire series. This cycle was to be his masterpiece exploring the fortunes and misfortunes of the New England Puritan, Irish Harford family. This project was part of O'Neill's obsession with family stories, particularly his own, and his reaction to the Depression and the growing political turmoil in Europe.

Through most of his life, O'Neill had rejected the materialism and superficiality of American life. His plays were populated by down-and-out characters who were filled with doubt about American society, their families and friends, and themselves. The shock of the Great Depression to the American psyche only confirmed what O'Neill had long thought about Americans: They were delusional with their own success. The marginal characters of his plays reflected the underworld of the Gilded Age and Roaring Twenties that had become all too real during the 1930's.

In the summer of 1939, O'Neill stopped working on the cycle and probed into his own private history. O'Neill wrote to friends and agents that he was working on two plays, both set in 1912. One was a memory of his days in the New York Bowery, *The Iceman Cometh*, and the other was his semiautobiographical masterpiece *Long Day's Journey into Night*, which was not completed until 1941. He began writing *The Iceman Cometh* in June, 1939, and it was completed in late November. All the while, he worked on scenes for *Long Day's Journey into Night*. O'Neill felt *The Iceman Cometh* was too depressing to be staged in 1939 with war in Europe and the Depression still lingering in the United States. He demanded that the intensely personal *Long Day's Journey into Night* not be staged until after his death. Shortly before his death in 1953, O'Neill burned the play cycle that had consumed him through the 1930's.

American playwright Eugene O'Neill, seated with his wife Carlotta Monterey, stares into the camera in this 1931 photo. (Time & Life Pictures/Getty Images)

Impact O'Neill's mastery in creating American tragedy revolutionized the 1920's theater. Though he received the highest literary honors in the 1930's, he lived and continued writing in isolation, giving shape and scope to his last produced works. The decade was not a publicly productive period for O'Neill, and the Depression and the beginning of World War II fed and reaffirmed his tragic perception of humanity.

Tyler T. Crogg

Further Reading

Diggins, John Patrick. *Eugene O'Neill's America: Desire Under Democracy*. Chicago: University of Chicago Press, 2007. Analysis of O'Neill's works as political visions and understandings of American history.

Gassner, John. *O'Neill: A Collection of Critical Essays*. Englewood Cliffs, N.J.: Prentice-Hall, 1964. Accessible essays analyzing specific plays and O'Neill's style, structure, and characters.

Gelb, Arthur, and Barbara Gelb. *O'Neill*. New York: Harper & Brothers, 1962. One of the most penetrating biographies of O'Neill.

Raleigh, John Henry. *Twentieth Century Interpretations of "The Iceman Cometh."* Englewood Cliffs, N.J.: Prentice-Hall, 1968. Analysis of O'Neill's play written in 1939, and some letters by and interviews with O'Neill on its significance.

Shaughnessy, Edward L. *Down the Nights and Down the Days: Eugene O'Neill's Catholic Sensibility*. Southbend, Ind.: University of Notre Dame, 2000. Exploration of the Roman Catholic ideas and attitudes of O'Neill and his works.

See also Group Theatre; Hellman, Lillian; Kaufman, George S., and Moss Hart; Muni, Paul; Nobel Prizes; Odets, Clifford; Sherwood, Robert E.; Theater in the United States.

■ Organized crime

Definition   Organizations operating illegal
enterprises or extorting money by means of
criminal tactics

Organized crime had been a presence in many American cit-
ies since the late nineteenth century. During the 1930's, it
made significant changes in the operation of its illegal en-
terprises. These changes allowed criminal organizations to
strengthen their holds on certain forms of illicit activity and
further enmesh themselves in legitimate businesses, unions,
and political affairs, especially at the local and state levels.

When the decade of the 1930's opened, headlines
about organized crime activities were commonplace
in the newspapers of most major American cities,
most prominently in New York and Chicago, home
to the country's best-known gangster, Al Capone. He
was but one of a group of men who dominated underworld activities at the time. A decade of Prohibition had allowed many criminal groups to add illegal
alcohol sales to their other illicit activities. In 1931,
however, Capone was arrested and sent to prison for
tax evasion, effectively removing him from the scene
in Chicago. Furthermore, in 1933, the Eighteenth
Amendment was repealed, ending Prohibition. The
legalized sale of alcohol drastically reduced an important source of revenue for organized crime. Nevertheless, while the rest of the country suffered
through several more years of the Great Depression,
the 1930's proved to be one of the most prosperous
decades for organized crime in the United States.

Organized Crime's New Structure   During the first
two years of the 1930's, organized crime was rocked
by some of the most violent internecine struggles
ever witnessed in the United States. By the end of the
1920's, Italians dominated organized criminal activities in most major cities, although other ethnic
groups were active, particularly the Irish, Jews, and
African Americans. As early as 1928, leaders of Italian criminal organizations in large American cities
had tried to reach some accord among themselves
about limiting intergroup violence, but no substantial action was taken until after the murders of New
York crime bosses Giuseppe Masseria on April 20,
1931, and Salvatore Maranzano on September 10,
1931. These men had been leaders of the two most
prominent Italian "families" in New York. Maranzano's assassination was directed by Lucky Luciano,
a rising star in organized crime circles, and carried
out by both Italian and Jewish mobsters.

The death of these kingpins ushered in a period
of great prosperity for organized crime. Luciano
brokered an arrangement among the five remaining Italian families in New York and brought together the heads of criminal groups from other major cities to form an informal syndicate. The
commission, as it was known by its members, consisted of representatives from the five major crime
families in New York and heads of crime groups
from Buffalo, New York; Chicago, where Capone
had been replaced by Frank Nitti; and later, Detroit,
Kansas City, and Los Angeles. This divided up organized crime geographically and laid ground rules
for managing the activities from which organized
crime traditionally made money: gambling, prostitution, extortion, and racketeering. The group was
empowered to settle disputes among the major criminal outfits in the country. Though the commission
did not include representatives from every major
city, its influence was felt indirectly in places such as
San Francisco, New Orleans, and even Hot Springs,
Arkansas. Although this accord did not end all brutality, it did reduce the level of violence committed
by one criminal group on members of rival organizations, which had been a characteristic of organized
crime in the previous decade.

Criminal Activities   Even though the repeal of Prohibition in 1932 eliminated one important source of
revenue for organized crime, the ability of criminal
groups to provide other illegal products and services, notably gambling and prostitution, allowed
them to maintain high revenues, draining the legitimate economy and the government of millions of
dollars. Many who had been bootleggers during Prohibition became legitimate liquor manufacturers
and distributors during the 1930's; that included
quite a few organized-crime leaders. Not everyone
made the transition successfully, however. A kingpin
among Prohibition-era bootleggers, William "Big
Bill" Dwyer spent most of the 1930's avoiding jail for
income tax evasion; he was finally convicted in 1939.
On the other hand, by 1930, Meyer Lansky had
emerged as the leading figure in Jewish organized
crime, after taking over for Arnold Rothstein, who
was assassinated in 1929. Lansky made his money in
the gambling industry and was by turns a bootlegger,
money launderer, and farsighted strategist who

helped establish organized crime in several locations outside New York City.

Behind the scenes, though, these men used customary criminal tactics to eliminate competition and strong-arm retailers into carrying their products. Operations such as these provided criminal groups with a way to launder money, disguising illegal profits by mingling them with earnings from legitimate businesses. Additionally, at the urging of Luciano, organized crime took up an activity that earlier leaders had considered off-limits: drug trafficking.

Throughout the 1930's, criminal organizations maintained and, in some cases, even strengthened ties with corrupt union officials. Unions representing teamsters, building trades, hotels and restaurants, and even the theater industry often had funds siphoned off to make payments to organized crime groups that ostensibly provided "protection services." These services included intimidating business owners who refused to hire unionized laborers or nonunion workers who attempted to break strikes. At the same time, Mafia leaders were able to operate with little fear of arrest because so many had helped elect politicians who would ignore their activities.

While African American crime groups did not share the same rigid hierarchal structure as found in Italian, Jewish, or Irish organizations, there were nevertheless a number of groups operating in cities such as New York, Philadelphia, Detroit, and Chicago. Predominant among illegal activities run by these groups was a form of numbers gaming known as "policy," in which participants bet on closing-day totals for large bank clearing houses. When these games proved to be financially lucrative to African American promoters, white gangs such as the one run by Dutch Schultz made several attempts to take them over. Schultz was able to use corrupt politicians and police to intimidate African American leaders in Harlem into turning over their operations to him.

Several of Luciano's close associates were instrumental in extending the reach of the New York crime syndicate far beyond the city limits. During the decade, Lansky developed a close relationship with Cuban dictator Fulgencio Batista y Zaldívar that allowed the syndicate to control gambling operations in Havana, an arrangement that lasted until Fidel Castro came to power in 1959. Sometime after 1936, Bugsy Siegel moved to the West Coast to extend the reach of East Coast organized-crime groups to that area. Over the next two decades Siegel managed operations that eventually resulted in the Mafia moving into Hollywood and Las Vegas. During the 1930's, Luciano's deputy Frank Costello established a business relationship with the young gangster Carlos Marcello in New Orleans, arranging for shipment of slot machines from New York to Marcello's fledgling criminal operation in the South. Owen "The Killer" Madden, not part of Luciano's crime syndicate but a feared gangster in his own right, left New York in 1935 to settle in Hot Springs, Arkansas, where he established a criminal network whose earnings came principally from gambling.

Law-Enforcement Efforts At the same time organized-crime leaders were expanding and consolidating their empires, law-enforcement officials in sev-

A victim of the organized crime hit on gangster Dutch Schultz lies head down on a blood-splattered table under a mirror cracked by bullet holes at the Palace Chophouse and Tavern in Newark, New Jersey, in 1935. (The Granger Collection, New York)

eral locales were stepping up activities to bring these criminals to justice. Over the years, many leaders of organized-crime groups had struck up cozy relationships with local politicians and law-enforcement officials, using both bribery and intimidation as means of shielding their organizations from prosecution. The situation was somewhat better on the federal level. Although J. Edgar Hoover systematically resisted efforts to have the Federal Bureau of Investigation become involved in pursuing organized crime, the U.S. Treasury had been active since the 1920's in disrupting criminal activities. Its prosecution of Capone in 1931 was one of several campaigns waged successfully against mob leaders. Under Harry Anslinger, the Federal Bureau of Narcotics led an active campaign to disrupt operations of organized crime, especially those engaged in selling illegal drugs.

Options for dealing with organized crime at the federal level were limited. Congress passed the Anti-Racketeering Act of 1934 to combat the use of interstate commerce by organized crime, specifically racketeering. The act proved to be too vague to be enforceable in many instances, however, and not until amendments were passed during the 1940's and 1950's did it became an effective tool for combating organized-crime activities crossing state borders.

As had been the case in previous decades, much of the activity mounted to stymie organized-crime groups during the 1930's was left to individual state governments. Some attempt was made by the state of New York to root out corruption in government caused by the association of politicians with known criminals. In 1930, Governor Franklin D. Roosevelt asked the judiciary to launch a probe into public corruption, and appellate court judge Samuel Seabury began a series of investigations that brought to light several links between long-time criminals and political figures throughout the state. His efforts eventually led to the resignation of New York City mayor James J. Walker, who had done little to hide his ties to organized-crime leaders.

In 1935, New York governor Herbert Lehman appointed Thomas E. Dewey as a special prosecutor charged with going after organized crime in New York City. Dewey's first target was Schultz, and although he was gunned down before Dewey could arraign him, other mob bosses soon felt the heat from Dewey's efforts. First among them was Lepke Buchwalter, a longtime extortionist. Dewey's most important coup, however, was the arrest and convic-

tion of Luciano, who was sent to prison in 1936 on charges of running a massive prostitution network. Luciano's deputy, Costello, stepped in to run operations for the imprisoned leader, however, and through a network of prisoners and corrupt prison officials, Luciano was able to get information to Costello and retain control of his operation from behind bars.

Impact Although the violence often associated with organized-crime activities has been portrayed as the greatest menace to society posed by these groups, the economic impact of criminal activities conducted by organized-crime elements most affected the United States. Viewed in that light, the 1930's marked the beginning of the period of greatest success for organized crime; during those years, individual groups made significant advances in organizational structure and inter-group cooperation. Key Mafia leaders in cities across the country developed systems for cooperating in conducting operations and sharing profits. Organized-crime elements infiltrated a number of unions, draining their coffers and helping to breed tension between union and management in a number of industries. Fledgling efforts by law enforcement began to make headway, but no federal or state agency was able to establish a program to arrest and convict leaders of criminal groups that was strong enough to be sustained when the United States began gearing up for World War II. That conflict quickly diverted law-enforcement resources from fighting organized crime, and the operating policies set in place during the 1930's by men such as Luciano and Costello allowed their outfits to flourish during the years when the United States was at war.

Laurence W. Mazzeno

Further Reading

Fox, Stephen. *Blood and Power: Organized Crime in Twentieth-Century America.* New York: William Morrow, 1989. Concentrates on the growth of organized crime after 1920; describes activities of criminals and law-enforcement officials during the 1930's.

Gage, Nicholas, ed. *Mafia, U.S.A.* Chicago: Playboy Press, 1972. Twenty-five essays on important figures in organized crime; several describe the organizational structure of various criminal groups operating in major American cities.

Peterson, Virgil. *The Mob: Two Hundred Years of Organized Crime in New York*. Ottawa, Ill.: Green Hill, 1983. Describes organized crime activities during the 1930's. Explains the relationship between leaders of criminal groups and elected officials and highlights efforts by state and federal officials to combat organized crime.

Raab, Selwyn. *Five Families: The Rise, Decline, and Resurgence of America's Most Powerful Mafia Enterprises*. New York: Thomas Dunne Books, 2005. Offers detailed accounts of the activities of the most important criminal organizations in New York City; includes a chapter summarizing the activities of these groups during the 1930's.

Reppetto, Thomas. *American Mafia: A History of Its Rise to Power*. New York: Henry Holt, 2004. Detailed account of the rise of organized crime, providing extensive information on its activities during the 1930's and efforts by law enforcement to curb its power.

Schatzberg, Rufus, and Robert J. Kelly. *African-American Organized Crime: A Social History*. New York: Garland, 1996. Includes a chapter describing organized-crime activities within African American communities in a number of American cities during the 1930's.

See also Anti-Racketeering Act of 1934; Capone, Al; Gambling; Luciano, Lucky; Ness, Eliot; Nitti, Frank; Prohibition repeal; Schultz, Dutch; Unionism.

■ Ott, Mel

Identification American baseball player
Born March 2, 1909; Gretna, Louisiana
Died November 21, 1958; New Orleans, Louisiana

Ott was one of the most dominant professional baseball players of the 1930's. His smooth swing helped him to be among the leaders in runs batted in (RBI) and home runs throughout the decade, and he played a major role in helping the New York Giants reach the World Series three times.

At 5 feet 9 inches and weighing a slight 170 pounds, Mel Ott did not have the body type of a Major League Baseball player, let alone a power hitter. However, he became one of the most prolific hitters in history.

As a sixteen-year-old, Ott began playing semipro ball for a lumber company in Patterson, Louisiana. The millionaire owner of the company saw Ott's potential and recommended that John McGraw, the manager of the New York Giants, take a look at the young catcher. When two men finally persuaded Ott to visit New York for a tryout, he did not disappoint. Even though Ott was young, McGraw signed him to a contract and kept him with the Giants rather than sending him to the minors.

McGraw switched Ott to the outfield to preserve his legs. For two years, Ott was used as a pinch hitter and as a part-time player, easing his way into the game. In 1928, at the age of nineteen, Ott became the Giants' regular right fielder. The following year, he became a sensation, hitting 42 home runs. In 1933, he helped lead the Giants to a World Series victory over the Washington Senators. Throughout the 1930's, Ott displayed excellent judgment at the plate and prowess in the field. He made the all-star team twelve times.

Impact Ott was the first National League player to hit 500 home runs and the first to have eight consecutive 100 RBI seasons. He became a player-manager and then a manager for the Giants before leaving baseball in 1948. In 1958, a drunk driver collided with the car in which Ott and his wife were traveling, killing him.

P. Huston Ladner

Further Reading

Martin, Alfred. *Mel Ott: The Gentle Giant*. Metuchen, N.J.: Scarecrow Press, 2003.

Stein, Fred. *Mel Ott: The Little Giant of Baseball*. Jefferson, N.C.: McFarland, 1999.

See also Baseball; Dean, Dizzy; Gehrig, Lou; National Baseball Hall of Fame; Negro Leagues; Ruth, Babe; Sports in the United States; Vander Meer, Johnny.

■ Ottawa Agreements

The Law Trade agreements providing for mutual tariff concessions and certain other commitments between Great Britain and Canada and other Commonwealth areas

Dates July 20 to August 20, 1932

The Ottawa trade agreements, which extended mutual trade by means of reciprocal preferential tariffs, benefited certain industries of the British Commonwealth nations. These sectors included cattle production, wheat farming, lumber and mills, fruit and vegetable farming, automobile manufacturing, and the nonferrous metals industry.

Negotiated in accordance with the provisions of the Import Duties Act of 1932, the Ottawa Agreements were the culmination of a series of imperial trade preferences, including Canada's unilateral grant of such preferences in 1897. There were twelve separate bilateral agreements: seven between the United Kingdom and Australia, the Union of South Africa (now known as the Republic of South Africa), New Zealand, India, Newfoundland, Southern Rhodesia (now known as Zimbabwe), and Canada; four agreements between Canada and the United Kingdom, the Union of South Africa, the Irish Free State (now known as the Republic of Ireland), and Southern Rhodesia; and one between New Zealand and the Union of South Africa.

Also during the conference, negotiations began on agreements between other members of the British Commonwealth, and substantial progress was made. These agreements were concluded at the Imperial Economic Conference, held at Ottawa, from July 21 through August 20, 1932, and signed at the closing session. The resolution adopted by the conference hoped to have financial results that were mutually beneficial to all the Commonwealth nations involved.

The agreements established a system of tariff preferences to counter the impact of the Great Depression. The tariffs provided for quotas of agricultural products, including poultry and eggs; meat, mostly live cattle and pig products, mutton, and lamb; fruits and vegetables; and cereals, including flour. Concessions were also made for metals and minerals from the Dominions to enter Great Britain free of import duties. In return, tariff benefits would be granted by the Dominions to imported British manufactured goods. Also, accommodations were made on duty-free entry, duties on foreign goods, preferential margins with respect to the rate of duty on U.K. goods, limits on new protective tariffs, allowances for "domestic competition" and tariff boards (except in South Africa and India), and customs administration.

The economic gains were helpful but not massive. Great Britain promised to impose no duties on food and other products produced within its Dominion countries, to increase duties and to impose quotas on certain goods imported from non-Dominion countries, and to continue duty-free or low-tariff arrangements for Dominion manufactures, such as Canadian automobiles.

The Ottawa Agreements gave Commonwealth countries larger shares of the British market but sections of the agreements were eventually modified. For example, the United Kingdom-Canada Agreement adopted certain changes in 1937 and 1938 and has made more modifications since 1945. After World War II, the benefits steadily eroded, and the agreements became increasingly dispensable with the prospect of British entry into the European Economic Community (EEC). Although the agreements were seriously reviewed during the 1961-1963 EEC discussions, they had little impact on the entry negotiations of 1971-1972 apart from the question of New Zealand dairy products. However, some mutual concessions still exist, and most of them can be traced to the Ottawa Agreements.

Impact The Ottawa Agreements effectively placed commercial relations between the United Kingdom and its dominions on a treaty basis. They negotiated better trade possibilities and more mutually favorable tariff advantages for the United Kingdom and certain countries within its dominions by the creation of reciprocal preferences, a definite advance toward closer economic association.

Martin J. Manning

Further Reading

Drummond, Ian M. *British Economic Policy and the Empire, 1919-1939.* New York: Barnes & Noble Books, 1972.
Riddell, Walter A., ed. *Documents on Canadian Foreign Policy, 1917-1939.* Toronto: Oxford University Press, 1962.

See also Agriculture in Canada; Business and the economy in Canada; Canada and Great Britain; Foreign policy of Canada.

■ *Our Town*

Identification　Play about a small American town
Playwright　Thornton Wilder
Date　First performed on January 22, 1938
Place　Play set in New Hampshire

Using a nearly bare stage to suggest the universal, Thornton Wilder presented in Our Town *a particular New Hampshire community, Grover's Corners, on particular dates decades before the play opened during the Great Depression. However, he emphasized not so much the simplicity of the rural United States as the value of the ordinary in human life in all places and ages.*

Reviving the use of simple sets, as in the ancient Greek theater, Wilder wanted to make playgoers imagine the specific and think about the general. First directed by Jed Harris, *Our Town* is a "meta-play," using the character of the stage manager to make introductions. The stage manager mentions Wilder as the author, names several actors, lays out Grover's Corners, and sets the date for act one—May 7, 1901.

Almost all the characters appear in that act, including the stage manager; the Gibbs family, which includes a physician, his wife, sixteen-year-old George, and eleven-year-old Rebecca; and the neighboring Webb family, which includes a newspaper editor, his wife, and their children, Emily and Wally. For the adults, the day entails work, at home or elsewhere, followed by church choir practice for the wives. For the youngsters, it entails school and homework. The day turns into a moonlit night. The act is peaceful and generally pleasant, but there is foreshadowing: The stage manager reveals that in 1930, Dr. Gibbs died, long outliving his wife, and that the paperboy, Joe Crowell, was headed toward an illustrious career in engineering but died in France during World War I. In addition, the audience ponders Simon Stimson, the choir director, whose alcoholism makes his future unpromising.

In act two, Emily and George marry; their wedding takes place on July 7, 1904. Like the first act, this act begins at dawn with milk and newspaper deliveries and then breakfast. Next, the stage manager takes the play back to June, 1903, just after high school has let out for the day and just after Emily and George have been elected officers of the class of 1904. That day becomes more special when the two neighbors realize they love each other. Following

the flashback, the stage manager returns the scene to the wedding day, when the playgoers observe the fear expressed by both George and Emily as they enter adulthood. Nonetheless, the couple marries; their witnesses are not only their friends and living relatives but also nature and millions of ancestors.

The last act begins in 1913 at the graveyard overlooking the town. In chairs sit the dead, including Mrs. Gibbs and Wally Webb, who both died naturally, and Simon Stimson, who hanged himself. In a New England version of purgatory, the dead grow indif-

---

Wilder on *Our Town*

In his preface to a 1957 volume containing three of his plays, Thornton Wilder sheds some light on his decisions regarding the staging of Our Town:

Our Town is not offered as a picture of life in a New Hampshire village; or as a speculation about the conditions of life after death (that element I merely took from Dante's *Purgatory*). It is an attempt to find a value above all price for the smallest events in our daily life. I have made the claim as preposterous as possible, for I have set the village against the largest dimensions of time and place. The recurrent words in this play (few have noticed it) are "hundreds," "thousands," and "millions." Emily's joys and griefs, her algebra lessons and her birthday presents—what are they when we consider all the billions of girls who have lived, who are living, and who will live? Each individual's assertion to an absolute reality can only be inner, very inner. And here the method of staging finds its justification—in the first two acts there are at least a few chairs and tables; but when she revisits the earth and the kitchen to which she descended on her twelfth birthday, the very chairs and table are gone. Our claim, our hope, our despair are in the mind—not in things, not in "scenery." Molière said that for the theatre all he needed was a platform and a passion or two. The climax of this play needs only five square feet of boarding and the passion to know what life means to us.

Source: Thornton Wilder, preface to *Three Plays* (New York: Harper & Brothers, 1957).

ferent to life in this world as the eternal within them gradually frees itself from Earth. The newest grave is for Emily, who has died of complications from childbirth. While the mourners sing "Blessed Be the Tie That Binds," she joins the other dead, and she eventually remarks on how unaware the living are. Then, against her mother-in-law's advice, Emily goes back to them, back to her childhood home on her twelfth birthday—February 11, 1899. As a cold dawn breaks, she returns to her parents' kitchen, where, as a visitor from the dead, she cannot be noticed. Her joy at rejoining the living turns into pain as she realizes how they do not genuinely see each other or know the wonder of ordinary life. Saying goodbye to the world she failed to appreciate when she was part of it, she returns to her grave, where George, under starlight, prostrates himself in sorrow. It is eleven o'clock in Grover's Corners, and the stage manager bids the audience good night.

Impact   After tryouts in Princeton and Boston, *Our Town* moved to New York, where, despite a few negative reviews, it ran from February 4 until November 19, 1938, winning a Pulitzer Prize the following May. After closing in New York, the show went on tour until February 11, 1939. Soon afterward, stock companies and amateurs were performing *Our Town* throughout the United States; it became a 1940 film and, following World War II, gained popularity abroad. For the 1930's, it was an unusual American play in its staging, but it has appealed through the years to generations.

Victor Lindsey

Further Reading

Konkle, Lincoln. *Thornton Wilder and the Puritan Narrative Tradition.* Columbia: University of Missouri Press, 2006.

Wilder, Thornton. *Our Town: A Play in Three Acts.* New York: HarperCollins, 2003.

_____. *The Selected Letters of Thornton Wilder.* Edited by Robin G. Wilder and Jackson R. Bryer. New York: HarperCollins, 2008.

_____. *Thornton Wilder: Collected Plays and Writings on Theater.* Edited by J. D. McClatchy. New York: Library of America, 2007.

See also   Hellman, Lillian; Kaufman, George S., and Moss Hart; Literature in the United States; MacLeish, Archibald; Odets, Clifford; O'Neill, Eugene; Rice, Elmer; Sherwood, Robert E.; Steinbeck, John; Theater in the United States.

■ Owens, Jesse

Identification   American track-and-field athlete
Born   September 13, 1913; Oakville, Alabama
Died   March 31, 1980; Tucson, Arizona

Owens dominated track-and-field competition during the 1930's, holding several world and Olympic records in the sprints and long jump. He won four gold medals at the 1936 Olympic Games in Berlin, Germany, countering attempts by Germany's Nazi government to politicize the event.

The youngest of ten children of poor Alabama sharecroppers, Jesse Owens, born James Cleveland Owens, picked cotton and attended school in a one-room schoolhouse. In 1921, the Owens family moved to Cleveland, Ohio, where Owens's father, Henry, and older brothers found jobs in a steel mill. Owens, nicknamed "Jesse" after a Cleveland teacher misunderstood his southern drawl, was older than his classmates and popular, but he struggled academically.

High School and College Records   At Fairmount Junior High School, Owens developed his track-and-field skills. Realizing Owens's enormous athletic potential, his coach Charles Riley taught him high-jumping techniques and a streamlined sprinting style. In 1928, Owens set junior high records of 6 feet in the high jump and 22 feet 11¾ inches in the long jump.

In 1933, the 5-foot 10-inch, 165-pound Owens graduated from East Technical High School, where he won seventy-five of seventy-nine sprint races. In Chicago that June, he led East Tech to a National Interscholastic Championship. Owens tallied a majority of his squad's points, tying the world record of 9.4 seconds in the 100-yard dash and setting interscholastic records in the 200-yard dash and broad jump.

Owens majored in physical education at Ohio State University, but worked full time in Columbus and never earned a bachelor's degree. He perfected his running and jumping skills under coach Larry Snyder and set numerous intercollegiate and Amateur Athletic Union (AAU) records. In 1935, at Madison Square Garden in New York, Owens shattered the 60-yard-dash world record. His 6.4 second mark lasted forty years.

The highlight of Owens's collegiate career came

at the Big Ten Conference Track and Field Championships in Ann Arbor, Michigan. Owens enjoyed the greatest single-day performance in track-and-field history on May 25, 1935, breaking five world records and tying another within a forty-five-minute span. Despite suffering back pain from falling down stairs a week earlier, he tied the world record of 9.4 seconds in the 100-yard dash. Ten minutes later, he demolished the broad jump world record with a leap of 26 feet 8⅓ inches. The mark lasted until 1960. Within the following twenty-five minutes, he obliterated world records in the 220-yard dash (20.3 seconds) and 220-yard hurdles (22.6 seconds) in a straightaway. Those times were automatically recognized as world records for the 200 meters.

Owens married Minnie Ruth Solomon of Cleveland on July 5, 1935, after publicity spread about a daughter whom he had fathered with her three years earlier. The AAU reprimanded him for accepting reimbursement of his travel expenses while serving as a page boy in the Ohio State House of Representatives. Owens was declared academically ineligible for the winter 1936 track-and-field competition but regained eligibility that spring.

The 1936 Olympic Games Owens dominated the sprints at the 1936 Olympic trials and made the U.S. Olympic track-and-field squad. Politics largely overshadowed athletics at the 1936 Olympic Games in Berlin, Germany. Adolf Hitler showcased his Nazi dictatorship and espoused his beliefs in Aryan supremacy. He boasted that his athletes would prevail, while the German press scorned "America's black auxiliaries." Around 100,000 spectators shouted "Heil Hitler" when the Nazi leader entered the Olympic Stadium.

Owens countered Hitler's supremacist propaganda, using his sheer grace and matchless speed to eclipse four Olympic records. In the 100-meter heats, he equaled Eddie Tolan's Olympic and world record of 10.3 seconds. Owens repeated the same record time in the finals, edging Ralph Horace Metcalfe for the gold medal. American newspapers falsely claimed that Hitler refused to congratulate Owens following that race. Olympic officials, however, already had ordered Hitler to stop greeting German winners at his box.

Owens's second gold medal came in the long jump after he nearly missed the finals because of a run-through and a foul on his first two jumps. Following advice from German competitor Lutz Long, Owens jumped well before the board on his last attempt and qualified for the finals. He outdueled Lutz for the gold, leaping an Olympic record 26 feet 5¼ inches. Owens earned his third gold medal in the 200 meters, defeating Matthew "Mack" Robinson by four meters. His time of 20.7 seconds established an Olympic record, the fastest time ever at the distance on a curve.

Owens's fourth gold medal came in the 4×100-meter relay. Foy Draper, Frank Wykoff, Sam Stoller, and Marty Glickman were originally scheduled to run for the American team, but Owens and Metcalfe replaced Stoller and Glickman. Owens established a

Sprinter Jesse Owens takes off from the starting blocks in a 200-meter race during the 1936 Summer Olympics, at which he won an unprecedented four track-and-field medals. (Library of Congress)

commanding lead for the American team, which triumphed in an Olympic record time of 39.8 seconds, besting Italy and Germany. Owens captured one more gold medal than the entire German track-and-field team and three more than any of the other 891 track-and-field contestants representing fifty-two nations.

The AAU suspended Owens from further amateur competition because he refused to complete a European barnstorming tour with his Olympic teammates. Owens sought to capitalize on his fame by racing against humans, horses, dogs, and automobiles, but he endured racial discrimination, job and business investment failures, and bankruptcy. He later served as a motivational speaker for athletic, business, religious, and civic groups and raised money for the U.S. Olympic Committee. Owens, who shunned the Civil Rights movement and opposed an African American boycott of the Mexico City 1968 Olympic Games, was elected a charter member of the National Track and Field Hall of Fame in 1974 and the U.S. Olympic Hall of Fame in 1983. He died of lung cancer.

Impact Owens soared far above track-and-field competitors, setting eleven world records. He and boxer Joe Louis ranked among the nation's first African American sports heroes, inspiring numerous minority youth. A 1949 *Ebony* poll named Owens the greatest African American athlete of all time. The Associated Press voted him the greatest track-and-field athlete of the first half of the twentieth century. Sportswriters later called his 1936 Olympic feat "the most significant sports story of the century."

David L. Porter

Further Reading

Baker, William. *Jesse Owens: An American Life.* Urbana: University of Illinois Press, 2006. Well-researched biography shows how Owens's graceful dominance, modest demeanor, and unique political significance made him the most legendary of all Olympic champions.

Edmondson, Jacqueline. *Jesse Owens: A Biography.* Westport, Conn.: Greenwood Press, 2007. Explores Owens struggles and hard-earned accomplishments, showing how he paved the way for other minority athletes.

Hart-Davis, Duff. *Hitler's Games: The 1936 Olympics.* New York: Harper & Row, 1986. Profiles Owens and the 1936 Olympics from a British perspective.

Mandell, Richard. *The Nazi Olympics.* Urbana: University of Illinois Press, 1987. Important account of the 1936 Olympic Games, showing how Owens feats impacted Hitler's politicized Games.

Owens, Jesse, with Paul Niemark. *Jesse: The Man Who Outran Hitler.* New York: Fawcett Gold Medal, 1978. Autobiography describes how Owens overcame adversity to become one of the greatest Olympic gold medalists, subsequently endured turbulent times, and nearly lost his religious faith.

Schaap, Jeremy. *Triumph: The Story of Jesse Owens and Hitler's Olympics.* Boston: Houghton Mifflin Harcourt, 2007. Well-researched, dramatic chronicle of Owens's journey to and glorious triumph at the 1936 Berlin Olympics.

See also African Americans; Louis, Joe; Olympic Games of 1936 (Summer); Sports in the United States.

P

Palko v. Connecticut

The Case U.S. Supreme Court ruling on the application to the states of the Fifth Amendment right to protection against double jeopardy

Date Decided on December 6, 1937

The Supreme Court's 8-1 ruling held that the Fifth Amendment right against double jeopardy was not a fundamental right and thus was not applicable to the states.

Frank Palka, whose name was spelled incorrectly as Palko on court documents, killed two officers while escaping from a burglary and was charged with first-degree murder. He was convicted of the lesser offense of second-degree murder and sentenced to life imprisonment. The state of Connecticut appealed the case, pursuant to a state statute that allowed the prosecution to appeal in certain criminal cases, and won a new trial. In the second trial, Palko was found guilty of first-degree murder and sentenced to death. Palko appealed the second conviction on the grounds that the second conviction violated his rightful protection against double jeopardy.

In *Palko*, the specific issue before the U.S. Supreme Court was whether the Fifth Amendment right against double jeopardy applied to the states through the due process clause of the Fourteenth Amendment. In writing the majority opinion, Justice Benjamin N. Cardozo held that the Fourteenth Amendment due process clause protected only those Bill of Rights guarantees that were deemed fundamental and were "of the very essence of a scheme of ordered liberty." Examples of such fundamental rights were freedom of thought and speech and the right to a jury trial in criminal cases, because without these rights, a fair system of justice would be impossible. In upholding Palko's conviction, the Court reasoned that double jeopardy was not a fundamental right. Palko was executed in Connecticut's electric chair on April 12, 1938.

Impact The *Palko* case represented the Court's struggle to find an appropriate test to extend the Bill of Rights to the states and relied on a subjective case-by-case approach. The decision was overturned in *Benton v. Maryland* in 1969, whereby the U.S. Supreme Court applied the protection against double jeopardy to the states.

LaVerne McQuiller Williams

Further Reading

Amar, Akhil R. *America's Constitution.* New York: Random House, 2005.
Lewis, Thomas T., ed. *U.S. Supreme Court.* Pasadena, Calif.: Salem Press, 2007.

See also Supreme Court, U.S.; *United States v. Carolene Products Co.*; *West Coast Hotel Co. v. Parrish.*

Panama Refining Co. v. Ryan

The Case U.S. Supreme Court ruling on the constitutionality of delegating legislative authority to the president

Date January 7, 1935

This case was the first of a series of Supreme Court decisions that invalidated some of President Franklin D. Roosevelt's major New Deal programs.

To stabilize falling oil prices during the Great Depression, section 9C of the National Industrial Recovery Act of 1933 granted the president the authority to prohibit the transportation in interstate and foreign commerce of petroleum and products thereof produced or withdrawn from storage in excess of the amounts permitted by state authority. Accordingly, on August 19, 1933, President Franklin D. Roosevelt approved a Code of Fair Competition for the Petroleum Industry, violations of which constituted a misdemeanor: a fine not to exceed one thousand dollars, imprisonment not to exceed six months, or both, and each day's violation deemed a

Chief Justice Charles Evans Hughes, pictured stepping out of his car after returning to Washington, D.C., from a vacation, wrote the opinion in the Panama Refining Co. v. Ryan *court case.* (Library of Congress)

separate offense. Panama Refining Company challenged the validity of section 9C as an unconstitutional delegation of legislative power to the president.

Chief Justice Charles Evans Hughes wrote the opinion of the Court, invalidating section 9C of the National Industrial Recovery Act as impermissibly delegating or granting legislative power to the president. Hughes dismissed the argument that Roosevelt acted in support of the public good during a time of national economic crisis, declaring that constitutional authority, not motives, is controlling in matters of law. Hughes pointed out that section 9C does not identify under what circumstances or conditions the president is to prohibit the interstate transportation of the petroleum products produced

in excess of the state regulations, establish the criteria to govern the president's promulgation of codes of fair competition, or provide any requirement of any finding by the president as a condition for issuing said codes. For these reasons, the U.S. Supreme Court ruled that section 9C gives the president unlimited and unconditional authority. The Congress, ruled the Court, is not permitted to abdicate or transfer to other branches its legislative powers. Congress must establish the legal standards that are to govern the president in administering or enforcing the law and cannot leave it wholly to the discretion of the president.

Justice Benjamin N. Cardozo dissented from the ruling, arguing that section 9C did establish standards that authorized the president to issue fair codes of competition for the petroleum industry. Cardozo pointed out that section 1 of the National Industrial Recovery Act expressed the desire of Congress to eliminate unfair competitive practices and that the president was authorized to prohibit the transportation in interstate commerce of oil produced in excess of state regulations if, in his judgment, the sale of such petroleum constituted unfair competitive practices. Section 9C of the National Industrial Recovery Act was declared unconstitutional, as was section 3 of the same act in the case of *Schechter Poultry Corp. v. United States* (1935).

Impact Although it was later generally acknowledged that the NIRA was not effective in dealing with the Great Depression, *Panama Refining* was seen as a political defeat for the Roosevelt administration. It also contributed to precipitating the 1937 confrontation between Roosevelt and the Supreme Court known as the court-packing plan.

Stefan Brooks

Further Reading

Leuchtenberg, William E. *Franklin D. Roosevelt and the New Deal, 1932-1940.* New York: Harper & Row, 2009.

Shales, Amity. *The Forgotten Man: A New History of the Great Depression.* New York: Harper, 2007.

See also *Carter v. Carter Coal Co.*; Great Depression in the United States; National Industrial Recovery Act of 1933; New Deal; Roosevelt's court-packing plan; *Schecter Poultry Corp. v. United States*; Supreme Court, U.S.

■ *Panay* incident

The Event   Japanese attack on a U.S. gunboat
Date   December 12, 1937
Place   Chang River (also known as Yangtze
 River), China

The gunboat Panay *had evacuated Americans from Nanjing (Nanking) as the Japanese surrounded the city. Anchored 27 miles upriver from Nanjing, the gunboat was sunk by Japanese aircraft, killing three and wounding forty-three. This incident further strained relations between Japan and the United States.*

The Japanese launched the second Sino-Japanese War in July, 1937, and quickly captured the cities of Beijing and Shanghai. As the Japanese forces closed in on Nanjing, the U.S. gunboat *Panay* evacuated the embassy staff and American citizens. The *Panay* was a part of the Yangtze Patrol, a group of gunboats specifically designed to protect American businessmen and missionaries along the river. The Americans boarded the *Panay* on December 11, and the gunboat moved upriver to avoid the fighting between Chinese and Japanese forces. The Japanese command was notified of the boat's new location. The *Panay* had three large American flags prominently displayed and lighted at night to prevent being mistaken for a Chinese vessel.

In spite of these precautions, Japanese naval aircraft attacked and sank the *Panay*. The *Panay* was also machine-gunned by a surface vessel. The Japanese high command insisted that the attack was an accident, that the *Panay* had been mistaken for a Chinese vessel. The evidence suggested otherwise.

President Franklin D. Roosevelt reacted by demanding an official apology and full restitution from the Japanese government. Roosevelt briefly considered ordering a naval response, but the American public opposed any military action. Almost immediately after the attack, the Imperial navy offered an apology for the event. The official Japanese government apology was not received until Christmas Day. The Japanese agreed to full restitution in the amount of more than $2.2 million.

Impact   While the *Panay* incident did not directly result in war between Japan and the United States, as the details of the attack became known, American public opinion turned against the Japanese and the isolationist faction in the United States. The incident indirectly led to support for increasing wartime preparations, such as the passage of the Vinson-Trammell Naval Bill in May of 1938, the largest naval appropriation bill ever passed to that time.

Ronald J. Ferrara

Further Reading

Bond, W. Langhorn. *Wings for an Embattled China.* Bethlehem, Pa.: Lehigh University Press, 2001.

Hixson, Walter L. *The American Experience in World War II.* New York: Routledge, 2003.

Icenhower, Joseph B. *The Panay Incident.* New York: Franklin Watts, 1971.

Koginos, Manny T. *The Panay Incident: Prelude to War.*

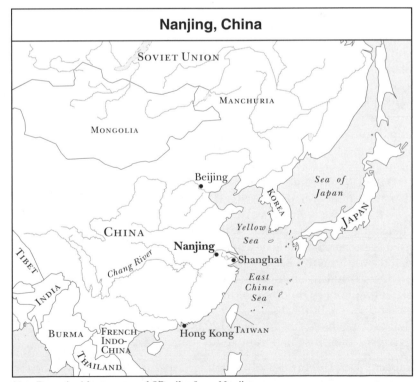

Nanjing, China

Note: Panay incident occurred 27 miles from Nanjing.

West Lafayette, Ind.: Purdue University Press, 1967.

See also   Asia; Foreign policy of the United States; Japanese military aggression; Manchuria occupation.

■ Parking meters

Definition   Mechanical devices used to regulate parking on city streets

Parking meters helped cities find enough space to accommodate the thousands of motorists who drove cars through their streets. Meters forced the turnover of valuable downtown parking spaces while providing much-needed revenue to the cities.

The age of the automobile brought the age of the parking problem. Without sufficient space alongside the curb or in parking lots, motorists could not leave their cars to patronize businesses. Those who did find parking spaces often parked in ways that slowed down the movement of traffic.

Oklahoma City pioneered the installation of parking meters in 1935. In the old parking system, the police traffic squad placed chalk marks on tires of parked vehicles and then rechecked them at the end of a given period. In the new system, workers placed a one-foot-tall parking meter, equipped with a clock, in each twenty-foot space. When a nickel was placed into a slot, a flag raised, indicating by a pointer the time allowed in that space. When the time limit was exhausted, the flag dropped out of sight, showing that the motorist had overstayed his or her time and was now subject to a traffic ticket.

Dallas, Miami, and other cities soon discovered that time limits for parking were more closely observed where meters were installed. The meters checked the overtime rigidly so that street space was used to the maximum. In curb space that accommodated two thousand cars, a strictly enforced hourly turnover could accommodate twenty thousand vehicles a day. Police could also monitor the flags more easily than chalk marks. In 1936, Dallas estimated that parking meters brought in $120,000, or enough to pay for their installation in about six months.

Impact   Despite protests by such groups as the American Automobile Association, more and more cities adopted parking meters. The meters reduced monopolization of parking spaces, gave motorists more space in which to maneuver, and earned a profit for cities.

Caryn E. Neumann

Further Reading
Hinckley, James, and Jon Robinson. *The Big Book of Car Culture: The Armchair Guide to Automotive Americana.* St. Paul, Minn.: Motorbooks, 2005.
Shoup, Donald C. *The High Cost of Free Parking.* Chicago: Planners Press, 2005.

See also   Automobiles and auto manufacturing; Business and the economy in the United States; Inventions; Transportation.

■ *Patterns of Culture*

Identification   Anthropological work on how cultures exhibit collective personality traits
Author   Ruth Benedict
Date   Published in 1934

One of anthropology's most influential and widely read books, Ruth Benedict's Patterns of Culture *has been translated into fourteen languages. The methodology established in this book was later used by Benedict to analyze Japanese national character during World War II for the U.S. government.*

Benedict was a founding member of the culture-and-personality school of American anthropology, which reached its zenith during the 1930's before falling out of fashion after World War II. Unlike Margaret Mead and others, however, Benedict argued that whole cultures have their own gestalt-like personalities, which she termed a "cultural configuration." For Benedict culture determined the fundamental personality characteristics of its members. She articulated these ideas most forcefully in her first book *Patterns of Culture* in 1934, which was for decades a best seller.

In *Patterns of Culture* Benedict compared three cultures: the Kwakiutl of the Pacific Northwest, the Dobu of Melanesia, and the Zuñi of the American Southwest. Combining her own ethnographic work on the Zuñi with observations made by seminal anthropologists Franz Boas (on the Kwakiutl) and Reo Fortune (on the Dobu) she characterized each soci-

The Diversity of Cultures

Ruth Benedict begins the third chapter of Patterns of Culture *with a discussion of the diversity of cultures around the world, using as an example the variety of reactions to the taking of a life:*

The diversity of cultures can be endlessly documented. A field of human behaviour may be ignored in some societies until it barely exists; it may even be in some cases unimagined. Or it may almost monopolize the whole organized behaviour of the society, and the most alien situations be manipulated only in its terms. Traits having no intrinsic relation one with the other, and historically independent, merge and become inextricable, providing the occasion for behaviour that has no counterpart in regions that do not make these identifications. It is a corollary of this that standards, no matter in what aspect of behaviour, range in different cultures from the positive to the negative pole. We might suppose that in the matter of taking a life all peoples would agree in condemnation. On the contrary, in a matter of homicide, it may be held that one is blameless if diplomatic relations have been severed between neighbouring countries, or that one kills by custom his first two children, or that a husband has right of life and death over his wife, or that it is the duty of the child to kill his parents before they are old. It may be that those are killed who steal a fowl, or who cut their upper teeth first, or who are born on a Wednesday. Among some peoples a person suffers torments at having caused an accidental death; among others it is a matter of no consequence. Suicide also may be a light matter, the recourse of anyone who has suffered some slight rebuff, an act that occurs constantly in a tribe. It may be the highest and noblest act a wise man can perform. The very tale of it, on the other hand, may be a matter for incredulous mirth, and the act itself impossible to conceive as a human possibility. Or it may be a crime punishable by law, or regarded as a sin against the gods.

Source: Ruth Benedict, *Patterns of Culture* (Boston: Houghton Mifflin, 1934).

ety as having a dominant personality, which she termed "Apollonian," "Dionysian," and "paranoid," respectively. These labels were borrowed from German philosopher Friedrich Nietzsche and Austrian psychoanalyst Sigmund Freud, who was influential in all of American intellectual life at this time. The peaceful Zuñi were said to be Apollonian because they kept their emotions under control and practiced moderation in all things. The extreme Kwakiutl were Dionysian, driven to excess in all aspects of their lives. The suspicious Dobu were described as paranoid because they were perpetually preoccupied with the sorcery they inflicted on each other.

Impact Immediately after the publication of *Patterns of Culture*, critics appeared, arguing that Benedict's analysis was skewed or reductionist. Nonetheless, the book stuck a chord in the United States during the 1930's. One reason for this was Benedict's indirect but powerful defense of cultural rela-

Anthropologist Ruth Benedict in 1934. (Library of Congress)

tivism—the unpopular idea of the time that there are no superior and inferior cultures. For example, if one believes that culture is simply the personality writ large, then it must follow that what is deviant in one culture is not deviant in another.

James Stanlaw

Further Reading

Benedict, Ruth. *Patterns of Culture.* Boston: Houghton Mifflin, 1934.

Modell, Judith. *Ruth Benedict: Patterns of a Life.* London: Chatto & Windus, 1999.

Young, Virginia. *Ruth Benedict: Beyond Relativity, Beyond Pattern.* Lincoln: University of Nebraska Press, 2005.

See also   Native Americans; Psychology and psychiatry; Racial discrimination.

■ Pauling, Linus

Identification   American physical chemist, molecular biologist, and peace activist
Born   February 28, 1901; Portland, Oregon
Died   August 19, 1994; Big Sur, California

Pauling helped to transform structural chemistry with his contributions in X-ray crystallography, quantum mechanics, and the nature of the chemical bond, and his work in molecular biology made him one of the founders of this significant field.

During Linus Pauling's adolescence and college life in Oregon, he developed an interest in chemistry in general and in the chemical bond in particular. As a graduate student at the California Institute of Technology (Caltech) he began to use the technique of X-ray diffraction to determine the structures of such substances as the molybdenum-and-sulfur mineral molybdenite, and as a Guggenheim Fellow in Europe he mastered the field of quantum mechanics and published one of his greatest papers, in which he used quantum-mechanical techniques to predict the physical properties of atoms and ions. When he returned to Pasadena, California, in 1927, he became assistant professor of theoretical chemistry at Caltech and created his coordination theory of the structures of ionic crystals, including silicate minerals, in which he developed rules enabling crystallog-raphers to ignore chemically unreasonable atomic arrangements and to construct likely configurations to be tested experimentally.

In 1930, with coauthor Samuel Goudsmit, Pauling published his first book, *The Structure of Line Spectra,* and he solved a problem that had plagued physicists and chemists: how to use quantum mechanics to account for the bonds in organic molecules. Pauling's solution was to mix or hybridize atomic orbitals into bond orbitals that could explain, for example, the tetrahedral arrangement of carbon-to-hydrogen bonds in the methane molecule. This led, in 1931, to the first of a series of papers on the nature of the chemical bond. In these papers he deepened chemists' understanding of the transition from ionic- to covalent-bond types, and he formulated such influential ideas as his electronegativity scale, which provided chemists with a quantitative measure of the ability of an element to attract bonding electrons.

Pauling also advanced his theory of resonance to explain the structures of such compounds as benzene, which, despite alternating single and double bonds, has a single interatomic distance between the carbon atoms. In resonance, the true state of a chemical system is neither of the component quantum states, but some intermediate one. He published his own experimental and theoretical studies, as well as those of other structural chemists, in his pivotal book, *The Nature of the Chemical Bond and the Structure of Molecules and Crystals: An Introduction to Modern Structural Chemistry* (1939).

Through interactions with geneticist Thomas Hunt Morgan and immunologist Karl Landsteiner, Pauling became increasingly fascinated with biological molecules, and by the mid-1930's, he had explained how, in blood, the oxygen molecules are bonded to the iron atoms of the hemoglobin molecule. This interest in hemoglobin as an oxygen-carrying protein molecule led to a general interest in the structure of proteins. With protein expert Alfred Mirsky, he published a paper explaining how protein molecules are coiled into specific configurations stabilized by hydrogen bonds. These hydrogen bonds are broken when the molecules are "denatured," for example, when their biological effectiveness is destroyed by heat. So impressed were officials of the Rockefeller Foundation by Pauling's research in the borderline field between chemistry and biology that they awarded him large grants to continue his studies on the "molecules of life."

Impact Pauling's achievements in structural chemistry and molecular biology during the 1930's had a profound influence on scientists in a variety of fields, including medicine and evolutionary biology. He built on these achievements to discover the first molecular disease: He proved that sickle-cell anemia is caused by a defective hemoglobin molecule. He also deepened his insights into protein structure by formulating three important amino-acid arrangements—the alpha helix, the beta pleated sheet, and the gamma helix. Furthermore, the discovery of the three-dimensional structure of deoxyribonucleic acid (DNA) would not have occurred in 1953 without the antecedent work of Pauling on chemical bonding and the structure of proteins. He also used his knowledge of chemistry and physics in his campaign against the testing of nuclear weapons in the atmosphere, for which he received the 1962 Nobel Peace Prize. His scientific achievements had earlier been recognized with a Nobel Prize in Chemistry (1954), making him the only person to have ever won two unshared Nobel Prizes.

Robert J. Paradowski

Further Reading

Goertzel, Ted, and Ben Goertzel. *Linus Pauling: A Life in Science and Politics.* New York: BasicBooks, 1995.

Hager, Thomas. *Force of Nature: The Life of Linus Pauling.* New York: Simon and Schuster, 1995.

Marinacci, Barbara, ed. *Linus Pauling in His Own Words.* New York: Simon and Schuster, 1995.

Pauling, Linus, Clifford Mead, and Thomas Hager. *Linus Pauling: Scientist and Peacemaker.* Corvallis: Oregon State University Press, 2001.

See also Chemistry; Medicine; Physics.

■ Peace movement

Identification Cause focusing on eliminating U.S. involvement in armed conflicts

The peace movement played a large role in keeping the United States from intervening in the Spanish Civil War and the Italian invasion of Ethiopia. It also postponed U.S. participation in World War II until Japan's attack on Pearl Harbor.

During the 1930's, the peace movement in the United States experienced one of its greatest periods of influence. Its success was related to American disappointment with the peace settlement that ended World War I. Many Americans had initially supported U.S. involvement in the war because they believed President Woodrow Wilson's claim that the conflict had been fought to preserve democracy and to end forever the need for further wars. Many of these same citizens were disillusioned when, in the war's aftermath, the victorious nations pursued nationalistic concerns rather than laying the foundations for a fair and just international system. This disappointment and a desire to avoid participation in future European conflicts led many Americans to embrace the peace movement during the 1930's.

Women were some of the greatest adherents of the peace movement during the 1930's. Women's peace activism was partly a relic of "separate spheres" ideology that not only declared women more caring, compassionate, and peace-loving than men but also suggested women's roles as mothers led them to abhor the human waste of war. Many women participated in peace activism through the Women's International League for Peace and Freedom (WILPF). Founded in 1915 by Jane Addams, the WILPF was a pacifist group that believed violence of any kind was unjustifiable. Other women joined the National Committee on the Cause and Cure of War, founded in 1924 by Carrie Chapman Catt. This more conservative organization supported military actions in certain circumstances, such as in a defensive war.

American clergy also embraced peace activism during the 1930's. Protestant, Roman Catholic, and Jewish religious leaders devoted more attention to the relationship between faith and peace than they ever had previously. Some joined organizations such as the Fellowship of Reconciliation, which had been founded in 1915 to push for political reforms based on ideals of Christian nonviolence, international brotherhood, and social justice. Meanwhile, the Catholic Worker movement, established in 1933 by Dorothy Day and Peter Maurin, attempted to lay the foundations necessary for world peace by engaging in activities such as feeding the hungry and providing shelters for the homeless.

College students were particularly active during the 1930's peace movement. Rejecting the mandatory Reserve Officers' Training Corps (ROTC) training taking place on numerous college campuses, many engaged in protests against war and fas-

This emblem of neutrality summarizes the message of the peace movement in the United States during the decade. (The Granger Collection, New York)

cism. Students also became some of the leading promoters of the peace movement by participating in peace caravans that traveled around the country raising awareness and attracting adherents to the cause.

Other supporters of the peace movement during the 1930's were American leftists. Socialists, communists, and unaffiliated radicals all viewed war as a consequence of an oppressive economic system. For them, peace activism was a way to challenge capitalism and prevent future wars that invariably affected the working classes more harshly than they did the upper classes.

Peace groups supported a variety of proposals during the 1930's that they hoped would diminish the chance of a future war. One of the most popular was disarmament, which called for a reduction in the number of weapons and other instruments of war maintained by nation-states. Another was neutrality legislation. Inspired by the Nye Committee's investigation of the munitions industry and the publication of *The Merchants of Death* (1934) by H. C. Engelbrecht and F. C. Hanighen, both of which argued that U.S. participation in World War I was largely the result of business owners wanting to profit from the sale of weapons, peace workers demanded the passage of laws to limit the influence of businesspeople on U.S. foreign policy. Their demands eventually led to the passage of the Neutrality Acts, which forbade the United States from selling armaments to belligerent nations, warned American citizens that they traveled at their own risk if they chose to sail on the ships of warring nations, and imposed a cash-and-carry policy for all American exports purchased by nations at war.

The influence of peace groups began to diminish with the rise of fascism in Italy and Germany during the mid-1930's. Although most peace activists were appalled by the oppressive and nationalistic characteristics of fascism and expressed unhappiness with efforts to appease fascist governments, they disagreed and were divided over how to respond to fascist aggression. Staunchly pacifist organizations focused on keeping the United States out of the impending war in Europe. They allied with isolationist organizations and supported preserving strict neutrality legislation. More conservative organizations supported President Franklin D. Roosevelt's foreign policies, including the peacetime draft and the act of providing aid to Great Britain and its allies once World War II broke out in Europe. They also began to argue that war to end oppressive systems such as fascism was justifiable.

The division of the peace movement led to a decline in membership for many peace groups. While some pacifist organizations stayed active during the 1940's, even after the United States joined the war, they never regained the prominence or influence they experienced at the beginning of the 1930's.

Impact The peace movement attracted a large and varied group of adherents during the 1930's. As these activists attempted to establish policies that would prevent U.S. participation in future wars, they were able to influence both public opinion and governmental actions. Disagreements about how to respond to the rise of fascism in Europe, however, led the movement to split during the mid-1930's.

Christy Jo Snider

Further Reading

Chatfield, Charles. *For Peace and Justice: Pacifism in America, 1914-1941*. Boston: Beacon Press, 1973. Study of the rise and decline of pacifism in the United States from the start of World War I until the entry of the United States in World War II.

Foster, Carrie. *The Women and the Warriors: The U.S. Section of the Women's International League for Peace and Freedom, 1915-1946*. New York: Syracuse University Press, 1995. Exploration of the founding and development of the U.S. section of the WILPF.

Howlett, Charles F., and Robbie Lieberman. *A History of the American Peace Movement from Colonial Times to the Present*. Lewiston, N.Y.: The Edwin Mellen Press, 2008. Examination of the efforts of peace activists and organizations to build an influential movement that would constrain U.S. military efforts.

See also   Addams, Jane; Day, Dorothy; Geneva Disarmament Conference; Isolationism; Neutrality Acts; Nye Committee; World War II and the United States.

■ Pearson, Drew

Identification   Muckraking American journalist
Born   December 13, 1897; Evanston, Illinois
Died   September 1, 1969; Washington, D.C.

During the early 1930's, Pearson anonymously coauthored two books that strongly criticized several prominent government officials and publicly exposed their wrongdoings in Washington, D.C. Pearson's aggressive, liberal reporting style drew a large following of supporters but angered many other people as well.

Born Andrew Russell, Drew Pearson began the 1930's as a foreign journalist for the *Baltimore Sun*,

Journalist Drew Pearson (left) listening to Brazilian government minister Oswaldo Aranha in 1939. (Time & Life Pictures/Getty Images)

reporting on the London Naval Conference and the Cuban Revolution. Soon thereafter, he became chief of the Washington, D.C., bureau of the *Baltimore Sun.* Despite Pearson's new position at the paper, editors of the *Sun* rejected his frequent proposals to investigate and publish several stories of misconduct in public life. In 1931, Pearson and reporter Robert S. Allen, from the *Christian Science Monitor,* anonymously published *Washington Merry-Go-Round,* a controversial book that criticized President Herbert Hoover, Congress, and other federal agencies and government leaders. The book became a best seller. After publishing a second book, *More Merry-Go-Round* (1932), Pearson and Allen were disclosed as the authors, and both were dismissed from their reporting positions.

In 1932, the two reporters negotiated a deal with Scripps-Howard's United Features to syndicate a daily newspaper column entitled "Washington Merry-Go-Round." The syndicated column began later that year in about a dozen papers. By the end of the decade, it was printed in more than 350 newspapers. Their investigation of the federal government was thorough. Pearson and Allen worked tirelessly and released their findings at strategic times when they could most greatly affect the operations of government.

Pearson and Constantine Brown, another newspaper reporter, coauthored *American Diplomat Game* (1935), a book on American diplomacy. In that year, Pearson and Allen also began a radio broadcasting program that expanded public awareness of their causes. They published *Nine Old Men* (1936) and *Nine Old Men at the Crossroads* (1937), their findings on the Supreme Court justices.

Cocolumnists, Pearson and Allen separated in 1942. Pearson continued "Washington Merry-Go-Round," which was later coauthored by Jack Anderson. In 1958, Anderson and Pearson published both *U.S.A: Second-Class Power* and *The Case Against Congress.* Pearson is credited for coauthoring two novels with Gerald Green: *The Senator* (1968) and *The President* (1970). Throughout his career, Pearson interviewed many prominent world leaders, investigated several presidents and their staff members, exposed corruption, published military secrets, and criticized several government agencies. His coast-to-coast newspaper column and radio broadcasts reached millions of people. In 1947, he was nominated for the Nobel Prize for his efforts in organiz-

ing the Freedom Train, a nationwide effort to collect food for war-torn countries in Europe. At the time of his death in 1969, Pearson's "Washington Merry-Go-Round" had been published in more than six hundred newspapers.

Impact In his crusade to deliver news, Pearson broke new ground in investigative reporting. Pearson was a strong advocate for civil liberties, was committed to world peace, and was opposed to militarism. His blunt, controversial, crusading approach to reporting delivered sensational news and resulted in a new form of media coverage. His pursuit of government figures whom he deemed to be in breach of just and lawful standards led other reporters to follow suit. Pearson's direct and honest style won respect as a powerful journalistic technique but also created much controversy. Attacks on political figures led to frequent legal suits for Pearson, who was sued for libel more than 120 times; he lost only one case.

Cynthia J. W. Svoboda

Further Reading

Klurfeld, Herman. *Behind the Lines: The World of Drew Pearson.* Englewood Cliffs, N.J.: Prentice-Hall, 1968.
Pilat, Oliver. *Drew Pearson: An Unauthorized Biography.* New York: Harper's Magazine Press, 1972.

See also Book publishing; Congress, U.S.; Crimes and scandals; Hoover, Herbert; Newspapers, U.S.; Supreme Court, U.S.

■ Pendergast, Thomas Joseph

Identification Kansas City, Missouri, politician
Born July 22, 1873; St. Joseph, Missouri
Died January 26, 1945; Kansas City, Missouri

During the 1930's, Pendergast may have been the most powerful city politician in the United States, and he played a major role in getting future U.S. president Harry S. Truman elected to the U.S. Senate.

Thomas Joseph Pendergast grew up about fifty-five miles upriver from Kansas City, Missouri. He moved to the city as a bookkeeper for several saloons owned by his older brother James, who was also a local Democratic politician, controlling a small ward in the

West Bottoms area. With his brother's patronage, Pendergast earned appointment as a deputy constable in the powerful first ward, where he found a talent for ward politics. In January of 1911, he married Carrie Snyder, with whom he would have three children. After his brother's death, Pendergast took over control of his brother's political organization in 1911 and the groundwork was laid for his rising political power.

Pendergast excelled at using middlemen to accomplish his bidding, binding individuals to him through personal favors when they were down on their luck or assisting them with relatively minor problems that appeared major at the time. He had a shrewd eye for talent and identified young men to place in key positions, including the state capitol. No one could get out the vote for local and statewide elections like the Pendergast organization. Consistently, Kansas City registered the highest voter turnout in the state, often exceeding 100 percent, the dead themselves rising to vote, as newspapers of the time wryly noted. However, all attempts to investigate voter fraud came up empty; the political machine controlled the police and judicial system. Most of the judges owed their jobs to Pendergast. The local business and civic community also acquiesced to the state of affairs, as many were either in Pendergast's debt or in fear of his influence and power.

John Lazia, an alleged crime boss on the north side of the city, served as the unofficial enforcer for the organization—although there was never enough firm evidence to tie him to Pendergast. During the Prohibition era, Kansas City had the reputation as a "wide-open town," with gambling establishments, free-flowing liquor, and a booming culture of jazz—the interconnectedness of these three aspects served as a mecca for criminal elements and flamboyant individuals and behaviors. Pendergast bet heavily on horses, amassing large debts.

By the early 1930's, Pendergast companies, some of which were held in others' names, such as Ready Mixed Concrete Company, Kansas City Concrete Pipe Company, Missouri Contracting Corporation, and Missouri Asphalt Products Company, were routine recipients of many city and state contracts. Any political candidate realized, in the vernacular of the day, that he had to pay a visit to "the Old Man at 1908 Main," where Pendergast ruled. He plucked individuals such as Truman from obscurity and placed them in office; they remained forever in his debt. Pendergast spared no expense in building a palatial residence at a cost of more than $125,000. It signaled to others that Kansas City was "Tom's Town," as many newspapers and others noted. Pendergast used political leverage to steer more than one-half of the New Deal jobs for Missouri to Kansas City, with his many companies also benefiting from federal construction projects.

An official with the U.S. Treasury's Bureau of Internal Revenue persuaded President Franklin D. Roosevelt that there was evidence that Pendergast had taken bribe money in 1935-1936 from 137 national fire-insurance companies operating in Missouri. Governor Lloyd C. Stark, who had been put into office by the Pendergast organization, wanted to run against Senator Truman in the 1940 primary. Stark disliked the whole business with Pendergast and learned of the possible federal interest. He went to visit Roosevelt, who realized that Stark would make a better political partner than Pendergast. Accordingly, the U.S. government built a case against Pendergast for income tax evasion and indicted him on April 7, 1939. He pled guilty and was fined ten thousand dollars and sentenced to fifteen months in Leavenworth Federal Penitentiary and five years' probation.

Impact   After Pendergast's 1939 income tax conviction, other indictments and convictions in federal courts followed throughout the year. These included a revelation that Kansas City had illegal heroin sales of $1 million a month during the 1930's. The Pendergast machine was dismantled, and cleanup of the city's affairs began to pass to a new generation of leaders.

Dennis W. Cheek

Further Reading

Ferrell, Robert H. *Truman and Pendergast.* Columbia: University of Missouri Press, 1997.

Hartmann, Rudolph H. *The Kansas City Investigation: Pendergast's Downfall, 1938-1939.* Columbia: University of Missouri Press, 1999.

Larsen, Lawrence H., and Nancy J. Hulston. *Pendergast!* Columbia: University of Missouri Press, 1999.

See also   Gambling; Music: Jazz; Organized crime; Prohibition repeal; Roosevelt, Franklin D.

■ People's Forests, The

Identification Nonfiction book calling for federal protection for disappearing American forests
Author Robert Marshall
Date Published in 1933

The People's Forests was one of the first popular books to describe the beauty of forests in the United States and to argue that their recreational value outweighed their commercial value. Its author, U.S. Forest Service employee Robert Marshall, contended that the federal government should purchase and manage forest land before the last remaining bits of true wilderness disappeared forever.

When Marshall, a conservationist and bureaucrat, began working for the U.S. Forest Service, the prevailing attitude at the agency was that forests, beautiful and inspiring though they may be, should be preserved only in places where there was no practical commercial use for them. The Forest Service's role was to sell or lease forest land to timber companies, and there was little thought of buying and preserving the wilderness for its own sake.

Within the organization, Marshall began arguing that the forests should be preserved. He enjoyed long hikes in the wilderness and believed that all citizens should have the opportunity to be alone in the forest. After writing government documents arguing for preservation, he took his case to the people with a well-written, passionate, and statistics-laden book, *The People's Forests*. Step by step, he described the history of the forests, from the first awe-inspiring encounters the Pilgrims had, through the Industrial Revolution and its high demands for wood, to the 1930's, when few swathes of uncut, "virgin" forest remained.

Impact *The People's Forests* was widely read and discussed. With public support, Marshall was able to exert strong influence when, in 1937, he became head of the newly created Division of Recreation and Lands in the U.S. Forest Service. However, after his death in 1939, the federal government did little to protect the forests until the Wilderness Act of 1964 was passed, using the arguments Marshall had promoted thirty years earlier.

Cynthia A. Bily

Further Reading

Glover, James M. *A Wilderness Original: The Life of Bob Marshall.* Seattle: Mountaineers, 1986.
Sutter, Paul. *Driven Wild: How the Fight Against Automobiles Launched the Modern Wilderness Movement.* Seattle: University of Washington Press, 2002.
Wellman, J. Douglas. *Wildland Recreation Policy: An Introduction.* New York: John Wiley & Sons, 1987.

See also Civilian Conservation Corps; John Muir Trail; National parks; National Wildlife Federation; Wilderness Society.

■ Perkins, Frances

Identification U.S. secretary of labor, 1933-1945
Born April 10, 1880; Boston, Massachusetts
Died May 14, 1965; New York, New York

Perkins was the first woman to hold a cabinet post, serving as secretary of labor for President Franklin D. Roosevelt. Working with Roosevelt, she was instrumental in drafting vital New Deal legislation, including the Social Security Act and the Fair Labor Standards Act.

Born Fannie Coralie Perkins, Frances Perkins was the daughter of Frederick W. Perkins, a businessman, and Susan E. Bean. Perkins graduated from Mount Holyoke College in 1902. After teaching at various schools, she moved to Lake Forest, Illinois, to teach at Ferry Hall, a woman's college. She changed her first name to Frances and, in her free time, helped out at Chicago Commons and Jane Addams's Hull House, settlement houses in nearby Chicago.

Volunteer work persuaded Perkins that her future was not in teaching but in helping the poor. In September, 1907, she was hired as the general secretary for the Philadelphia Research and Protective Association, working with immigrant girls. She relocated to New York City in 1909 to study economics and sociology at Columbia University. After receiving a master's degree in 1910, Perkins began working for the National Consumers League. On March 25, 1911, after witnessing women hurling themselves from upper-story windows to escape the fire at the Triangle Shirtwaist manufacturing company, she vowed to make workplaces safer and more humane, particularly for women and children.

Perkins began cultivating politicians, such as Robert F. Wagner and Alfred E. Smith, who had power to make changes. When she married Paul Caldwell Wilson, an economist, in 1913, many were shocked

U.S. secretary of labor Frances Perkins arriving at the White House to attend a special cabinet meeting called by President Franklin D. Roosevelt in September, 1938. (Library of Congress)

when she retained her maiden name. Although Perkins had stopped working, she continued her volunteer work and helped Smith successfully campaign for governorship of New York. Smith appointed Perkins to the New York Industrial Commission. When Smith was defeated for reelection in 1920, Perkins lost her post; however, when Smith was reelected in 1922, 1924, and 1926, she rejoined him, working on labor policies and attempting to improve workplace conditions.

Smith decided to run for president, endorsing Franklin D. Roosevelt as his successor as governor. Roosevelt won the election and appointed Perkins industrial commissioner. Over the following four years, she worked closely with Roosevelt, encouraging him to embrace far-reaching social programs. Aware of the effects of the deepening Depression, Perkins pushed Roosevelt to develop an unemployment insurance system. She also became the foremost national authority on unemployment statistics and used these numbers to aid Roosevelt in his campaign for president. After Roosevelt was elected president in 1932, he asked Perkins to join his cabinet as secretary of labor. Perkins agreed after proposing a series of reforms she wanted to work toward. Her first priority was unemployment. Prohibition of child labor, an eight-hour workday, and a minimum wage, as well as old-age insurance, were other concerns.

Women rejoiced at Perkins's appointment. Male labor leaders were "keenly disappointed." Nonetheless, Perkins, always intense and full of energy, went to work. She transformed the Department of Labor and had a key role in planning initiatives, including the Federal Emergency Relief Act. She was at the center of discussions that led to the National Recovery Administration and, later, the National Labor Relations Act. She persuaded the president to support legislation leading toward the Social Security Act of 1935, described by *The Washington Post* as the "New Deal's most important act."

Perkins was often the center of controversy, and her refusal to use her powers to deport a West Coast strike leader led to impeachment proceedings against her in early 1939; however, the judiciary committee found no grounds for proceeding. Continuing slander against Perkins decreased her effectiveness. She planned to retire but stayed, at Roosevelt's urging, when he won his fourth term.

Perkins retired on May 23, 1945, after aiding President Harry S. Truman through the transition period. In June, 1946, Truman appointed her to the U.S. Civil Service Commission; Perkins finally retired in 1953. In subsequent years, she taught classes at various universities and wrote. She died in 1965.

Impact Perkins broke the gender barrier in government by serving on a number of important commissions, leading to an appointment to Roosevelt's cabinet. Throughout her career, she worked toward making life better for Americans by supporting politicians who could make things happen and by giving them the ideas to push toward meaningful legislation.

Marcia B. Dinneen

Further Reading

Downey, Kirstin. *The Woman Behind the New Deal.* New York: Doubleday, 2009.

Martin, George. *Madam Secretary, Frances Perkins.* Boston: Houghton Mifflin, 1976.

Perkins, Frances. *The Roosevelt I Knew.* New York: Viking, 1946.

See also   Addams, Jane; Fair Labor Standards Act of 1938; Income and wages in the United States; National Labor Relations Act of 1935; National Recovery Administration; New Deal; Roosevelt, Franklin D.; Smith, Alfred E.; Social Security Act of 1935.

■ Petrified Forest, The

Identification   Play about people held hostage in a small diner
Author   Robert E. Sherwood
Dates   First performed on January 7, 1935; film version 1936

Between 1920 and 1933, the prohibition of alcohol sales created a new type of American criminal and icon: the gangster, whose organization grew out of the illegal distribution of alcohol. The Petrified Forest *features a psychologically complex gangster and other characters who find that the Great Depression has turned their goals into impossible dreams.*

The Petrified Forest was the first major success for Sherwood, who later won three Pulitzer Prizes. Humphrey Bogart, who was one of the stars of both

The principal actors in the 1936 film The Petrified Forest, *from left to right: Leslie Howard, Dick Foran, Bette Davis, and Humphrey Bogart—look surprised and suspicious as they stare to the left of the camera.* (The Granger Collection, New York)

the stage and film versions, had been a successful Broadway actor during the 1920's, but he turned to film during the Great Depression when ticket sales for plays declined dramatically. The film version was Bogart's breakthrough role, making him a movie star. It also featured the well-known film actors Leslie Howard, who also had been in the stage version, and Bette Davis.

The story revolves around three main characters: Gabby, the waitress in her family's diner, who wishes she could leave the desert of Arizona and live among artists in France; Alan Squier, a disillusioned writer who sees no future for art; and Duke Mantee, a gangster whose bitterness seems grounded in some personal disappointment. The modern world, it becomes clear, has no important role for any of these lonely people to play. Individual courage and the capacity for love are the only things that keep the human race from spiraling into savagery.

Impact   *The Petrified Forest* reveals many of the social conflicts of the 1930's, as various characters reflect on the roles of capitalism, patriotism, social class, and the arts. The film is a classic example of the American gangster film and a precursor to the film-noir genre that flourished during the 1940's.

Cynthia A. Bily

Further Reading

Alonso, Harriet Hyman. *Robert E. Sherwood: The Playwright in Peace and War.* Amherst: University of Massachusetts Press, 2007.

Brown, John Mason. *The Worlds of Robert E. Sherwood—Mirror to His Times, 1896-1939.* New York: Harper & Row, 1965.

Shuman, R. Baird. *Robert E. Sherwood.* New York: Twayne, 1964.

See also   Davis, Bette; Film; Gangster films; Great Depression in the United States; Literature in the United States; Organized crime; Prohibition repeal; Theater in the United States.

■ Philippine Independence Act of 1934

The Law   Federal law establishing the parameters for the eventual transformation of the Philippine Islands into an independent, sovereign state

Also known as   Tydings-McDuffie Act; Public Law 73-127; Philippine Commonwealth and Independence Act

Date   Approved on March 24, 1934

The law resolved several issues regarding the status of the Philippine Islands and Filipinos in relation to the United States. Among the issues were when and how the Philippines would become independent, the immigration status of Filipinos who were in the United States and those who wanted to emigrate from the Philippine Islands to the United States, and the status of American military forces in the Philippines.

At the conclusion of the Spanish-American War in 1898, Spain ceded control of the Philippine Islands to the United States for $20 million in the Treaty of Paris. However, before the war began, the Philippines were in revolt against Spain and declared independence from Spain on June 12. The United States refused to recognize the Philippine Republic and tried to assume control over an independent state. The Philippine Republic declared war in 1899 and fought until 1902, when Philippine president Emilio Aguinaldo surrendered. However, fighting in outlying provinces continued until 1913.

As the United States set up rule over the Philippines under the terms of the Philippine Organic Act of 1902, which permitted two resident commissioners to the U.S. House of Representatives, bitterness remained over the squelching of Filipino independence. In 1916, the Philippine Organic Act was superseded by the Philippine Autonomy Act, which promised eventual independence and granted some autonomy to Philippine political institutions, allowing the election of provincial governors, members of an assembly, and members of a senate.

In 1916, Manuel Quezon, who drafted the Autonomy Act while resident commissioner, was elected senator and later senate president. In 1919, he led a delegation to Washington, D.C., lobbying for Philippine independence.

In December, 1932, Congress passed the Hare-Hawes-Cutting Act, which established a framework for independence that included provisions for

American military and naval bases in the Philippines and imposed quotas and tariffs on exports from the Philippines. The act was vetoed by President Herbert Hoover, but it was overridden and went into law. However, the Philippine senate rejected the law. Accordingly, the Philippine Independence Act of 1934 corrected Hare-Hawes-Cutting and was approved by Congress, the president, and the Philippine senate.

Under the terms of the act, the Philippine legislature convened a constitutional convention to establish a basic law that would prevail for the next decade, when independence was to be granted. The United States was given the right to station naval bases in the Philippines two years beyond independence and to call upon the Philippine armed forces to serve in the American armed forces if so needed. Filipinos who had been recruited to work in the United States were classified as alien subjects, ineligible for citizenship, though afforded consular representation. A quota of fifty Filipinos was established for Filipino workers to immigrate to the United States, thereby stopping the emigration of spouses to join their husbands in the United States.

Impact Passage of the law calmed unrest in the Philippines regarding American rule over the islands, which became the Commonwealth of the Philippines in 1935. Quezon was elected president. Consular offices were established in American cities close to where most Filipinos lived. In 1935, the Filipino Repatriation Act afforded free passage for Filipinos to return to the Philippines, whereupon they could only return after applying under the newly restrictive quota, a law that was declared unconstitutional in 1940.

In 1944, when Philippine independence had been promised, the Philippine islands were in the middle of World War II, occupied by Japanese military forces. After the war, Congress passed the Philippine Independence Act of 1946, finally decolonizing the Philippines. Many insurgents in Muslim areas of the Philippines never recognized American sovereignty and believed that their own claims to independence would be granted by the new Republic of the Philippines.

Michael Haas

Further Reading

Agoncillo, Teodoro A. *History of the Filipino People.* 8th ed. Quezon City: University of the Philippines Press, 1990.

Quezon, Manuel. *The Good Fight.* New York: AMS Press, 1974.

Zulueta, Francisco M., and Abriel M. Nebres. *Philippine History and Government Through the Years.* Mandaluyong City, Philippines: National Book Store, 2005.

See also Asian Americans; Congress, U.S.; Naval forces; Philippine Islands; Supreme Court, U.S.; World War II and the United States.

■ Philippine Islands

Identification Archipelago bordered by the South China Sea to the west, the Philippine Sea to the east, and the Celebes Sea to the south

A colonial territory of the United States since 1898, the Philippine Islands yearned for political independence during the 1930's. American recognition of the Philippines in 1935 as a self-governing commonwealth was a triumph for the Filipino people overshadowed by fears of economic destabilization and Japanese expansion.

Relations between the United States and the Philippine Islands were often strained during the 1930's. Historically, the stated rationale for U.S. involvement in the Philippines was to foster economic development and prepare the islands for democratic independence. The United States originally attained control of the Philippine Islands after the Spanish-American War in the Treaty of Paris of 1898. After quelling a bloody, proindependence, Filipino insurgency from 1899 to 1902, the United States created a new legal system, appointing an American governor-general to administer the affairs of the islands. In the decades that followed, a strong proindependence movement emerged that defined the Philippine Islands during the 1930's.

Movement for Independence, 1930-1935 From the time of its establishment in 1907, the Nacionalista Party dominated politics in the Philippines. Two of its party leaders, Manuel Quezon and Sergio Osmeña, shaped the future of the islands during the 1930's. Although the Nacionalista Party platform called publicly for immediate independence, Quezon and Osmeña quietly postponed the push for political sovereignty during the 1920's, attempt-

Philippines

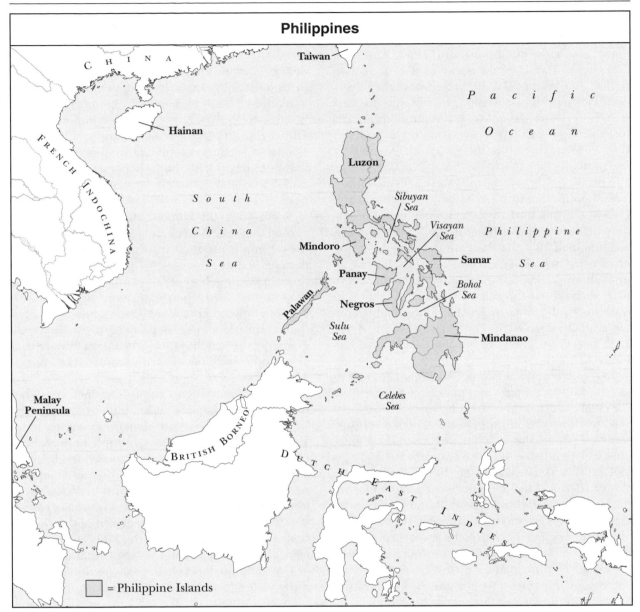

= Philippine Islands

ing to develop the islands' economic infrastructure before separation from the United States.

In 1930, while apprehensive of economic turmoil and foreign threats that would arise with independence, the Filipino citizenry made passionate demands for political sovereignty. In February of that year, approximately two thousand Filipinos participated in a rally for independence in Manila. Acting on this national fervor, the general assembly of the Philippines sent a delegation to Washington, D.C., to negotiate a timetable on independence.

As the Philippines lobbied for its political freedom, the U.S. Congress already favored independence for the territory. Specifically, many isolationist politicians favored separation to stop immigration from the Philippines and to prevent economic competition with the islands. With this purpose, in December, 1932, the U.S. Congress passed its first legislation on Filipino independence, the Hare-Hawes-Cutting Act. Subject to ratification by the Filipino general assembly, the bill made the Philippines a self-governing commonwealth and granted complete independence after ten years. In turn, the act stipulated that the U.S. would retain its military and naval bases in the Philippines and keep an American governor in Manila for the duration of the transition period. On January 17, 1933, four days after President Herbert Hoover vetoed the bill with the view that the territory was not yet economically prepared for sovereignty, Congress overrode the president's veto and sent the bill to the Filipino legislature for approval.

The bill met resistance in Manila. This was largely a result of the political rivalry between Quezon and Osmeña. From 1931 to 1932, Osmeña led the Filipino delegation in Washington, D.C., while Quezon was sidelined, ill with tuberculosis. Fearful of losing influence, Quezon argued that the Hare-Hawes-Cutting bill would damage the Filipino economy and violate its national sovereignty in its preservation of American military bases. The Filipino assembly, consequentially, rejected the Hare-Hawes-Cutting Act in 1933, and Quezon set out for new talks in Washington, D.C.

In these new negotiations, Quezon sought to hasten the date for Filipino independence but preserve the economic benefits the Philippines received as a U.S. territory. While largely unreceptive to Quezon's influence, the U.S. Senate passed the Philippine Independence Act (also known as the Tydings-McDuffie Act) on March 24, 1934. The new law, almost identical to its predecessor, stipulated that the United States would remove its military bases after independence and later negotiate the possibility of a naval base. Furthermore, the law set stringent restrictions on immigration from the Philippines, classifying all Filipino natives in the United States as aliens and implementing an annual immigration quota from the former territory at fifty people.

In spite of this, the Filipino general assembly unanimously approved the new law and convened a constitutional convention to create a new government in July, 1934. By February of the following year, the convention finished its new constitution with the approval of both the Filipino citizenry and President Franklin D. Roosevelt. In the autumn of 1935, the populace voted in elections for a new government, with Quezon running for president and Osmeña for vice president. The pair easily won the election. Shortly after, the Philippines was inaugurated as a self-governing commonwealth in front of 500,000 cheering Filipinos on November 15, 1935.

Economic Problems and Racial Tensions During the 1930's In 1930, the Great Depression dramatically increased American support for Filipino independence. After the October, 1929, stock market crash, isolationist politicians criticized the Philippines particularly as a costly dependency that hurt American businesses. Resenting the duty-free importation of Filipino sugar and coconut products, powerful American producers lobbied Congress to grant the islands independence and, then, enact costly tariffs on Filipino imports to prevent economic competition.

For its part, the Filipino elite were gravely concerned that such American measures would destroy the economic productivity of the Philippines. After decades of duty-free trade, Filipino economic development was largely dependent on the United States. For example, the United States alone bought 90 percent of Filipino exports in 1934. Although the Philippine Independence Act would phase in tariffs gradually, the new Filipino government worried that any implementation of tariffs would derail the islands' progress.

Equally unnerving to Filipino leaders, xenophobic sentiments against Asian immigration in the United States caused tensions in the first years of the 1930's. Many Filipinos, free to resettle in the American mainland before 1934, had moved freely to the United States; more than fifty-six thousand Filipinos resided on the American mainland by 1930. These immigrants often experienced discriminatory treatment from Caucasians, which aggravated race relations and provoked anger in the Philippines. At the peak of these tensions in the fall of 1929 and winter of 1930, Filipino laborers were the victims of at least thirty violent attacks in the United States. In the years that followed, the U.S. Congress not only sought to strengthen immigration restrictions but also launched a repatriation campaign to return Filipino immigrants to the Philippines, financing the voluntary repatriation of more than two thousand Filipinos from 1934 to 1940.

Japanese Threat, 1935-1940 After 1935, President Quezon was greatly concerned over the threat of an expanding Japanese empire. Japan had invaded Manchuria in 1931 and embarked on a full-scale invasion of China six years later. With American war planners viewing the Philippines as too expensive to defend, Quezon was fearful that the United States would abandon the Philippines in a war with Japan. General Douglas MacArthur, however, disagreed, stressing the importance of the islands for American security. MacArthur assured the Filipino government that it could repel any invasion and helped prepare a Filipino defense force of 400,000 reservists from 1936 to 1938. In spite of this, Quezon, disillusioned with the possibility of repelling any massive invasion, engaged the Japanese diplomatically during the late 1930's, traveling to Tokyo in 1937 and 1939.

Impact   As the 1930's closed, President Quezon utilized strong executive powers in the Filipino constitution to assume almost total control of the Philippines. Urgently seeking to guarantee Filipino neutrality in any conflict with Japan, Quezon petitioned President Roosevelt in 1939 to grant independence early to the Philippines by 1940. The American leader refused. In the last days of 1939, the foreboding shadow of an expanding Japanese empire was cast on the Philippine Islands.

Brandon Kyle Gauthier

Further Reading

Brands, H. W. *Bound to Empire: The United States and the Philippines.* New York: Oxford University Press, 1992. Scholarly and readable, this work utilizes government documents to analyze Filipino-American relations from the Spanish-American War into the 1990's.

Dolan, Ronald, ed. *Philippines: A Country Study.* Washington, D.C.: Library of Congress, 1993. First sixty-five pages of this book offer a unique and succinct summary of Filipino history from 1521 to 1990.

Golay, Frank H. *Face of Empire: United States-Philippine Relations, 1898-1946.* Madison: University of Wisconsin Press, 1998. Published in cooperation with the University of Manila; analysis of how American involvement shaped the future of the Philippines.

Karnow, Stanley. *In Our Image: America's Empire in the Philippines.* New York: Random House, 1989. Detailed summary of American involvement with the Philippine Islands from the 1890's to the 1980's.

Ngai, Mae M. "From Colonial Subject to Undesirable Alien: Filipino Migration in the Invisible Empire." In *Impossible Subjects: Illegal Aliens and the Making of Modern America.* Princeton, N.J.: Prince-

ton University Press, 2004. Analysis of Filipino immigration to the United States during the 1920's-1930's.

Schirmer, Daniel B., ed. *The Philippines Reader: A History of Colonialism, Neocolonialism, Dictatorship, and Resistance.* Boston: South End Press, 1987. Collection of primary documents from Filipino history that is good for research purposes.

See also   Congress, U.S.; Great Depression in the United States; Immigration to the United States; Japanese military aggression; MacArthur, Douglas; Philippine Independence Act of 1934; Racial discrimination; Roosevelt, Franklin D.

■ Philosophy and philosophers

During the 1930's, the field of philosophy in the United States became more professionalized, academic, and specialized than it previously had been. As an academic discipline, it became increasingly technical; as a result, professional philosophers devoted most of their attention to addressing and solving technical problems about the nature of philosophy itself. At the same time, there were still "public philosophers" who bridged conceptual, philosophical concerns and broad social issues.

Beginning in the late eighteenth century and throughout much of the history of the United States, philosophy, although an academic discipline, was part of the broad intellectual and social life of the country. The political philosophy of the Enlightenment was openly and explicitly woven into the founding documents of the nation, such as the Declaration of Independence and the Constitution. During the first half of the nineteenth century, the movement that came to be called American Transcendentalism was widely known, in large part because of the writings of Henry David Thoreau (1817-1862) and Ralph Waldo Emerson (1803-1882). By the beginning of the twentieth century, however, philosophy in the United States had become less "public" and more academic. Just as other intellectual fields of study had become more technical and specialized, so, too, had philosophy.

Pragmatism   Entering the 1930's, the predominant and most influential school of philosophical thought in America was pragmatism. Beginning as early as the late 1860's with the works of Charles Sanders Peirce (1839-1914) and William James (1842-1910), pragmatism had become the philosophical tradition that was most identified with American intellectual life. Pragmatism was in part a response to, and rejection of, much of the history of Western philosophical thought. In particular, pragmatism rejected much of what was seen as "sterile" and abstract philosophical problems. The term "pragmatism" derives from the Greek word for "deed" or "action." Pragmatists emphasized the practical effects and consequences of holding some philosophical view. For example, a long-standing philosophical question was whether or not people's actions were determined by external causes or free will. James remarked that what mattered were the practical consequences of accepting one or another of these views. What difference would it make, he asked, if one truly believed in determinism or in free will? For example, would it make a difference in whether a person was seen to be responsible for his actions? Underlying this pragmatist attitude was the sense that a belief or claim is empty and meaningless unless there is some practical consequence that results from holding that belief. As James had put it: "A difference that makes no difference is no difference."

During the 1930's the leading pragmatist thinker was John Dewey (1859-1952). His writings were voluminous and spanned most major areas of philosophy, including metaphysics, epistemology, ethics, aesthetics, and political philosophy. Among his important works during this decade were *Logic: The Theory of Inquiry* (1938) and *Liberalism and Social Action* (1935). Dewey argued that the traditional philosophical concerns, such as the nature of truth or knowledge or goodness, were best understood as people's reflections upon and interactions with their changing environments. Standards and criteria for knowledge or goodness are not abstract, eternal truths; rather, they are statements of what has proven to be the best response to a particular environment. Theories, including philosophical theories about truth or knowledge or goodness, are merely "instruments" to help people flourish in the world. If an ethical principle (such as that individuals have rights that may not be violated by others) indeed helps people get along in the world, then it is justified.

Dewey famously suggested that the notion of "truth" should better be understood as "warranted assertability." That is, the concept of truth is taken to imply a constant, changeless reality, but what really matters is that one has justification for asserting something. Dewey's work was not only highly influential among professional philosophers, but also important with respect to public concerns, such as shaping much of educational theory and practice and offering a strong defense of the value of community in social and political life. He practiced his philosophical beliefs in concrete ways, such as working closely with Jane Addams (1860-1935), who founded Hull House in Chicago.

Logical Positivism   Although pragmatism was an important tradition in American philosophy, by the 1930's other schools of thought had challenged and rejected pragmatism. The most significant of these was what came to be called logical positivism. Like pragmatism, logical positivism rejected much of traditional philosophy. In particular, it rejected any claims that were not verifiable by empirical (sensory) means. Science, said the logical positivists, makes progress because its claims can be tested and verified (or else proven to be false). Because much of philosophy cannot be tested, philosophers continued to wrestle with the same issues for centuries without ever coming to any conclusions. Like the pragmatists, then, the logical positivists focused on eliminating "sterile" philosophy; unlike the pragmatists, however, they thought that practical consequences were not an important criterion for what made a belief or claim true or acceptable. They roundly criticized Dewey for wanting to replace the concept of truth with the notion of warranted assertability, saying that the history of science repeatedly showed that a particular view might be warranted but was nonetheless false. The logical positivists were largely European philosophers who had immigrated to the United States during the 1920's and 1930's. The most famous of them was Rudolf Carnap (1891-1970), who came to Chicago in the 1930's, having already established himself as a world-renowned thinker. The job of philosophy, Carnap said, was to identify which issues were legitimately scientific and which issues were legitimately philosophical. When dealing with philosophical issues, the job of philosophers was to analyze logically the nature of the language used in making their claims. Language was a central theme in two of Carnap's works during this decade, *The Unity of Sci-*

ence (1934) and *The Logical Syntax of Language* (1934).

One consequence of logical positivism was that less emphasis was placed on ethics and social/political philosophy than on more technical issues such as logic, language, and the philosophy of science. Because the logical positivists argued that the only meaningful claims were ones that could be empirically tested, claims about values, including all of ethics and social/political philosophy, were said to be either purely subjective or else within the realm of social sciences. For example, a claim such as "Abortion is legal" is simply a descriptive fact about laws in the United States; it can be verified. On the other hand, a claim such as "Abortion is wrong [or right]" is evaluative; no facts can be used to determine whether the statement is true or false, said the logical positivists.

A particularly important American logical positivist philosopher was Charles Stevenson (1908-1979) at the University of Michigan. Stevenson argued for what he called "the emotivist" view of ethics, which states that value claims (such as "X is good") are merely ways of stating one's emotional feelings about something. This was sometimes referred to as the "Boo-Hooray" view of ethics: "X is bad" really means that the speaker does not like X, and, in effect, says, "X . . . boo!"; "X is good" really means "X . . . hooray!" Because this view became so prominent among academic philosophers, the fields of ethics and social/political philosophy dimmed in importance until the work of John Rawls (1921-2002) in the 1970's. Outside of professional philosophy, however, these value-related fields were still of great concern. For example, the social activist and thinker W. E. B. Du Bois (1868-1963) was influential in raising awareness about racial equality and civil rights for minorities in the United States.

Other Philosophical Schools   Two important philosophical traditions that were developing in Europe during the 1930's slowly rose to prominence in America as well. The first of these was linguistic philosophy, which was especially popular among British philosophers. One version of this emphasis on language was called formal language philosophy. This school of philosophy argued, like logical positivism, that the job of philosophy was to analyze how language shaped people's concerns and to resolve philosophical problems by focusing on the logical

analysis of language. Natural, ordinary language, they said, led to confusion and conceptual problems; philosophers should follow the example of scientists, who make progress by exploring the underlying structures and forms of ordinary phenomena. An important philosopher in the formal language tradition was Bertrand Russell (1872-1970). The other version of this emphasis on analyzing language came to be known as ordinary language philosophy. The job of philosophy, according to this school of thought, was to analyze ordinary language, to see what assumptions and implications it carries, and to see how philosophical problems arise from the misuse of language. An important philosopher in this tradition was Ludwig Wittgenstein (1889-1951).

On the European continent, especially France and Germany, phenomenology and existentialism also became a major philosophical tradition. Particularly influential were the writings of Martin Heidegger (1889-1976) and, soon afterward, Jean-Paul Sartre (1905-1980). Their focus was on deep assumptions about the nature of existence. Some of these writings were very technical, such as Heidegger's writings on metaphysics, while others were very "practical," such as Sartre's writings on creating meaning in one's life by impassioned choices. Existentialism soon became a dominant school of thought, especially in the wake of World War II. During the 1930's in the United States, this branch of philosophy began to have an impact, first on professional philosophers and later on American culture generally.

Impact   Some philosophers of the 1930's made important contributions to American culture. Dewey had a significant impact on public education and political life, while Du Bois was influential in promoting racial equality and civil rights. However, much of philosophy and the concerns of philosophers were technical and academic. This professionalization of philosophy carried over into subsequent decades, and it was not until the late twentieth century that any professional philosopher had an impact comparable to Dewey's and Du Bois's on general American culture. By the 1980's, however, some philosophers, such as Rawls and Richard Rorty, once again openly focused on the importance of philosophy in American intellectual and practical life.

David Boersema

Further Reading

Harris, Leonard, Scott L. Pratt, and Anne S. Waters, eds. *American Philosophies: An Anthology.* New York: Wiley-Blackwell, 2002. Scholarly exploration of the development and practice of philosophy throughout American history, including explanations of the schools of thought relevant to the 1930's.

Kuklick, Bruce. *A History of Philosophy in America, 1720-2000.* New York: Oxford University Press, 2003. Includes sections on the "Age of Pragmatism" and "professional period" that describe the diversity and cultural shifts in the field of philosophy during the 1930's.

Lachs, John, and Robert Talisse, eds. *American Philosophy: An Encyclopedia.* New York: Routledge, 2007. Offers profiles of major philosophers and descriptions of important philosophical movements.

Marsoobian, Armen T., and John Ryder, eds. *The Blackwell Guide to American Philosophy.* New York: Wiley-Blackwell, 2004. Provides information on influential philosophers and major trends and themes in philosophy through the years.

Smith, John E. *The Spirit of American Philosophy.* Albany: State University of New York Press, 1983. Discusses in detail the work and lives of Peirce, James, and Dewey.

Stuhr, John, ed. *Classical American Philosophy: Essential Readings and Interpretive Essays.* New York: Oxford University Press, 1987. Focuses on Peirce, James, and Dewey and the period from 1870 to the end of World War II.

See also Addams, Jane; Civil rights and liberties in the United States; Communism; Dewey, John; Du Bois, W. E. B.; Education; *Story of Philosophy, The.*

■ Photography

Definition An art form that uses light-sensitive media to make permanent images of objects

Photography was used in a number of ways during the 1930's: for documenting the homeless and the plight of the farmers during the Depression, for photojournalism in newspapers and magazines, for advertisements, and for art. Before the 1930's, most photography was black and white and was taken with cameras with fairly large negatives. Smaller 35-millimeter cameras, color photography, and flashes began to be used during the 1930's.

Introduced during the latter part of the nineteenth century, 35-millimeter (35mm) film was used for most commercial movies throughout the twentieth century. In 1934, Kodak began packaging in metal containers 35mm film to be used in small still cameras to make twenty-four to thirty-six exposures on one roll. The film was available as black and white and, starting in 1935, as Kodachrome color slide film.

Equipment and Film Kodak and some other vendors produced fairly economical 35mm cameras, such as the Retina, so that black-and-white pictures and color slides were available to amateur photographers at reasonable prices. Many professional photographers also liked the small 35mm cameras, with which pictures could be taken unobtrusively and rapidly for a given photo shoot. Professionals were especially drawn to more expensive 35mm cameras, such as the Leica and Contax, because they had good lenses, and the photographers could quickly change the shutter speed and lens opening to produce the best exposure of the film.

However, the small size of the 35mm film meant it was not ideal for producing sharp blowups. Therefore, most professionals continued to use larger cameras with larger film. These cameras included Graflex, which used sheet film with negative sizes from 2¼ inches by 3¼ inches up to 8 inches by 10 inches; the Rolleiflex twin lens reflex, with 2¼ inches by 2¼ inches on roll film; and various view cameras that used sheet film from 4 inches by 5 inches up to 20 inches by 24 inches.

Flashbulbs were first used during the early 1930's. Flashes were useful to newspaper photographers, for example, because they could rapidly expose pictures in darker places. However, the harsh front lighting was not flattering for pictures of people. Later, multiple flashes were used simultaneously to produce more flattering pictures. Flashbulbs had to be thrown away after one exposure, but electronic flashes that could be used many times came into use during the late 1930's.

Documentary Photographs Documentary photographs convey information about people, buildings, and other factual matter. These photos are not necessarily artistic, although many can be classified as such. Examples of the subjects of documentary photographs during the 1930's include migrant workers, steelworkers, farmworkers, young children

Margaret Bourke-White, one of the foremost photographers of the Depression era, risks injury for a shot off the decorative facade of the Chrysler Building in 1934. (Time & Life Pictures/Getty Images)

working in factories, and unemployed persons during the Great Depression.

Some of the most notable documentary photographers during the 1930's were Dorothea Lange, Margaret Bourke-White, Ben Shahn, Walker Evans, and Berenice Abbott. The government's Resettlement Administration employed Lange, Shahn, and Evans, among many other photographers, starting in 1935, to document the plight of farmworkers and other unemployed persons. The Resettlement Administration provided financial and housing assistance to farmers and farmworkers who were impoverished by the Depression and the Dust Bowl.

Lange produced some of the most dramatic photos of the homeless, unemployed, and migrant workers using a Graflex camera. Her photographs included pictures of workers living in tent camps, along the highway in old cars, and at work.

Shahn, who also was a painter, used a 35mm Leica camera with a right-angle viewer to photograph his subjects unobtrusively. He took most of his photos in the southeastern states; his subjects included striking mine workers and their quarters, prisoners, and cotton pickers.

Using a camera with 8-inch by 10-inch negatives, Evans documented sharecroppers in the South in their homes, workplaces, and churches and also photographed their belongings. Many of his subjects looked directly into the camera. The photographs drive home the extreme poverty of the subjects, most of whom are thin, have no shoes, and wear dirty, ragged clothing.

Bourke-White also captured many images of the poor using her Graflex camera. She coproduced a book with writer Erskine Caldwell called *You Have Seen Their Faces* (1937), which exposed the plight of southern farmers. Bourke-White also was a regular contributor to *Life* magazine.

Abbott was a renowned New York City photographer who used a Century Universal camera, which produced 8-inch by 10-inch, black-and-white negatives. She produced many photos of New York that captured the look and spirit of the city during the 1930's.

Photojournalism Photojournalism refers to the use of photographs in magazines and newspapers to illustrate a story about a person or event. Beginning in the mid-nineteenth century, illustrations were included in many publications; initially, these were drawings or paintings. As the technology became more widely available, photography supplanted drawn illustrations. Magazines could produce higher quality photos than newspapers could.

Journalistic photographs can include critical moments in sporting events, natural disasters, people involved in a crime, or celebrities. Often using small cameras, photojournalists must be able to rapidly recognize and record an important moment in time. One example of this was the 1937 *Hindenburg* disaster. The dirigible had crossed the Atlantic Ocean and was about to land in Lakehurst, New Jersey. A few photographers were present to record the landing for their newspapers. The dirigible was filled with hydrogen, a low-density but flammable gas. It burst into flame while attempting to land and, within a few seconds, it fell to the ground. The photographers' pictures of the inferno became classic images. One photographer with a view camera had film holders with two negatives, one on each side, which he had to rapidly insert into the camera for each exposure. In the chaos of the crash, he only exposed one negative in each holder, then threw the holder on the ground so he could quickly expose the next negative from another film holder. The photographs were rushed to the major newspapers in New York City and published with a minimal amount of writing.

Before the 1930's, many pictures had been published in illustrated news magazines, especially in Europe. *Time* and *Fortune* magazines began to publish photographs during the early 1930's. *Life* magazine published its first issue on November 23, 1936, and the magazine was an instant success. *Life* was dedicated to photographic essays with minimal writing. Its first issue featured an eleven-page story about the workers who built a large dam near Fort Peck, Montana, and the desert tent cities in which they lived. Another photojournalistic magazine called *Look* began shortly after *Life*.

Other magazines, such as *Vogue* and *Vanity Fair*, debuted during the early twentieth century. These lifestyle magazines, which showcased glamorous photographs of celebrities and fashions, became important cultural influences during the 1930's. One of the most outstanding photographers for these magazines was Edward Steichen. He produced brilliant black-and-white and color photographs, and his photographic essays on actors eloquently captured their character.

Art Photographs and Straight Photography Art and straight photography include pictures taken for the beauty of the subject and often resemble landscape paintings. Ansel Adams was one of the most famous landscape photographers of the twentieth century, and many of his black-and-white photographs were taken during the 1930's. Adams used an 8-inch by 10-inch view camera with a small lens opening to ensure that the prints were in focus. He took most of his pictures in the Western United States in places such as Yosemite Park, where he also promoted conservation. Adams taught and wrote a number of books to illustrate his methods for taking and printing photographs. He encouraged photographers to learn the development process, from exposure of the film to the final print, so that they could visualize the final photograph before taking it.

Adams was a member of a band of photographers that called itself Group f/64; f/64 is a tiny lens opening used to increase the sharpness range in photographs. Famous landscape photographers Edward Weston and Imogen Cunningham were among other members of the group.

Color Photography Color photography was attempted as early as the nineteenth century. However, producing color prints was much more complicated than producing black-and-white pictures.

Kodachrome slide film was used by some professional photographers when it was introduced during the mid-1930's. Eliot Porter, for example, made his own color prints from the Kodachrome transparencies. Eliot Elisofon used color filters to control the appearance of Kodachrome. Advertising also began to make use of color during the 1930's. However, Kodachrome was used mainly by amateurs because many professionals felt that the color produced by Kodak film was unnatural. Kodachrome was increasingly used after the 1930's; later, many more color films were introduced, such as Ektachrome, Fujichrome, and Ektacolor.

Impact Small 35mm cameras in various styles continued to be used long after the 1930's. Many amateurs were attracted to the small, economical 35mm cameras, which also took good pictures. The use of flashbulbs and, later, the electronic flash and artificial speed lights produced lighting that allowed pictures to be taken in more diverse settings.

Photography's spread and the advent of photojournalistic magazines such as *Life* brought news and culture to life for people worldwide. Photographs compellingly documented the plight of displaced farmworkers, the beauty of the natural world, and newsworthy events such as the *Hindenburg* disaster. The spread of affordable 35mm cameras and film also made it possible for average people to document their own lives.

Robert L. Cullers

Further Reading

Adams, Ansel, and Andrea Gray Stillman. *Ansel Adams: Four Hundred Photographs.* Boston: Little, Brown, 2007. Compilation of Adams's iconic photographs.

Newhall, Beaumont. *The History of Photography.* Boston: Little, Brown, 1982. Illustrated book chronicles the development of photography from the early nineteenth century to about 1980.

Pollack, Peter. *The Picture History of Photography.* New York: Harry N. Abrams, 1969. Describes the major developments in the history of photography and profiles some of the most outstanding and influential photographers.

Pultz, John. *The Body and the Lens.* London: Calmann and King, 1995. Documents how pictures of people have been taken since the beginning of photography.

Rosenblum, Naomi. *A History of Women Photographers.* Paris: Abbeville Press, 1994. Abundantly illustrated book about the history of women photographers. Includes brief biographies of some of the more renowned women photographers.

_____. *A World History of Photography.* New York: Abbeville Press, 1984. Contains more than eight hundred pictures with sections on portraits, landscapes, documentation, photojournalism, and art photography.

See also Adams, Ansel; Lange, Dorothea; *Life* magazine; *Look* magazine; Magazines; Newspapers, U.S.

■ Physics

Between 1930 and 1939, the center of excellence in both experimental and theoretical physics shifted from Europe to the United States, driven by the growing maturity of U.S. scientific institutions and the emigration of European scientists fleeing from Nazism in Germany, fascism in Italy, and Stalinism in the Soviet Union.

By 1930, the atomic nature of matter was almost universally accepted by physicists and chemists. The atom was known to consist of a heavy, dense nucleus with a positive electric charge surrounded by light, mobile, negatively charged electrons. The chemical identity of an atom was known to be determined by the number of electrons surrounding the nucleus, and hence by the number of positive charges in the nucleus. The nuclei of a chemical element varied in mass, with different varieties identified as different isotopes. Radioactivity was recognized as the spontaneous transmutation (radioactive decay) of the nuclei of one chemical element into another. Natural radioactivity was either of celestial origin in the form of cosmic rays or the product of radioactive decay. Cosmic rays were known to be charged particles of energies far greater than anything coming from radioactive decay. Beyond that, little was known for certain.

Radioactive decay produced three types of particles. Alpha rays had been identified as the nuclei of helium atoms, beta rays as electrons, and gamma rays as electromagnetic radiation similar to x-rays but much more penetrating and energetic. Alpha particles were used to transmute nuclei artificially and explore the physics therein, but progress was hampered by the small number of particles and limited ranges of energy available from natural radioactive sources. As early as 1919, Ernest Rutherford, a British physicist acknowledged worldwide as the dean of nuclear research, suggested replacing weak natural sources of radioactivity with electrical particle accelerators operating at a million volts.

Pure Physics Rutherford's dream came true during the 1930's. In 1929, Ernest Orlando Lawrence of the University of California at Berkeley invented the cyclotron and birthed the era of "big science." By 1932, Lawrence and M. Stanley Livingston succeeded in building a cyclotron with the equivalent of Rutherford's coveted one million volts of accelerating potential. It was powerful enough to produce artificial radioactive isotopes in quantity. Throughout the 1930's, Lawrence kept building bigger and more powerful machines. At the end of the decade, he received a grant of $1.15 million from the Rockefeller Foundation to build a cyclotron designed to work at the equivalent of 100 million volts of accelerating potential. Throughout the decade, the United States held the lead in both number and size of cyclotrons, making the U.S. physics community the most productive in the world.

In 1930, Carl David Anderson at the California Institute of Technology began a study of cosmic rays using the cloud chamber as a detector. On August 2, 1932, Anderson captured a cloud-chamber photograph showing the passage of a positron, the antimatter equivalent of the electron. This particle had been theoretically predicted in 1931 by the British physicist Paul A. M. Dirac. In 1937, Anderson and his associate Seth Neddermeyer discovered another particle in cosmic rays, the muon. Originally thought to be a new particle associated with the strong force that holds the nucleus together, it proved to be related to the weak force that controls beta decay.

James Chadwick in Great Britain discovered the neutron in January, 1932. Isotopes are known to be variations of an element with the same number of protons but differing numbers of neutrons in the nucleus. About that same time, at Columbia University, Harold C. Urey isolated a heavy form of hydrogen, called deuterium, with a nucleus composed of one proton combined with one neutron. The simplest type of nucleus with an inner structure, deuterium opened the door to understanding the nucleus. Lawrence used it as the accelerating particle in his cyclotrons; the extra neutron produced a wealth of intriguing nuclear reactions. Deuterium's most notorious application occurred during the 1950's in thermonuclear weapons. In 1938-1939, J. Robert Oppenheimer used Albert Einstein's theory of general relativity to predict the gravitational collapse of massive stars into neutron stars and black holes, which remained undiscovered by astronomers until the 1960's and 1970's.

Applied Physics In 1930, Lawrence Hyland of the Naval Research Laboratory realized that aircraft can be detected by the reflection of radio waves. Leo C. Young suggested the use of radio pulses with long intervals between. The distance to the target is the speed of the radio waves multiplied by one-half of the time it takes for the reflected pulses to return to the transmitter. Not only can objects be detected by radio reflection, but also their distance and bearing can be determined. The technique was christened "radar," short for radio detection and ranging. By 1936, Young could detect aircraft two and one-half miles distant; by 1938, he had developed equipment suitable for use at sea.

In the decade, numerous advances in nuclear medicine occurred. The radioactive isotopes produced by cyclotrons were cheaper than radium and offered physicians a range of therapeutic options. Most of Lawrence's funding for cyclotron research during the 1930's came from organizations interested in the medical use of radioactive isotopes. Eventually, the cyclotrons themselves were used for medical research. In 1937, Lawrence and his brother, John, a medical doctor, used neutron therapy to cure their mother of an inoperable cancer.

In 1939, pure physics and applied physics converged dramatically with the discovery in Germany of the nuclear fission of uranium. That same year, Edwin Mattison McMillan and Phillip Abelson produced the artificial element neptunium by the neutron bombardment of uranium, a result confirmed in early 1940. Emilio Gino Segrè and Glenn Theodore Seaborg produced the next transuranic element, plutonium, using Lawrence's 60-inch cyclotron. The fissionable isotope of uranium is less than 1 percent of natural uranium, but the more abundant isotope can be converted to fissionable plutonium. The physics communities in Britain and the United States immediately recognized the possibility of making nuclear explosives of unprecedented destructive power. The best physicists in the United States, both native and foreign-born, spent the World War II years turning that potential into reality.

Politics and Economics The evolution of physics in the United States during the 1930's was heavily influenced by politics in Europe and economics in North America. Academic positions in Europe were scarce and highly competitive. Jewish physicists were further hampered by anti-Semitism. The United States, despite economic problems, welcomed distinguished European physicists to its universities. When Adolf Hitler became chancellor of Germany in 1933, anti-Semitism escalated from repressive to dangerous. One of Hitler's first governmental acts, the dismissal of Jews from all government posts, threw hundreds of scientists of Jewish descent out of work. Emigration was frequently the best, if not the only, option. These circumstances were not unique to Germany. Benito Mussolini's Italy and Joseph Stalin's Soviet Union also drove many brilliant physicists away. Many found refuge in the United States, bringing knowledge and experience at the cutting edge of nuclear physics with them.

The list of distinguished physicists settling in the United States during the 1930's is long. Some were already world renowned. George Uhlenbeck and Samuel Goudsmit, authors of the theory of electron spin, emigrated from Holland in 1927. Einstein, the creator of special and general relativity, emigrated in 1932. George Gamow, the first to explain radioactive decay, emigrated from the Soviet Union in 1934. Enrico Fermi, developer of neutron bombardment for the production of artificial radioactive isotopes and author of the theory of nuclear beta decay, came to the United States from Italy in 1939.

Others made their historic discoveries after arrival in the United States. Eugene P. Wigner emigrated from Hungary in 1930; in 1936, he authored the theory of neutron absorption. Hans Albrecht Bethe emigrated from Germany in 1935; in 1938, he solved the mystery of energy production in stars.

The poor economy in the United States triggered a major expansion in the number of domestically trained physicists. Graduating students found jobs difficult to obtain during the Depression. In response, many more of them than in pre-Depression years remained in school to pursue advanced degrees. The rate at which American universities awarded doctorates in physics doubled. Almost all of the graduates were men. American women rarely entered physics in this decade, in contrast to other scientific fields, where they made significant contributions.

Nobel Prizes In 1934, Urey received the Nobel Prize in Chemistry for the separation of deuterium from deuterium oxide (heavy water). In 1936, An-derson shared the physics prize for the discovery of the positron. In 1937, Clinton Joseph Davisson shared the physics prize for demonstrating the wave nature of matter. Fermi received the 1938 prize in physics for the production of artificial radioactive isotopes while still a resident and citizen of Italy; he used the trip to Stockholm to collect the prize as an opportunity to escape to the United States. In 1939, Lawrence received the physics prize for the invention of the cyclotron.

Others received the prize in later years for important work completed during the 1930's. McMillan and Seaborg shared the 1951 chemistry prize for the synthesis of transuranic elements in 1939. Bethe received the physics prize in 1967 for his 1938 work on energy production in stars. Wigner shared the 1963 physics prize for numerous contributions to theoretical atomic and nuclear physics, his 1936 work on neutron absorption among them.

Impact Between 1930 and 1940, the number of pages published in *The Physical Review*, the premier professional journal of physics in the United States, grew by 150 percent, reflecting the growth of theoretical and experimental physics research in the nation. This concentration of talent, coupled with a greatly expanded research infrastructure, proved of immense importance to the United States in World War II, ultimately providing two powerful weapons: radar and nuclear explosives.

The purely academic research in nuclear physics during the 1930's led directly to the development of the atom bomb during World War II. After the war, development continued on the hydrogen bomb. The threat of nuclear war severely constrained U.S. foreign policy and military planning for decades. Postwar economic prosperity and the pressures of the Cold War kept research budgets high. The community of physicists assembled during the 1930's and the students they trained throughout the 1930's and 1940's kept the United States at the leading edge of physics research for the following two decades. As Europe and Japan slowly recovered from the war, the Soviet Union was the only significant competitor.

Billy R. Smith, Jr.

Further Reading

Gamow, George. *Thirty Years That Shook Physics: The Story of Quantum Theory.* New York: Dover Books,

1966. Explains difficult scientific concepts to general readers; one of the best books on atomic and nuclear physics.

Heilbron, John L. ed. *The Oxford Guide to the History of Physics and Astronomy.* New York: Oxford University Press, 2005. Starting point for any investigation of the history of physics.

Kevles, Daniel J. *The Physicists: The History of a Scientific Community in Modern America.* Cambridge, Mass.: Harvard University Press, 1995. Covers the history of physics in the United States from 1800 to 1995.

Pais, Abraham. *Inward Bound: Of Matter and Forces in the Physical World.* New York: Oxford University Press, 1986. Excellent history of atomic and nuclear physics research from 1895 to 1983.

_____. *Niels Bohr's Times, in Physics, Philosophy, and Polity.* New York: Clarendon Press, 1991. Covers Bohr's contribution to the history of physics in the twentieth century.

See also Black hole theory; Chemistry; Cyclotron; Einstein, Albert; Electron microscope; Medicine; Neutron star theory; Nobel Prizes; Nuclear fission; Positron discovery.

■ Pittman-Robertson Act of 1937

The Law Federal excise tax on firearms and ammunition to fund state wildlife conservation and shooting-range development
Date Signed into law on September 2, 1937
Also known as Federal Aid in Wildlife Restoration Act

One of the most effective American conservation laws, the Pittman-Robertson Act protected the habitats of a wide variety of game and nongame species. Consistent with the decade's faith in affirmative government, hunters and the gun business taxed themselves to promote conservation and safety.

At the request of sporting and firearms organizations, Senator Key Pittman of Nevada and Representative A. Willis Robertson of Virginia sponsored the Pittman-Robertson Act to dedicate the 10 percent federal excise tax on long guns and ammunition to conservation and safety. The act designated conser-

vation and firearms safety projects to be 75 percent funded by federal grants and 25 percent by state grants. The act stipulated that the 25 percent from the state did not have to be cash but could be in the form of services, materials, and so on. Funds are allocated to states based on population, geographic size, and the number of hunters.

Most of the act's funds are used to acquire, manage, or protect game habitat and migration areas. For example, projects reward farmers for protecting prairie potholes, which are used as watering stations by migratory birds. The act also pays for state scientific studies of wildlife populations. Hunter safety education and the development of shooting ranges open to the public are also supported by the act.

In order to receive grants, states must use hunting license fees for the administration of the state fish-and-game department and not divert the fees to other uses. Some states spend funds on programs directly administered by the state fish-and-game department, while others make the funds available as grants for citizen-initiated projects. Handguns, bows, and arrows were later added to the act's excise tax, which increased to 11 percent.

Impact The Pittman-Robertson Act has helped millions of people take hunter education courses and practice firearms safety at target ranges. Its designated lands are used by hikers, campers, and other outdoor enthusiasts. Among the animals that have greatly increased in numbers and range as a result of the act are black bears, mountain lions, bobcats, pronghorn antelope, wapiti (American elks), white-tailed deer, desert bighorn sheep, beavers, wild turkeys, and many migratory and predatory birds.

David B. Kopel

Further Reading

Buck, Susan. *Understanding Environmental Administration and Law.* 3d ed. Washington, D.C.: Island Press, 2006.

Musgrave, Ruth. *Federal Wildlife Laws Handbook with Related Laws.* Lanham, Md.: Government Institutes, 1998.

See also Migratory Bird Hunting and Conservation Stamp Act of 1934; National parks; National Wildlife Federation; Recreation; Wilderness Society.

■ Pluto discovery

The Event   Identification of an object orbiting
   farther from the Sun than Neptune
Date   February 18, 1930
Place   Lowell Observatory, Flagstaff, Arizona

*At the time, the discovery of Pluto was considered to be the
first discovery of a planet by an American. Pluto's small size
and similarity to comets sparked a long debate over the definition of a planet.*

Johannes Kepler's recognition that planets moved
in elliptical orbits around the Sun coupled with Sir
Isaac Newton's demonstration that
the gravitational force explained
this motion allowed astronomers
to calculate the orbits of planets
and compare the predicted positions with observations. Two astronomers, John Adams in England and Urbain Le Verrier in
France, suggested independently
that irregularities in the orbits of
Saturn and Uranus required an
eighth planet. Their calculations
of its orbit led to the discovery of
Neptune in 1846, in almost the exact position they predicted. However, small irregularities remained,
suggesting a ninth planet.

Percival Lowell, a diplomat from
a wealthy Boston family, established an observatory in Flagstaff,
Arizona. Lowell, who was interested in mathematics and astronomy, conducted several searches
for this ninth planet beginning in
1905. Planets move relative to the
stars, so Lowell compared photographic images of the same star
field taken several nights apart.
Initially, he simply placed the images next to each other for comparison. In 1911, he purchased a
"blink comparator," which alternately displayed the two images, so
an object that moved appeared to
jump back and forth, making his
planet search more efficient.

Lowell's death, in 1916, brought his search to a
halt as legal issues over his estate were resolved. The
search resumed in 1927 under the leadership of
Vesto Melvin Slipher, Lowell's former assistant who
was appointed director of the Lowell Observatory.
Lowell's brother, A. Lawrence Lowell, the president
of Harvard University, assisted Slipher in purchasing
a 13-inch telescope for the search. However, the
Lowell Observatory could not afford to hire another
professional astronomer. As the project was set to resume, Slipher received a letter from Clyde William
Tombaugh, a twenty-two-year-old who lived on a
farm in western Kansas. Tombaugh, who could not
afford a college education, was an amateur astrono-

Searching for Planet X

In many ways, Clyde Tombaugh was like his astronomer hero William Herschel, who discovered Uranus unexpectedly during a
routine sky survey in 1781. Both were dedicated amateur astronomers and skilled telescope makers who devoted hours to tedious observations. Tombaugh, however, was only twenty-four
years old when he discovered Pluto, whereas Herschel was in his
early forties when he made his discovery. Furthermore, Tombaugh's yearlong search for Planet X lasted much longer than
that of either Herschel or Johann Galle, who discovered Neptune
in 1846 on the first night he looked for it, lying less than 1 degree
from its predicted position.

The search for Pluto was complicated by the fact that its orbit
is highly eccentric—sometimes even passing inside the orbit of
Neptune—and has a large inclination of about 17 degrees from
the mean plane of the other planets. It is now known that Percival
Lowell's predictions for the position of Pluto were based on
faulty calculations, and its discovery within 6 degrees of the predicted location was only a coincidence. Fortunately, Tombaugh
did not limit his observations to the predicted area of the sky or
to the region close to the mean orbital plane of the planets.

When James Christy discovered Pluto's moon, Charon, in
1978, it was conclusively demonstrated that the mass of Pluto was
far too small to cause observable deviations in the orbits of Uranus and Neptune; thus the two larger planets' orbits could not be
used to predict Pluto's position. In the 1990's, several icy objects
much smaller than Pluto were discovered just beyond Pluto's orbit in the Kuiper comet belt with periods of about 300 years, compared to Pluto's 248-year period. In 2006, Pluto was redesignated
as a dwarf planet because it did not conform to the International
Astronomical Union's revised definition of a planet.

mer who built his own telescopes. His astronomical observations impressed Slipher, who invited Tombaugh to join the observatory staff.

On clear nights when the Moon was not visible in the sky, Tombaugh would expose a photographic plate, then rephotograph the same star field several days later. He used the blink comparator that Lowell purchased to search for moving objects. The job was tedious, requiring great concentration in order not to miss one blinking spot on the 14-by-17-inch plate, but Tombaugh was dedicated to the effort.

On February 18, 1930, Tombaugh found what he was looking for, comparing images taken on January 23, 1930, and January 29, 1930. He examined another plate, taken during poorer weather on January 21 and confirmed his discovery of an object orbiting the Sun well beyond the orbit of Neptune. The Lowell Observatory announced the discovery on March 13, 1930, Percival Lowell's birthday and the anniversary of William Herschel's discovery of Uranus. Initially, Pluto was believed to be the missing planet, but the orbital irregularities required Pluto to be about the mass of Earth. Since Pluto appeared as a point not resolvable in large telescopes, it was small. The discovery of Pluto's moon, Charon, in 1978, made it possible to calculate Pluto's mass, which was less than 0.25 percent of Earth's mass.

The inner planets—Mercury, Venus, Earth, and Mars—are rocky objects, while the outer planets—Jupiter, Saturn, Uranus, and Neptune—are composed primarily of hydrogen and helium. Pluto, which is bright because of the high reflectivity of its icy surface, is not similar to either group of planets, appearing more like a huge comet. In 1992, astronomers David Jewitt and Jane X. Luu discovered 1992 QB1, an icy object orbiting in the "Kuiper Belt," outside the orbit of Neptune, where many comets are thought to originate. Many more of these icy objects were soon discovered; Pluto was the most easily observable.

Impact Determined in 1989 during the Voyager 2 spacecraft flyby, Neptune's mass explained its orbital irregularities, eliminating the need for a ninth planet. In 2006, the International Astronomical Union grouped Pluto with other large Kuiper Belt objects as "dwarf planets." Because Pluto is extremely difficult to observe from Earth, NASA's New Horizons spacecraft planned to study Pluto in 2015 and observe several other Kuiper Belt objects.

George J. Flynn

Further Reading

Levy, David H. *Clyde Tombaugh: Discoverer of Planet Pluto.* Tucson: University of Arizona Press, 1992.

Minard, Anne. *Pluto and Beyond: A Story of Discovery, Adversity, and Ongoing Exploration.* Flagstaff, Ariz.: Northland Books, 2007.

Tombaugh, Clyde W., and Patrick Moore. *Out of the Darkness: The Planet Pluto.* Harrisburg, Pa.: Stackpole Books, 1980.

See also Astronomy; Chemistry; Physics; Radio astronomy.

■ Polio

Definition Highly contagious human disease caused by a virus
Also known as Poliomyelitis; infantile paralysis

Polio was one of the most feared and devastating diseases of the first half of the twentieth century with nearly eighty thousand paralytic cases, most of them affecting children, reported during the 1930's alone. There was no vaccine, effective treatment, or cure available.

Poliomyelitis, or polio, is a disease caused by the poliovirus. The virus usually infects only the small intestine, causing a mild illness characterized by headache and nausea. Sometimes no symptoms develop. In one in about three hundred cases the virus invades the central nervous system, causing motor neuron destruction and paralysis. The majority of deaths are caused by paralysis of the respiratory muscles. The infection spreads via food, water, various objects, and humans who have become contaminated by fecal matter.

Small outbreaks of polio were reported in Europe during the mid-nineteenth century, but the first epidemic in the United States was in 1894. There were 123 cases reported in Otter Valley, near Rutland, Vermont. In 1909, Karl Landsteiner discovered that polio was caused by a virus. By 1910, polio had become a major health concern in the United States as several epidemics affecting both the poor and the wealthy were reported.

In 1921, thirty-nine-year-old Franklin D. Roosevelt was stricken with the disease. During the later 1920's, Roosevelt and his law partner, Basil O'Connor, purchased a resort in Warm Springs, Georgia, and converted it into a rehabilitation center for polio patients. O'Connor and Roosevelt eventually turned the resort into a nonprofit foundation, the Georgia Warm Springs Foundation, which raised money to provide care and therapy for polio patients. After Roosevelt became president of the United States, the main means of fund-raising was through national parties and balls held on the president's birthday. In 1938, Roosevelt created the National Foundation for Infantile Paralysis to replace the old foundation and appointed O'Connor as the director. Hollywood giant Eddie Cantor was a strong supporter of the foundation and referred to the foundation's fund-raising campaign as the March of Dimes after the newsreel *The March of Time*. Cantor used his radio program to launch the fund-raising effort, and soon many other Hollywood celebrities joined Cantor's campaign.

By the mid-1930's, research on a vaccine for polio was well underway. In 1935, Maurice Brodie and William H. Park made an attempt to inactivate the virus without damaging its ability to stimulate antibody formation. In the same year, John A. Kolmer developed another vaccine using a live virus that was chemically attenuated. The two experimental vaccines were tried with disastrous results. Several children became paralyzed and at least ten died.

In 1938, a National Foundation for Infantile Paralysis Committee on Scientific Research was established. Priorities were reordered to focus on the basic biology of the poliovirus, but later monies were distributed to various vaccine research programs. Grant money from the foundation led to the development of the Jonas Salk and Albert Bruce Sabin vaccines and the eventual eradication in 1979 of polio from the United States. Foundation monies were also expended to develop and distribute the iron lung, a machine that aided the breathing of polio victims whose respiratory muscles were affected.

Impact Polio was one of the most devastating and feared diseases to affect the United States in the first half of the twentieth century. More than one-half million people, primarily children, were stricken with the disease. Polio spread across all socioeconomic boundaries. From the 1930's through the 1960's, medical science focused on finding a cure, a treatment, and a vaccine for polio. With the assistance of Hollywood celebrities, Roosevelt, the most famous American polio victim, drew the spotlight to the disease. Fund-raising efforts led to the development of effective vaccines during the mid-1950's. Although polio has been eradicated from the United States and the developed world, more than one thousand cases are still reported each year from undeveloped countries.

Charles L. Vigue

Further Reading

Oshinsky, David M. *Polio, An American Story*. New York: Oxford University Press, 2005.

Silver, Julie K., and Daniel Wilson. *Polio Voices: An Oral History from the American Polio Epidemics and Worldwide Eradication Efforts*. Westport, Conn.: Praeger, 2007.

Wilson, Daniel J. *Polio (Biographies of Disease)*. Portsmouth, N.H.: Heinemann, 2009.

See also Health care; March of Dimes; Medicine; Roosevelt, Franklin D.

■ *Porgy and Bess*

Creators George Gershwin (musical score); DuBose Heyward and Ira Gershwin (libretto)

Identification Opera about African American life during the 1920's

Dates First performed in 1935

Many people consider George Gershwin's Porgy and Bess *to be the most popular American opera ever produced. Several of its songs became classics. In addition, its sympathetic, if perhaps a bit stereotypical, portrayal of African Americans in the South both reflected and influenced the typical Anglo-American view of black culture at the time.*

For many years, Gershwin had considered writing a "popular American opera." After looking at several different texts for the basis of the work, Gershwin settled on DuBose Heyward's novel *Porgy* (1924), which had already been turned into a play and performed by the Theatre Guild (which also, incidently, did the first performance of the opera). Gershwin started writing the opera in earnest in 1934, finishing the first draft by January, 1935, and the short score by September, 1935.

Todd Duncan (right) looking over his shoulder at Anne Brown in the original production of George Gershwin's musical Porgy and Bess. *(Archive Photos/Getty Images)*

The story is set in "the recent past" on the islands off South Carolina and features an almost entirely black cast. Much of the plot concerns lost love—through violence of man, as when Crown kills Robbins; violence of nature, as when a hurricane kills the parents of a young baby; or violence of thought, as when Sportin' Life persuades Bess to go to New York, leaving Porgy alone again—and how society nonetheless carries on.

The work was first performed in Boston on September 30, 1935, and subsequently, after some cuts, on Broadway on October 10, 1935. It received mixed reviews, particularly regarding its mix of musical styles, but subsequent revivals have secured its place in history.

Impact Gershwin's *Porgy and Bess* has continued to be performed, discussed, studied, and imitated. Several tunes, including "Summertime" and "It Ain't

Necessarily So," became so popular in their own right that they crossed over to other genres, becoming hits for the likes of John Coltrane and Miles Davis. Furthermore, following Gershwin's example, other composers, of both classical and Broadway music, have successfully produced works that straddle the realms of opera and musical.

Lisa Scoggin

Further Reading

Alpert, Hollis. *The Life and Times of Porgy and Bess: The Story of an American Classic.* New York: Knopf, 1990.

Pollack, Howard. *George Gershwin: His Life and Work.* Berkeley: University of California Press, 2006.

Rosenberg, Deena. *Fascinating Rhythm: The Collaboration of George and Ira Gershwin.* New York: Dutton, 1991.

See also African Americans; Broadway musicals; Gershwin, George; Jews in Canada; Music: Classical; Racial discrimination; Theater in the United States.

■ Pornography

Definition Published materials in either print or visual form judged to be offensive to accepted moral standards

The concept of pornography was judicially narrowed during the 1930's, giving greater scope to writers wishing to explore socially controversial subjects. Placing the emphasis on the author's intent and on explicit language or imagery within a total work provided a more clearly defined approach to evaluating individual works, simplifying the process of determining what was pornography and reducing the amount of public attention given to the topic in general.

For Americans during the 1930's, the idea of pornography was paradoxically both clearly categorized and ambiguous. The widely used *Reader's Guide to Periodical Literature* referred anyone interested in pornography to the heading "immoral literature and pictures," clearly marking out these creative products as potentially suspect and injurious to accepted definitions of decency and morality. The underlying and most problematical concept with pornography was defining the particular aspects of any work that could be seen as immoral or obscene.

The decade opened with the adoption of two significant documents applicable to regulating pornography. Section 305 of the Tariff Act of 1930 targeted both citizens who ordered obscene materials from overseas and the businesses that imported them. Incoming parcels were to be randomly checked by U.S. Customs officials at ports of entry, and any questionable items were to be reviewed. Depending on the ruling, goods were then either released to the importer or sent to the assistant deputy commissioner of customs. If the second review agreed with the first that an item was obscene, the item was sent to the local U.S. district attorney, who was to initiate forfeiture proceedings. This law was attacked as constituting prior restraint and as violating the First and Fifth Amendment rights of the importers.

On March 31, 1930, the board of directors of the Motion Picture Producers and Distributors Association adopted a code developed by Father Daniel A. Lord of St. Louis University that both identified subjects inappropriate for depiction in film and established moral standards that films should work to promote (based in part on Roman Catholic theology). No provision was made for the enforcement of the code and studios throughout the 1930's continued to make films that pushed its limits.

All states had laws in place covering the publication, distribution, exhibition, possession, advertising, or importation of obscene materials, with several specifically prohibiting the showing of such goods to minors and all defining pornography as a misdemeanor or, less often, a felony. Some states exempted literature used by medical schools, druggists, and scientific publications. Penalties usually were a fine or imprisonment, the latter ranging from thirty days to up to five years. Perhaps the most severe law was Mississippi's, which specified that each day obscene items were offered for sale would be treated as a separate offense.

Court decisions figured prominently in the public dialogue on obscenity during the 1930's, not always with consistent results. In 1930, Mary Ware Dennett, author of the pamphlet *The Sex Side of Life*, had her conviction reversed, on grounds that her work treated the topic seriously. In 1931, the Supreme Court in the case of *Near v. Minnesota* struck down a state law that could have been applied to obscene publications, stating it to be too restrictive and extending the freedom of the press provision of the First Amendment to the state level. While the targeted publication in this case was a politically and culturally biased paper, the ruling prevented state "nuisance laws" from being potentially applied to actual pornography. The idea that pornography posed a significant and insidious threat to American society was emphasized in a statement issued by the Catholic bishops at their meeting in Washington, D.C., in 1932. Their argument was that immoral literature had contributed to the erosion of traditional moral values, which had spawned the conditions that caused the Great Depression.

The case with the most lasting impact regarding the public's view of pornography, both during the 1930's and for the rest of the twentieth century, was *United States v. One Book Called "Ulysses"* (1933). The legal dispute was set up by New York publisher Random House in an effort to overturn an earlier ruling that had kept Irish author James Joyce's novel *Ulysses* (1922) out of the U.S. market for a decade. The French edition of the work (with critical commentary pasted inside the cover) arrived in the United States and was judged obscene by U.S. Customs. The seizure was contested by Random House. Judicial examination of Joyce's complex novel resulted in a ruling that the determination of pornographic content lay in the impact the complete work would have on the average reader as well as the stated intent of the author. This was a significant departure from the prior practice of citing individual quotations as evidence that a work qualified to be labeled as pornographic or obscene.

Impact The definition of pornography changed significantly during the 1930's. Works of art were to be taken as a whole, and their value judged on their overall content. This change in law and attitude allowed for American access to works of art that had previously been censored.

Robert Ridinger

Further Reading

Black, Gregory. *Hollywood Censored: Morality Codes, Catholics, and the Movies*. New York: Cambridge University Press, 1994.

De Grazia, Edward. *Girls Lean Back Everywhere: The Law of Obscenity and the Assault on Genius*. New York: Random House, 1992.

Moscato, Michael, and Leslie LeBlanc, eds. *The United States of America v. One Book Entitled "Ulysses" by James Joyce: Documents and Commentary—A Fifty-

Year Retrospective. Frederick, Md.: University Publications of America, 1984.

Vanderham, Paul. *James Joyce and Censorship.* New York: New York University Press, 1998.

See also Book publishing; Civil rights and liberties in the United States; Literature in the United States; Medicine; *Near v. Minnesota*; Religion in the United States; Sex and sex education; *Ulysses* trial.

■ Positron discovery

The Event Discovery of the first experimental proof of the existence of positrons
Dates August-September, 1932
Place California Institute of Technology, Pasadena, California

The positron was the fourth subatomic particle discovered and proved the existence of antimatter.

Prior to the 1930's, physics had undergone radical change. Even the ultimate constituent of matter was unknown, as the discoveries of both the electron and the proton showed that the atom itself consisted of small particles. Equations in Paul A. M. Dirac's relativistic quantum mechanics, derived in 1928, predicted that each particle would have a "twin" with the opposite charge; this twin was eventually called "antimatter." However, no such particles had been detected at that time.

One place where subatomic particles could be detected was in cosmic rays—high-energy radiation emanating from outer space. Working under cosmic-ray researcher and Nobel laureate Robert Andrews Millikan, California Institute of Technology researcher Carl David Anderson designed an experiment to determine the nature of cosmic radiation. He sent balloons into the atmosphere equipped with cloud chambers. These instruments could photographically track particles that passed within them. The tracks determined the mass of a particle, and as the cloud chambers were equipped with strong magnets, the curvatures of the tracks determined whether a particle was positively or negatively charged.

Initial results seemed to show a few particles with the mass of an electron, but the positive charge of a proton, a particle nearly two thousand times heavier. After making additional instrument refinements, on August 2, 1932, Anderson obtained a photograph showing unambiguously a positively charged particle with the mass of an electron. He quickly announced to the world the discovery of a new particle, the "positive electron," later known as the positron.

Impact Anderson's initial claim was met with skepticism. However, in early 1933, British researchers Patrick M. S. Blackett and Giuseppe P. S. Occhialini confirmed Anderson's results, thereby also confirming both Dirac's equations and the existence of antimatter. Later work also showed that a high-energy photon could instantaneously change into an electron/positron pair, energy changing into mass as Albert Einstein's $E = mc^2$ predicted. For his work, Anderson shared the 1936 Nobel Prize in Physics.

George R. Ehrhardt

Further Reading

Crease, Robert P., and Charles C. Mann. *The Second Creation: Makers of the Revolution in Twentieth-Century Physics.* Rev. ed. New Brunswick, N.J.: Rutgers University Press, 1996.

Kevles, Daniel J. *The Physicists: The History of a Scientific Community in Modern America.* New York: Alfred A. Knopf, 1977.

Segrè, Gino. *Faust in Copenhagen: A Struggle for the Soul of Physics.* New York: Penguin, 2007.

See also Astronomy; Cyclotron; Nobel Prizes; Physics.

■ Post, Wiley

Identification Aviator
Born November 22, 1898; Grand Saline, Texas
Died August 15, 1935; near Point Barrow, Alaska

Post was one of the most famous pilots in aviation history. During the 1930's, he established the speed record for solo flight around the world and pioneered the art of high-altitude flying.

Wiley Post saw his first airplane at a county fair in 1913 and decided to become an aviator. While working as a mechanic in the oil fields in 1926, Post lost his left eye in an accident. Having trouble with depth perception, he internalized how to gauge distances through long hours of practice. During the late 1920's, he purchased his own airplane, taught student pilots, and performed as a skydiver.

Aviator Wiley Post in front of his plane after winning a Los Angeles-to-Chicago airplane race. (Hulton Archive/Getty Images)

After becoming the personal pilot for wealthy oil-man F. C. Hall, Post was allowed to use Hall's airplane, a Lockheed Vega nicknamed *Winnie Mae,* when Hall did not need it. After making several important modifications to the *Winnie Mae,* Post, and navigator Harold Gatty, departed from Roosevelt Field on Long Island on June 23, 1931, to establish a speed record for flight around the world. Making fourteen stops along the way, they completed the trip in a record time of eight days, fifteen hours, and fifty-one minutes. The two became instant national heroes.

Post's next goal was to be the first pilot to fly solo around the world. With a Sperry gyroscope, a device named for Elmer Ambrose Sperry, and a radio direction finder aboard the *Winnie Mae,* Post left Floyd Bennett Field, Long Island, on July 15, 1933. After eleven stops that included some necessary airplane repairs, he completed the trip in a record time of seven days, eighteen hours, and forty-nine minutes.

During the next year, Post developed the first pressure suit for flying at high altitudes. Reaching heights as high as fifty thousand feet, he established air speed records. In 1935, while flying with his friend Will Rogers in Alaska, an airplane malfunction led to a crash that killed both men.

Impact Post established himself as one of the world's foremost aviators when he became the first pilot to fly solo around the world. His development of the first practical pressurized pilot suit and subsequent substratospheric flights that led to the discovery of the jet stream were significant milestones in advancing the science and theory of flight.

Alvin K. Benson

Further Reading

Simons, David. *The History of Flight: From Aviation Pioneers to Space Exploration.* New York: Parragon, 2005.

Sterling, Bryan B., and Frances N. Sterling. *Forgotten Eagle: Wiley Post, America's Heroic Aviation Pioneer.* New York: Carroll & Graf, 2002.

See also Airships; Aviation and aeronautics; Earhart, Amelia; Goddard, Robert H.; Inventions; Physics; Rogers, Will; Transportation; Travel.

■ Postage stamps

During the 1930's, both the American and the Canadian governments issued increasing numbers of commemorative stamps, many of which had designs with political overtones.

In general, ordinary postage stamps are of two types: definitives, or regular, and commemoratives, honoring someone or something. There are also special stamps: airmail, postage due, special delivery, and others. Early U.S. postage stamps always contained the portraits of George Washington or Benjamin Franklin, the first postmaster general. During the 1860's, other presidents were added, and by the beginning of the twentieth century, a number of commemorative series had been issued.

During the 1930's, the post office issued 211 stamps, starting with the seal of the Massachusetts Bay Company and ending with an Alexander Graham Bell stamp. The notable commemoratives included the national parks series of 1935 and the presidential series of 1938 called the "Prexies." Because living persons cannot by law be pictured on U.S postage or currency, the series did not include President Franklin D. Roosevelt or Herbert Hoover, the only living former president at the time. All others were depicted in numerical order. Postage for some items, such as postcards and various weights, included one-half-cent stamps, and the post office minted one-half and one-and-one-half cent stamps. In the Prexies, the one-half-cent stamp depicted Benjamin Franklin; the one and one-half-cent stamp, Martha Washington; and the four and one-half-cent stamp, the White House. The design of the Prexies was the result of a competition announced in June, 1937. More than eleven hundred designs were submitted. Elaine Rawlinson of New York won the first prize of five hundred dollars. Her design, a simple bust of the presidents, was used on the stamps.

President Roosevelt was an enthusiastic stamp collector, and he advised Postmaster General James Aloysius Farley on ideas for designs. Other stamps during the 1930's included the Charleston, South Carolina, stamp; a reprint of definitives from the 1920's; a Red Cross stamp; and a victory at Yorktown stamp, depicting Washington, the French marshal the comte de Rochambeau, and the admiral the count de Grasse. In 1935, Farley ordered a special souvenir printing on uncut sheets of the 1934 stamps, including the National Parks stamp.

The U.S. Postal Service also minted thirteen airmail stamps during the 1930's. The *Graf Zeppelin* series of three stamps issued in 1930 involved some controversy. It included three stamps valued at $0.65, $1.30, and $2.60. The total for the set was more than the average family made in a week. Few were sold and most were destroyed.

Canadian definitives usually had a picture of the reigning monarch. During the 1930's, Canada released sixty-six general issue stamps. Thirty-two definitives depicted George V and six depicted George VI, who became king in December, 1936. None pictured Edward VIII because he abdicated before stamps could be minted. The 1935 George V issue was the "dated die issue" because of the small size of the date repeated on George VI's initial stamp in 1937. Three stamps in 1939 marked the royal visit to Canada: The one-cent stamp depicted the princesses Elizabeth and Margaret Rose, the two-cent stamp depicted the Ottawa War Memorial, and the three-cent stamp depicted George VI and Queen Elizabeth. A 1932 commemorative series for the Imperial Economic Conference of that year included a three-cent stamp depicting George V; a five-cent stamp of the Prince of Wales, the future Edward VIII; and a thirteen-cent allegory stamp of the British Empire, with Britannia sitting between the Eastern Hemisphere and the Western Hemisphere. The Arch issue of 1930 was a one-cent reissue of George V with an arched frame around the numeral. Canadian provinces historically minted their own stamps, but by the 1930's, only Newfoundland, which was not yet part of Canada, did so.

Impact Roosevelt chose his New York campaign manager Farley as postmaster general. He performed well generally, turning the U.S. Postal Service into a profitable operation and facilitating airmail. However, he committed a blunder as far as stamp collectors are concerned with his special reprints of twenty stamps designed for the president and Harold Ickes, secretary of the interior, both stamp collectors. When the public collectors learned of this they protested and the post office was forced to issue many more reprints. In the following decade, both the American and the Canadian postal services minted many more stamps, both definitives and commemoratives, every year and were much more conscious of stamp collectors.

Frederick B. Chary

Further Reading

Boggs, Winthrop S. *The Postage Stamps and Postal History of Canada.* Lawrence, Mass.: Quarterman, 1974.

Cullinan, Gerald. *The United States Postal Service.* New York: Praeger, 1973.

United States Postal Service. *The Postal Service Guide to U.S. Stamps.* New York: Collins, 2008.

See also   Air mail route scandal; Coinage; George VI's North American visit; Ickes, Harold; National parks.

Presidential elections. See **Elections of 1932, U.S.; Elections of 1936, U.S.**

■ Prohibition repeal

The Event   Repeal of the Eighteenth Amendment's prohibition of alcoholic beverages

Dates   Twenty-first Amendment passed by Congress on February 20, 1933, and ratified on December 5, 1933

The federal government opted to overturn the Eighteenth Amendment, which had prohibited the making, selling, and distribution of alcohol in the United States. This unprecedented decision turned the alcohol business, which had been dominated by such organized crime figures as Al Capone, from an illegal racket into a legitimate business opportunity.

In 1919, the necessary number of state legislatures ratified the Eighteenth Amendment to the Constitution, creating a national prohibition of alcohol within one year of its passage. The ratification of the Eighteenth Amendment to the U.S. Constitution ushered in a historical period in the United States known as Prohibition. Based on this amendment, manufacturing, distributing, and selling any type of alcoholic beverage anywhere within the United States became a federal crime.

Temperance Movement   Passage of the Eighteenth Amendment was the direct result of a social and moral campaign in the country known as the temperance movement, which had its financial backing from the Anti-Saloon League. This group was made up of wealthy, morally conservative businesspeople and politicians who were strongly opposed to alcohol usage. This particular movement called for more active involvement by the government to ensure that alcohol was banned outright because it only led to immoral behavior. In fact, various women's and Christian organizations, such as the Women's Christian Temperance Union, played crucial roles in bringing about Prohibition. Proponents truly believed that banning alcoholic beverages would alleviate or even eliminate many social problems, particularly poverty, crime, and mental illness, which, by consequence, would lead to a major reduction in taxes. The Eighteenth Amendment was written by lawyers associated with temperance organizations and put into law by the federal Volstead Act in 1919, the same year in which the amendment was ratified. Its passage was celebrated by alcohol prohibitionists throughout the country as much as it was protested by alcohol supporters.

Backlash   The idea that spawned the temperance movement backfired. Public support for the law was never strong throughout the 1920's. To get around the ban on alcohol, many Americans joined local clubs known as speakeasies, at which illegal alcoholic beverages were served at inflated prices. Crime rates soared during the Prohibition era, as organized-crime figures made millions of dollars on illegal alcohol sales. Additionally, corruption and illegal activities crossed over into various local and state governments; public servants ranging from police officers to well-known politicians also profited from the illicit alcohol business. Illegal empires resulting from bootlegging cropped up during this time. The American Mafia spread through numerous cities, most notably Chicago and New York.

Throughout the late 1920's, Prohibitionists continued to argue that Prohibition would work if enforcement was increased. However, this was not the case. In actuality, the longer Prohibition remained, the more tax dollars were used to deal with the federal law's negative impact on the American public. Law-enforcement agencies at every level of American government were investing expensive resources to combat Prohibition-related crimes. To complicate matters further, federal, state, and local agencies often disagreed about who was primarily responsible for enforcing various laws relating to Prohibition. State and federal court dockets became overcrowded with cases resulting from such disputes, and jails were filled with people convicted of Prohibition-related crimes. Not surprisingly, growing numbers of Americans supported repealing the Eighteenth Amendment to end Prohibition. Their demands led to the framing of the Twenty-first Amendment to the U.S. Constitution.

Rethinking Prohibition   Throughout the late 1920's and into the early 1930's, support for Prohibition diminished among voters and politicians alike. Supporters of repeal believed that the Constitution should not be involved with issues relating to public morals and that alcohol control and taxation should be state and local government responsibilities. Influential and politically connected businessmen created the Association Against the Prohibition Amendment, asking for the immediate repeal of the Eighteenth Amendment. Additionally, women had been granted the right to vote in 1920 and some strongly advocated the repeal of Prohibition, because many believed that the effects of Prohibition were destroying families. One such female activist, Pauline Sabin, who founded the Women's Organization for National Prohibition Reform in 1929, argued that repeal would protect families from the

Bar patrons in New York City saluting the repeal of the Eighteenth Amendment by way of the twenty-first Amendment, which ended the prohibition of alcohol in 1933. (The Granger Collection, New York)

moral corruption and crime that were direct results of the illegal alcohol business. This organization alone boasted a membership in the hundreds of thousands.

As the early 1930's progressed, the number of repeal organizations and the demand for repeal increased. Moreover, the issue of repeal became a major political tool for elections when in 1932 the Democratic Party included a provision for the repeal of Prohibition; a move that many believe helped secure the victory of Democratic presidential candidate Franklin D. Roosevelt. Estimates indicate that by this particular presidential election, close to three-fourths of American voters, along with an estimated forty-six states, favored repeal.

Repeal As more and more Americans began to publicly oppose Prohibition, the political push for repeal also grew. However, repealing a constitutional amendment was not an easy process. Although the U.S. Constitution outlines two methods for ratifying constitutional amendments, only one method had been used up to that point in history. This process called for ratification by the state legislatures of three-fourths of all the states. However, federal lawmakers knew that many state legislators were hesitant to go against the temperance movement, so they opted to propose the formal repeal of Prohibition using state conventions, the other ratification method established by Article V.

On December 6, 1932, Senator John Blaine of Wisconsin submitted a resolution to Congress proposing a formal submission to the states of a new amendment to repeal the Eighteenth Amendment. On February 20, 1933, Congress voted for the passage of the Twenty-first Amendment, and on the following day, the amendment was sent to the state governors to be disbursed and decided on at individual state conventions. The Twenty-first Amendment is the only amendment that has been ratified through the use of the state convention process.

Of additional historical significance was the fact that the federal government, as part of the Twenty-first Amendment, stipulated that each state should be able to establish its own laws regarding alcohol, further permitting more individual powers to the states. While the states deliberated on the issue, President-elect Roosevelt asked Congress to amend the

Eighteenth and Twenty-first Amendments

The Eighteenth Amendment to the U.S. Constitution, passed on January 16, 1919, outlawed the use, sale, and distribution of alcohol in the United States. The Twenty-first Amendment, ratified on December 5, 1933, repealed the Eighteenth Amendment, ending national Prohibition but retaining the right of individual states and territories to control alcoholic beverages.

Eighteenth Amendment

Section 1. After one year from the ratification of this article the manufacture, sale, or transportation of intoxicating liquors within, the importation thereof into, or the exportation thereof from the United States and all territory subject to the jurisdiction thereof for beverage purposes is hereby prohibited.

Section 2. The Congress and the several States shall have concurrent power to enforce this article by appropriate legislation.

Section 3. This article shall be inoperative unless it shall have been ratified as an amendment to the Constitution by the legislatures of the several States, as provided in the Constitution, within seven years from the date of the submission hereof to the States by the Congress.

Twenty-first Amendment

Section 1. The eighteenth article of amendment to the Constitution of the United States is hereby repealed.

Section 2. The transportation or importation into any State, Territory, or possession of the United States for delivery or use therein of intoxicating liquors, in violation of the laws thereof, is hereby prohibited.

Section 3. This article shall be inoperative unless it shall have been ratified as an amendment to the Constitution by conventions in the several States, as provided in the Constitution, within seven years from the date of the submission hereof to the States by the Congress.

Volstead Act to permit the sale of beer containing 3.2 percent alcohol or less. Within nine days, Congress complied and legalized beer. On December 5, 1933, less than one year after the Twenty-first Amendment was submitted for ratification, the required thirty-six states had ratified the amendment. At 7:00 P.M. that same evening, President Roosevelt signed the proclamation officially ending Prohibition. Federal Prohibition laws were immediately repealed. Some U.S. states, however, continued Prohibition within their jurisdictions. In fact, almost two-thirds of all states adopted some form of local alternative that enabled residents in political districts to vote for or against local Prohibition. However, by 1966, all states had repealed their state-level Prohibition laws, giving the ultimate power regarding alcohol consumption and distribution to counties and municipalities at the local level of government.

Impact With the passage of the Twenty-first Amendment, alcohol laws changed throughout the United States. During the thirteen-year period that alcohol was prohibited in the United States, many social problems became manifest, especially crime. By repealing the Eighteenth Amendment and giving individual states the right to create and enact their own laws regarding alcohol, the government hoped to address many of the social problems that were created by passage of the original Prohibition legislation.

The end of national Prohibition took most of the alcohol trade away from criminal organizations, but many of these organizations had grown so strong under Prohibition that they continued to operate by shifting to other illegal activities. Another legacy of Prohibition was the unanswered question of the propriety of government to legislate morality.

Paul M. Klenowski and Dwight Vick

Further Reading

Behr, Edward. *Prohibition: Thirteen Years That Changed America.* New York: Arcade, 1997. Provides a detailed historical overview of how Prohibition changed the United States for the worse. Highlights specific examples of criminal organizations that were conceived because of the illegal alcohol business.

Engdahl, Sylvia. *Amendments XVIII and XXI: Prohibition and Repeal.* Detroit, Mich.: Greenhaven Press, 2009. Concise work offering a comprehensive yet clear look at how both the Eighteenth and the Twenty-first Amendments had such a dramatic impact on the American public during the 1920's and 1930's.

Kyvig, David E. *Repealing National Prohibition.* Chicago: University of Chicago Press, 1979. Provides a comprehensive overview of how Prohibition impacted the United States, especially economically and socially, during the 1920's and 1930's. Detailed explanations of the illegal consequences of Prohibition provide a better understanding of its impact on crime in the United States during this time.

Rose, Kenneth D. *American Women and the Repeal of Prohibition.* New York: New York University Press, 1997. Discusses how American women helped spark a movement for the repeal of Prohibition. Highlights specific women's groups in the light of the passage of the Twenty-first Amendment.

Severn, William. *The End of the Roaring Twenties: Prohibition and Repeal.* New York: Julian Messner, 1969. Overview of the changes in the United States because of Prohibition. Highlights the impact of the passage of the Twenty-first Amendment on the American people.

Thorton, Mark. *The Economics of Prohibition.* Salt Lake City: University of Utah Press, 1991. Looks at who profited from the illicit sale of alcohol during Prohibition. Provides details regarding how alcohol spurred the foundation of the Mafia in the United States.

See also Anti-Racketeering Act of 1934; Capone, Al; Congress, U.S.; Luciano, Lucky; Ness, Eliot; Nitti, Frank; Organized crime; Schultz, Dutch.

973.917

The thirties in America